Rethinking Fiscal Policy afte

Before the financial crisis, fiscal policy often played a secondary role to monetary policy, with the manipulation of interest rates to hit inflation targets being the main instrument of macroeconomic management. However, after the financial crisis and the subsequent euro crisis, fiscal policy has been brought back to the fore. In the past, the limited understanding of the effects of fiscal policy, neglect of monetary-fiscal interactions, faulty institutional set-ups or ignorance of market expectations often led to bad policies. This book, written by a team of leading economists, seeks to address the current oversight of fiscal policy and to upgrade our understanding and conduct of fiscal policy, presenting a well-balanced diagnosis and offering several important lessons for future fiscal analysis and policy-making. It is an essential read for academics and graduate students focused on the current debate over fiscal policy, as well as policymakers working on day-to-day policy issues.

ĽUDOVÍT ÓDOR is a member of the Council for Budget Responsibility in Slovakia and Vice Chair of the Network of EU Independent Fiscal Institutions. In the past, he has served as a member of the Bank Board and Executive Director responsible for research at the National Bank of Slovakia, as an advisor to the Prime Minister, and as Chief Economist at the Ministry of Finance of the Slovak Republic. His book with Miroslav Beblavý and David Cobham, *The Euro Area and the Financial Crisis*, was also published by Cambridge University Press.

Rethinking Fiscal Policy after the Crisis

Edited by
ĽUDOVÍT ÓDOR
Council for Budget Responsibility, Slovakia

CAMBRIDGE
UNIVERSITY PRESS

CAMBRIDGE
UNIVERSITY PRESS

University Printing House, Cambridge CB2 8BS, United Kingdom

One Liberty Plaza, 20th Floor, New York, NY 10006, USA

477 Williamstown Road, Port Melbourne, VIC 3207, Australia

314-321, 3rd Floor, Plot 3, Splendor Forum, Jasola District Centre, New Delhi - 110025, India

79 Anson Road, #06-04/06, Singapore 079906

Cambridge University Press is part of the University of Cambridge.

It furthers the University's mission by disseminating knowledge in the pursuit of education, learning and research at the highest international levels of excellence.

www.cambridge.org
Information on this title: www.cambridge.org/9781316613689
DOI: 10.1017/9781316675861

First published 2017
First paperback edition 2019

A catalogue record for this publication is available from the British Library

Library of Congress Cataloging in Publication data
Names: Ódor, Ľudovít, editor.
Title: Rethinking fiscal policy after the crisis / Ľudovít Ódor, Council for Budget Responsibility, Slovakia.
Description: New York : Cambridge University Press, [2017] | Includes bibliographical references and index.
Identifiers: LCCN 2016050853 | ISBN 9781107160583 (hardback : alk. paper)
Subjects: LCSH: Monetary policy. | Global Financial Crisis, 2008-2009. | Fiscal policy. | Financial institutions–Management.
Classification: LCC HG230.3 .R48 2017 | DDC 339.5/2–dc23 LC record available at https://lccn.loc.gov/2016050853

ISBN   978-1-107-16058-3 Hardback
ISBN   978-1-316-61368-9 Paperback

Contents

Figures

Tables

Boxes

Contributors

Roel W.M.J. Beetsma, *University of Amsterdam*

Agustín S. Bénétrix, *Trinity College*

Michael Bordo, *Rutgers University and NBER*

Claudio Borio, *BIS*

Fabrizio Coricelli, *Paris School of Economics and CEPR*

Boris Cournéde, *OECD*

Xavier Debrun, *International Monetary Fund*

Falilou Fall, *OECD*

Carlo Favero, *Bocconi University and CEPR*

Riccardo Fiorito, *University of Siena*

John Fitzgerald, *Trinity College*

Jerry R. Green, *Harvard Business School*

Juan Carlos Hatchondo, *Indiana University*

Harold James, *Princeton University*

Madina Karamysheva, *Bocconi University*

Chrsitian Kastrop, *OECD*

Gábor P. Kiss, *Magyar Nemzeti Bank*

Richard C. Koo, *Nomura Research Institute*

George Kopits, *Woodrow Wilson International Center for Scholars*

Laurence J. Kotlikoff, *Boston University*

Philip R. Lane, *Trinity College and Central Bank of Ireland*

Eric M. Leeper, *Indiana University and NBER*

Marco Lombardi, *BIS*

Leonardo Martinez, *International Monetary Fund*

Francesco Molteni, *European University Institute, Florence*

Annabelle Mourougane, *OECD*

Ľudovít Ódor, *Council for Budget Responsibility and CEU*

Athanasios Orphanides, *MIT Sloan School of Management*

Klaus Schmidt-Hebbel, *Catholic University of Chile*

Raimundo Soto, *Catholic University of Chile*

Charles Wyplosz, *The Graduate Institute, Geneva*

Fabrizio Zampolli, *BIS*

Acknowledgements

This volume is based on the 'Rethinking Fiscal Policy after the Crisis' conference organised by the Slovak Council for Budget Responsibility in Bratislava on 10–11 September 2015. Most of the chapters were presented and discussed at the conference. The book greatly benefited from contributions by the following discussants and session chairs: Balázs Égert, Daniele Franco, Július Horváth, Michal Horváth, Lucio Pench, Ivan Šramko and Michael R. Wickens.

1 | Introduction and Overview

ĽUDOVÍT ÓDOR

Serious discussion of fiscal policy has almost disappeared. A reading of the literature on macroeconomic theory and policy would lead you to believe that there is only one policy goal – the control of inflation – and that task is assigned to monetary policy. Fiscal policy is either impossible or undesirable or both.

Robert M. Solow (2002), p. 1

The financial crisis and its global repercussions came as a wake-up call for macroeconomists and policymakers all over the developed world. According to the pre-crisis consensus, it could not happen. After all, we knew how to conduct macroeconomic policy, and the Great Moderation was proof that we had mastered our job relatively well. We were wrong. Eight years after the fall of Lehman Brothers, the developed world is still struggling with lacklustre growth and rising public indebtedness poses serious questions over fiscal sustainability in many countries. Moreover, ageing societies represent a substantial headwind for both growth performance and debt reduction policies. In this environment, we should think hard about how to adjust our understanding of the economy and upgrade the frameworks we use to analyse macroeconomic policies.

The main goal of this book is to contribute to this debate by rethinking several aspects of fiscal policy. In particular, it is argued that significant improvements in the institutional set-up and analytical toolkit of fiscal policy are indispensable to avoid policy mistakes in the future.

1 Fiscal Policy in the Backseat

The two decades prior to the crisis were all about monetary policy. There was a widespread belief that so long as inflation was stable, actual output could not be too far away from its potential ('divine coincidence'). In other words, one primary target (low inflation) and one instrument (short-term interest rate) were sufficient for stabilization purposes. And the profession believed that 'the quiet revolution' (Blinder, 2004a) in central banking made it possible to pursue close-to-optimal policies. The world achieved consensus on monetary policy (Goodfriend, 2007). Advances in macroeconomic modelling and the Volcker disinflation enabled convergence between monetary theory and actual policymaking. Flexible inflation targeting pursued by independent central banks has become the state-of-the-art monetary policy framework. Transparency gradually replaced secrecy and simple rules as guideposts defeated complete discretion.

Fiscal policy played a secondary role in the literature on macroeconomic stabilization. As Blanchard et al. (2010) describe, if monetary policy could maintain a stable output gap, there was little reason to use another instrument. Moreover, as the quote by Solow at the beginning of this chapter illustrates, there was widespread scepticism about the use of fiscal policy for macroeconomic stabilization. First, forward-looking models with rational expectations had Ricardian equivalence as their built-in feature and thus questioned the effectiveness of fiscal policy for stabilization purposes. Second, the political economy literature (Drazen, 2000) pointed out that politicians have many motives other than welfare maximization for the median voter. Third, the recognition of long implementation lags made fiscal policy impractical as a stabilization tool in normal business cycles. In the light of these developments, the major policy recommendation was to stay away from discretionary fiscal policy and let automatic stabilizers do their job (together with monetary policy). Blinder (2004b) made an attempt to issue at least a warning by stating that 'there are circumstances under which the lessons of Lord Keynes are best not forgotten'; however, he himself was cautious in arguing against the consensus (Blinder presented the 'case against the case against' and not 'the case for' discretionary fiscal policy).

The almost unlimited belief in the power of monetary policy to stabilize output had an unfortunate consequence, namely that fiscal policy was left under less scrutiny by the financial markets and the profession in general. Although secular upward trends in debt levels hinted in the direction of a serious deficit bias, attempts to pursue counter-cyclical policies failed, especially in good times.

1.1 Wake-Up Call

The crisis has brought fiscal policy back to the front pages of newspapers for several reasons. First and most importantly, the financial crisis and the subsequent deep recession pushed standard monetary policy to its limits on both sides of the Atlantic. Central banks, after hitting the zero lower bound on interest rates, had to come up with an alphabet soup of unconventional policy measures to avoid the collapse of economic activity. Many had doubts as to whether this would be sufficient, so policymakers had little choice but to turn to fiscal policy.

Second, many advanced countries had no adequate fiscal space to absorb the consequences of the Great Recession without serious financing problems. The euro-area countries in particular found themselves suddenly in the middle of a sovereign debt crisis. The need to bail out the financial sector and massive losses of revenues (no longer supported by financial boom) rapidly escalated debt levels, forcing several countries to seek international financial assistance. Moreover, the euro area also lacked some important institutional aspects to deal with the crisis, most notably resolution schemes and the lender-of-last-resort functions.

Third, neither the actual fiscal positions nor academic policy advice were prepared for the crisis. Limited understanding of the effects of fiscal policy, neglect of monetary-fiscal-financial interactions or ignorance of market expectations often led to policy advice by international organizations and prominent economists that was based more on conventional wisdom than on sound analysis.

1.2 Can We Do Better?

Despite the recent difficulties with monetary policy, there remains a striking gap between the ways in which monetary and fiscal policies are conducted. As Ľudovít Ódor and Gábor P. Kiss (Chapter 7) document, independent central banks, inflation targets, transparent communication of objectives and policy and monetary research all contributed to a much better understanding and execution of monetary policy. On the other hand, fiscal policy still relies on old-fashioned models, lacks clear objectives and is conducted in a very opaque environment. The huge gap between monetary and fiscal policy is understandable to some extent. Fiscal policy cannot be delegated to technocrats in its entirety ('no taxation without representation') because of the large distributional impacts which lie at the core of the political process.

On the other hand, a substantial part of the difference in the treatment of monetary and fiscal policy is not justified (here, we focus only on macroeconomic aspects of fiscal policy). One line of criticism relates to the institutional set-up. In order to achieve fiscal discipline, Wyplosz (2005) explicitly argues in favour of adopting a similar approach to inflation targeting, used by central banks to reach monetary discipline. Another strand of criticism targets the analytical approaches used in fiscal policy advice. Leeper (2010) talks about monetary science and fiscal alchemy, although in Chapter 2 of this volume he admits that fiscal analysis is intrinsically hard – 'darned hard'.

To sum up, we can and should do much better in institutional and analytical aspects of fiscal policy. This book brings fresh ideas to both areas. Part I sets the stage by describing the frontiers of fiscal policy. Part II focuses on institutional aspects of fiscal policy both in general terms and in the euro area in particular, where fiscal issues seem to be the most serious ones. Part III offers the reader interesting thoughts on new analytical perspectives in fiscal policy. Part IV is about the comeback of discretionary fiscal policy.

2 Frontiers of Fiscal Policy

Much of the existing fiscal analysis is less helpful than it could be. At least, this is a conclusion presented by Eric M. Leeper in Chapter 2. Although he displays a lot of sympathy with fiscal analysts in recognizing that fiscal research is harder than monetary research, he nevertheless sees huge room for improvement in the former. After colourfully illustrating fiscal 'alchemy' through examples from economic headlines, he constructively sets up a fiscal research agenda to improve upon current practices. Several ingredients seem to be essential for fiscal analysis to lose the 'alchemy' label and join monetary policy in the 'science' camp. The most important items on Leeper's to-do list are the following. First, we need a modelling framework which combines all important aspects of fiscal policy into one coherent analytical framework. Joint analysis of fiscal policy, monetary policy and financial stability, explicit treatment of the stabilization-versus-sustainability trade-off and political economy considerations are all elements without which a decent understanding of fiscal trends is simply not possible. Second, contrary to the current practice, fiscal policy needs to incorporate much more heterogeneity. Fiscal policy requires modelling many different tax and expenditure instruments and their impacts on a wide variety of economic agents. It also highlights the importance of including demographic structure and trends in policy analysis. Third, in most macroeconomic models, government debt serves merely as a vehicle for private saving and tax smoothing. In reality, debt might perform many additional roles: liquidity, collateral or maturity transformation. Ignoring these other purposes might substantially decrease the policy relevance of fiscal analysis.

The delegation of monetary policy to independent technocrats was possible mainly because of the limited distributional impacts of monetary policy over normal business cycles. This is, however, no longer true for the large-scale asset purchases which central banks are conducting under the banner of unconventional monetary policy. As Athanasios Orphanides argues in Chapter 3, at the zero lower bound on interest rates, some central bank balance-sheet policies may be effectively equivalent to fiscal operations. During the crisis, central banks provided preferential treatment to some entities, but not to others. Orphanides points out that the Federal Reserve used its 'fiscal' discretionary power to support some sectors of the economy (construction) and bailed out some firms, but not others. The European Central Bank proved to be an effective central bank during the crisis, but only for some members of the euro area. Orphanides' chapter shows how thin the line between monetary and fiscal policy is in crisis times. He understands the criticism both central banks received from politicians during the crisis, and advocates the setting of clear ex ante rules and boundaries for crisis management in order to maintain the independence which central banks need for their effective action. Otherwise, as Goodhart (2010) notes, 'the idea of the Central Bank as an independent institution will be put aside'.

3 Better Institutions for Better Policies

The three decades of a secular upward trend in government debt in OECD countries prior to the crisis discredited pure discretion in fiscal policy and introduced the term 'deficit bias' to the fiscal literature. One of the most important questions in practice was how to design effective constraints for fiscal policy action. The first line of attack came in the form of fiscal rules, usually embedded in fiscal responsibility laws or treaties. As Wyplosz (2005, p. 64) highlights, the record is not satisfactory: 'rules are either too lax or too tight and then ignored.' To address the weaknesses of rule-based frameworks, many countries started to complement fiscal rules with independent fiscal institutions to allow for discretion in the short run, while preserving sustainability in the long run.

3.1 Fiscal Frameworks in General

Chapter 4 looks at fiscal rules adopted around the world. Klaus Schmidt-Hebbel and Raimundo Soto identify conditions under which some countries decided to adopt constraints on their fiscal policies in the form of numerical fiscal rules. They define six categories of potential determinants: political and institutional variables, monetary regimes, degree of financial development, level of economic activity, costs of fiscal rules and fiscal performance indicators. The results are the following. Institutional and political conditions contribute significantly to the likelihood of having a fiscal rule in place. From monetary policy regimes, inflation targeting helps explain the presence of rules. This is understandable, since fiscal dominance might seriously undermine the effectiveness of reaching inflation targets. Both financial and overall economic development increase the likelihood of having a rule. On the other hand, costs associated with fiscal rules – as measured by the volatility of government revenues – have the opposite effect. Finally, better fiscal conditions contribute significantly to having a national fiscal rule in place. This raises the delicate question of reverse causality. It may well be that only countries with good fiscal performance adopt fiscal rules.

In Chapter 5, Roel W. M. J. Beetsma and Xavier Debrun introduce an important channel through which fiscal councils might operate (in addition to easing trade-offs associated with fiscal rules). Asymmetric information between voters and elected policymakers is at the heart of their model. Because of a lack of information, voters find it difficult to distinguish between bad luck and bad policy and between good luck and good policy. If this is the case, society might benefit from the presence of an independent fiscal institution tasked with minimizing the noise surrounding signals of competence of the incumbent government. Importantly, the fiscal council's positive value added in taming the deficit bias applies regardless of the type of government (competent or not). The second part of the chapter looks at the important preconditions which the existing fiscal councils should have in place in order to effectively reduce the noise in signals of competence. The conclusion is encouraging. Using the comprehensive IMF dataset on fiscal councils, Beetsma and Debrun show that strong majority of fiscal councils exhibit features – political independence and functions – that allow them to clarify existing signals about fiscal policy.

3.2 Fiscal Discipline in the Euro Area

No current monetary union arrangement illustrates the importance of ensuring fiscal discipline better than the euro area. Its management of the crisis, one could argue, also leaves much to be desired. The natural question is: what should be done to increase the European single currency's resilience to future crises? Economists might have somewhat different views on the nature of the optimal medicine.

Some would agree that a fully fledged fiscal union (something like the United States of Europe) would, at least in theory, go a long way towards solving most of the problems. In the current political environment, however, only a small minority of member states would be willing to transfer more sovereignty to Brussels. If the first-best solution is unattainable, is the euro project doomed to failure, or are there other options to ensure fiscal discipline? In Chapter 6, Charles Wyplosz argues that the fiscal policy problem in the euro area can be solved without further integration. In his view, compulsory adoption of effective fiscal discipline frameworks by member countries should replace the several-times-discredited Stability and Growth Pact. At the national level, these frameworks should combine intelligent fiscal rules and independent fiscal councils apt at combining rule and discretion. At the collective level, the implementation of national frameworks should be monitored by an independent European fiscal council vested with the power to bring cases to the European Court of Justice. The no bail-out clause should also be restored to eliminate moral hazard. In addition, Wyplosz argues that legacy debts should be significantly reduced in order to allow countries to pursue counter-cyclical fiscal policies.

In Chapter 7, Ľudovít Ódor and Gábor P. Kiss also advocate a decentralized and depoliticized fiscal framework in the euro area. The current European framework is plagued by extreme complexity, inconsistency between the various elements and non-existent enforcement. Paradoxically, there are so many rules that the final verdict is often a discretionary decision of the Council. Ódor and P. Kiss call for a clear separation of accountability between the Union and the national level. The first line of defence against irresponsible fiscal policy behaviour should be at the local level, using better indicators, home-grown fiscal rules and fiscal councils. Their design should, however, meet commonly agreed minimum standards. Under this model, if a member state operates with no significant fiscal risks, no yearly intervention from the Union level is necessary. At the European level, the European Commission and an independent euro-area fiscal watchdog should ensure compliance with minimum standards, focus on countries breaching European limits (represented by a single fiscal rule) and avoid pro-cyclicality at the Union level. A decentralized framework is thus theoretically sounder and practically more enforceable than the current web of complicated rules and procedures. Ódor and P. Kiss also note that completing the banking union and creating ex ante sovereign resolution schemes are necessary pre-conditions for any successful reform of the European fiscal architecture.

In Chapter 8, Michael Bordo and Harold James also agree that the euro area is still far away from a new political equilibrium that shifts towards greater fiscal federalism. In contrast to the minimalistic approach advocated by Wyplosz, Bordo and James propose a series of measures which amount to 'partial fiscalization'. Their rationale is quite simple, and based on the historical analogy between the US and EU: in order to achieve further integration, voters should first see the value added of a common action. Europe should focus on win–win situations which would increase cross-border ties and thus represent a 'strong cement to the union'. These partial fiscalizations might come in the form of reaping efficiency gains from a collective action or as insurance mechanisms at the Union level. Bordo and James provide a number of examples, among which the most prominent are banking union, capital markets union, common social security, energy union or, for example, common defence policy. Using the trade negotiations analogy they advocate for a 'big bang' strategy, where individual measures are not implemented sequentially, but rather as a comprehensive reform package.

There is a widespread consensus that the severity of the euro-area debt crisis was amplified by the rather hesitant crisis management of the authorities. Their 'too little, too late' behaviour was criticized extensively in the media. With the benefit of hindsight, George Kopits, in Chapter 9, looks at the effectiveness of the steps euro-area officials took before and during the crisis and presents the most important lessons for future crisis prevention and management. Kopits identifies the two main mistakes prior to the crisis in the failure of the peer pressure mechanism to guarantee the enforcement of fiscal rules and in the ECB's uniform treatment of government bonds as (riskless) collateral. After the crisis hit, several member states suffered from a sudden stop in financial markets. In these cases, crisis management has to focus on three issues: access to liquidity or financing renewal, macro-fiscal adjustment and structural measures. The authorities delivered satisfactory action in none of these areas. One can question the initial strong resistance to debt restructuring, the optimistic design of adjustment packages and the insufficient implementation of structural reforms. According to Kopits, some of the lessons have already been internalized. Stronger macroeconomic governance and more centralized financial sectors are prime examples. On the other hand, modifications to the fiscal framework have been rather modest.

4 New Analytical Perspectives

Even the most carefully designed fiscal frameworks and best-intended policy advice have little value added if we use the wrong metrics to measure fiscal performance. We need to know the diagnosis before recommending a cure. In Chapter 2, Eric M. Leeper sketches out a future research agenda for fiscal policy in general terms. According to Leeper, fiscal analysis might substantially benefit from calculating 'fiscal limit' distributions by integrating economic and political economy considerations. In Part III of this book we look at other promising analytical tools and concepts. We have at least three strong candidates for inclusion in the emerging post-crisis consensus on the essential ingredients of a fiscal toolbox: the balance sheet perspective, the relevance of financial cycles to fiscal cycles and the importance of sovereign default models.

4.1 Balance Sheet Analysis

It is easy to find in the literature highly critical articles, dating back as far as thirty years, on the deficiencies of the commonly used fiscal measures. Buiter (1983) advocated assembling comprehensive public sector balance sheets (including the central bank and the present value of future taxes and entitlements) in order to get a better understanding of fiscal trends. Kotlikoff (1986) pointed out that judging fiscal policy by government deficit figures only is a linguistic exercise and has nothing to do with economics.

'Statistics are like bikinis. What they reveal is suggestive, but what they conceal is vital.'[1] This quote attributed to Aaron Levenstein seems to be true also for public accounts. Fiscal gimmickry and creative accounting are the norm rather than the exception in many countries. Therefore, it is essential to look behind the official accounting numbers. In Chapter 7, Ódor and P. Kiss argue that only a comprehensive (inter-temporal) analysis of stock, flow and cash-flow data enables analysts to achieve more complete understanding of fiscal developments and to escape Goodhart's famous law.[2]

In Chapter 10, Jerry R. Green and Laurence J. Kotlikoff demonstrate that standard fiscal measures, including the deficit, taxes and transfer payments, are economically ill defined. Similarly, just as, a century ago, measures of time and distance were found to depend on one's reference point, many accounting exercises in fiscal policy have no absolute meaning and can be understood only in relation to other variables. In other words, they lack fundamental economic content and should be treated as mere labels. According to Green and Kotlikoff, economic theory provides a clear guide as to which measures are not invariant to the choice of the fiscal language. The infinite-horizon fiscal gap and generational accounting are the only options consistent with the fundamental inter-temporal budget constraint of the government. They present estimates of fiscal gaps for a number of advanced countries and show the difference in the ranking of countries based on this measure compared to traditional measures of deficit and debt. It is important to note that the infinite-horizon fiscal gap and the inter-temporal net worth of the government are different expressions of the same underlying principle, namely, taking into account all future flows in the public sector.

---

[1] www.oxfordreference.com/view/10.1093/acref/9780191804144.001.0001/q-oro-ed3-00016754?result=82&rskey=42Jyhf

[2] Goodhart's law is named after the economist Charles Goodhart. Its most popular formulation is: 'When a measure becomes a target, it ceases to be a good measure.'

The importance of comprehensive balance sheets or fiscal gaps is not just an academic debate completely detached from real policymaking. As John Fitzgerald and Philip R. Lane show in Chapter 11, governments often manage the public balance sheet during episodes of financial distress. Therefore, the stock of gross public debt is not a good measure of fiscal sustainability. Traditional analyses should be replaced by a more complete understanding of the public balance sheet. Fitzgerald and Lane focus on the role which asset acquisitions, liquidity management, debt management and central bank balance sheets might play in determining the 'true' fiscal health of the government. After analysing the case of Ireland, they offer a number of interesting lessons: the role cash reserves might play in times of rollover crises, the importance of a sufficiently diversified sovereign portfolio in the banking sector, the need to integrate central bank balance sheets into fiscal accounts and, for example, the potential benefits state-contingent debt securities might offer.

4.2 Fiscal Consequences of Financial Cycles

One of the most important lessons from the Great Recession is that there is a close two-way link between the health of the financial system and the fiscal position of the sovereign. Financial cycles have important fiscal consequences, and these were grossly underestimated prior to the crisis.[3] Booming credit and asset markets might generate a substantial amount of extra revenue and thus create an illusion that fiscal positions are fundamentally sound. Since financial cycles are usually much longer than business cycles, adjusting headline balances to the latter might not be sufficient to uncover the 'true' state of public finances. Prime examples are Ireland and Spain. Both countries had debt-to-GDP ratios around 30 percent in 2007 and cyclically adjusted net lending in surplus or close to zero.[4] In 2014, the debt figures in both cases were close to 100 percent of GDP. And as Fitzgerald and Lane show in Chapter 11, the dramatic increase in debt can be only partially

---

[3] Financial cycles are usually measured using asset price growth, credit growth, changes to leverage ratios (Geanakoplos, 2009) or movements in the debt service burden (Juselius and Drehmann, 2015).
[4] According to the EC Autumn 2008 Forecast, Ireland had cyclically adjusted net lending of −0.9 percent of GDP in 2007, while Spain had a surplus of 2 percent of GDP.

explained by the bank bail-out package (approximately one third). The rest has to do with cumulative deficits over the crisis years. Financial cycles acted as a distorting mirror in pre-crisis years, shrank the deficit significantly and confounded conventional methods when calculating the underlying fiscal balance.

In Chapter 12, Agustín S. Bénétrix and Philip R. Lane provide econometric evidence for the significance of financial cycles to budget balances over and above the output cycle. They approximate financial cycles by net capital flows (as captured by current account balances) and domestic credit creation. Bénétrix and Lane find empirical evidence that external imbalances are fiscally destabilizing and that credit booms are associated with improvements in the government fiscal balance in the short run. Therefore, it may be the case that the fiscal impact of the financial cycle should be incorporated into the design of numerical fiscal rules and the monitoring role of independent fiscal councils.

Chapter 13 nicely complements the empirical findings in Chapter 12. Claudio Borio, Marco Lombardi and Fabrizio Zampolli ask two additional questions. First, what are the channels by which financial cycles affect fiscal variables? Here, the authors focus separately on the damage financial busts can cause and the 'flattering effect' of financial booms. The former usually has the following manifestations: bail-out costs, output and employment collapse with long-term consequences, compositional effects, exchange rate movements or, for example, interest rate effects. On the other hand, financial booms sap productivity as they occur, misallocate resources and often lead to currency appreciation. The second question Borio et al. ask is how fiscal positions can be adjusted in order to take into account the effects of financial cycles. Building on previous work, they propose a simple filter to calculate 'finance-neutral' output gaps. One of the most promising features of their method is robustness. Compared to traditional filtering techniques, the finance-neutral output gap is estimated for the United States with greater precision and much better real-time properties.

4.3 *Sovereign Default Models*

Government bond risk premia have returned to the radar screens of policymakers in advanced countries, especially in Europe. The substantial increase in debt levels without the possibility of inflating debt away pushed a number of countries in the euro area to the brink of sovereign default. Greece, Portugal and Ireland had to seek international assistance to refinance their debt. It is not surprising that analysing probabilities of default and sovereign risk premia became a central issue in both the academic and policymaking circles. Models of sovereign default can be very helpful in understanding the mechanisms behind the risk premia movements. In contrast to conventional sustainability analysis, models of sovereign default feature endogenous sovereign spreads, a welfare criterion and endogenous borrowing policies. As Hatchondo et al. (2015) show, these models might play an important role also in the design of fiscal rules. Without a fiscal rule, the government cannot lower the level of sovereign risk by committing to lower levels of future debt issuances. Fiscal rules allow the government to solve the debt dilution problem and thus generate welfare.

Juan Carlos Hatchondo and Leonardo Martinez devote one section of Chapter 14 to an explanation of the usefulness of sovereign default models with long-term debt for policy analysis. In addition to that, they look at the specific problem of calibrating the cost of default in these models. They demonstrate how this cost can be calibrated to match average levels of sovereign debt and spread in the data. Hatchondo and Martinez also show that with one-period debt, it is impossible to match real-world levels of debts and spreads. This underscores the importance of modelling long-term debt, and thus the necessity to face the debt dilution problem.

5 The Comeback of Discretionary Fiscal Policy

The Great Recession was long and severe enough in many countries in order to assuage some of the objections against discretionary fiscal policy in normal times (such as long implementation lags). In addition to that, monetary policies hit the effective zero lower bound and the calls to use fiscal policy to stimulate the economy intensified. Moreover, unconventional monetary policy measures were in some cases effectively equivalent to discretionary fiscal policy (Chapter 3). However, not all countries were fortunate enough to enter the 'to stimulate or not' debate. Many countries with rising debt and sovereign risk premia had no other option but to put the need for counter-cyclical policies on hold for a while and had to present consolidation packages (either to calm markets down or satisfy international creditors). In Part IV of the book we look at discretionary fiscal policy from both the stimulation and consolidation points of view.

5.1 *Fiscal Multipliers*

When considering discretionary fiscal action, the first obvious question is: what are the macroeconomic effects of a discretionary fiscal policy? Here we come to the hotly debated topic of fiscal multipliers. When measured by the criterion expressed by Leeper (2010), fiscal policy comes closer to shedding its 'alchemy' label, since the simple question 'What is the fiscal multiplier?' is asked less frequently. The profession slowly moves towards a new consensus that it is meaningless to ask this question without specifying other details of the policy experiment. Multipliers depend on the choice of instrument, expected sources and timing of future fiscal financing, agent's expectations, monetary policy behaviour or, for example, actual economic conditions. There is no such thing as a unique fiscal multiplier independent of the actual economic and policy context.

There are two significant strands of the literature on fiscal multipliers. The first has its roots in fully specified dynamic optimizing models. The second focuses more on empirical evidence. It was not extraordinary in the past for model-based approaches to come to different conclusions on the size of multipliers using the same datasets. Leeper et al. (2015) decided to clear up this 'morass' by showing how model specification affects the size of multipliers *before* confronting the data. The prevailing monetary-fiscal regime, sources of fiscal financing or, for example, the degree of complementarity of government spending to private consumption all play an important role in determining multipliers.

In Chapter 15, Carlo Favero and Madina Karamysheva summarize the second strand of the literature, namely, the empirical approaches to calculating multipliers. They ask the same question that Leeper et al. asked in the case of model-based estimates of multipliers: what is behind the vast heterogeneity of estimates? To find an answer, they build a general, all-encompassing dynamic model based on fiscal stabilization plans. Although the model does not have a sufficient number of degrees of freedom to be estimated, it is nevertheless very helpful in understanding the identification strategies employed by different researchers. Almost all the specifications considered in the empirical literature so far are special cases of the general model developed by Favero and Karamysheva. In other words, the heterogeneity of results originates in the different choice of parameters and identification restrictions used by researchers to estimate fiscal multipliers.

5.2 Discretionary Fiscal Policy

No two recessions are alike. There is plenty of evidence in the literature that recessions after financial crises tend to be longer and deeper (e.g. Reinhart et al., 2012). It is hard for the economy to get back on track until the private sector has finished the process of deleveraging (getting rid of debt). Richard C. Koo, who coined the term 'balance sheet recession', argues in Chapter 16 that conventional economic wisdom breaks down in this type of slowdown. When private sector borrowers are underwater, the necessary condition for monetary policy to work is violated. Since households and firms focus on debt minimizing and thus are not ready to borrow even at zero interest rates, they are not capable of responding to interest rate movements.

Koo argues that standard macroeconomic textbooks take for granted the existence of borrowers. Therefore, we have no recipes for cases in which the main constraint on the economy is not the lack of lenders, but the absence of borrowers. This can happen for two reasons: if businesses are not able to find attractive investment opportunities or if borrowers are absent because of balance sheet problems. According to Koo, in the former case the role of the government is to adopt supply-side measures, while in the latter case, only sustained and sufficiently large fiscal stimulus can stabilize the economy. The size of private sector savings should be counterbalanced by an equal amount of government borrowing, otherwise the economy will struggle under the pressure of un-invested savings.

It is important to understand that – according to Koo – there is no reason to worry about financing the issuance of new sovereign debt in balance sheet recessions, since in the absence of private borrowers the financial sector will be ready to buy government bonds. The euro area is an exception, since domestic fund managers can easily buy bonds of other member states without facing exchange rate risk. Therefore, Koo proposes a mechanism (preferential risk weights) to force financial institutions to hold their own government bonds. This is in stark contrast with the current consensus that in order to eliminate the 'diabolic loop' between financial and sovereign risk, the home bias should be mitigated in Europe.

Although the exact timing of fiscal consolidation may be subject to debate, there is a relatively general consensus that 'for a long time to come, one of the priorities of macroeconomic policy will be slowly but steadily return debt to less dangerous levels, to move away from the dark corners' (Blanchard, 2014, p. 30). In Chapter 17, Christian Kastrop, Boris Cournéde, Falilou Fall and Annabelle Mourougane discuss fiscal consolidation strategies. They show the importance of the general political–economic context for the design of successful consolidation plans. Without taking into account the main trade-offs that politicians are facing, there is little hope of achieving sustainable adjustments. Kastrop et al. provide a ranking of potential consolidation instruments based on a qualitative assessment of their effects on various policy objectives: short-term growth, long-term prosperity and equity. In general, the most appropriate consolidation packages involve cutting subsidies and reducing pension outlays while increasing inheritance, capital gains and other property taxes. The good news is that many OECD countries have significant scope to meet fiscal challenges without the necessity to use the most harmful instruments (based on the three above-mentioned criteria): spending cuts in the area of education, health care and family policies or hiking social security contributions.

Kastrop et al. raise two other very important issues. First, it is not necessary to increase tax rates or abolish spending programmes if countries are able to harvest efficiency gains. Improving the quality of public finances should therefore be high on the agenda of every government. There is significant scope to enhance the delivery of essential public services, such as health care and education, while saving resources. On the tax side, more effective tax collection and base broadening can mitigate the negative growth impact of consolidations. Second, Kastrop et al. advocate a rule-based framework to guide fiscal consolidation strategies. They propose the following ingredients: prudent debt targets coupled with a budget balance rule over the medium run, complemented by an expenditure rule as an operational target (a similar proposal for Central European countries was made in Ódor and P. Kiss, 2011).

Advocates of discretionary policies usually assume that there is enough flexibility on the expenditure side of the budget and a sufficient number of worthwhile projects on the waiting list available for implementation. In his book *Dead Men Ruling*, Steuerle (2014) warns that this assumption might not always be valid. There is a clear declining trend in the non-mandatory part of the budget in the United States. In other words, current budgets are increasingly affected by past decisions and the room for manoeuvre for current politicians is extremely limited. In Chapter 18, Fabrizio Coricelli, Riccardo Fiorito and Francesco Molteni use a new measure of discretionary expenditures. They distinguish discretionary from non-discretionary spending by evaluating the persistence and volatility of expenditure components. Clearly, discretionary expenditures should be less persistent and more volatile than mandatory spending. By using this metric, the authors show that only about one third of total expenditure is ready to be used for the purposes of counter-cyclical discretionary fiscal policy in OECD countries. Coricelli et al. also point to the puzzling fact that there has been little use of discretionary expenditures to counteract the Great Recession, especially in Europe.

6 Conclusions

Every crisis is an opportunity to learn something new. Although the tuition cost was too high this time around and the profession's reputation suffered, one positive side-effect of the Great Recession is that serious fiscal policy analysis is now better integrated into macroeconomic research and policymaking. This book is proof that despite the still large gap between the conduct of monetary and fiscal policy, the latter has started to catch up quickly both in analytical and institutional terms.

At the end of this résumé, let me offer a list of seven elements I personally see as an integral part of the emerging new consensus on the macroeconomic aspects of fiscal policy: (1) understanding the consequences of monetary-fiscal interactions is key to the design of macroeconomic policies; (2) models without heterogeneity of agents and fiscal instruments are of limited use; (3) the long-term view, including contingent liabilities and proper risk assessment, is important; (4) synergies between home-grown fiscal rules and fiscal institutions might be more effective in combating the deficit bias; (5) fiscal rules should be smart in combining a long-term anchor (debt target) and short-term flexibility (expenditure rules); (6) political economy considerations should be an important part of any policy analysis and (7) discretionary fiscal policy should be brought back onto the radar screen of analysts and policymakers, either because of long recessions or due to consolidation needs to create adequate fiscal space in the long run.

Bibliography

Blanchard, O. (2014). Where danger lurks. *Finance & Development*, **51** (3), 30.

Blanchard, O., Dell'Ariccia, G. and Mauro, P. (2010). *Rethinking Macroeconomic Policy*. IMF Staff Position Note, 12 February 2010.

Blinder, Alan S. (2004a). *The Quiet Revolution: Central Banking Goes Modern*. New Haven, CT: Yale University Press.

(2004b). *The Case against the Case against Discretionary Fiscal Policy*. CEPS Working Paper No. 100, June 2004.

Buiter, Willem H. (1983). Measurement of the public sector deficit and its implications for policy evaluation and design. *Staff Papers, IMF*, Vol. 30, 306–49.

Drazen, A. (2010). *Political Economy in Macroeconomics*. Princeton: Princeton University Press.

Geanakoplos, J. (2009). *The Leverage Cycle*. Cowles Foundation Discussion Paper No. 1715.

Goodfriend, M. (2007). How the world achieved consensus on monetary policy. *Journal of Economic Perspectives*, **21**(4), 47–68.

Goodhart, C. A. E. (2010). *The Changing Role of Central Banks*. BIS Working Papers, No. 326, November 2010.

Hatchondo, J. C., Martinez, L. and Roch, F. (2015). *Fiscal Rules and the Sovereign Default Premium*. CAEPR Working Paper No. 010–2015.

Juselius, M. and Drehmann, M. (2015). *Leverage Dynamics and the Real Burden of Debt*. BIS Working Paper No. 501.

Kotlikoff, Laurence J. (1986). Deficit delusion. *The Public Interest*, **84**, 53–65.

Leeper, Eric M. (2010). Monetary science, fiscal alchemy. Proceedings – Economic Policy Symposium – Jackson Hole, Federal Reserve Bank of Kansas City, pp. 361–434.

Leeper, Eric M., Traum, N. and Walker, T. B. (2015). *Clearing Up the Fiscal Multiplier Morass: Prior and Posterior Analysis*. NBER Working Paper No. 21433.

Ódor, L. and Kiss, G. P. (2011). *The Exception Proves the Rule? Fiscal Rules in the Visegrád Countries*. MNB Bulletin, June 2011.

Reinhart, Carmen M., Reinhart, Vincent R. and Rogoff, Kenneth S. (2012). Public debt overhangs: advanced-economy episodes since 1800. *Journal of Economic Perspectives*, **26**(3), 69–86.

Solow, Robert M. (2002). *Is Fiscal Policy Possible? Is It Desirable?* Presidential address to the XIII World Congress of the International Economic Association, Lisbon, September.

Steuerle, C. E. (2014). *Dead Men Ruling: How to Restore Fiscal Freedom and Rescue Our Future*. New York: The Century Foundation Press.

Wyplosz, C. (2005). Fiscal policy: institutions versus rules. *National Institute Economic Review*, **191**: 64–78.

PART I

Frontiers of Fiscal Policy

2 | *Fiscal Analysis Is Darned Hard*

ERIC M. LEEPER

1 Introduction

After decades of neglect, the global financial crisis and recession of 2008 brought fiscal policy analysis to the forefront of researchers' and policymakers' minds.[1] The reasons are severalfold. First, the crisis rapidly drove monetary policy interest rates down close to their lower bound, which led central banks to undertake large-scale asset purchases as a means to further stimulate economies. Some aspects of those purchases bore striking resemblances to fiscal actions. And with central banks out of interest rate ammunition, fiscal authorities felt more pressure to adopt stimulative policies. Second, many countries that did adopt large fiscal expansions, within only a few years, reversed course to implement equally large fiscal consolidations. Third, beginning in 2010 and extending to the present day, several European countries developed severe sovereign debt troubles whose consequences were felt throughout Europe.

These dramatic fiscal developments led researchers and policymakers alike to realize how little we know about the macroeconomic effects of fiscal actions – a realization that is producing large and growing literatures on nearly every aspect of fiscal policy. Euro-area countries, which have been most buffeted by go-and-stop fiscal policies and sovereign debt crises, have been at the vanguard of reforming fiscal institutions in the hope of delivering better analysis and policy decisions.

Each country in the eurozone must now create a fiscal council with a mandate to serve as an independent assessor of fiscal developments. Councils also must have a public voice with which to speak out on public finances. While fiscal councils can elevate, and have elevated, public discourse on fiscal policy, they are a complement to, not a

---

[1] I thank Ľudovít Ódor and Torsten Slok for helpful comments.

substitute for, fresh analytical and empirical work designed to provide inputs into policymaking.

1.1 Seven Reasons

This chapter argues that fiscal analysis is intrinsically hard – darned hard – for a variety of reasons.[2] Many of these reasons either do not apply to or are glossed over by monetary policy analyses to make fiscal analysis *harder* than conventional monetary analysis.[3] To be concrete, I offer seven reasons:

1. Fiscal policy generates confounding dynamics so that fiscal actions affect the economy at both business cycle and much lower frequencies. Most central banks maintain – in both their communications and their formal models – that the Phillips curve is vertical in the long run, so that a type of long-run neutrality obtains. In New Keynesian models, for example, the natural rates of output and employment are independent of monetary policy shocks and monetary policy's choice of rule. This permits monetary analysis to focus on "short" horizons of a few years and on small fluctuations around a steady state that is invariant to monetary policy. Changes in tax rates and government infrastructure and human capital investments can have permanent impacts. Even fiscal financing decisions can have very long-lasting effects (e.g., Leeper, Plante, and Traum, 2010; Uhlig, 2010; Leeper, Traum, and Walker, 2015). When fiscal actions operate at all frequencies, it can be difficult to disentangle their effects in time-series data.

2. Heterogeneity plays a central role in transmitting fiscal changes. Heterogeneity comes in several guises. Economies are populated by many kinds of agents who react differently to fiscal policy changes. Policy instruments themselves are heterogeneous, with many types of government expenditures and taxes. Each instrument is likely to trigger different macroeconomic dynamics, raising the question of

---

[2] To limit the scope of the chapter, I focus primarily on the *macroeconomic* implications of aggregate fiscal choices.

[3] To be clear, "harder" in my context means that some of the simplifying assumptions that render monetary policy analyses tractable cannot plausibly be maintained when studying fiscal policy. Faust (2005) formalizes the concept of "hard" and applies it to monetary policy.

what thought experiment underlies statements about the effects of "increasing taxes" or "cutting spending."

3. It is well understood that fiscal impacts depend on the prevailing monetary-fiscal policy regime and on expectations about future regimes. This argues that fiscal analyses must integrate monetary policy and think through the consequences of beliefs about alternative future policy regimes.[4] It also argues that fiscal analysis that abstracts from monetary policy behavior can yield misleading interpretations and predictions.

4. Fiscal variables are strongly endogenous. Endogeneity arises not only from "automatic stabilizers" built into tax codes and spending programs, but also from macroeconomic stabilization efforts – which create countercyclicality – and political economy considerations – which create procyclicality. With endogenity comes identification problems that have not been satisfactorily resolved in the empirical literature.

5. Fiscal actions carry with them inside lags, between when a new policy is initially proposed and when it is passed, and outside lags, between when the legislation is signed into law and when it is implemented.[5] That institutional structure informs the nature of fiscal information flows. When agents react to fiscal news before the news appears in fiscal variables, conventional econometric methods will deliver misleading inferences. The key to solving this problem lies in nailing down agents' information sets (see Leeper, Walker, and Yang, 2013). Forward guidance of monetary policy can create similar issues, but the problems are less severe because in this respect monetary signals, whose information flows are not institutionally enforced, are noisier than fiscal signals.[6]

6. Supranational policy institutions influence fiscal decisions in many countries. Because those institutions often have significant leverage, their influence is out-sized and frequently decisive. As we witnessed

---

[4] In the eurozone, one might argue that European Central Bank decisions are exogenous with respect to a given country's fiscal choices, which permits some degree of simplification. But reflecting on the ECB's role in the sovereign debt crisis and its large-scale asset purchases, this argument carries some important caveats.

[5] I modify the language in Friedman (1948).

[6] Rondina and Walker's (2014) heterogeneous beliefs, when applied to agents' expectations of fiscal actions, introduce an additional source of confounding dynamics.

in the wake of the 2008 recession, the International Monetary Fund's fiscal advice fluctuated from year to year. And many countries adopted fiscal policies that also fluctuated. It is less common for these institutions to apply pressure on central banks.

7. Fiscal choices are inherently political because they have direct distributional consequences and are taken by elected legislative bodies. Analyses that abstract from political economy considerations, perhaps by solving the conventional Ramsey problem for optimal policy, are likely to have difficulty matching observed behavior. They also tend to offer policy advice that is politically difficult to follow. Monetary policy has been more insulated from political pressures with the institution of independent central banks endowed with specific – and generally narrow – objectives. No analogous narrowing of fiscal objectives appears to be on the horizon.

These factors conspire to make fiscal analysis darned hard. And analyses that do not confront that hardness are often of little help in reaching sound fiscal decisions.

I draw on the experiences of many countries to illustrate the difficulties of fiscal analysis. The experiences include actual analyses, actual fiscal outcomes, and actual fiscal policy advice. I will then sketch a broad analytical framework within which to study fiscal issues and cite examples within that framework that have borne fruit.

This chapter's critiques have a constructive goal. By pointing out the shortcomings of existing fiscal analyses, the chapter aims to provoke researchers to improve upon these methods to create more useful frameworks for fiscal policy analysis.

2 Seven Illustrations

This section is intentionally provocative. It uses examples torn from the economic headlines that suggest a need to develop approaches to fiscal analysis that can provide more informative inputs to policymakers – inputs that shed light on the tradeoffs that decisionmakers face.

2.1 Long-Term Government Debt Projections

Fiscal sustainability studies tend to be more akin to accounting exercises than to economic analyses. It is not a caricature to describe the exercises as following these steps: (1) establish the current state of government indebtedness; (2) arrive at a view about what current tax and spending policies – or past policies – imply about how fiscal deficits depend on the state of the economy; (3) posit paths for economic variables on which deficits depend – output growth, unemployment, interest rates, inflation, and so forth; and (4) use a fiscal accounting identity to recursively derive the path for government debt given the information contained in steps (1) to (3).

Because this procedure takes the path of the economy as evolving independently of any fiscal developments, it is commonplace for projections to show an exploding path for debt-to-GDP ratio, while the rest of the economy evolves benignly. Figure 2.1 is a typical example. The top panel plots actual US debt as a percentage of GDP, along with the Congressional Budget Office's (CBO's) long-term projections in its 2010 and 2015 projections. In 2010 (dashed line) the CBO ran projections out to 2083, with the ratio reaching over 900 percent at the end of the projection period; by 2015 (dashed-dotted line) the CBO was truncating its projection in 2054, noting that beyond that year the ratio exceeds 250 percent.

Figure 2.1's bottom panel graphs the paths that the 2010 projection assumes for the unemployment rate, real interest rate, GDP growth rate, and inflation rate. After recovering from the 2008 recession, these series settle in at 4.8 percent, 3.0 percent, 2.2 percent, and 2.0 percent. But the CBO's narrative belies the benign assumed paths for the macroeconomic variables. A small sampling from Congressional Budget Office (2015, p. 4): "At some point, investors would begin to doubt the government's willingness or ability to meet its debt obligations, requiring it to pay much higher interest costs to continue borrowing money"; "The large amounts of federal borrowing would drain money away from private investment ... The result would be a smaller stock of capital, and therefore lower output and income..."; "The large amount of debt would restrict policymakers' ability to use tax and spending policies to respond to unexpected challenges, such as economic downturns or financial crises."

Because none of these outcomes are depicted in the CBO's reported projections, policymakers are left to conjecture about the economic mechanisms that underlie the dire macroeconomic predictions and speculate about the tradeoffs that those mechanisms create. In a

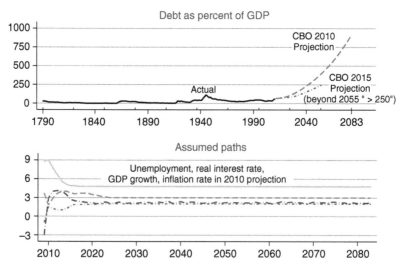

Figure 2.1: US Congressional Budget Office long-term projections, 2010–85

Notes: projections of debt-to-GDP ratio (top panel) in percent and underlying assumptions (bottom panel) about the paths of unemployment rate (solid line), real interest rate (dashed line), real GDP growth rate (dashed-dotted line), and consumer price inflation rate (short dashed-dotted line) in annual percent.

Source: Congressional Budget Office (2010, 2015)

phrase, policymakers need *economic analysis*, rather than accounting exercises.[7]

Conventional long-term fiscal projections violate Stein's (1989, p. 1) law: "If something cannot go on forever, it will stop." Simply acknowledging that law points us in the right direction. It forces us to ask what

---

[7] Long-term fiscal projections like those in Figure 2.1 are not unusual. The Bank for International Settlements, for example, conducted a similar analysis for a range of advanced economies, reporting very similar figures (Cecchetti, Mohanty, and Zampolli, 2010). Although the CBO has regularly performed analyses that include the budgetary feedback of macroeconomic effects, that analysis has not featured in baseline projections like those in Figure 2.1. With the passage of the concurrent resolution on the budget for fiscal year 2016, the CBO is required "to the greatest extent practicable, to incorporate the budgetary impacts of macroeconomic effects into its 10-year cost estimates for 'major' legislation" (Congressional Budget Office, 2016). Remarkably, this "dynamic scoring" requirement has been extremely controversial because it needs the analyst to specify a complete macroeconomic model, which necessarily carries with it many assumptions about economic behavior. This argument is specious: Static scoring also carries many (usually implicit) assumptions, most of which are utterly implausible (see Leeper and Yang, 2008).

might happen once the unsustainable policies stop. Of course, no one *knows* what future policies will be adopted, but we do know that current policies will not persist. We can also deduce, within the context of a formal economic model, the class of future policies that are sustainable. With additional work, we might be able to whittle the sustainable policies down to a set of policies that, if economic agents today believed they would be implemented, are consistent with the equilibrium we now observe. Policymakers could then assess how alternative future resolutions to the long-run fiscal stress reflected in Figure 2.1 would feed back to the present to pose decision makers with tradeoffs.[8]

Some readers may object that the research program I propose requires modelers to ponder the imponderables about alternative future policies. This is true. But any dynamic economic analysis requires analogous assumptions about the future. The CBO's projections take a stand both on future policies – they will be whatever current policies are – and on future transmission of fiscal choices to private behavior – there will be none. There is no way to avoid making bold assumptions in long-run analyses. It makes sense to examine a broad range of plausible alternative policies.

2.2 Latvia's Fiscal Consolidation

In the recent financial crisis, Latvia became a symbol either of "successful crisis resolution" (Ålund, 2015) or of a "depression-level slump" (Krugman, 2013b). That observers can come to such diametric conclusions underscores a difficulty of fiscal analysis.

During the financial crisis, all three Baltic countries opted for internal rather than external devaluation, but only Latvia implemented severe cuts in government spending. Between 2008 and 2010, Latvian government consumption fell by 20 percent in real terms and by almost a third in nominal terms (Di Comite et al., 2012). As Prime Minister Dombrovskis later commented to Bloomberg: "It's important to do the [fiscal] adjustment, if you see that adjustment is needed, to do it quickly, to frontload it and do the bulk already during the crisis" (McLaughlin, 2012). This argument is buttressed by political

---

[8] Examples of research that takes a step in this direction include Davig, Leeper, and Walker (2010, 2011) and Richter (2015).

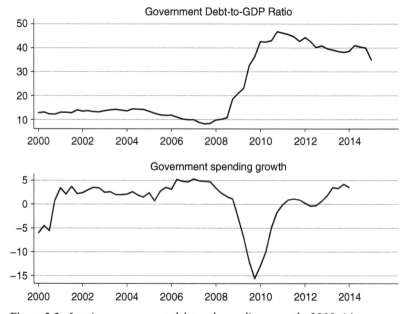

Figure 2.2: Latvian government debt and spending growth, 2000–14

Notes: central government consolidated gross debt as a percentage of GDP (top panel); percentage change in final consumption expenditures of general government (bottom panel).

Source: Central Statistical Bureau of Latvia, www.csb.gov.lv/en/dati/statistics-database-30501.html

economy reasoning: "Hardship is best concentrated to a short period, when people are ready to sacrifice" (Åslund and Dombrovskis, 2011, p. 3). But another rationale often invoked is credibility: Because it is difficult for fiscal policy to pre-commit, credible policy requires rapid implementation, rather than gradual phase-in.

Latvian government consumption expenditures grew relatively rapidly during the boom years before the crisis (Figure 2.2). Despite that growth, government debt had fallen to 10 percent of GDP by 2008 (top panel), well within the Maastricht treaty limit for admission to the euro area.[9] But, as it did in most countries, the recession brought with it rapidly growing debt, particularly as a share of declining GDP. Without getting into the timeline of events, prodded by IMF demands

---

[9] The Euro Area Council approved Latvia's admission on July 9, 2013.

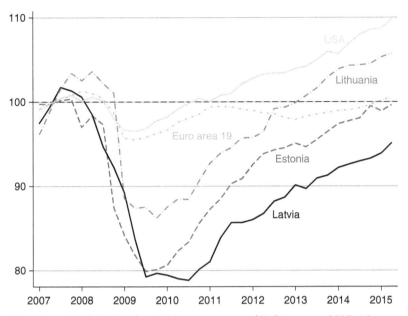

Figure 2.3: Real GDP index, USA, euro area, and Baltic states, 2007–15

Notes: 2007 = 100, chain-linked reference year 2010.

Source: Eurostat and US Bureau of Economic Analysis, ec.europa.eu/eurostat/data/data base; www.bea.gov/national/index.htm#gdp

for deficit reduction, in December 2008 the Latvian government undertook substantial fiscal reforms: Real public spending was cut by 25 percent; public wages were reduced by 25 percent in nominal terms; local governments were compelled to implement similar wage cuts; value-added taxes were increased from 18 to 21 percent. Left untouched were pensions, though they were frozen in nominal terms at 2009 levels, and the flat income tax and low corporate profit tax rates were maintained.[10]

The outcomes for the real economy are striking. Figure 2.3 reports the levels of real GDP for the three Baltic countries, along with a nineteen-country euro-area aggregate and the United States for comparison. The economic downturn was evidently far more severe and prolonged in Latvia than in the other areas. As of the second quarter of

[10] Excellent accounts of the timeline of events and other details appear in Åslund and Dombrovskis (2011), Di Comite et al. (2012), and Blanchard, Griffiths, and Gruss (2013).

2015, Latvian real GDP remained five percent below its 2007 level, while in the euro area and Estonia the level has recovered; Lithuania's GDP is almost 6 percent higher and that of the United States is nearly 10 percent above 2007 levels.

My purpose is not to assess whether Latvia adopted "good" or "bad" policies; there is plenty of debate about that already.[11] Instead, I want to highlight two key aspects of the arguments in favor of severe fiscal consolidation. First is the claim that frontloading is essential. Conventional optimal policy would call for smooth and gradual adjustment of government expenditures, just as it calls for gradual adjustment of tax rates. Of course, optimal policy prescriptions usually do not incorporate the typically short-lived nature of governments, particularly in parliamentary systems. It would be instructive to learn what kinds of political dynamics imply that frontloading fiscal adjustment is optimal.

Second is the closely related and oft-touted assertion that fiscal authorities cannot pre-commit, so reform-minded governments have little choice but to take drastic actions over short horizons. I think this assertion overstates the pre-commitment problem, which can lead policymakers to treat frontloading as a *fait accompli*. Many features of conventional fiscal policy entail substantial pre-commitment: The structure of the tax code is typically given until it is changed; social safety-net programs may be indexed to inflation; pension systems – particularly defined benefit programs – commit to payouts; and multi-year infrastructure spending projects commit to expenditure flows, to mention just a few. Each of these *requires an explicit legislative action* to undo, so the default is to maintain the previous commitment. These are all elements of the social contract between the "government" – writ large – and the "people"; a contract that transcends the particular group of individuals currently in power.

Monetary policy also faces a pre-commitment problem, as Kydland and Prescott (1977) and Barro and Gordon (1983) have neatly shown. Central banks could mimic fiscal authorities and respond to this problem by, for example, raising or lowering the policy interest rate by

---

[11] An assessment of policies seems to hinge on immeasurables, such as Latvia's potential output, as well as on seemingly innocuous assumptions, such as the choice of base year for the real GDP index in Figure 2.3. See Blanchard, Griffiths, and Gruss (2013) and the discussions of that paper by Forbes (2013) and Krugman (2013a).

500 basis points at a time, on the grounds that future monetary policy committees might opt not to follow through. Of course, central banks don't do this, because drastic swings in interest rates are rarely optimal. Instead, we have created institutional conditions – central bank independence – and constraints – clearly articulated objectives and accountability – designed to deliver consistent monetary policies.

Fiscal rules to which policymakers are held accountable could go a long way toward alleviating time-inconsistency problems. And fiscal policy councils have arisen to hold policymakers' feet to the fire when they seem inclined to go astray. But we could also imagine more fundamental institutional reforms that might be more effective, such as placing some aggregate aspects of fiscal choices in the hands of technocrats rather than elected officials, as Leeper (2011) suggests.

2.3 Low Inflation in Sweden and Switzerland

There is a tendency, among both academics and policymakers, to treat monetary policy in isolation from fiscal policy. This tendency has led a number of countries to adopt inflation targets for monetary policy without imposing compatible restrictions on fiscal behavior. Few inflation-targeting countries have asked, even *ex post*, whether their fiscal policy behavior is consistent with their adopted inflation target.

In recent years, two prominent inflation-targeters – Sweden and Switzerland – have had a hard time getting their inflation rates *up* to their targets. Sweden aims to keep inflation around 2 percent, while Switzerland shoots for 2 percent or less. Figure 2.4 reports that since the financial crisis, both countries have experienced persistently below-target rates of consumer price inflation (top panel).[12] By the end of 2015, the two central banks had aggressively pursued monetary stimulus through interest rate policy: Sveriges Riksbank set its repo rate at

---

[12] The figure reports annual CPI inflation rates for all items, not core inflation, because both countries couch their inflation targets in terms of broad inflation. Swedish inflation is particularly sensitive to interest-rate movements that transmit directly into this measure of inflation and both countries' rates vary with energy prices.

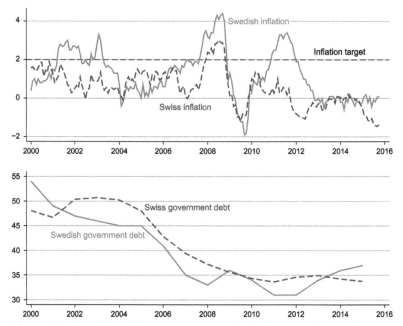

Figure 2.4: Swedish and Swiss consumer price inflation and central government debt, 2000–15

Notes: consumer price inflation (top panel), annual rates; central government debt (bottom panel) as percent of GDP. Sweden has a 2 percent inflation target and Switzerland aims for 2 percent or below.

Source: Statistics Sweden, Swedish National Debt Office, and Swiss National Bank, www.statistikdatabasen.scb.se/pxweb/en/ssd/?rxid=34d518b7-102f-4875-8789-87fa216 793fd; www.riksgalden.se/en/aboutsndo/Central-government-debt-and-finances/Central-government-debt-an-overview/; data.snb.ch/en/topics

−0.35 percent and the Swiss National Bank set a range for its three-month libor rate at between −1.25 and −0.25 percent.

But these countries stand out in another way as well: in the wake of the global recession, when most countries saw government debt as a share of the economy rise sharply, Swedish and Swiss fiscal policies engineered either flat or declining debt-to-GDP ratios. This pattern of debt is still more surprising because in 2009 real GDP fell by 5.2 percent in Sweden and 2.1 percent in Switzerland.

Governments in the two countries will argue that they were simply following their fiscal rules – a surplus target in terms of net lending in

Sweden and a debt break in Switzerland.[13] Viewed through that narrow prism, presumably fiscal policies have been successful. But that prism does not refract the light that emanates from the central bank's inflation target. Questions that are not being asked by policymakers in the two countries include: Can the two central banks even achieve their inflation targets in the face of these fiscal rules? Is there any causal connection between the low levels of government debt and the chronically low inflation rates?

2.4 Japan's Confused Priorities

Japan has become the poster child for inconsistency in macroeconomic policies, and these inconsistencies have been well documented (see, e.g., Hausman and Wieland, 2014; Ito, 2006; Ito and Mishkin, 2006; Krugman, 1998). Japan's economic performance reflects this: since 1993, inflation has averaged 0.21 percent, economic growth has averaged 0.84 percent, and government debt has risen from 75 to 230 percent of GDP. Abenomics was heralded as the end of stop-and-go policies and the beginning of policies designed to re-inflate the economy through monetary expansion, fiscal stimulus, and structural reform.

To partially address concerns about fiscal sustainability, Japan raised the consumption tax from 3 to 5 percent in 1997. This did little to retard growth in government debt. Despite decades of economic malaise in Japan, the IMF applied substantial pressure on the country to move forward with planned tax hikes. April 2014 saw the consumption tax rise to 8 percent. Figure 2.5 records the consequences. Consumption, which had been growing at 3 percent, plummeted to −3 percent, and stopped falling only late in 2015 (top panel). GDP followed a similar pattern. Meanwhile, after a year or two of positive inflation in consumer prices, prices have stopped rising (bottom panel).

An IMF country report from July 2014 continued to beat the fiscal austerity drum:

The consumption tax rate increase in April to 8 percent was a major achievement, but is only a first step toward fiscal sustainability ... The

---

[13] In principle, rules of this sort ensure fiscal sustainability and free fiscal policy to pursue other objectives, at least in the short term. In practice, the rules effectively take fiscal policy off the table as a factor in macroeconomic stabilization.

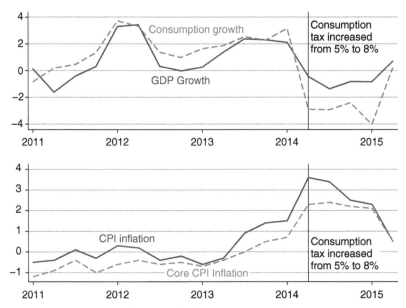

Figure 2.5: Japanese real GDP and consumer price inflation, 2011–16

Notes: GDP figures, expenditure approach (top panel, solid line), and private final consumption expenditures (top panel, dashed line); Japanese consumer prices, all items (bottom panel, solid line) and consumer prices, all items non-food, non-energy (bottom panel, dashed line). All data are growth rates compared to same quarter of previous year, seasonally adjusted.

Source: OECD Statistics, http://stats.oecd.org/

second consumption tax rate increase in 2015 to 10 percent with a uniform rate should be confirmed. Raising the tax rate further at a moderate pace would help establish fiscal policy credibility … A post-2015 fiscal consolidation plan is urgently needed … Options … include gradually increasing the consumption tax to at least 15 percent. (International Monetary Fund, 2014b, pp. 14–15)

In the event, Japan postponed the scheduled 2015 tax hike until 2017.

Apparently, the policy objectives of Japan and of the IMF conflict. While the Abe government seeks to fight deflation and escape secular decline, the IMF's concern centers on debt reduction. Conflict as fundamental as this screams out for careful study.

Obsession with the level of Japanese government debt is puzzling. There are no clear signs that the high levels of debt have caused any economic problems – interest rates and inflation remain low and the

Japanese government has no difficulty selling new debt.[14] More important, Japanese debt is denominated in yen and Japan – unlike countries in the eurozone – controls its own monetary policy. Japan need not face a tradeoff between fiscal stabilization and fiscal sustainability because it can address both its deflation and its high level of government debt simultaneously: The government needs to convince its people that there are no plans to raise taxes or cut spending to back new debt issuances. If Japanese bond holders, most of whom are Japanese institutions and people, are persuaded that future primary surpluses will not rise, Japanese bonds will become less attractive. As bond holders substitute out of bonds and into buying goods, aggregate demand will rise, bringing with it current and future price levels. Higher price levels, together with the associated lower bond prices, reduce the real market value of outstanding debt.[15]

To shift expectations in this way, the Japanese government must be consistent in both its communication and its actions. Such consistency would be a substantial change from past policy behavior.

2.5 Spanish Sovereign Risk

The increase in sovereign risk premia on Spanish government debt that began in 2010 took many observers by surprise. After the realization of the true state of public finances, the Greek situation seemed understandable – it was clearly in trouble. But Spanish government debt had been on a downward trajectory for more than a decade, reaching a mere 35.5 percent of GDP in 2007 before the financial crisis. As in most countries, it rose with the crisis, to hit 60 percent in 2010 – still seemingly a manageable level.

One story behind the increased risk premia in Spain is "contagion," a term with many possible meanings. According to one policymaker,

---

[14] Although production of investment goods for manufacturing in Japan has been flat or declining since 1990.
[15] This is merely an application of the fiscal theory of the price level: See Leeper (1991), Sims (1994), Cochrane (2001), and Woodford (2001). See Section 3.3 for further discussion.

financial contagion refers to a situation whereby instability in a specific market or institution is transmitted to one or several other markets or institutions. There are two ideas underlying this definition. First, the wider spreading of instability would usually not happen without the initial shock. Second, the transmission of the initial instability goes beyond what could be expected from the normal relationships between markets or intermediaries, for example in terms of its speed, strength or scope. (Constâncio, 2010, p. 110)

Constâncio (2010) goes on to say that contagion entails an externality that cannot be well priced by financial markets.

Beirne and Fratzscher (2013, p. 2) define "contagion" as "the *change* in the way countries' own fundamentals or other factors are priced during a crisis period." These fundamentals may be observable – risk premia in neighboring countries – or unobservable – herding behavior by market participants.

The first definition would seem to call for policy authorities to intervene, if possible, to force the responsible parties to internalize the externality. But the authors of the second definition are more circumspect about the normative implications of their notion of "contagion."

Section 3.2 on the *fiscal limit* discusses a type of fundamental that is largely unexamined in the sovereign risk literature, so I shall not explore that concept in detail here. Instead I will present a broader set of data than is typically studied that, together with the fiscal limit, may point to a reason for the increase in Spanish risk premia.

The top panel of Figure 2.6 records Spanish and euro-area inflation rates (left scale) and Spain's unemployment rate (right scale) from 1998 through the middle of 2015. For reference, the middle and bottom panels of the figure show Spanish government debt as a percentage of GDP and the yield spread between ten-year Spanish and German government bonds. From 1998 through 2008, Spanish inflation consistently exceeded euro-area inflation, with the difference averaging one percentage point over the period. It is reasonable to posit that in the face of this chronic difference, investors might grow concerned about Spain's competitiveness going forward. Reduced competitiveness would bring with it weak economic growth, lower revenues, and higher government expenditures. So fears about Spain's competitive position would translate into an expectation of lower Spanish primary surpluses. All else constant, a downward shift in the expected present value of surpluses would reduce Spain's capacity to support government debt.

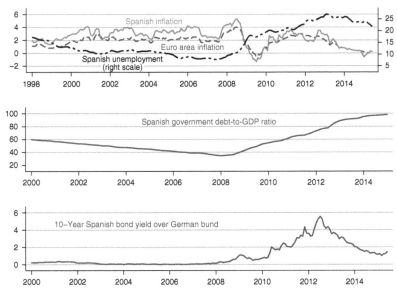

Figure 2.6: Spanish inflation, government debt and sovereign spread, 2000–16

Notes: Spanish (top panel, solid line) and euro-area (top panel, dashed line) Harmonized Index of Consumer Prices, growth rate over same month of previous year, not seasonally adjusted; Spanish harmonized unemployment rate (top panel, dashed-dotted line), total, ILO definition, not seasonally adjusted; Spanish central government debt as percentage of GDP (middle panel), Maastricht definition; yield spread is the difference between Spanish and German long-term interest rates for convergence purposes (bottom panel), ten-year yield.

Source: Eurostat and European Central Bank, http://ec.europa.eu/eurostat/data/database; http://sdw.ecb.int/

Then the crisis hit. Spanish unemployment rose dramatically and with it came a higher debt-to-GDP ratio. At the same time that the country's ability to support debt fell, the level of debt rose. In any model of sovereign default, this would increase the probability of default and raise Spanish bond yields.

As it happened, the global recession also brought Spanish inflation in line with the eurozone. Coupled with a decline in Spanish unemployment beginning in 2013, the improvement in competitiveness and growth prospects reduced the yield spread over German bunds.

This is by no means a rigorous analysis. But it highlights interactions among nominal developments, real economic activity, and fiscal outcomes that do not feature in conventional sovereign risk analyses.

2.6 *Waffling Policy Advice*

An unusually large degree of uncertainty accompanied the financial crisis – uncertainty about both the sources and the macroeconomic consequences of the crisis. That uncertainty flowed into policy actions and policy advice. Nothing illustrates the degree of policy uncertainty that prevailed between 2009 and 2013 more clearly than the see-sawing fiscal advice that the IMF proffered to countries.

A chronology of IMF fiscal advice tells the story:

October 2008:	Called for "timely" and "targeted" fiscal stimulus, always with a reminder to "safeguard the medium-term consolidation objectives." (International Monetary Fund, 2008, p. xvii)
July 2009:	"Fiscal policy should continue to support economic activity until economic recovery has taken hold (and, indeed, additional discretionary stimulus may be needed in 2010). However, the positive growth impact of fiscal expansion would be enhanced by the identification of clear strategies to ensure that fiscal solvency is preserved over the medium term." (Horton, Kumar, and Mauro, 2009, p. 3)
November 2010:	The IMF's *Fiscal Monitor* bore the self-explanatory title "Fiscal Exit: From Strategy to Implementation." (International Monetary Fund, 2010)
June 2011:	"The pace of fiscal adjustment is uneven among advanced economies, with many making steady progress, others needing to redouble efforts, and some yet to begin." (International Monetary Fund, 2011, p. 2)
January 2012:	"Given the large adjustment already in train this year, governments should avoid responding to any unexpected downturn in growth by further tightening policies, and should instead allow the automatic stabilizers to operate, as long as financing is available and sustainability concerns permit. Countries with enough fiscal space, including some in the Euro Area, should reconsider the pace of near-term adjustment." (International Monetary Fund, 2012, p. 1)

| October 2014: | "Hesitant recovery and persistent risks of lowflation and reform fatigue call for fiscal policy that carefully balances support for growth and employment creation with fiscal sustainability." (International Monetary Fund, 2014a, p. ix) |
| April 2015: | "Countries with fiscal space can use it to support growth ... Countries that are more constrained should pursue growth-friendly fiscal rebalancing" (International Monetary Fund, 2015, p. ix) |

In the course of writing this, I came across an independent evaluation of the IMF's fiscal advice by Dhar (2014). That evaluation, which is much broader and more detailed than my synopsis, draws on many IMF sources different from those cited above, but arrives at similar conclusions. It more diplomatically states:

[The IMF] had been urging countries to plan for such stimulus starting in early 2008 ... [T]he IMF in 2010 endorsed the shift from fiscal stimulus to consolidation that was initiated in the United Kingdom in 2010, the United States in 2011, and recommended that each Euro Area economy including Germany engage in fiscal consolidation by 2011 at the latest, inter alia to enhance investor confidence. The call for fiscal consolidation turned out to be premature ... In 2012, the IMF began to reassess its views on fiscal policy and subsequently called for a more moderate pace of fiscal consolidation if feasible. (Dhar, 2014, p. vii)

Of course, the IMF is not the only policy organization that waffles about fiscal policy. The American Recovery and Reinvestment Act (ARRA), implemented in 2009, was a fiscal stimulus of about 5.6 percent of GDP spread over a decade and comprised a mixture of tax reductions and spending increases, particularly on infrastructure. Within six days of signing the act into law, President Obama was pledging to reduce the fiscal deficit by half by the end of his first term in office (Phillips, 2009).

The pattern seems to be to undertake fiscal stimulus and then immediately promise to reverse it. Economic theory tells us that this is likely to be counterproductive. Theory instructs that policy should either stimulate or not. Fiscal expansions that are *not* backed by promises of reversals have large and persistent impacts in economies that issue nominal debt and control their own monetary policy (see Leeper, Traum, and Walker, 2015 for estimates using US data).

Missing from both the IMF statements and President Obama's pledge is an appreciation of the role of expectations in fiscal dynamics. Cutting taxes today and promising to raise them tomorrow anchors expectations on a Ricardian experiment: In some models this policy is neutral; in all models the reversal attenuates the stimulus's effects. In practice, it is hard to tell how private sector fiscal expectations are anchored, particularly when it is commonplace for policymakers to send these kinds of mixed messages (see discussions in Leeper 2009, 2011).

This issue highlights the poorly understood tension between fiscal stabilization and fiscal sustainability. If people believe that fiscal finances are sufficiently feeble, is it even possible for fiscal actions to stabilize the macro economy? Faced with this tradeoff, most policy-makers and advisors opt for sustainability as the safest route to follow, removing fiscal policy as a player in macroeconomic stabilization.

2.7 Demographics and Political Economy

Nearly all the world's countries are aging. But demographics differ sharply across countries. The top panel of Figure 2.7 plots old-age dependency ratios for China, Japan, Western Europe, and the United States.[16] Japan is the oldest country by this measure, but Western Europe is close behind. Today the United States is older than China, but that relationship will reverse in about two decades.

Many economic implications flow from an aging population, including persistent shifts in saving rates, real interest rates, the composition of consumption, and relative prices.[17] But a robust consequence of these demographic shifts is that older citizens have a much higher propensity to vote than do younger citizens.[18] Because different age cohorts have different preferences over tax and spending policies, demographic changes are likely to generate slowly evolving changes in fiscal rules and outcomes.

---

[16] Old-age dependency is the population over 64 years old as a percentage of working-age population, which is those aged 15–64. It roughly reflects the number of aged people that each worker supports.

[17] See Faust and Leeper (2015) and references therein for further discussion.

[18] For example, File (2014) reports that the 2012 US presidential election produced turnout rates of 45.0 percent (ages 18–29), 59.5 percent (ages 30–40), 67.9 percent (ages 45–64), and 72.0 percent (ages 65 and above).

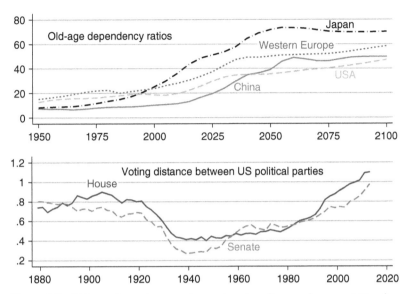

Figure 2.7: Old-age dependency ratios and voting distance between US political parties

Notes: old-age dependency ratios in various countries/regions (top panel), population older than 64 years as a percentage of working-age population, ages 15–64, medium variant projections and US political polarization (bottom panel), difference in party means derived from voting data.

Source: United Nations Population Division's World Population Prospects, https://esa .un.org/unpd/wpp/, and http://voteview.com/political_polarization_2014.htm

Figure 2.7's bottom panel illustrates that democracies do not always operate smoothly. The figure graphs the voting distance between the two major political parties in the United States across Congresses from 1879 to 2014 for both houses of Congress. Voting distance is a measure of political polarization. During the Great Depression and World War II, the parties came together to find common cause, but polarization has grown since the 1960s and in recent years has reached all-time highs.[19] Political polarization can make it more difficult for governments to reach consensus on fiscal agendas, increasing fiscal uncertainty.

---

[19] McCarty, Poole, and Rosenthal (2006) is the underlying source for the data, which are available for download at http://voteview.com/political_polarization_ 2014.htm.

The political economy dynamics implied by the data in Figure 2.7 are too often absent from analyses of fiscal policy. It is impossible to understand eurozone monetary and fiscal policies without grasping the underlying political economy. The 2012 "fiscal cliff" and 2013 government shutdown in the United States were political rather than economic decisions. Optimal policy prescriptions that fail to take account of demographics are likely to seem sterile and irrelevant, which is unfortunate, because some of the logic of optimal policy transcends political considerations. Fiscal analysis could be made more relevant – and hence be more influential – if it were to integrate and impose political constraints, in addition to the usual economic constraints.

3 A Fiscal Research Agenda

The preceding illustrations are intentionally chosen to induce researchers to ask, "Can we do better?" I think we can do better and, in fact, there are examples in the literature that contain some of the ingredients that are essential to more useful fiscal analysis.

In this section, I sketch a research agenda for improving fiscal analysis. The agenda includes three overriding criteria:

- rigorous analytics and tight connections to data,
- full integration of monetary and fiscal policies and perhaps also financial policies,
- incorporation of the sources of disparate confounding dynamics highlighted in Section 2.

Because I am fantasizing about this agenda, I will not feel constrained by tractability.

3.1 Essential Ingredients

Any model that is useful for macro policy analysis must be *general equilibrium*. I say this fully acknowledging the limitations that this imposes. General equilibrium should be taken to mean that the elements deemed to be critical for understanding how fiscal policy transmits to the aggregate economy are derived endogenously. For example, the analysis discussed in Section 2.1, which simply posits paths for output, interest rates, and inflation, does not satisfy this definition of general equilibrium.

Fiscal sustainability can quickly become a bugaboo in any fiscal analysis, being invoked as an unmodeled rationale to "do more" (or less) on the fiscal front. To grapple with this bugaboo, models of fiscal policy need to include an explicit *fiscal limit* that yields insights into the tradeoffs between stabilization and sustainability. There are many ways to model the fiscal limit, and in Section 3.2 I discuss one way that is well grounded in theory.

To date, the vast majority of macroeconomic fiscal analyses have employed representative-agent models or environments in which there is some, often trivial, form of *heterogeneity*.[20] In contrast, micro-oriented public finance places distributional consequences of fiscal changes front and center. Dynamic models of fiscal policy often adopt an overlapping-generations framework to incorporate intragenerational heterogeneity (e.g., Auerbach and Kotilikoff, 1987; Altig et al., 2001). While this set-up captures important aspects of heterogeneity, it tends to do so by restricting attention to deterministic models, making it impossible to address the central issue of uncertainty. Recent advances in computational techniques open the door to handling both heterogeneity and uncertainty (Holter, Krueger, and Stepanchuk, 2015 and McKay and Reis, 2015, to mention two examples).

As Section 2.7 suggested, *demographic* developments have potentially very large and persistent impacts on fiscal analysis. Modeling demographics requires heterogeneity, but this is an area in which important progress is being made in fiscal analysis (Ferrero, 2010; Katagiri, Konishi, and Ueda, 2015). Section 2.7 also highlighted the *political economy* repercussions of demographic change – phenomena that are not yet well understood.

It goes without saying that a full understanding of fiscal policy requires modeling the *many different fiscal instruments* employed by government. The list includes multiple types of taxes – labor, capital, consumption, profits – and many kinds of spending – consumption, investment, transfers. As obvious as this ingredient is, many macro models base their fiscal analyses on a single income tax rate or

---

[20] For example, positing that a fixed fraction of households live hand-to-mouth or that two groups of agents differ only in their rates of time preference. Todd Walker has proposed to me a useful metric for the degree of heterogeneity in a dynamic model: The number of distinct saving functions across agents in a model.

government spending that is completely wasteful – restrictions that are important for policy implications.

In most macro models, government debt serves merely as a vehicle for private saving and tax smoothing. In actual economies, *government debt serves additional roles*: liquidity, collateral, and maturity transformation (see, e.g., Yun, 2011; Williamson, 2014; Eiben, 2015). US treasuries are a critical source of collateral in repurchase agreements, giving fiscal financing a direct role in credit creation, and figuring into the financial crisis in an important way (Gourinchas and Jeanne, 2012; Gorton and Ordoñez, 2013, 2014). This line of work suggests that modeling the economic roles played by government debt can fundamentally alter our understanding of the fiscal transmission mechanism by highlighting the linkages between fiscal policy and financial stability.[21]

Eventually, we will want to include interactions between fiscal policy and *financial stability*. In addition to the considerations just discussed, the fiscal authority is, after all, the lender of last resort, which is the ultimate financial stability tool. But the use of fiscal policy for these purposes can have political economy consequences, as we have seen in many countries in the aftermath of the financial crisis. Those consequences will interact with the government's ability to harness fiscal tools for macro-stabilization purposes.

I now selectively elaborate on these ingredients.

3.2 The Fiscal Limit

A government's decision to honor its debt obligations is most often more about its *willingness* than about its *ability*, as Eaton and Gersovitz (1981) emphasize. Eaton and Gersovitz spawned a literature in which the government makes a strategic decision to default, weighing costs of default against the benefits of not having to repay. Recent work has aimed to quantify the default decision (see Aguiar and Gopinath, 2006 and Arellano, 2008, to name early examples).

Although among academics strategic default has become the dominant approach to sovereign debt studies, for policymakers the line of

---

[21] Gourinchas and Jeanne (2012), for example, argue that shortages of safe assets such as short-term government bonds can create financial instability and Eiben (2015) shows that increases in the supply of government bonds can improve the efficiency of capital allocation to raise welfare.

work is not terribly helpful. Policymakers are interested in answers to questions such as "if policy continues on the current track, will government debt become risky?" or "what sorts of fiscal reforms can reduce the riskiness of government debt and provide fiscal policy with room to engage in stabilization actions?" Strategic default models, as currently specified, cannot address these questions, for obvious reasons: Those models do not include specifications of fiscal behavior – tax and spending rules – which can be intervened upon to predict the consequences of alternative rules.

The IMF has developed the idea of "fiscal space," defined as the distance between current debt and a computed debt limit. Ghosh et al. (2012) estimate reduced-form fiscal rules, following Bohn (2008) and Mendoza and Ostry (2008), and then ask: if countries were to continue this past behavior indefinitely, what is the maximum level of debt that can be sustained? Ghosh et al. (2012) deliver point estimates for fiscal space – 172.2 percent for Australia, 81.3 percent for France, 50.8 percent for the United States and "unsustainable"[22] for Greece, Iceland, Italy, Japan, and Portugal – and then compute probabilities of a given amount of fiscal space by using the standard errors from the estimated fiscal reaction functions.[23] Like the CBO approach discussed in Section 2.1, the IMF's procedure is essentially an accounting, rather than an economic, exercise. And like the strategic default literature, the exercise cannot address the questions that most press policymakers.

Bi's (2012) concept of the *fiscal limit* offers the modeling flexibility to provide useful inputs to policymakers. Whereas the IMF and the CBO approaches focus on the "backward" representation of debt – as the accumulation of past deficits – Bi's idea emphasizes the "forward" representation: the value of debt depends on the expected present value of primary surpluses. This provides an immediate link between sovereign debt risk premia, which reflect debt's current value, and expected economic fundamentals that affect revenues and spending in the future.

Bi (2012) and Bi and Leeper (2012) employ formal non-monetary models in which labor is productive and is taxed at a proportionate rate. Private sector decisions are optimal and expectations are rational. The model implies a Laffer curve and revenues are maximized at the

---

[22] "Unsustainable" presumably means that a country has negative fiscal space.

[23] As the discussion below argues, this is "uncertainty" associated with sampling error, but has little to do with uncertainty about future economic fundamentals.

state-dependent tax rate that pushes the economy to the peak of the curve. Government transfers fluctuate between stationary and non-stationary regimes to reflect the rapid growth in old-age benefits associated with aging populations and periodic fiscal reforms. In the non-stationary regime, transfers grow as a share of GDP – a state that cannot persist indefinitely, but contributes to rapid debt accumulation and an increase of the tax rate toward the peak of the Laffer curve. Fiscal reform is a move from the non-stationary to the stationary transfers regime.[24]

The fiscal limit answers the question: "Given the economic environment, what is the distribution of government debt that can be supported without significant risk premia?" The fiscal limit distribution emerges from the distribution of the expected discounted value of future maximum primary surpluses, where maximum surpluses come from driving tax revenues to the peak of the Laffer curve and driving expenditures to some minimum level.[25] The fiscal limit has several important features:

- Because it depends on realizations of shocks now and in the future, the fiscal limit is a probability distribution. Uncertainty in the economy means that there is no magic threshold for debt that, when crossed, triggers sovereign default or economic collapse.
- The fiscal limit is forward-looking: It depends on expected future policies and how credible those policies are.
- It depends on private behavior – consumption-saving and labor-leisure choices; policy behavior – current and expected; and the fundamental shocks to the economy – possibly including disturbances emanating from the political process.

Sovereign default probabilities depend on the current level of debt *relative to the position of the fiscal limit distribution.* High current

---

[24] Those papers do not model how the transfers regime is determined, treating transfers as following a recurrent Markov chain with exogenous transition probabilities.

[25] Political economy considerations come strongly into play in the calculation of maximum surpluses. In many countries – the United States, for example – it is likely to be politically infeasible to reach the Laffer curve peak because of low voter tolerance for high tax rates. In other countries – Sweden, for example – substantially reducing social benefits might not be politically viable. Hatchondo and Martinez (2010) is a thoughtful discussion of the interaction between politics and sovereign default.

debt may be associated with minimal default risk if the fiscal limit distribution implies the economy can easily support still more debt. And low current debt may nonetheless carry with it substantial risk of default when the economy cannot generate sufficiently large future surpluses.

Figure 2.8 plots fiscal limit distributions and associated risk premia from a model in Bi and Leeper (2012) that was calibrated to Greek data. Vertical lines mark a debt-to-GDP level of 170 percent for reference. The top row of the figure shows the fiscal limit cumulative distribution function conditional on current productivity (left panel) and on the current transfers regime (right panel). Persistently high productivity raises current and future primary surpluses to shift the distribution to the right and reduce the probability of default at any given level of debt, while persistently low productivity brings the limit in to raise the default probability.

When transfers policy resides in the stable regime, and is expected to remain there for some period, the distribution lies to the right, permitting the economy to support high levels of debt. The opposite is true when transfers are currently unstable and expected to remain so for a while: Growing transfers reduce the present value of surpluses to shift the limit in. As the lower row shows, risk premia rise the more the distribution lies to the left.

The figure highlights the state-dependent nature of the fiscal limit. Realizations of fundamental shocks today – shocks to technology or to the transfers regime, in this case – can shift the distribution substantially, which, when the prevailing level of debt is close to the limit, can have strong effects on risk premia.

Not only is the fiscal limit state-dependent, it is also highly country-dependent. If this model were calibrated to data in a different country, Figure 2.8 could look quite different. Slovakia's fiscal council – the Council for Budget Responsibility – applied Bi's (2012) model to the Slovak economy (Múčka, 2015). A critical aspect of that application is the modifications of the model to accommodate features of the Slovak economy: Growth in transfers that corresponds to demographic dynamics in Slovakia, countercyclicality of transfers and procyclicality of government purchases, switches in the transfers process that reflect the political cycle in Slovakia, and, most importantly, a distribution for technology shocks derived from Slovakia's empirical distribution for the output gap. That empirical distribution places substantial mass on

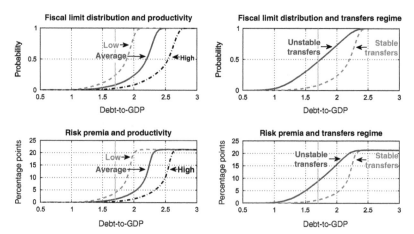

Figure 2.8: Fiscal limit cumulative density functions calibrated to Greek data
Notes: derived from peak of labor Laffer curve with constant government purchases, conditional on current transfers regime. Vertical lines at 170 percent debt-to-GDP.
Source: Bi and Leeper (2012)

large negative realizations of the gap. The Council used this setup to ask: "Is the Maastricht debt limit safe enough for Slovakia?" The answer: no. In normal times, the 60 percent limit is associated with a modest default probability of about 10 percent, but in the face of a bad draw from the lower tail of the technology distribution, that probability rises precipitously to around 40 percent. In light of this analysis, the Council recommended that the Slovakian government adopt a debt limit below the Maastricht level.[26]

Several useful extensions to Bi's (2012) model suggest themselves. Many countries, particularly in Europe, rely heavily on value-added taxes. Conventional models, like that of Trabandt and Uhlig (2011), do not impose a natural upper bound on tax revenues from such taxes, so an alternative to Bi's Laffer-curve criterion needs to be applied. Consumption taxes, like capital taxes, introduce intertemporal considerations into the revenue consequences of changes in tax rates – considerations that also pose challenges to the Laffer-curve reasoning. To my knowledge, very little work examines the spending side to bring political economy dynamics into the fiscal limit calculus.

---

[26] Bi and Traum (2012, 2014) take the fiscal limit idea to data to estimate fiscal limits for some European countries.

3.3 Integrating Nominal Considerations

Despite the long-standing tradition of studying fiscal policy in isolation from monetary policy – and vice versa – we must confront the fact that we do not live in that compartmentalized world. To put a sharper point on this, *any predictions about the impacts of fiscal actions are conditioned – often implicitly – on assumptions about monetary policy behavior.*[27] It is impossible to fully understand the euro-area sovereign debt crisis without bringing the ECB into the picture (Panico and Purificato, 2013; Chang, 2015). It is well established that government spending multipliers depend on how aggressively the central bank adjusts interest rates in response to inflation (Christiano, Eichenbaum, and Rebelo, 2011; Leeper, Traum, and Walker, 2015). The consequences of a debt-financed fiscal expansion hinge on whether fiscal or monetary policy adjusts to finance the debt (Gordon and Leeper, 2006).

The nature of the fiscal–monetary interactions depends on the composition of government debt between nominal and real (inflation-indexed) bonds. Because the vast majority of debt that governments issue is denominated in nominal units – euros, dollars, yen – it is important to understand the difference between real and nominal debt. Real debt is a claim to real goods, which the government must acquire through taxation. This imposes a budget constraint that the government's choices must satisfy. If the government does not have the taxing capacity to acquire the goods necessary to finance outstanding debt, it has no option other than outright default.

Nominal debt is much like government-issued money: it is merely a claim to fresh currency in the future. The government may choose to raise taxes to acquire the requisite currency or it may opt to print up new currency, if currency creation is within its purview. Because the value of nominal debt depends on the price level and bond prices, the government really does not face a budget constraint when all its debt is nominal. Some readers may object to the idea that a government does not face a budget constraint, but the logic here is exactly the logic that underlies fiat currency. By conventional quantity theory reasoning, the central bank is free to double or halve the money supply without fear of violating a budget constraint because the price level will double or

---

[27] The reverse is also true, as Wallace (1981) shows.

halve to maintain the real value of money. The direct analog to this reasoning is that the government is free to issue any quantity of nominal bonds, whose real value adjusts with the price level, without reference to a budget constraint. Of course, by doing so, the government is giving up control of the price level.

Member nations of the euro area issue debt denominated in euros, their home currency, but because monetary policy is under the control of the ECB rather than individual nations, the debt is effectively real from the perspective of member nations. The United States issues indexed debt, but it comprises only 10 percent of the debt outstanding. Even in the United Kingdom, which is known for having a thick market in indexed bonds, the percentage is only about 20. In the euro area, Japan, Australia, and Sweden, 5 percent or less of total debt issued is indexed.

To clarify how nominal debt changes interactions between fiscal and monetary policies, it is helpful to establish some notation. Suppose there is a complete maturity structure for government bonds so that $B_t(t+j)$ is the nominal quantity of zero-coupon bonds outstanding in period t that matures in period $t+j$ whose dollar price is $Q_t(t+j)$. The bond-pricing equation is

$$Q_t(t+j) = \beta^j E_t\left(\frac{U_c(C_{t+j})}{U_c(C_t)}\frac{P_t}{P_{t+j}}\right) \tag{1}$$

where $0 < \beta < 1$ is the discount factor, $U_c(\cdot)$ is marginal utility, and P_t is the aggregate price level. Denote the real discount factor by $m_{t,t+j} \equiv \beta^j \frac{U_c(C_{t+j})}{U_c(C_t)}$. Let B_{t-1} denote the nominal value of the bond portfolio outstanding at the beginning of period t.[28]

Every dynamic model implies an equilibrium condition that links the market value of debt to expected discounted future primary surpluses:[29]

$$\frac{B_{t-1}(t)}{P_t} = E_t \sum_{j=0}^{\infty} m_{t,t+j} S_{t+j} \tag{2}$$

[28] The portfolio is defined as $B_{t-1} \equiv B_{t-1}(t) + \sum_{j=1}^{\infty} Q_t(t+j)B_{t-1}(t+j)$.
[29] Condition (2) may be derived either from the household's or the government's budget constraint by imposing the bond-pricing relationships, the household's transversality condition, and market clearing. See, for example, Woodford (2001) for a careful derivation.

where S_{t+j} is the real primary surplus in period $t + j$. Cochrane (2005, p. 502) calls (2) "the valuation equation for government debt," to emphasize that debt's value depends not only on expected backing through surpluses, but also on the current price level, current bond prices, and expected real discount factors.

In countries that both issue nominal debt and control their own monetary policy, an expansion in nominal debt can be *unbacked* by future surpluses. With no expected change in future taxes, households perceive that their higher debt holdings raise their financial wealth, which raises demand for goods. If prices are perfectly flexible, higher demand transmits directly into a higher current price level and lower bond prices – that is, higher expected inflation – which reduces the real value of debt to coincide with the expected present value of surpluses. This mechanism, dubbed the "fiscal theory of the price level," is explained in Leeper (1991), Sims (1994), Woodford (1995), and Cochrane (1999). When prices are sticky, higher demand transmits into a mix of real and nominal variables.

Bi's (2012) fiscal limit from Section 3.2 can be generalized by embedding it in a broader DSGE model that includes monetary policy and some form of nominal rigidities so that purely nominal disturbances propagate to affect real variables. If a monetary policy expansion reduces real interest rates and real discount rates, then it raises the present value of a given stream of surpluses to shift out the fiscal limit. Even if the real effects of the monetary expansion are fleeting, so that real discount rates fall only in the short run, the impact on the position of the fiscal limit can be substantial.[30]

In the wake of the financial crisis, central banks around the world decreased policy interest rates dramatically and rates remained low for many years. Short-term real interest rates were negative in many countries. As interest rates "normalize" and return to historic levels, real discount rates will also rise back to historic levels. With fixed surpluses, the higher real discount rates will reduce the present value of surpluses and shift fiscal limit distributions. In the euro area, this

---

[30] To see this, note that the discount factor $m_{t,t+j}$ may be written as

$$m_{t,t+j} = \beta \frac{U_c(C_{t+1})}{U_c(C_t)} \beta \frac{U_c(C_{t+2})}{U_c(C_{t+1})} \cdots \beta \frac{U_c(C_{t+j})}{U_c(C_{t+j-1})} = \frac{1}{1+r_t} \frac{1}{1+r_{t+1}} \cdots \frac{1}{1+r_{t+j-1}} \text{ where}$$

r_t is the real discount rate between t and $t + 1$. Because each $m_{t,t+j}$ that appears on the right side of (2) includes $1/(1 + r_t)$, even a one-period decline in the real discount rate can change the present value a lot.

normalization of monetary policy may trigger further sovereign debt crises, because member nations have no alternative but to raise surpluses yet again and reduce aggregate demand.[31] Their only alternative is to default on outstanding debt.

Outside the euro area, countries have two options. They could choose to raises surpluses and reduce aggregate demand. But they could, instead, opt not to adjust surpluses. This would reduce the value of outstanding debt by raising inflation and bond yields. It is to this latter adjustment that Section 2.4 alludes in the Japanese context, because it solves both solvency and deflation problems.

Policy analysts are aware of this fiscal consequence of normalization. The Congressional Budget Office (2014), for example, projects that net interest costs will quadruple from 2014 to 2024 to reach 3.3 percent of GDP in 2024. In the United States, the typical response of Congress when interest payments chew up a large fraction of expenditures is fiscal reform. But there is little about Congressional behavior in recent years that is "typical." And in the absence of fiscal reforms to finance higher debt service, the Federal Reserve's efforts to rein in inflation by raising interest rates are likely to be thwarted.

3.4 Modeling Government Debt

Fiscal analysis that treats government debt as merely a saving vehicle that smoothes consumption and taxes is likely to miss important interactions among fiscal policy, monetary policy, and financial stability. One class of interactions arises from the maturity structure of government bonds. If bonds at different maturities generate different service flows, then the bonds will be imperfect substitutes and changes in the maturity structure will affect the macro economy. Despite new empirical research that tries to quantify the effects of the large-scale asset purchases in which major central banks engaged after the crisis, we have very little theory to guide those empirical explorations.

Recent theoretical work may help to fill this void. Williamson (2014) permits exchange to be facilitated by an array of assets, including

---

[31] An equivalent "backward" way of describing the adjustment is that as interest rates rise, debt service increases, requiring higher taxes or lower spending to cover additional interest on the debt, if the level of debt is to remain fixed.

government bonds, money, and credit. When asset market constraints bind, government bonds carry a liquidity premium and bonds bear a low rate of return. The constraint binds whenever government bonds are scarce. In Williamson's setting, fiscal policy sets the value of government debt exogenously and monetary policy determines the composition of that debt – between money and bonds – via open-market operations. The model delivers the striking conclusion that when the constraint binds, lower nominal interest rates reduce output, consumption, and welfare, so it is not optimal for monetary policy to move to the zero lower bound.

Eiben (2015) models the collateral role that government debt plays. This is designed to capture, without explicitly modeling, the essence of the repurchase market in which government securities are an important component of collateral on short-term loans between financial institutions. Government debt supplies liquidity services by overcoming financial frictions to facilitate portfolio reallocation. Plentiful government debt allocates physical capital to the highest productivity uses, raising welfare.

Yun (2011) shows that when roles such as these for government debt are embedded in an otherwise conventional New Keynesian model, conditions for determinacy of equilibrium can change from conventional wisdom. This suggests that monetary and fiscal policy design could change in important ways.

In most models used to study fiscal and monetary policy, a Modigliani–Miller irrelevance theorem holds for the maturity structure of government debt. Debt maturity matters, however, under the fiscal theory (Cochrane, 2001). Long debt permits any inflationary consequences that arise from equilibrium condition (2) to be spread over the term of the debt, permitting debt to serve as a shock absorber. Sims (2013), Leeper and Zhou (2013), and Leeper and Leith (2016) find that in the presence of long debt, the optimal mix of monetary and fiscal policies always entails some adjustment in inflation rates to shifts in fiscal needs, overturning the standard result that there is no role for inflation in ensuring fiscal sustainability (Schmitt-Grohé and Uribe, 2007; Kirsanova and Wren-Lewis, 2012).

One useful side effect of the financial crisis has been to push macro-economists away from Friedman's (1956) sharp focus on money and monetary policy, which has found modern voice in the graduate textbooks by Woodford (2003) and Galí (2008). Instead, by considering an array of assets and explicitly modeling both monetary and fiscal policies, the new research is closer to Tobin's (1961) more nuanced views of macroeconomic equilibrium.

3.5 Embracing Heterogeneity

Perhaps the most exciting recent developments in macroeconomic modeling lie in the broad area of integrating heterogeneity into general equilibrium models with aggregate shocks. Advances in both analytical and computational methods have opened doors to studying welfare costs of business cycles, tax policy, firm heterogeneity, monetary policy, housing, information dispersion, household default, mortgage markets, and worker flows (Storesletten, Telmer, and Yaron, 2001; Heathcote, 2005; Bloom, 2009; Gornemann, Kuester, and Nakajima, 2012; Iacoviello and Pavan, 2013; Rondina and Walker, 2014; Gordon, 2015; Guler, 2015; Michaud, 2015).

As Section 3.1 mentions, demographic dynamics are an important source of heterogeneity for fiscal analysis. Changes in birth rates, longevity, and dependency ratios have implications for saving rates, consumption patterns, labor market participation rates, relative prices, labor shares of income, real interest rates, and fiscal variables – government spending and revenues. Several papers have built on Gertler's (1999) life-cycle model to study the macroeconomic impacts of demographic dynamics in environments that treat demographics as deterministic (Carvalho and Ferrero, 2014; Kara and von Thadden, 2015; Katagiri, 2012).

But demographic "news" seems to arrive periodically, with major consequences for fiscal variables, as Nishimura (2012) and Katagiri, Konishi, and Ueda (2015) demonstrate. Figure 2.9 plots actual and projected birth rates (top panel) and life expectancy (bottom panel) for Japan. Projections are from official Japanese agencies. Evidently, over a thirty-year period, while the birth rate was steadily declining, forecasters continued to predict reversion toward the replacement rate. Although less pronounced, actual longevity consistently exceeds projections. Taking the difference between actual and projected as the "news," the figure implies that very substantial surprises arise from demographics. These surprises have both short-term implications for fiscal expenditures and long-term implications for labor productivity and consumption patterns, creating what Faust and Leeper (2015) call

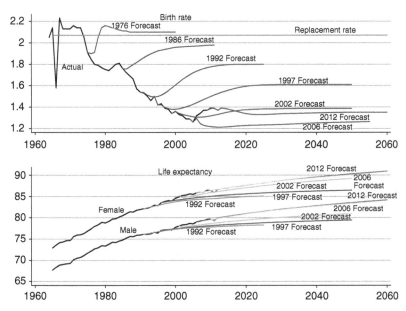

Figure 2.9: Actual and projected Japanese fertility rates and life expectancy, 1960–2060

Source: Japanese Ministry of Health, Labour and Welfare and National Institute of Population and Social Security Research, adapted from Nishimura (2012)

"disparate confounding dynamics" that make it difficult to separate trend and cycle in macro variables.

Economies subject to changes in fertility rates, retirement ages, and life expectancy carry broad implications about which representative-agent models are silent. Marginal propensities to consume vary across age cohorts, to impart drift to aggregate consumption functions. Consumption bundles also vary over the life cycle, which causes relative prices between consumption components to change persistently. As the population ages, labor supply declines, reducing the marginal product of physical capital and returns to investment. At the same time, an aging population reduces aggregate saving and the population's willingness to absorb government debt. Policy and non-policy disturbances asymmetrically affect age cohorts to generate redistributive effects. Finally, an aging population can inject a negative trend into long-term real interest rates, with implications for monetary policy that is run off of the New Keynesian notion of the "neutral real interest rate." Each of these effects poses challenges to analysts and policymakers alike.

A potentially high-impact line of research would integrate heterogeneous demographic dynamics with DSGE models of monetary and fiscal policies. Such research would provide valuable inputs to long-term fiscal decisions.

4 Rethinking Optimal Policy

In an environment that contains the ingredients I have sketched, it is no longer obvious how to conduct "optimal policy" analysis. Relative sizes of age cohorts evolve over time and with those evolving cohorts come gradual shifts in societal preferences. Before turning to what these shifts mean for optimal policy, let us first review what monetary and fiscal authorities state are their objectives.

4.1 Monetary vs. Fiscal Objectives

Central banks typically have a shortlist of objectives, in addition to ensuring financial stability.[32]

Federal Reserve: "maximum employment, stable prices, and moderate long-term interest rates."

Bank of England: "price stability – low inflation – and, subject to that, support the Government's economic objectives."

European Central Bank: "Without prejudice to the objective of price stability, to support the general economic policies of the Union."

Reserve Bank of New Zealand: "maintain a stable general level of price."

Among these central banks, with the exception of New Zealand, multiple mandates are the rule. While the Bank of England and the ECB seem to have lexicographically ordered mandates, no particular weights are given to the components of the triple mandate under which the Fed operates. Nonetheless, it is clear that price stability and possibly real stability are the aims of monetary policy.

---

[32] Sources for the objectives of monetary policy can be found on the respective central banks' web pages.

Fiscal authorities, in contrast, are all over the map. In addition to fiscal sustainability, their objectives can take up several pages.[33]

United States: "Maintain a strong economy and create economic and job opportunities by promoting the conditions that enable economic growth and stability at home and abroad, strengthen national security by combating threats and protecting the integrity of the financial system, and manage the U.S. Government's finances and resources effectively."

United Kingdom: "maintaining a stable macroeconomic framework with low inflation; improving the quality and cost effectiveness of public services; increasing the productivity of the economy and expanding economic and employment opportunities for all, through productive investment, competition, innovation, enterprise, better regulation and increased employability; promoting a fair and efficient tax and benefit system with incentives to work, save and invest; maintaining an effective accounting and budgetary framework and promoting high standards of regularity, propriety and accountability; securing an efficient market in financial services and banking with fair and effective supervision; arranging for cost effective management of the government's debt and foreign currency reserves and the supply of notes and coins; promoting international financial stability and the UK's economic interests and ideas through international cooperation as a way of increasing global prosperity including seeking to protect the most vulnerable groups."

Sweden: "to create as much welfare as possible by promoting high and sustainable economic growth and employment, welfare that extends to everyone, and stable resource utilisation."

New Zealand: "To address fiscal sustainability, governments must: achieve and maintain prudent public debt levels; ensure that, on average, Crown operating expenses do not exceed Crown operating revenues; achieve and maintain levels of Crown net worth to provide a buffer against shocks; manage fiscal risks facing the Crown prudently; consider the likely impact of fiscal strategy on

---

[33] This list draws on web pages from the US Department of the Treasury (2007, 2015), HM Treasury (2009a,b, 2014), Swedish Government (2011), New Zealand Treasury (2003), New Zealand Government (2015), Australian Treasury (2008), Swedish Ministry of Finance (2008).

present and future generations. To address economic stability, governments must: have regard to the interaction between fiscal policy and monetary policy. To address fiscal structure, governments must: when formulating revenue strategy, have regard to efficiency and equity, including the predictability and stability of tax rates; ensure that the Crown's resources are managed effectively and efficiently."

Various governments: "improve living standards; promote a sound macroeconomic environment; reduce labor market exclusions; encourage global economic growth; predict and prevent economic and financial crises; deliver conditions for business success; combat climate change; reduce poverty at home and abroad; equalize income distribution; build infrastructure; reduce smoking; minimize deadweight losses."

Whereas monetary policy objectives are narrowly focused and, for the most part, time-invariant, fiscal policy objectives cover tremendous ground and can vary with the government in power. Having many objectives, whose internal consistency is unchecked, is equivalent to having no verifiable objectives.[34] While this is to be expected in democratic societies in which fiscal policies are highly politicized, it makes it quite difficult to hold fiscal decisionmakers accountable for their actions. A clear message from the vast list of stated fiscal objectives is that the connection between them and optimal fiscal policy exercises is, at best, tenuous.

A large fraction of optimal policy papers – including by the present author – solve an uninteresting problem. They posit a representative-agent model and then seek to choose policies to minimize fluctuations around a steady state – efficient or not – subject to consumer optimization, budget constraints, and market clearing. Lucas (1987) taught that the welfare gains from eliminating business cycle fluctuations in consumption are tiny, a quantitative result that extends to recent New Keynesian models. Despite this, many researchers in academia and at central banks continue to treat central banks as if they are solving this optimization problem.

I think it is clear that fiscal authorities are not solving a problem that looks anything like this canonical optimal policy problem. Aside from

---

[34] Leeper (2009, 2011) discusses the difficulty of anchoring fiscal expectations in an environment with time-varying and unverifiable fiscal objectives.

ensuring solvency and providing some automatic stabilizers, it is not obvious that fiscal authorities are solving *any* macroeconomic problem. Instead, fiscal choices appear to be driven by distributional considerations – income and wealth distribution, tradeoffs between supporting the aged and investing in the young, distortions induced by tax rates that land differentially on agents, and so forth. I have nothing to add to the distributional aspects of fiscal choices.

But I do want to raise the question of whether we can create an institutional environment in which fiscal policy can contribute to macroeconomic stabilization. At present, this does not seem to be the case. Sovereign debt troubles in the GIIPS countries have been used as an excuse to consolidate in *all* euro-area countries, even ones that cannot see their fiscal limits with a telescope. Arbitrary targeting rules for net lending or government debt and constitutional requirements to balance budgets have been adopted without much reference to macroeconomic objectives. What are the opportunity costs of such stringent rules?

4.2 Social Contracts

Modern societies are grounded in social contracts between the people and their government. It is the fulfillment of these contracts by both parties that holds societies together. To an extent that is underappreciated, fiscal policies are an essential aspect of social contracts. After all, through taxation, the people have acceded to turn over resources to the government. Of course, the contract specifies what the people receive in exchange for those resources.

Social contracts in many countries are under threat. The kinds of promised expenditures that underlie explosive debt projections in the United States and nearly every other advanced economy are being renegotiated. At the same time, investments in infrastructure and education that would benefit future workers are being reduced to accommodate payments to the elderly. Our societies do face long-run fiscal stresses. Those stresses have been met with too much political vitriol and too little economic analysis.

Alternative resolutions to long-run fiscal stress need to incorporate the potential costs of breaking or substantially altering the social contract. These costs are not typically embedded in formal models, but they are foremost in the minds of policymakers. Useful analysis will bring those concerns explicitly into the calculations.

Okun's (2015) classic essay on the tradeoff between equality and efficiency is a good place to start to think about how to bring the idea of social contracts into fiscal analysis. He points out that American society chooses to accept "far more inequality in the distribution of its economic assets than in the distribution of its sociopolitical assets" (p. 118). And a major cost of equalizing incomes and wealth is the sacrifice of some economic efficiency. Okun wrote this in the mid-1970s after two decades with little change in income distribution. As Piketty and Saez (2003) document for the United States and Alvaredo et al. (2013) show for Australia, the United Kingdom, and Canada, the share of income going to the top 1 percent has followed a U-shape over the past century.[35] This shift in income distribution raises the question of whether the (implicit) social contract that Okun describes will begin to fray. Contracts are more likely to fray once we recognize that the potentially large fiscal changes to address long-run fiscal stresses will probably affect the lower deciles of the income distribution disproportionately.

5 Concluding Remarks

This is a daunting research agenda. But it is daunting only because fiscal analysis is darned hard. And the analysis is hard because fiscal actions affect every aspect of an economy and fiscal decision-making is complex.

Much existing fiscal analysis is less helpful than it could be. This sad state of affairs is due in large part to governments' massive underfunding of fiscal analysis. Central banks the world over have research staffs who are encouraged to make original contributions that are published in professional journals. Few ministries of finance have made similar investments. Fiscal policy councils, which have the potential to make valuable contributions to policymaking, are typically similarly underfunded and cannot maintain research staffs. Even large "fiscal councils," such as the US Congressional Budget Office, claim to have insufficient resources – and a lack of remit – to engage in original

---

[35] Data underlying these results are updated and available at https://eml/ berkeley.edu/saez and www.wid.world. Alvaredo et al. (2013) point out that the pattern of income inequality is more L-shaped in continental Europe and Japan.

research. They also seem unable to incorporate the insights that academic research has to offer, as Section 2.1 argues.

Although high-quality analysis does not seem to underlie macroeconomic fiscal choices, as it often does for monetary policy, there is reason for optimism. All of the *desiderata* that I list for useful fiscal analysis appear in one form or another in the academic literature. Over time they will be increasingly integrated into single frameworks to permit the kind of careful analysis that fiscal choices deserve.

Fiscal councils, even underfunded ones, can contribute to accelerating this process. Councils facilitate dialog between academic economists and policymakers. They can also encourage the use of frontier research methods to address practical policy problems. Compared to just a decade ago, the level of fiscal discourse in some countries operates on a higher intellectual plain. These are promising developments that confront the intrinsic difficulties in fiscal analysis to yield fresh policy insights.

Bibliography

Aguiar, M. and Gopinath, G. (2006). Defaultable debt, interest rates and the current account. *Journal of International Economics*, **69**(1), 64–83.

Altig, D., Auerbach, A. J., Kotlikoff, L. J., Smetters, K. and Walliser, J. (2001). Simulating fundamental tax reform in the United States. *American Economic Review*, **91**(3), 574–95.

Ålund, A. (2015). *Revisiting the Latvian and Greek Financial Crises: The Benefits of Front-Loading Fiscal Adjustment*. CASE Network Studies & Analyses No. 477, Center for Social and Economic Research, Warsaw.

Alvaredo, F., Atkinson, T., Piketty, T. and Saez, E. (2013). The top 1 percent in international and historical perspective. *Journal of Economic Perspectives*, **27**(3), 3–20.

Arellano, C. (2008). Default risk and income fluctuations in emerging economies. *American Economic Review*, **98**(3), 690–712.

Åslund, A. and Dombrovskis, V. (2011). *How Latvia Came through the Financial Crisis*. Washington, DC: Peterson Institute for International Economics.

Auerbach, A. J. and Kotlikoff, L. J. (1987). *Dynamic Fiscal Policy*. Cambridge, MA: Cambridge University Press.

Australian Treasury (2008). *The Treasury: Who We Are and What We Do*. Sydney: Australian Government.

Barro, R. J. and Gordon, D. B. (1983). A positive theory of monetary policy in a natural-rate model. *Journal of Political Economy*, **91**(4), 589–610.

Beirne, J. and Fratzscher, M. (2013). *The Pricing of Sovereign Risk and Contagion during the European Sovereign Debt Crisis*. European Central Bank Working Paper No. 1625, December.

Bi, H. (2012). Sovereign risk premia, fiscal limits and fiscal policy. *European Economic Review*, 56(3), 389–410.

Bi, H. and Leeper, E. M. (2012). *Analyzing Fiscal Sustainability*. Manuscript, Indiana University, October.

Bi, H. and Traum, N. (2012). Estimating sovereign default risk. *American Economic Review Papers & Proceedings*, 102(3), 161–6.

(2014). Estimating fiscal limits: the case of Greece. *Journal of Applied Econometrics*, 29(7), 1053–72.

Blanchard, O., Griffiths, M. and Gruss, B. (2013). Boom, bust, recovery: forensics of the Latvia crisis. *Brookings Papers on Economic Activity*, Fall, 325–71.

Bloom, N. (2009). The impact of uncertainty shocks. *Econometrica*, 77(3), 623–85.

Bohn, H. (2008). The sustainability of fiscal policy in the United States. In R. Neck and J.-E. Sturm, eds., *Sustainability of Public Debt*. Cambridge, MA: MIT Press, pp. 15–49.

Carvalho, C. and Ferrero, A. (2014). *What Explains Japan's Persistent Deflation?* Manuscript, University of Oxford, August.

Cecchetti, S. G., Mohanty, M. S. and Zampolli, F. (2010). *The Future of Public Debt: Prospects and Implications*. BIS Working Paper No. 300, Monetary and Economic Department, March.

Chang, M. (2015). *The Rising Power of the ECB: The Case of the Single Supervisory Mechanism*. Paper prepared for the biennial conference of the European Union Studies Association, March 5–7, Boston.

Christiano, L., Eichenbaum, M. and Rebelo, S. (2011). When is the government spending multiplier large? *Journal of Political Economy*, 119(1), 78–121.

Cochrane, J. H. (1999). A frictionless view of US inflation. In B. S. Bernanke and J. J. Rotemberg, eds., *NBER Macroeconomics Annual 1998*, vol. 13, Cambridge, MA: MIT Press, pp. 323–84.

(2001). Long term debt and optimal policy in the fiscal theory of the price level. *Econometrica*, 69(1), 69–116.

(2005). Money as stock. *Journal of Monetary Economics*, 52(3), 501–28.

Congressional Budget Office (2010). *The Long-Term Budget Outlook*. Washington, DC: US Congress, June.

(2014). *The Budget and Economic Outlook: 2014 to 2024*. Washington, DC: Congressional Budget Office, February.

(2015). *The Long-Term Budget Outlook*. Washington, DC: US Congress, June.

(2016). Does CBO do "dynamic scoring"? www.cbo.gov/faqs#dynamic

Constâncio, V. (2010). Contagion and the European debt crisis. In *Public Debt, Monetary Policy and Financial Stability*, Banque de France Financial Stability Review, vol. 16, pp. 109–21.

Davig, T., Leeper, E. M. and Walker, T. B. (2010). "Unfunded liabilities" and uncertain fiscal financing. *Journal of Monetary Economics*, 57(5), 600–19.

(2011). Inflation and the fiscal limit. *European Economic Review*, 55(1), 31–47.

Dhar, S. (2014). *IMF Macroeconomic Policy Advice in the Financial Crisis Aftermath*. Background Paper 14/07, Independent Evaluation Office of the IMF, October 8.

Di Comite, F., Giudice, G., Lendvai, J. and Toming, I. (2012). *Fiscal Consolidation in the Midst of the Crisis*. European Commission, DG ECFIN, March 1.

Eaton, J. and Gersovitz, M. (1981). Debt with potential repudiation: theoretical and empirical analysis. *Review of Economic Studies*, 48(2), 289–309.

Eiben, R. S. (2015). *The Bond Liquidity Premium and Fiscal Policy: A Re-examination*. Manuscript, Indiana University, October.

Faust, J. (2005). *Is Applied Monetary Policy Hard?* Manuscript, Federal Reserve Board, March, http://e105.org/faustj

Faust, J. and Leeper, E. M. (2015). "The Myth of Normal: The Bumpy Story of Inflation and Monetary Policy," in *Inflation Dynamics and Monetary Policy*. Federal Reserve Bank of Kansas City Economic Conference Proceedings, 2015 Jackson Hole Symposium, www.kansascityfed.org/publications/research/escp/symposiums/escp-2015

Ferrero, A. (2010). A structural decomposition of the US trade balance: productivity, demographics and fiscal policy. *Journal of Monetary Economics*, 57(4), 478–90.

File, T. (2014). *Young-Adult Voting: An Analysis of Presidential Elections, 1964–2012*. US Census Bureau, Department of Commerce, April.

Forbes, K. J. (2013). Comment on "Boom, bust, recovery: forensics of the Latvia crisis," by Blanchard, Griffiths, and Gruss. *Brookings Papers on Economic Activity*, **Fall**, 372–81.

Friedman, M. (1948). A monetary and fiscal framework for economic stability. *American Economic Review*, 38(2), 245–64.

(1956). The Quantity Theory of Money – A Restatement. In M. Friedman, ed., *Studies in the Quantity Theory of Money*, pp. 3–21. Chicago, IL: University of Chicago Press.

Galí, J. (2008). *Monetary Policy, Inflation, and the Business Cycle*. Princeton, NJ: Princeton University Press.

Gertler, M. (1999). Government debt and social security in a life-cycle economy. *Carnegie-Rochester Conference Series on Public Policy*, 50, pp. 61–110.

Ghosh, A., Kim, J. I., Mendoza, E. G., Ostry, J. D. and Qureshi, M. S. (2012). Fiscal fatigue, fiscal space and debt sustainability in advanced economies. *The Economic Journal*, 123(566), F4–F30.

Gordon, D. B. and Leeper, E. M. (2006). The price level, the quantity theory of money, and the fiscal theory of the price level. *Scottish Journal of Political Economy*, 53(1), 4–27.

Gordon, G. (2015). Evaluating default policy: the business cycle matters. *Quantitative Economics*, 6(3), 795–823.

Gornemann, N., Kuester, K. and Nakajima, M. (2012). *Monetary Policy with Heterogeneous Agents*. Federal Reserve Bank of Philadelphia Working Paper No. 12–21, September.

Gorton, G. and Ordoñez, G. (2013). *The Supply and Demand for Safe Assets*. NBER Working Paper No. 18732, January.

—— (2014). Collateral crises. *American Economic Review*, 104(2), 343–78.

Gourinchas, P.-O. and Jeanne, O. (2012). *Global Safe Assets*. BIS Working Paper No. 399, December.

Guler, B. (2015). Innovations in information technology and the mortgage market. *Review of Economic Dynamics*, 18(3), 456–83.

Hatchondo, J. C. and Martinez, L. (2010). The politics of sovereign defaults. *Federal Reserve Bank of Richmond Economic Quarterly*, 96(3), 291–317.

Hausman, J. K. and Wieland, J. F. (2014). Abenomics: preliminary analysis and outlook. *Brookings Papers on Economic Activity*, **Spring**, 1–63.

Heathcote, J. (2005). Fiscal policy with heterogeneous agents and incomplete markets. *Review of Economic Studies*, 72(1), 161–88.

HM Treasury (2009a). *Budget 2009, Building Britain's Future: Economic and Fiscal Strategy Report and Financial Statement and Budget Report*. London: The Stationery Office.

—— (2009b). *HM Treasury Group Departmental Strategic Objectives: 2008–2011*. London: HM Treasury.

—— (2014). *Annual Report and Accounts 2013–14*. London: Controller of Her Majesty's Stationery Office.

Holter, H. A., Krueger, D. and Stepanchuk, S. (2015). *How Does Tax Progressivity and Household Heterogeneity Affect Laffer Curves*. Manuscript, University of Pennsylvania, February.

Horton, M., Kumar, M. and Mauro, P. (2009). *The State of Public Finances: A Cross-Country Fiscal Monitor*. IMF Staff Position Note SPN/09/21, July 30.

Iacoviello, M. and Pavan, M. (2013). Housing and debt over the life cycle and over the business cycle. *Journal of Monetary Economics*, **60**(2), 221–38.

International Monetary Fund (2008). *World Economic Outlook*. Washington, DC: IMF, October.

(2010). *Fiscal Monitor – Fiscal Exit: From Strategy to Implementation*. Washington, DC: IMF, November.

(2011). *Fiscal Monitor Update – Staying the Course on Fiscal Adjustment*. Washington, DC: IMF, June 17.

(2012). *Fiscal Monitor Update – As Downside Risks Rise, Fiscal Policy Has to Walk a Narrow Path*. Washington, DC: IMF, January 24.

(2014a). *Fiscal Monitor – Back To Work: How Fiscal Policy Can Help*. Washington, DC: IMF, October.

(2014b). *Japan: 2014 Article IV Consultation – Staff Report*. IMF Country Report 14/236, July.

(2015). *Fiscal Monitor – Now Is the Time: Fiscal Policies for Sustainable Growth*. Washington, DC: IMF, April.

Ito, T. (2006). Japanese monetary policy: 1998–2005 and beyond. In *Monetary Policy in Asia: Approaches and Implementation*. Bank for International Settlements, pp. 105–32, www.bis.org/publ/bppdf/bispap31.pdf

Ito, T. and Mishkin, F. S. (2006). Two decades of Japanese monetary policy and the deflation problem. In A. K. Rose and T. Ito, eds., *Monetary Policy Under Very Low Inflation in the Pacific Rim, NBER–EASE*, vol. 15. Chicago, IL: University of Chicago Press, pp. 131–93.

Kara, E. and Von Thadden, L. (2015). Interest rate effects of demographic changes in a new-Keynesian life-cycle framework. *Macroeconomic Dynamics*, **20**(01), 120–64.

Katagiri, M. (2012). *Economic Consequences of Population Aging in Japan: Effects through Changes in Demand Structure*. IMES Discussion Paper No. 2012-E-3, Bank of Japan, March.

Katagiri, M., Konishi, H. and Ueda, K. (2015). *Aging and Deflation from a Fiscal Perspective*. Manuscript, Bank of Japan, June.

Kirsanova, T. and Wren-Lewis, S. (2012). Optimal feedback on debt in an economy with nominal rigidities. *The Economic Journal*, **122**(559), 238–64.

Krugman, P. (2013a). Comment on "Boom, bust, recovery: forensics of the Latvia crisis," by Blanchard, Griffiths, and Gruss. *Brookings Papers on Economic Activity*, Fall, 381–4.

(2013b). Latvia, once again. *The New York Times*, January 2, http://krugman.blogs.nytimes.com/2013/01/02/latvia-once-again.

Krugman, P. R. (1998). It's baaack: Japan's slump and the return of the liquidity trap. *Brookings Papers on Economic Activity*, **2**, 137–87.

Kydland, F. and Prescott, E. C. (1977). Rules rather than discretion: the inconsistency of optimal plans. *Journal of Political Economy*, **85**, 473–92.

Leeper, E. M. (1991). Equilibria under "active" and "passive" monetary and fiscal policies. *Journal of Monetary Economics*, **27**(1), 129–47.

(2009). Anchoring fiscal expectations. *Reserve Bank of New Zealand Bulletin*, **72**(3), 7–32.

(2011). Monetary science, fiscal alchemy. In *Macroeconomic Challenges: The Decade Ahead*, Federal Reserve Bank of Kansas City Economic Conference Proceedings, 2010 Jackson Hole Symposium, pp. 361–434.

Leeper, E. M. and Leith, C. (2016). Understanding inflation as a joint monetary-fiscal phenomenon. In J. B. Taylor and H. Uhlig, eds., *Handbook of Macroeconomics*, vol. 2. Amsterdam: Elsevier Press.

Leeper, E. M., Plante, M. and Traum, N. (2010). Dynamics of fiscal financing in the United States. *Journal of Econometrics*, **156**(2), 304–21.

Leeper, E. M., Traum, N. and Walker, T. B. (2015). *Clearing Up the Fiscal Multiplier Morass*. NBER Working Paper No. 21433, July.

Leeper, E. M., Walker, T. B. and Yang, S.-C. S. (2013). Fiscal foresight and information flows. *Econometrica*, **81**(3), 1115–45.

Leeper, E. M. and Yang, S.-C. S. (2008). Dynamic scoring: alternative financing schemes. *Journal of Public Economics*, **92**, 159–82.

Leeper, E. M. and Zhou, X. (2013). *Inflation's Role in Optimal Monetary-Fiscal Policy*. NBER Working Paper No. 19686, November.

Lucas, Jr., R. E. (1987). *Models of Business Cycles*. Oxford: Basil Blackwell.

Mccarty, N., Poole, K. T. and Rosenthal, H. (2006). *Polarized America: The Dance of Ideology and Unequal Riches*. Cambridge, MA: The MIT Press.

McKay, A. and Reis, R. (2015). The role of automatic stabilizers in the U.S. business cycle. *Econometrica*, **84**(1), 141–94.

McLaughlin, K. (2012). Euro area must take austerity pain now, Dombrovskis says. *Bloomberg*, May 7, www.bloomberg.com/news/articles/2012-05-07/eu-must-take-austerity-pain-now-to-end-crisis-dombrovskis-says

Mendoza, E. G. and Ostry, J. D. (2008). International evidence on fiscal solvency: is fiscal policy "responsible"? *Journal of Monetary Economics*, **55**(6), 1081–93.

Michaud, A. M. (2015). *A Quantitative Theory of Information, Worker Flows, and Wage Dispersion*. Manuscript, Indiana University, May.

Múčka, Z. (2015). *Is the Maastricht Debt Limit Safe Enough for Slovakia? Fiscal Limits and Default Risk Premia for Slovakia*. Council for Budget Responsibility, Working Paper No. 2/2015.

New Zealand Government (2015). *An Introduction to New Zealand's Fiscal Policy Framework*. Wellington: The Treasury.

New Zealand Treasury (2003). *Objectives, Targets and Instruments for Crown Financial Policy*. Wellington: New Zealand Treasury.

Nishimura, K. G. (2012). *Ageing, Finance and Regulations*. Keynote Address at the Joint Forum Meeting, Tokyo, November 14–15.

Okun, A. M. (2015). *Equality and Efficiency: The Big Tradeoff*, 2nd edn, Washington, DC: Brookings Institution Press.

Panico, C. and Purificato, F. (2013). *The Debt Crisis and the European Central Bank's Role of Lender of Last Resort*. Political Economic Research Institute Working Paper No. 306, University of Massachusetts Amherst, January.

Phillips, M. (2009). *Owning Up to What We Owe*. February 23, www.whitehouse.gov/blog/2009/02/23/owning-what-we-owe

Piketty, T. and Saez, E. (2003). Income inequality in the United States, 1913–1998. *Quarterly Journal of Economics*, **118**(1), 1–39.

Richter, A. W. (2015). Finite lifetimes, long-term debt and the fiscal limit. *Journal of Economic Dynamics and Control*, 51, 180–203.

Rondina, G. and Walker, T. B. (2014). *Dispersed Information and Confounding Dynamics*. Manuscript, Indiana University, October.

Schmitt-Grohé, S. and Uribe, M. (2007). Optimal simple and implementable monetary and fiscal rules. *Journal of Monetary Economics*, **54**(6), 1702–25.

Sims, C. A. (1994). A simple model for study of the determination of the price level and the interaction of monetary and fiscal policy. *Economic Theory*, 4(3), 381–99.

(2013). Paper money. *American Economic Review*, **103**(2), 563–84.

Stein, H. (1989). Problems and not-problems of the US economy. *The AEI Economist*, June, 1–8.

Storesletten, K., Telmer, C. I. and Yaron, A. (2001). The welfare cost of business cycles revisited: finite lives and cyclical variation in idiosyncratic risk. *European Economic Review*, 45(7), 1311–39.

Swedish Government (2011). *The Swedish Fiscal Policy Framework*. Stockholm: Regeringskansliet.

Swedish Ministry of Finance (2008). *Guidelines for Central Government Debt Management 2009*. Stockholm: Government Offices of Sweden, www.regeringen.se/sb/d/10494/a/115541.

Tobin, J. (1961). Money, capital, and other stores of value. *American Economic Review*, 51(2), 26–37.

Trabandt, M. and Uhlig, H. (2011). The Laffer curve revisited. *Journal of Monetary Economics*, **58**(4), 305–27.

Uhlig, H. (2010). Some fiscal calculus. *American Economic Review*, **100**(2), 30–34.

US Department of the Treasury (2007). *Strategic Plan: Fiscal Years 2007–2012*. Washington, DC: Department of the Treasury.

  (2015). Duties & functions of the US Department of the Treasury, www .treasury.gov/about/role-of-treasury/Pages/default.aspx

Wallace, N. (1981). A Modigliani–Miller theorem for open-market operations. *American Economic Review*, **71**(3), 267–74.

Williamson, S. D. (2014). *Scarce Collateral, the Term Premium, and Quantitative Easing*. Federal Reserve Bank of St. Louis Working Paper No. 2014–008A, March.

Woodford, M. (1995). Price-level determinacy without control of a monetary aggregate. *Carnegie-Rochester Conference Series on Public Policy*, **43**, 1–46.

  (2001). Fiscal requirements for price stability. *Journal of Money, Credit, and Banking*, **33**(3), 669–728.

  (2003). *Interest and Prices: Foundations of a Theory of Monetary Policy*. Princeton, NJ: Princeton University Press.

Yun, T. (2011). *Transmission Mechanisms of the Public Debt*. Manuscript, Seoul National University, October.

3 | Fiscal Implications of Central Bank Balance Sheet Policies

ATHANASIOS ORPHANIDES

1 Introduction

In the aftermath of the 2008 global financial crisis, central banks have been called on to undertake unprecedented responsibilities well beyond ordinary monetary policy operations aiming to preserve price stability. In large part, this reflects the ability of central banks to rapidly generate the equivalent of *fiscal* resources, through the creation of high-powered money. These resources could be used for asset purchases and bailout operations without the delays associated with fiscal deliberations in democracies and served a useful role in containing some adverse effects of the crisis. In the process, it was also revealed that the power of a central bank's balance sheet can be more massive and awe-inspiring than was the prevailing understanding before the crisis.

Although monetary arithmetic ultimately links fiscal and monetary policy (Sargent and Wallace, 1981), prior to the crisis the fiscal implications of central bank policies tended to be seen as relatively minor and escaped close scrutiny. This served a useful political role: Underemphasizing the fiscal consequences of central bank decisions could more easily sustain support for an independent central bank with discretionary powers and a price stability mandate. During the crisis, however, near-zero interest rates blurred the line separating fiscal and monetary policy and bailout operations drew attention to fiscal consequences and distributional implications of balance-sheet policies. This, in turn, raised questions about the institutional division of labor between independent central banks and elected governments.

The response to the crisis by the Federal Reserve and the ECB, the central banks of the world's two largest economies, included discretionary decisions with immense distributional effects that could be seen as incompatible with the role of unelected officials in democratic societies. For both central banks, issues arose with decisions that resulted in the preferential treatment of specific sectors of the economy

71

or specific private interests. In the case of the ECB, support to different euro-area member states appears to have been decidedly uneven during the crisis, as a result of discretionary decisions.

After a review of the historical antecedents and the pre-crisis consensus regarding the institutional design of central banks and their policies, this chapter examines some of the decisions taken by the Federal Reserve and the ECB during the crisis in the context of their role as independent central banks in a democratic society. The examples discussed draw questions that challenge the legitimacy of the use of discretion: Is the proper function of an independent central bank in a democratic society to use its discretion and decide which sectors of the economy deserve the support of its balance sheet and which don't? Does an independent central bank have the legitimacy to discriminate in favor of specific private interests and against others? In a monetary union, does the central bank have the legitimacy to take discretionary decisions that favor specific member states over others, or decisions that penalize member states for what the central bank views as moral hazard-induced actions by democratically elected governments?

The chapter concludes with a discussion about the potential resolution of the legitimacy problem that has arisen due to central bank actions during the crisis.

2 Historical Antecedents and the Pre-Crisis Consensus

Reflecting on modern central banks, certainly central banks operating in Europe and North America, we can identify price stability, economic stability, and financial stability as their key goals and the reason for their existence as independent policy institutions. The typical textbook treatment would discuss monetary policy as aiming to achieve these objectives without discussion of the fiscal consequences of central bank decisions in pursuit of these goals.

However, this is not an accurate reflection of the origins of central banking; nor does it do justice to the intimate potential links between central bank policies and the fiscal affairs of the state.[1] Financing the state, particularly during war, was perhaps the single most important

---

[1] Goodhart (2010) provides a brief review of the changing role of central banks over time. Orphanides (2014a) discusses the evolving role of the Federal Reserve.

early factor in the development of central banking. One of the oldest central banks, the Bank of England, was founded in 1694 and was granted monopoly on note issuance to provide financing to King William III. Napoleon Bonaparte founded Banque de France in 1800 to facilitate his government's finance. In North America, the Federal Reserve Board was founded in 1913 to provide an elastic currency in response to financial crises, so state financing was not an explicit reason for its founding. Nonetheless, the Federal Reserve's most important task during the first years of its operations was none other than to facilitate the financing of World War I.

Controlling the issue and use of currency is a powerful economic weapon that can be used during times of peace and war to extract resources from the economy and, on occasion, even to wage economic warfare. Seigniorage, the real value accruing to the issuer of currency notes, can be a significant source of fiscal revenue, an invisible tax. In modern economies with low and stable inflation, seigniorage is small, but it need not be negligible. Seigniorage can easily exceed 1 percent of GDP per year in economies with high inflation. During the early 1980s, seigniorage exceeding 5 percent of GDP was documented in countries such as Mexico and Russia.[2] Empirical estimates suggest that seigniorage can be maximized at inflation rates exceeding 100 percent per year, which suggests obvious tradeoffs, given the detrimental effects of high inflation to growth and welfare.[3]

In addition to extracting seigniorage through inflation, the central bank balance sheet can be used to secure favorable financing terms for government debt. The cost of financing for the government can be reduced with financial repression, through regulation of the financial sector. Financial repression also entails tradeoffs, as the redirection of resources for the benefit of the government restricts credit to the private sector that could have been otherwise allocated to investment. Like seigniorage, financial repression can be detrimental to growth and welfare.

A sovereign nation in control of money issuance can have immense power over the fiscal resources that can be extracted through the central bank. The debasement of money can be systematically abused,

[2] See Hawkins (2003) for historical information regarding seigniorage and central bank profit distributions.
[3] Fischer et al. (2002) present empirical estimates of the seigniorage-maximizing inflation rate and discuss the welfare tradeoffs involved.

a problem that has been well recognized in the history of central banking. In 1824, David Ricardo identified the issue as follows:

It is said that Government could not be safely entrusted with the power of issuing paper money; that it would most certainly abuse it; and that, on any occasion when it was pressed for money to carry on a war, it would cease to pay coin, on demand, for its notes; and from that moment the currency would become a forced Government paper. There would, I confess, be great dangers of this, if Government – that is to say, the Ministers – were themselves to be entrusted with the power of issuing paper money. (Ricardo, 1824)

Ricardo drew important lessons regarding the governance of the central bank. In his view, the institution entrusted with the issuance of money should be kept independent of the government in order to safeguard the value of money and avoid the potential abuse associated with its issuance.

The pre-crisis consensus on central bank design captured Ricardo's reasoning by recognizing both the need for central bank independence from the fiscal authority and the need to protect the central bank from becoming the de facto source of financing for the government – the latter taking the form of the "no monetary financing" clause seen in central bank legislation.

In democracies, ensuring that central banks remain independent from the elected government provides a solution to the dynamic inconsistency problems associated with intertemporal tradeoffs. Price stability without financial repression encourages growth and improves welfare in the long run. On the other hand, faster money creation offers short-term gains: It can raise employment and increases seigniorage. The costs come later, with lower credibility and higher prices. Higher prices also reduce the real value of nominal government debt. The incentives for governments wishing to improve their odds of re-election are to focus on the shorter end of the spectrum of the cost–benefit analysis. By maintaining a long-term focus, an independent central bank with a price stability objective and the support of a market-based economy, refraining from financial repression, can better facilitate growth and welfare over time.

Monetary policy decisions always have *some* fiscal implications and distributional consequences. By influencing the path of real interest rates over time, monetary policy decisions have an impact on the intertemporal fiscal burden of the government and on the relative returns enjoyed by savers and lenders in the economy. However, under ordinary circumstances, and as long as monetary policy aims to ensure price stability and economic stability, these effects can be ignored as an unavoidable side effect, of secondary importance, of policies aiming at society's broader good.

Central bank policies could and normally should aim to minimize any distributional effects and credit allocation distortions introduced by their policies to avoid encroaching on matters that are incompatible with the role of unelected officials in democratic societies. Overall, the central bank should encourage free markets to allocate capital efficiently and promote growth and welfare over time, without engaging in operations that might suggest a bias in favor of regions or sectors of the economy, even though some distributional effects may be unavoidable.

3 The Power of a Central Bank's Balance Sheet

In the aftermath of the 2008 global financial crisis, central banks have been called on to undertake unprecedented responsibilities well beyond ordinary monetary policy operations. Central banks were overburdened and seen as "the only game in town" (Orphanides, 2013). In large part, this reflected the ability of central banks to act quickly – specifically, to generate the equivalent of *fiscal* resources rapidly through the creation of high-powered money (currency and reserves). In part, central banks acted to fill a void created by the hesitation of *fiscal authorities* to act in a resolute manner, but in doing so they tested the limits of democratic legitimacy.[4] Central banks certainly averted the worst of outcomes feared at the beginning of the crisis, but their actions during the crisis also revealed that the power of a central bank's balance sheet can be more massive and awe-inspiring than was the prevailing understanding before the crisis, at least outside the circles of central bank policy experts.

Actions were wide-ranging. Central banks engaged in unconventional monetary policy, including the purchase of public and private assets and the expanded provision of liquidity at low interest rates upon presentation of collateral drawn from a broadened base – collateral that

---

[4] Buiter (2014) and Tucker (2015, 2016) present expositions of the legitimacy and accountability challenges that have been exposed as a result of central bank actions over the past several years.

would not have qualified for pre-crisis operations. Central banks also engaged in preferential lending operations, lending to government-related or other entities at terms not available to others in the economy. Perhaps most controversial, in some cases central banks became the central actors in bailout operations, lending to potentially insolvent private firms or government entities with compromised market access.

Examined in isolation, none of these operations should be seen as necessarily peculiar or problematic. However, many of the decisions taken by central banks during the crisis were not simple applications of established rules or principles, but rather were of a discretionary nature. Given the fiscal dimension and distributional consequences of such discretionary decisions, these balance-sheet policies raise questions about the governance and accountability of independent central banks in a democratic society.

3.1 Unconventional Monetary Policy

When policy interest rates are lowered near zero, additional monetary policy accommodation can be provided, if needed, by expanding the central bank's balance sheet.[5] Asset purchases become a crucial monetary policy tool. Purchasing government bonds – what is known as quantitative easing (QE) – has been recognized as an extension of conventional monetary policy easing at the zero lower bound at least since the 1930s.[6] QE lowers real interest rates at longer maturities than those constrained by the zero lower bound, thereby easing monetary conditions despite the constraint on short-term rates.

---

[5] See Clouse et al. (2003) for a review of unconventional policy easing options at the zero lower bound. In addition to QE, these options include alternative ways to increase the central bank balance sheet as well as exchange rate and communication policies that influence expectations of future policy actions. It should be noted that the zero lower bound is not a hard constraint exactly at zero. The constraint is due to the existence of currency notes that earn a nominal zero return. Central banks can engineer slightly negative rates but some may also opt to stop cutting rates somewhat above zero. The reference to the zero lower bound is about the "effective" bound chosen by a central bank depending on the specific institutional setting and tradeoffs it may face. This need not be fixed as a central bank may adjust its "effective" lower bound with experience. During the crisis the ECB initially stopped at slightly positive rates but subsequently reconsidered its bound and moved to slightly negative rates.

[6] Clouse et al. (2003) and Orphanides (2013) provide historical references.

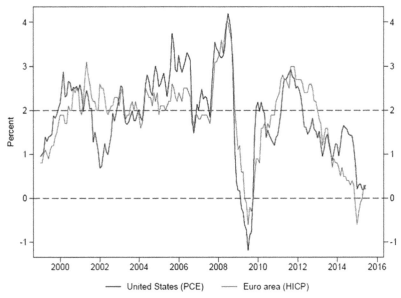

Figure 3.1: Fed vs. ECB: Inflation, 1999–2015
Notes: Monthly data. Headline PCE (Fed) and HICP (ECB).

As overnight interest rates may be constrained near zero, the extent of monetary policy easing is no longer reflected in policy rates alone. The size of the central bank's balance sheet becomes a useful summary indicator of policy accommodation, similar to the role of the overnight rate under ordinary circumstances. As with conventional easing, of course, no single indicator is sufficient to capture the degree of monetary accommodation in the economy.

The experience of the Federal Reserve and the ECB since 2008 serves as an illustration. Figures 3.1 through 3.5 outline a comparison of the conditions faced by and the policies pursued by the Fed and the ECB. Figures 3.1 and 3.2 compare headline and core inflation, respectively. As can be seen, the crisis and subsequent recession created disinflationary pressure in the two economies. It may be recalled that both of these central banks have an inflation objective close to 2 percent, using the PCE index for the Fed and the HICP for the ECB. Core inflation stayed below the inflation objectives of these two central banks. Conventional easing proved insufficient and additional unconventional easing became necessary. Figure 3.3 compares overnight rates in the United States and the

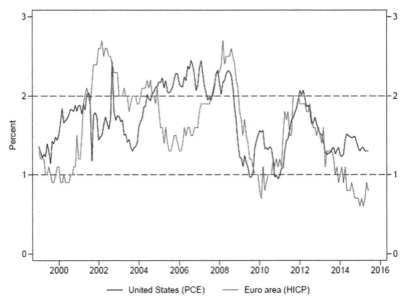

Figure 3.2: Fed vs. ECB: Core inflation, 1999–2015

Notes: Monthly data. Headline PCE excluding food and energy (Fed) and HICP excluding energy and unprocessed food (ECB).

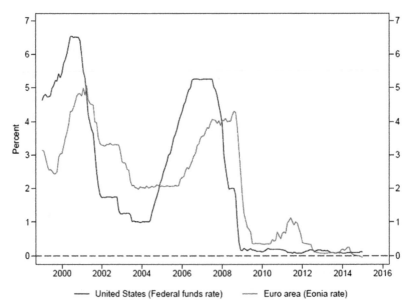

Figure 3.3: Fed vs. ECB: Overnight interest rate, 1999–2015

Notes: Monthly data.

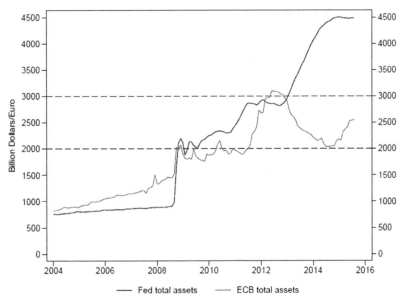

Figure 3.4: Fed vs. ECB: Balance sheet size, 2004–15
Notes: Billions of dollars (Fed) and euros (ECB).

euro area, while Figure 3.4 compares the size of the balance sheets of the Fed and the ECB. Before the crisis, movements in the overnight rate captured changes in monetary policy, while the balance sheets of the two central banks were nearly flat. By contrast, since the crisis, while rates have been close to zero for both central banks, the size of their balance sheets changed dramatically. Although balance-sheet increases have an accommodating role that is not reflected in over-night rates, this accommodation may be seen in longer rates that are not constrained by the zero lower bound. Figure 3.5 highlights this by showing the yields on ten-year government bonds for the United States and Germany.

3.2 Fiscal Operations during the Crisis

In some respects, central bank balance-sheet policies may be effectively equivalent to fiscal operations. First, at the zero lower bound, money is equivalent to short-term government paper. Liquidity can be injected in the economy with the Treasury issuing additional zero-interest-rate bills or the central bank raising the quantity of high-powered money,

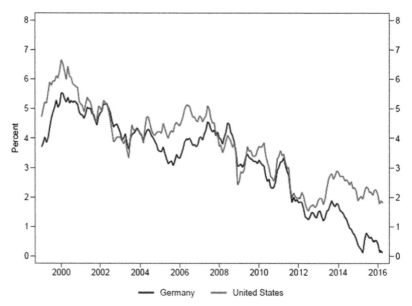

Figure 3.5: Effectiveness of unconventional policy easing in the United States and Germany, 2007–16

Notes: Yields of ten-year government bonds.

also earning zero interest. At the zero lower bound, high-powered money and treasury bills are near perfect substitutes, so these two policies may be indistinguishable from each other. By necessity, monetary and fiscal policies become much more closely linked at the zero lower bound than during periods when interest rates are clearly above zero.

Second, bailout operations aiming to restore the health of the financial sector are effectively fiscal operations. Provision of credit by the central bank to some private or government-related entities may sustain entities that would have otherwise collapsed. Central bank bailout operations are equivalent to governmental provision of fiscal support to troubled entities.[7]

---

[7] Such operations are often undertaken by central banks in their role as lender of last resort, which need not necessarily have a fiscal component. When emergency lending is provided at a "high rate" against "good collateral," that is strictly in accordance to Bagehot's (1873) principles, it does not involve a fiscal transfer. Bailout operations with a fiscal component invariably violate some aspect of Bagehot's principles.

A major issue with fiscal operations is that they have potentially large distributional effects. Such effects may be unavoidable during a crisis, but this does not reduce the scope for potential controversy associated with them.

During the global financial crisis, central banks provided preferential support to some entities but not to others. Balance-sheet policies had (and continue to have) immense distributional effects. This can raise questions when the central banks involved appear to provide preferential support on the basis of discretionary decisions or tailor-made "rules" adopted and adjusted during the crisis, rather than on the basis of principles and rules that are clear ahead of time – before the identity of the beneficiary becomes known.

The power to engage in distributional policies was not the intended purpose of central banks' independence. The purpose was to protect price stability over time. In democracies, distributional matters should fall squarely in the domain of elected governments. Unfortunately, a number of the fiscal operations implemented during the crisis appear to fall into the category that raises questions. Indeed, some distributional effects arising from central bank discretionary decisions during the crisis appear to have had no clear basis on rules that were in place before the crisis, which raises serious governance questions about the operation of independent central banks.

The next two sections review some specific examples of policy decisions that raise questions for the Fed and ECB.

4 Distributional Issues: Federal Reserve

As already mentioned, a central bank can enlarge its balance sheet by purchasing assets to provide unconventional monetary policy accommodation when this is needed for the aggregate economy. But the choice of what to purchase can provide preferential treatment to specific sectors of the economy over others. The Fed traditionally attempted to stay clear of such preferential treatment by doing all its monetary policy operations with US government bills and bonds. Plain QE could have been pursued during the crisis when the zero lower bound was reached and the Fed determined that additional accommodation was still needed. As part of its toolkit of unconventional monetary policy easing, however, the Fed decided to engage in additional asset purchases. Specifically, it decided to purchase large quantities of

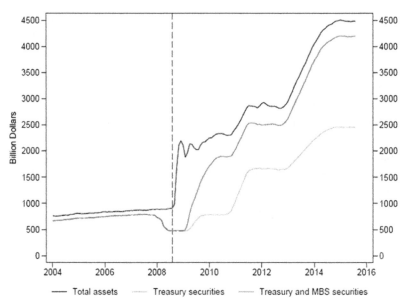

Figure 3.6: The balance sheet of the Federal Reserve, 2004–16

Notes: Decomposition of balance sheet into three categories of assets: Treasury securities, mortgage-backed securities (MBS) and others.

housing-related mortgage-backed debt (MBS). As Figure 3.6 shows, MBS holdings became a very important part of the Fed's balance sheet. This policy could be defended by noting that the housing sector had been disproportionately hurt by the crisis. Boosting the housing sector would help the economy overall. This may be true, but it does not change the fact that the Fed's decision to buy MBS rather than simply implementing QE through purchases of long-dated government debt was equivalent to a massive subsidy to the housing sector over other sectors of the economy, and that it disproportionately benefited holders of mortgage-backed securities over holders of other financial assets. This may have been effective as monetary policy, but this is a separate issue. The question raised is more fundamental: Whether it is the proper function of an independent central bank in a democratic society to use its discretion and decide which sectors of the economy deserve the support of its balance sheet and which do not.

It is interesting to note that, compared to other central banks, the Fed has rather limited authority on how to use its balance sheet for asset purchases. Congress has placed limits on the Fed, which can purchase only US government and US government-guaranteed assets. The authority to purchase MBS resulted from 1960s legislation by Congress that was meant to encourage the Fed to buy government-guaranteed debt, in an effort to advance financing of pet projects. The political dimension of the problem is unmistakable. Why face contentious discussion over the budget in Congress if the Fed could quietly achieve the same fiscal objective? An interesting example of this authority, as revisited in Haltom and Sharp (2014), was the financing of the construction of the Metro system in Washington, DC. The Washington Metropolitan Area Transit Authority (WMATA) was established in 1967 for that purpose and issued debt to fund the system's construction. By purchasing that debt, the Fed ended up financing the project, thereby vastly improving the efficiency of commuting in Washington, DC for residents of the metropolitan area, which included Congressional staff as well as the staff of the Federal Reserve Board.

This is not to say that investment in the Washington metro in the 1970s or support of the US housing market in the 2010s was not a worthwhile cause. The question simply is whether it is appropriate for an independent central bank, rather than the fiscal authority of a democratic state, to use its discretionary authority to decide what is worthwhile to support and what is not. Once it had been freed from the politicization it faced during the 1960s, and up until the crisis – a period spanning decades – the Fed had provided an answer to this question: It decided *not* to use its discretionary authority to finance pet projects or favor specific sectors of the economy.

An even more controversial aspect of balance-sheet operations pertains to bailout operations that may suggest preferential treatment to specific private interests. As with any central bank, the Federal Reserve has the authority to serve as a lender of last resort – to provide loans backed by collateral to private entities under stress. In the case of the Fed, this authority was not limited to banks or even financial institutions. Under Article 13(3) of the Federal Reserve Act, the Board of Governors had the power to provide credit to virtually anyone, as long as it judged that conditions were unusual and exigent. As Meltzer (2013) points out, however, the Fed never announced a lender-of-last-resort policy and, during the crisis, acted in a manner that shifted bailout costs to taxpayers – an outcome stemming from the too-big-to-fail doctrine.

It is very difficult to judge crisis decisions after the fact. To the extent that decisions follow clear principles and reflect the information available at the time as well as possible, even decisions that prove problematic after the fact could be justified and proper. A fundamental difficulty with ex post evaluation of crisis decisions is that counterfactuals may be hard to construct. Debates on such matters as the differential treatment of Bear Stearns and Lehman during 2008 cannot be authoritatively settled with any amount of data, since the relevant counterfactuals are not available.[8] The issues are complex. The evaluation of an institution's solvency – a pre-condition for providing emergency lending—can be subject to honest mistakes.

Internal consistency and uniformity of different support decisions can be evaluated with greater confidence. Conditional on the decision to provide lending to too-big-to-fail institutions, for example, additional questions pertain to the terms of the lending arrangement. Is it legitimate for the central bank to use its discretionary power to decide on a case-by-case basis whether a specific firm will be allowed to secure financing at favorable terms while another firm would not be allowed similar terms?

An interesting case for the Fed relates to its treatment of non-bank financial institutions under stress. We may call this the Goldman vs. AIG comparison.[9] Both Goldman and AIG were non-bank financial corporations, not eligible for the usual discount window operations to which Federal Reserve member banks had access before and during the crisis. In both cases, the Fed used its discretionary powers to provide lending. However, the lending was not provided on the same terms; nor could the difference in terms be explained on the basis of some rule or framework that had been developed before the crisis. In one case, the Fed protected the owners of the private entity by providing inexpensive credit. In the other, Fed actions effectively destroyed the value of the owners' stakes in the private entity. In both cases the institutions were bailed out, but the distributional consequences for stakeholders were vastly different.

---

[8] Reinhart (2011) provides a thoughtful analysis of the dynamic inconsistency problems in the Bear–Lehman episode.

[9] For this comparison, "Goldman" simply serves as the representative of the numerous investment banks that were generously supported by the Fed with similar favorable terms that were not made available to AIG.

AIG stakeholders filed a lawsuit against the Federal Reserve. As a result, in this case information from legal rulings has become available for some of the pertinent issues. A recent legal ruling determined that the Federal Reserve acted inappropriately (Kessler, 2015). Specifically, Judge Thomas C. Wheeler ruled that "The Government's unduly harsh treatment of AIG in comparison to other institutions seemingly was misguided and had no legitimate purpose, even considering concerns about 'moral hazard.'"

Effectively, the ruling suggested that the Fed erred in discriminating against the interests of AIG stakeholders. To reiterate, the issue at hand is not the treatment of either AIG or Goldman in isolation. The issue is whether Fed decisions exhibited reasonable uniformity and consistency. Ultimately, some protection of equal treatment of the stakeholders of both Goldman and AIG could have been expected. Inexpensive credit could have been provided to both or to neither, with similar terms. The owners could have been protected or forced to lose their stakes in the companies in both cases or in neither case. The troubling question in this case is whether it is appropriate for an independent central bank in a democratic society to use its discretionary authority to decide which stakeholders of which private entity to wipe out and which to support. Does an independent central bank such as the Fed have the legitimacy to discriminate in favor of Goldman and against AIG? Should such discretionary authority be available to an independent central bank in a democracy? Don't such decisions fall squarely under the purview of elected governments?

5 Distributional Issues: ECB

As difficult as the Fed's choices discussed in the previous section may have been, the ECB has been facing far more difficult choices associated with the distributional consequences of its balance-sheet policies. The ECB faces unique challenges as it was created to serve as the central bank for the euro area as a whole, which consists of the economies of all member states of the euro area but has no fiscal counterpart in the euro area. The ECB is also unique in that it is effectively unaccountable to any government and has immense discretionary powers, far greater than those of the Federal Reserve – powers that could be used well or could be abused. Gaps in the design of the euro area, including gaps that were well understood before the introduction of the euro, put the ECB in an impossible position during the euro-area crisis.[10]

The lack of a corresponding fiscal authority presents a challenge for the ECB, and especially for the operations that entail taking unusual risks on its balance sheet, as would have been expected to be encountered during the crisis. Should such risks be managed in a discretionary manner, on a case-by-case basis, depending on which member state benefits and which is harmed? The ECB can easily take decisions to favor specific member states over other member states in the euro area, or specific sectors and institutions in a specific member state over sectors and institutions in other member states. These powers stem from the European Union Treaty, which cannot be corrected without the unanimous consent of all EU member states. The ECB problem is therefore far more serious than any issues that might arise with the Federal Reserve. If any euro-area government manages to exert undue influence at the ECB, it may advance its own interests to the detriment of interests of other euro-area member states through the common central bank and without obvious mechanisms for correction.

It goes without saying that the euro-area crisis has been a nightmare for the ECB. As is well known, euro-area governments took a series of decisions after the global financial crisis started that have created an existential crisis for the euro area. Questions persist as to whether the euro will survive or whether some member states will be forced by others to abandon it. The ECB has a clear primary mandate – price stability, and subject to that to provide support to the objectives of the European Union, as specified in the Treaty. But in light of the existential concerns about the euro, should the ECB be expected to focus on its primary mandate or on crisis management? If there is a conflict between these two, should the ECB respect its mandate or should it yield to politics whenever the existence of the euro comes under threat? Should tradeoffs regarding the survival of the euro be ignored or dominate decisions, including decisions regarding monetary policy aiming to attain price stability for the euro area?

Views on these questions can reasonably vary. One view is that dedication to the mandate is appropriate. Another view holds that preserving the euro area could be more important, even if this means

---

[10] See Sims (1999, 2012) for a discussion of institutional problems facing the ECB due to the absence of a fiscal counterpart.

politicizing the ECB in a manner incompatible with the Treaty. A review of ECB decisions during the crisis suggests that the ECB did not escape immersion in decisions with horrendous distributional effects across euro-area member states – distributional effects that were clearly not envisaged when the ECB was given virtually unchecked discretionary powers.[11]

Numerous dimensions can be examined to see the differences in how various member states have been treated by the ECB during the crisis. Questions can be raised regarding the effectiveness of unconventional monetary policy and crisis-response measures across member states. The ECB serves as the central bank for all member states of the euro area, so an obvious question is whether support has been similarly beneficial across member states. Put differently: Has the ECB ensured equal treatment across different member states?

One relevant dimension relating to the effectiveness of unconventional monetary policy is the support the ECB provided to government debt markets. Another dimension regards support of the banking sectors across member states. It could be argued that on both fronts, ECB support to different member states has been decidedly uneven during the crisis.

Consider the effectiveness of unconventional monetary policy. This has been very problematic, with some member states experiencing tightening of monetary conditions during the crisis exactly when the ECB would have been expected to provide easier monetary policy instead. The result has been a monetary policy that contributed to deep recessions in some member states, while others enjoyed near-ideal monetary conditions.[12]

Figure 3.7 compares the yields on ten-year government bonds in two of the largest member states, Germany and Spain. As mentioned earlier, ECB unconventional monetary policy reduced the yields of German government bonds in a manner similar to the reduction of US government bond yields engineered by the Fed. This benefited

---

[11] The way in which a "rules-based institution," such as the ECB would like to be, enjoys virtually unchecked discretion may appear paradoxical. This simply reflects the power the ECB has to set its own operational rules and the discretion to adjust them or selectively waive them.

[12] Obviously, the horrendous outcomes in the euro area are not primarily the result of ECB policies, but of the political dynamics of the member states and the flawed design of the euro area. Eichengreen (2015), Kopits (Chapter 9 of this volume), Orphanides (2015), Wolf (2014), and Wyplosz (2014) offer expositions of various dimensions of the broader problem.

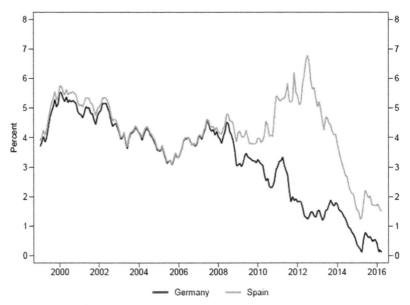

Figure 3.7: Effectiveness of unconventional policy easing in Germany and Spain, 2007–16

Notes: Yields on ten-year bonds.

Germany tremendously but was not reflected in monetary conditions faced by some other countries. Although they share the same currency, monetary conditions in Spain have been considerably tighter than those in Germany in the past several years. This reflects a number of factors, including decisions by euro-area governments. However, the wide gap in the cost of financing between Germany and Spain that developed during the crisis is not unrelated to ECB decisions. As explained by Buiter and Rahbari (2012) and De Grauwe (2011), the deterioration observed in 2010 and 2011 related to the unclear role of the ECB in government bond markets – specifically the extent to which the ECB was willing and/or able to appear as a lender of last resort to member state governments – similar to the role the Bank of England could be seen as serving for the UK government.[13] This largely

---

[13] The comparison with the Bank of England is particularly useful because the UK is a member state of the European Union. The mandate and legal framework of the Bank of England, including importantly a prohibition of monetary financing, is similar to that of the ECB, in accordance to the European Union Treaty.

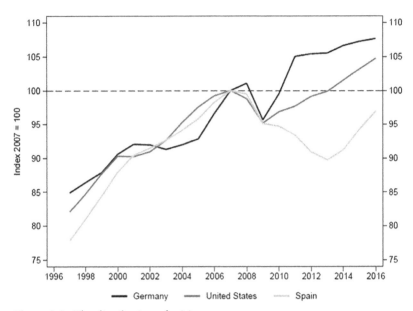

Figure 3.8: The distribution of crisis costs

Notes: Real GDP per person, index 2007 = 100. Observation for 2016 reflects projections as presented in the IMF World Economic Outlook, April 2016.

depended on ECB discretionary decisions.[14] Similarly, the partial convergence of monetary conditions observed since summer 2012 could be largely attributed to the ECB's discretionary decisions relating to the outright monetary transactions (OMT) program.[15]

The difference in the relative stances of monetary policy has had important consequences for the different economic outcomes observed across euro-area member states since the beginning of the euro-area crisis. Figure 3.8 presents a comparison of real GDP per person in Germany and Spain, also superimposing the United States as a benchmark for comparison. As can be seen, the relatively tight monetary policy conditions in Spain and relatively easy conditions in Germany have been associated with a notably better economic performance in Germany relative to that in Spain.

Once again, it is important to recognize that *some* distributional effects across regions, states, etc. may be the unavoidable consequence

---

[14] See also Gros (2012) and Kopf (2011) for a pertinent discussion of this period.
[15] Pill and Reichlin (2014) provide a detailed discussion of the OMT and its effects on government bond markets.

of policy decisions made for the common good on the basis of a pre-determined framework and rules. An issue arises when the distributional effects are not the result of applying a clear framework decided before the crisis, but rather the outcome of discretionary decisions that may be tailor-made to favor some sectors/states and discriminate against other sectors/states.

In the case of the euro area, a troubling aspect of the crisis has been that the distribution of potential benefits and losses appears to have become an unduly important factor in discretionary decision-making, with little regard to the principle of equal treatment that one would have expected to prevail in a democratic society.[16]

Returning to the comparison of the ECB and the Federal Reserve, it is quite clear from Figure 3.4 that from mid-2012 to the end of 2014, the ECB pursued a contractionary monetary policy – shrinking its balance sheet – while the Fed pursued an expansionary one. From Figure 3.2, which compares core inflation in the two economies, we can see that as a result of its tight policies, core inflation in the euro area has been systematically below the ECB's objective. In contrast, the Fed has achieved a better outcome. The difference could not be attributed to unforeseen developments or mere forecast errors, as the tightness of ECB policy over this period was evident in real time (Orphanides, 2014d). During the course of 2014, while the ECB was reducing the size of its balance sheet, it was also revising downwards its inflation forecasts. For example, the forecast of 2016 inflation fell from 1.5 percent in March 2014 to 1.3 percent in December 2014, well below the ECB's definition of price stability.

A question that arises is: What arguments could possibly justify the ECB's inappropriately tight policy over this period? Related to this, what is the mandate of the ECB? One might have thought that the mandate of the ECB was already clear: To maintain monetary conditions that are appropriate for the euro area as a whole and, subject to that, contribute to the other noble objectives of the EU Treaty. And yet, in December 2014, when the ECB reluctantly decided to consider reversing its inappropriately tight policy stance, a member of the ECB Governing Council who is also a state official for a euro-area member state reportedly opposed the decision, noting that "We have a monetary

---

[16] See Orphanides (2014b, c) for examples of specific decisions that raise these questions.

policy that is too expansive for Germany" and, furthermore, "Extremely low interest rates caused countries' willingness to implement structural reforms to tail off" (Carrel, O'Donnell and Martin, 2014).

This raises numerous questions about ECB monetary policy. Did the ECB maintain an inappropriately tight monetary policy for the euro area because changing course would have been inconvenient for a specific member state? Did the ECB maintain an inappropriate policy for the euro area as a whole in order to push the elected governments of some member states to implement structural reforms that some other member state thought should have been implemented? More generally, under what conditions, if any, is it legitimate for the ECB to implement monetary policy with undue influence from one member state, when in so doing it fails to achieve its primary mandate of ensuring that inflation in the euro area is close to 2 percent?

It is also of interest to note that even when it embarked on a form of QE in 2015, the ECB used its discretion to deviate from its established principle of loss-sharing in a very significant manner, with important distributional consequences. The issue regards the pooling of risks in the common monetary policy of the ECB. The principle established when the ECB started operating (well before the crisis) was that risks pertaining to monetary policy operations in the euro area would be shared. Potential profits and losses would be shared according to the capital key of the National Central Banks (NCB) of the member states. During the crisis, when the ECB decided in 2010 to embark on purchases of government debt for *selected* member states as part of its Securities Market Programme (SMP), risks were pooled, as usual.[17] However, purchases of government debt by the ECB proved controversial in Germany and the ECB was subject to multiple lawsuits.

In taking the decision to embark on QE, the ECB decided that rather than pool risks, purchases of government debt should be segmented across national borders inside the euro area. Each NCB would be purchasing the debt of its own government separately and would be responsible for any profits and losses from those purchases. The ECB would also purchase some non-government bonds for which risks would be pooled, to give the appearance of partial risk sharing for

---

[17] The SMP was initiated in May 2010. It entailed purchases of government debt of Italy, Spain, Portugal, Ireland, and Greece with the stated aim to restore an appropriate monetary policy transmission mechanism in member states under stress.

the overall decision. The account of the January 2015 meeting reveals arguments in the discussion:

Members discussed the appropriate modalities of risk sharing related to the purchases of securities issued by euro area governments and agencies and European institutions. On the one hand, arguments were made in favour of full risk sharing so as to counter perceptions of a lack of unity. Full risk sharing would also underline the singleness of monetary policy. On the other hand, in view of concerns about moral hazard it was argued that a regime of partial loss sharing would be more commensurate with the current architecture of Economic and Monetary Union and the Treaties under which the ECB operates. (ECB, 2015b)

The decision suggests that even though it was acknowledged that the normal loss-sharing regime was more consistent with the single monetary policy, concerns about "moral hazard" dominated. The account failed to clarify what these concerns were, but the reference was probably to potential actions of euro-area governments. To the extent that the moral hazard fears that caused the ECB to deviate from normal loss-sharing procedures did indeed refer to elected governments, it would have been of interest to also provide some explanation as to the legitimacy of the ECB taking upon itself the responsibility of "protecting" the euro area from moral hazard-induced actions by the democratically elected governments.

Understanding this decision outside the broader political tensions of the euro area is impossible. Even though the euro was supposed to be irrevocable, it is common knowledge that not all government officials in all member states respect this commitment and that some want to maintain the option to threaten other member states with exit from the common currency. Maintaining the possibility that some member states will potentially exit the currency union has tremendous distributional effects that benefit those member states that are perceived as relatively stronger, e.g. Germany, and harm member states perceived as weaker, e.g. Spain. Indeed, this is a key determinant of the respective governments' relative financing costs.[18] As an independent institution, the ECB could have decided to pursue the best monetary policy for the euro area as a whole, taking for granted the irreversibility of the euro and the responsibility of the governments to maintain it – that is, to

---

[18] See Dany et al. (2015) for a calculation of the monetary benefit accruing to Germany from sustaining the crisis.

respect the Treaty, at least until the governments specifically changed the prevailing framework. Had the ECB acted in this manner, spreads of euro-area governments would have been compressed, as the leverage of any government to use the threat of euro exit against other governments would be lower.

In the event, with its QE decision, the ECB signaled that it wished to account for the possibility of states leaving the euro area and protect its balance sheet against such eventualities. With the procedure adopted, when a member state leaves the euro area, the ECB would be fully protected from the possible loss on its balance sheet in the case that the exiting country's exchange rate weakens. With its decision, the ECB opted to reinforce spreads among government debt of different member states. Effectively, the ECB used its discretionary power to introduce an implicit tax on member states perceived as weak and a subsidy on member states perceived as strong. Needless to say, this decision reinforces a dynamic that raises the odds that a member state will be forced to leave the currency area – hardly consistent with the ECB's mandate.

Questions regarding the distributional consequences of ECB decisions during the crisis are not limited to monetary policy. More controversial have been decisions relating to the management of the euro-area crisis, when ECB interventions provided the appearance that it was aligned with the political objectives of specific member state governments against the political objectives of other member states. The design of the euro area effectively gives the ECB complete discretion on maintaining monetary stability or allowing a panic to materialize in each one of the member states that have joined the euro. Among others, the ECB has the discretion to decide the conditions it believes appropriate to declare that government debt issued by a member state should not be considered trustworthy and does not qualify as collateral for monetary policy operations in the euro area. The ECB also interprets its powers to include the discretionary authority to terminate lender-of-last-resort operations in any state whose government is considered untrustworthy, or any state that refuses to implement specific conditions that are promoted by some other member state.

One could question whether the intent of the writers of the European Union Treaty was to give such immense discretionary powers, with little if any accountability, to a body of unelected officials. The fact remains that the ECB not only has such powers but, to the surprise of many, has exercised these discretionary powers in a manner that has raised questions during the crisis. As an illustration, it suffices to revisit one example: The February 2015 decision to suspend the eligibility of Greek government debt as ECB collateral (ECB, 2015a). This decision was taken shortly after a new left-wing government was elected in Greece and in the middle of political negotiations on an IMF/EU program. The decision, which was widely seen as supporting the political interests of certain elected euro-area governments against the elected Greek government, was heavily criticized by outside observers. For example, it prompted *The Economist* to identify a new role for the ECB in the political discussions pertaining to the crisis: "The Enforcer." The subtitle of this article explained that it was about "How the European Central Bank can dictate terms to the Greek government" (*The Economist*, 2015). In an editorial in the *New York Times*, Paul Krugman pondered whether the ECB would clarify its proper role or act as "Germany's debt collector" (Krugman, 2015).

This was not the first time the ECB had intervened in a manner that could be seen as decidedly political and one-sided (in the sense of promoting the interests of one member state over the interests of another member state) during the crisis.[19] However, it was the occasion that attracted the widest attention, no doubt due to the unconventional, anti-establishment negotiating positions professed by the newly elected Greek government. In this case it could be argued that the newly elected Greek government was provocative and misguided. Perhaps *someone* in the euro area had to make an intervention of *some* sort. A possible defense for any politically motivated decision taken by a central bank is that it may aim to serve the "common good." In the case of the euro area, given the unparalleled discretion and lack of accountability that is enjoyed by the ECB, many decisions could be potentially justified as allowable within the context of the EU Treaty. This raises the question: Is it legitimate for the ECB to use its discretionary power to decide on a case-by-case basis which elected government of which member state should be cut to size for the benefit of other member states, and perhaps

---

[19] In a paper prepared for the European Parliament's Committee on Economic and Monetary Affairs, Whelan (2015) discusses the ECB's role in Greece in 2015 as well as its role in Ireland in 2010. Whelan identifies the ECB's "confused" lender-of-last-resort role as a reason why the ECB may appear to be overly involved in political developments and potentially act beyond its legal mandate.

what the ECB views as the "common" good? Is this compatible with our understanding of democracy in Europe?

In summary, the ECB proved to be an effective central bank during the crisis, but only for *some* member states of the euro area. Use of its balance sheet had immense distributional consequences. For some member states, ECB actions reflected both the crisis response and unconventional monetary policy measures expected from the central bank of any economy. For other member states, ECB actions reflected neither the crisis response nor unconventional policy measures expected from a country's central bank.

These outcomes were not pre-ordained by rules that had been agreed when the euro area was created. They were the outcome of discretionary decisions during the crisis. These decisions included numerous aspects that ordinarily would be seen as technical issues, such as determination of collateral eligibility, asset purchases, provision of emergency liquidity assistance, loss-sharing arrangements, etc. In many cases, it could be argued that alternative discretionary decisions could have ensured less unequal implications for member states. However, the ECB had the discretionary power to change the rules as it saw fit during the crisis, with the result of benefiting some member states and discriminating against others. Despite their fiscal consequences and highly unequal distributional consequences, most of the decisions taken were likely within the legal powers of the ECB, given the immense discretion that is granted to the ECB by the EU Treaty. Is such discretionary authority compatible with the democratic principles of Europe? Should any unelected and unaccountable institution maintain such discretionary power?

6 After the Crisis

Central bank actions in the aftermath of the global financial crisis have likely protected the global economy from the worst of possible outcomes that could have materialized. However, by becoming the "only game in town" and using their discretionary powers, central banks revealed the immense power of their balance sheet and the fact that, during a crisis, the fiscal implications of their actions are much greater than had previously been commonly understood.

In the cases of both the Federal Reserve and the ECB, discretionary authority was employed to implement fiscal operations with immense distributional consequences. These distributional aspects of central bank balance-sheet policies raise troubling questions regarding the discretionary power granted to independent central banks, when the original intent of central bank independence was primarily to ensure the maintenance of price stability.

How should this be resolved going forward? In democratic societies, independent central banks do not have the legitimacy and should not have the authority to make discretionary decisions with immense distributional fiscal consequences, such as have been observed during the crisis. It could be argued that actions taken by both the ECB and the Fed during the crisis overstepped the legitimacy of these institutions.

The main difficulty emanates from discretionary actions. While discretion can allow for good outcomes when employed to tackle unforeseen complications in an efficient manner, it can also lead to disastrous results, leveraging specific interests to the detriment of others in a manner that is inconsistent with the functioning of democracy. If central bank independence is to be maintained going forward, strict rules and boundaries may need to replace current discretionary powers, as argued by Goodfriend (2014) and others. Unless the discretionary powers of central banks are curtailed and accountability is improved, it is hard to see how the fiscal and distributional consequences of central bank actions can be tolerated for long in our democracies. The alternative, as Goodhart (2010) suggests, would be that "The idea of the Central Bank as an *independent* institution will be put aside."

Bibliography

Bagehot, Walter (1873). *Lombard Street: A Description of the Money Market*. London: H.S. King & Co.

Buiter, Willem (2014). *Central Banks: Powerful, Political and Unaccountable?* CEPR Discussion Paper No. 10223, October. http://ssrn.com/abstract=2526351

Buiter, Willem and Rahbari, Ebrahim (2012). The European Central Bank as lender of last resort for sovereigns in the eurozone. *Journal of Common Market Studies*, 50(2), 6–35.

Carrel, Paul John O'Donnell and Martin, Michelle (2014). ECB's Weidmann says monetary policy too expansive for Germany. *Reuters*, December 5, www.reuters.com/article/us-bundesbank-weidmann-idUSKCN0JJ0V12 0141205

Clouse, James, Henderson, Dale, Orphanides, Athanasios, Small, David and Tinsley, Peter (2003). Monetary policy when the nominal short-term interest rate is zero. *Topics in Macroeconomics*, 3(1), doi: https://doi .org/10.2202/1534-5998.1088

Dany, Geraldine, Gropp, Reint E. and von Schweinitz, Gregor (2015). Germany's benefit from the Greek crisis. *IWH Online*, 7/2015, www.iwh-halle.de/d/publik/iwhonline/io_2015-07.pdf

De Grauwe, Paul (2011). The governance of a fragile eurozone. *Revista de Economía Institucional*, 13(25), 13–41, July/December (in Spanish), www.scielo.org.co/pdf/rei/v13n25/v13n25a02.pdf

The Economist (2015). The enforcer: How the European Central Bank can dictate terms to the Greek government. February 7, www.economist .com/news/finance-and-economics/21642210-how-european-central-bank-can-dictate-terms-greek-government

Eichengreen, Barry (2015). *Hall of Mirrors: The Great Depression, the Great Recession, and the Uses – and Misuses – of History*. New York: Oxford University Press.

European Central Bank (2015a). *Eligibility of Greek Bonds Used as Collateral in Eurosystem Monetary Policy Operations*. Press release, February 4, www.ecb.europa.eu/press/pr/date/2015/html/pr150204.en.html

(2015b). *Account of the Monetary Policy Meeting of 21–22 January 2015*. February 19, www.ecb.europa.eu/press/accounts/2015/html/mg150219 .en.html

Fischer, Stanley, Sahay, Ratna and Végh, Carlos (2002). Modern hyper- and high inflations. *Journal of Economic Literature*, 40(3), 837–80, http:// dx.doi.org/10.1257/002205102760273805

Goodfriend, Marvin (2014). Lessons from a century of FED policy: why monetary and credit policies need rules and boundaries. *Journal of Economic Dynamics and Control*, 49, 112–20, http://dx.doi.org/ 10.1016/j.jedc.2014.09.005

Goodhart, Charles (2010). *The Changing Role of Central Banks*. BIS Working Paper No. 326, November, www.bis.org/publ/work326.pdf

Gros, Daniel (2012). On the stability of public debt in a monetary union. *Journal of Common Market Studies*, 50(2), 36–48.

Haltom, Renee, and Sharp, Robert (2014). *The First Time the Fed Bought GSE Debt*. Federal Reserve Bank of Richmond Economic Brief, EB14-04, April, www.richmondfed.org/publications/research/economic_brief/ 2014/eb_14-04

Hawkins, John (2003). *Central Bank Balance Sheets and Fiscal Operations*. BIS Papers, No. 20, www.bis.org/publ/bppdf/bispap20d.pdf

Kessler, Aaron (2015). Ex-A.I.G. chief wins bailout suit, but gets no damages. *The New York Times*, June 15, www.nytimes.com/2015/06/16/

business/dealbook/judge-sides-with-ex-aig-chief-greenberg-against-us-but-awards-no-money.html

Kopf, Christian (2011). *Restoring Financial Stability in the Euro Area*. CEPS Policy Brief 237, March, www.ceps.eu/book/restoring-financial-stability-euro-area

Krugman, Paul (2015). A game of chicken. *The New York Times*, February 6, www.nytimes.com/2015/02/06/opinion/a-game-of-chicken.html

Meltzer, Alan (2013). What's wrong with the Fed? What would restore independence? *CATO Journal*, **33**(3), 401–16.

Orphanides, Athanasios (2013). *Is Monetary Policy Overburdened?* BIS Working Paper No. 435, December, www.bis.org/publ/work435.htm

(2014a). The need for a price stability mandate. *CATO Journal*, **34**(2), 265–79.

(2014b). The euro area crisis: politics over economics. *Atlantic Economic Journal*, **42**(3), 243–63.

(2014c). Are rules and boundaries sufficient to limit harmful central bank discretion? Lessons from Europe. *Journal of Economic Dynamics and Control*, **49**, 121–5.

(2014d). *ECB Policy and Fed Normalization*. CEPR Policy Insight No. 74, November, http://cepr.org/sites/default/files/policy_insights/PolicyInsight75.pdf

(2015). The euro area crisis five years after the original sin. *Credit and Capital Markets*, **48**(4), 533–63.

Pill, Huw and Reichlin, Lucrezia (2014). *Exceptional Policies for Exceptional Times: The ECB's Response to the Rolling Crises of the Euro Area, and How It Has Brought Us towards a New Grand Bargain*. CEPR Discussion Paper No. 10193, October, http://ssrn.com/abstract=2510050

Reinhart, Vincent (2011). A year of living dangerously: the management of the financial crisis in 2008. *Journal of Economic Perspectives*, **25**(1), 71–90.

Ricardo, David (1824). Plan for the Establishment of a National Bank, reprinted in: R.McCulloch (ed.), *The Works of David Ricardo*, London: John Murray, 1888, http://oll.libertyfund.org/title/1395/83017

Sargent, Thomas J., and Wallace, Neil (1981). Some unpleasant monetarist arithmetic. *Quarterly Review of the Minneapolis Federal Reserve Bank*, **Fall**, 1–17.

Sims, Christopher (1999). The precarious fiscal foundations of EMU. *De Economist*, **147**(4), 415–36.

(2012). Gaps in the institutional structure of the euro area. *Public Debt, Monetary Policy and Financial Stability*, Financial Stability Review No. 16, Banque de France, April, www.banque-france.fr/uploads/tx_bdfgrandesdates/FSR16-20-04.pdf

Tucker, Paul (2015). *The Pressing Need for More Complete Central Bank Policy Regimes*. Paper presented at the BIS Research Conference, Lucerne, June 26, 2015.

 (2016). *The Political Economy of Central Bank Balance Sheet Paper*. Paper presented at the Federal Reserve Bank of New York, May 4, 2016.

Whelan, Karl (2015). *The ECB and Financial Assistance Programmes: Has ECB Acted Beyond Its Mandate?* Paper prepared for the session of the Monetary Dialogue, the Committee on Economic and Monetary Affairs (ECON) of the European Parliament, November 2015, https://polcms.secure.europarl.europa.eu/cmsdata/upload/bb7ffa74-62b1-4e00-92b5-402bd3c19ad2/WHELAN_FINAL.pdf

Wolf, Martin (2014). *The Shifts and the Shocks: What We've Learned – and Have Still to Learn – from the Financial Crisis*. New York: Penguin Press.

Wyplosz, Charles (2014). The eurozone crisis: a near-perfect case of mismanagement. *Economia Marche Journal of Applied Economics*, **XXXIII**(1): 1–13.

PART II

Better Institutions for Better Fiscal Policy

4 | *Fiscal Rules in the World*

KLAUS SCHMIDT-HEBBEL AND
RAIMUNDO SOTO

1 Introduction

Rules and restrictions that govern the conduct of fiscal policy have been adopted in a few industrial countries for a long time.[1] However, only since the 1990s has adoption of fiscal rules started spreading worldwide, as part of significant reforms of fiscal frameworks in many industrial and emerging/developing countries (Figure 4.1).

Reforms of fiscal institutions and fiscal rules are motivated by objectives that are related to the changes in monetary institutions and policies that preceded central bank reforms. In the case of fiscal rules, the objectives that motivate their adoption comprise strengthening fiscal solvency and sustainability (i.e. attaining sustainable levels of government deficits and public debt), contributing to macroeconomic (or cyclical) stabilization (i.e. reducing fiscal policy pro-cyclicality or raising policy counter-cyclicality), making fiscal policy design and execution more resilient to principal-agent and other political economy problems that cause deficit bias, and improving intergenerational fairness.

The latter objectives are shared by most fiscal policymakers worldwide. So why do some countries adopt fiscal rules while others do not? Answering this question boils down to identifying the conditions under which some countries decide to adopt fiscal rules and maintain them over time. In particular, which political and institutional conditions are behind policymakers' decisions to tie their own hands? Are fiscal rules more likely to be associated with particular monetary and exchange rate regimes, or with deeper financial market development and more

---

[1] We would like to thank our discussant Daniele Franco, as well as Michael Bordo, Xavier Debrun, Charles Wyplosz, and other participants at the Slovak Council of Budget Responsibility Conference on "Rethinking Fiscal Policy after the Crisis," Bratislava, September 2015, for helpful comments. We are particularly indebted to Ľudovít Ódor for excellent and constructive comments made during the conference and our post-conference draft. The usual disclaimer applies.

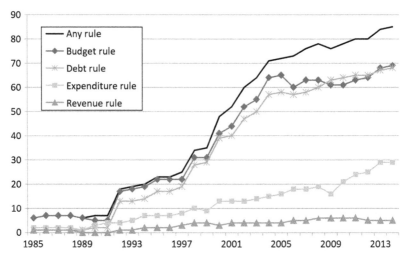

Figure 4.1: Number of countries with fiscal rules in place, 1985–2014

Source: IMF Fiscal Rules Dataset, 2015, www.imf.org/external/datamapper/FiscalRules/
fiscal_rule_database.zip

openness? Are richer countries more likely to adopt fiscal rules? Do
costs of fiscal rules – for example, large revenue volatility – inhibit
having fiscal rules in place? Are countries more likely to keep fiscal
rules in place when they exhibit stronger fiscal policy performance?
These are the key issues addressed by this chapter.

There are few previous empirical studies identifying institutional and
economic variables explaining why countries adopt and maintain fiscal
rules. This chapter extends significantly those previous studies that can
be found. The model used here is broader in its specification, focusing
on six categories of potential determinants for the choice of *de jure*
fiscal rules, addressing the particular questions we raised above. The
sample size is larger, comprising an annual data panel sample of
115 countries (of which eighty-nine had a fiscal rule in place during a
sub-period of the sample period) and spanning thirty-nine years
(1975–2013). Empirical estimation is based on different models suited
to the econometric issues relevant to discrete-variable estimation.

Section 2 reviews the literature on the objectives, benefits, and costs
of adopting fiscal restrictions and rules, as well as the categories of
fiscal rules. Against this background, Section 3 reviews the previous
policy and empirical literature on fiscal rules and discusses a

framework of potential determinants that explain why countries adopt and maintain fiscal rules. Section 4 discusses econometric models and presents empirical results. The final section concludes.

2 Fiscal Rules and Restrictions

2.1 Objectives, Benefits, Costs, and Enforcement of Fiscal Rules and Restrictions

Rules that govern the conduct of fiscal policy have long been adopted. In the eighteenth and nineteenth centuries, some forms of fiscal rules – known as golden rules – were prevalent in a few countries (Basseto and Sargent, 2006). In the late twentieth century, however, adoption of fiscal restrictions and rules started spreading around the world.

This paradigm shift in fiscal frameworks followed the revolution in monetary policy institutions and rules that took place in the 1980s and 1990s. Reforms of central banks and their monetary policy frameworks were politically motivated by the 1970s Great Inflation and intellectually grounded in the rational expectations revolution in macroeconomics. This was reflected in theoretical work in support of independent central banking and the welfare dominance of rules over discretion (Kydland and Prescott, 1977; Barro and Gordon, 1983; Cukierman, 1992). Under the influence of the latter theories and the policy experience of the independent Fed and Bundesbank, many countries have established independent and accountable central banks since the 1980s. The newly independent central banks were entrusted with the conduct of monetary policy under conditions of transparency and accountability, in order to raise policy effectiveness, increase economic efficiency, and strengthen democratic accountability. The ways in which monetary policy decisions are made have also been made more systematic since the 1980s. As "discovered" in the 1990s, starting with the seminal work by Taylor (1993) on what was subsequently named the Taylor rule, monetary policy decisions are modeled as monetary policy rules.

Coming back to fiscal policy, few countries had fiscal rules and fiscal policy restrictions in place before the 1990s. Yet the failures of discretionary fiscal policies and the lack of appropriate fiscal institutions – and the demonstration effects of successful rule-based monetary policies conducted by independent central banks – have led since the 1990s to wide adoption of fiscal restrictions and fiscal rules, and deep reforms of fiscal policy frameworks, in industrial and emerging/developing countries alike. Only four countries had fiscal rules in place in 1982. This had increased to forty-eight by 2000 and reached eighty-five in 2014 (the last year in the IMF's database on fiscal rules; IMF Fiscal Rules Dataset, 2015).

Why do countries tie the hands of their fiscal policymakers by putting in place fiscal rules and restrictions that limit the degree of fiscal policy discretion? Reforms of fiscal institutions and fiscal rules are motivated by objectives that are similar to those that inspired changes in monetary institutions and policies. In the case of fiscal policy, democratically elected governments tend to have biases toward excessive deficits and debt. Fiscal discretion often leads to fiscal insolvency (Wyplosz, 2005). Fatás (2005) summarizes the literature by listing four main biases in fiscal policy: those that lead to fiscal policy volatility, to fiscal policy pro-cyclicality, to unsustainable deficits and budget plans, and to intergenerational unfairness.

The latter deficit biases could be a result of time inconsistency on the part of the discretionary fiscal policymaker who decides in favor of his short-term objective (output stabilization) and against his long-term objective (debt sustainability) (Wyplosz, 2005; Morris et al., 2006). Political economy models of fiscal policy explain deficit biases due to common pool problems (Fatás, 2005; Krogstrup and Wyplosz, 2006), principal-agent problems, the aim of constraining successor governments with different budgetary preferences (Alesina and Tabellini, 1990), and asymmetric information between voters and politicians (Beetsma and Debrun, in Chapter 5 of this volume).

Coordination problems between discretionary fiscal and monetary policymakers can lead to bad equilibria, reflected in excessive fiscal deficits and high inflation (Bennett and Loayza, 2002). The imposition of rules and restrictions on both monetary and fiscal authorities is called for to avoid bad equilibria. In monetary unions where member countries retain fiscal sovereignty, fiscal deficit bias is likely to be exacerbated (Tornell and Velasco, 2000). Moral hazard in the monetary union members' conduct of sovereign fiscal policy is intensified due to the heightened likelihood of bailout by other member countries or by the common central bank to avoid a banking crisis (Buti and Guidice, 2004; De Grauwe, 2006). However, a monetary union may also induce more fiscal responsibility, as the union may act as an agent of restraint over the conduct of fiscal policy (Collier, 1991) or may dilute the strategic influence of fiscally irresponsible members (Masson and Pattillo, 2002).

Our reading of the literature leads us to identify four general object-ives of fiscal rules, restrictions, and institutions, in order to overcome the failures that characterize the behavior of fiscal policy under discre-tion. The first is to strengthen fiscal solvency and sustainability by attaining sustainable levels of government deficits and public debt. The second is to contribute to macroeconomic (or cyclical) stabilization by reducing fiscal policy pro-cyclicality or raising policy counter-cyclicality. The third is to strengthen fiscal policy design and execution and make them more resilient to government failures by strengthening the political economy of fiscal policy decisions and budgetary procedures. The fourth and final is to improve intergenera-tional equity.

The benefits of fiscal rules and restrictions are reaped by attaining the latter policy objectives. However, imposing fiscal rules and restric-tions may also have costs, derived from badly or too narrowly defined rules and institutions. Excessively narrow rules without escape clauses may find fiscal policy straitjacketed when macroeconomic and/or budget shocks of an unexpected type or magnitude materialize (Hughes-Hallett and Lewis, 2005; Cimadomo, 2012). Compliance with the rules during unforeseen events could have large macroeco-nomic costs, forcing the policymaker either to incur in the latter or to suspend the enforcement of the rule. For example, the EU's uncondi-tional Stability and Growth Pact (SGP) ceilings on fiscal deficit and debt levels were almost systematically violated during and after the 2008–9 global financial crisis. This led to the adoption of a new set of fiscal rules and procedures (the "six-pack," "two-pack," and fiscal compact). Therefore, countries that face very high levels of macroeco-nomic and budget volatility could refrain from adopting fiscal rules and restrictions in order to preserve more flexibility under fiscal policy discretion.

The EU's aforementioned eurozone experience leads to a distinction between *de jure* fiscal rules and restrictions and their enforcement. Fiscal rules are commitment devices that strengthen fiscal policymakers who want to be fiscally prudent (Drazen, 2004; Schick, 2004). Fiscal rules are likely to embody stronger signals of commitment to current and future fiscal discipline than current words or actions. This may be particularly relevant for developing and emerging economies (Kopits,

2004) or for a monetary union without a fiscal union, such as the euro area (see also Chapters 6, 7, and 9 in this volume). However, fiscal rules do not necessarily stand in the way of those who are predisposed to violate them – unless they are backed by enforcement mechanisms, including penalties on deviating behavior.

Enforcement of fiscal rules and restrictions requires compliance, which has to be assessed ex post and not only ex ante (Morris et al., 2006). Many fiscal rules and restrictions feature explicit monitoring of the fiscal authority by an independent domestic agency (the comptroller's office, a fiscal council), a supranational body (such as the EU, in the case of EU member countries), or, at a weaker level, international financial institutions and private sector analysts. High levels of transparency and accountability in preparing and executing the government budget – and its compliance with fiscal rules and restrictions – are major instruments for effective public monitoring of compliance.

Hence, the enforcement of fiscal rules and restrictions should take at least one of the following forms: exogenous enforcement, self-enforcement, and signaling to external players (Braun and Tommasi, 2004). Penalties for non-compliance should be sufficiently large to make it costly for politicians to violate fiscal rules and restrictions (Schick, 2004).

2.2 Fiscal Frameworks and Fiscal Rules

Fiscal rules are just one class of restrictions put on the conduct of fiscal policy. A modern institutional framework for the conduct of fiscal policy and financial management is based on the following components: a constitutional law and/or a fiscal responsibility law; procedural restrictions on budget presentation, adoption, and execution; modern financial management; requirements on accountability and public information on budget and financial management; a planning horizon that exceeds one year; rules for government asset and liability management; effective external control and auditing; a fiscal council and/or fiscal committee; a stabilization or sovereign wealth fund (for smoothing the impact of short-term volatility or an endowment fund for promoting long-term sustainability or intergenerational transfers), and – last but certainly not least – a fiscal rule for the budget (Ter-Minassian, 2010; Kumar et al., 2009; Schmidt-Hebbel, 2016).

One major condition to improve the likelihood of enforcement of *de jure* fiscal rules is the adoption of a full-fledged institutional framework for fiscal policy, with all the procedural and institutional components that were listed above. Many of the latter components are strongly complementary to fiscal rules; for example, deficit bias may be weakened by fiscal rules and fiscal councils separately, and this effect may be greater if both are present (Beetsma and Debrun, in Chapter 5).

A second condition is that the balance between benefits and costs of fiscal rules could be improved by following some design guidelines. Policy experience and the literature suggest that fiscal rules should be well defined, geared to their policy objectives, transparent, simple, flexible, consistent with budgetary and macroeconomic reality, enforceable, and efficient. Certainly no rule will satisfy perfectly all these desirable features (Kopits and Symansky, 1998; Morris et al., 2006), but they should be taken into account in the art of designing fiscal rules (and other fiscal restrictions), considering the policy objectives.

Fiscal rules apply to different government levels and come in different shapes and forms. National governments establish national rules on their budgets, in contrast to sub-national rules established at state or provincial level. Supranational rules are established at the level of a union of sovereign states, such as the EU.

Fiscal rules are quantitative constraints on fiscal policy that are based on numerical targets set for a given fiscal indicator or budget aggregate. Numerical targets can be set unconditionally (e.g., the EU's Maastricht Treaty unconditional debt and deficit ceilings) or may be conditional on certain macroeconomic aggregates (e.g., government spending targeted to estimates of potential GDP levels and of long-term commodity prices or commodity fund assets, as in Chile and Norway).

Different types of fiscal rules can be distinguished by the budgetary aggregate to which they are applied. The rules have different properties with regard to their objectives, operational guidelines, and transparency, as discussed by Kumar et al. (2009) and Schaechter et al. (2009). The four main categories of rules are the following (Schaechter et al., 2012):

(i) Debt rules that set an explicit limit or target on public debt in percent of GDP.
(ii) Budget balance rules that set an explicit limit or target on the budget balance in percent of GDP. The targets can be set on the

overall budget balance, the primary budget balance (excluding net interest payments), or the recurrent budget balance (this is the golden rule, which targets the overall balance net of capital expenditure). The budget balance measure can be specified as actual balance, cyclically adjusted or structural balance, or "over the business cycle balance."

(iii) Expenditure rules that set limits on total, primary, or current spending. They are set in absolute or growth terms, or in percent of GDP.

(iv) Revenue rules that set ceilings or floors on government revenue. They are set in absolute or growth terms, or in percent of GDP.

The latter types of fiscal rules have different advantages and disadvantages, discussed in detail by Schaechter et al. (2012). For example, debt and balance rules provide a close link to the policy objective of debt sustainability, but do not allow for cyclical stabilization (they may even contribute to fiscal policy pro-cyclicality). In contrast to the latter, expenditure and revenue rules can contribute to limiting the size of government and to cyclical stabilization, but are not directly linked to debt sustainability. Hence it is not surprising that many countries combine two or more fiscal rules.

In this chapter we focus on the determinants of *de jure* national fiscal rules in the world. For this purpose, we will use the IMF world database on fiscal rules (www.imf.org/external/datamapper/Fiscal-Rules/matrix/matrix.htm), which identifies separately and jointly if a country has one or more fiscal rules in place. We will not analyze fiscal rules applied at supranational level, even though national rules may sometimes be adopted as a result of a supranational commitment (e.g. as a member of the EU). We also will not analyze fiscal rules applied at sub-national (state or provincial) levels, due to the lack of systematic information on their potential sub-national determinants. Finally, we focus on *de jure* rules due to the absence of reliable and systematic information on how strictly fiscal rules are enforced.

3 Understanding Adoption of Fiscal Rules: Previous Findings and a New Framework

In this section we briefly review the previous literature on fiscal policy rules, focusing on empirical cross-country panel studies. Then we address key questions on potential determinants of adoption and maintenance of fiscal rules, which lead to a selection of regressors for the policy choice. Finally, we discuss some issues related to variable frequency and causality between fiscal rule choice and its potential determinants.

3.1 Previous Literature

There is a rising body of descriptive and empirical country and cross-country studies on fiscal rules, their design, and related institutional issues, as well as on the fiscal, macroeconomic, welfare, and growth effects of different fiscal rules (a few examples include Debrun and Kumar, 2007; Kumar et al., 2009; Ter-Minassian, 2010; Anderson and Minarik, 2006; Deroose, Moulin and Wierts, 2006; Maliszewski, 2009).

There are few previous empirical studies using international panel data to identify institutional and economic variables explaining adoption of fiscal rules. Among those that do exist, Calderón and Schmidt-Hebbel (2008a) estimate a model for the likelihood of having a fiscal rule in place, using an unbalanced panel dataset constructed by the authors (extending the database compiled by Kopits and Symansky, 1998, and others) on fiscal rules for seventy-five countries (of which twenty-four have fiscal rules) spanning the period 1975–2005. Their results (based on pooled, fixed-effect, and random-effect logit estimation, and pooled and fixed-effect probit estimation) show that a larger budget balance, lower population dependency ratio, lower expenditure pro-cyclicality, and greater government stability raise the likelihood of having a fiscal rule in place.

Kumar et al. (2009) present panel data results for the likelihood of adopting a fiscal rule and for having a *de jure* fiscal regime in place based on a sample of sixty-eight countries (of which two thirds have fiscal rules) covering the period 1985–2008. Results obtained using an exponential hazard model that identifies the probability of switching to a rule in any given country and year indicate that the likelihood of adopting a rule is raised by a higher primary budget balance and a lower public debt ratio, and is also affected by various macroeconomic performance variables. Additional results, based on a conditional fixed-effects logit model that identifies the probability of having a fiscal rule in any given country and year, show that the likelihood of having a fiscal rule in place responds to the same variables that helped explain the adoption of the rule.

Finally, Elbadawi et al. (2015) present panel data results for the likelihood of adopting fiscal rules for a sample of 100 countries and for the period 1975–2008. This study's findings show that several fiscal, macroeconomic, political, and regime-related variables contribute to the likelihood of having a fiscal rule in place.

In this chapter we significantly extend previous empirical research by broadening the framework that may explain why countries adopt and maintain fiscal rules. We also extend the database for our empirical work.

3.2 A Framework for Explaining Why Countries Adopt and Maintain Fiscal Rules

There is no narrow theoretical framework that explains the choice of macroeconomic policy regimes. Hence, most empirical studies of the determinants of macroeconomic regime choice are based on a narrative about objectives pursued by policymakers, (pre-) conditions that facilitate adoption of a particular regime, consistency with regimes in other policy areas (e.g. inflation targeting and exchange rate floats), and/or structural features that require or facilitate adoption of a particular regime. This is the case for empirical studies of determinants of exchange rate regimes (Levy-Yeyati and Sturzenegger, 2010; Calderón and Schmidt-Hebbel, 2008b), monetary policy regimes (Calderón and Schmidt-Hebbel, *What Drives the Choice of Inflation Targets in the World*, unpublished manuscript, Central Bank of Chile, 2008), and fiscal regimes based on fiscal rules (Calderón and Schmidt-Hebbel, 2008a; Kumar et al., 2009).

This chapter follows the latter literature, significantly extending the previous studies on fiscal rules. We identify six categories of potential determinants of choosing fiscal rules: political and institutional variables; monetary and exchange rate regimes; financial market development measures; the level of economic development; costs of fiscal rules; and fiscal policy conditions. We select the most representative measures available for the variables in each category.

3.2.1 Political and Institutional Variables
We identify four potential determinants of fiscal rules among political and institutional variables and then discuss their expected signs.

Fiscal rules are very likely to be the outcome of particular political regimes and institutions. By constraining fiscal policymakers in the design and execution of the budget, in a way that is relatively transparent and subject to open monitoring, fiscal rules reflect more transparency, stronger democratic accountability, less discretion, and less corruption. Therefore, our first political determinant is a standard measure of democracy.

At the constitutional level, the distinction between federal and unitary government is likely to make a difference in the adoption of fiscal rules. In federal countries, the fiscal sovereignty of federal governments is weaker than that enjoyed by central governments in unitary countries. The vast literature on fiscal federalism attests to the important differences in the conduct and outcome of fiscal policy between federal and unitary countries (e.g. Feld and Schnellenbach, 2010). We expect federal governments to be more likely to adopt fiscal rules than unitary governments, because they strengthen their bargaining position with respect to the federated states or provinces.[2] For this reason, we include a binary dummy variable for federal governments.

There is evidence suggesting that rules reflect an implicit contract between governments and voters. In other words, they signal a government commitment to maintain mutually agreed standards of fiscal discipline (Debrun and Kumar, 2007). Therefore, we include a measure of political risk and checks and balances.

As the political instability of governments makes it difficult to precommit to rules, fiscal rules are more likely to be adopted and continued over time under conditions of government stability.[3] Hence we include a government stability measure as a potential regressor.

3.2.2 Exchange Rate and Monetary Regimes

Two types of exchange rate regime are likely to affect adoption of fiscal rules. A super-hard exchange rate regime in the form of absence of a national currency due to the use of an international currency as a result

---

[2] Federal states tend to complement adoption of fiscal rules at the federal (or national) level with adoption of sub-national rules at state or provincial levels (Kumar et al., 2009).

[3] This argument is analogous to the inclusion of government stability measures as determinants of counter-cyclical fiscal and monetary policies in international panel data studies (e.g. Calderón et al., 2012).

of monetary union membership is likely to raise the likelihood of adoption of supranational fiscal rules that are then implemented at the national level. This is to reduce the incidence of moral hazard in member countries' conduct of sovereign fiscal policy, as discussed in Section 2 above. Therefore, we include monetary union membership as a regressor.

While there is literature that links the choice of exchange rates to fiscal performance, it focuses on the impact of government deficits and public debt levels on the success of fixed, intermediate, and floating exchange rates. The conventional view (e.g. Giavazzi and Pagano, 1988 and Frenkel et al., 1991, among others) is that pegs provide more fiscal discipline than floats. If governments adopt a lax fiscal policy under a fixed exchange rate, this would lead to a speculative attack on reserves and, consequently, result in currency devaluation. Because the eventual collapse of the peg would imply a large political cost for the policymaker, fixed regimes impose discipline on fiscal authorities.

However, political economy arguments provide the opposite rationale. Tornell and Velasco (2000) stress that, under reasonable conditions (linked to governmental uncertainty about re-election and lack of access to capital markets), more fiscal discipline is attained under floats, where fiscal mismanagement leads to devaluation and inflation in the short term. Under pegs, unsustainable fiscal policy leads to higher debt and lower reserves in the short term, postponing the costs of devaluation and inflation to the future.

Hence we include as a second exchange rate regime measure a binary variable for a fixed exchange rate regime. Considering the arguments of the preceding literature, this measure's effect on the likelihood of having a fiscal rule in place is ambiguous.

Inflation targeting requires that central banks commit to a pre-announced, explicit target for inflation and develop a highly transparent set of rules for operating monetary instruments and providing information to the public. Moreover, there is significant theoretical and policy consensus that the absence of fiscal dominance is a precondition for the success of inflation targeting. In turn, fiscal dominance – the need to rely on central bank resources, ultimately seigniorage – is less likely when a government commits to a fiscal rule.

Minea and Villieu (2009) develop a theoretical model whereby inflation targeting provides an incentive for governments to improve institutional quality in order to enhance tax revenue performance.[4] Testing of this model by Lucotte (2012), using propensity score matching, indicates that inflation targeting has a significant positive effect on public revenue collection in thirteen emerging economies.

Hence we include a discrete variable for countries in which monetary policy is based on an inflation-targeting regime. We expect that an inflation-targeting regime increases the likelihood of having a fiscal rule in place.

3.2.3 Capital Account Openness and Financial Development

Financial development could have a positive influence on the likelihood of having fiscal rules in place through two channels. First, both domestic financial development and stronger integration into world capital markets increase governments' access to domestic and external debt financing and subject governments to closer scrutiny of fiscal sustainability on the part of financial market analysts and rating agencies. This strengthens the case for adopting fiscal rules that commit governments to fiscal prudence and solvency. Second, if domestic financial markets are deeper, and integration into world capital markets is full and comprehensive, governments will be more likely to access domestic or external funding during cyclical downturns. This reinforces governmental adoption of fiscal rules that minimize fiscal pro-cyclicality or strengthen fiscal counter-cyclicality.

Therefore, we include one variable that reflects domestic financial development and another that measures international financial integration or openness as potential determinants of having fiscal rules in place.

3.2.4 Overall Economic Development

We use per capita real GDP for controlling the overall level of development. Some studies focus on reverse causality, i.e. on the impact of fiscal rules on economic growth (e.g. Castro, 2011). Here we focus on the causality from the level of development to the likelihood of having a fiscal rule in place. This hypothesis embodies the stylized fact that governments in richer economies have more human and financial

---

[4] The result requires monetary policy to be set in advance of fiscal effort to collect taxes. In our case, this requirement is empirically valid: No country in the sample initiated national fiscal rules prior to setting up inflation targeting.

resources available to undertake the complex tasks of adopting, complying with, monitoring, and evaluating the operation of a fiscal rule.

3.2.5 Costs of Having Fiscal Rules in Place

The sacrifice of fiscal discretion may have costs. Adhering to fiscal rules may also have costs, in particular when rules are defined badly. Rules that are too narrowly defined, or rules without escape clauses, may lead fiscal policy to be straitjacketed when macroeconomic and/or budget shocks of an unexpected type or magnitude materialize, as discussed in Section 2 above.

Therefore, we include measures of budgetary uncertainty that may inhibit adoption of fiscal rules. Our measure is the coefficient of variation of government revenue, included as a separate regressor. This variable indirectly reflects the volatility of underlying macroeconomic variables – such as GDP, consumption commodity prices, imports, exports, and profits of state-owned enterprises – on which the tax and non-tax revenues of the government are based.

3.2.6 Fiscal Policy Conditions

Measures of the fiscal stance are potentially both determinants and consequences of fiscal rules. The attainment of sustainable, moderate levels of public debt and deficits is likely to be a pre-condition for adopting fiscal rules. On the other hand, fiscal rules embody hard commitment devices and restrictions that are likely to achieve lower deficit and debt levels once they are put in place.

Acknowledging potential bi-causality, we identify three variables related to fiscal policy strength and conduct that may exert an influence on fiscal rule choice. First, we consider the government budget balance as a measure of overall fiscal policy strength. We expect that a higher budget balance raises the likelihood of adopting a rule-based fiscal regime, as it is easier to adopt a disciplining device and stick to it when fiscal accounts are on a more sustainable footing (Debrun and Kumar, 2007). Intrinsically well-behaved governments adopt strict rules and institutions to reveal the nature of their unobservable preferences. However, in many papers on fiscal institutions and policy outcomes, the focus is on reverse causality (from institutions to outcomes): Because institutions are effective commitment devices, certain fiscal outcomes are observed. The determination of which causality prevails thus remains an empirical issue, and one that is beyond the scope of this chapter. In any case, we include the budget balance as a possible determinant of fiscal rule choice, noting its potential endogeneity.

Next we include the population dependency ratio, i.e. the ratio of the population under 15 and over 64 years of age to those falling within the age range 15–64. As the ratio rises, so does demand for higher government spending on social programs in support of the young and the elderly (for childcare, education, pensions, and health). This makes it more difficult for governments to commit to a fiscal rule, reducing the likelihood of putting one in place.

The analytical and empirical literature provides several explanations for the existence of pro-cyclicality in government expenditures. First, restricted government access to credit markets, particularly during recessions, precludes borrowing to weather temporary shocks or recessions (Gavin and Perotti, 1997; Agénor and Aizenman, 2000; Kaminsky et al., 2004). Second, citizens in countries with corrupt governments demand fewer taxes and more government benefits in good times, for fear that these rents will be appropriated by government officials (Alesina and Tabellini, 2005). Third, voracity effects arise from interest groups influencing government expenditure to raise their consumption more than output in response to favorable income shocks (Talvi and Végh, 2004). Empirical evidence suggests that weaknesses in political institutions and financial underdevelopment are the main determinants of fiscal pro-cyclicality in the world (Calderón and Schmidt-Hebbel, 2008b; Ilzetzki and Végh, 2008). We expect governments prone to pro-cyclical government expenditure to be less willing to subject themselves to the discipline of a fiscal rule. Therefore, we include a measure of fiscal pro-cyclicality.

4 Econometric Analysis and Empirical Results

The existence of one or more fiscal rules in a country can be appropriately modeled using discrete-variable econometric models, whereby the authorities' choice to implement such rules depends on a set of exogenous variables selected to represent the main determinants of the choice (Train, 2003). The dependent variable is thus a discrete variable of *a de jure* national fiscal rule taking value 1 if it is in place and 0 otherwise, as defined in the IMF database on fiscal rules (www.imf.org/external/datamapper/FiscalRules/matrix/matrix.htm). The IMF definition covers rules with targets fixed in legislation as well as fiscal arrangements for which the targets can be revised, but only on a low-frequency basis (e.g. as part of the electoral cycle), as long as they are binding for a minimum of three years. Thus medium-term budgetary frameworks or expenditure ceilings that provide multi-year projections but can be changed annually are not considered to be rules. Furthermore, the IMF considers only those fiscal rules that set numerical targets on aggregates that capture a large share of public finances and, at a minimum, cover the central government. Therefore, rules for sub-national governments or government sub-aggregates are not included here.

We use two types of measures of national rules: an aggregate measure of any rule in place and four particular types of rules, as summarized in Table 4.1. National rules fall into any of the four different types of rules (revenue, debt, expenditures, and budget balance rules) but supranational rules only cover the latter two categories. Some countries have national and supranational rules in place simultaneously. In the Appendix 1 (at the end of the book) we provide a precise definition of (and the corresponding data sources for) the set of independent variables as described according to the six aforementioned categories of potential rule determinants.

As mentioned, the existence of a fiscal rule in a country is modeled using a discrete (binary) variable taking a value of one if a rule is in place and zero otherwise. Therefore, we make use of non-linear, discrete-variable panel data models. These types of models raise several econometric issues related to the nature of the individual effects (fixed or random) and the specification of the underlying distribution of error term (logistic or normal).

Consider the log likelihood for a sample of size (N, T) of the general individual effects model:

$$\log \mathcal{L} = \Sigma_{i=1}^{N} \Sigma_{i=1}^{T} \log g(y_{it}, \beta x_{it} + \alpha_i, \theta)$$

where y_{it} is the variable of interest, x_{it} is a set of exogenous control variables, α_i is the individual effect (fixed or random), β is the vector of slope coefficients, and θ is an ancillary parameter (e.g. scale parameter or dispersion of disturbances). The properties of the estimators depend on whether function $g(.)$ is linear or non-linear.

The conventional wisdom in linear panel data models indicates that the fixed-effects estimator is to be used when the individual effects are thought to be correlated with the included control variables. On the other hand, the random-effects estimator is more parsimonious, and

Table 4.1: *Number of countries with national and supranational fiscal rules, 1985–2014*

	Countries with fiscal rules	National Rule Only					Supranational Rule Only					National and Supranational				
		Expenditure	Revenue	Budget	Debt	Any national	Expenditure	Revenue	Budget	Debt	Any supranational	Expenditure	Revenue	Budget	Debt	Any national and supranational
1985	6	2	1	6	1	6	0	0	0	0	0	0	0	0	0	0
1986	7	2	1	7	1	7	0	0	0	0	0	0	0	0	0	0
1987	7	2	1	7	1	7	0	0	0	0	0	0	0	0	0	0
1988	7	2	1	7	1	7	0	0	0	0	0	0	0	0	0	0
1989	6	1	0	6	1	6	0	0	0	0	0	0	0	0	0	0
1990	7	3	0	5	2	7	0	0	0	0	0	0	0	0	0	0
1991	7	4	0	5	2	7	0	0	0	0	0	0	0	0	0	0
1992	18	4	0	5	1	8	0	0	10	11	12	0	0	2	1	3
1993	19	5	0	6	1	10	0	0	10	11	12	0	0	2	1	3
1994	20	7	1	7	2	13	0	0	10	11	12	0	0	2	1	3
1995	23	7	2	7	2	13	0	0	13	13	15	0	0	2	2	4
1996	23	7	2	7	2	13	0	0	13	13	15	0	0	2	2	4
1997	25	8	3	7	4	16	0	0	12	12	14	0	0	3	3	5
1998	34	10	4	10	7	20	0	0	18	18	20	0	0	3	3	5
1999	35	9	4	10	8	21	0	0	16	18	19	0	0	5	3	6
2000	48	13	3	12	10	25	0	0	23	26	27	0	0	6	3	7
2001	52	13	4	15	11	29	0	0	23	26	27	0	0	6	3	7
2002	60	13	4	17	12	31	0	0	29	32	33	0	0	6	3	7
2003	64	14	4	20	15	36	0	0	28	32	33	0	0	7	3	8
2004	71	15	4	19	12	33	0	0	36	39	43	0	0	9	6	13
2005	72	16	4	20	13	34	0	0	36	40	43	0	0	9	5	12
2006	73	18	5	21	12	35	0	0	29	40	42	0	0	10	5	12
2007	76	18	5	22	11	37	0	0	30	42	44	0	0	11	5	13
2008	78	19	6	22	13	40	0	0	31	42	45	0	0	10	5	13
2009	76	16	6	20	16	38	0	0	32	43	46	0	0	9	4	12

Table 4.1: (*cont.*)

	Countries with fiscal rules	National Rule Only					Supranational Rule Only					National and Supranational				
		Expenditure	Revenue	Budget	Debt	Any national	Expenditure	Revenue	Budget	Debt	Any supranational	Expenditure	Revenue	Budget	Debt	Any national and supranational
2010	78	21	6	20	17	42	0	0	31	42	45	0	0	10	5	13
2011	80	24	6	22	18	46	0	0	31	41	44	0	0	10	6	13
2012	80	25	5	23	18	46	0	0	32	40	44	0	0	9	7	13
2013	84	26	5	26	19	49	0	0	29	39	43	0	0	13	9	17
2014	85	26	5	27	20	50	0	0	25	39	42	0	0	17	9	20

Source: IMF Fiscal Rules Dataset, 2015

thus preferred when there is no correlation between individual effects and control variables.

The estimators of non-linear panel data models do not follow such conventional wisdom. The fixed-effects estimator suffers from the incidental parameter problem (Neyman and Scott, 1948), which makes the estimator biased when the time-series dimension (T) is fixed even if the number of cross-sections is large ($N \to \infty$). This problem arises because, in general, the estimator of the parameters of interest (β) will depend on the estimator of individual effects (α_i) and the latter is only consistent when the sample is large in the time dimension (i.e. $T \to \infty$).[5]

However, when using the logistic distribution specification, the incidental parameter can be avoided altogether if the *conditional* fixed-effects logit estimator is used. This estimator focuses only on cases in

---

[5] Linear models avoid this problem by virtue of the Frisch–Waugh theorem (which separates estimation of the parameters of interest from estimation of the fixed effects) and recover the individual effects using the individual mean, which is a sufficient statistic for the individual effect.

which countries have either implemented or abandoned a fiscal rule and drops all others that either have never enacted a rule or have maintained one for the complete period. The latter do not provide useful information: there is no way to tell if an individual has any value of the fixed effect (α_i) if he does not change his behavior. The conditional logit estimator is consistent, but has a major shortcoming: By avoiding the estimation of the fixed effects, it precludes computation of the estimates of the probabilities for the outcomes. Therefore, this approach limits the analyst to infer only about β.[6] The fixed-effects probit model, on the other hand, is not recommended because estimators are biased and, in addition, it is computationally cumbersome (see Greene, 2001).

Thus, in applying the fixed-effects estimator to models with qualitative dependent variables based on panel data, the conditional logit model seems to be the preferred choice. Nevertheless, it requires strict exogeneity of the regressors, and stationarity over time. Because these conditions may be violated in economic data, the random-effects estimator is an attractive alternative. In panel data, the random-effects probit model is computationally tractable while the random-effects logit model is not. The only limitation of probit models is that they require normal distributions for all unobserved components – a feature that may characterize most unobserved, random components but could be absent in cases where dependent variables are truncated (e.g., prices must be positive).

We first test our models for countries having any type of fiscal rule in place (budget balance, expenditures, revenues, or public debt). We code our dependent variable in binary form, whereby a value of one is assigned if one or more of the four types of rules is in place and zero otherwise. We later investigate the determinants of each type of rule. Following the discussion on the properties of the different estimators, we focus on the random-effects probit estimator and the conditional fixed-effects logit estimator. Our sample, which is dictated by data constraints, comprises observations for 115 countries in the period 1975–2013. However, the number of effective data points used in the

---

[6] There is an extensive literature on semi-parametric and GMM approaches for some panel data models with latent heterogeneity (Honoré, 2002). Among the practical limitations of these estimators is that, although they provide estimators of the primary slope parameters, they usually do not provide estimators for the full set of model parameters and, thus, preclude computation of marginal effects, probabilities, or predictions for the dependent variable.

estimations varies due to missing information on independent variables.

Right-hand-side variables are lagged one period to reduce the risk of biasing the estimates as a result of potential simultaneity of regressors with fiscal rules. This is a popular – yet not always optimal – way of addressing the problem, as it presumes that lagged observations of the variables are appropriate instruments. To our knowledge, there is no better practical alternative in the context of panel data discrete-choice models.

The econometric results are presented in Table 4.2. Column (1) reports results for the random-effects probit model. The likelihood-ratio tests validate the model at 99 percent confidence level. Most parameters display the expected sign and are statistically significant at conventional significance levels. The exceptions are monetary union, inflation targeting, capital account openness, and the budget balance, which display the expected sign but are very imprecisely estimated. The only counter-intuitive result is that of fiscal pro-cyclicality, which displays the opposite sign and is highly significant. Using alternative measures of government pro-cyclicality measures (e.g., three-year rolling windows or alternative government expenditure aggregates) does not produce qualitatively different results.

It is unlikely that our results are affected by potential cross-correlation between regressors. As shown in Appendix Table A3, cross-correlations between the different regressors are in general very small, except in a few cases. As expected, there is high correlation between democracy levels and political checks and balances, and between economic development and the dependency ratio.

One important limitation of this first model is the limited availability of data for our measure of the sacrifice in fiscal policy discretion – a three-year moving average of the coefficient of variation of government revenues (as share of GDP) – in particular for the first half of the sample period. When using an alternative measure – a similar three-year moving average of fiscal balance – the sample size more than doubles.[7] The results are shown in Column (2) of Table 4.2.

The likelihood-ratio test validates the model at 99 percent confidence. Now almost all parameters display the expected sign and are

---

[7] The results are not affected qualitatively by choosing a five-year moving average of fiscal balances.

Table 4.2: *Baseline results for national fiscal rules, panel estimation, 1975–2013*

	Random-effects probit estimation		Conditional fixed-effects logit estimation	
	(1)	(2)	(3)	(4)
Democracy	0.136***	0.120***	0.160*	0.163**
	(0.048)	(0.036)	(0.092)	(0.074)
Federalism	3.332***	4.702***	–	–
	(0.868)	(1.400)		
Political checks and balances	−1.296*	−1.028*	−0.784	−1.147
	(0.798)	(0.511)	(1.591)	(0.954)
Government stability	0.169***	0.080**	0.238*	0.124*
	(0.065)	(0.037)	(0.128)	(0.069)
Monetary union	0.070	0.470	0.578	0.568
	(0.440)	(0.309)	(0.965)	(0.612)
Fixed exchange rate	−0.539	0.245	−0.020	0.712
	(0.410)	(0.239)	(0.852)	(0.484)
Inflation targeter	0.583	1.528***	−0.092	2.112***
	(0.423)	(0.229)	(0.792)	(0.416)
Capital account openness	1.430**	1.929**	1.969*	2.599***
	(0.614)	(0.364)	(1.235)	(0.730)
Financial development	0.578**	0.319*	0.586	−0.168
	(0.284)	(0.199)	(0.647)	(0.389)
Economic development	0.600*	1.369***	−0.435	4.681***
	(0.326)	(0.391)	(1.887)	(0.957)
Sacrifice cost of fiscal rules I (based on fiscal revenue)	−0.458 (2.353)	–	0.591 (4.231)	–
Sacrifice cost of fiscal rules II (based on fiscal balance)	–	−7.415* (4.480)	–	−12.8386 (8.549)
Government balance	−2.938	3.441**	−8.673	4.290
	(3.065)	(1.726)	(6.507)	(3.419)
Dependency ratio	−6.480***	−9.106***	−31.731***	−19.477***
	(2.444)	(1.663)	(8.733)	(3.725)
Pro-cyclicality of government expenditures	−0.923***	−0.407**	−1.307**	−0.706**
	(0.303)	(0.179)	(0.537)	(0.352)

Table 4.2: (*cont.*)

	Random-effects probit estimation		Conditional fixed-effects logit estimation	
	(1)	(2)	(3)	(4)
Constant	10.199	11.430*	–	–
	(9.724)	(6.775)		
Observations	1,291	2,875	381	1,251
Countries	107	115	26	43
LR statistic	653.25	917.44	–	–
Value	0.000	0.000	–	–
Log likelihood	−276.68	−516.44	−124.40	−292.12

Note: standard errors in parenthesis, (***,**,*) significant at 99%, 95% and 90% confidence, respectively.

significant at conventional significance levels. The exceptions are monetary union and the exchange system, which are very imprecisely estimated. Again, the counter-intuitive result for fiscal pro-cyclicality remains.

We now turn to our results based on conditional logit models. As mentioned, this estimator focuses only on cases where countries have switched, i.e. they have either adopted or discontinued a fiscal rule during the sample period. Hence the sample size declines significantly, in particular, for the model that uses the government revenue-based measure of the sacrifice in fiscal policy discretion. In fact, the results in Column (3) of Table 4.2 indicate that most parameters are estimated very imprecisely, and only those of democracy, government stability, capital account openness, and dependency ratio are significant at 90 percent confidence or more. The imprecision arises from the fact that the data correspond to only twenty-six countries due to missing observations, particularly for the variable used to measure the cost of fiscal rules (government revenue).

The estimation improves somewhat when using the budget balance-based measure of the sacrifice cost of fiscal rules, as shown in Column (4) of Table 4.2. Now we have data for forty-six countries and more than 1,250 observations and, therefore, estimations are more robust. The results can be summarized in two groups. First, this model reproduces the results of the random-effects probit model but estimates are significantly more imprecise; this is itself the result of focusing only on those countries that actually switch to having fiscal rules. That is the case of variables such as checks and balances, fixed exchange rates, and government budget balance, for which the size of coefficients is similar but standard errors are much larger. Second, variables that appeared to be highly correlated with fiscal rules in probit models are also highly correlated in the conditional logit model (e.g. democracy, inflation targeting, economic development, and dependency ratio). In this latter group we also find the counter-intuitive result for fiscal pro-cyclicality.

In sum, these estimates suggest that the random-effect probit estimator is preferred, as the results based on the latter seem to be very similar to those obtained using the conditional logit model but are statistically far more precise. In what follows we abandon the conditional logit estimator. Likewise, we concentrate on models that use the budget balance measure of the sacrifice cost of fiscal rules, in view of its wider coverage.

The economic significance of the results of the preferred specification cannot be directly assessed from the coefficients in Column (2), since the model is highly non-linear. Hence, we compute the marginal effects of these estimates, defined as the change in the (conditional) probability of the outcome variable when changing the value of a regressor, holding all other regressors constant. The marginal effects of the discrete right-hand-side variables are reported in panel A of Table 4.3. The marginal effects of two variables are negligible in size (country belongs to a monetary union and has a fixed exchange rate), but those of the other three variables are sizable. Of the latter, the most salient result is for federal countries, which on average have a 7.5 percent higher probability of having a fiscal rule than non-federal countries.

The results for the conduct of monetary policy are quite interesting. Relinquishing monetary policy – either because the country belongs to a monetary union and/or because it has a fixed exchange rate – does not seem to have any impact on the choice of implementing fiscal rules. However, countries that conduct monetary policy under inflation targeting display a 5 percent higher likelihood of having a fiscal rule in place.

At face value, the results of the marginal effects of discrete variables in Panel A seem to be small. In order to provide perspective on their importance, we compute the *predicted probability of having a*

Table 4.3: Marginal effects of the random-effects probit estimation

Panel A: discrete variables

	Country is federal	Country has fixed exchange rate	Country is in monetary union	Country uses inflation targeting	Country has an open capital account
Change in variable	From zero to one	From zero to one	From zero to one	From zero to one	From zero to one
Change in probability	7.5%	−0.1%	0.4%	4.9%	3%

Panel B: institutional continuous variables

	Democracy levels	Checks and balances	Government stability	Economic development	Dependency ratio	Financial development
Change in variable	From percentile 25% to percentile 75%	From percentile 25% to percentile 75%	From percentile 25% to percentile 75%	From percentile 25% to percentile 75%	From percentile 25% to percentile 75%	From percentile 25% to percentile 75%
Change in probability	0.2%	−1.4%	0.1%	2.8%	8.4%	0.2%

Panel C: government-related continuous variables

	Fiscal balance	Pro-cyclicality of gov. exp.	Cost of fiscal rule
Change in variable	From percentile 25% to percentile 75%	From percentile 25% to percentile 75%	From percentile 25% to percentile 75%
Change in probability	1.0%	−0.1%	−1.7%

Note: expected change in the probability of observing a fiscal rule in an economy.

fiscal rule for countries that do have such a rule and then take the cross-country average. The model predicts an average probability of 28 percent that a fiscal rule is in place for these economies. We repeat the exercise for countries that do not have a fiscal rule and obtain a prediction of 9 percent. Therefore, the nineteen-percentage-point difference between the two latter averages better reflects the marginal effects in Table 4.3.

Computing the rest of the marginal effects is less straightforward since these regressors are continuous variables. Hence we need to determine an appropriate change in the regressor in order to compute the expected change in probability. We decide to define the relevant change in the regressor when moving from percentile 25 to percentile 75 of the observed sample distribution for each variable. For example, for the fiscal balance ratio to GDP, a country at percentile 25 exhibits a fiscal deficit of 4.8 percent of GDP, while at percentile 75 it exhibits almost a balanced budget (a −0.2 percent deficit of GDP).

The estimated marginal effects for the group of institutional variables are presented in Panel B of Table 4.3. Regarding political variables, the likelihood of having a fiscal rule in place declines in countries with more accountable governments – as reflected by a larger degree of checks and balances. This is reasonable, since more political responsibility is expected to lead to less arbitrary and more predictable fiscal policies. Political participation (as measured by the democracy index) and political stability have minor effects on the probability of implementing fiscal rules. Higher economic development has a small impact on having a fiscal rule in place. However, among all institutional variables, a larger dependency ratio has the largest effect on the likelihood of a fiscal rule.

Finally, Panel C of Table 4.3 shows the marginal effects of variables that are related to fiscal policy. Countries with balanced fiscal accounts increase by a small amount the likelihood of implementing fiscal rules. However, this is a highly non-linear result. In Figure 4.2 we compute the change in probability for different levels of fiscal balances, from a deficit of 5 percent of GDP to a surplus of 5 percent of GDP. The figure reflects that there is almost no change in the probability of implementing a fiscal rule for countries with larger deficits. Only when countries move from a small deficit to a balanced budget and then to budget surpluses is the likelihood of adopting fiscal rules raised – but only up to a certain limit (4 percent of GDP).

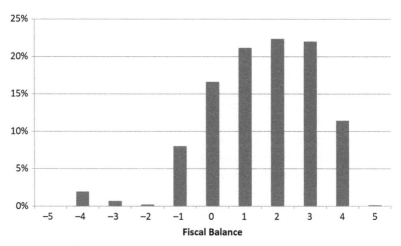

Figure 4.2: Change in the probability of adopting a fiscal rule
Note: by levels of fiscal balance (% of GDP).

Finally, while the pro-cyclicality of government expenditures is reported with a large estimated coefficient in our regression model, it actually has little effect on the probability of having a fiscal rule in place. The sacrifice cost of a fiscal rule has a small and negative effect on the likelihood of adopting a rule-based fiscal policy.

We now turn to the results of our model estimations for each type of rule. The main reason to focus on individual rules is that, a priori, there is no reason to assume that the determinants of adoption of different rule types are the same or that they could equally affect the probability of having one type of rule in place or another. The main limitation of our subsequent empirical search is that there are fewer observations of individual rules (as shown in Table 4.1) and therefore estimations could be less precise.

The analysis proceeds by comparing the role of each determinant on each type of rule (Table 4.4). Democracy is an important determinant of all categories of rule, but the coefficient is much larger for revenue and expenditure rules than for the other two rule categories. Regarding federalism, there is significant heterogeneity across rule types; this regressor is significant only for budget balance and public debt rules. Likewise, there is also heterogeneity in the case of the two other institutional variables. Government stability does not affect adoption of the two most popular fiscal rules (budget balance and expenditures) but is significant for the other types of rules. Checks and balances are

Table 4.4: *Results for national fiscal rules by rule type, panel estimation, 1975–2013*

	Budget balance rule	Expenditure rule	Revenue rule	Public debt rule
Democracy	0.104**	0.275***	0.393**	0.173***
	(0.047)	(0.062)	(0.142)	(0.049)
Federalism	7.089***	0.607	−1.270	3.811***
	(0.961)	(0.946)	(1.511)	(1.004)
Checks and balances	−1.148*	−2.225***	3.533	−1.340*
	(0.676)	(0.790)	(2.278)	(0.768)
Government stability	0.068	0.035	0.239*	0.245***
	(0.048)	(0.048)	(0.123)	(0.065)
Monetary union	−2.811**	0.051	−0.574	2.082**
	(1.361)	(0.348)	(0.532)	(0.967)
Fixed exchange rate	−0.357	0.317	1.164*	0.414
	(0.457)	(0.355)	(0.710)	(0.393)
Inflation target	1.813***	0.402	−0.426	3.653***
	(0.347)	(0.266)	(0.703)	(0.798)
Capital account openness	1.226**	2.488***	2.364**	−0.913
	(0.511)	(0.496)	(1.021)	(0.628)
Financial development	−0.142	−0.216	2.155***	0.015
	(0.304)	(0.253)	(0.632)	(0.298)
Economic development	1.655***	4.354***	0.758	−1.233***
	(0.383)	(0.569)	(0.774)	(0.357)
Cost of fiscal rules I	–	–	–	–
Cost of fiscal rules II	−6.418	−2.277	16.453	−8.321
	(5.799)	(6.555)	(17.387)	(7.423)
Government balance	8.197***	−3.482	−3.126	16.928***
	(2.432)	(2.212)	(6.584)	(3.263)
Dependency ratio	−16.433**	−1.325	3.258	−18.196***
	(1.914)	(1.946)	(6.242)	(3.368)
Pro-cyclicality of govmt. expenditures	0.212	−0.041	1.364**	−0.409
	(0.248)	(0.239)	(0.655)	(0.311)
Constant	32.108***	−44.722*	−48.850*	62.049***
	(7.950)	(9.137)	(28.071)	(10.078)
Observations	2,875	2,875	2,875	2,875
Countries	115	115	115	115
LR statistic	689.91	539.28	342.19	631.85
Value	0.000	0.000	0.000	0.000
Log likelihood	−304.55	−322.29	−78.82	−195.59

Note: random-effects probit model, standard errors in parenthesis, (***,**,*) significant at 99%, 95% and 90% confidence, respectively.

significant for three of the four types but are insignificant in the case of revenue rules. It ought to be acknowledged that there are very few countries in our sample that have implemented revenue rules, as shown in Table 4.1; hence, we are not very confident that the estimated model is statistically robust.

We now turn to monetary and exchange systems. Monetary union membership has a sizable and significant estimated coefficient for budget balance rules but a similar significant coefficient of opposite sign in the case of public debt rules. These contradictory results may explain the non-significant result obtained for this variable in adopting any rule, as reported in Table 4.2. The fixed exchange rate system continues to be statistically insignificant. Finally, inflation targeting has been instrumental in adopting budget balance and public debt rules but has had no effect in the case of expenditure rules.

We find an important effect of integration with international financial markets in determining the adoption of budget balance and expenditure rules, but none for the public debt rule. On the other hand, while we find the expected positive effect of economic development on adopting budget balance and expenditure rules, we find a somewhat surprising negative impact on public debt rules – as countries develop, their appetite for public debt rules declines.

Turning to fiscal variables, we note that the sacrifice cost of implementing fiscal rules is very imprecisely estimated for all type of rules, but displays the expected negative sign. This suggests that the significant estimate obtained for this variable in Table 4.2 is the result of increased precision when pooling together the data. A similar result obtains for the dependency ratio and the government budget balance.

Finally, and surprisingly, the counter-intuitive result for fiscal procyclicality of the aggregated fiscal rule models does not hold when looking at individual rules, since in all cases the estimated coefficient is statistically insignificant. This could indicate the need for further study of the extent to which the counter-intuitive result for fiscal procyclicality of the models in Table 4.2 is the result of aggregation biases or other econometric problems.

5 Concluding Remarks

Reforms of fiscal institutions and fiscal rules are motivated by several policy objectives, shared by most policymakers in the world. So why do some countries adopt fiscal rules while others do not? Answering this question boils down to identifying the conditions under which some countries decide to adopt fiscal rules and maintain them over time. In particular, which institutional conditions favor adoption of fiscal rules? Are rules more likely to be associated to particular exchange rate and monetary regimes, and to financial openness and development? Are richer countries more likely to adopt fiscal rules? Does revenue volatility inhibit having fiscal rules in place? Are countries more likely to keep fiscal rules in place when they exhibit stronger fiscal policy performance?

These are the empirical questions addressed by this chapter, using a large world panel sample of *de jure* national fiscal rules for 115 countries (of which eighty-nine have adopted fiscal rules) and spanning the period 1975–2013. We have tested our model both at the aggregate level (any national fiscal rule in place) and for four particular fiscal rules.

Our main result for aggregate national fiscal rules is drawn from our largest sample and based on the random-effects probit model. The results conform to our qualitative model of determinants of adopting and having a national fiscal rule in place. Institutional and political conditions (democracy, federalism, checks and balances, and government stability) contribute significantly to the likelihood of having a fiscal rule in place. While fixed exchange rate regimes do not contribute to explaining rules, one particular monetary regime – inflation targeting – does. Capital account openness and financial development contribute to having fiscal rules. And so does overall economic development. Our measure of the cost of having a fiscal rule in place – the volatility of government revenue – in fact inhibits having a rule. Finally, our three measures of fiscal conditions – budget balance, population dependency ratio, and government expenditure pro-cyclicality – contribute significantly to having a national fiscal rule in place.

The results presented here suggest several avenues for future research on fiscal rules in particular and the fiscal policy frame in general. First, considering that our results are based on the relatively recent history of fiscal rules, we would expect that conditions explaining past adoption and maintenance of rules are likely to change in the future. This would merit revisiting our research once a richer set of country-year data is made available in the future. Second, it would be most relevant to empirically assess the conditions under which *de facto* fiscal rules are adopted, or what explains compliance with *de jure* rules. Obviously this requires having available future measures of rule compliance. Third, beyond controlling for potential endogeneity of regressors – as was done in this chapter – it is of key interest to empirically assess the effectiveness of rules, i.e. to measure the fiscal and macroeconomic effects of having fiscal rules in place. Finally, both academics and policymakers have much more to learn – far more than what we know to date – about how fiscal rules interact with other components of a modern fiscal framework, such as fiscal councils.

Bibliography

Agénor, P. and Aizenman, J. (2000). *Savings and the Terms of Trade under Borrowing Constraints*. National Bureau of Economic Research, Working Paper No. 7743.

Alesina, F. and Tabellini, G. (1990). A positive theory of fiscal deficits and government debt. *Review of Economic Studies*, 57(3), 403–14.

(2005). *Why Is Fiscal Policy Often Procyclical?* Discussion paper no. 2090, Harvard Institute of Economic Research, CESifo Working Paper No. 1556.

Anderson, B. and Minarik, J. (2006). *Design Choices for Fiscal Policy Rules*. Paper for OECD Working Party for Senior Budget Officials GOV/PGC/SBO 4.

Arellano, M. and Bond, S. (1991). Some tests of specification for panel data: Monte Carlo evidence and an application to employment equations. *Review of Economic Studies*, 58(2), 277–97.

Barro, R. and Gordon, D. (1983). Rules, discretion and reputation in a natural rate model of monetary policy. *Journal of Monetary Economics*, 12, 101–21.

Bassetto, M. and Sargent, Thomas J. (2006). Politics and efficiency of separating capital and ordinary government budgets. *The Quarterly Journal of Economics*, 121(4), 1167–1210.

Bennett, H. and Loayza, N. (2002). Policy biases when the monetary and fiscal authorities have different objectives. In N. Loayza and K. Schmidt-Hebbel, eds., *Monetary Policy: Rules and Transmission Mechanisms*. Santiago: Central Bank of Chile, pp. 299–330.

Braun, M., and Tommasi, M. (2004). Subnational fiscal rules: a game theoretic approach. In G. Kopits, ed., *Rules-Based Fiscal Policy in Emerging Markets: Background, Analysis and Prospects*. New York: Palgrave Macmillan, pp. 183–97.

Buti, M. and Guidice, G. (2004). EMU fiscal rules: what can and cannot be exported. In G. Kopits, ed., *Rules-Based Fiscal Policy in Emerging*

Markets: Background, Analysis and Prospects. New York: Palgrave Macmillan, pp. 97–113.

Calderón, C. and Schmidt-Hebbel, K. (2008a). *The Choice of Fiscal Regime in the World.* Central Bank of Chile, Working Paper No. 487.

(2008b). *Business Cycles and Fiscal Policies: The Role of Institutions and Financial Markets.* Central Bank of Chile, Working Paper No. 481.

Castro, V. (2011). The impact of the European Union fiscal rules on economic growth. *Journal of Macroeconomics*, **33**(2), 313–26.

Chang, Y. (2003). Nonlinear IV Panel Unit Root Tests. *Unpublished manuscript*, Department of Economics, Rice University.

Chinn, M. and Ito, H. (2008). A new measure of financial openness. *Journal of Comparative Policy Analysis*, **10**(3), 307–20.

Cimadomo, J. (2012). Fiscal policy in real time. *Scandinavian Journal of Economics*, **114**(2), 440–65.

Collier, P. (1991). Africa's external economic relations, 1960–90. *African Affairs*, **90**(July), 339–56.

Cukierman, A. (1992). *Central Bank Strategy, Credibility and Independence: Theory and Evidence.* Cambridge, MA: MIT Press.

Debrun, X. and Kumar, M. S. (2007). *The Discipline-Enhancing Role of Fiscal Institutions: Theory and Empirical Evidence.* International Monetary Fund, IMF Working Paper No. 07/171.

De Grauwe, P. (2006). Flaws in the design of the Eurosystem? *International Finance*, **9**(1), 137–44.

Deroose, S., Moulin, L. and Wierts, P. (2006). National expenditure rules and expenditure outcomes: evidence for EU member states. *Wirtschaftspolitische Blätter*, **1**, 27–42.

Elbadawi, I., Schmidt-Hebbel, K. and Soto, R. (2015). Why do countries have fiscal rules? In R. Caballero and K. Schmidt-Hebel, eds., *Economic Policy in Emerging-Market Economies.* Santiago: Central Bank of Chile.

Fatás, A. (2005). *Is There a Case for Sophisticated Balanced-Budget Rules?* OECD Publishing, OECD Economics Department Working Paper No. 466.

Feld, L. P. and Schnellenbach, J. (2010). *Fiscal Federalism and Long-Run Macroeconomic Performance: A Survey of Recent Research*, http://ssrn.com/abstract=1566390

Ferrero, A. (2009). Fiscal and monetary rules for a currency union. *Journal of International Economics*, **77**(1), 1–10.

Frenkel, J., Goldstein, M. and Masson, P. (1991). *Characteristics of a Successful Exchange Rate System.* IMF Occasional Paper No. 82.

Friedman, M. (1968). The role of monetary policy. *The American Economic Review*, 58(1), 1–17.

Gavin, M. and Perotti, R. (1997). Fiscal policy in Latin America. In B. Bernanke and J. Rotemberg, eds., *NBER Macroeconomics Annual 12*. Cambridge, MA: MIT Press, pp. 11–70.

Gengenbach, C., Palm, F. C. and Urbain, J. (2008). *Panel Unit Root Tests in the Presence of Cross-Sectional Dependencies: Comparison and Implications for Modeling*. Research Memoranda 040, Maastricht: METEOR, Maastricht Research School of Economics of Technology and Organization.

Giavazzi, F. and Pagano, M. (1988). The advantage of tying one's hands: EMS discipline and central bank credibility. *European Economic Review*, 32(5), 1055–75.

Greene, W. (2001). *Fixed and Random Effects in Nonlinear Models*. Department of Economics, Stern School of Business, New York University, Working Paper No. EC-01-01.

(2009). Discrete choice modeling. In T. Mills and K. Patterson, eds., *The Handbook of Econometrics: Vol. 2, Applied Econometrics*. London: Palgrave, Part 4.2.

Heckman, J. (1981). Statistical models for discrete panel data. In C. Manski and D. McFadden, eds., *Structural Analysis of Discrete Data with Econometric Applications*. Cambridge: MIT Press, pp. 114–78.

Henisz, W. and Zelner, B. A. (2010). Measures of political risk database. *Unpublished manuscript*, The McDonough School of Business, Georgetown University.

Hlouskova, J. and Wagner, M. (2006). The performance of panel unit root and stationarity tests: results from a large scale simulation study. *Econometric Reviews*, 25, 85–116.

Honoré, B. (2002). Nonlinear models with panel data. *Portuguese Economic Journal*, 1(2), 163–79.

Hughes Hallett, A. and Lewis, J. (2005). *Fiscal Discipline before and after EMU - Permanent Weight Loss or Crash Diet?* Vanderbilt University Department of Economics, Working Paper No. 0516.

Ilzetzki, E. and Végh, C. A. (2008). *Pro-Cyclical Fiscal Policy in Developing Countries: Truth or Fiction?* National Bureau of Economic Research, Working Paper No. 14191.

Im, K. S., Pesaran, M. H. and Shin, Y. (2003). Testing for unit roots in heterogeneous panels. *Journal of Econometrics*, 115, 53–74.

IMF. (2006). *Inflation Targeting and the IMF*. Mimeo, prepared by Monetary and Financial Systems Department, Policy and Development Review Department, and Research Department.

(2010). *Annual Report on Exchange Arrangements and Exchange Restrictions*. Washington, DC: IMF.

Kaminsky, G., Reinhart, C. and Végh, C. (2004). *When It Rains, It Pours: Procyclical Capital Flows and Macroeconomic Policies.* National Bureau of Economic Research, Working Paper No. 10780.

Klein, M. W. and Shambaugh, J. C. (2008). The dynamics of exchange rate regimes: fixes, floats, and flips. *Journal of International Economics,* **75** (1), 70–92.

Kopits, G. (2004). *Rules-Based Fiscal Policy in Emerging Markets: Background, Analysis and Prospects.* New York: Palgrave Macmillan.

Kopits, G. and Symansky, S. (1998). *Fiscal Rules.* IMF Occasional Paper No. 162.

Krogstrup, S. and Wyplosz, C. (2006). *A Common Pool Theory of Deficit Bias Correction.* CEPR Discussion Papers, No. 5866.

Kumar, M., Baldacci, E., Schaechter, A., Caceres, A. C., Kim, D., Debrun, X., Escolano, J., Jonas, J. Karam, J. P., Yakadina, I. and Zymek, R. (2009). *Fiscal Rules – Anchoring Expectations for Sustainable Public Finances.* IMF Staff Papers, www.imf.org/external/np/pp/eng/2009/121609.pdf

Kwak, D. W. and Wooldridge, J. M. (2009). *The Robustness of the Fixed Effects Logit Estimator to Violations of Conditional Independence.* Mimeo, Department of Economics, Michigan State University.

Kydland, F. and Prescott, E. (1977). Rules rather than discretion: the inconsistency of optimal plans. *Journal of Political Economy,* **85**(3), 473–91.

Levy-Yeyati, E., Sturzenegger, F. and Reggio, I. (2010). On the endogeneity of exchange rate regimes. *European Economic Review,* **54**(5), 659–77.

Lucotte, Y. (2012). Adoption of inflation targeting and tax revenue performance in emerging market economies: an empirical investigation. *Economic Systems,* **36**(4), 609–28.

Maddala, G. (1987). Limited dependent variable models using panel data. *Journal of Human Resources,* **22**(3), 307–38.

Maliszewski, W. (2009). *Fiscal Policy Rules for Oil-Producing Countries: A Welfare-Based Assessment.* International Monetary Fund, Working Paper No. WP/09/126.

Masson, P. and Pattillo, C. (2002). Monetary union in west Africa: an agency of restraint for fiscal policies? *Journal of African Economies,* **11**(3), 387–412.

Minea, A. and Tapsoba, R. (2014). Does inflation targeting improve fiscal discipline? *Journal of International Money and Finance,* **40**, 185–203.

Minea, A. and Villieu, P. (2009). Threshold effects in monetary and fiscal policies in a growth model: assessing the importance of the financial system. *Journal of Macroeconomics,* **31**(2), 304–19.

Morris, R., Ongena, H. and Schuknecht, L. (2006). *The Reform and Implementation of the Stability and Growth Pact*. European Central Bank, Occasional Paper Series No. 47.

Neyman, J. and Scott, E. (1948). Consistent estimates based on partially consistent observations. *Econometrica*, **16**, 1–32.

Polity IV Project. (2010). *Political Regime Characteristics and Transitions, 1800–2010 Database*, www.systemicpeace.org/polity/polity4.htm

Ravn, M. O. and Uhlig, H. (2002). On adjusting the Hodrick–Prescott filter for the frequency of observations. *The Review of Economics and Statistics*, **84**(2), 371–5.

Reinhart, C. and Rogoff, K. S. (2004). The modern history of exchange rate arrangements: a reinterpretation. *The Quarterly Journal of Economics*, **119**(1), 1–48.

Schaechter, A., Kinda, T., Budina, N. and Weber, A. (2012). *Fiscal Rules in Response to the Crisis—Towards the "Next-Generation" Rules. A New Dataset*. IMF Working Paper No. WP/12/187.

Schick, A. (2004). Fiscal institutions versus political will. In G. Kopits, ed., *Rules-Based Fiscal Policy in Emerging Markets: Background, Analysis and Prospects*. New York: Palgrave Macmillan, pp. 81–94.

Schmidt-Hebbel, K. (2016). Fiscal institutions in resource-rich economies: lessons from Chile and Norway. In I. Elbadawi and H. Selim, eds., *Understanding and Avoiding the Oil Curse in Resource-Rich Arab Economies*. Cambridge: Cambridge University Press, pp. 225–84.

Taylor, J. B. (1993). Discretion versus policy rules in practice. *Carnegie-Rochester Conference Series on Public Policy*, **39**, 195–214.

Talvi, E. and Végh, C. (2005). Tax base variability and procyclical fiscal policy in developing countries. *Journal of Development Economics*, **78** (1), 156–90.

Ter-Minassian, T. (2010). *Preconditions for a Successful Introduction of Structural Fiscal Balance-based Rules in Latin America and the Caribbean: A Framework Paper*. Inter-American Development Bank, Discussion Paper No. IDB-DP-157

Tornell, A. and Velasco, A. (2000). Fixed versus flexible exchange rates: which provides more fiscal discipline? *Journal of Monetary Economics*, **45**(2), 399–436.

Train, K. (2003). *Discrete Choice Methods with Simulation*. Cambridge: Cambridge University Press.

von Hagen, J. and Eichengreen, B. (1996). Federalism, fiscal restraints, and European monetary union. *American Economic Review*, **86**(2), 134–8.

Wooldridge, J. (1995). Selection corrections for panel data models under conditional mean independence assumptions. *Journal of Econometrics* **68**(1), 115–32.

  (2009). Correlated Random Effects Models with Unbalanced Panels. Working Paper, Department of Economics, Michigan State University.

World Bank (2015). *World Development Indicators 2014*, www.grad uateinstitute.ch/md4stata.

Wyplosz, C. (2005). Fiscal policy: institutions versus rules. *National Institute Review*, **191**, 70–84.

5 | Fiscal Councils: Rationale and Effectiveness

ROEL W. M. J. BEETSMA AND
XAVIER DEBRUN

1 Introduction

In recent years, a rapidly growing number of countries have established independent institutions specifically aimed at promoting sound fiscal policies.[1] These agencies – which we label "fiscal councils" in the remainder of this chapter – vary greatly in terms of their mandate, tasks, and institutional models (see Debrun et al., 2009, 2013; Kopits, 2013, for comprehensive surveys). Although such heterogeneity complicates theoretical and empirical analyses, fiscal councils share broad features, such as an explicit mandate enshrined in legislation, an official "watchdog" role implying a direct contribution to the public debate on fiscal policy, and non-partisanship in their activities. The emphasis on non-partisanship is essential to distinguish them from ad hoc bi-partisan or multi-partisan advisory committees sometimes appointed by government to formulate policy recommendations on specific public finance or broader economic issues.

Although the literature often compares fiscal councils to independent central banks, the fundamental difference between them is that fiscal councils never have the discretion to set policy instruments.[2] They are at a minimum government-sponsored cheerleaders of fiscal discipline, and at best active facilitators of such discipline. This is clearly far from the role of decisionmakers deliberately insulated from politics to escape a time-inconsistency problem (Thomson, 1981; Rogoff, 1985).

The rise in fiscal councils around the world has coincided with rapidly escalating concerns about the longer-term sustainability of

Without implication, we are grateful to Jun Il Kim, Joana Pereira, and Andrea Schaechter for insightful comments on an earlier version of this chapter.

[1] By "sound," we essentially mean financially sustainable over the medium term, because this is the precondition for policymakers to deliver adequate amounts of public goods and services and to smooth the business cycle.

[2] Only one such institution (in Hungary) has formally a veto power on the budget.

public finances. In contrast to what was seen in the final three decades of the twentieth century, these concerns have not spared advanced economies, where preventing explosive public debt trajectories has become a challenge. More than five years after the global financial crisis of 2008–9 (GFC), public debt ratios are still at historical highs despite record low interest rates in many countries. The fiscal legacies of the GFC are only partly to blame for the erosion of fiscal credibility. Substantial liabilities had already been accumulated pre-GFC, and the intensifying demographic pressures on entitlement spending thwart efforts to rebuild robust fiscal positions.

The aim of this chapter is to analyze fiscal councils' effectiveness in encouraging fiscal discipline. Since experience with fiscal councils is arguably too limited to envisage a robust empirical analysis, we proceed in two steps.

First, we fill an important gap in the literature by proposing a simple theoretical model of fiscal policy with or without a fiscal council. Asymmetric information between voters and a politician is the central feature of the model. We show how a fiscal council can: (i) be in the interest of the elected official establishing it; and (ii) be effective in discouraging the deficit bias affecting the official's fiscal decisions, which raises social welfare. The fiscal council's capacity to improve the public's understanding of the quality of fiscal policy contributes to better aligning voters and policymakers' incentives and to taming the deficit bias affecting well-intended governments. Specifically, the model shows that a fiscal council's impact on fiscal performance is greatest when it is able to minimize the noise surrounding signals of the incumbent government's productivity in delivering public goods, which we summarize in the generic term "competence." Most importantly, the positive impact of the fiscal council applies regardless of the true type of government ("competent" or not).

Second, we map the main policy implications of the model into a set of core criteria that increase the likelihood that a council will effectively improve voters' ability to assess the competence of the incumbent government – the key factor in their voting decision. Using the latest vintage of the IMF dataset on independent fiscal institutions, we assess whether existing institutions have been designed to be effective or whether they are more likely to have been conceived as smokescreens.

The rest of the chapter is structured as follows. Section 2 briefly reviews the rationale for fiscal councils and the possible channels through which they influence fiscal outcomes. Section 3 discusses the model, while Section 4 maps the model's results into features of fiscal councils likely to boost their effectiveness. Existing fiscal councils are assessed along these criteria.

2 Fiscal Councils on the Rise

This section first documents recent trends in the establishment of fiscal councils. It then reviews arguments made in the literature to explain the rise in fiscal councils and provides some motivation for the model proposed in Section 3.

2.1 Deficit Bias and the Emergence of Fiscal Councils

Since the early 1970s, the conduct of fiscal policy has been characterized by a strong bias towards budget deficits. Looking at a sample of twenty-two advanced economies for which long fiscal time series exist, the frequency of general government deficits increased markedly over time and across countries (Figure 5.1). While in the 1960s about half of the countries recorded broadly balanced or in-surplus budget positions more than half of the time, only New Zealand and Norway managed such performance during the period 1990–9. The median number of deficit years per decade was between seven and nine years for all post-1970 sub-periods except the pre-GFC period (2000–8), when many countries benefited from rapidly increasing revenues on the back of asset price booms and relatively strong economic growth. The fiscal legacies of the GFC to this day are also very clear: thirteen out of the twenty-two countries in our sample have recorded or were expected to experience a deficit in every single year between 2009 and 2017.

While fiscal deficits often reflect adverse domestic and external shocks, their persistence in so many countries for so long and the protracted public debt buildup that follows suggest that some fundamental factors are at play. Figure 5.2 provides a useful historical perspective. Never in peacetime has public debt reached the levels seen today among the G7 economies. If debt ratios are expected to decline in the next few years, it is mostly due to abnormally low borrowing costs for these countries. Should interest rates move back to their historical average, debt ratios would,

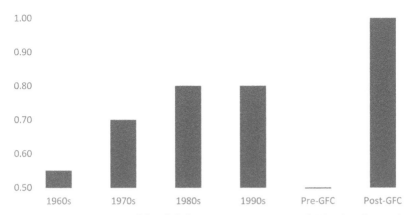

Figure 5.1: Frequency of fiscal deficits over 0.5 percent of GDP in advanced countries

Note: Median OECD country. The sample covers Australia, Austria, Belgium, Canada, Denmark, Finland, France, Germany, Greece, Iceland, Ireland, Italy, Japan, The Netherlands, New Zealand, Norway, Portugal, Spain, Sweden, Switzerland, the United Kingdom, and the United States. Observations for 2015–17 reflect IMF forecasts (World Economic Outlook database, June 2015).

Sources: Mauro et al. (2013), *World Economic Outlook*, OECD, and national authorities

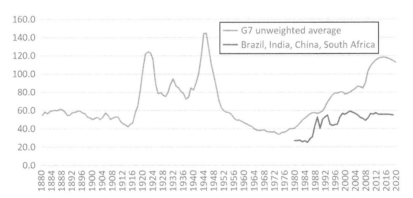

Figure 5.2: Public debt in G7 and selected emerging market economies, 1880–2020

Note: as a percent of GDP.

Sources: Abbas et al. (2010) and *World Economic Outlook*

all else equal, be sharply on the rise. Note that a number of emerging economies with market access also exhibit a clear upward trend in their public debt-to-GDP ratios despite relatively stronger economic growth.

A vast theoretical and empirical literature suggests that weak public financial management and distorted political incentives are the main culprits for the deficit bias. Political distortions include policymakers' tendency to focus on the consequences of their discretionary actions in the short term, paying insufficient attention to the medium and the long term. Moreover, distributive conflicts entail the "common pool" problem: That is, the basic tendency for any given political constituency to use the available resources for their exclusive benefit without regard to the overall budgetary position. In addition, the deficit bias can also reflect time inconsistency. For instance, it can be difficult for governments to credibly commit to saving revenue windfalls in good times because of strong spending pressures that inevitably arise when abundant resources are available.

Faced with nervous voters and financial markets, governments have actively sought to strengthen the institutional setup shaping fiscal policy decisions in the hope of shoring up the credibility of their commitments to financial sustainability. Not surprisingly, it was during one of the worst episodes of pervasive and persistent deficits – the 1990s – that advanced economies started to constrain fiscal discretion through fiscal rules. These consist of numerical limits on debts, deficits, or expenditure, and an explicit implementation mechanism expected to entail reputational and political costs to non-compliant governments. The appetite for rules spread to developing economies less than a decade later. Following the initial wave of fiscal rule adoption, many countries tried to further boost fiscal credibility through better-designed rules and by setting up fiscal councils to foster transparency and accountability. However, the emergence of fiscal councils has been much more gradual and really started in earnest after the GFC, reflecting in part provisions of the Treaty on Stability, Coordination and Governance in the (European) Economic and Monetary Union (Figure 5.3). Efforts to comply with the Treaty also explain why a significant number of fiscal councils have been explicitly mandated to strengthen and facilitate the implementation of fiscal rules, not to substitute them.

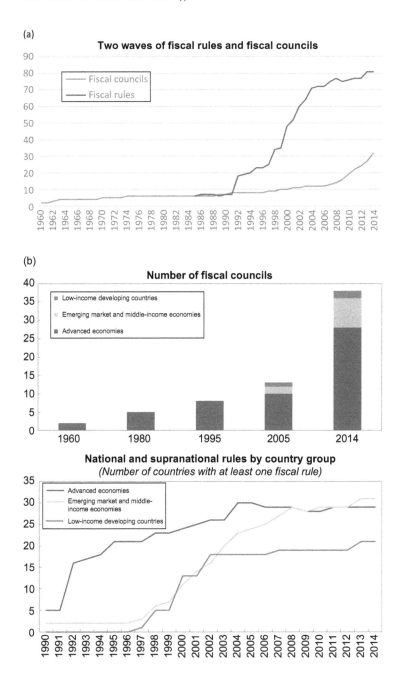

Figure 5.3: Number of countries with fiscal rules and fiscal councils

Sources: IMF (2015a, b): Fiscal Rules and Fiscal Councils Datasets (information current as of end 2014)

(c)

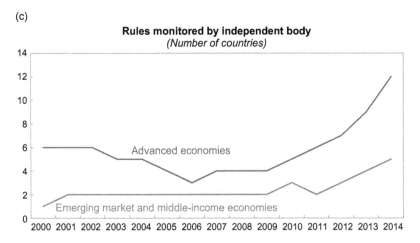

Figure 5.3: (*cont.*)

2.2 Institutions for Fiscal Credibility?

The widespread reliance on institutional reforms to boost fiscal credibility contrasts with long-standing doubts about the actual impact of institutional arrangements on policy outcomes. Objections to the effectiveness of institutions aimed at constraining macroeconomic policy discretion were originally articulated in the debate on central bank independence, and they apply to fiscal councils. One major critique – directly echoing McCallum (1995) – is that theoretical derivations of optimal fiscal institutions simply assume their effectiveness. Indeed, institutions are modeled as incentive schemes for policymakers and their credibility is often taken as given. Proponents of institutional reforms invariably reply that institutions are essentially defined by the high costs of changing them so that they are intrinsically more credible than discretionary policies. In the end, there is a clear need to be explicit about policymakers' incentives to set up and preserve such institutions, including the mechanisms through which bypassing or changing institutions could entail costs for policymakers (Jensen, 1997).

Another critical view on the effectiveness of institutions is set out by Posen (1995), who argues that in a democracy, institutions can only be sustained if they reflect deeper social preferences or permanent features of the political system. That argument again implies that institutions *per se* do not change underlying incentives. In the context of central bank independence, Posen (1995, p. 271) concludes that "both central bank independence and a coalition in society committed to protecting that independence are necessary to achieve the low inflation heretofore ascribed to central bank independence; either alone is insufficient."

Thus the question of why fiscally profligate governments would adopt discipline-enhancing mechanisms such as fiscal rules and fiscal councils remains open. As noted by von Hagen (2013, pp. 50–1), fiscal councils "can help improve fiscal performance if and only if the government agrees that there is a problem of weak fiscal performance and something must be done about it." This has direct implications for any attempt to establish an empirical link between institutions and performance. The risk of reverse causality looms large because the governments that adopt strong institutions are likely to be precisely those that would spontaneously stick to sound public finances in the first place (see Debrun et al., 2008; Fabrizio and Mody, 2006; Krogstrup and Wälti, 2008).

Importantly, however, these critiques do not necessarily imply a lack of effectiveness of fiscal institutions, because they have been developed in response to theories that assume (i) that the public knows the true motivation and competence of the government (complete information) and (ii) that institutions can only be effective if they somehow "tie the hands" of politicians by acting as binding constraints on their actions (or even by acting on their behalf on the basis of a predetermined mandate, like today's central banks).

In the plausible case where voters do not know the true level of competence and commitment of politicians, institutions can play a signaling role. Specifically, the very fact that an elected official would have no incentive to tie her own hands suggests that setting up discipline-oriented institutions could be a signal of underlying preferences or competence.[3] In other words, fiscal institutions exist to inform the public about the genuine preferences or competence of the government, and as such they can help align the incentives of policymakers and the public. To the extent that the information asymmetry between voters and policymakers is a source of bias – for example, because it increases political instability and shortsightedness in decision-making –

---

[3] Stéclebout-Orseau and Hallerberg (2007) develop a full-fledged model of the signaling role of independent watchdogs.

the effectiveness of institutions (i.e. their positive effect on fiscal discipline or welfare more broadly) can come from their signaling (or signal-enhancing) role.[4] This is the spirit of the theoretical model developed in Section 3, which focuses on how institutions can improve voters' assessments of government's competence (as defined above).

Our model contrasts with the conventional exposition of the case for fiscal councils. The literature often builds the case for fiscal councils on a comparison with monetary policy delegation. The typical narrative is articulated as follows (see e.g. Wyplosz, 2011). First, there is a review of the many reasons why fiscal policy tends to systematically deviate from a socially optimal solution, with an emphasis on common pool problems, short-termism, and time inconsistency. Second, fiscal policy rules are deemed ineffective in containing the deficit bias, largely because of low compliance (see Cordes et al., 2015) and frequent changes. The main reason is that the simplicity required for their smooth operation reduces their appropriateness when uncommon conditions prevail. For example, deficit ceilings fail to trigger discipline in good times – when compliance is more likely to result from automatic stabilizers than conscious actions – but bind in bad times, forcing undesirable pro-cyclical contractions. Third, there comes a call to our sense of déjà vu to draw a parallel with the case for central bank independence, which is also based on the idea of an expansive bias affecting unconstrained discretionary policies and on the manifest failure of rigid rules (e.g., caps on the growth of certain monetary aggregates) to address that bias.

We now turn to the description of the model.

3 A Simple Model of a Fiscal Council

This section presents a simple model aimed at rationalizing the potential existence of fiscal councils (FC). As discussed in Section 2, our basic premise is that an FC can contribute to mitigating problems of asymmetric information between elected officials and voters. In principle, this could be asymmetric information about the competence of the

---

[4] Debrun (2011) proposes a formal illustration of that argument. Of course, the possibility for incompetent or intrinsically profligate policymakers to adopt similar institutions opens the possibility of fiscal institutions being mere smokescreens in a non-trivial number of cases (Milesi-Ferretti, 2004; von Hagen and Wolff, 2006; and Debrun and Kumar, 2008).

government or about policies themselves, for instance because the executive branch may have more information about the true state of the public finances than the parliament or the public at large.

The model presented in this section emphasizes the first aspect of fiscal councils. The algebra is kept as simple as possible to better bring out the key intuitions. We make two essential assumptions. First, there is a political distortion (myopia) giving rise to sub-optimally high deficit levels. Second, a fiscal council is effective in helping voters to assess the exogenous and unobservable level of competence of the government.[5] In that setting, we show that a fiscal council can raise social welfare either by helping voters to elect competent governments more often or by directly encouraging elected policymakers – regardless of their competence – to select deficits closer to the social optimum. That second channel is of particular interest because it shows that an official watchdog with no direct policy lever can enhance fiscal discipline by strengthening the government's incentive to signal a high level of competence through a lower deficit.

3.1 Basic Setup

There are two periods. We assume a representative individual featuring a quasi-linear utility function defined over public good provision in the two periods:

$$E_0[u(g_1) + g_2],$$ (1)

where g_1 and g_2 are spending on public goods in periods 1 and 2, respectively, and $u(.)$ is a strictly increasing, concave function. Utility in the second period is linear because it simplifies the algebra substantially and avoids introducing effects arising purely from risk aversion. These technical simplifications are immaterial for the existence of a sub-optimal debt bias.

There are two political parties, which we label as L (liberal) and C (conservative), although ideology is not a factor in the model. Public spending in period t is selected by the political party that is in power in

---

[5] Recall that "competence" is a generic term capturing the efficiency in delivering public goods and services. It is the only criterion voters can use to differentiate two political parties competing for power, and therefore, the only determinant of voting decisions.

that period. A party only benefits from public spending if it is itself able to deliver the public good. For convenience, and without loss of generality, we assume that party L is in power in the first period. Hence, the utility of party L at the start of the game is:

$$E_0[u(g_1) + \Delta_L g_2], \tag{2}$$

where the indicator function Δ_L is 1 when L is in power in period 2, and zero when it is not. Regardless of the party, policymakers have individual levels of efficiency at generating public goods (or competence) λ when they take office in period 2. This level of competence is uncertain to all players at the start of the game. Competence is drawn from a binary distribution as follows:

$$\lambda_L, \lambda_C = \begin{cases} \overline{\lambda}, \text{with probability } 0.5 \\ \underline{\lambda}, \text{with probability } 0.5 \end{cases}. \tag{3}$$

where $\overline{\lambda} > 0$. Hence, the unconditionally expected competence level of a party is zero.

The economy is an endowment economy with exogenous amounts of resources that can be transformed into public goods in a more or less efficient way, depending on the competence of the government in charge. The resource constraints in the two periods can be written as:

$$\begin{cases} g_1 = 1 + b \\ g_2 = 1 - b + \lambda_2 \end{cases} \tag{4}$$

where b is the public debt (or deficit in this two-period setup) and we have used the fact that the party in power in the first period is L and the party in power in the second period is unknown at the start of the game.

A fiscal council may be established by a decision of "society" (a representative individual/the legislature) or the government. There is an important difference between the two cases. If it is society's prerogative to establish the FC, then that decision does not provide any information about the competence of the government. However, if it is the government's prerogative to establish an FC, then this decision could in itself provide information about the government's competence. The reason is that the fear of being exposed as incompetent might discourage a government to establish an FC, making the decision to do so a potential signal of competence.

We study both cases. For the case in which society decides to institute an FC, we assume that this decision comes first in the game. Then, the government learns its own competence level, after which it selects the debt level. Next, voters receive a signal about the competence level of the government. This is followed by the election and, finally, the second-period outcomes materialize. Hence, under this timing debt can potentially act as a signal of the government's competence.

For the case in which the government itself chooses whether or not to install an FC, we assume the following timing. First, the government learns about its competence level. Then, it simultaneously decides on whether to establish (or not) an FC and on the debt level. Then, voters receive the signal about the competence of the government. This is followed by elections; finally, the second-period outcomes materialize. The cases in which the government would choose to establish (or not) an FC and set the debt level before it knows its competence level are clearly less interesting because those decisions could not convey any information about competence.

The competence signal received by voters is noisy:

$$\delta = \lambda + \alpha\mu, \text{ where } \mu \sim N\left(0, \sigma_\mu^2\right) \tag{5}$$

where μ is independent of λ. Hence, we have that: $\left(\delta|\lambda = -\bar{\lambda}\right) \sim N\left(-\bar{\lambda}, \alpha^2\sigma_\mu^2\right)$ and $\left(\delta|\lambda = \bar{\lambda}\right) \sim N\left(\bar{\lambda}, \alpha^2\sigma_\mu^2\right)$.

Obviously, the mean of the signal's distribution depends on the government's competence. This is where the FC comes into play. Through economic analysis and public communication about fiscal policy, a fiscal council can help the general public and all stakeholders in the budget process to infer the competence of the government. For instance, the FC can issue reports summarizing and clarifying information that would otherwise be buried in official documentation or distorted by ideologically charged arguments exchanged in the political arena. The watchdog role that is common to all FCs thus arguably contributes to reduce the noise around the public debate about fiscal policy, thereby enhancing the signal about government competence. In the terms of Equation (5), this means that $\alpha = 1$ in the absence of an FC, while $0 \leq \alpha < 1$ if an effective FC is in place. Overall, an effective FC makes it more likely that a positive (negative) signal reflects true competence (incompetence).

Two intuitive assumptions help streamline the remainder of the analysis.

Assumption 1: *Public debt must always be repaid in full (or assets liquidated) in period 2.*

Allowing for default would significantly complicate the analysis with little benefit for the core argument, because borrowing costs would have to factor in default probabilities. Assumption 2 is related to the no-default conjecture and concerns marginal period utilities.

Assumption 2: *The highest debt level a government can choose in period 1 is $1 - \bar{\lambda}$, which is characterized by $u'(2 - \bar{\lambda}) < 1$.*

The underlying intuition is as follows. Because the government must be able to face its obligations even in the case of a bad realization of the competence variable in period 2 ($\lambda_2 = -\bar{\lambda}$), the maximum amount of public debt that can be issued and spent in period 1 is $1 - \bar{\lambda}$. Otherwise, there would be an unconditional probability of default in period 2 of at least 50 percent. The public consumption path when public debt is maximized by an incompetent government is therefore $g_1 = 2 - \bar{\lambda} > 0$ and $g_2 = 0$.[6] In that case, it seems intuitive to assume that the marginal utility associated with a large public consumption in period 1 is strictly smaller than the marginal utility of zero public consumption in period 2, which is by definition constant equal to 1. In practice, Assumption 2 implies that an extreme "starve-the-beast" strategy cannot be an interior solution of a government maximization program.[7]

3.2 Establishing an FC is Society's Choice

This case is particularly interesting because the choice of debt can be used by the government to signal its competence. However, the eventual outcomes depend on the type of equilibrium that materializes. Under a "pooling equilibrium," the incompetent government tries to "mimic" the competent government by choosing the same debt level

---

[6] Note that if the government is competent, $g_2 = 2\bar{\lambda}$, although this does not change the inequality between period marginal utilities.

[7] Such a strategy would be extreme because the government would find it optimal to accumulate such a high level of debt in period 1 that there would be at least a 50 percent chance of government shutdown (zero public consumption) in period 2.

that the latter would also choose. Hence, in equilibrium, the only remaining information that voters can exploit to infer something about the government's competence is the signal δ. In a "separating equilibrium" the two types of government choose different debt levels and the voting public can infer the competence level from the specific choice of the debt level. Hence, the signal δ does not carry any additional information about competence.

3.2.1 Pooling Equilibrium

If δ is the only relevant piece of information that voters can use to extract information about the government's competence, then re-election takes place when the signal δ is greater than or equal to zero. Hence, the likelihood of re-election that the government perceives when it has to choose its debt level is $\Pr(\lambda + \alpha\mu \geq 0 | \lambda_L)$. If the incumbent is incompetent, i.e. $\lambda_L = -\bar{\lambda}$, its perceived re-election probability is:

$$\Pr\left(\lambda + \alpha\mu \geq 0 | \lambda_L = -\bar{\lambda}\right) = 1 - \Pr\left(\mu/\sigma_\mu < \bar{\lambda}/\left(\alpha\sigma_\mu\right)\right) = 1 - \Phi\left(\bar{\lambda}/\left(\alpha\sigma_\mu\right)\right)$$

(6)

where $\Phi(.)$ is the cumulative distribution function of the standard normal density function. Clearly, the perceived re-election probability of the incompetent government is increasing in α. If the incumbent is competent, i.e. $\lambda_L = \bar{\lambda}$, its perceived re-election probability is:

$$\Pr\left(\lambda + \alpha\mu \geq 0 | \lambda_L = \bar{\lambda}\right) = 1 - \Pr\left(\mu/\sigma_\mu \geq -\bar{\lambda}/\left(\alpha\sigma_\mu\right)\right) = 1 - \Phi\left(-\bar{\lambda}/\left(\alpha\sigma_\mu\right)\right)$$

(7)

This expression falls if α increases. Hence, conditional on a given debt level, an incompetent government would be worse off in the presence of an FC (i.e. $0 \leq \alpha < 1$), while a competent government would be better off.

There potentially exists a multiplicity of pooling equilibria associated with different ways in which the off-equilibrium probabilities about the type of government are formed. We focus on a candidate pooling equilibrium that we consider plausible. The candidate equilibrium debt level is the one that maximizes the competent incumbent's expected utility, assuming that voters cannot infer the type of government from the chosen debt level (precisely because an incompetent government would choose the same debt level). That is, we look for the value of b that maximizes:

$$u(1 + b) + \left[1 - \Phi\left(-\bar{\lambda}/(\alpha\sigma_\mu)\right)\right]\left(1 - b + \bar{\lambda}\right),$$

where the term in square brackets is the likelihood of re-election of an incumbent which knows it is competent. The first-order condition is:

$$u'(1 + b) = \left[1 - \Phi\left(-\bar{\lambda}/(\alpha\sigma_\mu)\right)\right]. \tag{8}$$

The solution exists and is unique. We denote it by $b^{c,p}$.

A potential equilibrium needs to be supported by a proper set of beliefs about the government's competence level when a specific on-equilibrium or off-equilibrium action is taken. Consistent with this being a pooling equilibrium, voters believe the incumbent is competent with probability one half if $b = b^{c,p}$. In the case of an off-equilibrium action $b \neq b^{c,p}$, we assume that voters believe that the incumbent is incompetent. Does such a pooling equilibrium indeed exist? To this end, we need to check that, given the way the beliefs are formed, none of the two government types have an incentive to deviate from setting $b = b^{c,p}$.

First, does the *incompetent* government have an incentive to deviate? If it deviates, then voters infer that the incumbent is incompetent and, hence, it will certainly not be re-elected. Knowing this, the optimal deviation is to maximize $u(1 + b)$ over b under the restriction that debt must always be repaid. This implies $b = 1 - \bar{\lambda}$ and utility to the incumbent of $u(2 - \bar{\lambda})$. Hence, an incompetent incumbent mimics $b = b^{c,p}$ if

$$u\left(1 + b^{c,p}\right) + \left[1 - \Phi\left(\bar{\lambda}/(\alpha\sigma_\mu)\right)\right]\left(1 - b^{c,p} - \bar{\lambda}\right) \geq u(2 - \bar{\lambda}), \tag{9}$$

where the left-hand side is the expected utility under not deviating.

Second, does the *competent* government have an incentive to deviate? If it deviates, the voting population is led to believe that it is incompetent. When it deviates, it would deviate in an optimal way, maximizing the objective $u(1 + b)$. This again yields $b = 1 - \bar{\lambda}$, and utility $u(2 - \bar{\lambda})$. Hence, the competent government sets $b = b^{c,p}$ if:

$$u\left(1 + b^{c,p}\right) + \left[1 - \Phi\left(-\bar{\lambda}/(\alpha\sigma_\mu)\right)\right]\left(1 - b^{c,p} + \bar{\lambda}\right) \geq u(2 - \bar{\lambda}) \tag{10}$$

Notice that the left-hand side of (10) exceeds that of (9) and, hence, (9) is the more restrictive condition.

We can now state:

Proposition 1: If condition (9) holds, a pooling equilibrium exists in which:
(i) along the equilibrium path, both the competent and incompetent incumbent set $b = b^{c,p}$; (ii) the voting

> population believes that if $b = b^{c,p}$ the incumbent is
> competent with probability one half, while if $b \neq b^{c,p}$ it
> believes that the incumbent is incompetent.

This equilibrium has some interesting characteristics. From (8) we observe that the equilibrium debt level $b^{c,p}$ is increasing in α, meaning that the debt level decreases with the precision of the signal δ. The establishment of an FC thus lowers the equilibrium debt level. The question is whether this reduction is welfare-improving. To answer this question, observe that the socially optimal debt level, i.e. the debt level that maximizes the representative individual's utility and which we denote by b^*, follows from the first-order condition $u'(1 + b^*) = 1$. Hence, $b^{c,p} > b^*$, and the introduction of an FC brings the equilibrium debt level closer to the socially optimal debt level. This raises social welfare because the latter is strictly concave in the debt level. Summarizing, we can state:

Proposition 2: In the pooling equilibrium described above, the introduction of a fiscal council lowers the equilibrium debt level, bringing it closer to the socially optimal debt level.

As far as social welfare is concerned, we can formulate Proposition 3:

Proposition 3: In the pooling equilibrium described above, the FC enhances social welfare via two different channels: (i) it leads both types of government to select a debt level that is preferable from a social perspective; and (ii) the greater precision of the signal δ raises the likelihood that a competent government is elected, while it reduces the re-election prospects of an incompetent administration.

A direct consequence of the second channel in Proposition 3 is that the expected amount of public goods produced in the second period is higher under an FC.[8] To unveil this second channel, observe that in a pooling equilibrium there is no other information than the realization $\bar{\delta}$ of the signal δ that the voters can use to assess the competence of the incumbent. Hence, voters re-elect the incumbent government if, given the signal, expected second-period resources under the incumbent

---

[8] If we were to change the timing, and assume that the government selects its debt level before it observes its competence, then debt would be independent of the government's competence, and only the second channel in Proposition 3 would be present.

exceed expected second-period resources under the other party C, which is deemed competent with probability ½. Voters choose the incumbent if $E_1[1 - b + \lambda_L|\delta = \bar{\delta}] \geq E_1[1 - b + \lambda_C]$, that is if $E_1[\lambda_L|\delta = \bar{\delta}] \geq 0$, because $E_1[\lambda_C] = 0$. The subscript "1" on the expectations operator indicates that the expectation is taken just before period 2 starts, i.e. just before the election in the second period. Using Bayes' rule, we can write this condition as

$$E_1[\lambda_L|\delta = \bar{\delta}] = -\bar{\lambda} \Pr(\lambda_L = -\bar{\lambda}, \delta = \bar{\delta}) + \bar{\lambda} \Pr(\lambda_L = \bar{\lambda}|\delta = \bar{\delta}) \geq 0.$$

Working this out, we obtain:

$$E_1[\lambda_L|\delta = \bar{\delta}] = \frac{-\bar{\lambda} \exp\left[-\frac{1}{2}\left(\frac{\bar{\delta}+\bar{\lambda}}{a\sigma_\mu}\right)^2\right] + \bar{\lambda} \exp\left[-\frac{1}{2}\left(\frac{\bar{\delta}-\bar{\lambda}}{a\sigma_\mu}\right)^2\right]}{\exp\left[-\frac{1}{2}\left(\frac{\bar{\delta}-\bar{\lambda}}{a\sigma_\mu}\right)^2\right] + \exp\left[-\frac{1}{2}\left(\frac{\bar{\delta}+\bar{\lambda}}{a\sigma_\mu}\right)^2\right]} \geq 0. \quad (11)$$

Hence,

$$E_1[\lambda_L|\delta = \bar{\delta}] \, (<) = (>) \, 0, \text{if } \bar{\delta} \, (<) = (>) \, 0.$$

This means that, conditional on a positive (negative) signal, the electorate believes that the incumbent's competence exceeds that of its competitor, so that the incumbent is re-elected (voted out of office). In the limit case of $\delta = 0$, which effectively occurs with probability zero, we assume that the incumbent is re-elected.

Taking into account the electoral choice conditional on the signal, the expected competence level in period 2 is:

$$\Pr(\delta > 0) \times E_1(\lambda_L|\delta > 0) + \Pr(\delta < 0) \times 0 = \frac{1}{2} E_1(\lambda_L|\delta > 0) > 0 \quad (12)$$

The presence of a fiscal council makes the signal less noisy. Hence, conditional on a positive signal, the expected competence level of the incumbent is higher. The welfare gain materializing through the second channel results from the fact that a negative signal is more likely to lead to the dismissal of an incompetent government, while a positive signal raises the likelihood that a competent government remains in office.

3.2.2 Separating Equilibrium

We now explore whether a *separating equilibrium* exists and, if so, what its properties could be. Such an equilibrium exists if the incumbent government finds it optimal to select different debt levels depending on its level of competence and given the way voters form their beliefs about competence when they observe the debt level. As we illustrate below, no plausible separating equilibrium exists in our simple setup.

The search for a separating equilibrium starts with characterizing different candidate equilibrium debt levels $b^{i,s}$ and $b^{c,s}$ chosen by the incumbent administration depending on its competence. If the debt level conveys information about competence, then it is realistic to assume that voters believe with probability 1 that the incumbent is incompetent if it deviates from $b^{c,s}$. Because setting a debt level different from $b^{c,s}$ leads to certain electoral defeat (and a complete ignorance of the future), an incompetent government would simply maximize $u(1+b)$. Such a government would thus spend the highest amount possible in period 1, choosing the highest debt consistent with the no-default assumption: $b^{i,s} = 1 - \bar{\lambda}$. The utility of the incompetent government playing $b^{i,s}$ would thus be $u(2 - \bar{\lambda})$. By playing $b^{c,s} \left(\neq b^{i,s} \right)$, a competent incumbent would be re-elected with certainty. In that case, the optimal debt level maximizes the expected utility $u(1+b) + (1 - b + \bar{\lambda})$ and $b^{c,s}$ satisfies the first-order condition $u'(1 + b^{c,s}) = 1$, which coincides with the socially optimal debt level. We can now formulate Proposition 4.

Proposition 4: There exists no separating equilibrium with distinct choices $b^{i,s}$ and $b^{c,s}$ for the incompetent and competent incumbent, respectively, and with voter beliefs that assign a probability zero (one) to the incumbent being competent if debt deviates from (equals) $b^{c,s}$.

The exclusion of this a priori plausible candidate equilibrium directly follows from Assumption 2 above. Since $b^{c,s}$ solves $u'(1 + b) = 1$, it is strictly smaller than the maximum amount of debt consistent with solvency (which, in our candidate equilibrium, would be $b^{i,s} = 1 - \bar{\lambda}$ with $u'(2 - \bar{\lambda}) < 1$). It is now clear that even an incompetent government cannot benefit from accumulating debt beyond $b^{c,s}$ because it would forfeit re-election and, with it, lose the total utility generated in period 2 in exchange for a strictly inferior utility gain on any additional unit of public consumption provided in period 1. Thus the fact that an incompetent government has no incentive to choose $b^{i,s} \neq b^{c,s}$ proves Proposition 4.

3.3 Installing an FC Is the Prerogative of the Government

In the analysis so far, society chooses whether or not to set up an FC. As a result, that decision is not per se a signal about the competence of the government. In this subsection, we consider the case in which the government itself can create the FC.[9] For this exercise to be relevant, we now assume that the government knows about its competence before any policy decision is made, so that both choices – creating an FC and setting the debt level – can convey information about competence to voters. We restrict the analysis to a pooling equilibrium, when a government – regardless of its true competence – could be led to pick a debt level closer to the social optimum so as not to appear incompetent.

Equation (7) showed that for a given debt level, the competent government is better off in the presence of an FC. Therefore, it seems natural to look for a pooling equilibrium in which both types create an FC and choose a level of public debt $b^{c,p}$ that maximizes the competent government's expected utility in the presence of an FC, knowing that the incompetent type would pick the same debt level. We can state:

Proposition 5: If the government can establish an FC, a pooling equilibrium exists in which the incumbent establishes an FC and chooses a debt level $b^{c,p}$, with the voters' beliefs about the two types along the equilibrium path given by $\Pr(\lambda_L = -\bar{\lambda}|\delta = \bar{\delta})$ and $\Pr(\lambda_L = \bar{\lambda}|\delta = \bar{\delta})$, as calculated above according to Bayes' rule, and voters assigning an off-the-equilibrium-path (i.e. when the choice is made not to install an FC) probability of competence of zero.

Under this pooling equilibrium, the government's choice to install an FC effectively yields no extra signal beyond that provided by the realization of δ. Beliefs are updated in the same way as when society establishes the FC and outcomes are also the same. Once again,

---

[9] This conjecture is not only relevant for cases where the fiscal council was created by executive decisions (e.g., Belgium), but also in parliamentary systems where the executive and legislative branches have the same political color and generally work hand in hand.

creating an FC is welfare-improving because public debt ends up closer to the social optimum and because it provides a more precise signal about government competence, which helps voters make a better-informed decision at the ballot box.

4 Are Existing Fiscal Councils Built to Work?

The limited experience with FCs, and their considerable heterogeneity across countries, make it difficult to assess their effectiveness empirically.[10] In our view, the effectiveness of an FC depends on two main preconditions. The first is that the mandate and tasks of the council specifically aim at addressing the most relevant sources of deficit bias (von Hagen, 2013; Debrun et al., 2013). The second dimension is that the council should be equipped to ensure that all public information about the budget is a clear signal of politicians' genuine intent and actions. Our model elaborates only on the second precondition. This "signal enhancement" capacity of the FC will also be the focus of this section.

We build a simple summary index assessing the likelihood that existing fiscal councils can mitigate the asymmetry of information between the public and politicians.

4.1 Enhancing the Signal: An Index

To find out whether fiscal councils have what it takes to reduce the noise-to-signal ratio of budgetary information, we build a simple summary index based on relevant features of existing institutions. The construction of the index primarily reflects our judgment as to what characteristics reported in the IMF Fiscal Council dataset are likely to help the council ensure that the right information reaches the right people (voters, members of parliament, and other stakeholders in the budget process).

The advantage of the index is to be able to compare FCs for which little or no track record exists with FCs that have been around for a long time. The practical relevance of such exercise is immediately

---

[10] There is nevertheless some evidence of a link between the existence and features of fiscal councils and fiscal performance, based on dynamic panel regressions (see Debrun et al., 2008, 2013; Debrun and Kinda, 2014; and Nerlich and Reuter, 2013).

relevant in the European Union, where the Treaty on Stability, Coordination and Governance, which came into force in January 2013, explicitly requires that an "independent body" be designated or established at the national level to monitor fiscal policy. Such body should in particular verify compliance with national fiscal policy rules and produce (or at least assess or validate) the macroeconomic and budgetary forecasts used for budget preparation in each euro-area member state (Article 3, para. 2).[11] While it seems clear that a well-designed fiscal council qualifies as such an "independent" body, the concept is vague enough to leave the door open to merely "decorative" institutions with no real value for the conduct of fiscal policy. A low score on our "signal enhancement capacity" (or SEC) index should raise alarm bells regarding that risk. The presumption underlying this exercise is indeed that by looking at the design features of a council, one should be able to infer with reasonable precision whether they were conceived as mere smokescreens or genuine attempts to reduce informational asymmetries.

The SEC index is calculated for most countries reported in the IMF dataset, except for those where too much information is missing. It encompasses four main dimensions:

- *A broad mandate (sub-index M)*. The mandate of the council should encompass the main sources of informational asymmetry between the public and the government, such as the accuracy of budgetary forecasts, the uncertainty about long-term pressures stemming from entitlement systems, the inaccurate costing of policy initiatives, the opacity of intergovernmental fiscal relations in highly decentralized or federal systems, etc.
- *The ability to communicate to the public (sub-index C)*. The value of a signal is to be heard by all relevant stakeholders. The publication of freely accessible reports and their impact on the public debate about fiscal policy – the IMF dataset provides a staff assessment of media impact – are the main aspects of this dimension. Beyond these two aspects, one should ideally form a view on a council's communication strategy. A good communication strategy is essential to project an image of non-partisanship and technical competence, and to

---

[11] Similar requirements can be found in the EU Directive on "requirements for budgetary frameworks" of November 2011 and one of the Regulations of the so-called "two-pack," which came into force in May 2013.

translate in simple terms the complexities underlying fiscal policy measures and, possibly, the tradeoffs implied by alternative courses of action.

- *The possibility to directly interact with participants in the budget process (sub-index B).* FCs can be given direct channels of influence on budgetary choices. These include the use of its macroeconomic and budgetary forecasts for budget preparation, the obligation for governments to explain why official forecasts deviate from the FC's own or why the government chooses to ignore the FC's advice, or the possibility for the FC to meet regularly with decisionmakers. All these aspects are documented in the IMF dataset.

- *Independence from politics (sub-index PI).* Independence is essential to guarantee the signal-enhancing value of the council's activities. Depending on the political context, all possible safeguards should be put in place to dispel the perception that the council is somehow embroiled in the political fray. For new institutions without a pre-existing reputation, legal guarantees on the professionalism and independence of their staff and management in performing their statutory tasks are a must. However, working independently also requires human and financial resources commensurate to the tasks and insulation from political manipulations. Resources perceived as insufficient or vulnerable to political pressures can clearly undermine the signaling value of the council's activity, and thereby its effectiveness.[12] At the same time, one must acknowledge that maintaining solid bridges between the Ministry of Finance and the fiscal council is key for the effectiveness of the latter. In that regard, free access to information – including potentially confidential information – is critical for the fiscal council to be able to perform its tasks.

We calculate two variants of the SEC. The first is a simple average of the score S_i obtained for all four sub-indices $i \in \{M, C, B, PI\}$ with the score calculated such that $S_i \in [0, 1] \forall i$. The simple average presumes that each dimension is in its own right equally *sufficient* to give to the

---

[12] It has been argued that independence also requires prohibiting the council from playing a normative role in the public debate—e.g., by making policy recommendations or comparing alternative policy paths. There are, however, reasons in specific political contexts to mandate the council to issue recommendations (see Debrun et al., 2013). Our assessment of independence thus simply ignores this aspect.

FC a signal-enhancing role. The higher the score, the greater the FC's potential to enhance signals about fiscal policy. A second variant of the SEC gives political independence the status of a *necessary* condition for effectiveness: without it, there cannot be any signal enhancement, regardless of the council's official tasks and capacities. In that case, we define the aggregate index as:

$SEC = S_{PI}^* \sum_i S_i/3$, where S_i is the score obtained for each sub-index $i \in \{M, C, B\}$. Each S_i has been defined as follows:

- S_M is the simple average between the FC's requirement to perform ex post analysis (0 or 1) and a fraction representing the number of specific ex ante tasks out of a possible total of seven. These include the preparation of forecasts, the assessment of forecasts, the preparation of policy recommendations, the assessment of long-term sustainability, an assessment of the adequacy of fiscal policy, the costing of measures, and the monitoring of fiscal rules.
- S_C is the simple average between two dummy variables capturing the free publication and dissemination of reports on a website and IMF staff assessment of the FC's impact in the media (1 if high, 0 if low).
- S_B is the simple average of dummy variables indicating various means through which the FC can interact with players in the budget process, namely the systematic (but not necessarily compulsory) use of the FC's forecasts for budget preparation, the compulsory use of these forecasts, a comply-or-explain requirement for the government, formal consultations or hearings for FC management, and the possibility to block the budget process.
- S_{PI} is the product of two simple averages. The first combines individual scores on the existence of legal guarantees of independence, an assessment of the operational independence of the council, and formal guarantees of access to information. If none of these three conditions exist, we consider that all other aspects of independence are irrelevant. The second combines scores assessing managerial independence (i.e. safeguard on the council's budget; the right to select, employ, and pay staff; a term in office strictly greater than four years; appointment by parliament or another authority than the government; impossibility of being reappointed), the availability of a staff commensurate to the tasks of the FC, and the characteristics of the senior management (i.e., possibly non-citizen of the country, academics, and established public finance experts).

4.2 Results

Both the unweighted and independence-contingent indices point to significant heterogeneity among fiscal councils in terms of their a priori ability to provide clear and consistent signals about fiscal policy (Figure 5.4). In absolute terms, 75 percent of FCs exhibit unweighted scores ranging between 0.5 and 1 (the "perfect score"), suggesting that they often have many of the features expected from effective institutions. Although cross-country dispersion is larger when independence is given greater prominence, the rankings are broadly similar regardless of the index, suggesting that fiscal councils that were particularly well equipped to clarify policy signals were also given the political independence to do so. This is evident from Figure 5.5, which plots a summary index capturing the remit, tasks, and public output of the council against the aggregate score on independence from politics (S_{PI}). The scatter diagram also allows assessment of the quality of FCs' design in terms of the combination between the two indicators.

In Figure 5.5, we identify four quadrants, using the cross-country averages for each index as demarcation lines. This definition of quadrants (in relative rather than absolute terms) gives a better idea of any skewness in the joint distribution of these two main dimensions. The better-designed institutions are located in the north-east quadrant, which we extended to the shaded rectangle to capture borderline cases (within ½ a standard deviation below the mean for each index). By that simple metric, almost two thirds of fiscal councils appear to be relatively well designed. The number falls to one half if one does not allow for borderline cases, but this still points to the broad tendency for FCs to be conceived and designed as signal enhancers.

By contrast, a quarter of the fiscal councils in the sample are well into the south-west quadrant, identifying institutions with little independence and often limited capabilities to effectively perform a signaling function. Only two of the institutions in our sample belong to the north-west quadrant that would identify relatively independent institutions with a limited remit. Similarly, two institutions exhibit a broad set of roles and functions but enjoy a degree of independence that could hinder their ability to perform these tasks in an effective manner.

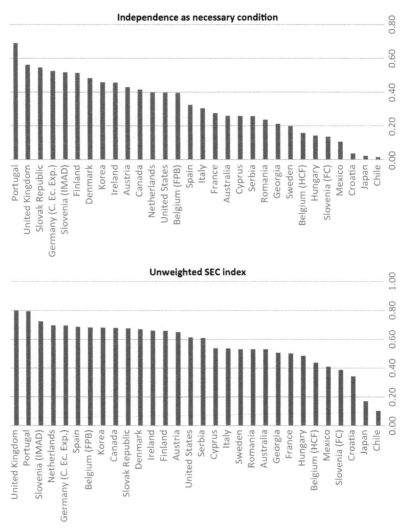

Figure 5.4: Fiscal councils' signal enhancement capacity: An index

Notes: The sample includes the countries identified in IMF (2015b) as having a fiscal council, except for Estonia, Germany (Advisory Board to the Stability Council), Greece, Kenya, Latvia, Lithuania, Luxembourg, South Africa, and Uganda, for which too much information is missing. The entry for Germany refers to the German Council of Economic Experts, an institution created in 1963 and that only performs some of the functions of fiscal councils. The German institution corresponding to the mainstream definition of a fiscal council is the Advisory Board to the Stability Council, created in 2015, but it is not covered in the dataset.

Sources: IMF (2015b) and authors' calculations and corrections

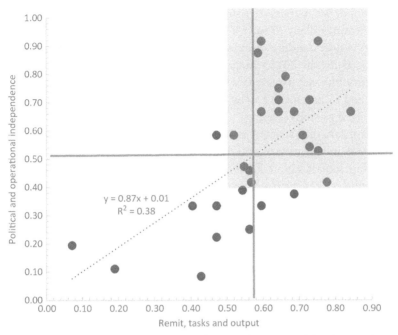

Figure 5.5: Independence and signal-enhancing functions of fiscal councils
Source: IMF (2015b) and authors' calculations and corrections

5 Conclusions

This chapter took stock of the current debate on the role of fiscal councils in enhancing fiscal policy credibility. First, we developed a simple theoretical model of fiscal policy with or without a fiscal council to provide foundations for the potential influence of merely advisory institutions on the conduct of fiscal policy, and in particular the alleviation of the deficit bias. Asymmetric information between voters and elected policymakers is the central feature of the model. The model suggests that society benefits most from a fiscal council when it is able to minimize the noise surrounding signals of competence of the incumbent government. Doing so raises social welfare through two channels: A fiscal council can increase the likelihood of electing competent governments, and a fiscal council can discourage excessive deficits. Importantly, that second channel's positive impact of the fiscal council on taming the deficit bias applies regardless of the true type of government (competent or not).

Second, we mapped the story suggested by the model into a set of core features likely to raise a council's capacity to effectively improve voters' understanding of existing signals about the adequacy of fiscal policy. Using the 2015 vintage of the IMF dataset on independent fiscal institutions, we assessed whether existing institutions have been designed to be effective or whether they are more likely to have been conceived as smokescreens.

It appears that a strong majority of fiscal councils exhibit features – political independence and functions – that allow them to clarify existing signals about fiscal policy. A number of institutions would nevertheless benefit from stronger guarantees of independence to join the group of potentially highly effective councils, including through increased and secure resources and guaranteed access to information.

Bibliography

Abbas, Ali, Belhocine, Nazim, El Ganainy, Asmaa and Horton, Mark (2010). *A Historical Public Debt Database.* IMF Working Paper No. 10/245, Washington, DC: International Monetary Fund.

Cordes, Till, Kinda, Tidiane, Muthoora, Priscilla and Weber, Anke (2015). *Expenditure Rules: Effective Tools for Sound Fiscal Policy?* IMF Working Paper No. 15/29, Washington, DC: International Monetary Fund.

Debrun, Xavier and Kumar, Manmohan S. (2008). Fiscal rules, fiscal councils and all that: commitment devices, signaling tools or smokescreens? In *Fiscal Policy: Current Issues and Challenges*, Proceedings of the 9th Banca d'Italia Workshop on Public Finance, June 2008. Rome: Banca d'Italia.

Debrun, Xavier, Moulin, Laurent, Turrini, Alessandro, Ayuso-i-Casals, Joaquim and Kumar, Manmohan S. (2008). Tied to the mast? The role of national fiscal rules in the European Union. *Economic Policy*, **54**, 297–362.

Debrun, Xavier, Hauner, David and Kumar, Manmohan S. (2009). Independent fiscal agencies. *Journal of Economic Surveys*, **23**, 44–81.

Debrun, Xavier (2011). *The Theory of Independent Fiscal Agencies: Where Are We? And Where Do We Go from There?* Economic Policy Papers (Wirtschaftspolitische Blätter), 1–2011: 559–70. Also available as IMF Working Paper No. 11/173.

Debrun, Xavier, Kinda, Tidiane, Curristine, Teresa, Eyraud, Luc, Harris, Jason and Seiwald, Johann (2013). *The Functions and Impact of Fiscal Councils.* IMF Policy Paper, www.imf.org/external/np/fad/council/.

Debrun, Xavier and Kinda, Tidiane (2014). *Strengthening Post-Crisis Fiscal Credibility – Fiscal Councils on the Rise. A New Dataset.* IMF Working Paper No. 14/58. Washington, DC: International Monetary Fund.

Fabrizio, Stefania and Mody, Ashoka (2006). Can budgetary institutions counteract political indiscipline? *Economic Policy*, **21**, 689–739.

International Monetary Fund (2015a). *Fiscal Rules Dataset*, www.imf.org/external/datamapper/FiscalRules/map/map.htm

(2015b). *Fiscal Councils Dataset*, www.imf.org/external/np/fad/council/

Jensen, Henrik (1997). Credibility of optimal monetary delegation. *American Economic Review*, **87**, 911–20.

Kopits, George (ed.) (2013). *Restoring Public Debt Sustainability: The Role of independent Fiscal Institutions*. Oxford: Oxford University Press.

Krogstrup, Signe and Wälti, Sebastien (2008). Do fiscal rules cause budgetary outcomes? *Public Choice*, **136**, 123–38.

Mauro, Paolo, Romeu, Rafael, Binder, Ariel and Zaman, Asad (2013). *A Modern History and Fiscal Prudence and Profligacy.* IMF Working Paper No. 13/5. Washington, DC: International Monetary Fund.

McCallum, Bennett (1995). Two fallacies concerning central bank independence. *American Economic Review*, **85**, 207–11.

Milesi-Ferretti, Gian Maria (2004). Good, bad or ugly? On the effects of fiscal rules with creative accounting. *Journal of Public Economics*, **88**, 377–94.

Nerlich, Caroline and Reuter, Wolf Heinrich (2013). *The Design of National Fiscal Frameworks and Their Budgetary Impact.* ECB Working Paper No. 1588, Frankfurt: European Central Bank.

Posen, Adam (1995). Declarations are not enough: financial sector sources of central bank independence. *NBER Macroeconomics Annual*, **10**, 253–74.

Rogoff, Kenneth (1985). The optimal degree of commitment to an intermediate monetary target. *Quarterly Journal of Economics*, **100**, 1169–90.

Stéclebout-Orseau, Eloise, and Hallerberg, Mark (2007). Who provides signals to voters about governance competence on fiscal matters? The importance of independent watchdogs. *European Economy-Economic Papers*, **275** (April), 243–68.

Thomson, Earl (1981). Who should control the money supply? *American Economic Review*, **71**, 150–61.

von Hagen, Juergen (2013). Scope and limits of independent fiscal institutions. In George Kopits, ed., *Restoring Public Debt Sustainability: The Role of independent Fiscal Institutions*, Oxford: Oxford University Press, pp. 32–53.

von Hagen, Juergen and Wolff, Guntram (2006). What do deficits tell us about debt? Empirical evidence on creative accounting with fiscal rules in the EU. *Journal of Banking and Finance*, **30**, 3259–79.

Wren-Lewis, Simon (2013). Comparing the delegation of monetary and fiscal policy. In George Kopits, ed., *Restoring Public Debt Sustainability: The Role of Independent Fiscal Institutions*, Oxford: Oxford University Press, pp. 54–74.

Wyplosz, Charles (2011). Fiscal discipline: rules rather than institutions. *National Institute Economic Review*, **217**, R19–R30.

6 Fiscal Discipline in a Monetary Union without Fiscal Union

CHARLES WYPLOSZ

1 Introduction

It was always understood that the Economic and Monetary Union required fiscal discipline to be rigorously enforced in each and every member country. Indeed, the Delors Committee Report (1989) devotes considerable space to developing the now classic case for monetary dominance. The sovereign debt crisis has been a stunning confirmation of the overriding importance of fiscal discipline. The combination of large public debts and high budget deficits triggered a crisis, and the crisis was contagious. Monetary policy dominance has been challenged. From bailing out crisis countries to absorbing vast quantities of public debt instruments, the ECB has repeatedly been drawn into territories that were dangerously close to fiscal policy dominance. This led to considerable hesitation on the part of the ECB, which resulted in harmful delays. Governments were visibly in disarray. Summits were repeatedly called but failed to calm financial markets. Wyplosz (2014) argues that most summits even worsened the crisis, because governments did not display a grasp of the situation.

One would expect the governments to undertake a comprehensive assessment of the fiscal discipline framework, the Stability and Growth Pact, which failed to deliver. This is not what happened. The official, knee-jerk reaction was to "strengthen" the pact, without ever stopping to ask exactly what went wrong and what other options were available. Even more unsettling is that the governments rushed to the "strengthening" mode without acknowledging the essential role of the no-bailout clause (Article 125 of the Treaty on the Functioning of the European Union), which was set aside from the beginning of the crisis. This chapter argues that, following a new intergovernmental treaty (Treaty on Stability, Coordination and Governance) and new legislation (the so-called "six-pack" and "two-pack"), fiscal discipline is still not reliably established in the eurozone.

Transferring some elements of fiscal policy sovereignty from member countries to the eurozone is often seen as the only way of establishing fiscal discipline. That may well be true, but the current political environment makes this solution impossible at this stage. Accordingly, this chapter asks whether, short of sovereignty transfers, there exists an alternative to the Stability and Growth Pact. Section 2 looks at the reasons that lie behind the poor performance of the Stability and Growth Pact. Drawing on these lessons, Section 3 develops a set of proposals to redesign the eurozone's fiscal framework. Section 4 looks at various criticisms and responses. Section 5 concludes.

2 The Stability and Growth Pact: A Hopeless Failure

The Maastricht Treaty takes due note of the need to establish fiscal discipline. Its response rests on two components: the Excessive Deficit Procedure (EDP) and the no-bailout rule. The EDP is formalized as the Stability and Growth Pact, which is designed to enforce the 3 percent limit on deficits and the 60 percent limit on public debt (compared to GDP). The pact came into force when the euro was launched in 1999.

Figure 6.1 shows that the only year in which no member country's deficit exceeded 3 percent of GDP is 1998, the year before the start of the eurozone, when the 3 percent limit was one of the conditions for acceptance into the monetary union.[1] Afterwards, the deficit limit was breached by at least one country every single year. This means that the Stability and Growth Pact was never effective in constraining deficits in all countries. The deterioration over the period following the creation of the euro shows that the deficit limit was only binding when it mattered, namely as a criterion for admission to the eurozone. Member countries took the admission test very seriously but, once in, the pact was obviously disregarded as a binding constraint, and the associated sanctions were simply not credible enough to ensure compliance. In fact, no sanction was imposed over the first fifteen years of the euro.

As is well known, the pact was "put in abeyance" when the two largest countries, France and Germany, faced the threat of sanctions in

---

[1] It is also known that some countries resorted to "creative accounting" to pass the 3 percent test.

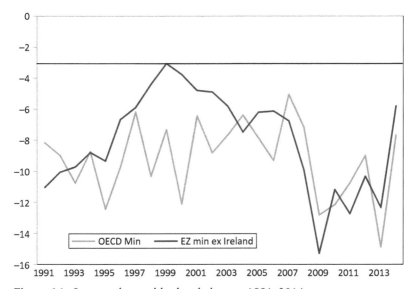

Figure 6.1: Lowest observed budget balances, 1991–2014

Note: The lowest ratio of budget balance to GDP is selected each year among the eurozone countries and among the rest of the OECD countries. Ireland is excluded because its 2010 deficit (32.5% of GDP) is a large outlier.

Source: *Economic Outlook*, OECD

2003. This episode was followed by a reform in 2005, designed to introduce some flexibility. One interpretation is that the pact was too rigid and called for sanctions when prevailing conditions justified deficits in excess of 3 percent. Alternatively, the reform could be seen as a fix designed to minimize the risk of sanctions because they are too politically difficult. As argued in Eichengreen and Wyplosz (1998), both interpretations are correct. The reform started a process of making the pact more complex and multi-faceted, thus injecting the possibility for the enforcer, the European Commission, to interpret its implementation. This was achieved by adding to the deficit and debt limit criteria the cyclically adjusted balance, the depth and duration of downturns, and deficit-augmenting structural reforms.

For the pact, the sovereign debt crisis was a debacle. It made obvious that the pact had failed to deliver and was ill adapted to serious exogenous shocks. This prompted another revision, finalized in 2013. This time, the intention was to strengthen the pact – a 180-degree turn from the aims of 2005. Like before, however, the chosen route was to make the pact even more complex and subject to judgment by the Commission. The revision included a slew of additional criteria, multi-year planning, the creation of a European semester officially designed to involve national parliaments early on in budget design and negotiations, and a decision procedure (reverse qualified majority voting) designed to make it more difficult for governments to overturn a Commission recommendation. The very complexity of the new version makes it even more prone to politicization, as was evidenced in the autumn of 2014 when France earned yet another respite for failing to meet its objectives.

A budget rule faces the usual challenge of finding the proper balance between rule and discretion. If too tight, it is bound to become counterproductive in specific situations. If too lax, it will always be ignored for political convenience. The two revisions can be seen as successive attempts at striking the right balance. However, rather than clarifying what the proper balance should be, these revisions have muddied the waters by relying on increasing complexity. Complexity can be a step toward discretion, as in the first revision, but the intent of the latest revision was the opposite. These unsuccessful oscillations betray a superficial approach to the rule vs. discretion debate, rooted in the unique institutional characteristic of the eurozone.

3 An Alternative Approach to Fiscal Discipline

Within a monetary union, fiscal discipline is a common good. More precisely, it is a necessary condition for its lasting existence. This necessity was well understood early on when Economic and Monetary Union was at the planning stage. Unfortunately, the chosen solution, the Stability and Growth Pact, was designed without the help of the relevant economic principles. The need for collective bank supervision and resolution was not even recognized. When the crisis made this need all too obvious, the banking union was set up, but only partially. These shortcomings are now recognized but, again, economic principles are treated lightly. The emerging conventional wisdom is to call for "more Europe." More Europe would certainly help in solving these problems, but this is a view that ignores political reality. This section argues that it is possible to use economic principles to find solutions that are constrained by political feasibility.

3.1 The Constrained Optimum View

Policymakers' reaction to the eurozone crisis is to call for more centralization, as recently summarized in the Five Presidents' Report (Juncker et al., 2015). There is little doubt that a truly federal arrangement stands to make a revamped Stability and Growth Pact operational. This would involve transferring to the European level a significant part of national sovereignty in budgetary matters.

The question is about feasibility and acceptability. A new treaty would be required. It would either reduce – possibly eliminate – the authority of national parliaments over national budgets, or transfer significant parts of national budgets to the eurozone level. This would concern public expenditures but also taxation, according to the basic implication of fiscal federalism principles (Oates, 1972). National policymakers, both governments and parliaments, are most unlikely to relinquish spending powers. Citizens are highly likely to refuse taxation by powers that are not directly elected as national parliaments are, according to the deeply felt principle of "no taxation without representation." It may well be, and in many ways it is highly desirable, that in some distant future Europe will adopt important federal features. At this stage of the history of European integration, however, such a step is effectively ruled out, as exemplified by the failure to adopt a "European Constitution" in 2005, even though there was precious little transfer of sovereignty involved.[2] It follows that the idea that fiscal discipline can be achieved in the eurozone through a further strengthening of the Stability and Growth Pact is simply illusory.

From its beginnings, critics of the common currency have pointed out that there is no example of a successful monetary union without an underlying political union.[3] The European common currency has always been an experiment that claims that this line of reasoning is not compelling. While a political (or fiscal) union would indeed be likely to "solve the euro problem," there is no proof that it is the only solution. Formally, a monetary-cum-political union may be the first

---

[2] The vagueness of the Five Presidents' Report implicitly recognizes the validity of this judgment.

[3] The seminal contribution is Feldstein (1997). Other lasting monetary unions have existed for decades in Africa and in the Caribbean, but they concern developing countries without significant financial sectors. Many small states also operate with a foreign currency.

best in some unspecified sense. However, the impossibility of achieving a political union at this juncture suggests looking for a second best, a constrained optimum. Indeed, the experiment itself and the current challenge call for the design of a sustainable monetary union subject to a "no fiscal and no political union" constraint.[4] It might be that there is no viable second-best solution, but this is the question raised in this chapter. The answer must include an in-depth analysis of the requirements of a monetary union and the search for methods that effectively deal with these requirements.

3.2 The Case of the Banking Union

A good example of how to make the monetary union robust without a political or fiscal union is the banking union. Even before the launch of the euro, the need for collective banking, supervision, and resolution had been duly identified (Begg et al., 1998). The reasoning can be summarized as follows. Bank failures may require the urgent injection of cash, possibly in very large amounts if the bank is big or if a systemic failure is looming. Governments cannot mobilize this kind of amount in a matter of hours, but central banks can. The ECB may therefore be called into playing the role of emergency lender of last resort. Lending in last resort always involves the risk of significant losses. Furthermore, emergency lending must be set up in a way that minimizes or even eliminates such losses. Effective action requires in-depth and up-to-date knowledge of the situation of each and every bank. Procedures must have been thought through ahead of time and the financing of potential losses must have been agreed in advance. Within a monetary union where taxpayers are national, this requires common banking regulation, supervision and resolution procedures, backed by collective resources. When this point was made, it was deemed too politically sensitive to be addressed. The result was that "a crisis is now much more likely" (Begg et al., p. 4).

This political sensitivity goes to the heart of the unique feature of a monetary union. Governments are typically prone to defend national champions, including in banking. To that effect, they want to regulate

---

[4] A separate issue is whether this solution, or indeed the first best one alluded to, is more desirable than no monetary union. This issue has been hotly debated for decades, without reaching a consensus.

and supervise their own banks. When a bank fails, its resolution may be more or less "friendly," transferring the risks and potential costs to taxpayers. In that environment, the common central bank is paralyzed. This is what happened. Furthermore, if banks operate across borders, which is what a monetary union is expected to promote, explicit agreements are needed on all these issues. The solution can only be full centralization, which requires governments to give up the protection of their banks.

It is easier to achieve the required arrangements in a federal state with federal resources, but it can be arranged without a political (or fiscal) union. The banking union is an exercise in constrained optimality. It has been achieved, but not completely, since the Single Resolution Mechanism is only partially centralized and the Single Resolution Fund remains to be operational. As a result, a new systemic crisis within the eurozone still remains a distinct possibility. The problem is not the absence of a political union but remaining protectionist tendencies, possibly fuelled by political capture.

3.3 The Case of Fiscal Discipline

As previously noted, fiscal discipline is a well-recognized requirement of a monetary union. This calls for a rule that applies to all member states. The fact that a rule must be open to interpretation – the discretion leg of the challenge – immediately raises the issue of who is in charge of interpreting the rule. It has to be a person or a body that does not suffer from the deficit bias and that has the expertise and independence to pass judgment in analytically challenging situations.[5] This evidently disqualifies governments, which are structurally subject to the deficit bias. At the same time, budgetary decisions go to the heart of the functioning of democracies, meaning that the person or body that interprets the rule must be legitimate. Over recent years, many countries have established independent fiscal councils composed of independent experts that are made accountable for their judgments. Details vary from country to country, but the general principle is everywhere the same.[6]

Within the eurozone, the situation is much more complicated, because budgets remain in the realm of national sovereignty. The

---

[5] On the deficit bias, see e.g. Krogstrup and Wyplosz (2006).
[6] See Debrun et al. (2009), IMF (2013), Kopits (2013) and Ódor (2014).

Commission plays the role of a fiscal council but it has no legitimacy to instruct member governments regarding fiscal policies – and, yet, this is the task that it has been given by the Stability and Growth Pact. Even as an advisory body, the Commission is far too political to win legitimacy. Thus, we face a fundamental legal contradiction in the European Treaties between national sovereignty and the mission of the Commission. There will not be any effective fiscal discipline in the eurozone until this fundamental contradiction is resolved.

These points are implicitly recognized in the Treaty on Stability, Coordination and Governance (TSCG) adopted in 2012. The treaty calls for all eurozone countries to establish a rule, "if possible" inscribed in their constitutions, along with a national fiscal council. In addition, the Five Presidents' Report calls for the creation of a European fiscal council, thus acknowledging the limits of the European Commission. The treaty can be seen as yet another layer designed to strengthen the Stability and Growth Pact, and this is indeed how it came about. In that case, it does not deal with the contradiction explained above. Another way to see the treaty is as a replacement for the Stability and Growth Pact. In that case, it would mean that fiscal discipline is decentralized to the national level, where sovereignty lies. In this view, the effectiveness of the combination of a constitutional budgetary rule and an independent council would establish fiscal discipline at the level of each member country, complemented by an independent European Fiscal Board that would monitor national implementation of the requirements. By making the Stability and Growth Pact useless, this approach would eliminate the fundamental contradiction previously described.

The policymakers' refusal to move in that direction reflects in part their innate reluctance to officially recognize that the pact is a failure and in part the Commission's innate opposition to any decentralization, instinctively perceived as a loss of power. Calls for a political or fiscal union are appealing because they can be cast as the unconstrained optimum. Yet, if that objective is not achievable at this stage, we need to look at the constrained optimum: How to achieve fiscal discipline given that member states remain sovereign in budgetary matters?

One answer is the decentralization of fiscal discipline through effective national budget frameworks. Viewed in this way, a solution emerges naturally. Each member state adopts a constitutional fiscal rule and establishes an independent fiscal council. The rule must be simple. As argued above, a complex rule that combines a large number of requirements opens the door to manipulation, as a government will always try to game the rule by fulfilling some (weak) requirements while violating other (strong) requirements. The rule must build on recognized principles and on the considerable amount of experimentation accumulated over many years and decades.[7]

The 3 percent deficit and 60 percent (of GDP) original rule of the Stability and Growth Pact was set without any theoretical backing. Being arbitrary, from the start it lacked credibility and it was easy to challenge and circumvent it. It is clearly desirable to start with the elementary question: What is fiscal discipline? The theoretical answer is uncontroversial: fiscal discipline requires the fulfilment of the government budget constraint. The difficulty starts with the recognition that the budget constraint is intertemporal and forward-looking. It can be subsumed by the transversality condition, namely that the present value of the debt remains bounded at a suitable horizon. For a government, whose lifetime is in principle finite, implementing the principle is challenging and requires an approximation. Additionally, the bound must be specified.

A reasonable and implementable simplification is as follows. First, regarding the bound, we know that there is no agreement on what is a possible maximum, and even less on what is the optimal size of the public debt. Reinhart and Rogoff (2010), among others, identify a debt-to-GDP ratio of 90 percent as a threshold above which growth is impaired, but this result is challenged by Panizza and Presbitero (2014). Even so, there are good reasons to believe that it is desirable to keep this ratio below, say, 100 percent, possibly quite a lot less, as argued in Section 4.2 below. Most eurozone countries need to lower their debts. Second and consequently, the transversality condition can be translated as requiring that the debt-to-GDP ratio does not increase and, in many cases, that it be put on a declining long-term trend over the duration of a cycle. This is a simple rule, which inevitably calls for interpretation.

Note the important differences between this rule and the Stability and Growth Pact. First, it involves only one target, the debt-to-GDP ratio. It does not involve hard-to-measure and controversial targets

---

[7] For a review of existing rules around the world, see Bova et al. (2015). For an analysis of rules, see Wyplosz (2012).

such as the cyclically adjusted budget deficit. Second, it does not rely on any arbitrary number applied to each and every country irrespective of its situation, including the existing debt. Third, the objective is a trend, not an annual target that is bound to be unrealistic in the presence of shocks. Fourth, the horizon is a business cycle, allowing for the fiscal multipliers to kick in and, if need be, for discretionary policy action. Fifth, and crucially, responsibility for enforcing the rule lies with the national authorities, which must respect their own constitutions.

As previously argued, any rule must be interpreted. This should be the role assigned to national fiscal councils. These councils must be independent, with all the necessary safeguards. To work efficiently, they should include a small number of members whose appointments must be exclusively based on demonstrated competence. In line with existing best practice (Kopits, 2013), their mandate should include the following:

- determining the long-run debt target;
- evaluating the annual budget proposal before it is submitted to parliament;
- verifying the conformity of the executed budget with the earlier law;
- proposing deviations from the trend according to the general economic situation.

Ideally, the national fiscal councils would have some decision power, but this does not seem to be the case with the existing budgets, probably because it would violate the time-honored practice of empowering the parliament with full authority. An interesting halfway measure is the Dutch solution whereby the council agrees with each newly elected government on the debt path for the duration of the legislature, which then becomes a binding requirement (Bos, 2008).

The decentralized solution does not require any new treaty. Indeed, it is already mandated by the TSCG. However, the implementation of the TSCG varies from country to country. In the absence of an evaluation of implementation, casual evidence is that some countries have adopted rigorous frameworks while others have exploited the many loopholes of the TSCG to put in place weak frameworks.

This observation suggests that, given the collective need for national fiscal discipline, the decentralization approach would need to include safeguards not present in the TSCG. Five of them come to mind. First, the independent European fiscal council should evaluate the quality of the budget rule and its assessment should be formally considered by the European Council. Second, the European fiscal council should monitor the work of the national councils and make public its assessments. Third, the European fiscal council should be informed of nominations to the national councils and make public its assessments. Fourth, if a country violates its own constitutional provisions, a procedure should make it possible to bring the case to the European Court of Justice. Finally, and most importantly, the no-bailout clause already enshrined in the Treaties should be strengthened to eliminate the ambiguities that made it possible to treat it as lightly as has been the case during the crisis.

The no-bailout clause is a crucial component of the eurozone. A strong no-bailout clause stands to provide the right incentives to governments in two ways. First, it is meant to discourage any calculation that a country may allow its public debt to grow to the point where it becomes unsustainable, only to obtain support from other countries frightened by the risk of a crisis. Second, if credible, the no-bailout clause is bound to affect how financial markets evaluate and price national public debts. As is well known, the risk premia on all member countries were infinitesimal up until the sovereign debt crisis started to pick up steam. It is widely reported that the markets did not believe that the clause would be adhered to and, therefore, discounted any risk of default. Thus market discipline – the imposition of risk premia that raise the cost of deficit financing – failed to strengthen the incentives faced by governments to act in a responsible way. Would markets have reacted differently if the clause had been fully credible? The evidence from federal states such as the United States, Canada, and Australia is that they do indeed impose risk premia on sub-central governments whose debts are not perceived as safe.[8]

Another possible reason why risk premia were negligible while debts were accumulating is that the ECB has long been dealing in public debt instruments as if they were safe. It is only when markets imposed risk premia that the ECB started to require haircuts. A simple solution is for the ECB to apply the US Fed's practice of not dealing with sub-central debt instruments. In the absence of a "federal debt," the ECB can issue its own debt instruments to serve as exclusive assets on the interbank market.

---

[8] Ter-Minassian (2007) discusses the evidence and provides references.

Whether these safeguards require a new treaty is beyond the scope of this chapter, as detailed legal knowledge would be required. Ideally, they could be worked into a revamped Stability and Growth Pact, which does not require a new treaty. The really difficult issues concern the authority of the European Court of Justice and the restoration of the no-bailout clause.

4 Potential Drawbacks of the Constrained Optimum

The previous section argued that fiscal discipline can be achieved in the eurozone in the absence of any political or fiscal union. In many ways, the suggested solutions are inspired by existing arrangements in federal states, the United States being a prime example. This section examines whether the absence of any federal state may create difficulties or generate side effects in the eurozone.

4.1 Counter-cyclical Policies

The standard view is that the absence of a federal state rules out the decentralization of fiscal discipline in the eurozone. That view is argued in four steps. Step one asserts that fiscal rules prevent governments from adopting counter-cyclical policies. Step two notes that, in a monetary union, fiscal policy is the only macroeconomic management tool that remains available at the national level. Step three argues that the existing large public debts effectively remove the ability to use fiscal policy during downturns. Step four observes that in federal states where sub-central governments are subject to rigorous and effective fiscal rules, the central government is in charge of counter-cyclical fiscal policy (and the central bank conducts counter-cyclical policies as well).

Each step of the argument is misleading at best, and possibly wrong. The next section deals with the third step and will argue that, indeed, something must be done about the legacy debts. This section focuses on the remaining three steps.

The first step is actually wrong. Some old-style fiscal rules indeed lead to pro-cyclical policies. This is the case, for example, with the balanced budget rules in place in many US states. With no local demand-management instruments, the states depend on transfers from the federal level when it comes to cushioning local or asymmetric shocks. This leads to the conclusion that the eurozone is fundamentally different from the United States, since its "federal" budget is minimal (less than 2 percent of GDP). This conclusion ignores that fiscal rules have become considerably more sophisticated to allow for macroeconomic stabilization. For example, the "debt brake" adopted in 2001 in Switzerland allows for counter-cyclical policies (Bodmer, 2006). Furthermore, the *raison d'être* of fiscal councils is precisely to inject judgment into the implementation of rules.

The second step is correct, but it implies that the ability to use national fiscal policies counter-cyclically must be preserved. This is in fact an indictment of the Stability and Growth Pact as applied during the crisis years 2010–14. If anything, it is a powerful argument in favor of decentralization.

The third step too is correct, but its usual implication can be turned on its head. That large debts make it nearly impossible to conduct fiscal policies at the national level is one conclusion. Another is that national fiscal policies are so important that the debt overhang must be eliminated. This issue is examined in the following section.

The last step is as superficial as it looks convincing. It is true that there is no central government in the eurozone, but that only means that aggregate fiscal policy is lost. The issue, however, is not about *aggregate* policy, but about *decentralized* fiscal policy. It can even be asserted that if each member country conducts optimal fiscal policies from a purely national perspective, there is no need to be concerned about the aggregate stance. Popular suggestions that we must coordinate fiscal policies or that we need a "Eurozone Finance Minister" are unjustified. A version of this discussion is that the eurozone is not the United States, where a large federal budget allows for transfers across states that automatically cushion idiosyncratic shocks. Studies of federal stabilization in the United States invariably report small effects, suggesting that they absorb about 10 percent of the relevant shocks – a most modest effect.[9]

The conclusion is that, once fiscal discipline is achieved at the national level, eurozone member countries will be able to use the fiscal policy instrument at the national level as needed for macroeconomic stability. There will be no need for the centralized instruments set up after the crisis (the strengthened Stability and Growth Pact, the Macroeconomic Imbalance Procedure, the European semester, and the like),

---

[9] A review of these studies is in Hepp and von Hagen (2009).

nor for further sovereignty transfers (fiscal policy coordination, a European Finance Minister, etc.). All that is needed is the restructuring of existing public debts.

4.2 Legacy Debts

Figure 6.2 shows that public debts are close to or above 100 percent of GDP in eight eurozone member countries. They are close to or above the Maastricht limit of 60 percent of GDP in four other countries. As noted in Section 3.3, these levels are inefficient and can be crippling, for a number of reasons that can be usefully restated. First, debt service requires adequate taxation, which is always distortionary. At this stage, ultra-low borrowing costs partly conceal this fact, but, and this is the second point, the eventual normalization of interest rates stands to disturb precarious budgets. More generally, large public debts magnify the destabilizing effects on national budgets of fluctuations in interest rates and economic growth. Third, large debts hamper the

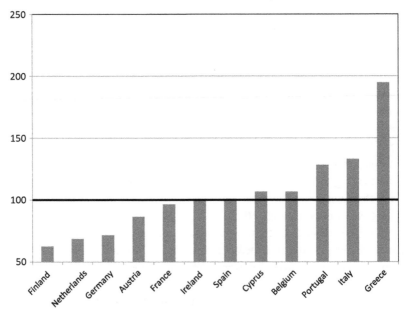

Figure 6.2: Public debts in the euro area
Note: percent of GDP.
Source: AMECO online, the European Commission

ability to conduct counter-cyclical fiscal policies. Fourth, much-needed economic reforms are invariably costly for the budget when they require Pareto-compensating transfers.[10] Large debts stand in the way of much-needed reforms. Fifth, financial markets are known to be fickle. This means that debts that were long considered sustainable can be suddenly deemed unsustainable, which is precisely how the sovereign debt crisis began at the end of 2009 and then spread within the eurozone. Large debts are a permanent threat to economic stability, unless the central bank is known to be ready to act as lender of last resort, as the Fed and the Bank of England unofficially, but not unexpectedly, did in the wake of the global financial crisis. The reason why the ECB refrained from acting as lender of last resort is that doing so in effect would have mutualized debts across member countries. Thus – and this is the sixth reason to fear large debts – in a monetary union, large debts are a collective threat with many dysfunctional implications. This is of course the fundamental reason why fiscal discipline is crucial in a monetary union.

Thus, the recent crisis, coming on top of protracted fiscal indiscipline in many countries, leaves a number of countries with large, inefficient, and dangerously high public debts. Among other adverse consequences, it makes the decentralized solution – national fiscal discipline frameworks along with fiscal policy sovereignty – unconvincing. The official answer to large legacy debts is to call for a slow attrition of public debts inherited from the past. As Eichengreen and Panizza (2014) observe, this requires many countries to run primary budget surpluses as large as 5 percent of GDP for a decade; looking at history, they find no evidence that this is doable. If it is attempted, it will bring about economic misery with incalculable political consequences.

The alternative is to restructure the legacy debts. This alternative is often considered as a major source of moral hazard. Restructuring existing debts, it is argued, will provide an incentive for many governments to again run up debts in the expectation that they will end up being restructured. Debt accumulation is a two-way moral hazard: Borrowers and lenders alike must be discouraged. This is precisely what the decentralized solution described in Section 3 achieves. Strong national fiscal frameworks – smart fiscal rules and independent fiscal councils – eliminate the borrower moral hazard. The restoration of the

---

[10] This point is developed in details in Delpla and Wyplosz (2007) (in French).

no-bailout rule, if credible, will eliminate the lender moral hazard and bring in market discipline.

Moral hazard apart, it is also asserted that public debts cannot be restructured. This assertion rests on two misconceptions. First, public debt restructuring is presented as an exceptional and dangerous procedure. As noted by Reinhart and Rogoff (2010), debt restructuring is a fairly mundane event, one for which considerable experimentation has been accumulated. It is well known how to do that. Second, financial and/or public institutions hold much of the eurozone's public debts. It is feared that a restructuring would dangerously hit financial institutions, possibly triggering a new financial crisis of huge proportions. In addition, it is believed that restructuring must necessarily impose costs on taxpayers in the low-debt countries.

These two fears are unwarranted. There are ways of restructuring public debts without imposing losses on bondholders and without involving transfers from low-debt to high-debt countries, as shown in Corsetti et al. (2015) and Pâris and Wyplosz (2014). The latter shows how this can be done. In a nutshell, the solution is to actually reschedule, not to write debts down. Existing debts can be purchased at face value, hence imposing no loss to anyone, and transformed into very long duration claims on each country's share of central bank seigniorage. Simple calculations suggest that seigniorage provides enough resources to reschedule, over decades, very sizeable portions of existing debts. Various provisions designed to eliminate borrower moral hazard can be added to strengthen the decentralized fiscal discipline framework.

Deep debt restructuring is therefore possible. The welfare case is compelling. Not only does it deal effectively with the many adverse consequences of large public debts, but it also re-establishes the ability to conduct decentralized counter-cyclical fiscal policies. It is a precondition for the fiscal discipline framework described in Section 3, and therefore for the survival of the euro.

4.3 Contagious Crises

A strict imposition of the no-bailout rule means that a government that does not abide by fiscal discipline will stand alone to face the consequences of its policies – and this will include those of its predecessors. As is well known, the reason why the decision was taken to bail out

Greece in 2010 was the fear of contagion. In the event, in spite of four bailouts (in chronological order, Greece, Ireland, Portugal, and Cyprus), contagion did happen. The reason was that the bailouts came in the form of loans, thus adding further debts to previously existing debts. We cannot know what would have happened if the no-bailout rule had been enforced, leaving each country to seek standard assistance from the IMF if needed. Thus, we do not know whether decentralized fiscal discipline backed by the no-bailout rule can be a source of crisis contagion.

The answer hinges on whether the combination of decentralized fiscal discipline and debt restructuring stands to eliminate forever the risk of a sovereign debt crisis in the eurozone.[11] One possibility is that a credible no-bailout rule is likely to trigger market defiance at much lower debt levels. Indeed, Reinhart and Rogoff (2010) report that public debts become unstable at levels as low as 40 percent of GDP in developing countries that borrow in foreign currencies, thus making any central bank bailout impossible.

Indeed, any rule, no matter how well crafted, may fail under unexpected circumstances. It is necessary therefore to admit that accidents can always happen, and to plan for such occurrences. Imagine that a eurozone member country faces a sovereign debt crisis. The logic of the decentralized framework is that no eurozone country or institution may provide any support, so the country is forced to default, possibly with IMF assistance. This could create extreme hardship for some of its lenders, including systematically important banks. The no-bailout logic that lenders must face the consequences of their decisions should apply. This is also the logic of the banking union. If large banks fail, they should be resolved.

Bank resolution, however, may trigger a crisis in other countries. This can be the consequence of a drain on public finances in the bank's host countries, or it can be a matter of general defiance regarding lending to eurozone governments. This possibility, no matter how remote, calls for four measures.

First, as recommended by the Basel Committee on Banking Supervision and proposed by the European Commission, bank regulation should establish limits on individual banks' exposure to particular

---

[11] Skeptics need only to study the history of the United States since the adoption in 1841 of the no-bailout principle, as described by Henning and Kessler (2012).

countries. Given the contagion risk within the eurozone, specific limits should also apply to aggregate holdings of all member countries' public debts. Well-designed limits would go a long way toward thwarting the risk of contagion.

Second, one channel for implicit bailout is the ECB's holding of national debt instruments. If a country defaults, the ECB may well suffer losses. The normal practice of the ECB is not to buy debt instruments but to operate reverse swaps so that it should not bear any loss. If the value of the debt declines, however, the ECB must call in for more collateral, which may be difficult in the midst of a crisis. Anyway, by the end of QE, the ECB will hold large amounts of public debts and it may take many years to download these legacy stocks. In the steady state, it should consider limiting its dealing to its own debt instruments. In the meantime, it could start exchanging public debts for its own debt.

The third measure is actually partly in place. The banking union is meant to make debt resolution possible. Unfortunately, as noted in Section 3.2, the resolution process is far too unwieldy to be operational. Preventing contagion is an additional reason to complete the process.

Finally, the banking union needs a large and mutualized fund available for bank rescues to prevent contagion. This instrument exists. With resources totaling €500 billion, the European Stability Mechanism (ESM) should be able to deal with severe contingencies. However, in its present form, it is not suited to the task. It can only lend to governments, which in turn may use the borrowed funds to resolve banks. However, this means increasing the public debt, hence making the crisis already underway deeper and more contagious, as markets can start gambling on the next likely country to succumb. In addition, ESM loans require that a Troika program be in place. This is incompatible with bank resolution in an emergency. In order to deal with the bank contagion channel, the ESM would need to be able to deal directly with banks and should be directly linked to a suitably integrated Single Resolution Mechanism.

5 Conclusions

European monetary union has always been an original experiment. The abandonment of monetary sovereignty by otherwise independent countries is bound to be challenging.[12] A key issue, well identified from the start, is the collective requirement that member countries be fiscally disciplined while budgetary sovereignty is firmly entrenched at the national level. These two features have not been reconciled, which has resulted in a calamitous crisis. The crisis further brought to the fore a number of additional, deeply buried challenges, such as the absence of solidarity or deep divergences of views regarding the role of monetary policy.

The original sin of European monetary union is undoubtedly the reliance on the Stability and Growth Pact to establish fiscal discipline. The cardinal sin was the *de facto* dismissal of the no-bailout clause when it became binding for the first time. Paradoxically, the potentially effective instrument, the no-bailout clause, was abandoned while the flawed instrument, the pact, was not just retained but further "strengthened." From the point of view of fiscal discipline institutional arrangements, the eurozone is much weaker now than it was before the crisis. It is further weakened by the large public debts that affect a sizable number of countries.

One of the European Founding Fathers, Jean Monnet, asserted that integration would largely come in steps taken in response to crises.[13] This prophecy still drives the thoughts of policymakers. This explains the numerous calls from political leaders to go to the next level and achieve some form of fiscal union and to mutualize existing debts, at least partially. Independently of their inherent merits, however, these calls are deeply divisive, which throws doubt on the question of whether they can solve the vital fiscal discipline problem at this stage.

This chapter evaluates the ongoing debates through the prism of optimization. It regards fiscal union as an unconstrained optimum. A benevolent dictator, informed by the monetary unions at work in numerous federal states, would indeed choose this solution. Fortunately, a dictator does not rule Europe. There was a time, perhaps, when benevolent leaders could force decisions onto unconcerned citizens, the adoption of the euro being a case in point. These times, however, are long gone, in part as a result of the disastrous

---

[12] Other significant sovereign transfers include the Single Market and trade.
[13] The Banking Union is one case where the prophecy materialized.

mismanagement of the crisis.[14] As a consequence, decisions must now be made under constraints that reflect public opinions. Quite understandably, fiscal union is controversial within each member country and across countries. The chapter therefore took as its departure point the assumption that further integration is ruled out for the time being. This assumption can be challenged, of course. Yet it is a worthwhile exercise to examine whether constrained optima exist.

Can the fiscal policy problem be solved without further sovereignty transfers? The apparent absence of any precedent leads to a widely shared negative answer. This assessment ignores that current federal states were gradually built over time. It is also based on a paucity of efforts to develop constrained optima.

This chapter presents a worked-out constrained optimum. Its main feature is member countries' compulsory adoption of effective fiscal discipline frameworks that already exist in many countries. At the national level, they combine intelligent fiscal rules and independent fiscal councils, apt at combining rule and discretion. At the collective level, they provide for supervision of the implementation of national frameworks, combining an independent European fiscal council with the possibility of bringing cases to the European Court of Justice. The chapter also calls for a restoration of the disqualified no-bailout rule and examines a number of side effects of such an arrangement.

Several criticisms can be raised against this approach. A first criticism is that the proposed constrained optimum will not be effective, i.e. that it is not an optimum. A second criticism is that such a solution is politically impossible, i.e. that the constraint is not tight enough. A third criticism is that a less constraining optimum can be reached, for example with the now strengthened Stability and Growth Pact. These are all worthy criticisms. The main aim of this chapter is to contribute to a debate on which constraints must be accepted and what the optima are under various plausible constraints. The key insight can be summed up in the following question: If a constrained optimum exists, why aim at an unrealistic unconstrained optimum?

---

[14] Funke et al. (2015) also show that financial crises have deep political implications.

Bibliography

Begg, David, de Grauwe, Paul, Giavazzi, Francesco and Uhlig, Harald (1998). *The ECB: Safe at Any Speed? Monitoring the European Central Bank 1*. London: CEPR.

Bodmer, Frank (2006). The Swiss debt brake: how it works and what can go wrong. *Schweizerische Zeitschrift für Volkswirtschaft und Statistik*, **142** (3), 307–30.

Bos, Frits (2008). The Dutch fiscal framework: history, current practice and the role of the Central Planning Bureau. *OECD Journal on Budgeting*, 8(1), 7–48.

Bova, Elva, Kinda, Tidiane, Muthoora, Priscilla and Toscani, Frederik (2015). *Fiscal Rules at a Glance*. International Monetary Fund, www.imf.org/external/datamapper/fiscalrules/Fiscal%20Rules%20at%20a%20Glance%20-%20Background%20Paper.pdf.

Corsetti, Giancarlo, Feld, Lars P., Lane, Philip R., Reichlin, Lucrezia, Rey, Hélène, Vayanos, Dimitri and Weder di Mauro, Beatrice (2015). *A New Start for the Eurozone: Dealing with Debt*. London: CEPR.

Debrun, Xavier, Hauner, David and Kumar, Manmohan S. (2009). Independent fiscal agencies. *Journal of Economic Surveys*, **23**(1), 44–81.

Delors Committee Report (1989). *Report on Economic and Monetary Union in the European Community*. Luxembourg: European Commission.

Delpla, Jacques and Wyplosz, Charles (2007). *La fin des privilèges*. Paris: Hachette Litérattures.

Eichengreen, Barry and Panizza, Ugo (2014). *A Surplus of Ambition: Can Europe Rely on Large Primary Surpluses to Solve Its Debt Problem?* CEPR Discussion Paper No. 10069.

Eichengreen, Barry and Wyplosz, Charles (1998). The Stability Pact: minor nuisance, major diversion? *Economic Policy*, **26**, 67–113.

Feldstein, Martin (1997). The political economy of the European Economic and Monetary Union: political sources of an economic liability. *Journal of Economic Perspectives*, **11**(4), 23–42.

Funke, Manuel, Schularick, Moritz and Trebesch, Christoph (2015). *Going to Extremes: Politics after Financial Crises, 1870–2014*. CEPR Discussion Paper No. 10884.

Henning, C. Randall and Kessler, Martin (2012). *Fiscal Federalism: US History for Architects of Europe's Fiscal Union*. Working Paper No. 12-1, Peterson Institute for International Economics, Washington, DC.

Hepp, Ralph and von Hagen, Juergen (2009). Fiscal federalism in Germany: stabilization and redistribution before and after unification. *Publius: The Journal of Federalism*, **42**(2), 234–59.

IMF (2013). *The Functions and Impact of Fiscal Councils.* International Monetary Fund, Policy Paper, www.imf.org/external/np/pp/eng/2013/071613.pdf

Juncker, Jean-Claude, Tusk, Donald, Dijsselbloem, Jeroen, Draghi, Mario and Schulz, Martin (2015). *Completing European's Economic and Monetary Union.* European Commission, https://ec.europa.eu/prior ities/sites/beta-political/files/5-presidents-report_en.pdf

Kopits, George (ed.). (2013). *Restoring Public Debt Sustainability: The Role of Independent Fiscal Institutions.* Oxford: Oxford University Press.

Krogstrup, Signe and Wyplosz, Charles (2006). A common pool theory of deficit bias correction. *European Economy*, **275**, 1–29.

Oates, Wallace (1972). *Fiscal Federalism.* New York: Harcourt Brace Jovanovich.

Ódor, Ľudovít (2014). *Another Quiet Revolution?* Discussion Paper No. 5/20, Council for Budget Responsibility, Bratislava.

Panizza, Ugo and Andrea Presbitero (2014). Public debt and economic growth: is there a causal effect? *Journal of Macroeconomics*, **41**, 21–41.

Pâris, Pierre and Wyplosz, Charles (2014). *PADRE: Politically Acceptable Debt Restructuring in the Eurozone.* Geneva Report on the World Economy Special No. 3. London: CEPR.

Reinhart, Carmen and Rogoff, Kenneth (2010). Growth in a time of debt. *American Economic Review*, **100**(2), 573–8.

Ter-Minassian, Teresa (2007). Fiscal rules for subnational governments: can they promote fiscal discipline? *OECD Journal on Budgeting*, **6**(3), 1–11.

Wyplosz, Charles (2012). Fiscal rules: theoretical issues and historical experiences. In A. Alesina and F. Giavazzi, eds., *Fiscal Policy After the Crisis.* Chicago: Chicago University Press, pp. 495–530.

   (2013). *Europe's Quest for Fiscal Discipline.* European Economy Economic Papers, No. 498.

   (2014). The eurozone crisis: a near-perfect case of mismanagement. *Economia Marche Journal of Applied Economics*, **33**(1), 2–13.

7 | Lost in Complexity

Towards a Decentralised and Depoliticised Fiscal Framework in Europe

Ľ U D O V Í T   Ó D O R   A N D   G Á B O R   P .   K I S S

1 Introduction

A proper fiscal framework should ensure long-term sustainability while avoiding pro-cyclical fiscal behaviour. In its current form, the European fiscal framework fails on both fronts. Fine-tuning the already complex system is not, in our view, a viable alternative; one has to design a fundamentally new institutional set-up, where account-abilities are clearly defined. Path-dependency should be abandoned and basic theoretical and empirical lessons respected. We propose a decentralised and depoliticised framework, which is theoretically sounder and practically more enforceable than the current web of complicated rules and procedures. Moreover, it also exploits synergies between fiscal rules and independent fiscal institutions at both the national and European levels.

The financial and sovereign debt crises have shaken the very foundations of the euro area. In order to calm financial markets, European governments and institutions have adopted a wide variety of reforms and measures to avoid the break-up of the currency union. These trial-and-error and learning-by-doing methods were sometimes successful, but did not always achieve the desired outcomes. Hence there is clear consensus among economists and policymakers that additional steps are necessary to increase the euro area's resilience to future crises. In what is known as the 'Five Presidents' Report', Juncker et al. (2015) call for progress on four fronts: genuine economic union, financial union, fiscal union and political union. The main objective of this chapter is to contribute to the debate by identifying the weaknesses

Useful comments and suggestions from Michal Horváth, Geert Langenus, Lucio Pench and participants at the CBR conference in Bratislava are gratefully acknowledged. This chapter represents the views of the authors and does not necessarily reflect those of the CBR and the MNB.

of the current European fiscal framework and proposing an alternative – more robust – solution.

At the heart of the sovereign debt crisis in Europe lies the fundamental contradiction between bail-outs and fiscal sovereignty inside a monetary union. One cannot have both at the same time. With the benefit of hindsight, it is clear that absent resolution mechanisms and strong links between bank and sovereign risks were the main factors behind the bail-outs in the initial phase of the crisis. Since then, major progress has been made to set up resolution schemes and to present a roadmap towards a banking (financial) union. These are absolutely necessary building blocks of any successful currency union. Creditors and shareholders have to bear a large part of losses stemming from the insolvency of banks or even sovereigns. The question we investigate in this chapter is: what kind of fiscal framework can better ensure fiscal discipline in the euro area?

Important lessons can be learned from the functioning of existing federations. The degree of central control varies considerably within them. One extreme possibility is reliance purely on market discipline, i.e. having a credible no-bail-out policy (like in the United States). The other extreme is full solidarity between Member States, when bail-out is widely expected. It should be noted that the design of area-wide fiscal rules is heavily dependent on the approach chosen. In the former case, almost no monitoring by the centre is necessary (see Wyplosz in Chapter 6), while if one chooses the latter approach, very detailed rules and coordinated fiscal policy are unavoidable in fighting moral hazard. The current situation in the euro area is somewhere between these two extremes. Europe is balancing between the low credibility of the no-bail-out clause in the Treaty and the need to avoid free-riding. Irrespective of the final model chosen, we argue that a fundamental redefinition of accountability between the centre and national authorities would be necessary in any case. In our view, Europe needs a decentralised fiscal framework to ensure fiscal discipline in the long run.

Our motivation is threefold. First, in our view it is necessary to better align theory and the actual design of fiscal rules and institutions. The fundamental conflict between using one-size-fits-all approaches and taking into account country specificities has often led to reliance on escape clauses, special regimes and 'other factors'. As a result, Europe has ended up with a complex web of sometimes contradictory rules and procedures (Ódor, 2014a). Paradoxically, the system relies on so many rules that in many cases the final verdict is in fact a discretionary decision by the European Commission/Council.[1] Second, the division of labour between the community and national levels is blurred. There is no clear separation of accountability and responsibility. The European framework combines a non-credible no-bail-out principle, Member States' sovereignty over budgetary issues, the Stability and Growth Pact (SGP), and several funds, such as the ESM or EFSF. In our view, it is necessary to define when and under what conditions the intervention from the centre is warranted. Moreover, current discussions about a stronger fiscal union will add another layer of challenges – namely, the question of proper design of fiscal rules and institutions at the community level. It is also important to limit political influence in applying rules and procedures as far as is possible. Third, current fiscal indicators allow fiscal gimmickry, and real-time evaluation of structural budget balances is more art than science. More appropriate methodological tools are available in the literature, but their application is often hampered by the current institutional set-up.

The solution to these three fundamental problems that we propose in this chapter is similar to the arrangement advocated by Wren-Lewis (2003). The first line of defence against irresponsible fiscal policy behaviour should be at the local level, using home-grown fiscal rules and independent fiscal institutions.[2] Their design, however, should fulfil commonly agreed minimum standards. If a Member State operates with no significant fiscal risks and if spill-over effects are unlikely, no yearly intervention at the community level is necessary. The community level in our proposal is represented not only by the European Commission, but also by an independent fiscal watchdog for the euro area. These institutions should, in our view, focus primarily on avoiding free-riding and aggregate pro-cyclicality and supervising countries not respecting European fiscal rules.

A decentralised fiscal framework is also more compatible with the current situation in the European Union, where as yet not all Member States have introduced the single currency. For member countries outside the euro area, it would be hard to accept more central

---

[1] Despite the introduction of more rules, the actual decision of the EC is still difficult to predict.

[2] In this paper, we use the terms 'fiscal councils' (FCs) and 'independent fiscal institutions' (IFIs) somewhat interchangeably.

budgetary oversight. In the rest of the chapter, we focus on the euro area only.[3]

The chapter is organised as follows. Section 2 discusses the foundations on which our reform proposal is based. Section 3 briefly describes the main building blocks of our proposal for a more transparent and efficient European fiscal framework. Section 4 contains a more detailed description of the various national elements of the proposed framework, while Section 5 discusses those parts of the framework which require action at the euro-area level. The final section concludes.

2 Foundations of a New European Fiscal Framework

Before we present our proposal for a decentralised fiscal framework, it is necessary to put the question of fiscal responsibility into a wider context (the overall architecture of the EMU) and to define the basic objectives we want to achieve. Our main goals are the following:

- better alignment of theory and practice in fiscal policymaking;
- full utilisation of synergies between fiscal rules and independent fiscal institutions;
- compatibility with a more complete design of the EMU;
- better balance vis-à-vis the set of criteria defined by Kopits and Symansky to assess the quality of fiscal rules.

The first two objectives are mainly about incorporating the most important lessons from the literature (both purely academic and policy-oriented) into the design of fiscal frameworks. The last two are specific to the euro area. By recognising the flaws in the initial set-up of the EMU and comparing the Stability and Growth Pact to a well-known set of criteria for fiscal rules, one can obtain a more complete picture of problems to be resolved. We now look at those objectives in more detail.

2.1 Theory and Practice in Macroeconomic Aspects of Fiscal Policy

Changes to the conduct of monetary policy (MP) have been enormous in the past few decades. Despite recent challenges after hitting the zero

---

[3] However, in order to avoid repetition we sometimes use 'European' instead of 'euro area'.

lower bound (ZLB), Blinder rightly calls this development a 'quiet revolution' (Blinder, 2004). Independent central banks, inflation targets, transparent communication of objectives and policy and monetary research all contributed to a much better understanding and execution of monetary policy. On the other hand, the more important macro policy tool from a social welfare point of view – fiscal policy (FP) – is still conducted on an ad hoc basis and in a very opaque environment in many countries. Leeper (2010), for example, talks about 'monetary science and fiscal alchemy'.

The quiet revolution in central banking has occurred because of the depoliticisation of some aspects of monetary policy. The Great Inflation of the seventies was the main trigger, when the public realised the cost of high inflation. Now we are in a period of 'Great Debt' and, similarly, the public sees the costs of permanently high debt. This may lead to a greater appetite to adopt changes. The question is where to draw a borderline between technocratic work and political decisions. According to Wyplosz (2002, p. 15), 'it is important to distinguish between the macroeconomic side of fiscal policy, which resembles monetary policy, and its allocative and structural aspects, which require indeed political oversight'. In monetary policy there is a consensus that independent central banks can target inflation fairly well on a medium-term horizon by setting short-term interest rates. Moreover, simple rules can help to fight time-inconsistency problems (Kydland and Prescott, 1977) while at the same time mimicking optimal policy from a theoretical point of view. We argue that these successful elements in the conduct of monetary policy might also play a useful role in the case of fiscal policy. Table 7.1 provides a simple comparison of the current state of monetary and fiscal policy conduct.

Are the differences between the conduct of the two policies due to the different nature of fiscal policy (comparing apples to oranges) or do the gaps simply reflect a lack of reforms in fiscal policymaking? The short answer is: both are true. In our view, there are two major inherent differences between MP and FP. First, fiscal policy has many instruments with possible large distributional effects (standard MP[4] has also distributional 'side effects' mainly via the inflation channel,

---

[4] However, it should be noted that many unconventional monetary policy measures also have significant distributional aspects, especially those which target special asset markets. See Brunnermeier and Sannikov (2012).

Table 7.1: *Comparing monetary and fiscal policy*

	Monetary policy	Fiscal policy
Understanding the economy	New micro-founded models	Models from the seventies dominate in practice
Institutional set-up	Independent central banks	Political decision-making
Objectives	Inflation targets	No clear consensus; some notion of sustainability
Operational rules	Short-term interest rates as an instrument and simple rules (optimal policy)	Tax smoothing in theory vs. ad hoc fiscal rules in practice
Dynamic behaviour and expectations	Firmly anchored inflation expectations, importance of time-inconsistency	Importance of fiscal expectations recognised mostly in crisis times
Communication	Open communication, high transparency	Fiscal gimmickry is the rule, not the exception
Theory vs. practice	Convergence	Important differences prevail

Source: Ódor (2014b)

but usually these are limited in size, especially over the business cycle).[5] Second, FP has many supply-side effects. These two aspects make the separation of technocratic work and political process much harder than is the case in MP (see also Leeper in Chapter 2). The traditional 'taxation without representation' has to be clearly respected; however, there can still be ample scope for IFIs to clarify the effects of policies or, for example, to better coordinate the macroeconomic effects of MP and FP when the economy is close to the ZLB. In other words, we argue in this chapter that the above-mentioned two major differences do not justify the large gaps between the conduct of MP and macro-economic aspects of FP. On the other hand, it is important to bear in mind those differences when designing better fiscal frameworks.

Now we turn to the main lessons from *theory* with regard to fiscal policy. It is far beyond the scope of this chapter to provide a full literature review; our aim is to focus on major lessons only. As far as the optimal level of public debt is concerned, there are no clear-cut

---

[5] Among other distributional aspects of standard monetary policy, the exchange rate channel or the availability of credit could be mentioned.

recommendations for policymakers. It is, however, clear from the literature that optimal sovereign debt trajectories are country-specific and depend on a complex array of variables. On the one hand, higher public debt can bring the economy to the optimal capital level and increase welfare. Furthermore, it allows consumption smoothing by lifting liquidity constraints on some households. Another benefit of higher debt is the deepening of domestic capital markets. On the other hand, increasing levels of government debt are obviously not without costs. Higher market interest rates can crowd out private investments, distortionary taxation used to finance debt reduces welfare, and lower wages in equilibrium can be also mentioned as a cost. As Vogel (2014) illustrates, wealth inequality can also be an important factor affecting optimal debt levels. Therefore, it is not surprising that optimal values of debt in theoretical models vary between a substantial negative amount (accumulation of assets) and a large positive value.

Another very important theoretical lesson is that, after a shock to the debt level, it is not optimal to make an immediate and complete adjustment. Instead, debt should function as a shock absorber;[6] therefore, efforts should be made to achieve tax smoothing (Barro, 1979). Kirsanova et al. (2007) show that in many models, optimal fiscal policy would involve steady-state debt following a random walk in response to shocks. However, a pre-requisite for this is a benevolent policy-maker, a pre-shock debt level that is not excessively high (i.e. adequate fiscal space is available) and market expectations that are well anchored even after the shock. Otherwise, a sudden increase in risk premia may easily lead to a loss of confidence in the government debt markets. In other words, designing optimal consolidation paths is also a difficult exercise, where strict fiscal rules with no space for discretion are unlikely to help.

A new strand of the literature focuses more on debt sustainability and government defaults rather than optimal debt levels. For example, Bi and Leeper (2013) calculate 'fiscal limits' as probabilistic distributions (instead of fixed debt-to-GDP ratios) dependent on Laffer curves and economic shocks. Sovereign default probabilities cannot be ignored and expectations about future policy are also crucial in understanding the evolution of fiscal limits (see also Leeper in Chapter 2).

---

[6] Debt levels are therefore not suitable for the purposes of operational fiscal rules. However, they can be useful as long-term anchors for fiscal policy.

The problem with theoretical considerations is that they often assume a benevolent policymaker. The reality is, however, much more complicated. From a *practical* point of view, we know that countries often have persistent deficits and rapidly increasing debt levels even in normal times. The literature calls this phenomenon 'deficit bias'. There can be many reasons for such behaviour (Calmfors and Wren-Lewis, 2011): myopia, informational asymmetries, impatience, electoral competition or, for example, common-pool theory. The important point here is that the most important reasons for 'fiscal alcoholism' are often country-specific or even time-varying. For example, different degrees of credibility, forms of governance and political set-ups all require tailor-made solutions.

Both theoretical (optimal debt trajectories, fiscal limits and speed of debt adjustments) and practical (source of deficit bias) considerations point towards the need for country-specific fiscal rules. One-size-fits-all solutions can easily be sub-optimal at individual country level.

In this chapter we state that the elimination of the deficit bias (in as efficient a manner as possible) should be the most important policy objective of FP (but, of course, not the only one; for example, coordination of fiscal and monetary policy is also crucial, especially in crisis times). This goal implicitly contains anchored fiscal expectations, predictability and counter-cyclicality of policies and sustainability of some fiscal stock variable, i.e. gross debt, net debt or inter-temporal net worth ('taxpayers' equity'). Deficit bias is interpreted here in a very broad sense, including all potential factors allowing the government to create permanent deficits (non-transparency, implicit liabilities, fiscal illusion, etc.). As Portes and Wren-Lewis (2014) show, the severity of the deficit bias is an important variable when designing fiscal rules. Without such a bias it is much easier to follow optimal policy (tax smoothing).

What are the best instruments to fight the deficit bias while at the same time respecting theoretical lessons? In a general sense, it is some mix of fiscal rules and independent fiscal institutions, which constrain the behaviour of policymakers. The detailed design depends very much on the source of the bias. The next section deals with this question.

2.2 Synergies between Fiscal Rules and Fiscal Institutions

Fiscal frameworks usually mix together fiscal rules, fiscal institutions, transparency requirements and various technical procedures. This section briefly discusses the potential trade-offs when designing fiscal rules and the ways in which fiscal councils can mitigate them.

Our starting point is the well-known set of criteria defined by Kopits and Symansky (1998) to assess the quality of fiscal rules. Ideally, a fiscal rule should be well defined, transparent, adequate, consistent, simple, flexible, enforceable and efficient. Of course, since there are important trade-offs among these criteria, it is impossible to score highly on all aspects. The key point is to balance the fiscal rule along these characteristics to achieve the desired outcome. Kopits and Symansky do not attach weights to individual criteria.

Here we focus on four important trade-offs:

- flexibility vs. enforceability;
- simplicity vs. adequate definition;
- optimality vs. effectiveness;
- one-size-fits-all vs. adequacy (in a monetary union).

It is impossible to foresee all future states of the world. That is the reason why fiscal rules should be flexible enough to be able to cope with unexpected circumstances.[7] Significant shocks beyond the control of policymakers should be accommodated. For this reason, fiscal rules often contain exceptions, special regimes or escape clauses. On the other hand, overly frequent use of 'excuses' makes the rules non-binding most of the time (as in Europe). Fiscal councils might have an important role in easing this kind of trade-off. If the activation of escape clauses is delegated to an independent fiscal institution, the risk of throwing out the baby with the bathwater can be minimised.

Fiscal rules should also be well defined, to avoid ambiguities and ineffective enforcement. This usually requires a detailed description of indicators, procedures and institutional coverage. With more details specified, the rule becomes increasingly complex and hardly understandable for the general public. On the other hand, if rules are simple, the democratic accountability of policymakers is better ensured. If an independent fiscal institution is part of the fiscal framework, rules can be slightly more complex, since there is an independent body to check

---

[7] There are good reasons to use judgements in the case of monetary policy as well (Svensson, 2003).

compliance with them. Fiscal council communications towards the general public can be a useful substitute for simple fiscal rules.

Portes and Wren-Lewis (2014) emphasise the trade-offs between optimality and effectiveness. Public debt should be used as a shock absorber to mimic optimal policy. On the other hand, if a deficit bias is present, fiscal rules should also serve as a commitment device. In reality, it is hard to achieve both objectives – optimality and prevention of bias – at the same time. Fiscal councils might play an important role in combating the deficit bias, so optimal policies can be easier to follow.

In the euro area, there are fiscal rules at both the national and community levels. Centrally enforced rules have to be based on 'equal treatment' in order to be respected by national authorities and the general public. However, as we saw earlier, optimal policies and sources of deficit bias are country-specific, and in some cases time-varying. Therefore, European rules should *not* focus primarily on the local deficit bias or nationally optimal policy. Instead, central rules should limit free-riding behaviour by eliminating potential contagion from one Member State to another.[8] Here, an independent fiscal council at the central level might help to identify gross policy errors at the local level.

2.3 Compatibility with Other Pillars of a Currency Union

If one wants to design a proper fiscal framework for the euro area, focusing solely on fiscal policy issues is not sufficient. It is important to bear in mind the overall architecture of a currency union. In the case of Europe, it is not only the current set-up that is important, but also the likely future (more complete) version of the euro area. Here we mention three key factors. First, if risks in the banking (financial) sector are not dealt with early on and no quick resolution mechanisms are in place, taxpayers' money is usually used to bail out financial institutions, with far-reaching consequences for the fiscal position of a country (contingent liabilities). Second, the complexity of fiscal rules is heavily dependent on the division of responsibilities between the national and European level. The degree of credibility of the no-bail-

---

[8] Avoiding gross policy errors was the main reason behind establishing the original Stability and Growth Pact.

out clause and the sovereignty principle in fiscal matters are two important elements to consider when designing fiscal frameworks in monetary unions. Third, to ensure counter-cyclicality of fiscal policy at the aggregate level, one has to recognise the nature and size of risk-sharing mechanisms across Member States. In the same spirit in which the low credibility of no bail-out clauses leads to the need for more central control and less sovereignty, insufficient risk-sharing means a greater role for EU-level counter-cyclical fiscal policy. We look at these three important issues in turn.

2.3.1 Banking (Financial) Union

Many economists and policymakers have highlighted that the 'diabolic loop' between banks and sovereigns in the euro area should be eliminated. The size of contingent liabilities should be reduced by establishing a banking union. No fiscal framework can survive if massive public injections are necessary to save the banking system. Businesses in Europe rely too much on financing from banks, and banks exhibit substantial home bias with regard to sovereign risks. Capital market union, abolishment of zero risk-weights on sovereigns and introducing concentration risks on sovereign exposures would be important steps towards weakening the bank–sovereign nexus. Juncker et al. (2015), Corsetti et al. (2015) and Bundesbank (2015) describe these arguments in more detail. It is also important to build a credible backstop mechanism for the banking union.

2.3.2 Bail-Outs and the Sovereignty Principle

The usual theoretical argument in favour of strong fiscal frameworks is the well-known deficit bias. The set-up of a monetary union is more complicated, since common-pool problems can arise not only for local reasons but also at the level of the whole union. There are several ways in which federations are dealing with this 'common-pool squared' problem (Allard et al., 2013; Wyplosz, 2013). One extreme is to rely on pure market discipline. In this case, there is no formal coordination mechanism, but a strict and credible no-bail-out principle at the central level. The deficit bias at the local level is then usually dealt with through self-imposed fiscal rules or procedures. The US model is very close to this type of arrangement.

Another extreme is direct central control. The German set-up can be reasonably well approximated by this model. In this case bail-out is not

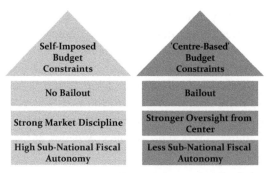

Figure 7.1: Two possible arrangements of fiscal discipline
Source: adapted from Allard et al. (2013)

prohibited, but the free-riding is contained by heavy involvement of the centre in local budgetary decisions through rules and procedures.

Despite recent improvements, the problem of the European framework is that, on the one hand, pure market discipline is not credible at the current juncture and, on the other, substantial involvement of the centre in national budget decisions is at odds with the national sovereignty principle guaranteed by the Treaty. Therefore, in the short run (when changes in the Treaty are not realistic), the only possibility has been overregulation with fiscal rules and stricter enforcement mechanisms (a move from a more market-controlled regime towards more oversight from the centre). In other words, this is the price Europe had to pay for the non-credibility of the no-bail-out principle and the failure of the former SGP. If substantial changes to the Treaty are not possible in the longer run, the pendulum will have to swing back towards more market discipline.

At this stage it seems unlikely that Member States are ready to give up a large part of their sovereignty in fiscal matters (see Wyplosz in Chapter 6 and Bordo and James in Chapter 8). Therefore, in order to move towards more market discipline, clear ex ante bail-in mechanisms and processes for orderly sovereign debt restructuring should be implemented (Bundesbank, 2015). On the other hand, ESM support for illiquid sovereigns and the OMT programme of the ECB should be strictly conditional on reform packages or even debt restructuring (Bundesbank, 2015). Moreover, Member States should not expect full sovereignty in the case of financial supports from the centre (in order to eliminate moral hazard).

2.3.3 Stronger Fiscal Union?

While there is relatively wide consensus regarding the need for a well-designed banking union in Europe,[9] strengthening the fiscal union is a very controversial topic. It is not possible to ignore this debate, since the need for counter-cyclical policy at the euro-area level cannot be completely neglected, especially because more severe home bias compared to the United States makes private risk-sharing less effective. In other words, the design of a European fiscal framework should ensure not only sustainability but also counter-cyclicality (especially in crisis times), and the latter is closely linked to a question of central budgets in a currency union. One can argue that to date the European framework has been more about sustainability and less concerned with pro-cyclical policy at the aggregate level.

2.4 Better Balance vis-à-vis the Kopits–Symansky Criteria

Apart from ensuring compatibility with the overall set-up of the monetary union, a thorough analysis of the strengths and weaknesses of the current fiscal framework is necessary. Although significant progress has been made since the crisis, the European fiscal framework itself has become overly complicated, non-transparent and almost unenforceable over the years. As Ódor (2014a) points out, comparing the end result with a well-known set of criteria (Kopits and Symansky, 1998), the European fiscal architecture scores relatively low on simplicity, consistency, definition and enforceability. The latter weakness has also been demonstrated by the current application of the new fiscal legislation: granting an arbitrary number of years for correction of excessive deficits (instead of 'one year as a rule'), introducing the 'investment clause' and defining more space for flexibility in the application of the SGP. Especially worrisome is the treatment of structural reform plans. Ex ante proposals can qualify for an extension of deadlines (European Commission, 2015).

Ódor draws six broad conclusions. First, when designing fiscal frameworks, systemic considerations should be preferred to incremental changes. It is important to notice that the effectiveness of the fiscal framework depends on many factors outside purely fiscal issues. Second, he criticises the idea of attaching correction mechanisms to unobservable variables. Third, some features of the new system can be

---

[9] With the exception of introducing common deposit guarantee schemes.

considered 'unnecessary ornaments'. For example, the expenditure benchmark, the investment clause and the debt reduction rule are good candidates for future simplifications. Fourth, IFIs might play an even more important role in the European fiscal architecture. Fifth, despite some progress, more emphasis should be placed on debt and sustainability. Finally, the appearance of unequal treatment and excessive flexibility should be avoided. This is especially important in the first years of application of the new rules. The SGP should mainly deal with fiscal goals; other objectives (growth) should be addressed primarily through new instruments (e.g. through the EU budget) or via National Reform Programmes.

3 A Decentralised and Depoliticised European Fiscal Framework

In this section, we use the conclusions from the previous section to propose a new fiscal framework for the euro area. In our view, a decentralised framework of fiscal responsibility is not only better aligned with theory, but also benefits more from synergies between fiscal rules and independent fiscal institutions (both at the European and national levels). In addition, it offers a more efficient division of labour between the community and the national levels with regard to fiscal responsibility. The new structure will achieve its objectives only if it takes into account country-specific conditions and is based on better fiscal indicators.

A similar set-up was advocated by Wren-Lewis (2003, p. 77): 'There is, however, an alternative path for reforming the Pact, which puts the emphasis back on subsidiarity. National governments should be allowed to establish and follow their own fiscal rules. If these rules are sufficient to ensure long term sustainability, then these governments should be exempted from the Pact.' The value added by this chapter is its discussion of this solution in the current context and its much more detailed description of a possible decentralised framework for fiscal responsibility in Europe.

As we stated earlier, it is not possible to separate the issue of fiscal frameworks from the question of the overall set-up of a currency union. Therefore, at the bottom of Figure 7.2 and Figure 7.3 we list two important pre-conditions to be met: a fully functional banking union and a stronger no-bail-out principle. One should, however, note that strengthening the no-bail-out clause is not possible without sound

Figure 7.2: Proposal for a new European fiscal framework

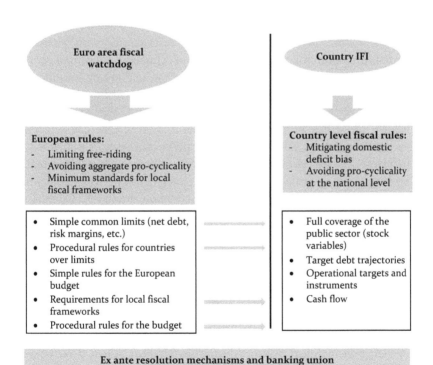

Figure 7.3: Separation of fiscal responsibilities in the euro area

macroprudential policies and an effective banking union. Even if the no-bail-out principle is unlikely to achieve full credibility, as is the case in the United States (at least in the medium run), the more losses are absorbed by shareholders and creditors, the easier is the design of fiscal rules at the community level.

The problem of deficit bias in currency unions arises both at the local level and at the whole-area level. In our view, the obvious approach would be to build a hierarchical system of responsibilities. When there is no sign of free-riding behaviour with potential contagion effects, the national level should be responsible for fighting against the local deficit bias. In that case, a country-specific, tailor-made solution should be designed (also more in line with theory).

Area-level rules and institutions should primarily focus on problems concerning common interest. High on this list is possible contagion, free-riding behaviour or, for example, counter-cyclical aggregate fiscal policy. In the case of a fully credible no-bail-out clause, centrally imposed fiscal rules on Member States are not even necessary (see Wyplosz in Chapter 6). If the euro area is successful in putting in place clear rules for burden-sharing, banking union and debt restructuring with a strong backstop mechanism, the current trend of legislating more and more complex fiscal rules can be reversed. In our view, in that case it would be sufficient to operate with one or two simple rules. These rules should *not* target yearly balances in national budgets. Instead, they should fight against the deficit bias occurring at the area level. One can imagine various possibilities suitable for this purpose: debt levels, sustainability indicators or, for example, sovereign risk indicators. It is important, however, to design rules not with a target level, but rather as a maximum value tolerated by the community (one common threshold). Countries operating below these thresholds would be free to conduct their fiscal policy if they respect minimum benchmarks (the universal 3 percent deficit limit can be abolished). However, after breaching the limits, oversight from the centre should step in. The sovereignty principle should be significantly reduced when exceeding the agreed limits.

It is also important to depoliticise budgetary decisions at the European level as much as possible. Unfortunately, many of the European Commission's current decisions are hard to interpret without taking into account political pressures from big Member States. That is the main reason why we advocate for a truly independent fiscal council at the European level.

In the next two sections, we discuss the local and European elements of the framework in more detail.

4 National Fiscal Rules and Institutions

As far as national fiscal frameworks are concerned, three ingredients seem to be necessary to mitigate the deficit bias: adequate indicators supporting sustainability and counter-cyclicality of policies, country-specific fiscal rules (probably even time-varying) and independent local fiscal institutions.

4.1 Better Indicators

For fiscal policy to operate properly, it needs to rely on a fiscal framework that keeps debt on an optimal path and at the same time avoids fiscal policy that is pro-cyclical (i.e. intensifies economic volatility).[10] These two fundamental goals can be achieved more easily if one chooses the right set of basic fiscal indicators. We argue that from this perspective, improvements in at least three areas are necessary to place fiscal architectures on more solid ground. First, a numerical fiscal rule will function properly and be enforceable only if it covers the full scope of discretionary fiscal policy. Second, a numerical rule should exclude impacts of all exogenous factors. As we will see, there is potential for significant methodological progress in this respect as well, although the uncertainty surrounding the potential GDP level and growth rate will nevertheless persist. Third, countries should also put more emphasis on optimal composition of public debt, cash flow and other medium-run solvency indicators. Independent fiscal institutions might play a very important complementary role in all three areas.

In this chapter we put a lot of emphasis on using the 'right' set of fiscal indicators based on best practices. As we are going to show in this section, currently used one-size-fits-all indicators in the EU have serious problems in filtering out all exogenous and temporary factors. In our opinion, these defects cannot be easily cured at the level of fiscal rules by introducing special regimes, safety margins, etc. A better strategy would be to use discretion not in the interpretation of rules,

---

[10] More detailed description of basic fiscal indicators can be found in Ódor and P. Kiss (2015). Here we rely heavily on the aforementioned paper.

but in the design of meaningful country-specific indicators. We will come back to this question in Section 5.

Carefully designed and policy-relevant fiscal indicators calculated by local fiscal councils are also important in order to escape Goodhart's law (Goodhart, 1975). In its most popular formulation, this law states that 'when a measure becomes a target, it ceases to be a good measure'. One solution to this problem is to use a battery of indicators including stock, flow and cash-flow measures. However, it is not irrelevant who reports these indicators. In order to be able to assess the 'true' state of fiscal policy in real-time, pure statistical constructs or one-size-fits-all methodologies might be sub-optimal. In our view, independent fiscal institutions are much better placed to design and evaluate policy-relevant analytical indicators.

Table 7.2 illustrates some of the weaknesses of currently used indicators in Europe.

Table 7.2: *Weaknesses of currently used fiscal indicators in Europe*

Main problems	Possible remedies
Partial coverage of discretionary action	– Use of public sector balance sheets – International accounting standards (substance over form) – Analytical indicators covering quasi-fiscal activities
Over-reliance on (extremely uncertain) real-time estimates of the output gap	– Robust estimates: battery of methods – Mainly ex ante evaluation or longer ex post horizons – Disaggregated methodology for structural budget balances – Bottom-up crosschecks
Not consistent and transparent identification of one-off and temporary measures	– Full disclosure of one-off items – Consistent methodology (only self-reversing measures are considered)
No adequate focus on cash-flow figures	– More emphasis on medium-term solvency – Sensitivity analysis of interest expenditures

Table 7.3: *Simple deficit decomposition*

	Permanent	Temporary
Exogenous	Part of structural deficit (P_1)	Medium-term cyclical component (T_1) Revenue windfall/shortfall (T_2) Surprise inflation/disinflation (T_3) Volatility of yields + lagged effects on interest expenditure (T_4) Long-term volatility (T_5)
Endogenous (discretionary)	Part of structural deficit (P_2)	Creative accounting and one-offs (T_6) Deviations from necessary investment level (T_7)

In international practice, a large number of fiscal indicators are used for setting targets, monitoring compliance and analysing developments. They are created for different purposes and their definitions reflect the differences in questions they are intended to answer. It is important to make the distinction between permanent and temporary components of the deficit. Similarly, the impacts of discretionary fiscal policy and exogenous factors should be separated. This is demonstrated in Table 7.3.

Ideally one needs to have an estimate of $P_1 + P_2$ in order to have a good understanding of fiscal trends. The current framework in Europe is far from this benchmark.

Now we turn to a more detailed discussion of stock and flow indicators. We argue that one needs a comprehensive analysis of stock, flow and cash-flow data in order to achieve a more complete understanding of fiscal developments and to escape Goodhart's law.

4.1.1 Stock Indicators (Balance Sheets)

The most used (by far) stock indicator is the level of (gross) public debt. A conceptual problem, however, is that it represents only one component of the government's balance sheet. Net debt is a key indicator for assessing medium-term solvency, but longer-term debt trajectories cannot be determined independent of the desirable level of other items in the balance sheet of the sovereign (i.e. capital stock). Therefore, changes to the inter-temporal net worth of the public sector (Buiter, 1993) might play an important role in aligning theory and practice in fiscal policy (see also Chapters 10 and 11 in this volume).

However, the estimation of net worth raises a large number of measurement and methodological questions. First initiatives have appeared in this area (Ódor, 2011 and 2014c), but introduction across all the EU Member States is not possible for the time being. Nevertheless, many of these criteria can be considered when setting the medium-term objectives (MTOs). It is also very important to constantly analyse contingent liabilities (including potential bail-outs of financial institutions). For example, the European Commission (2014) estimates the value of potential bank bail-out costs to be covered by individual countries' taxpayers. FCs could be relied on extensively in this respect, particularly as their independence and country-specific knowledge may be coupled with an interest in designing meaningful indicators, since they are in charge of checking that the objectives are set and delivered.

4.1.2 Cash-Flow Indicators

As in the case of private companies, basic stock and flow indicators are not sufficient to gain a complete picture of financial health. Cash-flow financing requirements and financing conditions can be used as starting points for the identification and management of fiscal risks. Basic cash data, debt redemption profiles or interest expenditure sensitivities can reveal information not available through gross debt figures or structural budget balances. Ódor (2014c) includes regular analysis of these variables in the risk assessment framework of the Council for Budget Responsibility. The new European fiscal framework goes in this direction when asking Member States to provide detailed debt issuance calendars.

Recent research at the intersection of macroeconomics and finance has brought a lot of dynamism into the analysis of the term structure of interest rates. Following Diebold and Li (2006), it is relatively straightforward to link small-scale yield factors models with parsimonious macroeconomic models. These approaches might be also helpful in analysing the permanent and temporary components of interest expenditures consistent with the equilibrium path of macroeconomic variables. For example, independent fiscal institutions could develop these relatively simple tools. This is especially important in periods of 'abnormally' low market interest rates or in situations where creditors have agreed to grant grace periods or accepted terms and conditions much below the market level.

4.1.3 Headline Deficits

The System of National Accounts records stocks and flows within a consistent framework. Consequently, it defines a deficit (b_{ESA}) as equal to the change in the stock of financial assets and liabilities, excluding effects from revaluation. On the other hand, it includes all the temporary components shown in Table 7.3:

$$b_{ESA} = P_1 + P_2 + T_1 + T_2 + T_3 + T_4 + T_5 + T_6 + T_7$$

The first important step in designing better measures of the headline deficit would be to filter out creative accounting (T_6) in order to eliminate bad incentives in the conduct of fiscal policy.

There are two possible solutions to replace the purely statistical approach, which is ineffective against creative accounting. One would be the adoption of international public sector accounting standards (IPSAS Board). The other would be the use of practical analytical indicators calculated by independent fiscal institutions. In the following we focus on the second option by describing two potential approaches currently used in international practice.

The CBO's methodology defines creative accounting as 'operations without significant economic impact' (Congressional Budget Office, 2002). The practical approach to this is a 'standardisation' of the budget deficit. A Hungarian body of experts (KESZT, 2010) has proposed a similar solution. In essence, the proposal is to generate – with simple adjustments – a 'normalised' cash-based indicator that excludes any creative accounting. This involves expanding the coverage of public finances to include public companies (T_{6a}) and the coverage of investments to include PPP projects as if the private partners in those projects were involved merely as the financing partner (T_{6b}), and spreading over time the non-transfer type capital revenues from sources other than the disposal of fixed assets, e.g. over the whole concession period (T_{6c}). It should be noted here that Magyar Nemzeti Bank has published such an analytical indicator regularly since 1998 (P. Kiss, 2011). This approach (b_{ADJ1}) requires significantly fewer data and imposes fewer methodological requirements; therefore it would be more practical and more transparent for some of the countries.

$$b_{ADJ1} = P_1 + P_2 + T_1 + T_2 + T_3 + T_4 + T_5 + T_7$$

An alternative direction (b_{ADJ2}) would be to eliminate creative accounting by identifying it from the stock side. This approach coincides with the OECD definition of creative accounting, which states that these operations have no effect on the net worth of the government (Koen and Van den Noord, 2005). As seen above, the analysis of net worth has appeared among the proposals (Ódor, 2011) and in the practice of the Council for Budget Responsibility. It has the advantage of being comprehensive: besides eliminating distortions that result from creative accounting, it is also able to identify the effects of changes in parameters affecting long-term expenditures (T_5), such as increasing retirement age. However, it may also have disadvantages, specifically the aforementioned valuation problem and the absence of the definition of a desired level of financial and non-financial assets. For this reason, it is unclear how capital spending should relate to the depreciation of the stock of fixed assets (T_7).

$$b_{ADJ2} = P_1 + P_2 + T_1 + T_2 + T_3 + T_4 + T_7$$

It should be noted that while b_{ADJ1} is a cash-based concept, b_{ADJ2} rests on accrual data.

4.1.4 Structural and Underlying Deficit

Structural budget balances are designed to filter out cyclical fluctuations and one-off and temporary measures. In the EU approach (s_{COM}), the impacts of each temporary measure are eliminated one by one from the structural deficit on the basis of consensus between the particular Member State and the Commission, although there are practical guidelines to be followed (Larch and Turrini, 2009). One criterion is that of size: only measures impacting over 0.1 percent of GDP may be filtered out. Another criterion concerns the time horizon: measures may apply to one year or a few years at most. A third one requires that the focus should be placed on current items rather than capital items. Finally, for reasons of prudence, items that increase the deficit should be omitted from the filtering exercise, or else they will be classified as 'temporary' by the Member States. Clearly, these practical considerations are not suitable for filtering out self-reversing measures and do not fulfil the requirements of theoretically sound principles, and as a consequence confusion of individual (I) and one-off measures could not have been avoided. In principle, distortive effects of creative accounting could have been corrected, but the criteria applied were only partly successful, if at all; the methodology does not treat quasi-fiscal activities properly, even though experience suggests that their impacts can be 'outsourced' only temporarily. Some capital revenue, for example concession payments, was filtered out from the deficit, but this was not spread over the whole concession period (T_{6c}):

$$s_{COM} = P_1 + P_2 + T_2 + T_3 + T_4 + T_5 + T_{6a} + T_{6b} + T_7 + I$$

An even more serious problem is that the cyclical component (T_1) is estimated with a weak and unstable methodology (P. Kiss and Vadas, 2006; Marčanová and Ódor, 2014). Cyclical adjustment has an inherent problem in that potential GDP is an unobservable variable, and its estimate may be revised at any time, in light of new GDP figures, due to endpoint uncertainty. An IMF methodology represents one kind of solution: it takes into consideration the historical correlation between short-term GDP revisions and long-term revisions in potential output to reduce the estimation error in potential GDP (Tereanu et al., 2014). Another possible solution is to find a method that minimises the joint uncertainty coming from the choice of model and from parameter updates with new data. Cheremukhin's (2013) method in the United States is an example. Nevertheless, since the possibility of significant revisions cannot be fully excluded, this could be managed with an escape clause to the fiscal rule. The Council for Budget Responsibility currently uses the methodology developed by P. Kiss and Vadas (2006) to cyclically adjust budgetary figures. The aggregate output gap used is a result of an 'estimate combination' (Ódor and Jurašeková Kucserová, 2014) utilising various methods and information sets. Robustness is very important when the final estimate can have substantial welfare implications (by triggering correction mechanisms).

Another problem is the inability of the commonly agreed methodology to filter out all exogenous effects. This even exists with the ECB method (Bouthevillain et al., 2001), which takes composition effects into account. If tax changes are adjusted to changes in discretionary measures as well as to the cyclical component estimated with the ECB method, there remains an unexplained (windfall/shortfall) component (T_2) (Morris et al., 2009). Two proposals have been put forward to resolve this, but neither has been used in practice. One would have eliminated the 'dividend' effect of inflation, which may have contributed to the fact that tax revenues differed from the forecasts (Buti and Van den Noord, 2003). This was computed as the difference between the officially projected rate of inflation and the rate of inflation that is consistent with normal capacity utilisation. This, however, would not have eliminated the effects of the housing market bubble, nor would it have estimated the short-term impacts of surprise inflation (T_3). By contrast, the other proposal suggested adjusting the absorption cycle itself (T_5) (Lendvai et al., 2011).[11] It used a somewhat arbitrary definition of 'absorption gap', although in theory it interpreted potential absorption as an indicator that is in line with potential output and the external position consistent with the fundamentals (the balance of payments). The disadvantage of this approach is that it determined the absorption gap to be a deviation with respect to norms rather than deviations from trends, as a result of which the correction lacked a zero mean. Moreover, the norms are period- and country-specific (Langenus, 2013).

We have seen above how adjusted headline indicators are able to eliminate the effects of creative accounting (T_6). However, adjustments to other factors may be needed as well. Factors exogenous to fiscal policy include natural disasters and the budgetary effects of court rulings. A backward-looking moving average may be proposed here; it will filter out only genuinely significant impacts and will not deviate the structural deficit from the actual deficits across the period as a whole (Hoffmann and P. Kiss, 2010).

Finally, some aspects of interest expenditures can also be regarded as temporary (T_4), especially after large shocks or regime changes. In order to estimate the transitory component, one can use the methodology mentioned in Section 4.1.2. As a result, an alternative structural balance can be defined (s_{ALT})

$$s_{ALT} = P_1 + P_2 + T_5 + T_7$$

The long-term orientation of the fiscal policy (u_{ALT}) can use the b_{ADJ2} indicator as a starting point, since it adjusts the deficit with the future costs of ageing (T_5). However, long-term volatility cannot be properly filtered out by using any cyclical adjustment methods. Convergence periods, absorption and financial cycles should also be taken into account.

---

[11] 'Absorption cycle' refers to booms and busts in absorption (national income minus the balance of trade) leading to swings in current account deficits around a sustainable level.

Table 7.4: *Better flow indicators*

	Current methodology	Alternative1	Alternative2
Headline deficit	$b_{ESA} = P_1 + P_2 + T_1 + T_2$ $+ T_3 + T_4 + T_5 + T_6 + T_7$	$b_{ADJ_1} = b_{CASH} - T_6$	$b_{ADJ_1} = b_{ESA} - T_6 - T_5$
Structural deficit	$s_{COM} = P_1 + P_2 + T_2 + T_3 + T_4$ $+ T_5 + T_{6a} + T_{6b} + T_7 + I$	$s_{ALT} = P_1 + P_2$ $+ T_5 + T_7$	
Underlying deficit			$u_{ALT} = P_1 + P_2$

The last temporary item unfiltered so far is the difference between actual and 'desirable' levels of investment (T_7). It is a difficult exercise, but international comparisons, analysis of amortisation or calculation of marginal products of capital might shed some light on this issue. A less ambitious approach would be to take into account only changes to the 'usual' (average) level of maintenance costs in the budget.

$$u_{ALT} = P_1 + P_2$$

Our proposal to calculate better headline and structural budget balance indicators is presented in Table 7.4.

4.2 National Fiscal Rules

As we have seen in Section 2, there are no one-size-fits-all optimal fiscal rules. Sustainable debt trajectories depend on many country-specific factors, such as openness, distribution of shocks hitting the economy, investment needs, credibility of policy regimes, market expectations, etc. Moreover, the source of the deficit bias also varies from country to country, since voters' preferences, political institutions and fiscal policy track records are inherently country-specific. Therefore, home-grown, tailor-made fiscal rules are, in principle, better suited to fight the deficit bias and mimic optimal policy than one-size-fits-all approaches.

While the design of local fiscal frameworks crucially depends on country-specific circumstances, it might be useful to characterise the potential main building blocks. Here, we describe three important elements in more detail: long-term debt trajectories as anchors, medium-term objectives and expenditure limits as instruments (see also Kastrop et al. in Chapter 17).

4.2.1 Debt Trajectories as Long-Term Anchors

Optimal debt trajectories should be based on analytical work (with the active participation of fiscal councils), but they also have to take into account political economy considerations. It is far from easy to combine long-term stability (anchor) with medium-term flexibility to avoid sub-optimal fiscal policy.

When designing fiscal rules with debt trajectories, the following seems to be necessary:

- analysis of the whole inter-temporal balance sheet of the public sector (including contingent liabilities);[12]
- calculation of country-specific fiscal limits, sound debt levels, fiscal space;
- considerations regarding the investment needs of the country;
- definition of escape clauses and automatic correction mechanisms;
- high power of the law.

The basic function of debt trajectories is to have a clear and commonly agreed long-term anchor for fiscal policy, written preferably in a constitutional law. To avoid medium-term pro-cyclicality, well-defined escape clauses are necessary, but with the active participation of independent fiscal institutions to ensure counter-cyclicality also in good times.

4.2.2 Medium-Term Objectives

As we highlighted in Section 2, debt trajectories should *not* be used as medium-term operational targets for fiscal policy. Instead, they should be 'translated' into the level of the structural/underlying deficit. Fiscal councils have to check the extent to which these objectives are consistent with debt trajectories embedded in higher-level legislation.

However, while structural or underlying deficits are relatively easy to construct ex ante, their ex post evaluation is problematic. It can be done only over a longer time horizon (at least a full business cycle); drawing conclusions in real time is almost impossible. That is the reason why we recommend using expenditure limits as operational instruments. In good times they limit over-spending, while in bad times they allow deficits to increase.

---

[12] Buiter (2003) calls for a definition of sovereign (public sector), where the central bank is also included.

4.2.3 Expenditure Rules

It is important to stress at the outset that expenditure ceilings should take discretionary revenue measures (DRM) into account to avoid politicisation of the concept (they should not limit the size of the government). Obviously, an appropriate escape clause should be defined, again with a monitoring role of fiscal councils. To avoid unpleasant surprises, the best practice would be to also include non-allocated buffers in expenditure limits with a size of tenths of percentages of GDP. Expenditure rules should cover multiple years by regulating the annual rate of growth in primary expenditures (excluding interest expenditure) or setting a spending cap for each year (Ódor and P. Kiss, 2011). Multi-annual expenditure limits can be useful only if they are binding under normal conditions and are not renegotiated each year.

If applied in a credible framework, the expenditure rule may also eliminate the distortions originating from tax volatility, as it adjusts the expenditure growth rate not with the change of cyclically adjusted revenue, but with the estimated effects of discretionary tax measures. The FCs may play an especially important role here, as they have appropriate information at their disposal to perform this task. As mentioned before, estimating potential GDP will also remain an unresolvable problem in this framework, even though it is the benchmark for expenditure growth. Its minor revisions may be solved with a spending reserve and major revisions with an escape clause.[13] Further investigations will be necessary to decide whether the rule should apply to total primary expenditure or whether intra-governmental transfers to municipalities and investment should be handled separately.

As has been seen, investment represents a special category, since it is closely related to a specific stock indicator and can be directly compared to the rate of depreciation. Savings in investment may be feasible in the short term, but this will not be acceptable for the purposes of either the structural deficit as a medium-term target indicator or the expenditure rule as an instrument. If the objective is, for instance, to prevent the stock of fixed assets from decreasing, then a shortfall of investment spending compared to the level necessitated by depreciation

---

[13] Its size may be determined in a country-specific way, similarly to the estimated safety margin for the MTO.

may be interpreted as temporary, and cannot be used for increasing current expenditure.

The treatment of inflation may nevertheless pose a problem in the case of the expenditure rule. In principle, inflation volatility may affect the primary balance as well. An example is the so-called inflation dividend, which is the budget revenue impact of the 'inflation gap', defined as the difference between the actual and the ECB targets for the euro-area countries (Buti and Van den Noord, 2003). An expected rise in inflation would, in fact, have an impact on the primary balance only if the government were to decide that it would not compensate for the loss in real value of expenditures from its extra revenues (P. Kiss, 2007). This, however, is not permitted under the expenditure rule, since it automatically increases the expenditure budget with the expected rate of inflation. The case of surprise inflation is different. The question here is whether the expenditure reserves are sufficient to offset the effect of the higher inflation and whether its compensation is obligatory. Another question is whether expenditures should be reduced in the event of, and consistently with, lower inflation, and the reserves thus increased.

4.3 Local Fiscal Councils

Today it is recognised almost universally that independent central banks, simple rules and a high degree of transparency play essential roles in monetary policy. Despite the fact that the crisis has engendered new problems in monetary policy as well, Ódor (2014b) considers it important that synergies between independent institutions and simple rules should also have a stronger role within fiscal policy. However, as fiscal policy has greater distribution effects than monetary policy, the scope of the role assigned to the independent FCs should be carefully considered. For example, it is not recommended that an FC be authorised to legislate.

One of the most important lessons from recent years has been the recognition that FCs are able to mitigate several of the trade-offs created when fiscal rules are defined (more in Section 2). The FC's theoretical role is normally subdivided into three specific areas:

1. the interpretation and communication of fiscal policy;
2. the evaluation and monitoring of the fiscal rules;
3. an analytical (expert) role.

The model proposed in this article covers each of those three areas. The FC fills the first function by estimating public sector net worth and evaluating the escape clauses. It performs the second role as it carries out ex ante and ex post assessments of compliance with the proposed fiscal rules. (Here, the important role of the 'comply or explain' principle should be emphasised.) And it fulfils the third function when it calculates the structural or underlying balance, estimates the effects of discretionary measures, or, as the case may be, defines benchmark debt trajectories.

Moreover, in our view, local councils are also better suited to monitor fiscal rules at sub-national level, a question often neglected when discussing the European fiscal architecture. This is especially important in countries with a highly decentralised fiscal policy (i.e. Spain or Belgium).

5 European Fiscal Rules and Institutions

In the proposal presented in Section 3, the European level would have three responsibilities: monitoring compliance with minimum standards defined for local fiscal frameworks, checking compliance with European fiscal rules and supervising countries over pre-agreed limits.

5.1 Minimum Standards for Local Fiscal Frameworks

One important role of the centre in a decentralised framework of fiscal responsibility would be the supervision of national frameworks. Rather than analysing national budgets every year, this would involve the definition of minimum standards applicable to national fiscal frameworks. An EU-level process would be triggered only in the case of gross policy errors at the national level. Minimum standards should ensure that essential basic principles are respected when national fiscal frameworks are designed. They should include:

- rules for transparency and data availability;
- requirements for presenting indicators covering the whole public sector;
- requirements for smart fiscal rules;
- requirements for effective medium-term budgetary frameworks;
- descriptions of the basic remit of local IFIs, including long-term sustainability reports, access to data and adequacy of resources;
- guarantees of independence of IFIs and 'comply or explain' rules.

The current reforms of the EU fiscal framework (the "six-pack", "two-pack" and Fiscal Compact) were an important step forward as far as transparency at the national level is concerned. The Directive on requirements for budgetary frameworks of the Member States placed more emphasis on reporting tax expenditures, contingent liabilities, public corporations, capital injections and other extra-budgetary operations. The new framework also addresses the macroeconomic forecasts on which the budget figures are based. According to the "two-pack", independent fiscal institutions should produce or endorse these assumptions. All these aspects of transparency should be part of minimum standards. To increase transparency even further, this list might be appended with more ambitious requirements such as publicly available datasets, methodologies and in-year evaluation of budgetary trends.

In order to limit creative accounting and fiscal gimmickry, minimum standards should also require the construction of balance-sheet indicators. Even if it is not possible to estimate all the elements of a theoretically defined comprehensive balance sheet (Buiter, 1993) and there are also valuation problems, best available estimates should be assembled in every Member State. In this way, bad incentives in fiscal policymaking could be substantially reduced. It is important to note that while the level of net worth is subject to substantial uncertainty, its change is somewhat easier to estimate.

While the choice of national fiscal rules in our framework would be a sovereign decision, it might be useful to define some common principles. There are already two such guidelines in the euro area: the Council Directive on requirements for budgetary frameworks of the Member States (2011/85/EU) and the Common Principles on national fiscal correction mechanisms. These represent an excellent starting point for defining minimum standards in this area. We consider the following as the most important requirements:

- clearly defined numerical rules covering the whole general government sector;
- binding medium-term targets in order to anchor expectations;
- clarification of the role of municipalities and sub-national governments in fiscal planning;
- clearly defined escape clauses;
- ex ante definition of correction mechanisms;

- compliance checked by independent bodies;
- the 'comply or explain' principle.

The fourth important category to be embedded in minimum standards is the basic remit of local fiscal councils (the OECD Principles for Independent Fiscal Institutions serve as an excellent benchmark). Five important areas could be considered: (i) macroeconomic and fiscal forecasts, (ii) checking compliance with fiscal rules, (iii) ex ante monitoring of budgets, (iv) benchmarking fiscal policies upon generally agreed objectives and (v) costing of major discretionary measures (at least in the tax-benefit system).[14]

It is important to ensure de facto independence of local fiscal councils. There should be strict professional requirements for the management of IFIs and procedures guaranteeing adequate financing in the medium term.

5.2 European Fiscal Rules

In a decentralised framework, and depending on the strength of the resolution mechanisms and the future design of a fiscal union, the euro area needs two types of fiscal rules. The first set should tackle potential free-riding behaviour in a monetary union. The second set should ensure counter-cyclical policy at the aggregate level.

5.2.1 Avoiding Free-Riding in a Monetary Union

Recent changes to the European fiscal architecture have brought unnecessary complexity to the landscape of fiscal rules.[15] Instead of focusing on gross policy errors (the initial objective of the SGP), the community level is now involved in fine-tuning of national budgets. In our view, this is not a sustainable solution. Rather, our proposal is to have a clear division of accountabilities between the centre and national authorities. The European level should focus on deficit bias arising at the community level (free-riding), while the primary role of national fiscal frameworks should be to fight against the deficit bias at local level.

---

[14] Examples of the generally agreed objectives in point (iv) would include long-term sustainability, intergenerational equity, redistribution, etc.

[15] Here we focus mainly on free-riding and ignore other negative externalities of high debts in a monetary union, such as overburdening monetary policy.

The stronger and more efficient the resolution mechanisms are, the less need there will be to interfere with national budgets. A prime example is the United States, where the strong and credible no-bail-out rule eliminates free-riding, so there are no fiscal rules imposed on individual states from the federal level. However, it seems to us that this solution is not feasible in the medium run in Europe, so we see some role for SGP-type agreements with an aim to correct gross policy errors. On the other hand, the current overregulation in terms of fiscal rules is clearly sub-optimal.

What kind of indicators can signal free-riding and potential contagion? We see three possibilities. The first option is to use some kind of a stock variable. The current limit on nominal gross debt is a good starting point. One can imagine various improvements by adding more assets and liabilities in the definition, but only if clear valuation principles and independent reporting are available. Various forms of net debt can serve this purpose relatively well. The main problem, however, is in the definition of 'dangerous' limits. As we argued earlier, one-size-fits-all rules in a diverse monetary union are sub-optimal. On the other hand, the status quo, with a 60 percent (of GDP) ceiling for gross debt, shows that, from a political point of view, agreeing on one number is relatively straightforward.

The second possibility we see is using sustainability gaps as limits (see Green and Kotlikoff in Chapter 10). Since these are expressed in relative terms, the problem of different optimal thresholds for different countries is mitigated. On the other hand, calculating infinite-horizon fiscal gaps is a tricky exercise. Fortunately, there is an agreed methodology at the European level, and countries are routinely evaluated based on this indicator. The level of the fiscal gap is reflected in the calculation of the medium-term objective (MTO) with a 1/3 weight.

The third option is reliance on the market valuation of debt instruments. This is often expressed as a margin over safe bonds. What can be constituted as a safe asset? We see two options, depending on the future strength of a fiscal union. If there is a stronger central budget with a possibility to issue debt instruments, the price of these 'Eurobonds' should be set as the benchmark (e.g. at ten-year maturity). In the case that there is no political support to further fiscal integration, one can create a benchmark from best-performing Member States (as in case of the Maastricht criteria). For instance, the arithmetical average of the three lowest sovereign yields is one possibility. Once a benchmark is calculated, a definition of a 'dangerous' spread should be set. Here, one can rely on past episodes of fiscal stress. As Hatchondo et al. (2015) state, 'since levels of debt tolerance are difficult to identify and vary both across countries and over time, and political constraints often force common fiscal rule targets across countries, these findings indicate that sovereign-premium limits may be preferable to debt limits'. One should also note that the euro-area crisis was effectively calmed by the ECB's decision to limit yields on sovereign bonds. On the other hand, procedures for countries breaching the sovereign-premium limit should be carefully designed, including thorough analysis of the underlying factors.

To sum up, with strong resolution schemes in place, European fiscal rules targeting free-riding behaviour can be radically simplified. All that is needed is a limit over which community-level authorities step in to interfere with the national budgetary process. Below these thresholds, national parliaments are free to choose their fiscal targets; however, above those limits national sovereignty should be substantially curbed. The European-wide limit should be set on some form of net debt, fiscal gap or risk margin on debt instruments.

5.2.2 Avoiding Aggregate Pro-Cyclicality

Sustainability is only one of the goals of fiscal policy in a monetary union. Counter-cyclical fiscal policy is also needed. Currently, there is an ongoing debate about delegating more fiscal power to the centre. The size of the European budget is small (1 percent of GDP) and focuses mainly on structural issues and the common agricultural policy (CAP). The budget is always balanced. In order to allow for more risk-sharing between countries, one can imagine a stronger role for central redistribution of funds and use of European-level automatic stabilisers or discretionary fiscal policy. According to Allard et al. (2013), a central budget with a few percentage points of EU GDP would be capable of much better risk-sharing between countries. As Bordo and James show in Chapter 8, the size of the federal budget in the United States was relatively limited for more than a century (3 percent of GDP).

If a stronger fiscal union is created, there will be a straightforward option for counter-cyclical aggregate fiscal policy, either via automatic stabilisers or through discretionary policy action in crisis times. The central authority would be able to issue debt against its revenues in bad times and pay it back in good times. One positive side effect would be the creation of safe assets for the financial sector. In this case, one or two simple fiscal rules would be sufficient to ensure the sustainability and counter-cyclicality of the EU budget. Balanced budgets over the cycle or a low debt limit are the most obvious options to consider.

A much harder task is to ensure counter-cyclicality at the aggregate level if there is no appetite for more centralisation. In a decentralised framework, the centre cannot force individual Member States to tighten or loosen their budgets. However, minimum standards should require counter-cyclicality of fiscal rules at the local level (by design).[16] The rest will be up to the monetary policy of the ECB, and to some extent common investment vehicles could also be used for this purpose. In normal times these arrangements might be sufficient.

In crisis times, a more coordinated approach inside the European Semester could be considered (as envisaged in the mandate of the European Fiscal Board). The independent fiscal watchdog at the euro-area level (in cooperation with national IFIs) would be in charge of triggering such mechanisms by issuing non-binding advice for every country. The 'comply or explain' principle might play a useful role also in this case. A major disadvantage of this approach compared to counter-cyclical policy via a stronger EU budget is in its very problematic practical implementation (measuring output gaps in real-time and fiscal multipliers with high precision is almost impossible) and the political controversy it would cause (at odds with the sovereignty principle). Past experience also shows that peer pressure alone is not very efficient in delivering EU-wide objectives.

5.3 European Fiscal Institutions

The most important argument in favour of a euro-area fiscal watchdog (EFW) is that currently there is too much political pressure on the European Commission to interpret fiscal rules in a flexible manner. This was also recognised in the Five Presidents' Report. On the other hand, Member States require detailed ex ante rules for every step in a surveillance procedure. It seems to be an impossible task to take

---

[16] Wyplosz, in Chapter 6, argues that legacy debts should be reduced significantly in order to create room for counter-cyclical fiscal policy in the most indebted member states.

country specificities into account on the one hand, and follow exact quantitative (one-size-fits-all) rules on the other. This is exactly the flexibility vs. enforceability trade-off we described in Section 2. As we have shown, independent fiscal institutions can help to ease this problem.

5.3.1 Role for a Euro-Area Fiscal Watchdog

It is impossible to design a complete fiscal rulebook for Europe which takes into account every conceivable future situation. The current trend should be reversed. The euro area needs *fewer* and simpler rules, not more of them. As Allard et al. (2013) highlight, existing federations use just a couple of central fiscal rules. In comparison, more than 100 pages are needed to meaningfully describe all the fiscal rules in Europe (European Commission, 2013). In a decentralised framework with strong resolution mechanisms and a complete banking union, radical simplification seems to be achievable.

If rules are simple enough at the European level (Section 5.2), a professional EFW can play a useful complementary role. If political pressures are less present, checking compliance with ex ante well-defined minimum standards (Table 7.5) is a fairly simple exercise. While judgement and discretion cannot be avoided, comparison with international standards and best practices would be sufficient. It would be similar to the functioning of the ESCB, where comparisons and common standards keep the quality of individual central banks' outputs relatively high.

As far as compliance with European fiscal rules is concerned, the three options mentioned in Section 5.2 require somewhat different

Table 7.5: *Basic roles for the European fiscal watchdog*

Task	Potential tools
Compliance with minimum standards	Country-specific recommendations, European Court of Justice
Limiting free-riding	Activation of escape clauses, 'comply or explain', participation in ex ante veto over national budgets
Avoiding aggregate pro-cyclicality	Recommendations, 'comply or explain', deficit targets

strategies. If free-riding is judged solely based on debt limits, a more extensive set of escape clauses is needed and hence there would be more room for discretion. In the case of infinite-horizon fiscal gaps, the evaluation of compliance is much harder (high sensitivity of results to some variables). Our preferred option is to base European rules on risk margins, since in that case identification is straightforward and the link between the value of the risk margin and potential contagion via financial markets is the strongest.

As far as minimum standards are concerned, the EFW would carry out a yearly evaluation exercise. When deviations are observed, these should be reflected in country-specific recommendations via the European Semester. In the case of serious non-compliance, there would be a possibility to ask the European Court of Justice to judge the matter (as in the case of the Fiscal Compact).

One very important task to fulfil would be the activation of escape clauses. Apart from that, the EFW should be in a position to issue direct recommendations to national authorities breaching European rules. Here the 'comply or explain' principle would apply. In most serious cases, the EFW would have a tool to recommend veto power over national budget plans.

In order to ensure counter-cyclical fiscal policy at the aggregate level in crisis times, the EFW would set the 'desirable' aggregate fiscal position based on the euro-area output gap. Furthermore, according to some proposals it might translate it to the individual country level (not a trivial exercise from our point of view). Again, the 'comply or explain' principle would be the main tool. In the case of a stronger fiscal union and EU budget, the EFW would also check the compliance with fiscal rules designed to constrain debt at 'federal' level. A stronger alternative would be to have deficit targets in the EU budget set by the EFW.

5.3.2 Setting up an EFW

Based on international experience, a small council (3–5 members) with a medium-sized secretariat seems to be the preferable alternative. Having too many council members would make the decision-making process cumbersome and the body would quickly lose its credibility. The selection of council members is also very important. One should seek an optimal balance between academics and policymakers.

Hands-on experience with budgets seems to be necessary as well. Council members should be selected via standard, internationally advertised job offers. The shortlisted candidates should also take part in public hearings in the European Parliament. After selecting the management, the council should be free to hire and fire staff members. The number of staff would depend on the mandate (approximately 30–50 analysts).

A substantial amount of the independence of fiscal councils is related to the source of financing. Here, we see two alternatives: the budget of the European Central Bank or the European Parliament. In both cases, it is recommended to have a pre-agreed medium-term budget limit. The actual use of finances would be the responsibility of the EFW; however, the accountability principle would require the establishment of a supervisory authority (strictly on budgetary matters; either from the ECB or the EP). We do not think that financing an independent euro-area fiscal watchdog from the ECB would be a form of monetary financing. Since the success of monetary policy heavily depends on fiscal policy (threat of fiscal dominance), ensuring fiscal sustainability should be a primary concern for the ECB as well.

5.3.3 Relationship with Other Institutions

In order to avoid duplicities and blurred responsibilities, two important sets of relationships should be clarified, vis-à-vis the European Commission and local fiscal councils.

Since the EFW would function in this set-up as an independent analytical body only, major decision-making processes should remain in the hands of the European Commission. However, there would be no role for the EC with regard to those Member States operating without gross policy errors. When non-compliance with pre-agreed limits is identified by the EFW, the EC should step in and issue recommendations. If these were not followed in the draft budget, ex ante veto power would be exercised (based on the recommendation from the EFW). The EFW can also be part of the 'Troika' to judge the sustainability of debt after measures are implemented (DSA).

There are important arguments why cooperation between the EFW and local fiscal councils would be beneficial for all parties involved. On the one hand, the EFW might use the outputs of a local IFI when judging an individual country's circumstances and measures. In this way it is possible to abandon one-size-fits-all methodologies and to focus on best possible estimates/methodologies instead. In our view, it is much better to use discretion in methodology than in the interpretation of fiscal rules (as is the case now). There are at least three important areas in which local IFIs can have a significant comparative advantage: calculation of structural budget balances, costing discretionary measures and identifying ex ante risks in draft budgets (especially on the expenditure side, including creative accounting techniques).

Local fiscal councils might also benefit from the presence of a euro-area fiscal watchdog. By evaluating minimum standards, the EFW would be a guardian of their independence. Moreover, by collecting international best practices and research outputs, cooperation with the EFW might also increase the quality of outputs of local IFIs.

However, it should be noted that it is of utmost importance that the independence of all councils involved are respected. Local fiscal councils should not be viewed as 'branches' of the EFW, but rather as home-grown, local institutions responsible for monitoring local fiscal rules.

5.3.4 EFB vs. EFW

The European Commission decided to establish an independent advisory European Fiscal Board in October 2015. While the institutional set-up and mandate of the EFB has significant overlaps with our proposal for the EFW, important differences prevail.

Our proposal is consistent with a decentralised fiscal framework. However, the EFB was set up to operate in the current centralised framework, following the current practices of the Commission by sharing the same legal background. Part-time members of the board can definitely play an important advisory role, but real-time evaluation of European fiscal trends is unlikely given the limited resources. Institutionally, the EFB is not independent. It was set up by the EC, with financing also from the Commission. Moreover, all the five members of the board were nominated by the EC and its secretariat is filled with Commission employees.

6 Conclusions

The architecture of the euro area is unfinished business in many respects. As the Five Presidents' Report shows, more work should be done to strengthen the fiscal pillar. We share this view and argue in this chapter that systemic considerations should be clearly preferred over further incremental changes to the already complex system. Our proposal goes beyond the goal of addressing current shortcomings in the Stability and Growth Pact. In our opinion, building a lasting and effective fiscal architecture in a currency union is not possible without close links to theory, international best practices and compatibility with other pillars of the union. Current strong political opposition to a full-fledged United States of Europe indicates that the fundamental conflict between bail-outs and the sovereignty principle can be resolved only in a decentralised framework of fiscal responsibility.

We propose a hierarchical fiscal system, where local and European responsibilities are clearly separated. No direct intervention from the central level is needed if contagion risk is low or non-existent. Deficit bias at the local level would be mitigated by country-specific fiscal rules and institutions based on better fiscal indicators. In our model, the role of the centre would be substantially simplified: checking compliance with minimum standards defined for local fiscal frameworks, monitoring compliance with much simpler European fiscal rules and supervising countries with gross policy errors. Both at the national and European levels, complementarity and synergy between fiscal rules and independent fiscal institutions would be exploited as much as possible.

It should be noted that our proposal does not deal with legal issues, although they can play an essential role, as current experience shows. We also do not analyse the transition from one regime to the other. Some features of the proposal could be implemented immediately, while others would need changes to the SGP and the related documents.

Bibliography

Aiyagari, S. R. and McGrattan, E. R. (1998). The optimum quantity of debt. *Journal of Monetary Economics*, **42**(3), 447–69.

Allard, C., Brooks, P. K., Bluedorn, J. C., Bornhorst, F., Christopherson, K., Ohnsorge, F., Poghosian, T. and IMF Staff Team (2013). *Toward a Fiscal Union for the Euro Area*. IMF Staff Discussion Note No. 09/13.

Barro, R. (1979). On the determination of the public debt. *Journal of Political Economy*, **87**(5), 940–71.

Bi, H. and Leeper, E. M. (2013). *Analysing Fiscal Sustainability*. Working Papers, No. 13–27, Bank of Canada.

Blinder, A. (2004). *The Quiet Revolution*. New Haven and London: Yale University Press.

Bornhorst, F., Dobrescu, G., Fedelino, A., Gottschalk, J. and Nakata, T. (2011). When and how to adjust beyond the business cycle? A guide to structural fiscal balances. *Technical Notes and Manuals*, IMF, April 2011.

Boskin, M. J., Robinson, M. S. and Huber, A. M. (1987). *Government Saving, Capital Formation and Wealth in the United States: 1947–1985*. NBER Working Paper No. 2352, August 1987.

Brunnermeier, M. K. and Sannikov, Y. (2012). Redistributive monetary policy. Federal Reserve Bank of Kansas City, *Proceedings – Jackson Hole Symposium*, pp. 331–84.

Buiter, W. H. (1993). Measurement of the public sector deficit and its implication for policy evaluation and design. *IMF Staff Papers*, 30(2), 306–49.

(2003). Ten commandments for a fiscal rule in the E(M)U. *Oxford Review of Economic Policy*, 19(1), 84–99.

Bundesbank (2015). *Approaches to Strengthening the Regulatory Framework of European Monetary Union*. Monthly report, March.

Buti, M. and Van den Noord, P. (2003). *Discretionary Fiscal Policy and Elections: The Experience of the Early Years of EMU*. OECD Working Papers, No. 351.

Bouthevillain, C., Cour-Thimann, P., Van den Dool, G., Cos, P. H., Langenus, G., Mohr, M., Momigliano, S. and Tujula, M. (2001). *Cyclically Adjusted Budget Balances: An Alternative Approach*. European Central Bank Working Paper No. 77, September 2001.

Calmfors, L. and Wren-Lewis, S. (2011). *What Should Fiscal Councils Do?* Department of Economics Discussion Paper Series, Oxford University.

Congressional Budget Office (2002). *The Standardized Budget and Other Adjusted Budget Measures*. April 2002.

Cheremukhin, A. (2013). *Estimating the Output Gap in Real Time*. Dallas FED Staff Papers, No. 22, December.

Cimadomo, J. (2008). *Fiscal Policy in Real Time*. European Central Bank Working Paper No. 919, July 2008.

Corsetti, G., Feld, P. L., Lane, R. P., Reichlin, L., Rey, H., Vayanos, D. and Weder di Mauro, B. (2015). *A New Start for the Eurozone: Dealing with Debt – Monitoring the Eurozone 1*. London: Centre for Economic Policy Research, ebook.

Denis, C., McMorrow, K. and Roeger, W. (2002). *Production Function Approach to Calculating Potential Growth and Output Gaps – Estimates for the EU Member States and the US*. Economic Papers, No. 176, September.

Diamond, J. and Schiller, C. (1993). Government arrears in fiscal adjustment programs. In Blejer, M. and Cheasty, A., eds., *How to Measure the Fiscal Deficit*. Washington, DC: IMF, pp. 113–46.

Diebold, F. X. and Li, C. (2006). Forecasting the term structure of government bond yields. *Journal of Econometrics*, **130**(2), 337–64.

European Central Bank (2015). *The Creation of a European Fiscal Board*, www.ecb.europa.eu/pub/pdf/other/eb201507_focus05.en.pdf? 0efbdc35fade6cb8462c6cbf418e69c8

European Commission (2000). *Public Finances in EMU – 2000*. Report of the Directorate for Economic and Financial Affairs, May 2000.

(2008). "Public Finances in EMU – 2008". *Brussels, European Economy* 3, http://ec.europa.eu/economy_finance/publications/pages/publication12832_en.pdf

(2013). *Vade Mecum on the Stability and Growth Pact*. Occasional Papers, No. 151, May.

(2014). *Assessing Public Debt Sustainability in EU Member States: A Guide*. Occasional Paper No. 200, September.

(2015). *Making the Best Use of the Flexibility within Existing Rules of the Stability and Growth Pact*. COM(2015) 12.

European Commission, Economic and Financial Affairs (2014). *Cyclical Adjustment of Budget Balances*, http://ec.europa.eu/economy_finance/db_indicators/gen_gov_data/documents/2014/ccab_spring_en.pdf

(2014). *Independent Fiscal Institutions in the EU Member States*, http://ec.europa.eu/economy_finance/db_indicators/fiscal_governance/independent_institutions/index_en.htm

Forni, L. and Momigliano, S. (2005). Cyclical sensitivity of fiscal policies based on real-time data. *Applied Economics Quarterly*, **50**(3), 299–326.

Godin, A. and Kinsella, S. (2013). Production function at the business end: the case of the European fiscal compact. *Global and Local Economic Review*, **17**(1), 153–79.

Goodhart, C. A. E. (1975). Problems of monetary management: the UK experience. *Papers in Monetary Economics*, Reserve Bank of Australia, I.

Hatchondo, J. C., Martinez, L. and F. Roch (2015). *Fiscal Rules and the Sovereign Default Premium*. CAEPR Working Paper No. 010–2015.

Hoffmann, M. and P. Kiss, G. (2010). *From Those Lying Facts to the Underlying Deficit*, MNB Bulletin, December.

Juncker, J. C. in close cooperation with Tusk, D., Dijsselbloem, J., Draghi, M. and Schulz, M. (2015). *Completing Europe's Economic and Monetary Union*, https://ec.europa.eu/priorities/sites/beta-political/files/5-presidents-report_en.pdf

KESZT (2010). A Költségvetési Elszámolások Szakértői Testülete (KESZT) javaslatai a költségvetési elszámolási szabályok (The recommendations of the Expert Body on Budgetary Accounting (KESZT) for changing budgetary accounting rules), www.freepress.nuzoka.com/download/000/297/reszletes.pdf.

Kirsanova, T., Leith, C. and Wren-Lewis, S. (2007). *Optimal Debt Policy, and an Institutional Proposal to Help in Its Implementation*, Paper prepared for a workshop organised by the DG Ecofin of the European Commission on the role of national fiscal rules and institutions in shaping budgetary outcomes, Brussels, 24 November 2006.

Koen, V. and Van den Noord, P. (2005). *Fiscal Gimmickry in Europe: One-off Measures and Creative Accounting*. OECD Working Paper No. 417.

Kopits, G. and S. Symansky (1998). *Fiscal Policy Rules*. Occasional Paper No. 162, International Monetary Fund.

Kydland, F. E. and Prescott, E. (1977). Rules rather than discretion: the inconsistency of optimal plans. *Journal of Political Economy*, **85**, 473–90.

Langenus, G. (2013). *Comments on Session 4: Fiscal Tools to Control Macroeconomic Risks and Imbalances: Experiences and Prescriptions*, 15th Workshop on Public Finance, organised by Banca d'Italia in Perugia, 4–6 April 2013.

Larch, M. and Turrini, A. (2009). *The Cyclically-Adjusted Budget Balance in EU Fiscal Policy Making: A Love at First Sight Turned Into a Mature Relationship*. Economic Papers, No. 374, March.

Leeper, E. (2010). *Monetary Science, Fiscal Alchemy*. NBER Working Papers, No. 16510, National Bureau of Economic Research, Inc.

Lendvai, J., Moulin, L. and Turrini, A. (2011). *From CAB to CAAB? Correcting Indicators of Structural Fiscal Positions for Current Account Imbalances*. Economic Papers, No. 442, April 2011.

Marčanová, M. and Ódor, L. (2014). *The "True" Deficit*. Council for Budget Responsibility, Working Paper No. 3/2014.

Morris, R., Braz, C. R., De Castro, F., Jonk, S., Kremer, J., Linehan, S., Marino, M. R., Schalck, C. and Tkacevs, O. (2009). *Explaining Government Revenue Windfalls and Shortfalls: An Analysis for Selected EU Countries*. ECB Working Papers, No. 1114, November.

Ódor, L. (2011). *Is It Worth Considering Net Worth? Fiscal Policy Frameworks for Central Europe*. Public Finance Workshop, Perugia, 31 March–2 April.

    (2014a). *The Good, the Bad and the Ugly – Lessons from the First Phase of Implementation of the New European Fiscal Framework*. Council for Budget Responsibility, Discussion Paper No. 3/2014.

    (2014b). *Another Quiet Revolution? Future Role of Independent Fiscal Institutions in Europe*. Council for Budget Responsibility, Discussion Paper No. 5/2014.

    (2014c). *Fiscal Risk Assessment at the CBR: A Conceptual Framework Council for Budget Responsibility*. Discussion Paper No. 1/2014.

Ódor, L. and J. Jurašeková Kucserová (2014). *Finding Yeti: More Robust Estimates of Output Gap in Slovakia*. Working Paper No. 1/2014, National Bank of Slovakia.

Ódor, L. and P. Kiss, G. (2011). *The Exception Proves the Rule? Fiscal Rules in the Visegrád Countries.* MNB Bulletin, June 2011.

(2014). Back to basics – good fiscal indicators for good fiscal institutions! *Financial and Economic Review*, **13**(4), 125–51.

(2015). *Gordian Knot or Ariadne's Ball of Thread?* Public Finance Workshop, Perugia, 2015, www.bancaditalia.it/pubblicazioni/altri-atti-con vegni/2015-beyond-austerity/Odor_Kiss.pdf.

P. Kiss, G. (2007). *Pain or Gain? Short-Term Budgetary Effects of Surprise Inflation – the Case of Hungary.* MNB Occasional Papers, No. 61.

(2011). *Moving Target Indication – Fiscal Indicators Employed by the Magyar Nemzeti Bank.* MNB Occasional Papers, No. 92.

P. Kiss, G. and Vadas, G. (2006). *Filling the Gap – Measurement of the Cyclical Effect on Budgets.* 7th Workshop on Public Finance, organised by Banca d'Italia in Perugia, 30 March–1 April.

Portes, J. and Wren-Lewis, S. (2014). *Issues in the Design of Fiscal Policy Rules.* Department of Economics Discussion Paper No. 704, University of Oxford.

Röhrs, S. and Winter, C. (2014). Reducing government debt in the presence of inequality. In Society for Economic Dynamics, 2014 Meeting Papers, No. 176.

Stella, P. (1993). Toward defining and measuring the fiscal impact of public enterprises. In M. Blejer and A. Cheasty, eds., *How to Measure the Fiscal Deficit*, Washington: International Monetary Fund, pp. 207–35.

Svensson, L. E. O. (2003). What is wrong with Taylor rules? Using judgment in monetary policy through targeting rules. *Journal of Economic Literature*, **41**(2), 426–77.

Tereanu, E., Tuladhar, A. and Alejandro, S. (2014). *Structural Balance Targeting and Output Gap Uncertainty.* IMF Working Papers, No. 14/107, June.

Vogel, E. (2014). *Optimal Level of Government Debt: Matching Wealth Inequality and the Fiscal Sector.* Working Paper No. 1665/ April 2014, European Central Bank.

Wren-Lewis, S. (2003). Changing the rules: why we should not accede to EMU's current fiscal regime. *New Economy*, **10**(2), 73–8.

Wyplosz, C. (2002). Fiscal policy: institutions versus rules. CEPR Discussion Paper No. 3238, Centre for Economic Policy Research.

(2013). *Europe's Quest for Fiscal Discipline.* European Economy – Economic Papers, No. 498, Directorate General Economic and Monetary Affairs (DG ECFIN), European Commission.

8 | Partial Fiscalization: Some Historical Lessons on Europe's Unfinished Business

MICHAEL BORDO AND HAROLD JAMES

1 Introduction

The British referendum on EU membership, combined with the discussion of a partial Greek exit from the euro, has raised in a suddenly acute form the question of the relationship between the EU and the eurozone. The new, acute crisis demands some innovative thinking to preserve – and extend – the central benefits of European integration, while thinking about additional areas that demand a cooperative rather than a confrontational solution.

The Maastricht Treaty basically assumes that all EU member countries will satisfy the membership criteria for the currency union and stipulates that they are then obliged to join. The opt-outs only relate to the United Kingdom and Denmark. The United Kingdom has been in a paradoxical position of championing the rather abstract case (with which probably a majority of economists agree) that a currency union requires a greater measure of fiscal integration than the EU or the eurozone currently possesses – US policymakers made very similar points – while, on the other hand, making it clear that it did not want to participate in that greater fiscal integration. In January 2012 (along with the Czech Republic) it voted not to accept the fiscal compact (Treaty on Stability, Coordination and Governance), on "legal grounds."

Brexit may thus in theory make a move to greater fiscal integration easier. At the time of the Maastricht discussions, many European policymakers, such as the influential Commission President Jacques Delors, simply assumed that the EU budget's share would rise to about 3 percent of GDP (by coincidence, that was about the share in peacetime of the US federal budget during the nineteenth century). Instead, the figure remained stuck at just over 1 percent (it has actually declined slightly since the 1990s). Denmark on its own is unlikely to want to remain an outlier, especially since the management of the currency since the global financial crisis of 2008 has been rather precarious.

There is a similarly strong case why Sweden might want to end its anomalous "out" position – for the same kind of reasons why Norway and Switzerland are finding it very hard to live with an independent currency and to devise an appropriate set of monetary and exchange rate policies. But, at the same time, the contemporary Greek experience should be a warning against thinking that there might be a new political equilibrium that shifts toward an obvious acceptance of greater fiscal federalism.

At the start of this decade, we identified three key problems facing the euro after ten years (Bordo and James, 2010): (a) the lack of a fiscal union (the architects of the euro had assumed that the European budget would rise as a share of GDP from about 1 percent to at least around 3 percent; (b) the absence of a banking union (the architects of the euro believed that some common banking supervision was needed to meet the financial stability requirements that followed from an integrated capital market with large cross-border financial institutions); (c) slow economic growth (the architects of the euro had had a naïve belief that market integration would set off a surge of economic growth).

We believe that we were prescient, in that all three elements contributed to the eurozone debt crisis, although at the time our views were greeted with considerable skepticism. Our analysis, however, raises the questions of how the euro area can get around these obstacles, and where the eurozone project will go in the aftermath of the debt crisis. Can lessons from history help? It is by no means clear that fiscal union on its own solves adjustment problems: For instance, the existence of an integrated monetary and fiscal regime in Italy after Italian unification did not promote equal growth throughout the new state, and for most of the next 150 years (with the exception of the 1950s and 1960s, and partially also of the 2000s) regional differences in wealth and income increased rather than decreased (Toniolo, 2013). So there is a legitimate question about the circumstances in which a commitment to greater fiscal integration has a growth-enhancing effect that builds rather than erodes integration.

In this paper, after looking at the historical record of fiscalization (which is mixed), we highlight a series of measures which amount to partial fiscalizations, some of which are currently being discussed. These fiscalizations are all understandable as a variety of insurance mechanisms, in which different risks for different participants are covered. Each taken by itself is likely to produce substantial objections from those who fear that somebody else's risks are being covered at their expense. The answer to such objections may be to think not of partial but of comprehensive reform packages.

2 The Historical Analogy between the EU and the United States

The creation of a monetary and fiscal union in the United States is often presented as the outstanding model for Europe (Sargent, 2011). Successive presidents of the ECB seem to endorse this advice. Accepting the Charlemagne Prize in Aachen, Jean-Claude Trichet (2011) said: "In a long term historical perspective, Europe – which has invented the concept and the word of democracy – is called to complete the design of what it already calls a 'Union'." His successor, Mario Draghi (2012), has been even more dramatic, demanding

the collective commitment of all governments to reform the governance of the euro area. This means completing economic and monetary union along four key pillars: (i) a financial union with a single supervisor at its heart, to re-unify the banking system; (ii) a fiscal union with enforceable rules to restore fiscal capacity; (iii) an economic union that fosters sustained growth and employment; and (iv) a political union, where the exercise of shared sovereignty is rooted in political legitimacy.

This advice seems appallingly radical to many, since almost every politician denies that there is any real possibility of creating a European state, and almost every citizen recoils at the prospect.

A great deal of the discussion of how European integration might operate – both in the past and in the future – has been driven by thoughts of how precedents on the other side of the Atlantic have worked. At the highest political level, such reflection concerns the constitution, where the US precedent has driven European leaders to contemplate (up to now rather unproductively) the possibility of realizing a European constitution. At the time of independence in 1776, the thirteen former colonies were widely thought of as independent and sovereign entities, and Americans did not want the United States simply to be another conventional state like France or Britain. The constitution was only drawn up in 1787, and really only completed in 1791 with the Bill of Rights. Modern European attempts to follow the eighteenth-century US constitutional path were suspended after the proposed constitutional treaty was rejected in referenda in France and the Netherlands in the summer of 2005. That was not, however, the end of the discussion. In the wake of the financial crisis, some – including Chancellor Merkel – suggested that in the long run, a new constitutional settlement is the only acceptable way to define the claims and obligations of member states. This argumentation is convincing. If the path laid out in this section is taken, in which monetary union is followed by the development of some measure of fiscal federalism, a constitutional solution laying out clearly the extent and limits of states' commitments would be an essential condition.

The aftermath of the recent financial crisis has driven another sort of European reflection on how a workable federal fiscal system arose in the United States: That came, again with a considerable lag after the Declaration of Independence, in 1790. Fiscal federalism actually took much longer to work its nation-building magic. It was not until the middle of the nineteenth century that "the United States is" became the accepted grammatical form (rather than "the United States are"). The federal state expanded beyond a rather modest peacetime share of 3 percent of GDP only in the middle of the twentieth century. Strikingly, that ratio of 3 percent was the size of the EU budget envisaged by European Commission President Jacques Delors at the time of the Maastricht Treaty, when the actual size of the budget was 1 percent, where it still lies (James, 2012); it might be noted, though, that in the nineteenth century, the public sector as a whole was of course much smaller than in the late twentieth or twenty-first centuries.

Those who (like Jacques Delors) would like to see Europe moving in a federal direction see the long (and often tumultuous) development of the United States as a precedent. But is it a helpful example or rather a grim warning? There are many episodes in the creation of a modern federal US state that hold analogies with the painful and politically contentious road to European integration.

In 1790, Alexander Hamilton created a currency union based on specie convertibility, created a fiscal union based on the consolidation of state debt into US bonds serviced by excise taxes collected by the federal government, and created a prototype central bank, the First Bank of the United States, that closely resembled the Bank of England (ten years later Napoleon similarly imitated the British example when he established the Banque de France).

Hamilton's eventually successful proposal for the assumption of state debt arising out of the War of Independence was certainly a decisive initial step in the creation of a real Union – and it accompanied the constitutionalization of the American experiment. But assumption did not produce a responsible system of state finance, and within the subsequent half-century there were numerous state-level defaults and a debate about new debt assumptions and/or new ways of blocking state indebtedness. The irresponsibility of states also gravely damaged the reputation of the federal government and made external borrowing prohibitively expensive.

Hamilton argued – against James Madison and Thomas Jefferson – that the war debt accumulated by the states in the War of Independence should be assumed by the federation. There were two sides to his case, one practical, the other philosophical. Initially the most appealing argument was that a federal takeover of war-related state debt was an exercise in providing greater security and thus reducing interest rates – from the 6 percent at which the states funded their debt to 4 percent. Hamilton emphasized the importance of a commitment to sound finance as a prerequisite to public economy: "When the credit of a country is in any degree questionable, it never fails to give an extravagant premium upon all the loans it has occasion to make" (Hamilton, 1790). Reduced borrowing costs and a lower drain on resources through the need to service debt would allow the state governments to "furnish new resources," to uphold public order and to protect the security of the union against foreign attacks. There would be concrete benefits, accruing "to every member of the community." Land values would increase from their postwar lows. The historical case looks like an attractive precedent for the Europeans of today, where proponents need to sell a solution as holding out gains for both debtors and creditors.

Hamilton also insisted on a stronger reason for following good principles than merely the pursuit of expediency. There existed, he stated, "an intimate connection between public virtue and public happiness." That virtue was considered in honoring commitments. Extended in a political body, it would build solidarity. Those principles made the fiscal union what he called "the powerful cement of our union" (Hamilton, 1790). The promise to honor obligations had already been clearly set out during the War of Independence as a foundation of a new American identity: In Congress's address to the states of April 18, 1781, it had stated that "A bankrupt, faithless Republic would be a novelty in the political world, and appear, among reputable nations, like a common prostitute among chaste and reputable matrons" (United States. Continental Congress, 1823, p. 357).

The state debt (estimated at $25m) at this time was smaller than the federal debt (also incurred almost entirely as a result of the war), with $11.7m of foreign-owned federal debt (on which default was at that time unthinkable) and $40.4m of domestically owned debt (for comparison, a modern estimate of GDP in 1790 is $158m: Mitchell, 1983).

The condition for success in the American case was that the Union raised its own revenue, initially mostly through new excises and federally administered customs houses that generated an amount equivalent to 10 percent of imports or around 2 percent of GDP (Perkins, 1994; Bordo and Végh, 2002). The logic of a need for specific revenue applies also in modern Europe, where the sources of funding for bank rescues or for a recapitalization fund should be clearly spelled out. This consideration has produced an initiative to impose a small levy or tax on financial transactions. In the longer horizon, the analogy with Hamilton's system would require a more extensively reformed fiscal system that might include a common administration of customs or of value added tax (with the additional benefit in both cases of eliminating a great deal of cross-border fraud).

Would an expansion of European federal fiscal capacity represent a massive transfer of power from member states to EU authorities? It is significant that the 1790 assumption of state debt occurred in the context of an understanding that federal powers should be few and limited. In Federalist paper 46, James Madison had made clear that central authority should be carefully circumscribed, and had concluded that "the powers proposed to be lodged in the federal government are as little formidable to those reserved to the individual States, as they are indispensably necessary to accomplish the purposes of the Union" (Madison, 1788).

There were two problems with the Hamilton proposals, both of which gave rise to immediate and violent political controversy. First, state debt had been extensively traded on a secondary market at a deep discount. Relatively few of the original purchasers, who had acted out of patriotism, still held the debt; instead, the debt had been bought up by speculators – financial intermediaries – who hoped that something like the Hamilton scheme might be realized. A settlement that imposed no haircut and treated the debt at nominal value would in effect be a reward for speculation. James Madison disliked the idea of what would be in effect a subsidy for northern financiers. But Hamilton argued that any discrimination between creditors based on the moment at which they had bought debt would be a breach of contract.

Second, some states had already made great efforts to pay down their wartime debt and would not benefit from the federal bailout. Virginia and Maryland in particular had largely paid off their debt, and the Virginian representatives in Congress consequently pressed for a precise calculation of the level of outstanding state debt (Mitchell, 1962, p. 70). Madison in particular pressed for compensation for states that had already discharged their debt. Politically, a straightforward debt assumption was unworkable.

Initially, assumption was rejected by Congress, with potentially catastrophic consequences. Thomas Jefferson, who was opposed to the Hamilton proposal, wrote to his fellow Virginian James Monroe about the possibility of failure as Congress was split: "Unless they can be reconciled by some compromise, there will be no funding bill agreed to, our credit will burst and vanish, and the States separate" (Mitchell, 1962, p. 81).

Eventually the Union was bought, at a price, and there was a compromise. Since the financial arrangement favored the northern states, the south and its landed elite needed a symbolic but also practical form of compensation. There were financial clauses that limited the liability of the southern states. The exposure to the common liability of Virginia, the most politically powerful state in the Union, was limited with a ceiling. Only this inducement moved Madison to drop his opposition and agree to assumption. But there was also a symbolic and political concession. The historic compromise also led to the capital being moved to the new site of Washington, on the border of Virginia and Maryland, rather than staying in Philadelphia. Some states, such as Georgia, opted out of the assumption.

The US experiment in federalized finance was not immediately successful from the point of view of driving economic growth in the young republic. Two important parts of Hamilton's financial architecture were not realized, or only realized imperfectly. First, he proposed a model of joint stock banking on a national scale, which ran into immediate opposition, and which curiously was much more influential in Canada than in the United States. Second, the proposal for a

Figure 8.1: Yield of ten-year US federal bonds, 1790–1914
Source: Global Financial Data

national central bank, based on the model of the Bank of England, was eventually blocked by political opposition. The charter of the First Bank of the United States was allowed to lapse in 1811; then, one generation later, the charter of the Second Bank of the United States was successfully opposed by Andrew Jackson after 1832.

The fiscal side did not bring long-lasting relief, either. Yields on US government debt fell immediately, showing the new confidence produced by the debt arrangement. By the beginning of 1792, they had fallen to 4.6 percent, but after that the cost of borrowing rose sharply again (Figure 8.1).

Neither did the Hamiltonian scheme of federal finance guarantee a peaceful commonwealth in the longer term. The immediate consequence of the new excise was a revolt in Pennsylvania (the Whiskey Rebellion of 1794 and, four years later, the Fries Rebellion). States were in the longer run divided over the shape of tariffs, which southern states saw as disadvantageous to them since they relied on cotton exports and the import of British manufactures. In fact, the fiscal union proved to be explosive rather than cementing, because by the 1830s the tariff dispute had become a constitutional struggle in which southern states claimed that the constitution was merely a treaty between states and that the south could resist federal laws that it deemed to be unconstitutional. The fiscal mechanism designed to allow servicing of a common liability raises inherently explosive distributional issues.

A fiscal mechanism's distributional consequences between states would also be a potentially divisive mechanism in contemporary Europe. The most popular suggestions in discussion today are a general financial transactions tax, which would fall heavily on major financial centers (and for this reason is resolutely blocked by the United Kingdom), or a European payroll tax, which would raise problems of different implementation and coverage in the various European states.

The fiscal union was also dangerous because it allowed states to recommence their borrowing. As with the dispute over the tariff, this problem became very apparent in the 1830s. As international capital markets developed in the first decades of the nineteenth century, American states used their new-found reputation to borrow on a large scale, and quite soon ruined their creditor status. The states borrowed to finance infrastructure projects, canals, and railroads. It was assumed that these improvements would lead to economic growth and would generate the tax revenues to service and amortize the debt (Wallis, Sylla and Grinath, 2004). It also may have been assumed that the federal government would bail out the states in the event of a default, as they did after the Revolution (Sargent, 2014).

At first, the North American states looked to British banks and investors as more appealing debtors than the newly independent South American republics, which just wanted to borrow in order to buy weapons. Agents of the American states swarmed over Europe in order to sell their debt. A key part of the argument for the foreign investors was that the American state borrowing was sanctioned and approved by the US government. A characteristic statement was that of the *London Morning Chronicle* in 1839 and 1840 that "persons desirous of investing money in any of the principal American securities will find on inquiry that we have never over-rated the honor and good faith which have always been shown by the United States government." Even "the newest and smallest states" were satisfactory for Washington (McGrane, 1933, p. 677).

In addition, the states' difficulties became acute because of banking issues. In the long-standing conflict about the Hamiltonian concept,

President Andrew Jackson launched a Bank War, in the course of which he vetoed the rechartering of the Second Bank of the United States, but also encouraged other banks to seek charters. The result was successful in achieving Jackson's immediate objective, in that it decentralized credit. But then the new banks immediately started to expand their lending, above all to the states and the political elites that had facilitated their establishment. The upshot was an orgy of bank credit to individual states, often structured in a complex way so that debt securities could be repackaged and sold on foreign markets.

When in 1841 the first state, Mississippi, reneged on its debt, disingenuously claiming that its law allowing state bond issuance had been unconstitutional, the major British bank involved in the issuance of American state debt in London, Barings, counseled against a panic response: "Is it wise for this single instance of dishonesty in a remote and unimportant state to endeavor to brand the whole of the United States as wanting in good faith? We think not" (McGrane, 1933, p. 683). But the foreign creditors also tried to push the US government into a new federal assumption of state debts, and the case was actively pushed by the Whigs (while Jacksonian Democrats saw the campaign as a conspiracy to get the American tax-payer to bail out individual states but, above all, the foreign creditors).

The practice of default spread in 1841–1842, with Florida, Michigan, Pennsylvania, Maryland, Indiana, Illinois, Arkansas, and Louisiana all announcing their unwillingness or inability to pay. At this time, a whole palate of responses was contemplated, ranging from defaulters' expulsion from the Union to the repetition of the Hamiltonian assumption. The situation was so precarious because of the international consequences: not just exclusion from the European capital markets needed to finance American development but also a real security threat. The federal government could not even sell bonds yielding 6 percent, while – as the US Treasury bitterly complained – 'nations with not a tithe of our resources, and with large public debts, have been able to effect loans at three percent per annum" (Bolles, 1885, p. 580). But the consequences of default also included the risk of international conflict, as Britain was widely thought to be willing to use naval and military power to enforce credit claims. As a response to the danger of military conflict with the principal creditor country, Congressman John Quincy Adams even introduced a proposal that the repudiation of any debt to foreigners be made "a violation of the

Constitution of the United States" and that any state involved in a war as a consequence of repudiation should cease to be a state of the Union (Scott, 1893, pp. 248–9).

Inevitably, the Hamiltonian option was floated again. In 1843, a congressional committee recommended a new assumption, on the grounds that the debts incurred had been mostly for infrastructure that was "calculated to strengthen the bonds of union, multiply the avenues of commerce, and augment the defenses from foreign aggression" (Scott, 1893, p. 251). But this proposal was rejected, primarily on moral hazard grounds: If states were freed of present debt, they would only be likely to get into debt very quickly again. The measure also would have imposed a clear and heavy cost on the non-indebted states. The outcome of the 1840s debate was laissez-faire: no federal intervention to punish defaulters, but also no bailout.

The fiscal space of the US federal government in the nineteenth century was very small, about 1–3 percent of GDP in peacetime – in other words, somewhere between the actual size of the EU budget today and the size envisaged by the visionaries of the late 1980s. The big innovation that led to the creation of a real fiscal union occurred in the aftermath of the Great Depression, but there were two parts of this story: First, an expansion of general fiscal activity, aimed at public goods that pulled the union together (water and dam projects and federal highways); second, a social security system that collected payments from individuals and created benefits for individuals, but where the resulting surpluses or deficits in strongly expanding or contracting states amounted to a fiscal stabilizer.

The Great Depression also produced the beginning of a banking union, with the Federal Deposit Insurance Corporation (FDIC) in 1934. Like the European banking union, it started in a modest and perhaps even disappointing way. In 1934, a relatively small share of deposits was protected by the FDIC, which had a limit of $10,000 per account. The Federal Reserve's Gold Settlement account, which provided reserves to deficit Reserve banks on the collateral of gold certificates, also protected member banks from asymmetric shocks to the extent that they had access to the Reserve Bank's discount window. This differed between Reserve Bank districts (Richardson and Troost, 2009). This arrangement financed inter-regional payments imbalances (Rockoff, 2004). In many ways it was a predecessor to the use of the Target II facility of the ECB (Bordo, 2014).

It was the legacy of the 1930s more than that of Alexander Hamilton that made the late twentieth-century United States more resilient, and in the aftermath of the housing bust and the global financial crisis, US states did not go through the severe traumas suffered by the EU members.

The implication taken from the US story was that Europe needed to imitate the American example. Europeans had already done that by creating integrated goods, capital, and labor markets, as well as in establishing the ECB and the euro. But they did not go all the way and create a fiscal union at the same time, because of fears over loss of sovereignty and one-way fiscal transfers (Art. 122 of the Maastricht Treaty). They also believed that following the discipline of the no-bailout clause (Art. 125 of the Maastricht Treaty) and market reforms would be enough. This omission came to haunt the framers during the 2007–2008 global financial crisis, when many countries ran large fiscal deficits which threatened their fiscal stability. The crisis came to fruition in 2010 after Greece revealed that its deficits and debt were much higher than originally stated. Despite the evidence that a fiscal union like that of the United States would have prevented much of the eurozone's distress, going very far in this direction is vehemently opposed by most member states, because it would involve a perceived surrender of sovereignty and because it would lead to permanent one-way fiscal transfers. With that said, we ask whether there are alternative paths to greater integration and stability.

3 Improvements in Fiscal/Governance Integration

There are many reforms – some of them being actively debated at present – that would make the EU work more effectively without requiring full fiscal integration. But at the heart of Europe's contemporary paradox is that it either needs more moves to establish a wider field of common areas of activity (implicitly or explicitly mechanisms for sharing public goods subject to certain conditions, in a manner analogous to insurance) or alternatively greater monetary flexibility.

3.1 Currency Innovation: The Meaning of Currency Union

The debate about currencies within the EU should include a greater willingness to think about alternatives. In 1992–1993, the EMS crisis almost destroyed the path to the euro, but the crisis was resolved by instituting greater flexibility through wider (15 percent) margins in the exchange rate bands. The modern equivalent to the band widening of 1993 would be keeping the euro for all members of the eurozone but also allowing some of them (in principle, all of them) to issue – if they needed it – national currencies. The countries that did that would find that their new currencies immediately traded at what would probably be a heavy discount. California adopted a similar approach at the height of the recent financial crisis, issuing IOUs when faced with the impossibility of access to funding. The success of stabilization efforts could then be read off from the price of the new currency. If the objectives were met, and fiscal stabilization occurred and growth resumed, the discount would disappear. In the same way, after 1993, in a good policy setting, the French franc initially diverged from its old level in the band but then converged back within the band. Such a course would not require the redenomination of bank assets or liabilities, and hence would not be subject to the multiple legal challenges that a more radical alternative would encounter. There would also be the possibility that the convergence did not occur. The two parallel currencies could then coexist for a very much longer time period. This is not a novel thought. One of the possibilities raised in the discussions on monetary union in the early 1990s was that there might be a common currency but not necessarily a single currency.

3.2 Minimizing Financial Vulnerability: Banking Union

The debate on banking union also needs to be recast. What is now termed a banking union – that is, common European regulation with some fiscal capacity for resolution in the case of failed banks – is a very belated but necessary completion of the monetary union. Even this step is only partial, and has excited a great deal of opposition from Germans who do not want to bail out Southern European banks. Thus, while there is European supervision, the resolution process is predominantly national. Critics have correctly identified the problem – that some sort of permanent fiscal mechanism is required in order to pay for the bailouts, and thus in fact implies a move to a real political union which regularly redistributes resources. But there is also a legitimate worry that the creation of an extended banking union would involve very large insurance commitments, which Europe's citizens are not necessarily already willing to take on. The current discussion – as set out for instance in the very helpful Four Presidents' Report of December 2012, and extended in June 2015 in the Five Presidents' Report – is set out very much in terms of an "insurance-type mechanism," but it is important to remember that insurance mechanisms are not suited to make long-term one-way transfers; rather, they have to represent a genuine sharing of risk (i.e. of conditions which, at the time of making the insurance contract, cannot be anticipated).

In a recent extended analysis of political economy trilemmas (Bordo and James, 2015), financial vulnerability provided the key linkage by which instability is transferred from the primarily technical domain of currency arrangements to the large, fundamentally political problems of democracy and the international order. Taking the fangs out of a dangerous financial system – for instance, moving along the path from a bank-based system to a greater orientation toward capital markets – is thus an important element in rectifying flaws. The critical issue is to find innovative institutional paths to ensure better financing of small and medium-sized enterprises – which are traditionally at the core of economic dynamism in Mediterranean countries, but also in Germany and in Baltic Europe.

Securitization – which is often, especially in the United States, presented as the villain of the 2008 crisis, because of the centrality of problems in the securitized mortgage market – may be the most hopeful solution. Combining and repackaging small enterprise loans – from different regions and from different kinds of economic activity – is an obvious step toward risk diversification. Of course, there can still be shocks that produce coordinated and generalized slowdowns, and that require macroeconomic responses. One of the problems of bank lending in many countries (in the United States but also in Europe) is that it has been increasingly directed toward property lending, and just served in consequence to drive up real estate prices, leading to a boom and eventual bust. It may also have been a source of increased wealth inequality in modern societies.

3.3 Becoming More American: The Capital Markets Union

Consequently, part of the transformation of Europe's economy should lie in a reduction of banks' role in financing business activity and increased access to capital markets, especially for small and medium-sized enterprises (SMEs). This has become part of the official European agenda for the capital markets union, sketched out in the green paper on the subject. Creating a genuine capital union will also require steps to ensure compatibility of products across national frontiers and provisions for greater transparency, including credit registries and credit ratings for SMEs. To date, small enterprise credit rating has been handled in a very different manner in different countries: in some cases, private providers take up the task; in others, central banks still play a major role. The Banque de France created its major credit register in 1946; Germany has a tradition of private associations, such as Creditreform, which was established in 1879 and has since internationalized its activity. There is also a requirement for convergence on legal procedures, notably bankruptcy: The idea of integrating capital markets thus requires really quite considerable steps in political and legal integration.

3.4 Shifting the Tax Base: Tax Union

Fourth, the debate about fiscal consolidation is in need of rethinking. One of the great controversies of the nineteenth-century United States revolved around Henry George's proposal for a land tax. In *Progress and Poverty* (1873), he explained that a great part of the gains from productivity were captured through rents of monopolists or land-owners. Competition policy – the limiting of monopoly power – has from the beginning been a core task of the European Economic Community/European Union. But the land-owning issue has not been the subject of thought or debate – until very recently.

The recent story of Europe has been a process of learning lessons about the appropriate character of the tax base. In the 1970s, with increased capital integration, many European countries discovered that they could not tax capital highly, as large companies would otherwise move their operations. Capital was too mobile, and smaller European countries in particular adopted low rates of corporate taxation which contributed to stronger and more dynamic economic performance. With increased mobility of people, the same limits are being reached for personal tax – as President Hollande found when he introduced a tax on the super-rich (over 1 million euros), which brought unexpectedly little revenue, and which he was obliged to scrap. The threat of the tax just precipitated the movement of high-earning French residents to other countries with lower tax environments. One solution – a common European tax rate – is hardly likely to lead to greater dynamism, and is incompatible with the principle of national democratic choice.

Taxing land more effectively has many obvious advantages. It is not easy to conceal land, and it is impossible to move it. Taxing under-utilized land (empty, neglected, and decaying houses) imposes a cost on the owners that they will try to avoid by selling their property to others who can make better use of it. Taxing urban land is an effective counter to the substantial rents that are created by planning restrictions in densely populated urban settings. Like any new tax, however, such an innovation would produce a politically powerful coalition of those property-holders fearing the costs of the scheme; it could only be real-ized with a broad coalition of other tax-payers (those on wages and salaries) who would look favorably on the consequences of tax relief.

3.5 Transfers without Politics: Welfare Union

Problems of transfers in a large unit are at the heart of the political process of building federations or federalism. The better way of discuss-ing transfers within a large and diverse political order is to think of them as individualized or personalized. In particular, a Europe-wide social security system would not only be a logical completion of the labor mobility requirements of the single European market, but would also indicate that the insurance principle is not just one which it is appropri-ate to apply to financial institutions. It would provide an important buffer in that booming areas would pay in more, and shrinking areas would draw out more – without these payments going through govern-ment bodies and appearing as transfers from north to south – whether in a country such as Italy or in the whole of the European area. Defusing the political problem requires less statehood, rather than necessarily requiring the erection of a European super-state. But, like the problem of designing better bank insurance, it also depends on making more adaptable labor markets so that the threat of large-scale unemployment swamping and destroying the insurance system is minimized.

3.6 Common Projects: Energy Union

The argument in favor of a European energy union – a genuine common energy market with common regulation – may even be stronger than the case that was successfully made in the 1980s and 1990s for a monetary union. Security concerns and worries about the extent of risk generate considerable pressure to implement dirigiste measures that may be counter-productive and harmful.

A coordinated approach to energy needs to address equally obvious problems that are often not recognized explicitly. Just as in the case of the European Union's overall "growth, stability, and cohesion" object-ives, the 1996 Internal Energy Market directive's goals of (a) secure, (b) environmentally compatible, and (c) competitive energy sources are in conflict with each other: Renewable energy may be environmentally sound, but is neither secure nor inexpensive; foreign supplies of oil and gas may be inexpensive at a point in time, but are subject to geopolit-ical risks. Policy choices need to provide a framework to guide the myriad choices of market participants, producers, and consumers, through a pricing mechanism that is accepted as fair and transparent. An economic argument can be made for security-oriented policies, such as renewable energy subsidies, that increase both current costs and self-sufficiency.

The difficulty in formulating a forward-looking energy policy arises from the issues in comparing different types of risk and drawing appropriate policy lessons. There are at least four different perceptions of risk – in CO_2 emissions and global warming, in nuclear energy, in security dependence on imported gas and oil, and in the vulnerability of grid delivery systems to periodic breakdown – and while all are clearly present, they tend to be seen in quite contrasting ways in different European countries, and consequently produce varied and mutually incompatible responses from national political authorities. Since public debate is often driven by single headlines, a nuclear accident such as Fukushima produces a greater sense of danger than the vaguer (but more certain) long-term threat of climate change. The risk of system breakdown only enters the political debate after a concrete instance. Politics thus tends to respond too late to threats.

A fundamental philosophical division is discernible in energy discus-sions, around the choice between long-term planning or fixing of prices in order to generate certainty about future signals on the one hand, and a response to short-term and noisy market signals on the other. The debate is most pronounced in the case of the two environmentally and politically most sensitive issues: gas pricing and nuclear energy. The greater the diversity of supply, and the more market alternatives exist (including different forms of energy), the more resilient the energy economy becomes against unanticipated events, including attempts to blackmail energy users. In other words, diversity of supply limits the power of the resource providers. Marketization can thus also provide a substantial impetus to improve political conditions in other parts of the world and reduce the monopoly rents that corrupt politicians extract in resource-rich countries.

There is a geographical divide in Europe between those countries that rely on spot markets and those that use long-term oil-indexed contracts to purchase and receive their natural gas supplies. Northwest Europe has spot markets, with LNG import facilities and hubs. Oil-indexed contract markets predominate in Central, Eastern, and Southern European countries, where only one or two suppliers provide gas to domestic markets and there is little gas-supply diversification. The geopolitical strategy of President Putin is based around a pipeline view of the world, rather than a LNG vision. The Ukraine–Russia crisis of 2014 may have resulted in a greater awareness of the security threat, an enhanced willingness to construct LNG facilities, and an expansion of the market principle of spot pricing as a result, rather than long-term indexation to other energy products.

Flexibilization is an important principle in wholesale markets, but it can also play a major part in promoting domestic energy efficiency. From a consumer point of view, a move to flexible pricing may be an increasingly attractive way of steering demand away from peak times, at which the production costs/marginal costs are high. Reducing extreme peaks of demand (and consequently of pricing) in an energy supply network that is pushing against capacity restraints requires a better linkage of supply systems that are still not fully integrated. The same is true for the potentially even bigger problem of smoothing peaks in green energy supply. If the national smoothing capacity becomes exhausted thanks to the closure of conventional power plants, as is regularly the case in Germany, there is a case for selling the excess electricity to other national energy markets and using their smoothing capacity.

Further improving the linkage requires a substantial investment in transmission systems. One response to the financial and debt crisis, which is also a crisis of European growth, is to demand higher levels of investment – both public and private – in Europe. The problem is that in the past, much public sector investment has been misdirected as a result of political bargaining processes. However, private investment has also been misdirected (above all in large construction booms). Investment in energy networks may offer appropriate incentives to private producers looking at innovative ways of producing new clean energy sources. Since the search for funding also coincides with a widespread sentiment that Europe should investigate large infrastructure investment projects, it may be conceivable to fund the new energy transmission channels, both electricity gridlines and gas pipelines, with public or a mixture of public and private funding. A security levy on energy supply might be an appropriate way of ensuring the fiscal sustainability of such investment.

3.7 Common Projects: People Union

One of the gravest security crises currently facing Europe is the outcome of the disintegration of neighboring regions: North Africa and the Middle East in the wake of the so-called Arab Spring and, more recently, the crisis in eastern Ukraine. Europe is confronting a humanitarian crisis as a consequence of the flight of refugees from civil war in Libya and Syria. ISIS is indeed trying to use the threat of further expulsions as a weapon against Europe.

The countries that are today on the front line of Europe's humanitarian struggle are, by chance, also the worst affected by the financial crisis: Greece, Italy, Spain. Responding to the distress of refugees is a European task, and the financial consequences of the refugee crisis cannot be left to the crisis-struck states, in which there is inevitably a political feeling that resources devoted to accommodating and even potentially integrating refugee populations can only come at the expense of citizens. Any adequate solution to the refugee challenge involves including or integrating them in a constructive way, at least for some time, into the host societies. It would necessarily involve substantial financial injections from Europe as a whole into the countries at the forefront of the refugee crisis. That could also be a source of new dynamism, and an answer to the problem of European ageing and decline.

At the same time, ensuring that people can move with dignity also requires the elaboration of a precise political program to stabilize the neighborhood of Europe. Europe cannot be an island in a sea of a humanitarian disaster. It needs to act effectively to end the chaos that is driving despairing people by the millions to a European safe haven.

3.8 Common Projects: Military Union

At the outset of the 1990s, in the face of the new security challenge created by the collapse of communism and the Soviet Union, many European leaders emphasized that they needed to find a way to permanently secure European peace. Even at the time, it was not quite obvious that a currency union was the best way to do this (it was rather a question of the central bankers having plans for a currency union in their drawers). Would not a common European army be a better course? In the nineteenth century, many people made the argument that universal military service was a central part of the project of nation-building. Jean-Claude Juncker recently triggered a storm of controversy when he made this suggestion, and critics emphasized the difficulty of expecting military sacrifice without much greater deepening of political community. On the other hand, common defense organization and procurement would certainly involve major savings, could generate a more effective capacity to project power, and might well indeed make a wider group of young people realize that they are Europeans.

3.9 Common Projects: Youth Union

But a similar argument could be made for encouraging other sorts of organized movement, such as a common social year (in a different country), but also cross-national apprenticeship schemes: indeed, this is an area that some German companies have looked at, with considerable success. Fostering youth mobility is probably a better way of moving to an integration of outlooks and attitudes, but also a dissemination of best practice across Europe. Countries with high levels of out-migration at some point in the past century (Ireland and Poland are the most striking examples) found that the return of young migrants who had increased their skill levels represented a major source of dynamism. In that sense, if the current crisis is promoting higher migration, it should not simply be a source of worry: in the long run, it may have a strengthening effect.

3.10 Thinking Globally: Global Union

The management of cross-national problems and the containment of nationalistic quarrels certainly require technical fixes. But more is also needed. The fatal loops that tie badly managed currencies to the destruction of the international economic and political order inevitably conjure up memories of the disasters of the 1930s, the Great Depression and the drive to war. Currency wars are now making a reappearance. Some observers believe that the rise in the exchange rate risks choking off an incipient strong US recovery. Unusually, Federal Reserve officials now sound worried about the currency. The unpleasantness created by the strong dollar additionally interacts with the vulnerabilities of the political system. The fierce debates about dispute settlement in the Trans-Pacific Partnership as well as in the Transatlantic Trade and Investment Partnership play into the hands of trade skeptics. We should remember that there can be global disaster, as well as merely European disaster.

Finding a politically legitimate mechanism for solving the problem of international adjustment was the unsolved problem of the twentieth century. In Europe and elsewhere it generated enormous conflict. There is an urgent need for ways of constructing currency stability that go beyond the narrow framework suggested by the optimum currency area (OCA) literature. Fixing this issue is a European but also a global agenda for the twenty-first century.

4 Potential Obstacles to Fiscalization

All of the areas of potential cooperation raise classic issues associated with the provision of public goods: the (many) gainers can often not see precisely how they will gain, while the (relatively few) well-organized losers know quite well what their losses would be and have powerful lobby activities dedicated to stopping the realization of the public good. The obstacles to change are multiple:

1. There is a great deal of worry associated with the prospect of temporary or longer-term replacement of the euro by any new secondary currency (as evidenced by the debate in Greece on possible "Grexit"). The possibility of an easy road to exit might set the stage for speculative attacks against other countries' bonds, so that the whole union would become more precarious.

2. Countries with small public sector banks that are heavily engaged in regional economies fear the consequences of a Europeanization of banking that might divert resources from those (politically important) regions. In the United States, a similar fear of banks acting as a drain on local economies was the source of early

opposition to Hamilton's idea of a national bank, and to the First and Second Banks of the United States.

3. The promotion of a better functioning capital market raises fears in the banking sector as a whole about a possible loss of privileges.

4. A Europeanization of some part of tax revenue raises fears in national parliaments, whose competences would be somewhat eroded by such a move.

5. A welfare union arouses fears of abuse and long-term one-way transfers: The United States dealt with this fear in the 1930s by constructing a social security system that made benefits largely dependent on the amount of in-payments.

6. National energy providers with partial or complete monopolies would see their positions eroded by a more complete energy union.

7. The perception that refugees are being settled locally raises numerous fears and concerns, and has already led to a sharp rise in hostility to the EU in many countries.

8. The prospect of a military union worries the providers of goods and services for national armies, even when there are clear efficiency gains to be realized.

9. Actions that try to engage young people in the labor force more actively encounter opposition from older workers, who fear that employment protection is being eroded.

10. Trade openness on a global level worries those who fear that they will have to compete with cheaply produced imported goods and services.

Realizing any of the potential gains from any of these partial fiscalizations thus requires some mechanism for negotiation in which potential losers can be either compensated by other insurance measures, or convinced that there are substantial potential gains that also make them beneficiaries.

5 The Trade Analogy

We suggest that the analogy from trade negotiations may be a useful way to think of solving the political side of some of Europe's problems. Trade negotiations were a largely successful exercise in the second half of the twentieth century, in which large welfare gains were realized in many areas. How did they work?

First, the breakthrough occurred in the 1930s, with the conceptual realization that negotiating fora that were too open to the assertion of particular interests stood in the way of the realization of generally beneficial outcomes. A landmark study (Schattschneider, 1935) examined the contribution of Congress to an unintended snowballing effect, in which thousands of extra positions were added to the Smoot–Hawley tariff, which was thus transformed from its original intention of providing some agricultural support into an extensive and complex industrial tariff. After the 1934 Reciprocal Trade Agreement Act, and after the Second World War, the authority to act in trade negotiations in the United States was delegated to the President (Irwin, 1998). In an analogous manner, European countries delegated trade authority at an early stage to a supranational institution in the European Economic Community. In all the controversies over European policy after 2010, no one has ever cast doubt on the effectiveness of the Commission as the voice of Europe in trade. Trade is an instance in which framing in terms of an over-arching interest (Olson, 1971) is required in order to realize potential gains.

Second, though, the appeal to an over-arching interest may not be enough. In practice, trade is often accompanied by auxiliary measures (Germans speak of "flankierende Massnahmen"). In trade negotiations going back to the nineteenth century, domestic policy packages were put together in which all players gain something but some lose more than others, so a compensation mechanism has to be created to make the deal go through. The Bismarckian welfare state is an early example, and can be understood as a compensation for the grain tariff, which raised food prices and thus hit workers who wanted some measure that would protect them. The same logic was at the heart of many compromises made on a national level in the aftermath of the Great Depression, both during the New Deal, where trade negotiations conducted through the RTA were compensated by deals that favored unions in the Wagner Act, but also especially in some smaller European states (the Swedish and Swiss examples are often discussed as examples: Gourevitch, 1984). After the Second World War, the major surges of trade liberalization also occurred at the same time as social reform packages: The Kennedy Round came at the same time as the Great Society.

The lesson from trade reform is in part a story of political framing, and in part a story of compensatory deals.

6 Conclusion

The possibility exists of a large variety of overall gains through partial fiscalization that would make the eurozone operate more effectively, and which would in practice produce a logic that would increase cross-border ties and thus represent a "strong cement of the union." In this chapter, we first identified greater currency flexibility as a potential way to ease the problem of whether reforms need to be accomplished at the EU or the eurozone level. We then briefly discussed banking union; capital markets union; a Europe-wide tax, possibly on property; a Europeanization of social security; an energy union; a Europe-wide response to the refugee crisis; common defense; a common approach to youth employment; and acting on a broader international stage to realize a global compact. Some of these proposals are already being partly implemented; others are the subject of intensive debate.

The obstacles to their realization lie in political rather than economic logic. All measures represent some variant of a common insurance, but taken individually, they insure only particular sectors. That is why they are more likely to be realized as a grand compact rather than as a series of incremental measures, each produced in response to a particular crisis (an approach that has been characteristic of the European process so far, and was identified by Jean Monnet as working to integration through crises). Their realization also requires a negotiation method that identifies over-arching or general interests rather than sectional preferences.

Bibliography

Bolles, Albert A. (1885). *The Financial History of the United States from 1789 to 1860*. New York: Appleton.

Bordo, Michael D. (2014). *Tales from the Bretton Woods*. NBER Working Paper No. 20270.

Bordo, Michael D. and Végh, Carlos A. (2002). What if Alexander Hamilton had been Argentinean? A comparison of the early monetary experiences of Argentina and the United States. *Journal of Monetary Economics*, **49**, 459–94.

Bordo, Michael D. and James, Harold (2010) A long-term perspective on the euro. In M. Buti, S. Deroose, V. Gaspar and J. Nogueria Martins, eds., *The Euro, The First Decade*. Cambridge: Cambridge University Press, pp. 37–71.

(2015). *Capital Flows and Domestic and International Order: Trilemmas from Macroeconomics to Political Economy and International Relations*. NBER Working Paper No. 21017.

Draghi, Mario (2012). *A European Strategy for Growth and Integration with Solidarity*. Conference organized by the Directorate General of the Treasury, Ministry of Economy and Finance – Ministry for Foreign Trade, Paris, November 30, 2012.

Friedman, Milton and Schwartz, Anna J. (1963). *A Monetary History of the United States: 1867–1960*. Princeton: Princeton University Press.

Goldenweiser, E. A. (1925). *Federal Reserve System in Operation*. New York: McGraw-Hill.

Gourevitch, Peter (1984). Breaking with orthodoxy: the politics of economic policy response to the depression of the 1930s. *International Organization*, **38**, 95–130.

Hamilton, Alexander (1790). *Report on Public Credit, January 9*, http://press-pubs.uchicago.edu/founders/documents/a1_8_2s5.html

Irwin, Douglas (1998). From Smoot–Hawley to reciprocal trade agreement: changing the course of US trade policy in the 1930s. In Michael D. Bordo, Claudia Goldin and Eugene White, eds., *The Defining Moment: The Great Depression and the American Economy in the Twentieth Century*. Chicago: University of Chicago Press, pp. 325–52.

James, Harold (2012). *Making the European Monetary Union*. Cambridge: Harvard University Press.

Kim, Namsuk and Wallis, John Joseph (2005). The market for American state government bonds in Britain and the United States, 1830–1843. *Economic History Review*, 736–64.

Madison, James (1788). (Publius). *The Influence of the State and Federal Governments Compared*. Federalist Paper No. 46.

McGrane, Reginald (1933). Some aspects of American state debts in the forties. *American Historical Review*, **38**, 673–86.

Meltzer, Allan H. (2003). *A History of the Federal Reserve I: 1913–1951*. Chicago: University of Chicago Press.

Mitchell, Brian (1983). *International Historical Statistics: The Americas and Australasia*. London: Macmillan.

Mitchell, Broadus (1962). *Hamilton: The National Adventure, 1788–1804*. New York: Macmillan.

Olson, Mancur (1971). *The Logic of Collective Action: Public Goods and the Theory of Groups*. Cambridge: Harvard University Press.

Perkins, E. J. (1994). *American Public Finance and Financial Services 1700–1815*. Columbus: Ohio State University Press.

Richardson, Gary and Troost, William (2009). Monetary intervention mitigated banking panics during the Great Depression: quasi experimental evidence from a Federal Reserve district border, 1929–1933. *Journal of Political Economy*, **1170**(6), 1031–73.

Rockoff, Hugh (2004). Deflation, silent runs and bank holidays in the Great Contraction. In Richard S. Burdekin and Pierre Siklos, eds., *Deflation: Current and Historical Perspectives*. New York: Cambridge University Press, pp. 31–60.

Sargent, Thomas J. (2011) *United States Then, Europe Now*. Nobel Prize speech, www.nobelprize.org/nobel_prizes/economics/laureates/2011/sargent-lecture.html

Schattschneider, E. E. (1935). *Politics, Pressures and the Tariff: A Study of Free Private Enterprise in Pressure Politics, as Shown in the 1929–1930 Revision of the Tariff*. New York: Prentice-Hall.

Scott, William A. (1893). *The Repudiation of State Debts*. New York: Crowell.

Toniolo, G., ed. (2013). *The Oxford Handbook of the Italian Economy since Unification*. New York: Oxford University Press.

Trichet, Jean-Claude (2011). *Building Europe, Building Institutions*. Speech on receiving the Karlspreis 2011 in Aachen, June 2, 2011.

United States. Continental Congress (1823). *Journals of the American Congress from 1774 to 1788*. Washington: Way & Gordon.

Wallis, John Joseph, Sylla, Richard and Grinath III, Arthur (2004). *Sovereign Debt and Repudiation: The Emerging Market Debt Crisis in the US States, 1839–1843*. NBER Working Paper No. 10753.

9 | *Managing the Euro-Area Debt Crisis*

GEORGE KOPITS

1 Introduction

The crisis that befell the euro area (EA) within the European Union (EU) in 2008 will provide rich material for policy analysis for many years to come. This crisis was a unique multidimensional experience affecting a group of sovereign countries bound together by a common currency, with wide-ranging implications and lessons for macroeconomic policies. Views on it cover a spectrum, from those that identify weaknesses in the financial system as the root cause of the crisis to those that attribute the crisis primarily to deficiencies in fiscal policy. Without attempting to settle the question of whether the euro crisis was mostly financial or fiscal, there clearly has been far more progress in correcting financial weaknesses than fiscal vulnerabilities in the wake of the crisis. Indeed, important lessons have yet to be learned and applied to the fiscal framework in paving the way to a viable currency union. Therefore, the present chapter is devoted mainly to major fiscal issues before and during the euro debt crisis, but takes fully into account relevant monetary and financial aspects as well.

On the basis of these considerations, answers are sought to the following set of questions. Was the crisis due to flaws in the design or the enforcement of the EU policy framework? Were the policy stances of vulnerable EA member governments sufficiently prudent prior to the crisis? What were financial markets' attitudes toward these countries? Were the EU institutions and the International Monetary Fund (IMF) fulfilling their surveillance role as regards EA government policies? Was the financing provided to crisis-hit countries adequate? Were the scale and composition of the macroeconomic adjustments in

Comments by Michael Bordo, John Fitzgerald, Ľudovít Ódor, Sergio Rebelo, Manuel Sebastiao, Ling Hui Tan, and Charles Wyplosz are gratefully acknowledged. Franz Loyola provided computational assistance.
The author alone bears responsibility for all views expressed.

these countries appropriate? What were some key structural measures envisaged and their pace of implementation? Last, what major lessons can be derived for future crisis prevention and management, on the road to closer unification?

The next two sections of the chapter focus on the pre-crisis period, from the inception of the Economic and Monetary Union (EMU) until the outbreak of the crisis. They trace the behavior of vulnerable EA member governments in the light of the EU policy framework and the oversight by supranational institutions. The three sections that follow examine the stabilization programs for Greece, Ireland, and Portugal under three pillars that typically constitute the remedy for a debt crisis: Adequacy of financing the imbalance, including through possible debt restructuring; size and quality of macroeconomic adjustment; and macro-critical structural reform. The final section explores lessons from the crisis, including the scope and outlook for establishing a fiscal and a banking union and supporting measures toward the prevention and remedy of future crises in the EA.

2 Well-Designed, Poorly Enforced Framework

Fiscal discipline and labor market flexibility, along with effective banking supervision, are necessary conditions for a well-functioning common currency area.[1] The basis for this view is that, as shock absorbers, these conditions should help offset asymmetric shocks among member countries, unless of course their economic structure is very similar and they are fully integrated into an optimal currency area – which rules out such shocks. In a monetary union, given inexorably fixed exchange rates among participating countries, disequilibria among member economies must be corrected primarily through fiscal and wage adjustments.

In a federal system, within a common currency area, subnational governments retain a greater or lesser degree of fiscal autonomy, albeit qualified by intergovernmental relations that may include various tax-transfer arrangements. To prevent free-rider behavior,

---

[1] As illustrated by recent developments in the EA, the fiscal condition becomes imperative when lacking an area-wide banking union consisting of effective banking supervision and uniform deposit insurance across member countries. Otherwise, impaired banks are eventually to be recapitalized directly or indirectly by the host government, compounding its debt burden.

subnational governments are typically subject to (often self-imposed) fiscal rules that limit budget deficits and indebtedness. Alternatively, or in addition to such rules, a critical determinant of subnational fiscal behavior is a statutory or implicit no-bailout provision – often overlooked by analysts who argue that a full-fledged fiscal union is indispensable for an optimum currency area.[2] Under the no-bailout provision, subnational governments are exposed directly to market pressures, reflected in a risk premium on their bonds relative to bonds issued by the national government (as, e.g., in Canada, the United States, and Switzerland). By contrast, if subnational governments are shielded by an explicit or implicit nationally guaranteed bailout, the risk premium charged in financial markets vanishes, as the interest yield on subnational bonds moves perfectly in tandem with the yield on corresponding national bonds (e.g., in Germany and Spain).

In a monetary union among sovereign countries, the need for fiscal discipline is underscored by nearly full fiscal autonomy and limited wage flexibility.[3] This, in fact, is the case with the EA, which is composed of a diverse group of economies, some of them with a history of fiscal profligacy and burdened by high public indebtedness. In this regard, the crisis of the early 1990s, which led to the near-collapse of the Exchange Rate Mechanism (ERM) of the European Monetary System (EMS), could be viewed as a dress rehearsal of the dynamics of such a crisis, if it were to occur in the EA. The ERM, initially with a narrow band around a central exchange rate, was to serve as an anchor for macroeconomic policies in the participating member states. However, because differences in fiscal and wage behavior, compounded by divergent cyclical positions, were inconsistent with the anchor, the ERM became untenable and the narrow band had to be abandoned. In most member countries facing a current account deficit, the bulk of the correction took place through exchange

---

[2] For instance, in a review of the conditions for an optimal currency area and of the empirical evidence on whether the EA meets these conditions, Pasimeni (2014) omits any mention of the no-bailout provision. Herein, the term 'bailout' denotes financial assistance without conditionality – unlike the widespread use of the term in the media in reference to any financial rescue operation, regardless of conditionality.

[3] Chari and Kehoe (2009) formalize, in theoretical terms, the need for fiscal rules in a monetary union.

rate depreciation, rather than adjustment in nominal wages or fiscal policy. A major lesson from the ERM crisis was that, without the exchange rate adjustment, and given the downward stickiness of nominal wages for regaining external competitiveness, the adjustment burden would have to fall largely on fiscal policy, as experienced during the recent euro crisis.

Against this backdrop, the EMU, established by the Treaty of Maastricht, envisaged a fiscal framework requiring member countries to abide by a set of fiscal rules, while subject to an explicit no-bailout clause – much like in a federal system, as outlined above. Member countries were bound by a deficit ceiling equivalent to 3 percent of GDP and an objective to keep, or reduce, the public debt to a ceiling of 60 percent of GDP, subject to financial sanctions upon noncompliance – waived if noncompliance was due to a sharp contraction in output. Besides these limits, member governments were required to maintain the budget in balance or surplus over the medium term. The no-bailout clause was intended to gain support for the monetary union in the large hard-currency member countries and to ensure that all member countries be exposed to market discipline as an additional safeguard.

Under the EMU, details of the fiscal framework were spelled out in the Stability and Growth Pact (SGP), which took effect from 1997 and was revised in 2005, 2011, and 2013, following episodes which revealed its principal shortcoming – namely, weak enforcement. The original design of the fiscal rules, enshrined in the Pact, was deemed as meeting seven out of the eight criteria of good practice: definition, transparency, adequacy, consistency, simplicity, flexibility, and efficiency.[4] The enforceability criterion, however, eventually proved to be the Pact's Achilles' heel.[5] Indeed, the SGP was undermined by

---

[4] This was the assessment of the EU fiscal rules by Buti and Giudice (2002) on the basis of the criteria formulated in Kopits and Symansky (1998). These criteria, discussed and endorsed by the IMF Executive Board, became widely accepted as the guide to good practice for fiscal rules.

[5] While agreeing on the weakness in enforcement, Wyplosz (Chapter 6) is critical of the numerical rules under the Pact for being arbitrary and not sufficiently flexible. Although arbitrary (as are all numerical fiscal rules, by their very nature), EU rules are internally consistent. Also, contrary to this criticism, the binding deficit ceiling has been flexible in accommodating significant output shocks. Given their tax progressivity, for most EU members, a 1 percent decline in GDP leads to roughly half a percent of GDP deterioration in the budget balance. Thus, it would

certain practices of the European Central Bank (ECB) and the Council of Economic and Financial Ministers (Ecofin), as well as its subset of EA member governments, the Eurogroup, which, as the ultimate arbiter, was in charge of enforcement through peer review.

From the outset, the ECB treated all EA-member sovereign bonds uniformly as riskless collateral in repurchase transactions, regardless of significant differences, for example, between Germany and Greece in their public debt-to-GDP ratios or in their ability to generate primary budget surpluses.[6] Although eventually a slight discount on lower credit-rated obligations was to be introduced, this practice was in stark contradiction of the Treaty's no-bailout clause. An additional, though justifiable, practice was the accumulation of residual external imbalances to be offset through the ECB's Target settlement system. These imbalances, which were significant and rising sharply from 2007 onward, could, however, turn into an off-budget subsidy in the event of sovereign default. At an extreme, this practice could also be viewed as a backdoor bailout, without conditionality, in an environment where each state retained fiscal sovereignty.[7]

Unlike the nominal stringency of the deficit rule, the SGP did not stipulate sanctions for insufficient surpluses during an upswing in economic activity. At most, in the spirit of the Pact, the Commission applied moral suasion to adopt a countercyclical contractionary fiscal stance to help offset the upswing, as in the case of Ireland in the early 2000s. This asymmetry in the letter of the Pact failed to prevent some EA members from adopting a procyclical expansionary fiscal stance during the so-called Great Moderation.[8] This is reflected in the structural deficit being in excess of the headline deficit (or surplus in the case of Ireland), when the output gap was mostly in positive territory or

---

take a sharp fall from trend GDP to push the budget from balance to excess deficit, which would anyway trigger a waiver under the EDP because of the contraction.

[6] See the analysis by Buiter and Sibert (2006).

[7] See Sinn (2014) for extensive documentation of this practice. From a monetary history perspective, Bordo (2014) argues that the EA would have collapsed in the absence of Target.

[8] This was in addition to the built-in procyclicality insofar as compliance with the deficit limit was determined ex post as percent of GDP instead of nominal terms. An unanticipated rise (drop) in GDP would allow for a commensurate rise (would have to be compensated with a commensurate cut) in the nominal deficit. See Coricelli and Ernani (2004) for various approaches to correct this deficiency.

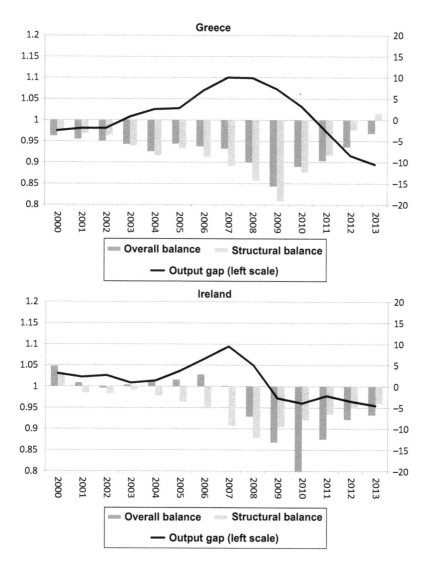

Figure 9.1: General government balance and output gap in the euro area countries, 2000–13

Note: in percent of actual or potential GDP

Source: IMF *World Economic Outlook* and author's estimates

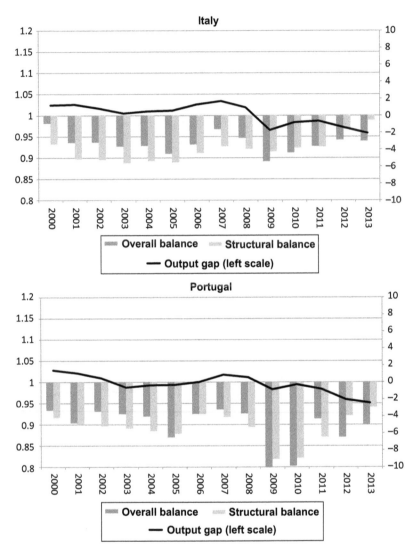

Figure 9.1: (*cont.*)

near zero, over much of the past decade. Thus measured, admittedly in hindsight, an expansionary stance is evident in Greece, Ireland, Italy, and Portugal (Figure 9.1).[9]

---

[9] Figure 9.1 reflects ex post estimates of the output gap which in certain cases differ markedly from methodologically inferior real-time estimates, discussed in footnote 23.

At the supranational level, the fiscal expansion of these countries was accommodated by monetary policy. By definition, the conduct of monetary policy by the ECB was uniform within the entire currency area, with a single reaction function determined by the relative weight of each member country, without regard to differences in inflation and growth rates among member countries. Thus, while appropriate for some core countries (Austria, Belgium, Germany), the monetary stance was too loose for peripheral high-inflation countries (Greece, Ireland, Portugal, Spain),[10] thereby exacerbating inflation in these countries – far beyond what could have been explained in terms of the Balassa–Samuelson effect. High price inflation, in turn, led to relatively high wages in both the private and public sectors, contributing respectively to the erosion in competitiveness for tradables and the rise in the government wage bill in these countries.

Fragmented and ineffective banking supervision across countries contributed also to the extension of easy credit to households and enterprises in some peripheral countries. Moreover, macroprudential regulation was unknown both at the national and the supranational levels. These deficiencies in the financial sector aggravated vulnerabilities, first by generating asset price bubbles, and then by imposing a considerable burden on public finances in the event of massive defaults. Not surprisingly, during the past decade, some of these countries experienced widening current account imbalances, driven by insufficient domestic savings.

On the fiscal front, the *deficit bias* and *procyclical bias* were reinforced by the demonstration effect of the failure of the Council and the Eurogroup to enforce sanctions against France and Germany, the largest member countries, under the excessive deficit procedure (EDP) for violation of the deficit ceiling – effectively ignoring the Commission's November 2003 recommendation to place these countries under enhanced surveillance. This event remained a testament to an essential flaw in the peer-review enforcement mechanism, as practiced by the Council. Arguably, it caused irreparable damage to the credibility of the Pact, enticing frequent breaches of the fiscal criteria

---

[10] Ahrend et al. (2008) and Mayer (2012) provide evidence on differences in monetary stance across selected EA member countries by applying the Taylor rule. See also FitzGerald (2006) for the implications of the one-size-fits-all EA monetary policy for Ireland and Spain.

by other EA member governments as well. For the most part, member governments failed to observe the deficit ceiling, or the mandatory decline in the debt ratio, or both.

In a further manifestation of the deficit bias, some countries tried to avert a breach of the deficit ceiling with stop-gap policy measures (starting with the introduction of a refundable income tax surcharge in Italy to qualify for entry in the EA) and accumulation of contingent liabilities (for instance, in the form of public–private partnership projects in Portugal) that would only show up in future deficits. Some governments also indulged in various creative accounting practices and misreporting.[11] In these circumstances, the fiscal reference values were met through repressed deficits, as predicted by Goodhart's law.[12]

In the extreme case of Greece, fiscal performance was aggravated by gross misreporting of national and public sector accounts. This was attributable to data manipulation under political influence – exacerbated by a culture of opacity – to meet the budget deficit reference value, first to qualify for entry into the EA, and then to demonstrate compliance with the SGP. On two occasions, after elections in 2004 and 2009, the authorities revealed that general government deficits and debt had been understated by a sizable margin. The second revelation spooked financial markets, reflected in a jump in the sovereign risk premium, which – together with the authorities' failure to take corrective action – resulted in a sudden stop in capital inflows the following year. Although in principle Eurostat was entrusted with the surveillance of macro-fiscal data, in fact it was only in 2009 that it gained authorization to investigate the veracity of data reported by national authorities.[13]

Continued failure to enforce EDP was accompanied by an *optimistic bias* in medium-term macro-fiscal projections by most EA member governments in yearly Stability Programs submitted to the European

---

[11] Creative accounting included cash-based recording of expenditure, off-budget transactions, and non-reporting of losses of certain state-owned enterprises. Alt, Lassen, and Wehner (2014) provide documentation and analysis of such practices.

[12] According to Charles Goodhart, a numerical indicator (such as a monetary aggregate target or a budget deficit ceiling) ceases to be reliable once it is declared an official policy target or rule. Along similar lines, Summers (2013) observed that a budget deficit repressed artificially has perverse consequences, much like repressed inflation achieved through price controls.

[13] See the informative assessment of Greek data in European Commission (2010).

Commission (EC).[14] The Programs were seen by some governments as fulfilling a reporting obligation that could soon be forgotten, rather than as a binding commitment to undertake policy measures that would lead to realization of the projected outcome. Governments' promises to exit the EDP became elusive policy goals that were not subject to accountability and enforcement.

In sum, in a number of countries, deficiencies in the enforcement of the fiscal framework – following strict observance of the Pact at the time of EA accession – enabled continued fiscal profligacy that can be traced back to before the introduction of the euro. These deficiencies were manifest in a significant deficit bias, procyclical expansionary bias, and optimistic bias. The confluence of fiscal expansion, monetary ease, and lax banking supervision contributed to widening external imbalances in peripheral EA member economies. In the event, they were rendered vulnerable to a sudden stop in capital inflows as the Great Moderation waned.

3 Pre-Crisis Complacency

The fiscal framework notwithstanding, since the launch of the EA, there was a widespread view in official and academic circles that individual EA member countries can run external deficits, and by implication fiscal deficits, without the risk of a financial or a fiscal crisis. According to a prominent public official,[15] external imbalances do not matter within a monetary union, as they tend to correct themselves automatically – reminiscent of the international specie-flow

---

[14] See Frenkel and Schreger (2013). Balassone, Franco, and Goretti (2013) discuss optimistic fiscal forecasts and planning in Italy over the period 1997–2008. There are several explanations for the optimistic bias. One is simply optimistic projections of key underlying macroeconomic variables (especially output and interest rates). Another consists of optimistic assumptions on spending control or effective tax elasticities. The third factor is time inconsistency of policy commitments to achieve the medium-term objective in compliance with the statutory deficit limit under the Pact.

[15] Constâncio (2000), the governor of the Bank of Portugal (currently ECB Vice President), expressed succinctly the prevalent view: "Without a currency of our own, we shall never again face the same balance of payments problems of the past. There is no macroeconomic monetary problem and no restrictive measures need to be taken for balance of payments reasons. No one analyses the macro size of the external account of the [state of] Mississippi or of any other region belonging to a large monetary union."

mechanism. The view was echoed by reputable scholars,[16] providing justification for the benign neglect of current account and fiscal deficits by EA member governments, by the EC and the ECB, and even by the International Monetary Fund (IMF). Not surprisingly, financial markets were lulled into complacency and member governments felt relatively immune to the need to abide by the fiscal framework. By the same token, there was hardly any concern about the loose monetary stance and lax banking supervision in the peripheral member countries.

Complacency in financial markets, however, cannot be attributed solely to the exuberant mood prevailing during the Great Moderation; more important were the contradictions and leniency in the implementation of the policy framework. Specifically, the ECB's uniform rating of EA sovereign bonds led investors to ignore the no-bailout clause and to bid up the price of bonds issued by high-debt member governments used as collateral, and thus make a profit from even a relatively small interest spread. As a result – and reinforced by the disappearance of the currency risk within the EA – the risk premium on sovereign bonds practically vanished and lost any link to the economic fundamentals of each member country until the beginning of the crisis in 2008 (Figure 9.2).

The rise in sovereign risk premiums – albeit cushioned somewhat by the unavoidable buildup of Target claims – continued well into the middle of 2012, until two important EA-wide policy measures were undertaken. One was the first significant step toward the creation of a banking union, at the June EU summit meeting. The other was the extension of credits by national central banks to commercial banks, under the Emergency Liquidity Assistance (ELA) program, in addition to the August 2012 announcement of Outright Monetary Transactions (OMT) by the ECB. The OMT program could be interpreted as a further softening of the no-bailout clause, even though financing would only be made available subject to conditionality.[17] In any case, as a

---

[16] See, for example, the theoretical and empirical analysis by Blanchard and Giavazzi (2002) with references mainly to Greece, Ireland, and Portugal. While recognizing the weight of public dissaving in external current account imbalances, they were somewhat guarded in extending this view to budget deficits.

[17] Arguably, these and other forms of EU financial assistance can be justified if a member state faces "difficulties or is seriously threatened with severe difficulties caused by exceptional occurrences beyond its control," under Article 103a of the Treaty, in effect overriding the no-bailout clause in Article 104.

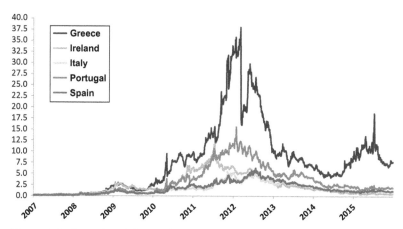

Figure 9.2: Sovereign risk premia in euro-area countries, 2007–15
Note: yield spread on ten-year government bonds, in percent.
Source: Thomson Reuters, *Datastream*

result, the risk premium on bonds issued by vulnerable EA member governments fell markedly, though not to pre-crisis levels.

Complacency, following the establishment of the EA, was also evident in the policy response of some member governments to the decline of risk premiums. As a consequence of the fall in the interest cost, highly indebted governments benefited from a windfall gain in their budgets and a corresponding sizable increase in fiscal space. But only some of them allocated this gain to a reduction in public debt, while most others squandered it by increasing primary expenditure (often in the form of generous across-the-board wage increases) or by cutting taxes.

This is illustrated by the case of member governments whose annual interest bill contracted by more than 1 percent of GDP from the establishment of the EMU through to 2005 (Figure 9.3). Whereas in Belgium, Finland, and Spain the interest saving was fully utilized to reduce the budget deficit, in Greece, Ireland, Italy, the Netherlands, and Portugal it was allocated to finance additional primary outlays or tax cuts, reflecting a continued deficit bias. As observed in the preceding section, in the case of Greece, Ireland, Italy, and Portugal, this was manifest also in a procyclical expansionary bias that exacerbated the vulnerability of these countries to potential shocks.

As noted, responsibility for monitoring compliance with the EU fiscal framework rests primarily with the EC as regards member

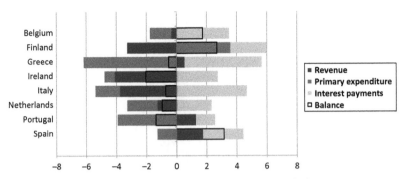

Figure 9.3: Net contribution to the general government balance in euro-area countries, 1998–2005

Note: cyclically adjusted, as percent of GDP.

Source: Banque Nationale de Belgique (2006)

country policies, and with Eurostat on public finance accounts and statistics. Yet the Council and the Eurogroup, as the ultimate authority, failed to enforce the Pact on several occasions, thereby serving as an instrument of peer protection rather than peer review.

The IMF has a well-defined surveillance function over public finances as part of its focus on each member's external balance, and ultimately on the stability of the international monetary system. Thus IMF oversight overlaps, but in no way substitutes, the mandate of the Commission. While IMF surveillance is supposed to monitor fiscal discipline and public debt sustainability in each member country, the EC's role is limited to observance of the fiscal framework per se, which is seen as paramount to preserving the integrity of the common currency area.

On the basis of the foregoing discussion, the track records of some EA member countries point to a number of deficiencies that merited attention by the EU institutions and the IMF: pronounced deficit bias, procyclicality bias, optimistic bias, and time inconsistency. The combination of these deficiencies contributed not only to a problem of debt sustainability, but eventually also to a liquidity crisis, exposing these countries to a fat-tail sovereign risk that was captured by financial markets only with a considerable recognition lag.

The quality of IMF surveillance of fiscal policy across the EA as a whole was mixed. While treating the EA common currency area – in essence, the result of a collective political action by participating governments – as a given, on several occasions the IMF staff weighed the advantages and disadvantages and flagged the challenges ahead in the enforcement of the fiscal framework.

Although there was no formal arrangement between the IMF and the ECB and EC on surveillance, it may have been implicitly understood that the IMF surveillance would strengthen the EU institutions in their oversight responsibilities insofar as the EC and ECB staffs had limited operational experience in monitoring macro-fiscal policymaking – notwithstanding both institutions' proven analytical capacity in the fiscal area. Conversely, it appears that at times, Fund staff may have felt that EU institutions, particularly Eurostat, had primary oversight responsibility in monitoring the national and public sector accounts of EU member countries. While supportive of the initial design features of the SGP, the IMF was correct in its criticism – albeit muted – of lax enforcement of the watered-down 2005 version.

Overall, the intensity of surveillance and exhortations by the Fund and the EU institutions was driven to a large extent by market pressures. They seemed complacent in the initial years as sovereign risk premiums narrowed and then vanished. This attitude turned into alarm only when financial markets experienced oscillations, and eventually turbulence, reflected in the gyrations of the sovereign risk premium.[18] Instead, the assessment of policies during surveillance should have addressed the fundamentals of fiscal policy and of the financial system – long before the shift in market sentiment – with a view to preventing possible shifts from an apparently good to a bad equilibrium, as seen from a multiple-equilibrium perspective.[19]

In particular, the supranational institutions could have exercised far more intense surveillance of highly indebted governments with a trail of past fiscal problems that exhibited a deficit bias. On this basis, countries that entered the EA with public debt in excess of economic activity, barely meeting the references values – countries such as

[18] A further shift in the IMF advice was the controversial advocacy of a fiscal stimulus in 2009 in response to the crisis-driven recession, which apparently encouraged governments in Portugal and Spain in the run-up to elections to incur budget deficits of to 10 percent of GDP, more than twice the deficits in the preceding year. Tanzi (2013) compared this advice (instead of recommending much-needed structural reform measures) to prescribing steroids to a patient suffering from a serious illness.

[19] An explanation and test of this shift in the EA can be found in De Grauwe and Ji (2013).

Greece, Italy, and Portugal – deserved special attention from the very start of their euro membership.[20]

While correctly endorsing the design of the EU fiscal framework, though critical of its enforcement, the Fund and the EC could have questioned the suitability of euro membership for some of the fiscally vulnerable countries—though without necessarily objecting to a member's choice of exchange rate regime. In particular, there was considerable evidence to argue that Greece was not ready to join the EA, on the grounds not only of insufficient real economic convergence (given markedly lower income levels and a different economic structure than the rest of the members), but also of the foreseeable difficulties in complying with the requirements of the fiscal framework (given past fiscal profligacy).

In addition, in the early years of EA membership, the Fund and the Commission seem to have missed opportunities to critically assess member countries that failed to allocate significant windfall gains from declining interest cost to a reduction in public debt, and concomitantly to create fiscal space for countercyclical action in the event of an economic downturn.

Although it was perhaps difficult to ascertain in real time a surge in economic activity over the past decade, in the wake of a brief downturn, insufficient attention was paid to the procyclical fiscal expansion pursued by fiscally vulnerable member countries. In general, despite occasional references to the structural budget balance, discussions with the authorities focused mostly on the headline balance. Similarly, the differential impact of the single monetary policy and uneven quality of banking supervision across EA countries merited closer surveillance.

In retrospect, the expansionary stance is evident not only in Greece, Italy, and Portugal, but also in Ireland and Spain. The latter two stood apart from the other countries in the sense that a root cause of their sizable macroeconomic imbalances was a financial bubble reflected mainly in a jump in real estate asset prices. While public finances were essentially sound, the bubble fed a seemingly favorable fiscal performance that masked a significant structural deficit that was not readily

---

[20] In Italy, the deficit reference value was met with recourse to various creative accounting maneuvers, including the introduction of a tax surcharge that was reimbursed following EA accession. See Spaventa and Chiorazzo (2000) and Reviglio (2001). For Greece, as discovered several years later, the reference value was reached through gross misrepresentation of fiscal data.

observable. The resulting boom in tax revenue, in turn, encouraged these governments to embark on a procyclical boost of expenditure on wages and pension benefits, as well as of tax subsidies.[21]

This problem was particularly pronounced for Ireland, where, in a departure from Ecofin's concern about the expansionary stance, in 2001 the Fund staff downplayed the issue in view of a headline budget surplus.[22] The staff had expressed misgivings about the evolving real estate boom underlying strong economic growth from the beginning of the past decade, but – relying on EC estimates of the output gap and structural balance, as well as a low public debt ratio – it felt that the fiscal accounts were broadly in equilibrium. In a reversal of this view, based on a methodological shift – revising the 2006 structural balance from a small surplus to a deficit of 7 percent of GDP – in 2009 the staff alerted the authorities to the need for fiscal consolidation. The new methodology sought to incorporate the ongoing asset price boom in the calculation of the output gap underlying the structural balance estimates.[23]

In the case of Spain, the effect of the financial bubble was perhaps more difficult to detect, for it manifested primarily in a rise in subnational government revenue from fees charged on construction and development permits, and only to a lesser extent in capital gains from the surge of real estate prices and thus a rise in income tax revenue. In all, the damage to the financial system and to the public sector accounts was milder, more gradual, and better managed in Spain than in Ireland.

The strong optimistic bias in budgetary projections incorporated in the medium-term Stability Programs did not receive sufficiently critical attention from the supranational institutions, as reflected, for

---

[21] This policy stance was best summarized by a widely quoted remark by Charlie McCreevy, former Irish finance minister: "When I have it I'll spend it. When I don't I won't."

[22] In a rare display of difference in official views between the EU and IMF surveillance, the Fund staff stated that "the rising budget surplus fed public desires for additional tax cuts and spending increases. Shaped by these circumstances, the 2002 Budget gave rise to an opinion by the European Council in February critical of the procyclical fiscal stance. Subsequent indicators point to a welcome slowing of the economy, however, reducing the potential risks from the fiscal stimulus" (IMF, 2001).

[23] In IMF (2009a) the staff adopted the approach reported in Kanda (2010), developed along the lines suggested earlier by Jaeger and Schuknecht (2004).

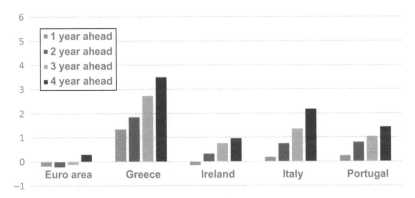

Figure 9.4: General government balance forecast errors, 2000–8

Note: in percent of GDP, calculated as the difference between forecast values for each year and actual values measured in the following year, so as to avoid the effect of subsequent data revisions.

Source: IMF *World Economic Outlook* and author's estimates

example, in IMF projections. From the euro's beginnings, IMF forecasts of the budget balance, as reported in the semiannual *World Economic Outlook*, exceeded the actual balance by a significant margin for Greece, Ireland, Italy, and Portugal – in contrast to the forecasts for the EA as a whole, which consistently tracked the actual balances (Figure 9.4). These projections can be interpreted as representing an endorsement of the optimistic bias exhibited by vulnerable member governments.

During much of the past decade, the Fund expressed far less concern about the reliability of fiscal accounts than warranted. In Greece, in 2006, the IMF staff went as far as declaring that "in recent years has made progress in meeting requirements of the fiscal transparency code … At the central government level, Greek budget processes give assurances of integrity about fiscal data through independent audit and recently strengthened statistical reporting."[24] The EC and the Fund openly criticized the quality of Greek public sector accounts for the first time in 2009.[25]

The IMF, with the support of EU institutions, could have stepped up the monitoring of public finances in the vulnerable economies,

---

[24] See IMF (2006).
[25] In 2010, the IMF found Greece in breach of members' reporting obligations under Article VIII, Section 5 of the Articles of Agreement.

shortening the consultation cycle, much before the onset of the crisis. Indeed, there was a strong case for applying enhanced surveillance to vulnerable EA members, given the weaknesses in fiscal policy, compounded in the case of Greece by unreliability of fiscal data. Enhanced surveillance was only considered with regard to Italy in late 2011.[26] Support from EU institutions for high-frequency and in-depth surveillance of some of these countries much before the crisis would have been most helpful as a preventive step.

In order to evaluate the Fund's potential role in averting a crisis, it is necessary to examine its role in assessing the sustainability and risk facing a member country's public finances.[27] A critical component of surveillance is in fact to help anticipate and communicate in a timely manner the probable impact of shocks on public finances, and to advise the government on mitigating or neutralizing the impact of such shocks. Insofar as is feasible, the objective should be to alert the authorities as to the country's vulnerability to a so-called fat-tail risk of outright default, which was ruled out as a possible outcome from the outset.

Since the early 2000s, Fund staff reports have included a debt sustainability analysis, consisting of a quantitative scenario of the public debt ratio over a medium-term horizon, in which the underlying drivers and macroeconomic assumptions are not always stated. In addition to a baseline scenario, an illustrative fan chart was provided with deviations from the baseline given an arbitrary change in the growth rate, interest rate, exchange rate, and realization of contingent liabilities.[28]

---

[26] As discussed by Leipold (2011), after the G20 meeting in Cannes, the IMF staff was instructed to monitor the implementation of measures promised by the Italian government through quarterly staff visits. However, the proposal was shelved following the demise of the Berlusconi government.

[27] This task is an integral part of Fund surveillance, as noted by IEO (2011, p. 3), insofar as it "consists of monitoring the global economy and that of member countries to help head off risks to international monetary and financial stability, alert member countries to potential risks and vulnerabilities, and advise them of needed policy adjustments."

[28] The original template (IMF, 2002) has been applied in most annual consultations with member countries until the present, though expanded (IMF, 2011) in coverage and including an assessment of debt structure and liquidity issues. For EA members, no exchange rate shock was simulated since they held hardly any non-euro denominated debt.

Given the arbitrary character and methodological limitations of the template, efforts have been underway for more than a decade within the Fund to develop more realistic and objective methods of sustainability-cum-risk assessment, drawing on macroeconomic and financial analysis.[29] In some variants, these initiatives sought to incorporate stochastic methods into the public sector balance sheet, incorporating the government's exposure to contingent liabilities. Such methods were available for application to vulnerable EA countries, yet ignored in the ongoing policy dialogue between the Fund and the national authorities in assessing fiscal risk.

A notable exception to the substandard approach to risk assessment was an IMF staff estimate of an intertemporal balance sheet of the public sector for Greece in 2009, calculated in terms of the present value of the future stream of major assets and liabilities, including contingent liabilities.[30] This exercise, subsequently abandoned, served to illustrate Greece's fiscal insolvency only about half a year before its loss of access to financial markets.

In all, prior to the crisis, the widespread complacency prevailing in financial markets permeated some member governments, EU institutions, and notably the IMF with regard to the risks facing the EA, especially vulnerable economies. This attitude was summed up in an external report on IMF surveillance: "Rather than fully exploiting its comparative advantage, based on its international experience, the IMF fell victim to a 'Europe is different' mindset."[31]

4 The Financing Quandary

Typically, if a country suffers a sudden stop in market financing of sovereign paper – as experienced by Greece, Ireland, and Portugal in 2010–11 – the loss of liquidity must be compensated with financing from various (mostly external) official and private sources. If concurrently the government is in default (or near default) on its obligations, it is granted debt restructuring, usually in the form of a rescheduling of

---

[29] Kopits (2014b) provides a review of this literature, as well as the results of a recent OECD survey of country practices as regards specific, general, and systemic fiscal risks.

[30] The IMF (2009b), however, fell short of subjecting the estimate to a formal Value-at-Risk (VaR) analysis, along the lines of Barnhill and Kopits (2004).

[31] See Pisani-Ferry, Sapir, and Wolff (2011).

existing liabilities, in some cases accompanied by debt relief (or haircuts) on those liabilities. (Increasingly, to this effect, anonymous private bondholders are bound by collective action clauses.) Thus an orderly process had been developed over the years in which financing, including through debt restructuring, became an integral part in the negotiation and design of any IMF-supported stand-by arrangement or extended arrangement.

More generally, financing the imbalance is one of three pillars of a stabilization program; the other two pillars are macro-fiscal adjustment (lacking other macroeconomic tools in the case of currency union) and macro-critical structural measures. The relative weight of each pillar depends on a number of factors, including the supply of funding, public debt sustainability, the size of the fiscal imbalance, and the extent of structural distortions. Each of the pillars is examined in this and the following two sections.

In the early phase of the crisis, as indicated, financial markets were spooked by developments in Greece and Ireland, as well as by the initial resistance of supranational institutions to provide unconditional stop-gap financing, which explains the jump and continued rise in sovereign yields in these countries. However, the upward pressure on spreads began to abate under the effect of multiple ECB facilities that provided mainly indirect financing to governments mainly through the banking system.[32] In addition to the steady buildup of Target claims, the ECB began to extend refinancing credit through Long-Term Refinancing Operations (LTROs), ELA credits, and purchases of government bonds through the Securities Market Program (SMP). However, it was not until 2012, with the announcement – albeit not the activation – of the OMT program by the ECB, that risk premiums declined significantly. In fact, the ECB became the principal source of financing for vulnerable EU member countries during much of the euro crisis.

In comparison to past crisis episodes, the stabilization programs introduced in Greece, Ireland, and Portugal can be characterized as among the most complex; they belong to a category of their own in a number of aspects, including the financing pillar.[33] Following the loss

---

[32] Sinn (2014) offers a detailed analysis of these facilities and their implications.

[33] The programs under scrutiny are: a three-year stand-by arrangement for Greece launched in 2010, replaced by a four-year extended arrangement in 2012; a three-year year extended arrangement for Ireland in 2010; and a three-year extended arrangement for Portugal in 2011.

of access to financial markets, in the first half of 2010, Greece became the first case in which it was incumbent on the EU institutions and the IMF, possibly with the cooperation of private creditors and in negotiation with the national authorities, to consider various forms and magnitudes of financing. Unlike in previous crises, a major challenge emerged for the various parties – occasionally operating with conflicting interests – to put together a financing package without recourse to debt restructuring.

Many observers expressed skepticism about the exclusion of debt restructuring for Greece, and to a lesser extent for Ireland and Portugal, given a convincing *prima facie* case on the basis of the sharp increase in the public debt ratio – by nearly one half in Greece and Portugal and nearly quadruple in Ireland – from 2007 through 2010. This resulted mainly from revenue loss due to a marked contraction of output and from the need to recapitalize the banking system owing to a surge in impaired assets. The general case for debt restructuring was further strengthened by fresh evidence on the growth-depressing effect of a high public debt ratio.[34]

Nevertheless, from the outset of the programs and well into the adjustment period, the EC, the ECB, and the crisis-hit governments (for reputational reasons) alike resisted any form of debt restructuring. The EU institutions and their major member governments were apparently opposed to debt restructuring because they wished to protect their banks' balance sheets, which held a sizable amount of such debt, as well as possibly to avoid violating the no-bailout provision.[35] The IMF, partly because of fear of contagion to EA members, went along with this position.

The programs approved for Greece, Ireland, and Portugal were constrained by the availability of official balance-of-payments support to EA member governments on the scale required in each case. The IMF was persuaded to lend unprecedented amounts far in excess of

[34] Estimates of the growth-depressing effect of public debt approaching 100 percent of GDP as reported by Reinhart and Rogoff (2009) were corroborated by Cecchetti et al. (2011) with robust estimates on a homogeneous sample of OECD countries over a recent period and encompassing a broad institutional coverage of the public sector.

[35] In the case of Ireland, opposition to the bail-in of private bank bondholders resembled the forced recapitalization of failed foreign-owned banks by the government in a Fund-supported adjustment program for Chile in the 1980s, documented in a seminal paper by Diaz Alejandro (1985).

country limits expressed in terms of membership quota. EC financing could be provided only by diverting some funds from earmarked windows and by drawing from the newly created European Financial Stability Facility (EFSF) and European Financial Stabilization Mechanism (EFSM), succeeded in 2012 by the European Stability Mechanism (ESM) as a permanent firewall for EA governments facing financial difficulties. But more importantly, as sovereign risk premiums continued to spike for the vulnerable countries over the course of 2011, a relatively generous debt restructuring agreement with private sector involvement – defined as voluntary, to avoid declaring a formal default by an EA economy – was approved for Greece the following year. These steps, as noted, were supported with significant backdoor financing from the ECB.

In order to justify the IMF's participation in the Greek rescue program, it was necessary to meet several criteria, including a high probability of public debt sustainability over the medium term. Given prevailing uncertainties regarding debt sustainability, the IMF sought to bolster the case for exceptional access by invoking a newly devised criterion of "high risk of international spillover effects."[36] But in an attempt to broadly conform to the debt sustainability criterion, the Fund prepared the prescribed medium-term baseline public debt scenario for Greece on the basis of an excessively optimistic set of macro-fiscal assumptions.[37] A similar exercise was repeated at the beginning of each of the other two programs as well, although, in retrospect, this was underpinned by somewhat more realistic assumptions.

The actual trajectory of the debt ratio was significantly higher than projected under the initial programs for both Greece and Portugal. Without the 2012 debt restructuring, by 2014 Greece's public debt would have exceeded the projected stock by at least another twenty percentage points of GDP, on top of the actual twenty-point overrun. In Portugal, the actual debt ratio exceeded the projected ratio by ten percentage points. By contrast, by the end of the adjustment program,

---

[36] On the Fund's Greek rescue operation, including insights into the inter-institutional and interpersonal dynamics, see a comprehensive discussion by Schadler (2013).

[37] Specifically, the underlying assumptions included a relatively rapid resumption in growth and a turnaround in the primary balance from deficit to surplus over the scenario period, all on the strength of structural reform measures yet to be launched; see IMF (2010).

the Irish debt ratio had actually been contained below the projected ratio (Figure 9.5) on a sustainable path.[38]

The upshot, for Greece in particular, was a continuous need for additional financing from the ELA facility. Any further restructuring of the Greek debt – since 2012 held primarily by EU governments – has been rejected by the EC and by major EA governments, apparently because of possible violation of the no-bailout clause. In the most recent departure from their previous position, on the basis of an unusually comprehensive analysis, the IMF staff questioned Greece's debt sustainability for the first time and recognized the need for some debt relief as a precondition for a new program.[39]

5 Constrained Adjustment

The EU/IMF-supported adjustment programs launched in 2010 by Greece and Ireland, and in 2011 by Portugal, upon loss of market access were subject to a number of critical internal and external constraints. First, unlike most other macroeconomic adjustment programs, these programs were constrained by a common hard exchange rate peg and rigid nominal wages,[40] which imposed an extraordinary adjustment burden on fiscal policy. Second, the programs were undertaken in the face of stagnant external demand and financial fragmentation, which acted as impediments to export performance and capital inflows. And third, the programs required unprecedented support and tutelage – in both magnitude and coordination – from the IMF, EC, and ECB. This arrangement, known as the Troika, posed a singular operational challenge to all three institutions.

Internally, the three programs differed in two important respects: local ownership and institutional constraints. The latter had important implications for the design and implementation of the adjustment's fiscal components, for the credibility of the authorities' policy commitments, and ultimately for the outcome of the adjustment effort.

---

[38] Projections have been rescaled to fit actual base-year data.

[39] See IMF (2015c, 2015d).

[40] In the context of accession to EMU, McKinnon (1999) advocated adoption of the so-called restoration rule, used under the gold standard, to allow for a temporary deviation from parity and imposition of capital controls by an EA member during a crisis episode. For a similar approach during the current EA crisis, see also Bordo and James (2013).

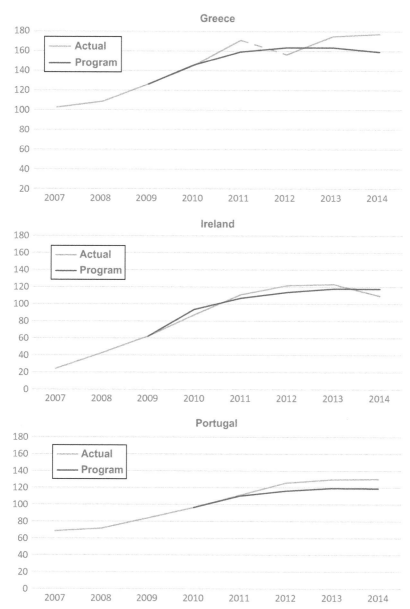

Figure 9.5: Actual and projected public debt in Greece, Ireland, and Portugal, 2007–14

Note: in percent of GDP

Source: IMF *World Economic Outlook*, staff reports, and author's estimates

In Ireland, from the outset of the crisis, there was deep and wide-spread local ownership of the adjustment effort, which the government had launched in 2010, before the official arrival of the Troika. Indeed, the authorities reacted with conviction in the face of an extraordinary rise in the budget deficit to over 30 percent of GDP and an increase of nearly 100 percentage points in the public debt ratio, only one fourth of which stemmed from the recapitalization of the banking sector, the rest coming from the fall in tax revenue and some increase in current expenditure in the wake of the extraordinary collapse of asset values.[41]

In Portugal, by the beginning of 2011, the government's initial denial of the crisis had given way to negotiation of an extended arrangement that was fully honored by the successor coalition government. The resulting implicit consensus among political parties as well as other stakeholders lasted until the fall of 2012, when the government made a failed attempt at shifting a portion of the payroll tax for social security from employers to employees – as a form of internal "fiscal devaluation" and to offset the budgetary cost of a constitutional court decision to annul an expenditure cut – without consulting social partners. This was followed by an equally unsuccessful proposal to shift part of the payroll tax to the value-added tax.[42] In response, opposition parties withdrew support for the program and pledged to reverse some fiscal measures if elected.

In Greece, following a period of denial that lasted well into 2010, the political leadership never fully identified with the program's policy requirements. To a greater or lesser degree, each government blamed the outside world for the hardships imposed by the fiscal adjustment – with occasional attempts made to blackmail the EU institutions and creditor governments. The lack of ownership throughout the program was a significant handicap for successful implementation.

Whereas in Ireland institutional constraints were minimal, in Greece they posed a major stumbling block for the design and execution of the fiscal adjustment. Despite being classified as an "advanced economy"

---

[41] See Donovan and Murphy (2013) on these estimates.

[42] Despite its conceptual attractiveness for improving external competitiveness – given a fixed exchange rate, low price inflation, and nominal wage rigidity – the attempted partial shift of the employers' payroll tax to employees or to VAT, inspired by Blanchard (2007), proved to be a classical failure in political economy. Such an approach had been tried with mixed success a few decades earlier in Italy; see the analysis in Kopits (1982).

by virtue of EA membership, Greece's institutional capacity in terms of the judicial process, tax administration, expenditure control, and statistical services was found to be below that of practically any other European economy. In Portugal, apart from some weaknesses in public financial management, several expenditure-reducing measures were struck down by the constitutional court, which interpreted them as contrary to the acquired rights of citizens, and especially of public employees, that were enshrined in the constitution.

Given the extent of the fiscal imbalances and the accumulated public debt, accompanied by a severe financing constraint (including absence of debt restructuring) and in the context of the hard peg and wage rigidity, all three countries faced a major fiscal adjustment requirement. Therefore, unavoidably, each program entailed a large-scale front-loaded budgetary consolidation, rendered onerous by the lack of market access and by a stagnant economic environment in major trading-partner countries. While the EU institutions insisted on compliance with the statutory deficit ceiling of 3 percent of GDP by the end of the program period, the Fund's objective was to restore public debt sustainability. The resulting fiscal targets represented a compromise between the two positions.

In both size and speed, the envisaged adjustment under each program ranked among the highest in recent decades.[43] Most observers felt that the adjustment was probably excessive, but inevitable. The apparent inevitability of the scale and procyclicality of the fiscal consolidation was attributable not only to the regional economic contraction, but also to limited financing from private and official sources. Nonetheless, some observers felt that the fiscal adjustment was too harsh.[44] Yet the debate over the size of the multipliers, though of interest from an academic point of view, was considered of limited practical relevance, given the need to meet a very large financing requirement, in part because early debt restructuring was discarded.

---

[43] See Tsibouris et al. (2006).

[44] Blanchard and Leigh (2013) found evidence that fiscal multipliers were underestimated and growth forecasts optimistic in the early phase of the recent crisis. Given the state-dependent nature of the multiplier, its assumed value seems to have been broadly appropriate for Ireland, the most open economy, and unrealistically low for Greece, a relatively closed economy, with Portugal somewhere between them.

Table 9.1: *Fiscal adjustment in Greece, Ireland, and Portugal, 2009–14*

	Greece	Ireland	Portugal
Primary balance, projection	14.5	13.5	10.0
Primary balance, actual	11.7	12.1	8.2
Revenue (excluding interest)	4.9	1.0	5.0
Expenditure (excluding interest)	−6.8	−11.1	−3.2

Note: percent of GDP.
Source: IMF, *World Economic Outlook* and staff reports

In both Greece and Portugal, the nominal deficit ceiling was frequently corrected downward in the course of the program in line with the observed GDP, which contracted more than was anticipated. This was tantamount to disallowing the operation of automatic stabilizers, thus aggravating the procyclicality of the fiscal stance, which in turn widened the nominal deficit and exacerbated the contraction – a self-defeating approach, much like the case of a dog chasing its own tail. By contrast, in the case of Ireland, no such revisions were undertaken during the program and the stabilizers were permitted to operate, possibly contributing to the fiscal correction and an earlier recovery.

Measured in terms of the primary fiscal balance, the adjustment since 2009 has been sizable: around 12 percent of GDP in Greece and Ireland and slightly over 8 percent of GDP in Portugal, in each case between 1 and 3 percentage points less than initially envisaged (Table 9.1). The correction was sharply front-loaded in Greece, where more than one half came during the first two years; the slowest correction was seen in Ireland. The composition of the fiscal consolidation varied across the three countries. In Portugal more than one half of the adjustment in the primary budget deficit came about in the form of increased revenue. By contrast, in Ireland almost the entire adjustment consisted of noninterest expenditure reduction. Thus, apart from in Ireland, the composition of the adjustment is likely to have had an unfavorable consequence on economic activity.[45]

A closer look at the composition reveals additional doubts regarding the quality of the adjustment in terms of longer-run effects on economic growth and public debt sustainability. It is well known that

---

[45] According to Alesina and Ardagna (2013), the higher the proportion of a fiscal adjustment in expenditure cuts, the more likely a favorable impact on activity.

increments in property taxes and indirect taxes on goods and services are less distortionary than hikes in income and payroll taxes; also, tax base broadening is preferable to statutory tax rate increases.[46] On the expenditure side, cuts in wages, pensions, and subsidies are preferable to those in productive investment; furthermore, rationalization of the work force – to retain productive employees – and targeting of social benefits can actually be favorable to growth.

From this perspective, the program design was in a number of instances harmful to growth, and, as a corollary, inimical to public debt sustainability. For example, in Greece and Portugal, reliance on cuts in investment, tax rate increases (instead of base broadening), and across-the-board wage freezes or reductions (instead of trimming the work force) – perhaps justified against a background of very generous wage awards in the previous decade – seems to have been favored by the authorities on political grounds, and endorsed at least tacitly by the Troika.

Along similar lines, in Portugal, the Troika backed the merger of certain defined-contribution private pension funds with the defined-benefit public pension system, thus compounding the future debt burden with additional contingent liabilities for the sake of a short-run reduction in the budget deficit. Also, to ensure compliance with the deficit ceiling, the authorities imposed a sharp increase in the effective income tax burden, apparently endorsed by the Troika.

Admittedly, when confronted with severe solvency and liquidity problems, policymakers may not be in a position to select an optimal tradeoff between quality and speed of adjustment. Yet, as indicated above, repressed deficits – through recourse to contrived short-run measures, rather than sound policies – are, just like repressed inflation, usually distortionary and self-defeating in restoring public debt sustainability.

6 Uneven Structural Reform

Structural reform measures comprised an integral component of the stabilization programs in Greece and Portugal but were relatively marginal in Ireland, mainly reflecting differences in institution-building

---

[46] See the evidence for OECD member countries in Kneller et al. (1999).

needs among the three countries. From the IMF's perspective, recommendations on structural reform, for the most part in the fiscal and financial areas, were to be determined by their likely contribution to medium- to long-run fiscal sustainability and economic growth, as well as by the objective of introducing internationally accepted good practice.[47] For EU institutions, which were responsible mainly for improving efficiency in the goods, services, and labor markets, structural conditionality was formulated to comply with EU single market regulations. Accordingly, in broad terms, whereas for the Fund most structural conditions were macro-critical, for the EU they were not.

For Greece, the importance of macro-critical structural reform cannot be overemphasized. By necessity it was a most ambitious undertaking both in scope and depth, and for the most part was met with relatively modest success. At the heart of the program, the reform measures covered the entire spectrum of public finances, including public financial management, taxation, and public pensions. In all these areas, progress, if any was made, was protracted, with frequent reversals and slippages, attributable to weak institutional infrastructure and high turnover of senior officials – including more than half a dozen finance ministers since the onset of the crisis. Lack of local managerial continuity and political interference prevented the completion of many tasks envisaged in the programs. For example, tax administration was without a head for more than a year; a highly competent head was removed after a year in office for unexplained reasons. Reform of public pensions is perhaps the only area where some lasting, though modest, progress was achieved toward unifying the excessively large number of pensions and reducing effective replacement ratios.

Considerable resistance was encountered to any steps aimed at improving competitiveness in the markets for goods and services, at improving efficiency in the investment environment, and at introducing greater flexibility in the labor market. Any initial gains in these areas were subsequently eroded. For example, legislation was enacted

---

[47] A highly successful Fund-supported extended arrangement undertaken by Turkey in the early 1980s, documented in Kopits (1987), was among the first adjustment programs with rich structural reform content. Without any of the constraints enumerated above, it was a model of expansionary fiscal adjustment, supported by adequate financing, the full arsenal of macroeconomic instruments, and total ownership by the national authorities.

to liberalize regulated professions and streamline investment approvals of investment proposals, only to be abandoned at the implementation stage.

A specific measure that stands out in the Greek case is the government's apparent commitment to privatization of state-owned enterprises. Although intended primarily to contribute to a one-off budget deficit reduction and to debt sustainability over time, it was also meant to confer lasting benefits in terms of efficiency in the corporate sector. But the lack of broader political support blocked this initiative during the program period and beyond.

Overall, in Greece, structural measures in the adjustment program are to be viewed as a means to building much-needed institutions that would pave the way to public debt sustainability. To sum up, the goal was a regime shift toward better governance in public finances, characterized by institutions that ensure transparency and predictability in fiscal policymaking.

In Ireland, practically all structural conditions were met in a timely fashion. In the fiscal area, important structural measures consisted in the adoption of a sound rules-based fiscal framework, the establishment of an independent fiscal council, and the development of an effective medium-term budgetary strategy. In the financial sector, the program called for winding down insolvent banks and subjecting intervened banks to strict capital and liquidity assessments, as well as for more effective banking supervision. In addition, steps were taken to ensure better enforcement of competition regulations and some reforms in the service sector and the labor market.

In Portugal, a number of structural measures were completed as envisaged, others extended beyond the horizon of the program, and a few have been reversed. The program called for improvements in public financial management and an expenditure review whose implementation was relatively slow. Specific legislative actions encompassed the amendment of the budgetary framework, local government finances, and public pensions. In addition, tax administration was to be streamlined in a number of key operational and structural aspects. Banking supervision and capital buffers were strengthened, but the resolution of failed banks has yet to be completed. Reforms initiated in the labor market and energy sector seem to have stopped, and in some instances reversed.

The success of a program hinges to a large extent on timely availability to the public of information on the design and implementation of the program, but even more importantly on the rationale for, and anticipated socioeconomic impact of, specific measures that affect the daily lives of citizens. The need for transparency and public outreach is crucial where local ownership is scant or altogether absent, especially as regards fiscal measures, since taxes and subsidies are most visible for the public and directly affect their welfare. On this score, the track record of the national authorities and the Troika has been mixed.

Ironically, the program's goals, rationale, and fairness were most transparent and best communicated in Ireland, where the degree of local ownership was the highest. Openness and frequent communication may have contributed significantly to the success of the program. From the very beginning of the crisis, government leaders regularly explained the fiscal strategy and policy measures and their likely impacts on households and enterprises, as well as the steps being taken to alleviate such impact. With the encouragement of national authorities, Troika representatives held press conferences at regular intervals to brief the public on progress under the program.

In Portugal, contact between the authorities and the public was less frequent, but intensified at a later phase in the program. Least successful, however, was the public announcement of the aborted shift of part of the social security contribution from employers to employees, and the subsequent hike in the personal income and payroll tax burden – called "brutal" by the finance minister himself – which was greeted with outrage by various stakeholders.

The lack of transparency was most pronounced in Greece, on several counts. The flow of information from the government to the general public on fiscal developments was rather infrequent and incomplete. This was paralleled by the lack of communication from the IMF and EU institutions. The information gap not only failed to generate local ownership of the program, but in some ways contributed to weakening it further.

A related shortcoming was the apparent lack of sufficient concern expressed by the IMF and EU institutions, as well as the national authorities, in addressing publicly the social costs of the program, as compared to a counterfactual no-adjustment scenario. The provision of estimates and communication of the distribution of the adjustment burden among various segments of the population, along with suggested targeted fiscal measures to alleviate hardship for those seriously affected, could have helped create greater support for the adjustment.

Estimates of favorable distributional effects of the adjustment pro-grams in Greece and Portugal should have been widely circulated.[48] Likewise, national authorities in general did not attempt to quantify or publicize the social and economic effects of the programs. As an exception, the Irish authorities published an initial appraisal of the impact of the pre-Troika fiscal adjustment and a package of measures intended to alleviate its effects on low-income households.[49] In Greece, independent estimates of the adjustment's distributional consequences were made available only recently.[50]

7 Quest for a Closer Union and Other Lessons

A number of lessons can be derived from the euro crisis for the prevention and cure of such crises in the future. Some of the lessons have already been internalized and remedial action has been taken by national and supranational authorities, with a view to strengthening macroeconomic governance, foremost in the context of a closer union in the financial sphere. By and large, governance within the EA can be said to be more robust than before the crisis, though with considerable scope for further improvement – especially on the fiscal front.

Substantial progress has been achieved in strengthening the financial system, starting with the 2012 summit meetings of European leaders with an agreement to create a banking union within the EA, extended on a voluntary basis to the rest of the EU membership as well.[51] The announcement was followed by the establishment of the Single Super-visory Mechanism (SSM) and the Single Resolution Mechanism (SRM).

The new institutions have taken over central supervisory functions through the application of stress tests to major banks within the EA and the resolution of insolvent banks, in cooperation with national banking supervisory authorities. They are also supported by a set of

---

[48] Micro simulations on the basis of a tax-benefit model, by Avram and others (2013), suggest that the net direct impact of the fiscal consolidation on household disposable income has been favorable, as measured by changes in the Gini coefficient.

[49] See Government of Ireland (2010), www.budget.gov.ie/The%20National%20Recovery%20Plan%202011-2014.pdf.

[50] See Parliamentary Budget Office (2014).

[51] For a detailed account, see Veron (2015).

banking regulations and directives under new EU legislation, including on capital adequacy requirements, recovery and resolution procedures, and deposit guarantees. However, the banking union remains incomplete without the establishment of a joint deposit insurance scheme. Although an essential component of the banking union and indispensable for the prevention of a future crisis, the proposed European Deposit Insurance Scheme (EDIS) is held in abeyance due to opposition by Germany and a few other member countries.[52]

In comparison to the steady progress toward a banking union, modifications of the fiscal framework have been rather modest. At the national level, most member governments have enshrined in their fundamental statutes (organic legislation or constitution) key elements of the reformed EU fiscal framework, namely the structural balance rule, with some variations. Many of them have also established an independent fiscal institution to monitor compliance with the rules, as well as independent macroeconomic forecasts as an input into, or control over, official budgetary forecasts – prescribed in the so-called "two-pack" that accompanies the amended SGP. The degree to which these fiscal watchdogs conform with best practice varies across countries.[53]

The extent of national ownership and effective political support for these innovations remains to be tested. Beyond the enactment of the rules-based framework in national legislation, in practice member governments need to adopt the framework in a simplified and transparent manner that places accountability at the decision-making level. For this purpose, it is necessary to distinguish between policy rules and operational rules, and between indicative and binding rules. Views are converging toward establishing a framework in which the principal policy rule is the debt ratio rule, while an expenditure rule is the binding operational rule – for which the finance minister or the budget director could held accountable – and the structural balance rule is to be treated as an indicative rule, given the difficulty of reliably estimating the latter in real time.[54] Such a framework is broadly compatible

---

[52] Such a scheme, with a timetable for implementation, has been proposed in the so-called Five Presidents' report by Juncker et al. (2015).

[53] See the analysis and country cases in Kopits (2013).

[54] See for example Ayuso i Casals (2012) and Carnot (2014) on the advantages of simple government expenditure rules. Kopits (2014a) proposed an approach based on the framework applied in Hungary in 2009–10, whereby a binding

with the reformed SGP, with the advantage of being more enforceable in practice. In most member countries, it is essential that this approach be accompanied by a political commitment to tackle structural reforms – to ensure sufficient fiscal space within the envelope of the medium-term objective (MTO) – incorporated in the concrete measures outlined by the government in its annual Stability Program.[55]

Presumably, rather than fearing financial or legal EU-level sanctions for noncompliance, member governments have become increasingly sensitive to market perceptions, reflected in sovereign bond spreads, as well as to evaluations by credit rating agencies, which since the outbreak of the crisis seem to be more alert to macro-fiscal fundamentals. Market pressures, however, have yet to be fully felt again beyond the eventual phase-out of the sovereign quantitative easing by the ECB that currently dampens spreads on government paper. In the meantime, governments should not succumb to the temptation of borrowing at low interest rates in order to resume the pre-crisis spending spree; instead, they should opportunistically replace high-cost with low-cost borrowing, as part of their debt management strategy. In any event, enhanced fiscal discipline and structural reforms should be undertaken not to avert possible sanctions from the financial markets or from the EU authorities, but to regain stability and growth.[56]

It is, however, at the level of EU institutions that the most important lessons of the crisis need to be learned and implemented. In the first place, the ECB has learned about the importance of differentiating among sovereign collateral by taking into account each government's

discretionary expenditure ceiling (net of mandatory components outside the immediate control of the decision-makers) was derived from the target debt ratio through a two-step algorithm. For options along these lines, see Andrle and others (2015).

[55] Coeure (2014) provides an overview of the structural reform tasks pending in member countries.

[56] Former state secretary Henriksson (2007), reflecting on Sweden's crisis episode of the early 1990s, expressed his country's predicament as follows: "A country with [public] deficit and debt problems is constantly monitored by the financial markets, by international organizations, by other countries ... Being closely monitored by the financial markets means that power shifts from the open chambers of the people's elected representatives to the closed rooms of the financial markets in London and New York ... Some people argue that it is undemocratic that markets have this power over elected representatives. This is a view I do not share. A country that each and every day has to borrow money, either to service the debt or to finance the deficit, is in the hands of its creditors."

credit rating. Hopefully, it will also manage to take into account cross-country inflation rate differences when formulating monetary policy. To be sure, it is now in charge of a unified macroprudential approach to systemic risk across member countries through the newly established European Systemic Risk Board (ESRB). A major challenge ahead will be to wind down quantitative easing as soon as the risk of deflation subsides. All these steps should contribute to sound fiscal policymaking. In addition, the ESM, as the principal financial tool of crisis management – including banking resolutions within the EA, in the context of the evolving banking union – can help alleviate the need for bank recapitalization by member governments.

The EC, under the Eurogroup, is expected to continue to play a pivotal role as guardian of the reformed SGP. The 2011–13 revisions, intended to strengthen the design of and compliance with the Pact (contained in the so-called "six-pack", "two-pack", and an intergovernmental treaty), included granting increased independence and inspection authority to Eurostat. In principle, the emphasis on the structural balance or surplus, replacing the balance or surplus over the cycle, allowing for overruns on account of structural reform measures, and adopting of a numerical yearly reduction in the debt ratio are welcome steps. In practice, the difficulty of measuring these metrics in real time may render them ineffective.[57] Moreover, the increased complexity of the rules poses a major challenge for compliance with the reformed fiscal framework.[58]

A promising tool of enforcement is the MTO to hold governments accountable to their commitments. Apart from the complexity of the existing framework, which will need streamlining for greater simplicity and transparency, the critical challenge for the EC will be effective enforcement of the framework through the European Semester, and ultimately rigorous peer review within the Eurogroup. The recent decision to allow the governments of France and Italy

---

[57] The reliability of real-time estimates of the structural balance for a large number of countries is questioned in Ley and Misch (2013).

[58] For a critical evaluation of the reformed framework, see Barnes, Davidsson, and Rawdanowicz (2012) and Koester, Mohl, and van Riet (2012). Two papers by the European Commission (2013a, 2013b) are intended to help navigate through the maze of rules, regulations, and practices which currently underlie the SGP.

further deferral of compliance with the MTO has been disappointing in this regard.

It is widely recognized by government leaders and policy analysts that the next major step for future crisis prevention and management in the EA (and possibly in the EU) is the creation of a fiscal union.[59] To be viable, the union should be grounded on two key principles of a federal structure: subsidiarity and solidarity (including through risk sharing).[60] For the EA, these principles should facilitate, at an aggregate level, the adoption of a countercyclical fiscal stance and the return to a satisfactory growth path even on the part of member countries that otherwise are unable to do so when restoring debt sustainability takes priority over fighting a recession.

Under the subsidiarity principle, each government function is assigned to the lowest level at which it can be performed most efficiently. This implies that international relations, defense, environmental protection, and immigration, with significant spillovers beyond national boundaries (much like monetary policy and banking regulation), should be carried out by a supranational authority, rather than by national or local governments.[61] To ensure fairness and efficiency, central outlays on international relations and defense would have to be financed with revenue from a uniform earmarked share of a broad-based tax, such as the value-added tax.

A logical extension of the subsidiarity principle is that macroeconomic stabilization should be assigned to the supranational authority, to counteract cyclical, regional, country-specific, or asymmetric shocks, regardless of their source. In this regard, the proposal for a fiscal union put forth in the recent report authored by the five EU presidents is a welcome initiative, envisaged as the next stage in the evolution of EMU.[62] Although it does not specify the responsible authority or the source of financing, the five presidents' proposal to centralize the fiscal stabilization function deserves immediate attention from EU

---

[59] See, for example, Allard et al. (2013).

[60] Finance Minister Schäuble endorsed subsidiarity as the guiding principle of further integration, in Lamers and Schäuble (2014).

[61] See Alesina, Angeloni, and Schucknecht (2005) on application of the subsidiarity principle. As an alternative, Bordo and James (Chapter 8) advocate unifying such functions under a "partial fiscalization" as a common insurance to member countries.

[62] See Juncker et al. (2015).

institutions and member governments alike. In the present circumstances, the yet-to-be-named authority could launch a large-scale, time-bound, and targeted fiscal stimulus within the EA region. This would include primarily, but not solely, public investment – surpassing by an order of magnitude the scope and resources of the European Investment Bank – and active labor market programs, with direct or indirect repercussions across member economies.[63]

Government expenditures aimed at macroeconomic stabilization would be financed with eurobonds issued by the supranational authority, without mutualizing existing legacy public debt. The interest cost would be minimal inasmuch as these bonds finance public spending during recessions, to be wound down during expansionary periods. Moreover, the ECB would not have to refrain from sizable acquisition of such bonds.

Centralizing the stabilization function in this manner is entirely consistent with the subsidiarity and solidarity principles. Recessionary conditions prevailing in some member countries have repercussions throughout the union. Social unrest and the emergence of extreme political movements in one member country cannot be ignored in other member countries, since they are likely to cause severe and long-lasting distress and instability in the EA as a whole. EA-wide stabilization would be a win–win solution, conferring widespread multiple benefits: A major euro-wide expansionary impulse and a strengthened institutional architecture, with negligible moral hazard for member governments. Highly indebted member countries would regain some fiscal space under the deficit ceiling, with room for implementing structural reforms that socially and politically may be difficult to undertake.

However, the challenge of transferring key functions from national governments to the supranational government cannot be underestimated. Such a fundamental step toward fiscal and political unification cannot be achieved without amending the Treaty. Merging defense budgets across member countries is bound to be a protracted process, even in the shadow of the confrontation with Russia over Ukraine. By comparison, an intergovernmental treaty on activating the common

---

[63] Centrally financed public expenditures would include major infrastructure and research and development projects, manpower training, and mobility and housing subsidies. By their nature, they would consist of outlays that not merely stimulate aggregate demand, but also, more important, contribute to long-term growth.

macroeconomic stabilization function in the EA might be relatively easy to reach, if subject to a fast-track procedure, in view of the need for averting a bleak economic and social outlook.

Nevertheless, given the constraints imposed by cultural and economic differences, it would be unrealistic to assume that major steps toward a closer political union in the EA can be accomplished in less than a generation. To be sure, completion of the banking union – by centralizing deposit insurance – should be feasible well within that interval. However, if the United States can serve as an example, it may take up to three generations to establish and enforce the necessary institutional framework for a stable fiscal union, under the criteria outlined above, with appropriate incentives and some risk pooling.[64] Admittedly, even under exceptionally fortunate circumstances, tensions and unresolved issues are likely to prevail among member states even beyond that period.

For the IMF, the lessons from the euro crisis are rather straightforward and for the most part ready for implementation. Having apparently abandoned the "Europe is different" mindset and the complacency that characterized the previous decade, the IMF is increasingly exercising bilateral surveillance of EA member states similarly to any other IMF member country, not only through annual consultations, but also through more candid transparency reports, including risk assessments.

Further progress is called for in the preparation of public debt sustainability and risk assessments. The standard fan chart was supplemented, effective 2013, by a recently developed risk assessment matrix (RAM) consisting of subjective staff views on the likelihood of specified shocks and their impacts on the economic and financial performance of the EA. Against its obvious shortcomings as an objective numerical indicator of risk,[65] the advantage of this approach is the ease with which it communicates the RAM in non-technical terms. A technically superior alternative approach would involve applying stochastic techniques that can capture quantitatively fiscal and financial systemic risks. Overall, comprehensive risk assessments should be driven not by market conditions but by in-depth analysis of fundamentals.

---

[64] In his Nobel lecture, Sargent (2012) provides a comprehensive economic analysis of the history of US fiscal unification in an embryonic federal context, spanning the period between the fiscal crises of the 1790s and the 1840s, but with relatively few lessons for the EA.

[65] For a description and some critical views on the RAM, see Robinson (2014).

As regards the rescue of crisis-hit EA countries, the Fund would do well in following uniform criteria and conditionality in the design of stabilization programs. The Fund's increasingly independent stance in recent negotiations over a new program for Greece can be viewed as evidence of a return to the well-tested conventional approach. In general, the Fund needs to calibrate programs taking into account the internal and external constraints that prevail in crisis-hit countries, recognizing the extraordinary burden of the adjustment placed on the public sector. In addition, it is necessary to step up efforts to communicate clearly the rationale and effects of policy measures undertaken in a program, especially where local ownership is missing.

Bibliography

Ahrend, R., Cournede, B. and Price, R. W. (2008). *Monetary Policy, Market Excesses and Financial Turmoil*. OECD Economics Department Working Paper No. 597.

Alesina, A., Angeloni, I. and Schucknecht, L. (2005). What does the European Union do? *Public Choice*, **123**(3–4), 275–319.

Alesina, A. and Ardagna, S. (2013). The design of fiscal adjustments. *Tax Policy and the Economy*, **27**, 19–68.

Allard, C., Koeva-Brooks, P. Bluedorn, J. Bornhorst, F. Christopherson, K. Ohnsorghe, F. and Poghosyan, T. (2013). *Toward a Fiscal Union for the Euro Area*. IMF Staff Discussion Note SDN/13/09, September.

Alt, J., Lassen, D. and Wehner, J. (2014). It isn't just about Greece: domestic politics, transparency and fiscal gimmickry in Europe. *British Journal of Political Science*, **44**(04), 707–16.

Andrle, M., Bluedorn, J., Eyraud, L., Kinda, T., Koeva-Brooks, P., Schwartz, G. and Weber, A. (2015). *Reforming Fiscal Governance in the European Union* IMF Staff Discussion Note SDN/15/09, May.

Avram, S., Figari, F., Leventi, C., Levy, H., Navicke, J., Matsaganis, M., Militaru, E., Paulus, A., Rastrigina, O. and Sutherland, H.(2013). *The Distributional Effects of Fiscal Consolidation in Nine EU Countries*. EUROMOD Working Paper Series EM2/13, Institute for Social and Economic Research, University of Essex, February 11.

Ayuso i Casals, J. (2012). *National Expenditure Rules: Why, How and When?* European Economy Economic Papers, No. 473, European Commission, December.

Balassone, F., Franco, D. and Goretti, C. (2013). Italy: what role for an independent fiscal institution? In G. Kopits, ed., *Restoring Public Debt*

Sustainability: The Role of Independent Fiscal Institutions. Oxford: Oxford University Press, pp. 250–69.

Banque Nationale de Belgique (2006). *Rapport annuel 2005*. Brussels, February.

Barnes, S., Davidsson, D. and Rawdanowicz, L. (2012). *Europe's New Fiscal Rules*. OECD Economics Department Working Paper No. 972.

Barnhill, T. and Kopits, G. (2004). Assessing fiscal sustainability under uncertainty. *Journal of Risk*, 6(4), 31–53.

Blanchard, O. (2007). Adjustment within the euro: the difficult case of Portugal. *Portuguese Economic Journal*, 6, 1–21.

Blanchard, O. and Giavazzi, F. (2002). Current account deficits in the euro area: the end of the Feldstein–Horioka puzzle? *Brookings Papers on Economic Activity*, 2, pp. 147–86.

Blanchard, O. and Leigh, D. (2013). *Growth Forecast Errors and Fiscal Multipliers*. IMF Working Paper No. WP/13/1, January.

Bordo, M. (2014). TARGET balances, Bretton Woods, and the Great Depression. *Vox EU*, March 21, http://voxeu.org/article/historical-lessons-target-imbalances

Bordo, M. and James, H. (2013). *The European Crisis in the Context of the History of Previous Financial Crises*. NBER Working Paper No. 19112, June.

Buiter, W. H. and Sibert, A. C. (2005). How the eurosystem's treatment of collateral in its open market operations weakens fiscal discipline in the eurozone. In National Bank of Poland, *Fiscal Policy and the Road to the Euro*, pp. 29–58.

Buti, M. and Giudice, G. (2002). Maastricht fiscal rules at ten: an assessment. *Journal of Common Market Studies*, 40, 823–48.

Carnot, N. (2014). *Evaluating Fiscal Policy: A Rule of Thumb*. European Economy Economic Papers, No. 526, European Commission, August.

Chari, V. V. and Kehoe, P. (2009). On the need for fiscal constraints in a monetary union. *Journal of Monetary Economics*, 54(8), 2399–408.

Cecchetti, S. G., Mohanty, M. S. and Zampoli, F. (2011). Achieving growth amid fiscal imbalances: the real effects of debt. In *Achieving Maximum Long-Run Growth*, symposium sponsored by the Federal Reserve Bank of Kansas City, Jackson Hole, Wyoming, August, www.kansascityfed.org/publicat/sympos/2011/Cecchetti_final.pdf, pp. 145–98.

Coeure, B. (2014). *Structural Reforms: Learning the Right Lessons from the Crisis*. Keynote speech, Economic Conference, Latvijas Banka, Riga, October 17, www.ecb.europa.eu/press/key/date/2014/html/sp141017.en.html

Constâncio, V. (2000). *Statement by Governor Vitor Constâncio at His Swearing-in Ceremony*. Bank of Portugal, Lisbon, February 23.

Coricelli, F. and Ercolani, V. (2004). Fiscal rules on the road to an enlarged European Union. In G. Kopits, ed., *Rules-Based Fiscal Policy in Emerging Markets: Background, Analysis and Prospects*. Basingstoke: Palgrave Macmillan, pp. 146–63.

De Grauwe, P. and Ji, Y. (2013). Self-fulfilling crises in the eurozone: an empirical test. *Journal of International Money and Finance*, **34**, 15–36.

Diaz Alejandro, C. (1985). Good-bye financial repression, hello financial crash. *Journal of Development Economics*, **19**, 1–24.

Donovan, D. and Murphy, A. (2013). *The Fall of the Celtic Tiger: Ireland and the Euro Debt Crisis*. Oxford: Oxford University Press.

European Commission (2010). *Report on Greek Government Deficit and Debt Statistics*. Brussels, January 8.

(2013a). *Building a Strengthened Fiscal Framework in the European Union: A Guide to the Stability and Growth Pact*. European Economy Occasional Papers, No. 150, May.

(2013b). *Vade Mecum on the Stability and Growth Pact*. European Economy Occasional Papers, No. 151, May.

European Parliament, Directorate General for Internal Policies (2014). *Committee Study on the Troika and Financial Assistance in the Euro Area: Successes and Failures*, prepared by A. Sapir, G. B. Wolff, C. de Sousa and A. Tazi, February.

FitzGerald, J. (2006). *The Experience of Monetary Union – Ireland and Spain*. Economic and Social Research Institute, Dublin.

Frankel, J. and Schreger, J. (2013). Over-optimistic official forecasts and fiscal rules in the eurozone. *Review of World Economics*, **149**(2), 247–72.

Henriksson, J. (2007). *Ten Lessons about Budget Consolidation*. Brussels: Bruegel.

Independent Evaluation Office of the International Monetary Fund (2011). *IMF Performance in the Run-Up to the Financial and Economic Crisis: IMF Surveillance in 2004-07*, Evaluation Report.

International Monetary Fund (2001). *Ireland: Staff Report for the 2001 Article IV Consultation*. SM/01/218, July 11.

(2002). *Assessing Sustainability*. May 28, www.imf.org/external/np/pdr/sus/2002/eng/052802.pdf.

(2006). *Greece: Report on the Observance of Standards and Codes (ROSC) Fiscal Transparency Module*. IMF Country Report No. 06/49, February.

(2009a). *Ireland: Staff Report for the 2009 Article IV Consultation*. IMF Country Report No. 09/195, June.

(2009b). *Greece: Selected Issues*. IMF Country Report No. 09/245, August.

(2010). *Greece: Staff Report on Request for Stand-by Arrangement*. IMF Country Report No. 10/110, May 10.

(2011). *Modernizing the Framework for Fiscal Policy and Public Debt Sustainability Analysis*. IMF Policy Paper, August 5.

(2013). *Greece: Ex Post Evaluation of Exceptional Access under the 2010 Stand-by Arrangement*. IMF Country Report 13/156, May 20.

(2015a). *Ireland: Ex Post Evaluation of Exceptional Access under the 2010 Extended Arrangement*. IMF Country Report 15/20, January.

(2015b). *Portugal: First Post-Program Monitoring Discussions*. IMF Country Report 15/21, January.

(2015c). *Greece: Preliminary Draft Debt Sustainability*. IMF Country Report No. 15/165, June 26.

(2015d). *Greece: An Update of IMF Staff's Preliminary Public Debt Sustainability*. IMF Country Report No. 15/186, July 14.

Jaeger, A. and Schuknecht, L. (2004). *Boom-Bust Phases in Asset Prices and Fiscal Policy Behavior*. IMF Working Paper No. WP/04/54, April.

Juncker, J.-C., Tusk, D., Dijsselbloem, J., Draghi, M. and Schulz, M. (2015). *Completing Europe's Economic and Monetary Union*. Brussels: European Commission, June.

Kanda, D. (2010). *Asset Booms and Structural Fiscal Positions: The Case of Ireland*. IMF Working Paper No. WP/10/57, March.

Kneller, R., Bleany, M. and Gemmel, N. (1999). Fiscal policy and growth: evidence from OECD countries. *Journal of Public Economics*, **74**, 171–90.

Koester, G. B., Mohl, P. and van Riet, A. (2012). *The New EU Fiscal Governance Framework: A Quantum Leap or Only Small Steps Ahead?* Paper presented at the ECB-IMF Conference on Reforming EU Fiscal Governance, Frankfurt, December 13–14.

Kopits, G. (1982). *Factor prices in industrial countries*. IMF Staff Papers, No. **29**, September, 437–66.

(1987). *Structural Reform, Stabilization, and Growth in Turkey*. IMF Occasional Paper No. 52, International Monetary Fund.

(2013). *Restoring Public Debt Sustainability: The Role of Independent Fiscal Institutions*. Oxford: Oxford University Press.

(2014a). Ireland's fiscal framework: options for the future. *Economic and Social Review*, **45**(1), 135–58.

(2014b). Coping with fiscal risk: analysis and practice. *OECD Journal on Budgeting*, **14**(1), 47–71.

Kopits, G., and Symansky, S. (1998). Fiscal Policy Rules. IMF Occasional Paper No. 162, International Monetary Fund.

Lamers, K. and Schäuble, W. (2014). More integration is still the right goal for Europe. *Financial Times*, September 1.

Leipold, A. (2011). Non sprechiamo l'occasione del Fondo. *Il Sole 24 Ore*, November 6.

Ley, E. and Misch, F. (2013). *Real-Time Macro Monitoring and Fiscal Policy*. Policy Research Working Paper No. 6303, The World Bank, January.

Mayer, T. (2012). *Europe's Unfinished Currency: The Political Economics of the Euro*. London: Anthem Press.

McKinnon, R. (1999). Toward virtual exchange-rate stability in Western and Eastern Europe with the advent of EMU. In M. Blejer and M. Skreb, eds., *Balance of Payments, Exchange Rates and Competitiveness in Transition Economies*. Norwell: Kluwer Academic Publishers, pp. 131–57.

Parliamentary Budget Office (2014). *Fiscal Adjustment: How Fair is the Distribution of the Burdens?* Athens: Hellenic Parliament.

Pasimeni, P. (2014). An optimum currency crisis. *The European Journal of Comparative Economics*, 11(2) 173–204.

Pisani-Ferry, J., Sapir, A. and Wolff, G. B. (2011). *TSR External Study – An Evaluation of IMF Surveillance of the Euro Area*. IMF, July 19.

Reinhart, C. and Rogoff, K. (2009). *This Time is Different: Eight Centuries of Financial Folly*. Princeton: Princeton University Press.

Reviglio, F. (2001). *Budgetary Transparency for Public Expenditure Control*. IMF Working Paper No. WP/01/08, January.

Robinson, D. J. (2014). *The IMF Response to the Global Crisis: Assessing Risks and Vulnerabilities in IMF Surveillance*. Independent Evaluation Office of the International Monetary Fund Background Paper BP/14/09, October 8.

Sargent, T. J. (2012). Nobel lecture: United States then, Europe now. *Journal of Political Economy*, **120**(1), 1–40.

Sinn, H. W. (2014). *The Euro Trap: On Bursting Bubbles, Budgets, and Beliefs*. Oxford: Oxford University Press.

Schadler, S. (2013). *Unsustainable Debt and the Political Economy of Lending: Constraining the IMF's Role in Sovereign Debt Crises*. CIGI Papers, No. 19, October.

Spaventa, L., and Chiorazzo, V. (2000). *Astuzia o Virtu'?: Come accadde che l'Italia fu ammessa all'Unione monetaria*. Roma: Donzelli Editore.

Summers, L. (2013). End the damaging obsession with deficits. *Financial Times*, January 21.

Tanzi, V. (2013). *Dollar, Euros and Debt*. New York: Palgrave Macmillan.

Tsibouris, G. C., Horton, M. A., Flanagan, M. J. and Maliszewski, W. S. (2006). *Experience with Large Fiscal Adjustments*, Occasional Paper No. 246, International Monetary Fund.

Veron, N. (2015) *Europe's Radical Banking Union*. Bruegel Essay and Lecture Series. Brussels: Bruegel.

PART III

New Analytical Perspectives

10 Problems with Deficit Accounting

JERRY R. GREEN AND LAURENCE J. KOTLIKOFF

1 Introduction

The Great Recession has created enormous interest in fiscal policy matters. Discussions about sovereign debt and deficit levels, stimulus measures and consolidation packages have filled the front pages of the newspapers and the top sections of media websites. Unfortunately, much of the discussions of fiscal positions, fiscal performance, fiscal policy have been exercises in linguistics that have nothing to do with economics and everything to do with bad accounting.

This chapter is a synthesis of an earlier paper written by Jerry R. Green and Laurence J. Kotlikoff,[1] and Kotlikoff's Testimony to the Senate Budget Committee on 'America's Fiscal Insolvency and Its Generational Consequences'. The chapter has two major objectives. The first is to provide a general proof that standard fiscal measures, including the deficit, taxes and transfer payments, are economically ill defined. Instead, these measures reflect the arbitrary labelling of underlying fiscal conditions. Analyses based on these and derivative measures, such as disposable income and private assets and personal savings, constitute the perusal of nomenclature, not the application of economics.

Economic theory is not just telling us what is meaningless, but is also crystal clear in teaching us what to measure, namely the infinite-horizon fiscal gap. Therefore, the second objective of this chapter is to illustrate the usefulness of this concept in uncovering the 'true' state of public finances. The infinite-horizon fiscal gap tells us whether the government has, over time, enough receipts to cover its projected spending. It equals the present value of all projected future expenditures less the present value of all projected future revenues.

---

[1] 'On the general relativity of fiscal language', in Auerbach and Shaviro, eds., *Institutional Foundations of Public Finance*, Harvard University Press, 2008. Permission for reprint granted by Harvard University Press. Licence Nr. 38458.

Section 2 introduces a very general model to show that for any real policy there are an infinite number of ways it can be reported, making the measured path of deficits in all future periods completely arbitrary. Section 3 provides a concrete illustration of this general model using Diamond's canonical model of government debt. Section 4 introduces the concept of the infinite-horizon fiscal gap. Section 5 provides estimates of fiscal gaps for the United States and other advanced countries, while Section 6 concludes.

2 General Relativity of Fiscal Language

The argument that any underlying fiscal policy can be reported as entailing any time path of deficit, taxes and transfer payments, and that these measures are, economically speaking, content-free, was originally advanced by Kotlikoff (1986). Auerbach and Kotlikoff (1987) and Kotlikoff (2002) provide formal treatments of the point, but neither provides a general proof of the proposition. This section provides such a proof. It posits a competitive, contingent claims economy that can accommodate uncertainty, information asymmetries, distortions, externalities, public goods, time-inconsistent policy, imperfect credit markets and incomplete/segmented markets.

Specifically, we show that one can report any time path whatsoever of government deficits independent of the general equilibrium of the economy. The reported time path of deficits requires mutually consistent reporting of the time paths of taxes and transfer payments. This consistency requirement means that the time paths of reported fiscal variables are determined relative to each other, rather than being determined independently.

Our method of demonstrating this proposition is to articulate the equilibrium of a fully general neoclassical model. In presenting this model, we make no reference to 'deficits', 'taxes' or 'transfer payments'. This, in and of itself, proves that these measures are arbitrary descriptive constructs, which have no more scientific bearing than does the choice of whether to use French or English as the language in which to discuss the model.

Our model differs from the classical private ownership model only in that it includes a government sector. Government policy is unconstrained in real terms. What we show, therefore, is that for any real policy there are an infinite number of ways it can be reported, making the measured path of deficits in all future period completely arbitrary.

In what follows, there are K agents, N states, M goods, V firms and H endowments. Goods include leisure. Endowments include time, various types of physical capital and natural resources. As in Arrow (1964), a state of the world is defined by a particular date, a particular resolution of uncertainty and a specification of all economically relevant variables. The terms p_s and q_s reference pre-policy producer and endowment price vectors in state s.

2.1 Profit Maximization

There are V firms, which may be operated by private agents, the government or both. Firm j's profit is

$$\pi_j \equiv \max_{y_{js}} \left(\sum_s p_s y_{js} - \sum_s q_s \phi_{js} + m_j \right), \tag{1}$$

where y_{js} is firm j's 1 x M vector of net goods supply in state s, ϕ_{js} is firm j's 1 x H vector of endowment demands and m_j is a function determining the government's net payment to firm j. Producers are atomistic and take producer prices, endowment prices and their net payment functions as given.

Firm j's constant returns production function is given by

$$f_j(y_{j1}, \dots, y_{jN}, \phi_{j1}, \dots, \phi_{jN}; Y_{-j1}, \dots, Y_{-jN}, \phi_{-j1}, \dots, \phi_{-jN},$$
$$X_1, \dots, X_N, Z_1, \dots, Z_N, \omega_1, \dots, \omega_N) = 0, \tag{2}$$

where Y_{-js} is a 1 x M x (V−1) vector of net supplies of firms other than j in state s, ϕ_{-js} is a 1 x H x (V−1) vector of state $-s$ endowment demands of firms other than j, X_s references the 1 x M x K vector of goods demanded by agents 1 through K in state s, Z_s references the 1x M vector of goods demanded by the government in state s and ω_s references the 1 x H vector of economy-wide endowments in state s. For future reference, we denote by Y_s the 1 x M x V vector of net supplies of firms 1 through V in state s and by $Y_{\phi s}$ the 1 x H x V vector of endowment demands of firms 1 through V.

Including the Y_{-js}'s, ϕ_{-js}'s, X_s's, Z_s's, ϕ_s's and ω_s's in (2) entertains the possibility of production externalities, consumption externalities, externalities from the use of economy-wide endowments and externalities arising from the levels of economy-wide endowments.

Firm j's net payment function, m_j, may depend on its own state-specific net supplies of goods and demands for endowments. But it may also depend on the state-specific net supplies and demands of other firms, the constellation of agents' state-specific demands, the constellation of government state-specific demands for goods and endowments and the economy's overall endowments. In other words, the firm's net payment function may depend on any real variable in the economy. This potential dependency, which may be highly non-linear, is expressed in

$$m_j = m_j(y_{j1}, \ldots, y_{jN}, \phi_{j1}, \ldots, \phi_{jN}; Y_{-j1}, \ldots, Y_{-jN}, \phi_{-j1}, \ldots,$$
$$\phi_{-jN}, X_1, \ldots, X_N, Z_1, \ldots, Z_N, \omega_1, \ldots, \omega_N). \tag{3}$$

2.2 Preferences

Let x_{is} reference the 1 x M vector of goods demanded by agent i in state s, X_{-is} reference the 1 x M x (K−1) matrix of goods consumed by agents other than i in state s and Z_s reference the 1 x M vector of goods consumed by the government in state s. The utility of agent i is given by

$$U_i = U(x_{i1}, \ldots, x_{iN}, X_{-i1}, \ldots, X_{-iN}, Z_1, \ldots, Z_N, Y_1, \ldots, Y_N,$$
$$\phi_1, \ldots, \phi_N, \omega_1, \ldots, \omega_N). \tag{4}$$

The arguments of these preferences accommodate consumer and producer externalities as well as externalities/public goods generated by producers' and government demands. These arguments can also determine commodity characteristics, such as average quality, that can be important determinants of demand and welfare in economies characterized by asymmetric information.

2.3 Private Budgets

The budget constraint of agent i is given by

$$\sum_s p_s x_{is} = e_i, \tag{5}$$

where e_i is the net resource function of agent i. The net resource function references the amount of resources the government arranges for agent i to be able to spend on state-specific claims. As indicated in (6), this function may depend not only on the agent's own demand for claims in states of nature but also on the claims of other agents, the production of each firm, the government's state-specific goods demands and the economy's state-specific overall endowments. This dependency may also be highly non-linear.

$$e_i = e_i(x_{i1}, \ldots, x_{iN}, X_{-i1}, \ldots, X_{-iN}, Z_1, \ldots, Z_N, Y_1, \ldots, Y_N, \omega_1, \ldots, \omega_N).$$
(6)

In addition to (5), agent i's demands are constrained by

$$x_{is} \in \psi(X_1, \ldots, X_N, Z_1, \ldots, Z_N, Y_1, \ldots, Y_N, \omega_1, \ldots, \omega_N).$$
(7)

Equation (7) can accommodate a variety of important restrictions on trade, including those arising because of incomplete/segmented markets and borrowing constraints.

2.4 Market Clearing

In equilibrium firms' supplies of goods in each state, s must cover agents' and government demands and the economy-wide supplies of endowments must cover firms' endowment demands.

$$\sum_j y_{js} = \sum_i x_{is} + Z_s,$$
(8)

$$\omega_s = \sum_j \phi_{js}.$$
(9)

2.5 The Government's Budget

Equations (1), (5), (8) and (9) imply

$$\sum_s p_s Z_s = \sum_s q_s \omega_s + \sum_j \pi_j - \sum_i e_i - \sum_j m_j.$$
(10)

The economy's overall resources consist of the value of its overall endowments plus the value of pure profits. These overall resources less the amount of net resources that the government provides to agents and firms must finance the government's demand for goods.

2.6 Government Policy

Government policy consists of a set of $e_i(\ )$ and $m_j(\ )$ functions as well as state-specific government product demand functions given by

$$Z_s = Z_s(X_1, \ldots, X_N, Z_1, \ldots, Z_N, Y_1, \ldots, Y_N, \omega_1, \ldots, \omega_N). \qquad (11)$$

As (10) indicates, these four sets of policy functions are not mutually independent.

2.7 Equilibrium

In equilibrium, households maximize (4) subject to (5) and (7), firms maximize (1) subject to (2), the government jointly chooses its $m_j(\ )$, $e_i(\ )$ and $Z_s(\ )$ functions consistent with (10) and the market clearing conditions (8) and (9) are satisfied.

2.7.1 Reporting Policy

Agent i's net resources, e_i, can be reported as reflecting the market value of a 1 x H vector of state-specific private endowments, a_{is}, proportionate holdings of firm j of θ_{ij}, less a 1 x K vector of state- and good-specific net tax functions, τ_{is}, that is,

$$e_i = \sum_s q_s a_{is} + \sum_i \theta_{ij} \pi_j - \sum_s p_s \tau_{is}. \qquad (12)$$

Since the elements a_{is} and agent i's reported share of firm profits will be described as constants, the τ_{is} functions must contain the same arguments as the e_i function; for example,

$$\tau_{is} = \tau_{is}(x_{i1}, \ldots, x_{iN}, X_{-i1}, \ldots, X_{-iN}, Z_1, \ldots, Z_N, \\ Y_1, \ldots, Y_N, \omega_1, \ldots, \omega_N). \qquad (13)$$

Note that in equilibrium endowment and producer price vectors depend on the same arguments as τ_{is}, namely $X_1, \ldots, X_N, Z_1, \ldots, Z_N, Y_1, \ldots, Y_N, \omega_1, \ldots, \omega_N$, so there is no need to list them in (13) as separate arguments.

Let Ω_s reference a 1 x H vector of reported government endowments in state s. Since endowments are held either by agents or the government, reporting, for agent i, endowments of a_{is} in state s also requires, for consistency, announcing a government net endowment vector Ω_s satisfying

$$\Omega_s = \omega_s - \sum_i a_{is}. \tag{14}$$

Combining (10), (12) and (14) yields the more conventional expression for the government's budget, namely

$$\sum_s p_s Z_s + \sum_s \sum_j m_{js} = \sum_s q_s \Omega_s + \sum_j \theta_{gi} \pi_j + \sum_s \sum_i p_s \tau_{is}, \tag{15}$$

where

$$\theta_{gi} = 1 - \sum_i \theta_{ij} \tag{16}$$

references the government's reported ownership share of firm j. Equation (15) can be described as the government financing its goods and its net subsidies payments to firms from its net worth (the sum of the first two terms on the right-hand side of (15)) plus its net taxation of agents.

Given an equilibrium, any party, be it a private agent or government official, is free to report any constellation of private endowments and corresponding government endowments she wants. Assume, for example, that there is a single endowment, namely capital, and that agent k reports private asset values of $\hat{a}_{is}$ for $i = 1, \ldots, K$ and $s = 1, \ldots, N$ and private firm ownership shares θ_{ij}. The corresponding announcement of government net tax payments by agent i in state s – denoted by $\hat{\tau}_{is}$, and government assets in state s, $\hat{\Omega}_{is}$, must satisfy (17) and (18).

$$e_i = \sum_s q_s \hat{a}_{is} + \sum_i \hat{\theta}_{ij} \pi_j - \sum_s p_s \hat{\tau}_{is}, \tag{17}$$

$$\hat{\Omega}_s = \omega_s - \sum_i \hat{a}_{is}. \tag{18}$$

If agent k is a fiscal conservative (liberal) and is reassured by contemplating a large government surplus (debt) and low (high) taxes, agent k can simply declare very low (high) values of private assets, $\hat{a}_{is}$, which will lead, according to (17) and (18), to high (low) reported values of $\hat{\Omega}_s$ and low (high) reported values of $\sum_s p_s \hat{\tau}_{is}$. Thus the reported levels of these fiscal variables are completely undetermined as individual magnitudes, but they are linked to each other by (17) and (18). In this sense these variables are mutually determined, but not individually determined. As we discuss below, however, many economic analyses in macroeconomics and public finance have used the levels of taxes or deficits as measurable, identifiable variables, as if these levels had an unambiguous, independent meaning.

Equations (17) and (18) complete the demonstration of the proposition that is our main objective, as stated at the beginning of this section. One can see from these equations that a change in $\hat{a}_{is}$ and a corresponding change in $\hat{\Omega}_s$ and $\sum_s p_s \hat{\tau}_{is}$ leaves the real value of i's net resources constant, while changing the reported government assets to any desired level. Of course, taxes and private assets need to be restated consistently. But there is no intrinsic meaning to the level of the deficit, the level of taxes paid, transfer payments received or private assets held. Stated differently, there is an infinite number of mutually consistent sets of fiscal labels that one can attach to any neoclassical model without providing the slightest economic insight concerning the model's true underlying fiscal policy, including the impact of that policy on the welfare of current and future economic agents.

2.8 Deficits

Time is one of many characteristics of our model's states of nature. If we consider two states, s_1 and s_2, that differ with respect to their measure of time, the difference in government net debt (the negative of government assets) between the two states constitutes their intervening deficit. Since one can report any size of debt or surplus for states s_1 and s_2, one is free to report any size deficit (reduction in net assets) across those two states and, indeed, across any two states that one wants. Hence, each agent is free to concoct whatever deficit and associated net tax payment times series, past or present, that one wants.

2.9 Tax and Transfer Payments

Net taxes are defined as gross taxes minus transfer payments. Given one's reported level of net taxes, one can report any level of gross taxes minus a corresponding level of transfer payment. Hence, gross taxes and transfer payments are just as ill defined as net taxes. The same holds for any measures that rely on gross taxes and gross transfer payments, such as average tax rates, the unfunded liabilities of transfer programs, disposable income or personal income/saving.

2.10 Intuition

There is an old joke in which a husband claims to be in charge of his household. As he puts it to his friends, 'I make the important decisions – I determine our household's foreign policy and let my wife handle everything else'. Knowing who is really in charge in a marriage is tough business, and determining who owns what can be even harder. Indeed, if the household resides in a community property state, it is impossible to allocate ownership. The husband and wife may have 'separate' bank and other accounts, but neither can withhold the corpus of 'their' accounts from the other. Indeed, a variant of the quoted joke is 'I own the money and my wife spends it'.

The private sector and the government are no different from a couple living under community property law. They jointly own everything and jointly determine how to spend it. Whether the government says: (a) 'It's all mine, but I'll let you (the private sector) have some'; (b) 'It's all yours, but I'll take whatever I'd like'; or (c) 'It's partly mine and partly yours, but I'll determine how much of mine to give you and how much of yours to keep' does not make an iota of economic difference.

3 Illustrating the Relativity of Fiscal Language

The canonical model of government 'debt' is Diamond's (1965) two-period life-cycle formulation. We now show how the above general formulation accommodates this model. Agents are assumed to consume a single good and leisure when young and old. Labour supplied by young and old is homogeneous. Output of the good, call it corn, is produced via constant returns to scale with capital and labour. There is neither population nor productivity growth. We normalize each cohort's population to unity. The endowment of time that can be used for work or leisure is 1 per generation per period. For simplicity, we assume the government makes no net payments to firms, but does have a demand for consumption of the economy's single good.

Let c_{yt}, l_{yt}, c_{ot+1} and l_{ot+1} stand, respectively, for consumption and leisure when young and old of the generation born at time t. The lifetime utility of the generation born at time t is given by

$$u_t = u_t\left(C_{yt}, l_{yt}, C_{ot+1}, l_{ot+1}\right). \tag{19}$$

Consider the economy as of time $t = 0$. The budget constraint facing the old at time 0 is given by

$$C_{o0} + W_0 l_{o0} = e_{o0}. \tag{20}$$

For generations born at time $t \geq 0$, the budget constraint is given by

$$C_{yt} + \frac{C_{ot+1}}{1 + r_{t+1}} + W_t l_{yt} + \frac{W_{t+1} l_{0t+1}}{1 + r_{t+1}} = e_t. \tag{21}$$

In (20) and (21) e_{o0} stands for the remaining lifetime net resource function of the old at time 0, and e_t is the lifetime net resource function of the generation born at time t. Each generation's net resource function can depend freely and in a highly non-linear way on its consumption and leisure decisions. And since each generation will consider how its consumption and leisure decisions affect its net resources both inframarginally and at the margin, this formulation fully accommodates distortionary policy.

The production function is

$$Y_t = F(K_t, L_t). \tag{22}$$

The government's demand for corn at time t is g_t. The economy's endowment of capital evolves according to

$$K_{t+1} - K_t = Y_t - C_{yt} - C_{ot} - g_t. \tag{23}$$

Labour supply is determined by

$$L_t = 2 - l_{yt} - l_{ot}. \tag{24}$$

Using (22) and (24), rewrite (22) as

$$K_{t+1} - K_t = F(K_t, 2 - l_{yt} - l_{ot}) - C_{yt} - C_{ot} - g_t. \tag{25}$$

In hiring capital and labour, firms equate marginal factor products to pre-policy factor prices; that is,

$$F_K(K_t, 2 - l_{yt} - l_{ot}) = r_t \ F_L(K_t, 2 - l_{yt} - l_{ot}) = W_t. \tag{26}$$

3.1 Policy

In equilibrium the government announces a time path of net resource functions – the terms e_{o0} and e_t – and a time path of corn demand, g_t, that satisfy (25) in each period given utility maximization subject to

(19) and (20), and given the determination via (26) of pre-policy factor prices.

3.2 Labelling

Suppose the economy is in dynamic equilibrium given government policy as determined by its net resource and spending functions. Denote by an upper bar this equilibrium's variables. Now consider announcing/reporting any time path of official debt, $\widehat{D}_t$ starting at time 0. If one reports $\widehat{D}_0$ as the amount of government debt prevailing at time 0, the corresponding report of private assets at time 0, $\widehat{a}_0$, is determined by (27) for $t = 0$. The consistent report of net taxes facing the elderly at time 0, $\widehat{\tau}_{ot}$, is determined by (28). The reported debt for time $t > 0$ determines $\widehat{a}_t$ from (27). This determines $\widehat{\tau}_{yt}$ from (29), and given $\widehat{\tau}_{yt}$, the reported value of $\widehat{\tau}_{ot+1}$ is determined by (30).

$$\widehat{a}_t = \widehat{D}_t + \overline{K}_t, \tag{27}$$

$$\overline{e}_{o0} = \widehat{a}_0(1 + \overline{r}_0) + \overline{W}_0 - \widehat{\tau}_{o0}, \tag{28}$$

$$\widehat{a}_{t+1} = \overline{W}_t(1 - l_{yt}) - \overline{C}_{yt} - \widehat{\tau}_{yt}, \tag{29}$$

$$\overline{e}_t = \overline{W}_t + \frac{\overline{W}_{t+1}}{1 + \overline{r}_{t+1}} - \widehat{\tau}_{yt} - \frac{\widehat{\tau}_{ot+1}}{1 + \overline{r}_{t+1}}. \tag{30}$$

3.3 Relationship to the General Formulation

In the above example, (20) and (21) are specific cases of (5), (24) is a specific case of (8) and the equation of economy-wide capital and time endowments with firm demands for these endowments in (26) is a specific case of (9).

Although we have presented this example assuming that all cohort members are identical, the example can readily be modified to include cohort-specific heterogeneity. One need simply apply an individual-specific subscript to each of the cohort-specific variables. Doing so does not rule out anonymous net resource functions. Subscripting net resources by an agent's identity does not imply that the function determining those resources (as opposed to the arguments of the function) is agent-specific. Hence, Mirrlees' (1971) optimal income 'tax' can be relabelled as freely as any other 'tax', with no alteration in his underlying optimal net resource function.

4 Infinite-Horizon Fiscal Gap

Before we turn to the definition of the infinite-horizon fiscal gap it is worth illustrating the problem with deficit accounting by two very simple, but revealing, examples. First, let us consider the almost $750 billion the government is collecting from workers under the heading of social security payroll taxes, and the future social security transfer payments these FICA contributions secure. The $750 billion could just as well be called government borrowing and the future transfer payments could just as well be called principal plus interest on this borrowing, plus a future tax (positive or negative) if the future payments do not correspond precisely to principal plus interest. This simple change in language would more than double the reported federal deficit. Indeed, were we to go back in time and re-label all past social security taxes as borrowing, official federal debt held by the public would not be $13 trillion (year 2014) but $38 trillion, which is 211 percent of US GDP.

Another way to clearly see the vacuity of standard fiscal accounting is to consider the two sets of cheques many old people receive from the US Treasury. The cheques look physically identical. They are both the same size and colour and have the same words in the same font. They usually differ only in their amount. This is how the old generation know that one set of cheques is for social security benefit payments and the other is for coupon payments on Treasury bonds. Despite the identical nature of their appearance, only the present value of the Treasury bond payments is included as part of government debt. The present value of the social security payments is not.

4.1 Fiscal Gap

Economic theory is unequivocal in telling us what not to measure when it comes to fiscal sustainability and generational policy. It is also crystal clear in telling us what to measure, namely the infinite-horizon fiscal gap. The infinite-horizon fiscal gap tells us whether the government has, over time, enough receipts to cover its projected spending. It equals the present value of all projected future expenditures less the present value of all projected future receipts.

The infinite-horizon fiscal gap has five important properties.

First, it puts everything on the books. All expenditures, regardless of whether they are called debt service, transfer payments or discretionary spending, are included in forming the present value of future outlays. It also puts all receipts on the books, including income the government receives on its real and financial assets.

Second, the infinite-horizon fiscal gap takes on the same value regardless of what internally consistent labelling convention is used to characterize fiscal outlays and receipts. In contrast, any finite-horizon fiscal gap, such as the seventy-five-year fiscal gaps calculated for the social security and Medicare programs, are, like the federal debt, creatures of nomenclature – that is, they can be set to any value one wants simply by choosing the right fiscal labels.

Third, a positive fiscal gap means the government is attempting to spend, over time, more than it can afford. Doing so violates what economists call the government's intertemporal budget constraint. Hence, a positive fiscal gap is a direct measure of the unsustainability of current fiscal policy.

Fourth, eliminating the infinite-horizon fiscal gap is a zero-sum game across generations. Hence, the fiscal gap tells us the fiscal burden that will be imposed on today's and tomorrow's children if current adults do not pay more to or receive less from the government. Understanding the fiscal burdens our kids could face from the fiscal gap is called generational accounting.

Fifth, the machinery of fiscal gap accounting tells us the size of the adjustment needed to balance the government's intertemporal budget constraint and how the magnitude of the requisite adjustments depend on the time at which the adjustment begins.

5 Fiscal Gaps in Advanced Countries

In this section, we first look at the evolution of the fiscal gap in the United States and then show how large are differences in country rankings when we use fiscal gaps and not gross debt values as proxies for fiscal soundness.

5.1 Fiscal Gap in the United States

The US fiscal gap currently stands at $210 trillion. This figure is the authors' calculation based on the Congressional Budget Office's July 2014 seventy-five-year Alternative Fiscal Scenario (AFS) projection. Constructing the infinite-horizon fiscal gap from the CBO's AFS projection takes less than five minutes. One simply needs to extend the

Table 10.1: *Percentage revenue increase or expenditure cut needed to eliminate the US fiscal gap*

Start year	Revenue increase	Cut in spending
2015	58.5	37.7
2025	64.4	40.4
2035	70.4	43.2
2045	77.0	46.5

Source: calculations by Laurence Kotlikoff based on CBO's 2014 Alternative Fiscal Scenario

CBO's projection into the future and engage, via spreadsheets, in some high-school algebra to form the appropriate present values of expenditures and revenues. Yet the CBO refuses to make the infinite-horizon fiscal gap calculation and continues to focus attention almost exclusively on official debt.

The size of the US fiscal gap – $210 trillion – is massive. It is sixteen times larger than official US debt, which indicates precisely how useless official debt is for understanding true fiscal positions. US GDP currently stands at $18 trillion. Hence, the fiscal gap represents almost twelve years of GDP. The fiscal gap can also be compared with the present value of the CBO's projection of GDP extended through the infinite horizon. Doing so indicates that the fiscal gap is 10.5 percent of GDP. This means we need to either reduce the time path of government expenditures by 10.5 percent of GDP or raise the time path of government revenues by 10.5 percent of GDP. Alternatively, we can enact a combination of spending cuts and tax increases that amount to 10.5 percent of annual GDP. This adjustment needs to begin immediately and continue forever. Waiting to adjust will leave current adult generations either fully or partially off the hook and make the fiscal burden on young and future generations that much larger.

Table 10.1 shows the requisite tax hike or spending cuts needed to eliminate the fiscal gap if such adjustments are postponed into the future. Waiting, for example, for a decade to permanently raise revenues requires a 64.4 percent tax hike starting at that date. Alternatively, spending would need to be cut not by 37.7 percent, but by 40.4 percent, starting in 2025. Obviously, the longer we wait to adjust, the worse the impact on our children and grandchildren. If, for example, we wait until 2035 before adjusting via tax hikes, we will sentence today's newborns to lifetime tax payments that are 70.4 percent larger than would arise under current law.

In 2013 the fiscal gap stood at $205 trillion. In 2014 it was $210 trillion. Hence the country's true 2014 deficit – the increase in its fiscal gap – was $5 trillion, not the $483 billion increase in official debt reported by the CBO.

Why did the fiscal gap increase so dramatically? A major reason is that the baby boom generation got one year closer to collecting what will ultimately be about $40,000 in social security, Medicare and Medicaid benefits per person per year. Hence, the present value of these obligations rose due simply to interest. Stated differently, the fiscal gap is, in effect, the nation's credit card bill, and, like our own credit card balances, the fiscal gap accrues interest. If we fail to pay interest on the fiscal gap it will get larger.

As indicated in Figure 10.1, the fiscal gap has risen dramatically over the past dozen years. This reflects interest accrual. But the major reasons for the growth in the fiscal gap from $60 trillion in 2003 to $210 trillion today are tax cuts, increases in Medicaid and Medicare benefit levels, additional defence spending and the introduction of Medicare Part D. In 2013 the US fiscal gap was reduced from $222 trillion to $205 trillion due to tax and spending legislation.

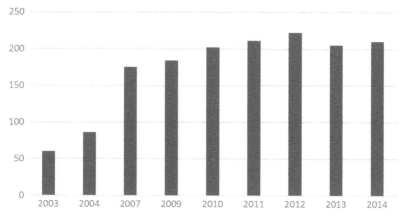

Figure 10.1: Historical US fiscal gaps, 2003–14

Note: in percent of GDP.

Source: Calculations by Laurence Kotlikoff based on CBO Alternative Fiscal Scenario Projections

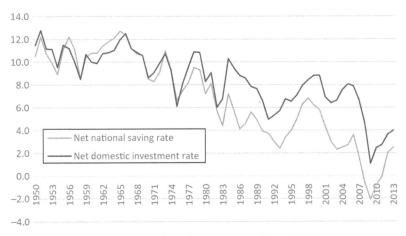

Figure 10.2: US net national saving and net domestic investment rates, 1950–2013

Note: in percent.

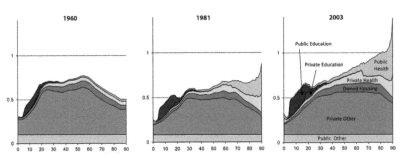

Figure 10.3: US consumption per capita by age, 1960, 1981 and 2003

Note: ratio to average labor income.

Source: courtesy of prof. Ronald Lee

US postwar generational policy is accurately characterized as 'take as you go'. Over the decades, Republican and Democratic Congresses and Administrations have taken ever larger amounts of resources from young workers and transferred them to old retirees. The resources taken from the young to give to the old were called, in the main, 'taxes'. And the young were effectively told: 'Don't worry. We are calling these resources taxes, but when you are old, you will receive massive transfer payments that more than make up for what you are paying now.'

The impact of this policy was predictable. Older generations consumed more, younger generations had no or little reason to consume

Table 10.2: *Fiscal gaps in major developed countries, 2012*

Country	Fiscal gap as a share of the present value of GDP
US	13.7
Germany	1.4
UK	5.4
Netherlands	5.9
France	1.6
Spain	4.8
Italy	−2.3
Sweden	1.7

Source: Laurence Kotlikoff calculation for the US and European Commission (http://ec.europa.eu/economy_finance/publications/european_economy/2012/pdf/ee-2012–8_en.pdf)

less and the national saving rate fell. Figure 10.2 documents the post-1950 decline in US saving rate, virtually all of which can be traced to increases in private consumption. And as Figure 10.3 shows, those within the household sector who consumed the most were older generations. This figure, provided by Professor Ronald Lee of the University of California at Berkeley, shows a dramatic increase over time in the absolute and relative consumption of the elderly.

Countries that save less invest less. And Figure 10.2 shows not just a remarkable postwar decline in the US net national saving rate, but also a remarkable postwar decline in net domestic investment rate. Given that investment is one of the key factors underlying real wage growth, it's not surprising that the average real wages of US workers have grown so little in recent decades. There are obviously other factors involved – relatively poor primary and secondary education, competition with foreign workers and competition with smart machines/robots, for example. But having a net domestic investment rate of 4 percent rather than 15 percent is a prescription for limited real wage growth.

5.2 Fiscal Gaps in Other Developed Countries

Table 10.2 compares the 2012 fiscal gaps in the United States with those in major European countries. The fiscal gaps for the EU countries were calculated by the European Commission. As is immediately clear, among the countries listed, the United States is in the worst fiscal shape by a considerable margin. It is also clear that there is little correspondence between official debt-to-GDP ratios and fiscal gaps measured as a ratio of the present value of future GDP. In 2012 both the United States and the Netherlands had debt-to-GDP ratios of roughly 70 percent, yet the US fiscal gap, scaled by the present value of GDP, was over twice that of the Netherlands. Or consider Italy, with its 127 percent 2012 debt-to-GDP ratio. Its 2012 fiscal gap is negative 2.3 percent of the present value of future GDP.

What explains Italy's negative fiscal gap? The answer is tight projected control of government-paid health expenditures, plus two major pension reforms that have reduced future pension benefits by close to 40 percent.

6 Conclusion

A century ago, everyone thought that time and distance were well-defined physical concepts. But neither proved to be absolute. Instead, measures/reports of time and distance were found to depend on one's direction and speed of travel, making our apparent physical reality, in the words of Einstein, 'merely an illusion'. Like time and distance, standard fiscal measures, including deficits, taxes and transfer payments, depend on one's reference point/reporting procedure/language/labels. As such, they too represent numbers in search of concepts that provide the illusion of meaning where none exists. Economists must accept this fact and acknowledge that much of what they have been writing and saying about fiscal policy has been an exercise in linguistics, not economics.

Economists have a professional obligation to ensure that the fiscal measures we present in our research and teach in our classes actually tell us about fiscal policy, not about accounting mistakes and the manipulation (with our assistance) of the fiscal truth by politicians. Fortunately, economic theory provides a clear guide to what measures are and are not invariant to the choice of fiscal nomenclature. The infinite-horizon fiscal gap and generational accounting provide meaningful metrics of whether an economy's fiscal policy is sustainable and the impacts on different generations of changes in fiscal policy. All we need to do is produce them, use them and teach them and, with time, fiscal discussions among ourselves, among the press, among our students and among the politicians will begin to connect to economic science and fiscal reality.

Bibliography

Arrow, Kenneth J. (1964). The role of securities in the optimal allocation of risk-bearing. *Review of Economic Studies*, 31, 91–6.

Auerbach, Alan J. and Kotlikoff, Laurence J. (1987). *Dynamic Fiscal Policy*. Cambridge: Cambridge University Press,.

Banks, James, Blundell, Richard and Smith, James P. (2001). Financial Wealth Inequality in the United States and Britain. Working Paper, Rand Institute, www.rand.org/content/dam/rand/pubs/drafts/2008/DRU2440.pdf

Barsky, Robert B., Mankiw, Gregory and Zeldes, Steven P. (1986). Ricardian consumers with Keynesian propensities. *The American Economic Review*, 76(4), 676–91.

Bell, Linda and Bosworth, Barry (2005). *The Decline in Household Saving: What Can We Learn from Survey Data*. Mimeo, The Brookings Institution, August.

Blanchard, Olivier (1985). Debts, deficits, and finite horizons. *Journal of Political Economy*, 93(2), 223–47.

Burnside, Craig, ed. (2005). *Fiscal Sustainability in Theory and Practice*. Washington, DC: The World Bank.

Engen, Eric M. and Hubbard, R. Glenn (2005). Federal government debt and interest rates. In Mark Gertler and Ken Rogoff, eds., *NBER Macroeconomics Annual 2004*, Cambridge: MIT Press, pp. 83–138.

Fischer, Stanley (1980). Dynamic inconsistency, cooperation, and the benevolent dissembling government. *Journal of Economic Dynamics and Control*, 2, 93–107.

Gale, William and Orsag, Peter R. (2004). Budget deficits, national saving, and interest rates. *Brookings Papers on Economic Activity*, 2, 101–210.

Hauner, David (2006). *Fiscal Policy and Financial Development*. IMF Working Paper No. WP/06/26, January.

Hayashi, Fumio (1987). Tests for liquidity constraints: a critical survey, invited paper, 5th World Congress of the Econometric Society, Cambridge, Mass. In T. Bewley, ed., *Advances in Econometrics II: Fifth World Congress*. Cambridge: Cambridge University Press, pp. 91–120.

Hubbard, Glenn and Engen, Eric (2005). Government debt and interest rates, In M. Gertler and K. Rogoff, eds., *NBER Macroeconomics Annual 2004*. Cambridge: MIT Press, 83–138.

Jaffee, D. M. and Russel, T. (1976). Imperfect information, uncertainty, and credit rationing. *Quarterly Journal of Economics*, 90, 651–66.

Kotlikoff, Laurence J. (1986). Deficit delusion. The Public Interest, 84 (Summer), www.kotlikoff.net/sites/default/files/deficit_delusion_0.pdf

Kotlikoff, Laurence J. (2002). *Generational Policy.* Cambridge, MA: MIT Press.

Mirrlees, James A. (1971). An exploration in the theory of optimal income taxation. *Review of Economic Studies,* **38**, 175–208.

OECD (1997). *Income Distribution and Poverty in Selected OECD Countries.* OECD Economic Outlook, December.

Slemrod, Joel, ed. (1994). *Tax Progressivity and Income Inequality.* Cambridge: Cambridge University Press.

Tabellini, Guido (1991). The politics of intergenerational redistribution. *Journal of Political Economy,* **99**(2), 335–57.

11 Fiscal Policy and Financial Distress: A Balance Sheet Perspective

JOHN FITZGERALD AND PHILIP R. LANE

1 Introduction

Governments actively manage the public balance sheet during episodes of financial distress. Under these circumstances, the stock of gross public debt is not a sufficient statistic for fiscal sustainability. In this chapter, we examine the roles of financial asset acquisition, liquidity management, debt management and the central bank balance sheet in determining the fiscal health of a government. We argue that a strategy of 'under-promising and over-delivering' is essential in restoring market access.

In fiscal analysis, the traditional focus has been on the gross stock of government debt and the general government fiscal balance. However, this can be an excessively narrow focus, especially in periods in which governments turn to more elaborate types of financial engineering. In general, it is desirable to analyse a more complete version of the public balance sheet, in order to assess properly the financial health of the government.

On the liability side, the face value of the aggregate gross stock of government debt is not a sufficient statistic. The composition of debt liabilities is crucial in relation to the present value of debt and funding risk, with maturity structure, the schedule of coupon payments and the identity of creditors (for instance, on-market debt versus official debt) all playing important roles. In addition, the government has implicit liabilities (for instance, unfunded pension commitments), contingent liabilities (for instance, explicit or implicit guarantees to the financial system) and deferred liabilities (for instance, future payment streams to the operators of PPP/PFI projects).

This chapter benefited from comments from the participants at the 'Rethinking Fiscal Policy After the Crisis' conference as well as Íde Kearney and Rossa White. We thank Rogelio Mercado and Jonathan Rice for research assistance. Lane thanks the Irish Research Council for grant support.

On the asset side, governments hold an array of financial assets and considerable non-financial assets (the public capital stock). In addition, through commercialisation, the claims on some non-financial assets can be transformed into financial assets (for instance, converting the water infrastructure network into a dedicated utility). Financial assets include cash balances, the assets of sovereign wealth funds and equity and debt claims on state-owned enterprises.

Taking a balance sheet perspective is helpful in analysing financial engineering initiatives such as privatisations and PPP projects. It is also especially important during periods of financial distress when the public balance sheet may be deployed to make interventions in the private sector (for instance, through bailouts of distressed corporates or financial institutions). Along another dimension, a sovereign's exposure to a funding crisis also depends on its treasury management, with pre-funding through the accumulation of cash balances providing a buffer during periods of erratic market access.

The full public sector balance sheet also incorporates the balance sheet of the central bank.[1] The scale of central bank balance sheets has expanded enormously in recent years. This provides scope for extra financial income (on the expanded set of financial assets held by the central bank) but also poses credit risks (if a central bank incurs losses on the collateralised assets it holds). The monetary–fiscal interactions through the public balance sheet represent another key analytical challenge. For instance, capitalising the present value of future monetary income has recently been discussed in the context of reducing the outstanding stock of gross government debt (Pâris and Wyplosz 2014, Corsetti et al., 2015).

The analysis of the public balance sheet should be viewed in the context of a more general 'balance sheet approach' (BSA) in analysing sustainability issues (IMF, 2015). In one direction, the risks associated with a high level of sovereign debt differ across countries with positive or negative net international investment positions. In the other direction, a low current stock of public debt many not be fiscally sustainable if other sectors are at risk of financial distress as a result of excessive leverage.

---

[1] For a monetary union, the balance sheet of the common central bank links the fiscal balance sheets of the member countries.

For instance, an external funding crisis or a domestic financial crisis may result in the transformation of the public balance sheet, via rescue operations that act to transfer assets and liabilities from the private sector to the government or to increase the contingent liabilities of the government through the provision of guarantees and insurance to private entities.[2] This may be the result of a publicly financed restructuring of the balance sheets of the banking system, the corporate sector and/or the household sector. In some cases, the costs of such bailouts may feed directly into the fiscal balance; in others, the main costs may remain off-balance sheet. In some cases, the government may also acquire foreign assets. Examples include the nationalisation of a bank with international operations or the establishment of an asset management agency that acquires non-performing (domestic and foreign) loans from the domestic banking system. The long-term horizon of the government means that it may be better able to withstand short-term declines in the market value of assets, although at the cost of increased direct risk to the taxpayer if the ultimate return on these assets fails to meet expectations.

In what follows, we explore some dimensions of taking a balance sheet approach to fiscal analysis. Our particular focus is on understanding the true fiscal dynamics of financially distressed sovereigns. We do not address other interesting balance sheet issues such as the role of unfunded liabilities like pay-as-you-go pension commitments or healthcare commitments.

In Section 2, we quantitatively examine the importance of financial operations for the dynamics of gross public debt. In Section 3, we turn to a case study of Ireland, which has experienced two major sovereign debt crises (1980s and 2010–13). Section 4 concludes by offering some directions for future research.

2 The Dynamics of Gross Public Debt

In this section, we investigate the contribution of financial asset acquisition to the dynamics of gross public debt. Rather than minimising gross debt (for a given path for the fiscal balance), governments may choose to acquire financial assets for a variety of reasons (as outlined above).

---

[2] This material is adapted from Lane (2010). See also Tirole (2015).

Equation (1) gives a decomposition of the change in the debt–output ratio between any two periods $N\text{-}t$ and N (Escolano, 2010):

$$d_N - d_{N-t} = \sum_{s=N-t}^{N-1} \frac{i_{s+1}}{1+\gamma_{s+1}} d_s - \sum_{s=N-t}^{N-1} \frac{\gamma_{s+1}}{1+\gamma_{s+1}} d_s$$

$$+ \sum_{s=N-t+1}^{N} P_s + \sum_{s=N-t+1}^{N} SFA_s \tag{1}$$

where d is the debt-to-GDP ratio, i is the average nominal interest rate paid on the debt, γ is the growth rate of nominal GDP, P is the ratio of the primary (non-interest) deficit to GDP and SFA is the stock-flow adjustment term.

The first two terms show the dependence of debt dynamics on the outstanding stock of debt. All else equal, a higher interest rate is associated with more rapid debt accumulation, while a faster rate of nominal GDP growth is associated with an improvement in the debt-to-GDP ratio by increasing the denominator in this ratio. In a given period, the net impact of these two terms depends on the sign of $(i_{s+1} - \gamma_{s+1})$: if the interest rate is higher than the growth rate, there is upward pressure on the debt ratio; conversely, if the interest rate is below the growth rate, there is downward pressure on the debt ratio.

The third term captures the contribution of the primary balance, while the final term is driven by factors that do not affect the fiscal balance but do operate on the stock of gross debt. In particular, the stock-flow adjustment term is affected by the acquisition of financial assets by the government. One basic type of financial asset is represented by a government's cash balances. For instance, a government may choose to 'over-fund' in a given period by issuing more debt than is required to fund the fiscal balance and repay maturing debt obligations, which adds to cash balances. Conversely, a government may avoid tapping market funding if it has sufficient cash balances to meet its financing requirements in a given interval. A second type of financial acquisition relates to corporate or bank rescue operations by which a government may issue debt (or run down cash balances) in order to acquire a debt or equity claim in a distressed entity.

Figure 11.1 illustrates the dynamics of cash balances for a selection of countries. The surge in cash holdings for the European periphery

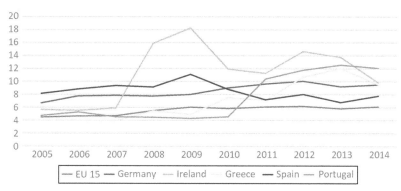

Figure 11.1: General government currency and deposit holdings, 2005–14
Note: in percent of GDP.
Source: Eurostat Sectoral Financial Accounts

countries during the crisis is quite striking and is consistent with an increased value of a cash buffer during periods of market turbulence, despite the high opportunity cost if sovereign bond yields are at elevated levels.

Table 11.1 shows the impact on the public balance sheet of governments' financial interventions during the financial crisis. Governments intervened through a number of mechanisms, including capital transfers to banks, public recapitalisation of banks, insurance schemes and liability guarantee schemes. In column (1), the fiscal net revenue/cost is shown: governments can earn revenues by charging fees for financial support and incur costs by making capital transfers and/or incurring losses on financial investments. Column (2) shows the peak value (scaled by GDP) over 2008–14 of financial assets acquired through intervention during the crisis, while column (3) shows the peak value of financial liabilities acquired.

Over the period 2008–14, column (1) of Table 11.1 shows that the cumulative net cost has been quite significant for a number of countries (Ireland, Greece, Slovenia and Cyprus in particular) but was relatively minor for other countries. For a wider set of countries, financial interventions generated significant expansions in the public balance sheet, even if the cumulative net fiscal cost was relatively low in a number of countries. Accordingly, the lesson from Table 11.1 is that governments may engage in significant financial engineering (acquisition of financial assets and financial liabilities) during a financial crisis,

Table 11.1: *Impact on public balance sheet of government interventions, 2008–14*

	(1)	(2)	(3)
	Net revenue/cost	Assets	Liabilities
Belgium	−0.4	6.1	6.5
Denmark	0.6	4.4	4.4
Germany	−1.3	10.2	11.8
Ireland	−25.6	11.3	38.9
Greece	−12.5	15.9	23.1
Spain	−4.4	2.4	4.9
France	0.1	0.5	0.4
Italy	0.1	0.3	0.3
Cyprus	−8.5	9.3	9.7
Latvia	−3.3	7.4	9.5
Lithuania	−3.0	0.1	2.8
Luxembourg	0.2	5.8	5.5
Hungary	0.1	2.1	3.2
Netherlands	−0.7	12.7	12.7
Austria	−3.1	7.6	8.4
Portugal	−2.9	8.1	11.1
Slovenia	−12.1	6.1	18.2
Sweden	0.2	0.6	0.2
United Kingdom	−0.4	9.7	9.7

Note: percentage of GDP. Column (1) refers to net revenue/cost (cumulative over 2008–14); columns (2) and (3) refer to peak levels of asset and liability acquisition over 2008–14.

Source: Eurostat – Supplementary Table for the Financial Crisis, http://ec.europa.eu/ eurostat/web/government-finance-statistics/excessive-deficit/supplemtary-tables-finan cial-crisis

even if the net impact on the fiscal accounts (as captured by net revenues/costs) can be quite low.[3]

Fitzgerald and Lane (2016) show the contributions of each term in explaining country-level fiscal dynamics over the periods 1998–2007, 2007–9, 2009–12 and 2012–14. In Table 11.2 we report regressions of each term on the initial stock of public debt (for the corresponding

---

[3] This point applies a fortiori if off-balance sheet interventions (such as guarantees) are included.

Table 11.2: *Cross-country variation in fiscal dynamics*

	A: 1998–2007			
	(1) Prim	(2) Int	(3) SFA	(4) Grow
α	−12.81	10.38***	24.82*	−20.45***
	(−0.24)	(3.11)	(1.95)	(−3.87)
$Debt_{98}$	−0.48	0.26***	−0.28	−0.08
	(−1.01)	(4.83)	(−1.38)	(−0.92)
R^2	0.01	0.47	0.07	0.03
Observations	28	28	28	32

	B: 2007–9			
	(1) Prim	(2) Int	(3) SFA	(4) Grow
α	4.31	2.57***	−0.58	5.88***
	(1.48)	(3.84)	(−0.23)	(3.61)
$Debt_{07}$	−0.02	0.04***	0.13**	−0.11***
	(−0.34)	(3.72)	(3.08)	(−3.92)
R^2	0.01	0.32	0.25	0.33
Observations	31	31	31	33

	C: 2009–12			
	(1) Prim	(2) Int	(3) SFA	(4) Grow
α	2.84	3.44***	1.89	−1.39
	(0.67)	(3.18)	(0.49)	(0.37)
$Debt_{09}$	0.06	0.07***	0.04	−0.12**
	(1.06)	(4.34)	(0.72)	(-2.37)
R^2	0.04	0.39	0.02	0.16
Observations	32	32	32	32

	D: 2012–14			
	(1) Prim	(2) Int	(3) SFA	(4) Grow
α	−2.67	1.94**	11.74**	−12.81***
	(−1.32)	(2.63)	(3.36)	(−3.4)
$Debt_{12}$	0.05**	0.04***	−0.18***	0.18***
	(2.08)	(4.68)	(−4.35)	(4.04)
R^2	0.13	0.42	0.4	0.35
Observations	31	32	30	32

Note: Regressions on initial debt-to-GDP ratio: (1) primary deficit, (2) interest payments, (3) stock-flow adjustment and (4) GDP growth term. Statistical significance is denoted as * for 10 percent, ** for 5 percent and *** for 1 percent confidence level.

period) in order to gain a sense of the relative importance of each term in the cross-country variation in debt dynamics.

During the 1998–2007 pre-crisis period, the cross-country evolution of gross debt ratios was positively linked to the scale of interest payments but not to the other underlying factors. A plausible interpretation is that debt stabilisation concerns were weak during this period, so that primary balances were not responsive to outstanding debt stocks.[4] There was no relation between initial debt levels and the growth term or the stock-flow adjustment term. The orthogonality of initial debt and the growth term is not consistent with models in which countries with faster expected growth trajectories rationally choose to run up debt levels.

Debt dynamics during the global financial crisis are captured in Panel B of Table 11.2. During this period, the cross-country pattern in the stock-flow adjustment term was destabilising in the sense that those countries with high initial debt levels also experienced larger stock-flow adjustments. The growth term was stabilising (in relation to the cross-country distribution) in that more indebted economies benefited from a larger growth impact on the debt–output ratio.

The results for the European debt crisis period (2009–12) are shown in Panel C of Table 11.2. During this period, the cross-country variation between initial debt levels and the growth term remained a stabilising force, while the other terms did not show a significant co-movement pattern with the initial debt level.

Finally, Panel D of Table 11.2 shows the results for the 2012–14 period. During this period, there was some disposal of financial assets by highly indebted countries, so that the stock-flow adjustment term negatively covaried with the initial stock of public debt. A second striking feature is the positive covariation between the growth term and the initial debt stock: the most indebted countries suffered relatively poorer growth performance (plausibly driven by the Greek experience).

The basic message from the analysis in this section is that the gross stock of public debt is not a sufficient statistic for the state of the public balance sheet. In one direction, bail-out operations and/or the accumulation of a cash buffer can induce growth in the stock of public debt in

---

[4] The response of the primary balance to the stock of public debt may also be nonlinear, with significant adjustment only in scenarios in which high debt levels trigger sustainability concerns. See also Eichengreen and Panizza (2016).

excess of the level required to fund the fiscal balance. In the other direction, gross debt can decline if the government disposes of financial assets or runs down cash buffers. More broadly, gross debt can also decline if a government creates new financial assets by capitalising various future revenue streams and/or through a privatisation pro-gramme. Accordingly, the expansion and contraction of the public balance sheet requires careful analysis in terms of assessing the impli-cations for fiscal sustainability and/or identifying optimal fiscal policy.

Finally, the composition of the gross stock of public debt also matters for sustainability in terms of maturity structure and the iden-tity of the investor base (domestic or foreign; bank or non-bank; private or official). All else equal, longer maturities and a 'sticky' investor base (buy-to-hold investors; committed investors) can be help-ful in minimising rollover risk.

In the next section, we examine this set of issues in the specific context of the Irish experience in managing its fiscal crises (1980s and 2008–13).

3 Lessons from Ireland

Over the past forty years, Ireland has undergone two major financial crises: the first in the 1980s and the second over the period 2008–12. In both cases, the ratio of national debt to GNP peaked at well over 100 percent (Figure 11.2). The first crisis was primarily due to

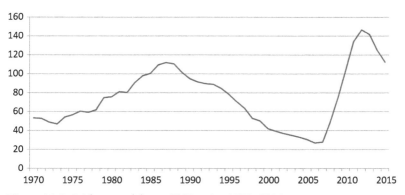

Figure 11.2: Irish gross debt-to-GNP ratio, 1970–2014

Note: CSO: National Income and Expenditure, Government Financial Statistics; ESRI: Databank.

extremely unwise fiscal policies pursued in the late 1970s and early 1980s and the financial sector remained largely unaffected. However, in the recent crisis, the problems in the public finances were massively increased by the collapse of the banking sector. The financial crisis magnified the costs to the government of achieving a resolution. Moreover, it contributed to a climate of fiscal uncertainty: at the time, it was very difficult to assess what would be the likely final cost to the government of fixing the broken banking system.

3.1 The Economic Crisis of the 1980s

Following the adoption of a very expansionary fiscal policy in the late 1970s when real interest rates were low, there was a major downturn in the economy in the early 1980s. This coincided with a big increase in real interest rates. The result was a crisis in the public finances, mirrored in a very large external deficit (Honohan, 1999). Government borrowing peaked at 16 percent of GNP in 1981 and 1982 and the current account deficit in 1981 was around 14 percent of GNP. There were serious concerns in those years about the sustainability of the rapidly rising debt. However, very deflationary budgets in 1983 and 1984 were implemented in an attempt to bring the situation under control (Kearney et al., 2000). This tough fiscal action convinced the markets that the situation was manageable.

In this crisis there was not a major problem with the banking system.[5] There was no housing bubble and the strict controls on the relatively closed domestic financial system meant that the banks did not suffer major problems of default in the recession. The counterpart to the government borrowing was the borrowing abroad to fund the current account deficit. The banks were not unduly exposed externally.

Reflecting the current account deficit, a growing share of the rising debt was funded abroad (Table 11.3). The small size of the Irish economy and the small market for Irish pound assets meant that much of the foreign borrowing was denominated in foreign currencies. However, there was also an extensive domestic market for Irish pound-denominated debt. The banks were required to hold approximately

---

[5] Nonetheless, there was a problem with one major bank which got into difficulties as a result of an unwise acquisition abroad. This required the state to guarantee its solvency but, in the end, there was not net cost to the government (Honohan, 1999). Also, the problem was contained within a single financial institution.

Table 11.3: *Holdings of Irish government debt, 1980–90*

	1980	1981	1982	1983	1984	1985	1986	1987	1988	1989	1990
Domestic:											
Banks	13.3	11.6	12.2	11.7	11.8	12.3	11.0	20.4	10.9	9.9	10.1
Private Sector	45.1	40.0	37.2	35.3	36.4	36.4	39.9	31.8	38.3	36.6	38.2
Central Bank	4.6	3.5	2.8	2.2	2.9	2.0	1.6	1.5	1.4	1.5	1.4
Foreign	37.0	44.9	47.8	50.8	48.9	49.2	47.6	46.3	49.4	52.0	50.3

Note: share of the total, in percentage. This includes bonds denominated in Irish pounds as well as borrowing abroad in foreign currencies.
Source: Central Bank of Ireland and ESRI databank

20 percent of their assets in government bonds. However, the bulk of the bonds held domestically were absorbed by the other domestic financial institutions – pension funds and insurance companies. With liabilities of the pension funds and the insurance companies denominated in Irish pounds, they sought to match their liabilities with Irish pound assets.

While the market operations by the Irish government were fully disclosed, there was one aspect of the government's treasury management operations which was only disclosed with a lag.[6] In 1985 and 1986, the government borrowed heavily abroad. The amount borrowed significantly exceeded the funding needs for the year. However, instead of lodging it with the Central Bank, where it would have appeared as a government deposit – which was the normal practice – it was, instead, held on deposit abroad. The amount held abroad on deposit at the end of 1986 amounted to 2.8 percent of GNP. Because it did not show up at the time in the government accounts, the situation looked slightly worse than it actually was.

When a new government came into office early in 1987, it cut expenditure very substantially, clearly bringing the fiscal crisis under control. At this point the government also disclosed this 'hidden' liquid

---

[6] In the 1980s, the debt was handled directly by the Department of Finance, However, in the late 1980s a special state agency, the National Treasury Management Agency (NTMA), was established, which has managed the national debt ever since.

asset. In turn, this significantly changed market sentiment: bond yields fell from 12.8 percent in January 1987 to 10.5 percent in December 1987. This relative lack of transparency contrasts with the recent crisis, where all significant information on the management of the national debt was disclosed in real time. In a context of huge uncertainty about the cost of the banking bail-out it was important to reassure financial markets through full disclosure of all available information. The experience gained in dealing with foreign financial institutions in the 1980s crisis was important – it provided a basis of expertise that was still available in the recent crisis. The National Treasury Management Agency (NTMA) was set up in 1990 to manage the debt, taking over the experienced staff from the Department of Finance.

The rapid decline in the debt ratio from the late 1980s onwards stemmed primarily from the rapid growth in GNP, especially in the period after 1993. The economic crisis of the 1980s had delayed a convergence to EU levels of output and income per head – a convergence which occurred instead in the 1990s.

As a result of the fiscal tightening implemented by successive governments, the level of government borrowing fell below 3 percent of GNP in 1989 and the deficit was effectively eliminated by 1996. However, while some surpluses occurred in later years, especially from sales of state assets, these played a very limited role in reducing the debt burden, as growth was so rapid over the 1990s.

While inflation had played a major role in reducing the debt burden in countries such as the United States and the United Kingdom in the immediate postwar years, inflation was relatively moderate over the 1990s, playing only a subsidiary role in reducing the burden of the debt.

3.2 Summary of the Impact of the Great Recession on the Public Finances

At the beginning of the current crisis, Ireland was in a strong position. As shown in Figure 11.3, the level of debt was very low and there were considerable liquid assets – cash, deposits and a portfolio of global equities and bonds. However, the bursting of the property bubble simultaneously caused a massive deterioration in the public finances and the collapse of the domestic banking system. A consequence of the problems in the domestic banks was that the government was dragged into the provision of massive support for the illiquid and insolvent banks.

Table 11.4: *Irish government borrowing, 2007–14*

	2007	2008	2009	2010	2011	2012	2013	2014
Including banks	−0.3	8.1	16.6	38.4	15.4	9.8	6.8	4.6
Excluding banks	−0.3	8.1	13.8	13.1	10.4	9.6	6.8	4.6

Note: percentage of GNP.
Source: CSO: Government Financial Statistics

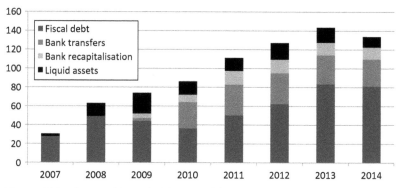

Figure 11.3: Composition of Irish gross debt, 2007–14
Note: CSO: National Income and Expenditure, Government Finance Statistics; NTMA
Annual Reports. In percentage of GNP.

Table 11.4 shows government borrowing both before and after the massive transfers to the banks. While the need to support the banking system was a very big factor in the rise in the debt, the biggest factor raising indebtedness over the period 2008–14 was the cumulative government deficit, excluding support to the banks. This amounted to 66 percent of GNP over the seven-year period. The transfers to the banks amounted to a cumulative 33 percent of GNP. In addition, part of the recapitalisation of the banks, amounting to 15 percent of GNP, was undertaken by the sovereign wealth fund the National Pension Reserve Fund (NPRF) and it did not appear in government borrowing – it was treated as a change in the asset composition of the NPRF. Thus the cumulative cost of supporting the banks over the seven years amounted to 48 percent of GNP.

Figure 11.3 shows the origin of the debt as a share of GNP, with the bulk of it being due to the cumulative deficits. It also shows the significant borrowing needed to build up the liquid assets of the government sector.

The management of the huge programme of borrowing that needed to be undertaken over a very short period was a complicated operation. The uncertainty about the magnitude of the problem, especially regarding the funding needs of the banking system, resulted in great uncertainty in financial markets. The fact that Ireland was only one of quite a number of countries that were suffering similar crises meant there was a serious danger of contagion.

Ireland began from a position of considerable experience of managing a very large debt. The state agency charged with managing the debt grew out of the experience of the 1980s and many of those working in the area had had first-hand experience of the searing experience of the 1980s.

One of the key concerns of financial markets is possible asymmetries of information – does the government know more about the size of the problem than they are disclosing? In the case of the 1980s, as discussed earlier, the government used a lack of transparency in government accounting to surprise markets positively. However, this time around, the use of standard Eurostat accounting rules made for much greater transparency.

3.3 Developing Credibility

The crisis had blown up very rapidly and it proved to be much more serious than anyone predicted. Forecasts for the public finances and the funding needs of the banking system in 2008–10 proved to be far too optimistic. Even more serious was the continuing upward revision in the estimated funding needs of the banking system. It was only with the publication of new stress tests of the banking system in March 2011 that a realistic ceiling on the cost of the banking crisis was established. All of this led to a major loss of credibility – a loss that took some considerable time to restore. The loss of credibility had a major cost in terms of higher risk premia on lending to Ireland.

The continuing upward revision in estimates of the potential costs of the banking system over the course of 2010 saw Ireland's access to funding drying up, and the result was its recourse to the support of the Troika in late November 2010. However, before assistance was sought from the Troika, the government had put in place an adjustment programme designed to bring government borrowing below 3 percent by 2015. The adjustment programme previously agreed with the EU

Table 11.5: *Actual and planned austerity measures in Ireland, 2008–15*

€bn	2008–2010	2011	2012	2013	2014	2015	2008–2015
Revenue	5.6	1.4	1.6	1.3	0.9	0.7	11.5
Expenditure	9.2	3.9	2.2	2.3	1.6	1.3	20.5
of which Capital	1.6	1.9	0.8	0.6	0.1	0.0	5.0
Total	14.7	5.3	3.8	3.5	2.5	2.0	31.8
Percent of GDP	9.2%	3.3%	2.3%	2.1%	1.5%	1.1%	19.5%

Source: Department of Finance Budgets. GDP figures revised based on CSO: National Income and Expenditure (2011) and Duffy et al. (2012).

Commission in 2009 had planned to reach this borrowing target by 2014 but, because of the additional burden of funding the banking sector losses, the time scale for meeting the borrowing target was extended to 2015.

The adjustment programme set out by the government in early November 2010 was accepted by the Troika in December 2010 without significant change. Thus it was the Irish government's plan, rather than a plan imposed from outside, that formed the basis for the ongoing fiscal adjustment. Up to that point, the forecasts for the public finances in the government's programme had proved to be overly optimistic. However, in drawing up the programme in late 2010, the then government aimed to under-promise.

Table 11.5 summarises the ex ante fiscal policy measures taken over the course of the crisis, including the measures pencilled in for 2015.[7] Together, the cumulative ex ante adjustment amounted to just under 20 percent of GDP. The composition of the large adjustments made over the period 2008–15 is shown in Table 11.5. Roughly two thirds of the measures involved cuts in expenditure and one third involved increased taxation. This contrasts with the adjustment in the 1980s, when the initial measures were heavily weighted towards increased taxation and cuts in capital expenditure (Honohan, 1999). Among the measures introduced this time round were cuts in public sector pay and cuts in welfare benefits.

---

[7] This is the effect of the measures taken, assuming no feedback from these measures to government revenue and expenditure.

Table 11.6: *Stability programme updates in Ireland and Spain, 2010–13*

Official deficit plans (percent of GDP)	2010	2011	2012	2013
Plan of: Spain				
Spring 2010	9.8	7.5	5.3	3.0
Spring 2011	9.2	6	4.4	3.0
Spring 2012	9.2	8.5	5.3	3.0
Latest	9.6	9.6	10.6	7.2
Plan of: Ireland				
Winter 2009	11.6	10	7.2	4.9
Winter 2010	—	10.6	8.6	7.5
Latest	10.6	8.9	8.1	7.1

Source: Stability Programme Updates for Spain and Ireland. Latest data for Spain from EU AMECO database; for Ireland Duffy et al. (2013)

Having consistently failed to meet fiscal targets over the previous three years, the government's programme published in November 2010 was deliberately very conservative. The aim was to put in place a programme of adjustment that was readily achievable, resulting in future outperformance. This policy has been pursued ever since in preparing fiscal forecasts.

This policy of under-promising and over-delivering in Ireland contrasted with that of Spain. The adjustment in the Spanish public finances planned in spring 2010 was more ambitious than that of Ireland (Table 11.6). While beginning with a deficit at a slightly lower level in 2010, the plan was to reduce the deficit to 3 percent of GDP by 2013. The outgoing government, in the spring of 2011, raised the bar for the incoming government, committing to reduce the deficit even more rapidly in 2011 and 2012. However, in spring 2012 the incoming Spanish government found that this time path of adjustment was not realistic and had to dramatically alter the plan.

In the case of Ireland, sure-but-steady progress since 2010 was rewarded with a steady fall in bond yields. In the case of Spain, it took longer to achieve such an outcome because of the initial under-performance relative to forecasts. While difficult to achieve politically, the lesson from these two examples of adjustment programmes seems to be that it is better to under-promise and over-deliver.

3.4 Keeping Liquid

The Irish authorities managing the national debt began the recent crisis with two major advantages: (i) the initial level of debt was very low, at under 25 percent of GNP at the end of 2007, as shown in Figure 11.3; and (ii) there was also a significant sovereign wealth fund, the National Pension Reserve Fund (NPRF).[8] The value of the NPRF plus the cash held by the government at the end of 2007 amounted to more than 15 percent of GNP so that the debt, net of liquid financial assets, was around 10 percent of GNP.

The lesson learned at the end of the 1980s crisis was that holding significant cash reserves greatly helped in managing the debt market. This preference for liquidity mirrors the decision in economies with independent currencies to hold substantial foreign reserves against possible capital market volatility (Jeanne and Rancière, 2011). As the crisis manifested itself in 2008, the NTMA built up its cash reserves very rapidly by undertaking extensive borrowing (Table 11.7). In addition, not shown here, there was the NPRF.

While the full magnitude of the problems facing the government was not apparent in the first half of 2008, nonetheless the NTMA had already built up significant holdings of cash and deposits by mid-year. Over the course of autumn 2008, further major borrowing was undertaken. Between the end of 2007 and the end of 2008, as well as funding the very large borrowing needs of the government, the NTMA increased holdings of cash and deposits by 11 percent of GNP. This policy continued over the course of 2009 so that by the end of the year holdings of cash amounted to 15.5 percent of GNP.

As shown in Table 11.7, initially quite a lot of the funding was short-term in nature. However, over the course of 2009 and the first quarter of 2010 this short-term funding was converted into borrowing at much longer maturities. The objective of this policy was to try and render the government secure from any wider crisis which might have impacted on the government's ability to borrow.

By early 2010, the NTMA had liquid assets equal to the then expected government borrowing needs for at least eighteen months, possibly to

---

[8] The bulk of the assets were held in equities which could, potentially, be liquidated relatively quickly. However, the high weighting on global equities also meant that the value of the NPRF was hard hit during the global financial crisis: it was not set up as a rainy day fund but as a long-term intergenerational savings vehicle.

Table 11.7: *Change in Irish national debt and liquid assets, 2008–10*

Change in debt and assets	2008				2009				2010			
	Q1	Q2	Q3	Q4	Q1	Q2	Q3	Q4	Q1	Q2	Q3	Q4
Total nat. debt	4451	8417	11260	8330	9932	11731	1832	1568	19639	−591	15524	4988
Long-term debt	−300	6947	−69	4720	11482	4273	3965	8706	20826	6392	13095	9046
Short-term debt	4750	1470	11329	3610	−1550	7458	−2133	−7138	−1186	−6983	2428	−4058
Liquid assets	2683	3888	7003	5741	5199	3607	−4787	−2313	3091	−6782	1804	−12018
Gov. borrowing	1768	4529	4257	2589	4733	8124	6619	3881	16548	6191	13720	17006

Note: CSO: Quarterly Government Debt (Maastricht Debt) for General Government. In million euros.

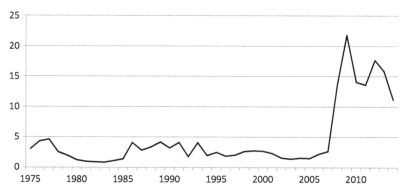

Figure 11.4: Irish government holding of cash and deposits, 1975–2014
Note: CSO: *National Income and Expenditure, Government Finance Statistics*; ESRI: Databank; Department of Finance: *Finance Accounts*. In percentage of GNP.

the end of 2011. However, while the NTMA had sought to protect against downside risks by borrowing well ahead of need, the size of the funding required to recapitalise the banks was even greater than the NTMA had provided for. This became apparent over the course of the summer of 2010 and the result was that it became impossible to borrow in the autumn of 2010 at any realistic interest rate.

While the government still held cash amounting to around 12 percent of GNP, because there was no realistic chance of undertaking further borrowing over the course of 2011 to fund the banks, it accepted the assistance of the EU and of the IMF in late November 2010. A further factor forcing the government to accept outside assistance was the discomfort expressed by the ECB at the amount of liquidity support it had to provide for the troubled banking system.

While, prior to the bail-out of December 2010, the NTMA had a clear strategy aimed at remaining exceptionally liquid, questions were raised as to whether the same strategy was appropriate once the EU and IMF long-term funding had been agreed. However, as shown in Figure 11.4, throughout the years that the EU/IMF programme was in place (2010–13), cash holdings remained very high. If the support from the EU/IMF had been unconditional in nature, once the programme had been agreed in December 2010, the funding would have been rather like an overdraft, available to draw down at will. Under those circumstances the cash could have been used in 2011 instead of drawing down the EU/IMF funding.

Table 11.8: *Government cash and deposits, 2005–14*

	2005	2006	2007	2008	2009	2010	2011	2012	2013	2014
Euro area-19	5.1	5.1	5.1	5.7	6.3	6.2	6.2	6.6	6.1	6.3
Belgium	2.7	2.5	2.8	4.6	4.4	4.7	4.7	4.5	4.3	4.5
Germany	6.7	7.8	7.9	7.8	8.0	9.0	9.6	10.0	9.2	9.5
Estonia	4.9	4.5	3.6	3.6	7.3	5.7	5.6	6.0	6.5	6.3
Ireland	5.7	5.5	5.9	15.9	18.3	11.9	11.3	14.6	13.7	9.8
Greece		4.0	3.9	5.5	5.0	7.5	7.1	10.7	12.0	9.5
Spain	8.1	8.8	9.4	9.1	11.1	8.8	7.2	8.0	6.8	7.8
France	3.2	1.4	1.4	2.2	3.1	2.1	2.9	2.6	2.1	2.0
Italy	3.9	4.5	3.6	4.1	5.2	5.8	4.5	4.7	4.8	5.4
Netherlands	3.8	2.5	3.0	3.0	2.9	2.3	2.2	2.3	1.7	1.7
Portugal	4.7	5.3	4.6	4.5	4.3	4.6	10.4	11.8	12.5	12.1
Sweden	1.8	2.5	2.2	3.1	2.5	2.0	2.8	2.7	2.4	4.3
United Kingdom	2.2	2.7	3.0	3.5	4.4	4.1	4.9	4.7	4.7	4.8

Note: as a percentage of GDP.
Source: Eurostat

However, because of the quarterly performance reviews, the government was nervous that, in the event of a dispute arising with the Troika, this source of funding would suddenly dry up. As a result, it continued to hold large reserves of liquid assets. In the event there were no disputes and the agreed funding was disbursed as expected. The cost of holding these precautionary balances amounted to around 0.5 percent of GNP in 2011 and 2012.[9]

As shown in Table 11.8, three of the countries that participated in EU/IMF programmes (Ireland, Portugal and Greece) gradually adopted rather similar policies on liquidity. As discussed, in the case of Ireland the huge increase in holdings of cash and deposits occurred at the very beginning of the crisis, to some extent anticipating the funding difficulties to come. In the case of Portugal the increase in liquidity occurred in 2011 and in the case of Greece in 2012, after the EU/IMF programmes were already in place. Portugal, like Ireland, still holds a large amount of cash which is available to smooth any temporary funding problems

---

[9] The difference between the average cost of EU/IMF funding and the deposit rate at the ECB.

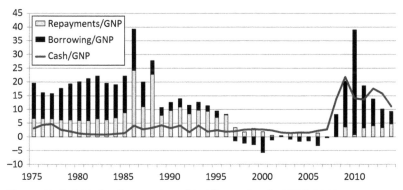

Figure 11.5: Irish funding needs and holdings of cash, 1975–2014

Note: CSO: *National Income and Expenditure, Government Finance Statistics*; ESRI: Databank; Department of Finance: *Finance Accounts*. In percentage of GNP.

that might arise in the immediate post-programme years. In the case of Greece, its holdings of liquid assets were not sufficient to ride out the disputes with the EU and the IMF in the first half of 2015 and the cash reserves are probably largely exhausted.

The one other country shown in Table 11.8 as holding large amounts of cash and deposits is Germany. This is surprising as the German economy is in a very strong position with sound and stable public finances. However, with low bond rates, the cost of remaining liquid is significantly lower than for Portugal, Ireland and Greece.

With the improvement in the public finances and the strong growth in the Irish economy, the question arises today as to whether the large holding of cash is still required. Over 2015 these holdings proved very useful, as they allowed the government to refinance the IMF borrowing at much lower cost when the opportunity arose. However, the holdings of cash today are more than enough to fund the government's needs (borrowing and rolling-over maturing debt). The Minister for Finance has indicated that the government will, as a result, gradually reduce this liquidity buffer.

3.5 Maturity Structure

As shown in Figure 11.5, in the 1980s crisis, as well as funding the very large government borrowing requirement, there was also a need to roll over a large amount of borrowing that matured each year. This posed major challenges for the authorities.

The experience of the past eight years has been rather different as the NTMA ensured that the debt maturity profile was longer and more regularly spaced: there was not a severe bunching of repayments. Having borrowed short-term in 2008, the NTMA managed to convert this borrowing into medium to long-term borrowing by early 2010, albeit at the cost of a high interest rate.

The borrowing from the EU and the IMF as part of the agreed programme was initially at a mixture of maturities. However, these provisions were subsequently revised for the borrowing from the EU, providing for longer-term maturities.[10] The fact that repayments were delayed till well after the ending of the programme meant that the funding needs for the period immediately after the end of the pro-gramme were manageable. This facilitated re-entry to the markets.

The first time the NTMA re-entered the markets was in the summer of 2012. On that occasion the NTMA swapped longer-dated bonds for bonds due to mature relatively early. This had the advantage that it showed an ability to begin funding on the open market again, as well as improving the maturity profile of the debt. The practice in the past has been that the NTMA tries to avoid bunching of debt repayments by swapping short-term debt for long-term debt. It is likely that they will return to this practice to smooth the rolling-over of existing debt in future years.

Figure 11.6 shows the maturity structure of government debt for a number of countries in 2014. Ireland and Portugal both have quite a high proportion of long-term debt. This has meant that their funding needs were limited in the years immediately following the ending of their programmes. Spain, by contrast, has a somewhat shorter matur-ity profile, as do countries such as Sweden and Slovakia.

3.6 Holders of Debt

Until the end of the 1980s, Irish banks were required to hold around 20 percent of their assets in the form of government debt. Because of the exchange risk, all of this debt was Irish government debt. However, with deregulation at the end of the 1980s, the banks were free to choose how much to hold. As shown in Figure 11.7, their holdings

---

[10] This extension of maturities followed on the provision of a similar revision to the terms of the lending to Greece.

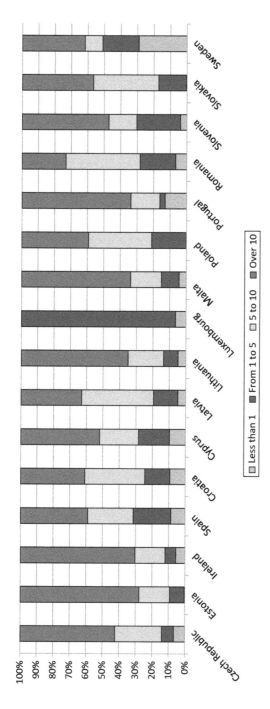

Figure 11.6: Maturity structure of government debt, 2014

Source: Eurostat

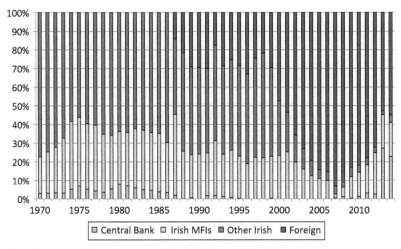

Figure 11.7: Irish government debt holdings, 1970–2014

Note: The absence of foreign holdings of Irish government debt up to the mid-1980s may reflect data problems.

Source: Central Bank of Ireland

were rapidly reduced at the time of the start of the EMU. With the ending of exchange risk from lending abroad, other investment opportunities opened up outside Ireland. In addition, the banking system rapidly increased its exposure to the Irish property market. As a result, by the beginning of the crisis, Irish banks held very little Irish government debt.

The domestic private sector, mainly pension funds and insurance companies, also held substantial amounts of Irish government debt up to the beginning of EMU. However, over the period 1999–2007, these companies greatly reduced their holdings of government debt, diversifying their portfolios of assets to include substantial holdings of foreign assets. This reflected the fact that prior to EMU they had been constrained to hold largely Irish pound assets to match their assets to their Irish pound-denominated liabilities.

Since 2008 there has been some increase in banks' holdings of Irish government debt. However, they still remain below the levels seen in the 1990s. The domestic private sector (pension funds and insurance companies) has continued to maintain very small holdings of Irish government debt. The increase in holdings by the Central Bank of Ireland reflects the Irish government's take-over of the insolvent banks' liabilities to the ECB. In 2013, these liabilities were converted into long-dated government bonds, which are gradually being sold off.

During the programme years 2010–13, the IMF had suggested that the government should have raised funding by issuing treasury bills to be taken up by the domestic banks. This strategy was adopted by a number of other countries facing funding difficulties. However, given the problems with the banking system, the Irish authorities believed that it would have been unwise to do so, as it would be seen to increase the interdependence of the state and the banking system.

While it is difficult to get good data on holdings of national debt on a similar basis to those for Ireland in Figure 11.7, it would appear that Ireland is unusual in the extent to which debt is held outside the country. This feature meant that, while the state proved to be seriously affected by the problems in the banks after 2008, the banks' balance sheets were not directly affected by the problems in the public finances.

3.7 Nature of the Financial Assistance

The financial assistance provided as part of the EU/IMF programme agreed at the beginning of December 2010 was of very considerable importance. At a time when the uncertainty about the government's liabilities through the banking system meant that it could not borrow at any sustainable rate, the financial assistance provided the necessary funding. The agreement on the programme of adjustment already put in place by the government also lent credibility to that programme, both abroad and domestically. The nature of the oversight was also helpful. The incoming government was free to alter the programme provided that the key parameters were left unchanged. The questioning by the Troika at their periodic visits helped sustain the commitment to sensible policies.

Unlike the other programmes agreed, in the case of the Irish programme exceptional support was provided by the non-euro area governments – the United Kingdom, Sweden and Denmark. This support was provided at low cost to the Irish government.

The initial terms agreed as part of the programme involved quite high interest rates charged by the EU. The formula used added a risk premium to the market interest rate at which the EU funds were raised. However, at a later date, as part of the second Greek programme, the interest rates were reduced for the programme countries to eliminate the substantial risk premium and the maturities of the loans were increased.

The loans provided by the IMF came at a significantly higher interest rate and the maturities of the loans were generally shorter than those eventually agreed for the EU funding. However, the IMF loans had the major advantage that the Irish government had the option of repaying the debt early if it so wished. With the dramatic fall in the interest rate facing the Irish government, since the end of 2013 nearly all of the IMF loans have been repaid and refunded on the open market. This has resulted in a major saving in interest payments. A similar policy is now being pursued by the Portuguese government, replacing IMF loans with normal borrowing.

A final complication with the Irish programme was the fall-out from the guarantee provided to the banks, in particular to the bank that proved to be insolvent. While that bank continued in operation it relied very heavily on liquidity assistance from the ECB, backed by a government guarantee of repayment. However, in 2013 the bank was wound up and the government guarantee was converted into government bonds. This left the Central Bank of Ireland holding the bonds, which will be sold off as monetary conditions permit.

The terms of the new bonds provided for very long maturities with a variable interest rate based on Euribor, plus a large premium, reflecting the premium then payable on Irish debt relative to German debt. Because the bonds were held at the risk of the Central Bank of Ireland rather than the ECB, the difference between the interest paid by the government and the interest paid by the Central Bank to the ECB means that, until the bonds are sold by the Central Bank, there is a substantial profit for the Central Bank of Ireland. This profit is duly paid to the bank's owner, the government.

The bonds have been sold by the Central Bank more rapidly than had been provided for in the minimum schedule agreed with the ECB. In turn, the Irish government has been able to refinance the bonds at the current very low interest rate. While the profit of the Central Bank is, as a result, reduced, because the bonds were due to be sold off long before their maturity date, the effect of the transaction is to substantially reduce the long-term cost of the borrowing. Thus the nature of the instrument agreed with the ECB and the EU in 2013, as part of the liquidation of the insolvent bank, has provided additional flexibility for the Irish government, allowing it to manage down the long-term cost of the crisis.

3.8 Managing the Government's Financial Assets

The guarantee provided by the government to the domestically owned banks in September 2008 effectively resulted in their nationalisation. Two insolvent banks were merged and then closed in 2013, and the remaining three institutions (after amalgamations) ended up in government ownership.

Already some of the shares in two of these banks have been sold. The redemption of preference shares and the sale of ordinary shares resulted in the repayment of over €4 billion to the taxpayer. However, the largest of the banks still remains in government hands, with a majority stake in a second bank and a minority stake in the third bank.

The banking system still has major problems with a high volume of non-performing loans. While provision has been made for the possible losses on these loans, they nonetheless continue to impact on the banks' performance. However, with output in the economy moving back towards potential, there has been a period of rapid growth. This has helped to move the banks back to profitability.

With the economy returning to reasonable growth and appropriate management of the banks, over the rest of the decade they may move towards more normal operating conditions. If this were to happen, the eventual sale of the remaining government stake in the banks could result in a significant further one-off reduction in the debt. The objective of government policy should be to try and maximise the eventual return from the sale of these state assets. However, even with favourable circumstances the eventual direct fiscal cost of the support for the banking system, illustrated in Figure 11.3, is still likely to be very substantial.

3.9 The Cost of Funding

When the NTMA began borrowing heavily and building up a buffer of liquid assets, the Irish long bond yield was not very much higher than it was at the time in Germany – although it was much higher than in Ireland after the crisis in 2014 (Figure 11.8).

However, as the public finances deteriorated and, in particular, as the problems with the domestic banking system loomed ever larger, the risk premium for Irish government borrowing continued to rise. In 2009 and into the beginning of 2010, the risk premium was

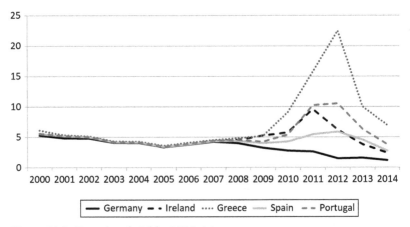

Figure 11.8: Long bond yields, 2000–14
Source: EU Commission, AMECO Database

manageable and the government continued to borrow as necessary on international markets. But over the course of 2010, as the problems with the banking system became clearer, the risk premium rose dramatically, so that in the autumn the government found it could no longer borrow at a realistic rate.

However, with the EU/IMF programme in place and with the publication of the stress tests on the banks in March 2011, it gradually became apparent to the financial markets that there was no more bad news hidden from view. The risk premium began to fall. But because of the availability of funding from the EU/IMF programme at an attractive interest rate, especially after the rates were revised down, the government had no need to access the financial markets in 2011 and 2012.

The decline in the risk premium occurred against the background of an unprecedented fall in German bond yields. With a decline in the risk premium in Ireland, and a similar but somewhat later decline in Portugal and Spain, nominal interest rates fell in Ireland, Spain and Portugal to levels significantly below those experienced in the pre-crisis years. This fall in interest rates, and the ability of Ireland and Portugal to access them, has played an important role in making high debt levels sustainable.

Previous episodes in which countries have found themselves heavily indebted have often been accompanied by relatively elevated interest rates. This had made debt levels over 100 percent of GDP difficult to

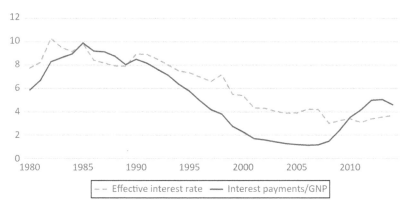

Figure 11.9: Irish national debt interest payments, 1980–2014
Note: as percentage of GNP and of debt outstanding.
Source: CSO, National Income and Expenditure and ESRI Databank

sustain. However, in the current situation the very low nominal interest rates are of significant benefit to indebted countries. As long as the low nominal interest rates persist, Ireland (and Portugal and Spain) will continue to replace maturing high interest-rate debt with new debt carrying a lower yield, further reducing the effective burden of the debt on the economy.

The effect of this process is that already the share of debt interest in GNP in Ireland is falling, having peaked in 2012–13 (Figure 11.9). Interest payments were 4.7 percent of the national debt (the effective interest rate) in 2007, whereas they had fallen to 3.8 percent by 2014. This reflects the relatively low interest rates available on the bulk of the debt issued since the crisis began.

Since EMU began, the burden of interest payments as a share of GDP has fallen pretty continuously in the case of Germany (Figure 11.10). Not surprisingly, the crisis saw a big increase in the share of GDP going on interest payments in the period 2008–12 in a range of other countries. However, the very low level of interest rates, combined with favourable rates under the EU/IMF programmes (especially for Greece), have seen the burden of debt interest fall back in Greece, Spain and Ireland.[11]

---

[11] As Portugal repays its debt to the IMF early, there will also be some reduction in the interest bill.

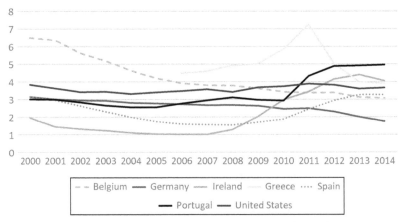

Figure 11.10: National debt interest payments in selected countries, 2000–14
Note: as percentage of GDP.
Source: AMECO Database

By 2014, the burden of the debt (measured by the burden of interest payments) in Ireland, Spain and Greece was very similar to that experienced in Belgium and the United States, and well below the levels previously experienced by Ireland in the 1980s and the early 1990s.[12]

4 Conclusions

We conclude by highlighting some important topics for future research in relation to the analysis and management of the public balance sheet.

First, the European sovereign debt crisis has underlined the value in mitigating the rollover risk of sufficient long maturities in the composition of debt issuance and adequate cash buffers. There is a substantial premium to being liquid when a crisis hits. It gives governments much more freedom to manoeuvre. In parallel to the debate on the optimal scale of official reserves for emerging economies, more work on the optimal scale of liquid public assets is warranted. In terms of political economy, the importance of demonstrating credibility in charting a course to fiscal sustainability is vital. To this end, a strategy of under-promising and over-delivering is more successful than excessively optimistic projections.

---

[12] However, the rate of inflation is also much lower.

Second, in terms of the composition of the investor base for sovereign debt, a challenge for a monetary union is to work out the appropriate role for the area-wide banking system as holders of sovereign debt. It is manifestly clear that excessive holdings of domestic sovereign debt by the domestic banking system sow the seeds of instability (see, among many others, Brunnermeier et al., 2011). At the same time, sovereign debt is an important category of liquid assets for banking systems. For a monetary union, designing financial regulations that encourage banks to hold an area-wide diversified portfolio of sovereign debt is an important priority.[13]

Third, in the context of sovereign crises, an important element in the composition of the investor base is the different characteristics of private sector creditors versus official sector creditors. Obtaining access to official funding can bring significant benefits in terms of funding stability and lower funding costs. It also holds the promise of 'soft' types of debt adjustments through renegotiation of the duration and coupon payments on official debt. However, the Greek experience suggests that more radical levels of debt restructuring are less likely vis-à-vis official creditors than vis-à-vis private creditors, for a variety of political economy reasons. Accordingly, troubled sovereigns (and, on the other side, potential official creditors) require a sophisticated understanding of the pros and cons of bail-out funding.

Fourth, the expansion of central bank balance sheets and, in particular, increased holdings of sovereign debt by central banks call for closer scrutiny of the interactions between the central bank balance sheet and the balance sheet of the wider public sector. Again, this is a more complex challenge for a monetary union, especially a monetary system that includes both a common central bank and a constellation of national central banks.

Fifth, it is plausible that there should be an expanded role for state-contingent debt securities. The literature on different varieties of GDP-indexed bonds is extensive.[14] However, in the context of providing support to the financial system during crisis episodes, working out the relative roles of nonlinear 'loss insurance' schemes versus plain-vanilla liability guarantees or the different forms of publicly funded recapitalisation is a high priority.

---

[13] See also Corsetti et al. (2015) and European Systemic Risk Board (2015).
[14] See, among many others, Borensztein and Mauro (2004).

Finally, with respect to interest rate risk, this time round the effective burden of a large debt is lower than in the past, because of low interest rates.

Bibliography

Borensztein, Eduardo and Mauro, Paolo (2004). The case for GDP-indexed bonds. *Economic Policy*, **19**(38), 165–216.

Brunnermeier, Marcus K., Garicano, Luis, Lane, Philip R., Pagano, Marco, Reis, Ricardo, Santos, Tano, NVan Nieuwerburgh, Stijn and Vayanos, Dimitri (2011). European Safe Bonds: ESBies. *Euro-nomics.com*, http://personal.lse.ac.uk/vayanos/Euronomics/ESBies.pdf

Corsetti, Giancarlo, Feld, Lars P., Lane, Philip R., Reichlin, Lucrezia, Rey, Hélène, Vayanos, Dimitri and Weder di Mauro, Beatrice (2015). *A New Start for the Eurozone: Dealing with Debt, Monitoring the Eurozone 1*. London: Centre for Economic Policy Research, ebook.

Eichengreen, Barry and Panizza, Ugo (2016). A surplus of ambition: can Europe rely on large primary surpluses to solve its debt problem? *Economic Policy*, **31**(85), 5–49.

Escolano, Julio (2010). A practical guide to public debt dynamics, fiscal sustainability, and cyclical adjustment of budgetary aggregates. *IMF Technical Notes and Manuals 10/02*.

European Systemic Risk Board (2015). *The Regulatory Treatment of Sovereign Exposures*, www.esrb.europa.eu/pub/pdf/other/esrbreportregulatory treatmentsovereignexposures032015.en.pdf?29664e3495a886d806863a ac942fcdae

Fitzgerald, J. and Lane, P. (2016). *Fiscal Policy and Financial Distress: A Balance Sheet Perspective*. Trinity College Dublin, Trinity Economic Papers.

Honohan, Patrick (1999). Fiscal adjustment and disinflation in Ireland: setting the macro basis of economic recovery and expansion. In F. Barry, ed., *Understanding Ireland's Economic Growth*. Basingstoke: Macmillan Press, pp. 75–98.

IMF (2015). *Balance Sheet Analysis in Fund Surveillance*. Policy Paper, www.imf.org/external/np/pp/eng/2015/061215.pdf.

Jeanne, O. and Rancière, R. (2011). The optimal level of international reserves for emerging market economies: a new formula and some applications. *Economic Journal*, **121** (September), 905–30.

Kearney, Ide, McCoy, D., Duffy, D., McMahon, M. and Smyth, D. (2000). *Assessing the Stance of Irish Fiscal Policy*. ESRI Series: Budget Perspectives 2001/1.

Lane, Philip R. (2010). External imbalances and fiscal policy. In Salvador Barrios, Servaas Deroose, Sven Langedijk and Lucio Pench, eds.,

External Imbalances and Public Finances in the EU. European Economy Occasional Paper No. 66.

Pâris, Pierre and Wyplosz, Charles (2014). *PADRE: Politically Acceptable Debt Restructuring in the Eurozone*. Geneva Special Report on the World Economy 3, ICMB and CEPR.

Tirole, Jean (2015). Country solidarity in sovereign crises. *American Economic Review*, **105**(8), 2333–63.

12 Financial Cycles and Fiscal Cycles

AGUSTÍN S. BÉNÉTRIX AND
PHILIP R. LANE

1 Introduction

The aim of this chapter is to examine the role of financial cycles in driving the cyclical behaviour of fiscal policy. Traditionally, the predominant focus in the fiscal cyclicality literature has been on how fiscal variables co-move with the output cycle (see Lane, 2003 and Alesina et al., 2008, among many others). However, the deterioration in fiscal positions that accompanied the global financial crisis has highlighted the sensitivity of fiscal outcomes to financial factors.[1]

In this regard, Bénétrix and Lane (2015) show that the decline in fiscal balances during the crisis was significantly correlated with the scale of financial imbalances during the pre-crisis years, even controlling for the variation in GDP outcomes. In particular, fiscal outcomes during the crisis are highly correlated with the scale of pre-crisis current account imbalances and credit growth.

There has been considerable research on the two-way inter-connections between financial crises and fiscal crises. For instance, taking a broad sweep of the historical evidence, Reinhart and Rogoff (2009) highlight that public debt levels grow rapidly in the wake of a banking crisis. In a related fashion, Honohan and Klingebiel (2003) document the mechanisms by which a banking crisis can generate a high fiscal burden. In the other direction, there are also negative feedback loops at work by which a weak sovereign can induce instability in the financial sector. For instance, Reinhart and Belen Sbrancia (2015) highlight that

We thank Torben Andersen, Xavier Debrun, Balázs Égert, Gernot Müller, Ľudovít Ódor, Ugo Panizza, Tack Yun and participants in several workshops and conferences for helpful discussions and comments on earlier versions of this work. Lane thanks the Irish Research Council for grant support. The views expressed in this chapter are personal and do not represent the views of the Central Bank of Ireland or the eurosystem.

[1] Discretionary stimulus programmes accounted for only a small proportion of the total decline in fiscal balances in most countries (Bénétrix and Lane, 2015).

financially challenged sovereigns often turn to financial repression measures. Alternatively, weak public finances can lead to financial instability through their impact on the balance sheets of financial institutions holding large stocks of public debt (Das et al., 2010; CGFS, 2011; Jordà et al., 2015). The interplay between fiscal crises and financial crises is a central theme in the current European debt crisis.

However, while much of the recent focus has been on the implications of financial crises for fiscal policy, it is also important to gain a better understanding of the role played by financial factors in determining fiscal outcomes during 'normal' times. In particular, financial cycles can induce volatility in fiscal balances. Furthermore, if the induced fiscal shocks are procyclical in direction, these may amplify macroeconomic imbalances and weaken the underlying capacity of the government to effectively respond upon the occurrence of a financial crisis.

Accordingly, the main contribution of this chapter is to examine whether financial variables influence the cyclical behaviour of fiscal variables. We focus on net capital flows (as captured by the current account balance) and domestic credit as key financial factors that may affect fiscal variables over the cycle. We report panel VAR models and regression estimates for a set of twenty-two advanced countries and thirty emerging market economies over 1980–2007.[2]

The structure of the rest of the chapter is as follows. Section 2 provides a conceptual framework for the analysis and relates our contribution to the previous literature. We turn to the empirical analysis in Section 3. Some policy implications are laid out in Section 4, while Section 5 concludes.

2 Conceptual Framework

An extensive literature has examined the behaviour of fiscal variables over the output cycle (see Bayoumi and Eichengreen, 1995; Gavin and Perotti, 1997; Lane, 2003 for early contributions). A theme in this literature has been to measure whether the fiscal balance and/or public spending has been inappropriately procyclical in some country groups and to identify the sources of such procyclicality.

---

[2] We end the sample in 2007, since the aftermath of the post-2007 crisis has not yet fully played out.

However, in some of the literature, it has also been recognised that simple measures of the output cycle are not sufficient to capture all sources of fiscal volatility. For instance, Bouthevillain et al. (2001) highlight that shifts in the distribution of income between labour income and profit income alter the composition of the tax base and thereby the level of revenues. Similarly, these authors also emphasise that different components of aggregate demand have different revenue implications (consumption versus exports, for example).

In relation to financial variables, Eschenbach and Schuknecht (2004) and Girouard and Price (2004) show that asset price cycles influence fiscal outcomes. A striking finding is that asset price booms not only raise revenues from asset-related taxes but also lead to generalised revenue growth, due to the wealth effect of increasing asset values on consumption. Findings of this type motivated research proposing methodologies to explicitly account for financial variables. For instance, Price and Dang (2011) propose a method to adjust the structural budget balance by equity prices and house prices. More recently, Borio et al. (2013, 2014, 2016) have suggested alternative measures for potential output and output gaps designed to account for financial factors.

Two recent papers have examined the role of the current account balance in influencing the fiscal cycle. Both Dobrescu and Salman (2011) and Lendvai et al. (2011) emphasise that a current account deficit should improve revenues from indirect taxes, since net capital inflows finance a higher level of domestic absorption. A primary focus of these studies is to derive an augmented cyclical adjustment for the fiscal balance that takes into account the mechanical impact of the current account balance on tax revenues. The objective is that such a corrected measure might better capture the true underlying structural fiscal position, net of both the output cycle and the current account cycle. Similarly, Liu et al. (2015) propose an empirical approach to estimate structural fiscal balances that explicitly account for the impact of asset price cycles.

Other financial variables may also influence fiscal outcomes. We focus on domestic credit growth. As was indicated in the introduction, Bénétrix and Lane (2015) find that pre-crisis credit growth is a strong indicator of the scale of fiscal deterioration during the 2008–9 crisis period. The interpretation is that credit expansion may have fuelled additional revenue growth during the pre-crisis period, which then melted away when the credit cycle went into reverse.

The influence of credit growth on fiscal outcomes is highly visible in the detailed Irish revenue data (Lane, 2007).[3] Credit growth affects revenues through several channels. First, the positive impact of credit growth on domestic asset and property prices improves revenues through the direct and indirect channels highlighted by Eschenbach and Schuknecht (2004), Girouard and Price (2004) and Addison-Smyth and McQuinn (2010). Second, credit growth may fuel a greater volume of asset market turnover, which raises revenues from asset transactions taxes. Third, if credit growth is associated with a shift in the composition of production towards the construction sector and other nontradables, this may alter the composition of the tax base to the extent that sectors differ in the distribution of income between wages and profits and in the composition of spending between domestic spending and exports. Fourth, credit growth may be associated with inflation and/or real exchange rate appreciation (an increase in the relative price of nontradables) and thereby raise revenues, since tax systems are not fully inflation-indexed.

We prefer to use credit growth rather than other domestic financial indicators, such as asset price indices (housing prices or equity prices).[4] First, the credit data are far more widely available and more easily comparable across countries.[5] Second, as is documented by Claessens et al. (2011), credit growth is highly correlated with house prices and equity prices, so that it may be a good general proxy variable. Third, credit growth may be more easily targeted by policymakers than asset prices. Fourth, the relation between credit growth and macroeconomic variables may be more stable than the relation between asset prices and macroeconomic variables.

In addition to the mechanical impact of financial variables on tax revenues, financial shocks may also operate through political economy channels. The fiscal cyclicality literature has emphasised

---

[3] Indeed, De Manuel and Raciborski (2015) show that corrections for the credit and house price cycles would have yielded different estimates of Ireland's fiscal stance in the years leading to the crisis.

[4] For a detailed assessment of the impact of housing prices or equity prices on specific revenue types see Price and Dang (2011).

[5] Although the availability of housing price indices is improving, the cross-country coverage is still relatively low and there are differences in the scope and definition of these indices. Stock market development varies widely across countries and over time, such that the representativeness of national equity price indices as a domestic financial indicator is open to question.

that political distortions may induce the discretionary component of fiscal policy to respond procyclically to output shocks, since the political equilibrium may exhibit a pattern by which an expansion in tax revenues induces matching increases in public spending or an offsetting reduction in tax rates (see Tornell and Lane, 1999; Talvi and Végh, 2005; Alesina et al., 2008 among others). Accordingly, the overall fiscal response to a shock may go in either direction, depending on the relative importance of the automatic and discretionary responses. The political economy literature is general in scope, such that the underlying shock might be an output shock, a terms of trade shock or a resource endowment shock, such as the discovery of oil.[6] By the same token, if a financial boom induces a revenue windfall, it may trigger similar political dynamics that result in increased public spending or discretionary tax cuts.

Accordingly, our main focus is on how the overall fiscal balance responds to the financial cycle. Our empirical specification generally follows the literature, but with the addition of financial variables to the fiscal equation.

3 Empirical Analysis

3.1 Descriptive Statistics and Correlations

As a prelude to the econometrics, Table 12.1 reports some descriptive statistics and autocorrelations. Panel A shows the mean, standard deviation and first autocorrelation coefficient for each variable for advanced countries and emerging economies. All variables are expressed as deviations from country means, so the focus is on within-country variation.

Panel B shows the matrices of bivariate correlations among the variables. In terms of the advanced country sample, the aggregate fiscal surplus is procyclical vis-à-vis both the GDP cycle and the absorption cycle. Not surprisingly, these correlations are considerably smaller in the case of the cyclically adjusted fiscal balance. The fiscal balance is positively correlated with both the current account and credit growth, with the latter presenting a stronger pattern. In terms of covariation with the output cycle and the absorption cycle,

---

[6] See Kaminsky (2010) on the impact of terms of trade shocks on fiscal outcomes.

Table 12.1: Descriptive statistics and correlations
Panel A: Descriptive statistics

	Advanced			Emerging		
	Mean	SD	Autocorrelation	Mean	SD	Autocorrelation
FBAL	−2.46	4.45	0.92	−2.26	5.07	0.81
CFBAL	−2.73	3.48	0.89			
GDP		2.69	0.78		6.73	0.79
ABS		3.64	0.73		7.59	0.63
CA	−0.31	4.85	0.90	−0.89	6.00	0.83
ΔDC	2.96	8.29	0.55	1.06	5.86	0.42

Panel B: Correlations

	Advanced					Emerging			
	FBAL	CFBAL	GDP	ABS	CA	FBAL	GDP	ABS	CA
CFBAL	0.88								
GDP	0.33	0.13				0.23			
ABS	0.28	0.10	0.90			0.17	0.77		
CA	0.20	0.15	−0.21	−0.39		0.03	−0.32	−0.51	
ΔDC	0.30	0.25	0.20	0.25	−0.25	0.17	0.26	0.31	−0.35

Note: de-meaned variables by country. FBAL is general government balance scaled by GDP. CFBAL is cyclically adjusted general government balance scaled by GDP. GDP and ABS are two alternative cycle measures. GDP is real GDP relative to trend, while ABS is real absorption (defined as GDP minus net exports) relative trend. To construct these deviations from trend, we take the residuals of OLS models regressing each cycle measure on a linear and quadratic trend. CA is current account balance scaled by GDP. ΔDC is the percentage point difference in private credit scaled by GDP.

the current account surplus is countercyclical, while credit growth is procyclical. Finally, faster credit growth is associated with a larger current account deficit.

These patterns are largely similar for the emerging economies. However, the correlations of fiscal variables with the financial variables are stronger for the advanced economies, while the correlations of these variables with the output and absorption cycles are weaker for the advanced economies.

3.2 Panel VAR Models

The next step to further study the link between financial and fiscal cycles is to look at the impact of financial cycle shocks on the short-term dynamics of different fiscal indicators. To this end, we estimate parsimonious panel VAR models using four endogenous variables and report the impulse-response functions associated with these shocks.

The fiscal indicator used in the baseline specification is the government general balance scaled by GDP, since our main focus is on aggregate fiscal measures. This allows the financial cycle to operate through discretionary fiscal responses as well as through the automatic stabilisers. Discretionary responses include general expenditure changes but also changes to the tax code and transfer programmes, which have the effect of altering the automatic stabilisers' sensitivity to the output cycle. In terms of evaluating policy performance, the aggregate fiscal variables may provide a better guide than the cyclically adjusted fiscal variables, since those are subject to large ex post revisions.[7]

The financial cycle is measured by two variables in this study. The first is the change in the ratio of private credit to GDP and the second is the current account balance scaled by GDP.[8] To allow for interactions with the rest of the economy, we include the GDP cycle as the fourth endogenous variable.

The model to be estimated in its structural form is given by

$$A_0 Z_{i,t} = A(L)Z_{i,t-1} + CX_{i,t} + \varepsilon_{i,t}, \tag{1}$$

where $Z_{i,t}$ is a vector including the endogenous variables and $X_{i,t}$ captures observed and unobserved sources of cross-country heterogeneity. It includes country-specific intercepts and the outstanding level of public debt scaled by GDP. The reason for including the latter is to

---

[7] In addition, it would be interesting to look at the behaviour of real-time estimates of cyclically adjusted fiscal variables, as in Beetsma and Guilodori (2010) and Cimadomo (2012). However, these real-time datasets are not available for a wide panel of countries or for a long time series.

[8] Clearly, domestic credit growth and the current account imbalance may be correlated variables, with shocks to the external balance affecting domestic credit and vice versa. In particular, Lane and McQuade (2014) show that international net debt flows are correlated with domestic credit growth, while there is no similar connection between international net equity flows and domestic credit growth. In the data, net debt flows dominate net equity flows.

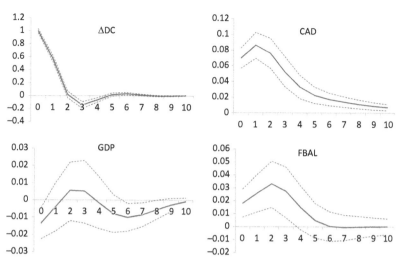

Figure 12.1: General government balance response to domestic credit shock

Notes: Solid lines are the point estimates of the impulse-response mean. Dashed lines represent the error bands. These are the 16th and 84th percentiles from Monte Carlo simulations based on 1,000 replications. *ΔDC* is the percentage point difference in domestic credit scaled by GDP, while *CAD* is the current account deficit scaled by GDP. *GDP* is the cycle of the real gross domestic product and *FBAL* is general government balance scaled by GDP.

account for the link between the stock of public debt and the fiscal balance.[9] Finally, $\varepsilon_{i,t}$ capture the structural shocks of the model.

We study the short-run dynamic effects of shocks to financial cycles on the fiscal balance by looking at the impulse-response functions generated by them. To this end, we implement a recursive approach for shock identification. We assume that financial cycles are exogenous to the fiscal balance and GDP within a window of one year. In addition, we treat the change in private credit as the 'most exogenous' financial cycle variable.[10] Thus, the recursive ordering for the

---

[9] A positive relation between debt and the primary fiscal balance is typically required to support non-explosive debt dynamics. See Bohn (1998), Ballabriga and Martinez-Mongay (2002), Galí and Perotti (2003) and Fatás and Mihov (2010).

[10] In robustness checks, we relax this assumption and estimate the dynamic effects of financial cycle shocks under the alternative assumption that the current account is the most exogenous variable. We find that our qualitative results are unaltered.

identification of these shocks is private credit, current account balance, GDP and the fiscal balance.

Figure 12.1 reports the dynamic responses of the four endogenous variables to a shock in domestic credit using a sample of twenty-two advanced countries. The size of the credit shock is equivalent to one percentage point of GDP.

Figure 12.1 shows that an acceleration in domestic credit improves the government balance contemporaneously and an improvement is also visible three years after the realisation of the shock. This is consistent with mechanisms by which credit growth is associated with a shift in economic activities to tax-rich sectors such as construction and/or a shift in the tax base, with an increase in asset values. From the fourth year onward, the response of this fiscal variable is statistically zero. Since credit negatively co-moves with the current account balance, shocks to the former are associated with current account deficits that emerge on impact and in each of the ten periods of the reported impulse-response horizon. Finally, the average response of the GDP cycle is statistically zero in most periods. The exceptions are the responses on impact and in years six and seven, where the responses are negative and statistically different from zero. However, Figure 12.1 shows that the magnitudes of these responses is small.

Figure 12.2 shows the impulse-response functions for a shock to net financial inflows, which is defined as an increase of one percentage point of GDP in the current account deficit. Strikingly, increases in net financial inflows are associated with deteriorations in the government balance. This contrasts with the findings of Dobrescu and Salman (2011) and Lendvai et al. (2011), who emphasise that increases in net financial inflows should increase revenues via indirect taxes, since larger current account deficits represent greater absorption and, therefore, larger a tax base for indirect taxation.

To shed more light on this, Figure 12.3 reports the impulse-response functions of models including revenues and expenditures as separate endogenous variables. These are reported together with the responses of the overall government balance from Figures 12.1 and 12.2. For a shock to domestic credit, the improvement in the fiscal balance is attributable to a reduction in expenditure and a small positive response of revenues. For a shock to the current account deficit, our model shows that the deterioration in the fiscal balance is the result of expenditure increasing more than revenues. This pattern is consistent

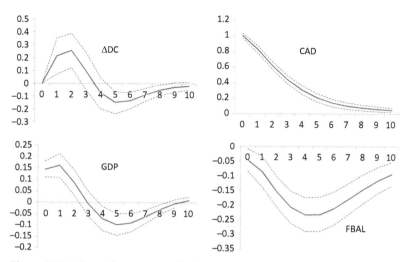

Figure 12.2: General government balance response to current account shock

Notes: Solid lines are the point estimates of the impulse-response mean. Dashed lines represent the error bands. These are the 16th and 84th percentiles from Monte Carlo simulations based on 1,000 replications. ΔDC is the percentage point difference in domestic credit scaled by GDP, while CAD is the current account surplus scaled by GDP. GDP is the cycle of the real gross domestic product and FBAL is general government balance scaled by GDP.

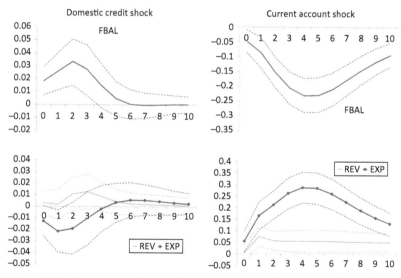

Figure 12.3: Revenue and expenditure responses to domestic credit and current account shocks

Notes: solid lines are the point estimates of the impulse-response mean. Dashed lines represent the error bands. These are the 16th and 84th percentiles from Monte Carlo simulations based on 1,000 replications. The first row reports the response of fiscal balances obtained from a four-variable panel VAR models including also the financial and GDP cycles. The second row reports the responses of government revenue and expenditure obtained from a five-variable panel VAR model. The financial and GDP cycle responses are omitted for presentation purposes.

with the presence of a 'voracity effect', whereby the political equilibrium response to a increase in revenues is a more-than-proportionate increase in public spending, as is laid out in Tornell and Lane (1999).

Taken together, Figures 12.1–12.3 suggest that the fiscal dynamics generated by shocks in financial cycles are mainly driven by government expenditure. This suggests that political economy mechanisms are at work in relation to the discretionary component of government spending, such that an exclusive focus on the mechanical impact of financial shocks on tax revenues would be misdirected.

So far, we have focused on the aggregate fiscal balance. In Section 2, we provided a set of reasons why it may be preferable to examining the general government balance. Still, we next turn to the cyclically adjusted balance to gain a better understanding of the effects of financial cycle shocks. Since this fiscal indicator already takes into account the GDP cycle, we would expect that it will react less to financial cycle shocks as its response will only capture the orthogonal contribution of these shocks, instead of also including those that operate by shifting GDP.

The first row of Figure 12.4 shows the responses of the cyclically adjusted government balance to changes in both financial cycle measures. For a credit shock, the qualitative response of the cyclically adjusted balance is very similar to the one for the unadjusted general government balance. For the current account deficit shock, the response of the cyclically adjusted fiscal balance is also negative. However, the magnitude of its response is smaller. This result provides further evidence that the financial cycle also has a direct impact on the short-term dynamics of the fiscal balance. Moreover, the cyclically adjusted balance's sensitivity to the current account and credit growth suggests that this is not an accurate measure of the 'permanent' component of the budget balance, since fluctuations in credit growth are associated with volatility in the cyclically adjusted budget balance. While this counter-cyclical pattern may provide some macroeconomic stabilisation, an approach that focuses only on the output cycle might mistakenly attribute a credit-driven improvement in the cyclically adjusted fiscal balance as a permanent increase in the underlying structural fiscal position.

The next exercise takes into account that credit and the degree of international financial integration grew more rapidly after the 1990s in advanced countries. To this end, we also focus on a more recent time period and estimate the baseline VAR model using data for 1990–2007. The impulse-response functions for the government

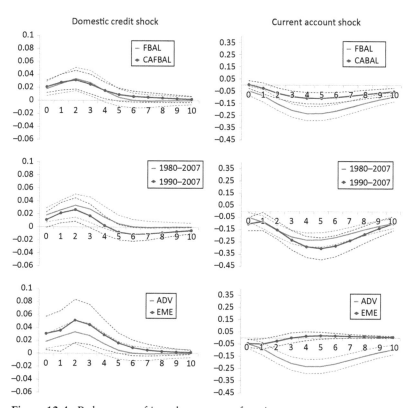

Figure 12.4: Robustness of impulse-response functions

Notes: Solid lines are the point estimates of the impulse-response mean. Dashed lines represent the error bands. These are the 16th and 84th percentiles from Monte Carlo simulations based on 1,000 replications.

balance are reported in the second row of Figure 12.4. In line with the baseline results, financial cycle shocks also affect the short-term dynamics of the fiscal balance. Although the point estimates of the mean responses suggest that the fiscal balance increases by less in response to credit shocks and reduces by more in response to current account shocks, these quantitative differences are statistically zero.

Finally, we compare the results of the baseline model with the fiscal responses of a model using thirty emerging economies. The aim of this exercise is to compare the previous results with countries that may be structurally different. For instance, emerging economies have lower income levels and less developed financial sectors and are less financially integrated with the rest of the world.

The final row of Figure 12.4 shows that emerging economies also exhibit an improvement in the fiscal balance in response to a credit shock. Although the point estimate of the mean response is larger than in the case of advanced economies, these are statistically similar. For the case of current account shocks, we find a qualitative difference in the response of the fiscal balance which is statistically significant: fiscal balances in advanced countries deteriorate much more than in emerging economies. The response in the latter group is slightly negative in years zero and one and then becomes statistically zero. For advanced countries, the fiscal balance is negative throughout the impulse-response horizon, with the largest deterioration between years four and five.

Overall, this section illustrates that shocks to the financial cycle affect the dynamics of fiscal balances directly and indirectly (through their impact on GDP). This finding is not confined to the aggregate general government balance. These shocks also affect the short-run dynamics of government revenues, expenditure and the cyclically adjusted government balance. In addition, these qualitative findings emerge in versions that just examine the latter period of the sample and, for the credit shock only, in emerging economies.

3.3 Regression Models

Next, we explore an alternative empirical approach, which focuses on understanding the relation between fiscal variables and financial variables in a set of panel regressions.

To this end, we examine the following regression model:

$$FISCAL_{it} = \alpha_i + \beta_i CYCLE_{it} + \gamma_i Z_{it} + \lambda_i DEBT_{it-1} + \rho_i FISCAL_{it-1} + \varepsilon_{it},$$
$$(2)$$

where $FISCAL_{it}$ is the fiscal variable of interest of country i in time t and the $CYCLE_{it}$ variable captures the cyclical state of the economy. The coefficient β_i captures the responsiveness of the fiscal variable to the output cycle. In the case where the fiscal variable of interest is the government balance, $\beta_i > 0$ indicates a countercyclical pattern and $\beta_i < 0$ a procyclical one.[11]

---

[11] In most of our specifications, the fiscal variable is scaled as a ratio to GDP. Accordingly, there is some terminological ambiguity about the meaning of cyclicality for such a ratio. For instance, a constant deficit-to-GDP ratio over the cycle may be termed acyclical in one sense but is procyclical in terms of

In terms of cyclical measures, we first examine the deviation of GDP from its trend value (expressed as percentage point deviations). The GDP trend is obtained as the predicted values of a model regressing GDP on linear and quadratic trends.[12] Second, we explore the deviation of absorption from its trend. Again, the trend is obtained from a regression model in which absorption is measured as the difference between gross national income and the current account surplus. Since both are derived from underlying stock positions, we treat the current account balance and credit growth as stationary variables, even if these may be quite persistent.

The Z_{it} vector comprises the financial cycle variables that are included individually or jointly as additional regressors. Since the output cycle is always included in the specification, these variables should only be important if financial factors have additional fiscal effects, over and beyond their influence on output dynamics. As before, we also include the lagged level of the public debt ($DEBT_{it}$). The final regressor is the lag of the fiscal variable, since fiscal variables typically exhibit considerable persistence.

We estimate (2) in two ways. We report fixed-effects panel estimates; in addition, we also report the mean group estimator developed by Pesaran and Smith (1995). The former is followed to account for unobserved heterogeneity across countries in the average fiscal values. In addition, the inclusion of country-specific constants means that our focus is on explaining the time series variation in the data, rather than the cross-sectional differences. The mean group estimator approach is followed to account for country-specific slope coefficients. More precisely, we allow for the covariation patterns between the fiscal indicator, the financial cycle and the other explanatory variables to differ across countries and report the mean group estimator to capture the 'typical' estimates.[13]

---

underlying dynamics, with revenue gains during upswings used to finance spending increases or tax cuts and revenue declines during downturns inducing spending cuts or tax rate hikes.

[12] An alternative could have been the use of output gap. However, these data are not available for the full time span for all countries.

[13] It is important to also account for this heterogeneity, as the effect of the financial cycle variables on the fiscal balance varies across countries. For instance, the range of the country-specific coefficients of the regression model including both financial cycle measures in Table 12.2 is $(-0.78, 0.55)$ for the current account balance and $(-0.59, 0.35)$ for credit growth.

Table 12.2 reports estimates of the specification laid out in Equation
(2) for a sample of twenty-two advanced countries, where the fiscal
measure is the general government fiscal balance. Columns (1)–(4)
report the estimates from panel data models with fixed effects while
columns (5)–(8) show the mean group estimates. These are the
unweighted cross-country averages of the intercept and slope
coefficients.[14]

Columns (1)–(3) show that the fiscal balance is mildly countercyclical vis-à-vis the output cycle and that, as expected, it is increasing in the
outstanding stock of public debt. In relation to the sensitivity to
financial factors, columns (1) and (2) show that neither the current
account deficit nor the change in domestic credit have a statistically
significant association with the general government balance when they
are included individually. However, the current account deficit exhibits
a statistically significant coefficient when both financial cycle variables
are included jointly in column (3). The negative sign of this coefficient
is in line with the dynamic response of the fiscal balance reported in
Figure 12.2. More precisely, an increase in net financial inflows is
associated with a deterioration in the government balance. As discussed before, under the hypothesis that a current account deficit
mechanically improves indirect tax revenues, one would expect an
opposite relation.

Column (4) of Table 12.2 reports the specification using the
absorption cycle instead of the GDP cycle. Here, it is striking that
the fiscal balance is acyclical with respect to the absorption cycle.[15]

These results are confirmed by the mean group estimates in
columns (5)–(8) that allow for cross-country heterogeneity in the
slope coefficients. As before, the coefficient of domestic credit is
statistically zero and the current account deficit is statistically significant when credit is also included as the explanatory variable. The
main difference with the panel data approach is that, as expected,
the fiscal cycle is mildly countercyclical vis-à-vis the absorption
cycle.

As in the previous section, we proceed exploring the covariation
patterns of government revenues and expenditure with the financial

---

[14] This is the standard implementation of Pesaran and Smith (1995).
[15] Dobrescu and Salman (2011) report panel regressions that look at the relation
between the absorption cycle and different fiscal measures. However, they do
not control for credit growth.

Table 12.2: *Regression results: general government balance in advanced countries*

	Panel data with FE				Mean group estimator			
	(1)	(2)	(3)	(4)	(5)	(6)	(7)	(8)
GDP_t^{CYC}	0.12**	0.09**	0.12**		0.15**	0.11**	0.16***	
	(0.04)	(0.03)	(0.04)		(0.06)	(0.05)	(0.06)	
ABS_t^{CYC}				0.03				0.06**
				(0.02)				(0.03)
CAD_t	−0.08		−0.09*		−0.11		−0.13*	
	(0.06)		(0.05)		(0.08)		(0.07)	
$\Delta DC_{(t,t-1)}$		0.01	0.02	0.01		0.01	0.01	0.02
		(0.02)	(0.02)	(0.02)		(0.02)	(0.02)	(0.02)
$DEBT_{t-1}$	0.02**	0.02***	0.02**	0.02***	0.03**	0.03***	0.03**	0.03***
	(0.01)	(0.01)	(0.01)	(0.01)	(0.01)	(0.01)	(0.01)	(0.00)
$FBAL_{t-1}$	0.86***	0.87***	0.84***	0.88***	0.63***	0.78***	0.66***	0.80***
	(0.03)	(0.03)	(0.03)	(0.03)	(0.06)	(0.05)	(0.06)	(0.05)
Obs.	615	614	613	614	615	614	613	614
R^2	0.76	0.76	0.76	0.75				

Notes: robust standard errors in panel data models and standard errors robust to outliers in mean group models are reported in parenthesis. Statistical significance of the point estimates is denoted as * for 10 percent, ** for 5 percent and *** for 1 percent confidence levels. These models are estimated using data for 1980–2007. $FBAL_t$ is general government balance scaled by GDP. GDP_t^{CYC} and ABS_t^{CYC} are two alternative cycle measures. GDP_t^{CYC} is real GDP relative to trend, while ABS_t^{CYC} is real absorption (defined as GDP minus net exports) relative to trend. To construct these cycles, we take the residuals from OLS regression models in which the explanatory variables for GDP and absorption are a linear and a quadratic trends. CAD_t is current account deficit and $DEBT_{t-1}$ is the outstanding level of public debt (both are scaled by GDP). $\Delta DC_{(t,t-1)}$ is the percentage point change in private credit scaled by GDP.

indicators. To this end, we take columns (3) and (7), which include both financial cycle variables from Table 12.2, and estimate similar regression models using revenues and expenditure as the dependent variable. Table 12.3 reports these estimates, with columns (1)–(3) showing the results for the panel data model and (4)–(6) reporting the mean group estimator.

In line with the regression models for the government balance and the impulse-response functions in the previous section, fiscal indicators covary more with the current account than with domestic credit. In addition, the table shows that revenues and expenditure positively

Table 12.3: *Regression results: general government revenues and expenditures in advanced countries*

	Panel data with FE			Mean group estimator		
	Bal	Rev	Exp	Bal	Rev	Exp
	(1)	(2)	(3)	(4)	(5)	(6)
GDP_t^{CYC}	0.12**	−0.05	−0.16**	0.16***	−0.07	−0.19***
	(0.04)	(0.04)	(0.07)	(0.06)	(0.04)	(0.05)
CAD_t	−0.09*	0.05*	0.13***	−0.13*	0.03	0.16**
	(0.05)	(0.02)	(0.04)	(0.07)	(0.05)	(0.08)
$\Delta DC_{(t,t-1)}$	0.02	−0.003	−0.02	0.01	−0.001	−0.03*
	(0.02)	(0.01)	(0.01)	(0.02)	(0.01)	(0.02)
$DEBT_{t-1}$	0.02**	0.01*	−0.01*	0.03**	0.03***	−0.02
	(0.01)	(0.00)	(0.01)	(0.01)	(0.01)	(0.01)
$FISCAL_{t-1}$	0.84***	0.88***	0.86***	0.66***	0.64***	0.74***
	(0.03)	(0.01)	(0.03)	(0.06)	(0.05)	(0.07)
Obs.	613	613	613	613	613	613
R^2	0.76	0.87	0.83			

Notes: robust standard errors in panel data models and standard errors robust to outliers in mean group models are reported in parenthesis. Statistical significance of the point estimates is denoted as * for 10 percent, ** for 5 percent and *** for 1 percent confidence levels. These models are estimated using data for 1980–2007. FISCAL is general government balance, revenues or expenditure scaled by GDP. GDP_t^{CYC} is real GDP relative to trend. This cycle measure is the residual from an OLS regression model in which the explanatory variables are a linear and a quadratic trend. CAD_t is current account deficit and $DEBT_{t-1}$ is the outstanding level of public debt (both are scaled by GDP). $\Delta DC_{(t,t-1)}$ is the percentage point change in private credit scaled by GDP.

covary with the current account, with the strongest pattern evident for expenditure. Table 12.3 gives further support to the previous finding showing that current account deficits are associated with fiscal deteriorations in advanced countries.

Although the point estimate of the current account coefficient on the revenue regressions is not statistically significant in the mean group estimator, it is positive and statistically significant in the panel data model. The latter result suggests that the potential impact of a current account deficit on revenues would be consistent with the sensitivity of taxation to the level of domestic spending, which is boosted by a current account deficit.

The positive covariation pattern between current account deficits and public spending supports the view that governments are more likely to spend such revenue windfalls rather than to accumulate a larger surplus. Moreover, the greater elasticity of spending than of revenue is consistent with the 'voracity effect' phenomenon whereby fluctuations in revenue trigger larger fluctuations in spending (Tornell and Lane, 1999).

For the case of changes in domestic credit shocks we find that, with the exception of the mean group model showing a negative and significant coefficient for government expenditure, the rest of the coefficients are small and statistically zero.

Following the structure of the previous section, we now look at the covariation patterns with the cyclically adjusted fiscal balance. As shown in Table 12.4, it is not too surprising that the output cycle has no systematic association with this fiscal indicator. In terms of the financial cycle variables, we do not find statistically significant patterns. The only exception is the significance of domestic credit in the specification that includes both financial cycle variables in column (3).

Next, we estimate the baseline model, but putting the focus on a more recent period (1990–2007) as well as looking at the emerging economy sample. Table 12.5 reports the estimates using data for this subperiod. The main difference with the baseline model is that the government balance is more countercyclical vis-à-vis both the GDP cycle and the absorption cycle, with most of these coefficients becoming statistically significant at the 1 percent confidence levels. As before, the coefficient measuring cyclicality vis-à-vis the absorption cycle is statistically zero in the panel model. However, this is strongly significant in the mean group estimates. For this sample period, none of the financial cycle variables are individually significant from a statistical point of view. However, the joint significance of the current account balance and credit in column (3) is different from zero at the 10 percent level. Finally, the sign of these point estimates does not change. These patterns are the same as in the baseline model estimated with the full period.

As before, we also look at the emerging economy sample to study whether the differences in the impact of the financial cycle between advanced and emerging economies that were previously reported still emerge in this estimation approach. Table 12.6 shows these estimates. Here, the fiscal balance does not show a significant covariation pattern

Table 12.4: *Regression results: cyclically adjusted general government balance in advanced countries*

	Panel data with FE			Mean group estimator		
	(1)	(2)	(3)	(4)	(5)	(6)
GDP_t^{CYC}	0.02	0.01	0.02	−0.01	−0.01	0.01
	(0.03)	(0.03)	(0.03)	(0.07)	(0.06)	(0.07)
CAD_t	−0.02		−0.03	−0.05		−0.10
	(0.04)		(0.03)	(0.07)		(0.08)
$\Delta DC_{(t,t-1)}$		0.02	0.02*		0.02	0.02
		(0.01)	(0.01)		(0.01)	(0.02)
$DEBT_{t-1}$	0.02**	0.02***	0.02**	0.02*	0.02***	0.01
	(0.01)	(0.01)	(0.01)	(0.01)	(0.01)	(0.01)
$CFBAL_{t-1}$	0.84***	0.83***	0.82***	0.55***	0.67***	0.54***
	(0.03)	(0.03)	(0.03)	(0.06)	(0.05)	(0.06)
Obs.	577	577	577	577	577	577
R^2	0.71	0.71	0.71			

Notes: robust standard errors in panel data models and standard errors robust to outliers in mean group models are reported in parenthesis. Statistical significance of the point estimates is denoted as * for 10 percent, ** for 5 percent and *** for 1 percent confidence levels. These models are estimated using data for 1980–2007. $CFBAL_t$ is cyclically adjusted general government balance scaled by GDP. GDP_t^{CYC} and ABS_t^{CYC} are two alternative cycle measures. GDP_t^{CYC} is real GDP relative to trend while ABS_t^{CYC} is real absorption (defined as GDP minus net exports) relative to trend. To construct these cycles we take the residuals from OLS regression models in which the explanatory variables for GDP and absorption are a linear and a quadratic trend. CAD_t is current account deficit and $DEBT_{t-1}$ is the outstanding level of public debt (both are scaled by GDP). $\Delta DC_{(t,t-1)}$ is the percentage point change in private credit scaled by GDP.

with either the current account deficit or domestic credit. In addition, the two financial cycle variables are jointly zero from a statistical point of view. The result for the current account deficit is in line with the evidence from the impulse-response function reported in Figure 12.4.

In summary, we find evidence that the fiscal cycle co-moves with the financial cycle under a regression-based estimation approach. In particular, the panel estimates (fixed effects and mean group) also show that there is evidence of a destabilising pattern between the current account balance and the fiscal balance, in the sense that a current account deficit is associated with an increase in public spending. In

Table 12.5: *Regression results: general government balance in advanced countries, 1990–2007*

	Panel data with FE				Mean group estimator			
	(1)	(2)	(3)	(4)	(5)	(6)	(7)	(8)
GDP_t^{CYC}	0.18***	0.16***	0.17***		0.38***	0.35***	0.40***	
	(0.06)	(0.05)	(0.06)		(0.07)	(0.07)	(0.08)	
ABS_t^{CYC}				0.05				0.22***
				(0.03)				(0.05)
CAD_t	−0.10		−0.11		−0.06		−0.08	
	(0.08)		(0.07)		(0.09)		(0.09)	
$\Delta DC_{(t,t-1)}$		0.01	0.02	0.01		0.04	0.03	0.01
		(0.02)	(0.02)	(0.02)		(0.02)	(0.03)	(0.02)
$DEBT_{t-1}$	0.02**	0.03**	0.03**	0.03**	0.08***	0.09***	0.08***	0.08***
	(0.01)	(0.01)	(0.01)	(0.01)	(0.03)	(0.02)	(0.02)	(0.02)
$FBAL_{t-1}$	0.80***	0.81***	0.78***	0.85***	0.40***	0.54***	0.43***	0.64***
	(0.04)	(0.04)	(0.05)	(0.05)	(0.07)	(0.08)	(0.08)	(0.09)
Obs.	396	396	396	396	396	396	396	396
R^2	0.72	0.71	0.72	0.70				

Notes: robust standard errors in panel data models and standard errors robust to outliers in mean group models are reported in parenthesis. Statistical significance of the point estimates is denoted as * for 10 percent, ** for 5 percent and *** for 1 percent confidence levels. These models are estimated using data for 1980–2007. $FBAL_t$ is general government balance scaled by GDP. GDP_t^{CYC} and ABS_t^{CYC} are two alternative cycle measures. GDP_t^{CYC} is real GDP relative to trend while ABS_t^{CYC} is real absorption (defined as GDP minus net exports) relative to trend. To construct these cycles we take the residuals from OLS regression models in which the explanatory variables for GDP and absorption are a linear and a quadratic trend. CAD_t is current account deficit and $DEBT_{t-1}$ is the outstanding level of public debt (both are scaled by GDP). $\Delta DC_{(t,t-1)}$ is the percentage point change in private credit scaled by GDP.

relation to credit growth, however, we are not able to confirm the previous finding that faster credit growth is associated with larger fiscal surpluses. By contrast, we find evidence that once credit and the current account are jointly included in the empirical specification, these are jointly significant from a statistical point of view.[16]

---

[16] We tested the joint significance of the current account balance and credit variables in the panel data models and rejected the null hypothesis of both coefficients being jointly zero in almost all the cases. The exceptions are the specifications revenues and emerging market countries.

Table 12.6: *Regression results: general government balance in emerging market economies*

	Panel data with FE				Mean group estimator			
	(1)	(2)	(3)	(4)	(5)	(6)	(7)	(8)
GDP_t^{CYC}	0.05***	0.03	0.04**		0.06**	0.04	0.04	
	(0.02)	(0.03)	(0.02)		(0.03)	(0.04)	(0.03)	
ABS_t^{CYC}				−0.00				−0.00
				(0.04)				(0.03)
CAD_t	−0.09		−0.08		−0.04		−0.08	
	(0.07)		(0.07)		(0.05)		(0.05)	
$\Delta DC_{(t,t-1)}$		0.01	0.03	0.02		0.05	0.09	0.07
		(0.02)	(0.03)	(0.02)		(0.06)	(0.06)	(0.06)
$DEBT_{t-1}$	0.00	0.01	0.01	0.01	0.02	0.02**	0.02**	0.04***
	(0.01)	(0.01)	(0.01)	(0.01)	(0.01)	(0.01)	(0.01)	(0.01)
$FBAL_{t-1}$	0.61***	0.69***	0.68***	0.69***	0.42***	0.50***	0.41***	0.51***
	(0.08)	(0.06)	(0.07)	(0.06)	(0.07)	(0.08)	(0.09)	(0.09)
Obs.	620	609	609	609	620	609	603	609
R^2	0.435	0.463	0.471	0.462				

Notes: robust standard errors in panel data models and standard errors robust to outliers in mean group models are reported in parenthesis. Statistical significance of the point estimates is denoted as * for 10 percent, ** for 5 percent and *** for 1 percent confidence levels. These models are estimated using data for 1980–2007. $FBAL_t$ is general government balance scaled by GDP. GDP_t^{CYC} and ABS_t^{CYC} are two alternative cycle measures. GDP_t^{CYC} is real GDP relative to trend while ABS_t^{CYC} is real absorption (defined as GDP minus net exports) relative to trend. To construct these cycles, we take the residuals from OLS regression models in which the explanatory variables for GDP and absorption are a linear and a quadratic trend. CAD_t is current account deficit and $DEBT_{t-1}$ is the outstanding level of public debt (both are scaled by GDP). $\Delta DC_{(t,t-1)}$ is the percentage point change in private credit scaled by GDP.

4 Some Policy Implications

In relation to the cyclical conduct of fiscal policy, there are several reforms that warrant consideration. First, the analysis in the preceding section suggests that the assessment of the cyclical fiscal stance should be broadened to take into account the financial cycle in addition to the output cycle. In this way, even if aggregate output is measured as being close to its potential level, surges in tax revenues from financial booms would be banked rather than used to boost public spending in a non-sustainable manner. In turn, running larger surpluses during financial booms would facilitate greater fiscal countercyclicality upon a reversal in financial conditions.

As has been widely advocated in recent years, the implementation of a formal fiscal framework may help improve fiscal effectiveness. A central element in such a framework is the specification of numerical fiscal rules. Typically, the set of fiscal rules includes a target for the cyclically adjusted fiscal balance. The potential sensitivity to financial factors of the real-time estimate of the cyclically adjusted fiscal balance suggests that such rules should be designed to take account of the financial cycle as well as the output cycle.

Given the complexity of estimating the current state of the financial and output cycles, the robustness of the set of rules is an important criterion in assessing the value of a rules-based approach. In such an environment, an independent fiscal council may play an especially valuable role in identifying the cyclical state of the economy and the distribution of macroeconomic risk factors (Lane, 2010a). Taken together, these considerations reinforce the importance of a well-designed institutional framework for the conduct of fiscal policy. While the literature on independent fiscal councils has largely focused on output stabilisation, such a council could also assess the appropriate fiscal stance in guarding against risks that may be embedded in the financial system.

Finally, the scope for the financial cycle to destabilise the fiscal position provides an additional rationale for preventive policies to minimise financial volatility. In relation to the current account, Summers (1988), Blanchard (2007) and Lane (2010b) describe the conditions under which policymakers may wish to target excessive imbalances, with a possible role for various fiscal instruments in external stabilisation. Similarly, there is a vast literature on the policy tools that are available to curb volatility in credit growth. In terms of implementation, the new economic governance proposals for member countries of the European Union put a premium on external and sectoral imbalances in assessing macroeconomic stability and the appropriate stance for fiscal policy.

5 Conclusions

This chapter has investigated the role of the financial cycle in driving the fiscal cycle. Although the results vary across specifications, we find

some empirical evidence that current account deficits are fiscally destabilising and that credit booms are associated with improvements in the
government fiscal balance in the short run. At a minimum, fiscal
outcomes' sensitivity to financial factors means that surveillance of
fiscal positions needs to go beyond the output cycle to also incorporate
the financial cycle. Moreover, it may be the case that the fiscal impact
of the financial cycle should be incorporated into the design of numerical fiscal rules and the monitoring role of independent fiscal
councils.[17] Also, the potential for financial cycles to destabilise the
fiscal position may provide additional motivation for preventive policies that can limit the macroeconomic impact of financial volatility.

In terms of the future research agenda, the estimates in this chapter
should be probed in further empirical analysis. In terms of mechanisms, the financial cycle affects fiscal outcomes through two types of
channels. First, there may be mechanical effects, by which financial
shocks affect the importance of different types of automatic stabilisers.
Second, financial shocks may induce discretionary fiscal responses.
Further work on the relative contributions of these two channels is
clearly warranted.

Furthermore, there may be non-linearities in the relation between the
financial cycle and the fiscal cycle. Accordingly, examining fiscal
behaviour during large financial booms and busts may be especially
revealing. Along another dimension, the prior literature has repeatedly
shown that the cyclical behaviour of fiscal policy varies across different
institutional and political environments. An investigation of how such
factors influences the fiscal impact of the financial cycle would be
interesting.

Data Appendix

The dataset covers the period 1980–2007 and includes annual data for
fifty-two countries. It is composed of twenty-two advanced countries
and thirty emerging market economies. The former group includes

---

[17] Recent contributions on this dimension include the work by Borio et al. (2013,
and in Chapter 13 of this volume); Liu et al (2015), outlining operational
approaches to the impact of asset price cycles in the calculation of output gaps
and structural balances; and De Manuel and Raciborski (2015), showing the
importance of the credit and house price cycles for the estimation of the output
gap in Ireland.

Australia, Austria, Belgium, Canada, Denmark, Finland, France, Germany, Greece, Iceland, Ireland, Italy, Japan, the Netherlands, New Zealand, Norway, Portugal, Spain, Sweden, Switzerland, the United Kingdom and the United States. The latter group is formed by Argentina, Brazil, Chile, China, Colombia, Czech Republic, Egypt, Estonia, Hong Kong, Hungary, India, Indonesia, Israel, Korea, Latvia, Lithuania, Malaysia, Mexico, Pakistan, Peru, Philippines, Poland, Russia, Singapore, Slovak Republic, Slovenia, South Africa, Thailand, Turkey and Venezuela.

Fiscal Variables

The source of the general government balance data varies across groups of countries. For the advanced country set, we use data from the OECD Economic Outlook (OECD EO), with the exception of Switzerland. For this we use the IMF World Economic Outlook, since it has better coverage than the OECD EO. For the emerging market economies group, we combine different sources. For China, Israel and Korea we use the OECD EO. For Chile, Egypt, India, Indonesia, Malaysia, Pakistan, Peru, Philippines, Singapore, South Africa, Thailand and Venezuela we use the World Bank World Development Indicators (WDI). For Czech Republic, Estonia, Hungary, Latvia, Lithuania, Poland, Slovak Republic and Slovenia we use the Annual Macro-Economic database from the European Commission (AMECO). For Turkey and Russia we use the Forecasts and Annual Indicators from the European Bank for Reconstruction and Development (EBRD). In addition, we fill missing data points for Czech Republic and Hungary using EBRD data. For Argentina, Brazil, Colombia and Mexico we use the Latin American and Caribbean Macro Watch Data Tool from the Inter-American Development Bank (IDB). In addition, we use this source to improve the series in Chile and Venezuela. Finally, Hong Kong's general government balance was obtained from national sources.

For the advanced country group, we also use alternative fiscal measures. These include the real general government balance, real general government revenues relative to trend, real general government expenditure relative to trend and the cyclically adjusted general government balance scaled by GDP. The source of the data is the OECD EO.

Other Variables

We use two alternative measures for the business cycle: real GDP relative to trend and real absorption relative to trend. The source of the former is the World Bank WDI. The latter is constructed as the difference between nominal GDP and net exports. The source of the latter is the IMF Direction of Trade Statistics (DOTS). We deflate nominal absorption using GDP prices. Our regression models use GDP and absorption relative to trend. As in the case of revenues and expenditure, these are the residuals of regression models using linear and quadratic trends as explanatory variables.

The current account balance is scaled by GDP and the source is the IMF World Economic Outlook. Private credit is private credit by deposit money banks and other financial institutions scaled by GDP. The source for this variable is the database on Financial Structure by Beck et al. (2015). Debt is the debt-to-GDP ratio obtained from the Historical Public Debt Database from Abbas et al. (2010) at the IMF.

Bibliography

Abbas, Ali, Belhocine, Nazim, ElGanainy, Asmaa and Horton, Mark (2010). *An Historical Public Debt Database*. IMF Working Paper No. 10/245.

Addison-Smyth, Diarmuid and McQuinn, Kieran (2010). Quantifying revenue windfalls from the Irish housing market. *Economic and Social Review*, 41(2), 201–23.

Alesina, Alberto, Campante, Filipe and Tabellini, Guido (2008). Why is fiscal policy often procyclical? *Journal of the European Economic Association*, 6(5), 1006–36.

Beck, T., Demirgüc-Kunt, A., Levine, R. E., Cihak, M. and Feyen, E. H. B. (2015). *Financial Development and Structure Dataset*. The World Bank, www.worldbank.org/en/publication/gfdr/data/financial-structure-database

Ballabriga, F. and Martinez-Mongay, C. (2002). *Has EMU Shifted Policy?* *European Economy*. Economic Papers, No. 166, February, Brussels.

Bayoumi, Tamim and Eichengreen, Barry (1995). Restraining yourself: fiscal rules and stabilization. *International Monetary Fund Staff Papers*, **42**, 32–48.

Beetsma, Roel and Giuliodori, Massimo (2010). Fiscal adjustment to cyclical developments in the OECD: an empirical analysis based on real-time data. *Oxford Economic Papers*, 62(3), 419–41.

Bénétrix, Agustín and Lane, Philip R. (2010). Fiscal shocks and the sectoral composition of output. *Open Economies Review*, 21(3), 335–50.

(2013). Fiscal cyclicality and EMU. *Journal of International Money and Finance*, **34**, 164–76.

(2015). International differences in fiscal policy during the global crisis. *Fiscal Studies*, **36**(1), 127.

Blanchard, Olivier (2007). Current account deficits in rich countries. *IMF Staff Papers*, **54**(2), 191–219.

Bohn, H. (1998). The behaviour of US public debt and deficits. *The Quarterly Journal of Economics*, **113**(3), 949–63.

Borio, Claudio, Disyatat, Piti and Juselius, Mikael (2013). *Rethinking Potential Output: Embedding Information About the Financial Cycle*. BIS Working Paper No. 404.

(2014). *A Parsimonious Approach to Incorporating Economic Information in Measures of Potential Output*. BIS Working Paper No. 442.

Borio, Claudio, Lombardi, Marco and Zampolli, Fabrizio (2016). *Fiscal Sustainability and the Financial Cycle*. Mimeo, BIS.

Bouthevillain, C., Cour-Thimann, P. Van den Dool, G. De Cos, P. H. Langenus, G. Mohr, M. F., Momigliano, S. and Tujala, M. (2001). *Cyclically Adjusted Budget Balances: An Alternative Approach*. ECB Working Paper No. 77.

Cimadomo, Jacopo (2012). Fiscal policy in real time. *Scandinavian Journal of Economics*, **114**(2), 440–65.

Claessens, Stijn, Kose, M. Ayhan and Terrones, Marco E. (2011). Financial cycles: What? How? When? In R. Clarida and F. Giavazzi, eds., *NBER International Seminar on Macroeconomics*. Chicago and London: University of Chicago Press, 303–43.

Claessens, Stijn, Pazarbasioglu, Ceyla, Laeven, Luc, Dobler, Marc, Valencia, Fabian, Nedelescu, Oana M. and Seal, Katherine (2011). *Crisis Management and Resolution: Early Lessons from the Financial Crisis*. IMF Staff Discussion Note No. 11/05.

Committee on the Global Financial System (2011). *Interactions of Sovereign Debt Management with Monetary Conditions and Financial Stability*. CGFS Papers, No. 42.

Das, Udaibir, Papapioannou, Michael, Pedras, Guilherme Ahmed, Faisal and Surti, Jay (2010). *Managing Public Debt and Its Financial Stability*. IMF Working Papers, No. 10/280.

De Manuel Aramendía, Mirzha and Raciborski, Rafal (2015). *Using Financial Variables to Estimate the Irish Output Gap: Do They Make a Difference?* Economic Brief 004, European Commission.

Dobrescu, Gabriela and Salman, Farhan (2011). *Fiscal Policy during Absorption Cycles*. IMF Working Paper No. 11/41.

Eschenbach, Felix and Schuknecht, Ludger (2004). Budgetary risks from real estate and stock markets. *Economic Policy*, **39**, 313–46.

Fatás, Antonio and Mihov, Ilian (2010). The euro and fiscal policy. In Alberto Alesina and Francesco Giavazzi, eds., *Europe and the Euro*. Chicago: University of Chicago Press, 287–324.

Galí, Jordi and Perotti, Roberto (2003). Fiscal policy and monetary integration in Europe. *Economic Policy*, 18(37), 533–72.

Gavin, Michael and Perotti, Roberto (1997). Fiscal policy in Latin America. *NBER Macroeconomics Annual*, 12, 11–70.

Girouard, Nathalie and Price, Robert (2004). *Asset Price Cycles, One-Off Factors and Structural Budget Balances*. OECD Economics Department Working Paper No. 391.

Honohan, Patrick and Klingbiel, Daniela (2003). The fiscal cost implications of an accommodating approach to banking crises. *Journal of Banking and Finance*, 27(8), 1539–60.

Jaimovich, Dany and Panizza, Ugo (2007). *Procyclicality or Reverse Causality?* IADB Working Paper No. 599.

Jordà, Oscar, Schularik, Moritz and Taylor, Alan (2015). Sovereigns versus banks: credit, crises and consequences. *Journal of the European Economic Association*, 14(1), 45–79.

Kaminsky, Graciela (2010). *Terms of Trade Shocks and Fiscal Cycles*. NBER Working Paper No. 15780.

Lane, Philip R. (2003). The cyclicality of fiscal policy: evidence from the OECD. *Journal of Public Economics*, 87, 2661–75.

(2007). Fiscal policy for a slowing economy. In Economic and Social Research Institute, *Budget Perspectives 2008*, pp. 5–25, www.esri.ie/pubs/BP200801.pdf

(2010a). Some lessons for fiscal policy from the financial crisis. *Nordic Economic Policy Review*, 1(1), 13–34.

(2010b). External imbalances and fiscal policy. In Salvador Barrios, Servaas Deroose, Sven Langedijk and Lucio Pench, eds., External Imbalances and Public Finances in the EU, European Economy Occasional Paper No. 66, pp. 17–30.

(2011). *Fiscal Policy and Financial Stability*. Mimeo, Trinity College Dublin.

Lane, P. R. and McQuade, P. (2014). Domestic credit growth and international capital flows. *Scandinavian Journal of Economics*, 116, 218–52. doi:10.1111/sjoe.12038

Lane, Philip R. and Milesi-Ferretti, Gian Maria (2011). The cross-country incidence of the global crisis, *IMF Economic Review*, 59(1), 77–110.

(2012). External adjustment and the global crisis. *Journal of International Economics*, 88(2), 252–65.

Lendval, Julia, Moulin, Laurent and Turrini, Alessandro (2011). *From CAB to CAAB? Correcting Indicators of Structural Fiscal Positions for*

Current Account Imbalances. European Economy Economic Papers, No. 442.

Liu, Estelle, Mattina, Todd and Tigran Poghosyan (2015). *Correcting "Beyond the Cycle": Accounting for Asset Prices in Structural Fiscal Balances*. IMF Working Paper No. WP/15/109.

Pesaran, M. Hashem and Smith, Ron P. (1995). Estimating long-run relationships from dynamic heterogeneous panels. *Journal of Econometrics*, 68(1), 79–113.

Price, R. and Dang, T. (2011). *Adjusting Fiscal Balances for Asset Price Cycles*. OECD Economics Department Working Papers, No. 868. Paris: OECD Publishing. doi:http://dx.doi.org/10.1787/5kgc42t3zqkl-en

Reinhart, Carmen M. and Rogoff, Kenneth S. (2009). *This Time is Different: Eight Centuries of Financial Folly*. Princeton: Princeton University Press.

Reinhart, Carmen M. and Belen Sbrancia, M. (2015). The liquidation of government debt. *Economic Policy, CEPR;CES;MSH*, 30(82), 291–333.

Summers, Lawrence H. (1988). Tax policy and international competitiveness. In Jacob Frenkel, ed., *International Aspects of Fiscal Policies*. Chicago: University of Chicago Press, pp. 349–86.

Talvi, Ernesto and Végh, Carlos (2005). Tax base variability and procyclical fiscal policy in developing countries. *Journal of Development Economics*, 78(1), 156–90.

Tornell, A. and Lane, Philip R. (1999). The voracity effect. *American Economic Review*, 89(1), 22–46.

13 Fiscal Sustainability and the Financial Cycle

CLAUDIO BORIO, MARCO LOMBARDI
AND FABRIZIO ZAMPOLLI

1 Introduction

The global financial crisis has reminded us of a few important lessons.

One is that severe financial crises are by no means confined to history or to less developed economies (e.g. Reinhart and Rogoff, 2009). Even in the most advanced economies, a prolonged financial boom, if unchecked, may end in a bust and a systemic banking crisis. And, when the bust occurs, the countries affected face deep recessions and several years of sluggish growth (Reinhart and Rogoff, 2009; BCBS, 2010; Jordà et al., 2013; Ball, 2014). The huge costs involved have hammered home a simple message: ignoring the build-up of financial imbalances, or failing to contain them, is no longer tenable (Borio, 2014a, 2016; BIS, 2014, 2015).

A second lesson is that financial crises can wreak havoc with public finances. Since the onset of the global financial crisis, public debt in many advanced economies has shot up to unprecedented peacetime levels and, in several cases, it is still rising. Even countries that were believed to be running prudent fiscal policies before the crisis found their fiscal sustainability rapidly called into question after the crisis erupted. Ireland and Spain are vivid examples. Their pre-crisis financial booms had made their fiscal accounts look much stronger than they actually were.

A third lesson is that there is a close two-way link between the health of the financial system and that of public finances. Private sector financial booms may eventually lead to a sharp deterioration of public finances when a financial crisis occurs, impairing the sovereign's ability to carry out countercyclical policies or act as a backstop for the

We thank Piti Disyatat, Balázs Égert, Mikael Juselius, Ľudovít Ódor and conference participants for comments and suggestions. Diego Urbina provided excellent statistical assistance. The views expressed in this chapter are those of the authors and do not necessarily reflect those of the BIS.

banking system. And weaker public finances may, in turn, cause financial instability, by sapping the strength of financial institutions' balance sheets (Das et al., 2010; CGFS, 2011; Jordá et al., 2016). This is particularly the case when these institutions hold large amounts of public debt. Thus, fiscal stress may both reflect and cause banking crises (Reinhart and Rogoff, 2009, 2013; Laeven and Valencia, 2013).

The close link between financial and fiscal risks calls for great prudence in managing public finances (e.g. Obstfeld, 2013). This is especially important, and difficult, in good times. It is then that policymakers may delude themselves that strong growth is here to stay – perhaps as a deserved reward for their policies – rather than seeing the poisoned chalice of an unsustainable domestic financial boom for what it is (Santos, 2014). Just like the private sector, governments may lull themselves into a false sense of security in the belief that debt tolerance has permanently increased. Even if they refrain from expansionary fiscal policy, they may thus fail to recognise the need to build sufficient buffers.

But how can one judge whether fiscal positions are prudent when a financial boom is in full swing and as events unfold – that is, in real time and not just with the benefit of hindsight? Typically, in order to measure the underlying fiscal position, policymakers seek to adjust fiscal balances for the business cycle, for one-off changes and for other temporary factors. The adjustment for the business cycle is normally based on standard measures of the output gap, which have traditionally been used to explain inflation – the well-known Phillips curve relationship. But as the pre-crisis experience reminded us once more, output may be above its potential or *sustainable* level even if inflation remains low and stable, boosted temporarily by a financial boom – unusually strong increases in credit and asset prices on the back of aggressive risk-taking. The boom masks the weakening of underlying fiscal strength. Policymakers may then be caught unprepared when the boom turns to bust. This is very much what has happened, again, in recent years.

This chapter takes one further step in tackling this complex issue. It builds on previous work that developed an alternative measure of potential output and the output gap to take into account the impact of financial factors – the so-called finance-neutral output gap (Borio et al., 2013, 2014). The method makes a simple modification to the Kalman filter problem associated with the popular Hodrick–Prescott (HP) filter in order to incorporate information about credit and property prices. Applying it, the authors find that it would have provided reliable signals that output was above potential pre-crisis. This is very much in contrast to traditional methods, which range from pure statistical filters to more elaborate approaches that combine a production function with a Phillips curve (e.g. Giorno et al., 1995; Beffy et al., 2006). Such methods have generally indicated that output was above potential only after the fact, as they have revised previous estimates of trends, de facto rewriting history – the notorious end-point problem. Indeed, such revisions have typically been quite large – often as large as the output gap itself (Orphanides and van Norden, 2002).

Here we take forward this previous work in two respects. First, we consider its strengths and weaknesses in the specific context of the cyclical adjustment of fiscal positions. Second, we sketch out ways in which this tool could be improved and become part of a more holistic approach to measuring underlying fiscal strength and ensuring adequate fiscal space.[1]

The rest of the chapter is organised as follows. Section 2 documents and discusses the potentially large impact that financial crises have on public finances. Section 3 describes how the finance-neutral output gap is computed and then proceeds to apply it to adjust fiscal positions, illustrating its properties with data for Spain and the United States. Section 4 discusses the limitations of the finance-neutral gap measure together with possible ways of overcoming them, and then sketches out how the tool might be part of a broader toolkit to evaluate financial strength. The conclusion highlights the key takeaways of the analysis.

2 Fiscal Balances over the Financial Cycle

2.1 The Damaging Effect of Financial Busts

Several studies have documented the behaviour of public debt around financial crises. Reinhart and Rogoff (2009, 2013) find that, in the

---

[1] Adjusting current fiscal balances for the financial cycle is key to assessing fiscal strength, but a full assessment requires that the resulting cyclically adjusted measures be complemented with measures of the fiscal gap or sustainable debt. The latter take into account not only current but also expected future expenditures and revenues as well as unexpected contingencies or risks (see e.g. Auerbach, 2011; Gosh et al., 2011). A discussion of these measures goes beyond the scope of this chapter.

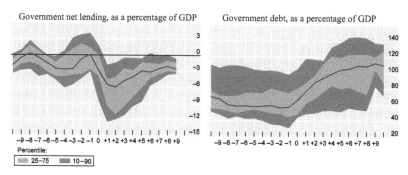

Figure 13.1: Government net lending ratio and debt, 2007–8

Note: Zero denotes the starting year of a crisis. Austria (2008), Belgium (2008), Denmark (2008), France (2008), Germany (2008), Greece (2008), Iceland (2008), Ireland (2008), Italy (2008), the Netherlands (2008), Portugal (2008), Spain (2008), Sweden (2008), Switzerland (2008), United Kingdom (2007), United States (2007).

Sources: L. Laeven and F. Valencia, *Systemic Banking Crises Database: An Update*, IMF Working Paper No. 12/163, June 2012; IMF, *World Economic Outlook*; OECD, *Economic Outlook*; BIS calculations

postwar period, (central) government debt almost doubles (86 percent increase) on average within three years from the onset of a crisis. Using a different data set limited to the period 1970–2011, Laeven and Valencia (2013) find somewhat smaller, but still sizeable, increases in public debt in advanced economies – some 24 percentage points of GDP – and smaller ones in emerging market economies – about 9 percentage points. In a sample spanning the period 1980–2006, Furceri and Zdzienicka (2012) document that the rise in public debt is quite persistent and depends on the severity of the crisis: in the case of crises that coincide with the largest output losses, the debt-to-GDP ratio surges by 37 percentage points over eight years.

The global financial crisis is no exception, even though it has mainly affected advanced economies (Figure 13.1). For one, there is a sizeable and persistent increase in deficits. Around the time the crisis broke out (2007 or 2008, depending on the country) the median fiscal balance fell by more than 5 percentage points within three years, to about 6 percent of GDP, with a quarter of the countries experiencing a much larger deterioration, to more than 10 percent (left-hand panel). Thereafter, the deficits narrowed only very slowly, remaining sizeable in many countries several years after the onset of the crisis.

In addition, the general government debt-to-GDP ratio soared (Figure 13.1 (b)). This ratio increased by more than fifty percentage points at the median, from around 60 percent at the onset of the crisis to more than 90 percent three years after – not far from the historical evidence uncovered by Reinhart and Rogoff (2013) and, for the most severe crises, by Furceri and Zdzienicka (2012). After nine years the ratio exceeded 110 percent and was even above 135 percent for 10 percent of the countries in the sample.

The steep post-crisis rise in public debt is usually driven by a number of factors.

First, the sovereign uses its fiscal space to support the repair of banks' balance sheets – what is often colloquially referred to as 'bailout fiscal costs'. The government's role is critical, ranging from supporting the recognition of losses and purchasing bad assets to recapitalising institutions, sometimes through temporary ownership. In some cases, the sovereign's support also extends to non-financial borrowers, including both corporations and households. From an ex ante perspective, this amounts to contingent liabilities that are generally not recognised in the fiscal accounts, except perhaps when they are explicit and subject to strict measurement and disclosure criteria.[2] Indeed, their recognition ex ante would be inconsistent with efforts to put in place credible no-bailout schemes, regardless of their ultimate effectiveness (e.g. Diaz-Alejandro, 1985).

These costs can be quite large but are difficult to estimate precisely, even ex post. Depending on the method and time horizon of the analysis, estimates for the same country and crisis often vary by a large amount.[3] That said, in many historical episodes such costs do not seem to have been the main driver of the rise in public debt (Laeven and Valencia, 2013; Reinhart and Rogoff, 2013).

Second, output and employment collapse and recover only slowly, sapping revenues and boosting non-discretionary spending and transfers whenever automatic stabilisers are in place. The evidence suggests that this is frequently the main factor in the steep post-crisis rise in

---

[2] For a detailed discussion of various types of contingent liabilities and historical episodes, see Bova et al. (2016).

[3] Moreover, over time countries may be able to recover some or most of the initial costs, in some cases even making a small net profit, provided they succeed in managing and resolving the crises effectively.

public debt.[4] Initial output losses – measured from peak to trough or from the peak to the point at which the growth rate returns to pre-crisis rates – are substantial, ranging from 6 percent to 14 percent on average across countries, against only 2 percent in an ordinary recession (i.e. a recession not accompanied by a financial crisis). In general, crises are followed by weak recoveries: it takes several years on average for activity to return to its pre-crisis peak. Above all, there is evidence that these losses are not entirely recouped in the subsequent recovery. Using a range of techniques, samples and controls, studies find *permanent* output losses of 7.5–10 percent.[5] Put differently, the evidence indicates that, even when growth returns to its pre-crisis long-term, output generally does not.

Third, for a given path of output and income, compositional effects may weaken public finances further. The collapse in asset prices, in particular, can play a key role. For example, panel regressions by Eschenbach and Schuknecht (2004) indicate that 30–40 percent of the deterioration of fiscal balances that took place in the United Kingdom and Sweden in the early 1990s was due to asset price effects, especially in the real estate market.

Fourth, much like asset price effects, exchange rates may play a similar role. This would be the case whenever debt is denominated in a foreign currency and, as often happens, the crisis coincides with sharp currency depreciation. Indeed, concerns of this nature have been behind attempts to reduce the sovereign's reliance on foreign currency borrowing in emerging market economies since the crises of the 1980s and 1990s (CGFS, 2007; Turner, 2012). Even when this is so, however, the sovereign may remain indirectly exposed to such currency mismatches if the private sector indulges in this practice: the sovereign may come under pressure to come to the rescue (e.g. BIS, 2010; Fischer and Yeşin, 2016).

---

[4] Reinhart and Rogoff (2013) document a strong rise in real government revenue in the three years leading to a banking crisis and a decline in the following three years.

[5] These studies are surveyed in BCBS (2010) and normally follow Cerra and Saxena (2008); for a more recent study, see Ball (2014). See also Box III.B in BIS (2014). Output losses in an ordinary recession are usually temporary, although this has been challenged recently (e.g. Blanchard et al., 2015; Martin et al., 2015).

Fifth, the one-off permanent loss of output may also go hand in hand with a long-lasting decline in trend output growth. Until recently, the literature had generally failed to find permanent effects on growth. But the impact may be persistent, even if sometimes difficult to disentangle from the one on the level of output. For example, recent research has found that, in the wake of financial crises, productivity growth may be badly damaged for many years (Borio et al., 2015b) – a point to which we return below.[6]

Sixth, the policy response may lead to a further deterioration in the fiscal position. For one, especially where the authorities have room for manoeuvre, they may respond to the crisis by increasing discretionary spending or cutting taxes to prop up aggregate demand. This was indeed the case in several countries in the wake of the global financial crisis (e.g. Carnot and de Castro, 2015). The response may be especially problematic in the longer term if it reflects an overly rosy assessment of the underlying fiscal strength. The stimulus may not be easily reversed in subsequent years, as worries of a faltering recovery and political economy pressures prevail.[7] Moreover, if the increase in the public debt-to-GDP ratio is not arrested, it may end up undermining trend growth. While no consensus exists, there is considerable evidence supporting this viewpoint (e.g. Cecchetti et al., 2011; Checherita-Westphal and Rother, 2012; Baum et al., 2013; Chudik et al., 2015; Woo and Kumar, 2015). Possible mechanisms include distortionary taxation, which may inhibit investment at least beyond certain thresholds (e.g. Jaimovich and Rebelo, 2012), and adverse effects on sovereign risk premia (see also below).[8] Finally, misguided attempts *not* to use fiscal space to repair balance sheets may backfire, delaying and weakening the economic recovery. A well-known case in

---

[6] See also the study by Reinhart and Reinhart (2015), which finds that the incidence of financial crises is negatively related to economic growth in a sample of more than sixty countries and more than 150 years. As pointed out by the authors, it is, however, unclear how far the relationship reflects reverse causation.

[7] Budina et al. (2015) find evidence of a debt bias and evidence that this bias is exacerbated by financial booms and busts.

[8] As debt rises, countries may get closer to their fiscal limits as perceived by investors, leading to a sharp (non-linear) increase in risk premia. Fiscal limits (i.e. the maximum government debt that can be sustained without appreciable risk of default or higher inflation) depend on how far a country is from the peak of the Laffer curve and how far authorities can cut expenditure without triggering a severe political backlash. The idea of fiscal limits has been formalised within a DSGE model by, for example, Bi and Leeper (2013) and Leeper (2013).

point is the difference between the rapid post-crisis recovery in the Nordic countries, where balance-sheet repair was prompt and thorough, and the protracted weakness in Japan, where balance-sheet repair was delayed for a decade following the reversal of their financial cycles in the late 1980s and early 1990s (Borio et al., 2010).[9]

The role of interest rates deserves a separate mention, as it is important but highly dependent on circumstances.

On the one hand, interest rates may rise in the aftermath of a financial crisis. This is more likely to be the case in countries exposed to a tightening of external funding conditions, possibly because of a weak external position, a large stock of debt denominated in foreign currency and/or limited fiscal space. The experience of several less developed economies is a case in point. The same may be true of countries with limited monetary policy room for manoeuvre, as the debt crisis in the euro area has shown. In these cases, interest rates may rise either because of attempts to defend the currency and prevent inflationary pressures or owing to a sharp increase in risk premia, as investors lose confidence in the sovereign's creditworthiness. In their historical study, Reinhart et al. (2012) report many examples of this kind.

On the other hand, where these constraints do not operate, central banks may have the leeway to ease very aggressively and, above all, persistently in response to the financial strains and the subsequent weak recovery. This is precisely what has happened in many jurisdictions following the global financial crisis, with central banks pushing interest rates all the way to zero, if not into negative territory, through a combination of adjustments in policy rates, forward guidance and large-scale sovereign bond purchases (e.g. BIS, 2015).

---

[9] Consistent with this, considerable evidence points to the importance of debt forbearance in Japan (e.g. Peek and Rosengren, 2005; Caballero et al., 2008); the reduction of capital and labour mobility compared with the pre-crisis period (e.g. Iwaisako, 2005); and the rise in the market share of inefficient firms (e.g. Ahearne and Shinada, 2005). Recent studies have also indicated that debt forbearance has been significant in some countries in the most recent post-crisis experience (e.g. Albertazzi and Marchetti, 2010; Bank of England, 2011; Enria, 2012). Japan's economic growth was also sluggish in the 2000s, but the main reason was probably demographics; by the early 2000s balance sheets had finally been largely repaired. In fact, output growth in terms of working-age population rose much more strongly than in the previous decade and was well above that of many advanced economies over the same period – for example, it was twice that of the United States (e.g. Borio et al., 2015b).

Clearly, the issues are very different in the two cases.

When interest rates rise, this adds immediately to the deficit and debt burden, to an extent that depends on the size of the debt outstanding and its contractual features (e.g. maturity and interest rate sensitivity more generally). At the same time, it also constrains the room for countercyclical fiscal policy, possibly quite tightly.[10] This may well be the reason why, despite the often *greater* severity of the crises, the fiscal position has historically deteriorated *less* sharply in emerging market economies than in their advanced counterparts.

When interest rates sink persistently to exceptionally low levels, fiscal positions may look much stronger than they really are, with policy-makers and investors overestimating sustainability.[11] This may provide an incentive to boost spending and/or cut taxes to sustain aggregate demand at the cost of weakening fiscal strength over the longer term. Large-scale purchases of sovereign debt by central banks add to this vulnerability: from the perspective of the consolidated public sector balance sheet, they amount to issuing liabilities indexed at the very short-term rate (bank reserves) while retiring longer-maturity debt (e.g. Borio and Disyatat, 2010). This increases the sensitivity of the debt service burden to the eventual normalisation of policy.

2.2 The Flattering Effect of Financial Booms

The flattering effect of financial booms on fiscal positions is, in many respects, the mirror image of the havoc wreaked by financial busts, especially when financial crises erupt. Potential output and potential growth are overestimated. Compositional effects, especially those associated with asset price booms,[12] boost revenues further. Nominal

---

[10] For instance, Alberola et al. (2016a) show that in Latin America worsening financing conditions induce fiscal contractions, leading to a procyclical bias in fiscal policy.

[11] Consistent with this view, rating agencies appear to give prominent weight to *current* debt service ratios in their sovereign ratings. Amstad and Packer (2015) find that the focus on current debt service measures explains some of the difference between the ratings assigned to advanced and emerging market economies.

[12] Asset price booms can affect personal and corporate income taxes as well as rental income through the sales or the accrual of capital gains. In addition, taxes are also paid on transactions. Since turnover intensifies during a boom, revenues tend to increase for a given level of asset prices.

exchange rates may tend to appreciate,[13] temporarily reducing the domestic currency equivalent of foreign exchange-denominated debt and the corresponding interest payments. Unnoticed, contingent liabilities to address balance-sheet repair build-up. And all this may encourage policymakers to relax fiscal policy further, exacerbating the familiar incentives linked to short horizons and political economy pressures (Santos, 2014).[14] Consistent with the flattering effect of financial booms, empirical evidence finds a positive impact of financial variables on fiscal balances over and above that of output (Eschenbach and Schuknecht, 2004; Price and Dang, 2011; Bénétrix and Lane in Chapter 12 of this volume).

More recent BIS research sheds further light on the reasons why potential output and growth may be overestimated during the boom and on the mechanisms involved in the lasting damage caused once the boom ushers in a banking crisis. That research produces three findings, based on a sample of more than twenty advanced economies and over some forty years. First, financial booms sap productivity growth as they occur (Cecchetti and Kharroubi, 2015) – an effect that is masked by their temporary boost to output (Drehmann and Juselius, 2015).[15]

---

[13] Empirical evidence indicates that the conjunction of credit booms with real exchange rate appreciation is a reliable leading indicator of financial crises (Borio and Lowe, 2002; Gourinchas and Obstfeld, 2012). In a low inflation environment, this tends to reflect a nominal currency appreciation. Even if nominal exchange rates remain relatively stable during a financial boom, stronger aggregate demand, especially towards non-tradables, may lead to higher price and wage inflation than in other economies, and/or poor productivity growth. The resulting loss of competitiveness can sow the seeds of future troubles.

[14] For example, when more resources become available, the common pool problem and the competition for them may intensify (e.g. Tornell and Lane, 1999). Thus, political economy incentives can explain not only why fiscal policy may be procyclical, especially in less developed economies (e.g. Lane, 2003; Talvi and Vegh, 2005), but also why even more developed economies may fail to insure themselves against the fiscal consequences of financial busts (e.g. Santos, 2014).

[15] There are many channels through which financial booms boost aggregate demand and output, including wealth, collateral, risk-taking and cash flow effects. To be sure, theoretically, housing wealth effects should tend to wash out in the aggregate, as the gains of those planning to scale down their consumption of housing services should be offset by those planning to scale up. But, because the marginal propensity to consume of the former is generally bigger, the net effect on consumption is generally positive and economically significant (e.g. Waldron and Zampolli, 2010).

For a typical credit boom, just over a quarter of a percentage point per year is a lower bound. Second, a good chunk of this, almost 60 percent, reflects the shift of labour to lower productivity growth sectors (Borio et al., 2015b). Think, in particular, of shifts into a temporarily bloated construction sector. The rest would be the impact on productivity growth that is common across sectors, such as the shared component of aggregate capital accumulation and of total factor productivity growth. Third, the subsequent impact of labour reallocations that occur during a boom is much larger if a crisis follows. The average loss per year in the five years after a crisis is more than twice that during a boom – around half a percentage point per year (Borio et al., 2015b). It is possible that the scarcity and misallocation of credit, alongside the slow repair of balance sheets, inhibit the transfer of resources across sectors needed to rebalance the economy. Put differently, the reallocations cast a long shadow. Taking the ten-year episode as a whole, the cumulative impact would amount to a loss of some four percentage points. Regardless of the specific figure, the impact is clearly sizeable.

But why should financial booms raise output above potential or sustainable levels without necessarily generating inflation? At least four reasons come to mind. One is that unusually strong financial booms are likely to coincide with positive supply-side shocks (e.g. Drehmann et al., 2012). These put downward pressure on prices while at the same time providing fertile ground for asset price booms that weaken financing constraints. A second reason is that the economic expansions may themselves temporarily weaken supply constraints. Prolonged and robust expansions can induce increases in the labour supply, either through higher participation rates or, more significantly, immigration. For instance, there was a strong increase in immigration into Spain and Ireland during the pre-crisis financial boom, not least to work in the construction sector that was driving the expansion. By adding new capacity, the unsustainable capital accumulation associated with the economic expansion may also weaken supply constraints. A third reason is that, as noted, financial booms may coincide with a tendency for the currency to appreciate, as domestic assets become more attractive and capital flows surge. The appreciation puts downward pressure on inflation. A fourth, underappreciated, reason is that, as just highlighted, unsustainability may have to do more with the sectoral and intertemporal misallocation of resources than with overall capacity constraints.[16]

3 Adjusting Fiscal Positions for the Financial Cycle

As the previous discussion indicates, there are obvious reasons to believe that the financial cycle has a first-order impact on fiscal strength and sustainability. We next illustrate a method for correcting fiscal positions for *one* of the many factors considered, albeit a key one: the behaviour of potential output, especially during financial booms. Before we adjust the fiscal balance, though, we need to spend a few words on explaining the specific statistical method used to estimate potential output, as developed in Borio et al. (2013, 2014).

3.1 The Finance-Neutral Output Gap

Borio et al. (2013) start from the premise that traditional measures of potential or sustainable output do not adjust for financial developments. The methods most commonly used in policymaking to make cyclical adjustments vary widely and use economic information to various degrees. At one end are univariate statistical filters, such as the popular Hodrick–Prescott filter, which distinguish trend from cycle based purely on the behaviour of output itself and assuming that the two components have certain statistical characteristics (such as that the cycle is of a certain length). At the other end are production function methods, in which potential output is defined as a function of production inputs. Given that production inputs, such as capital and labour, are also subject to cyclical fluctuations, these methods often involve the cyclical adjustment of those inputs, which can be performed with a univariate statistical filter or can be combined with additional theoretical restrictions, not least a Phillips curve (e.g. Giorno et al., 1995; Beffy et al.,

---

[16] This paragraph focuses on the way in which financial booms may lead to temporary and unsustainable increases in domestic supply or coincide with changes in the exchange rate that keep inflation down. Another possible explanation, as noted earlier, is that the link between inflation and domestic slack has become much weaker owing to other forces. One such force could be the globalisation of the real economy, as some evidence suggests (e.g. Borio and Filardo, 2007; Ciccarelli and Mojon, 2010; Bianchi and Civelli, 2013; Eickmeier and Pijnenburg, 2013).

2006). In between are methods that focus on fewer economic relationships, such as the determinants of inflation (the Phillips curve), the link between unemployment and output (Okun's law) and the like.[17] What is common to all of the procedures is that they either completely ignore financial factors or relegate them to a minor role. Based on the previous analysis, however, such an omission can be dangerous.

There is no unique way of incorporating the information that financial variables have for output fluctuations. Moreover, as compared with inflation, theory so far has provided less formal guidance. Because of this, Borio et al. (2013) opt for a more data-driven approach and allow the 'data to speak' as much as possible. The strategy is to make simple and transparent modifications to the HP filter, augmenting it with information from variables that are closely linked to the financial cycle. Here they follow Drehmann et al. (2012), who find that when the key concern is banking crises, the combined behaviour of credit and property prices is probably the most parsimonious way of describing the financial cycle, in turn confirming previous work about the leading indicator properties of these variables (Borio and Drehmann, 2009). This point is hinted at in Figure 13.2, which shows that both credit and property (house) prices grow very fast in inflation-adjusted terms in the years prior to the crisis but slow down considerably before it breaks out, with property prices tending to lead and actually starting to decline before the crisis.

The authors call the corresponding measure of deviations of actual output from its potential or sustainable level the 'finance-neutral' output gap. The term denotes the objective of filtering out the information that financial factors have for potential output.

Specifically, Borio et al. (2013) proceed as follows. The starting point is the HP filter, expressed in state-space form (e.g. Kuttner, 1994). The state equation governing the evolution of the *unobservable* (log) potential output y^* is:

$$\Delta y_t^* = \Delta y_{t-1}^* + \varepsilon_{0,t}. \tag{1}$$

---

[17] Even more theory-based are measures based on fully specified New Keynesian DSGE models in which potential output is defined as the hypothetical output that would prevail were prices and wages free to adjust instantaneously. Such methods, however, are not commonly explicitly used to derive standalone measures of potential output, not least as these are very volatile.

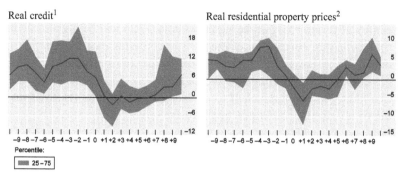

Figure 13.2: Credit and residential property prices growth, 1970–2011

Notes: Zero denotes the starting year of a crisis. [1] Argentina (1989, 1995, 2001), Belgium (2008), Brazil (1990, 1994), Chile (1976, 1981), Colombia (1998), Denmark (2008), France (2008), Germany (2008), Greece (2008), Hungary (2008), Iceland (2008), Indonesia (1997), Ireland (2008), Italy (2008), Japan (1997), Korea (1997), Latvia (2008), Malaysia (1997), Mexico (1981, 1994), the Netherlands (2008), Norway (1991), Peru (1983), Philippines (1997), Portugal (2008), Russia (2008), Slovenia (2008), Spain (1977, 2008), Sweden (1991, 2008), Switzerland (2008), Thailand (1997), Turkey (2000), United Kingdom (2007), United States (1988, 2007). [2] Belgium (2008), Colombia (1998), Denmark (2008), France (2008), Germany (2008), Iceland (2008), Italy (2008), Japan (1997), Korea (1997), Netherlands (2008), Norway (1991), Russia (2008), Spain (1977, 2008), Sweden (1991, 2008), Switzerland (2008), Thailand (1997), United Kingdom (2007), United States (1988, 2007).

Sources: L. Laeven and F. Valencia, *Systemic Banking Crises Database: An Update*, IMF Working Paper No. 12/163, June 2012; IMF, *World Economic Outlook*; OECD, *Economic Outlook*; BIS calculations

The measurement equation relates actual (log) GDP y to its potential:

$$y_t = y_t^* + \varepsilon_{1,t}. \tag{2}$$

The two noise terms are assumed to be normal iid, with zero mean and variances σ_0^2 and σ_1^2. The HP filter (applied to quarterly data) fixes the ratio $\lambda_1 = \sigma_1^2/\sigma_0^2$ (the so-called signal-to-noise ratio) to 1600, which corresponds to a business cycle length of roughly up to eight years. So far, this is entirely standard. The next, less standard step is to augment (2) with a set of additional explanatory variables x:

$$y_t - y_t^* = \gamma x_t + \varepsilon_{2,t}, \tag{3}$$

and, for simplicity, to calibrate the signal-to-noise ratio $\lambda_2 = \sigma_2^2/\sigma_0^2$ to match the same business cycle duration as assumed in the standard (non-modified) HP filter.

In doing this matching, there is a small technical wrinkle. In an infinite sample, this last step would simply be accomplished by fixing

$\lambda_2 = \lambda_1 = 1600$, as in the standard HP filter. But in finite samples, the empirical counterpart of the signal-to-noise ratio will be higher due to the strong autocorrelation of the cyclical component of output. So, to match the business cycle duration, Borio et al. (2013) propose to match the empirical counterparts of the signal-to-noise ratios linked to the two filters. This is equivalent to choosing λ_2 so that the relative volatilities of output around potential are the same:

$$\mathrm{var}\left(y_t - y^*_{(2),t}\right)/\mathrm{var}\left(\Delta^2 y^*_{(2),t}\right) = \mathrm{var}\left(y_t - y^*_{(3),t}\right)/\mathrm{var}\left(\Delta^2 y^*_{(3),t}\right), \quad (4)$$

where $y^*_{(2),t}$ and $y^*_{(3),t}$ are the potential output estimates from equations (2) and (3), respectively.

Technical details aside, the key point of the specification is that it does not 'force' the explanatory variables to shape potential output. That is, x does not appear directly in the state equation (1). Instead, explanatory variables only influence potential output estimates via their presence in the measurement equation (3), and hence in the likelihood function for observed output. In other words, they only contribute to the extent that they convey relevant information on the status of actual output with respect to its potential at the chosen frequency. In principle, *any* economic variable could do the job, not least the most popular candidate – inflation. As it turns out, however, the growth rates in (inflation-adjusted) credit and (inflation-adjusted) residential property prices perform quite well according to relevant criteria (see below). By contrast, as examined in detail in Borio et al. (2014), inflation performs poorly. This no doubt reflects the very weak link between domestic output gaps and inflation since at least the 1990s (e.g. Borio and Filardo, 2007; Kuttner and Robinson, 2008).

But what does 'performing well' mean in this context? Borio et al. (2013) mainly use three criteria: first, high statistical precision – that is, small confidence bands; second, good real-time properties – that is, small revisions as time unfolds and new data become available; third, in the absence of a formal model, 'reasonable' patterns – that is, a path that broadly accords with intuition.

On this basis, the finance-neutral gap appears to outperform traditional measures. Figure 13.3 illustrates this for the United States with respect to the last two criteria (see Borio et al., 2013 for statistical precision). The figure compares the real-time and full-sample performance of the finance-neutral output gap with those derived from the

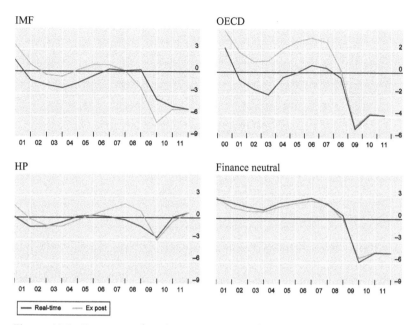

Figure 13.3: Ex post and real-time estimates of output gaps in the United States, 2001–11

Note: For each time t, the 'real-time' estimates are based only on the sample up to that point in time. The 'ex post' estimates are based on the full sample.

Sources: Borio et al. (2013); OECD, *Economic Outlook*; IMF; authors' calculations

traditional HP filter and the full production function approaches used by the IMF and OECD. Strikingly, *ahead* of the financial crisis, as the financial boom played itself out, the traditional measures indicated that output was *below, or at most close to* potential (grey lines). Only *after* the crisis, once the recession took place, did they recognise that, to varying degrees, output had been *above* its potential, sustainable level (black lines). By contrast, the finance-neutral measure is able to spot the unsustainable expansion in real time, pointing to a substantial positive gap between output and potential during the boom (grey line). More-over, the finance-neutral estimates are hardly revised as time unfolds and new data become available (the black and grey lines are very close). Thus, given what happened after the boom, the finance-neutral gap appears to provide much more useful information for policymakers concerning the sustainability of the output expansion.

In the *specific* example shown, two factors help explain the differ-ence in performance. For one, the traditional methods, *as applied here*,

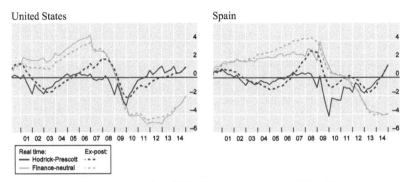

Figure 13.4: Finance-neutral and HP-filter output gaps, 2001–14
Sources: OECD; BIS calculations

are especially vulnerable to the end-point problem (Orphanides and Van Norden, 2002). One common reason is the reliance on the mechanical calculation of trends. For instance, the HP filter is applied directly to the output series, but in production function approaches it is not uncommon to use the HP filter or similar procedures to estimate the 'normal' level of the utilisation of factor inputs. In addition, the performance of inflation may well be another factor in traditional production function approaches in which a Phillips curve relationship is a key ingredient. Recall that inflation was generally low and stable ahead of the crisis, providing little signal from the underlying disequilibria.

That said, there is *no guarantee* that the finance-neutral gap will have good real-time properties (Borio et al., 2014). This depends on: (i) the financial explanatory variables having high explanatory power at the chosen business cycle frequency and (ii) these variables having stable means. We will return to some of these issues later, when we discuss the possible shortcomings of the approach.

For completeness, Figure 13.4 shows updated estimates of the finance-neutral output gap and the HP filter for the two reference countries used in the rest of this chapter – the United States and Spain. The estimates confirm the previous findings. They indicate similar patterns for the two countries and the superior real-time performance of the finance-neutral measure. They also highlight how the HP filter, tracing the actual behaviour of output, points to a quicker rebound relative to potential post-crisis. Indeed, implausibly, output is already above potential in 2012 (United States) and 2014 (Spain).

The shortfall narrows (United States) or stabilises (Spain) according to the finance-neutral estimates.

3.2 Cyclical Adjustment of Fiscal Balances

Having obtained a measure of the output gap that filters out the GDP fluctuations explained by financial cycle proxies, one can construct a corresponding measure of cyclically adjusted fiscal balances. Here we follow the methodology employed by the OECD (Girouard and André, 2005).

Define the cyclically adjusted fiscal balance as:

$$B^* = \left[\sum_{i=1}^{4} T_i^* - G^* + X\right]/Y^*, \tag{5}$$

where Y^* is the level of potential output, X is non-tax revenues,[18] G^* is the cyclically adjusted current primary government expenditures and T_i^* represents the cyclically adjusted revenues from the i-th tax category – personal and corporate income taxes, social security contributions and indirect taxes. To implement the adjustment, we can then use the elasticities of taxes and expenditures with respect to the output gap (denoted η_{Ti} and η_G respectively).[19] Hence, T_i^* and G^* are defined as:

$$T_i^*/T_i = (Y^*/Y)^{\eta_{Ti}}, \tag{6}$$

$$G^*/G = (Y^*/Y)^{\eta_G}. \tag{7}$$

Substituting into (5) yields:

$$B^* = \left[\sum_{i=1}^{4} T_i(Y^*/Y)^{\eta_{Ti}} - G(Y^*/Y)^{\eta_G} + X\right]/Y^*. \tag{8}$$

Naturally, estimates of the output gap play a key role in the adjustment defined in (8). This is shown in Figure 13.5, which compares cyclical adjustments based on the finance-neutral output gap with those based on the HP filter. In both cases, we rely on the estimates of expenditure and tax elasticities reported in Girouard and André (2005). The continuous line denotes the unadjusted balance, while the bars correspond

---

[18] If the adjustment was made on the primary balance, then this component would exclude net interest payments.

[19] Girouard and André (2005) actually use the unemployment gap for government expenditures. Here we stick to the output gap for ease of presentation and interpretation of the results.

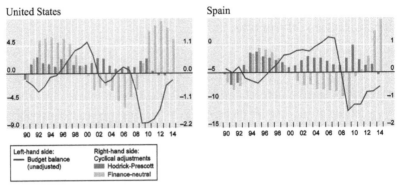

Figure 13.5: Cyclically adjusted fiscal balances, 1990–2014
Note: in real time, as a percentage of GDP.
Sources: OECD; BIS calculations

to the adjusted balance, in real time (grey) and ex post or based on the full sample (black).

The results are striking. While the adjustments to the fiscal position based on the HP filter point to a sound fiscal position in the years preceding the Great Recession, those based on financial cycle information paint a different picture. In the 2000s, the HP-filtered cyclical adjustments consistently *improve* the apparent fiscal strength for both the United States and Spain; those based on the finance-neutral measure consistently *worsen* it. Pre-crisis, the adjustment peaks at above 1 percent for the United States and is a bit lower for Spain. The pattern generally reverses post-crisis.

4 Current Limitations and Possible Ways Forward

In considering the limitations of the approach, it is worth distinguishing between two issues. The first has to do with the *specific method* of incorporating financial cycle information in the estimates of potential output, the second with the *omitted channels* through which the financial cycle influences the sustainability of fiscal positions. Consider each in turn.

4.1 Improving Estimates of Potential Output

The specific method illustrated above is simply one among a variety of possible ones. It has the advantage of a certain simplicity, parsimony and transparency. One could add that the proof of the pudding is in the eating: it works well as a means of identifying, in real time, key cases where it turned out ex post that problems were brewing.

The approach is based on a number of restrictive assumptions. For instance, to facilitate comparison with the traditional macroeconomic literature, the duration of the business cycle is fixed to be up to eight years – that is, the value of λ is set a priori. Likewise, it is assumed that the explanatory variables have a deterministic mean – a testable hypothesis that holds well enough in the cases examined and helps to explain the robustness of the estimates to the arrival of additional data as time unfolds. Moreover, the approach only slowly recognises the permanent loss of output that appears to be a stylised feature of financial crises. Typically, after a crisis both credit and property price growth are well below average. This, and the fact that the method constrains potential output to evolve slowly, implies that the size of the output gap is overstated for some time. As a result, so would be the fiscal space.

Some of these drawbacks could be addressed through statistical techniques. For instance, it is possible to estimate the frequency of common cycles through appropriate multivariate methods and to allow for structural breaks in the filter variables (e.g. Harvey and Trimbur, 2003).[20] It might also be feasible to allow for more discontinuous (non-linear) adjustments in the statistical properties of GDP. None of these approaches, however, is a panacea. Increasing the number of unobservable variables may lead to larger ex post revisions as more data become available. And purely statistical methods for detecting breaks would generally require a minimum set of post-break data to recognise the breaks with sufficient statistical confidence, reducing the tool's usefulness to policymakers in real time.

Addressing some of these shortcomings may require the policymaker to impose some form of a priori restrictions. This means bringing to bear information that goes beyond that included in the statistical properties of the variables over the relevant sample. For example, if a crisis occurs, it should be possible to make adjustments based on the fact that, as the historical record indicates, such episodes have tended to result in permanent output losses. There are many ways in which

---

[20] de Jong and Penzer (1998) provide diagnostic tests that can be used to test for structural breaks in multivariate filters. Strategies for modelling such breaks are discussed in Koopman et al. (2008).

this could be done, from ad hoc revisions based on the typical historical experience to the inclusion of judgemental elements supported more formally by Bayesian methods.

More generally, at the cost of simplicity, it is also possible to incorporate financial information in increasingly rich approaches, which vary in terms of the range and role of the financial variables themselves, the number of additional unobservable variables, the set of a priori theory-based restrictions and estimation methods. It is up to the policymaker to decide which method is more reliable and strikes a better balance between the trade-offs involved.[21] Again, the proof of the pudding is in the eating.

4.2 Dealing with the Omitted Channels

Estimating potential output and the corresponding elasticities of the various expenditure and tax items, even if done without error, is only one of the adjustments necessary to assess fiscal strength in the face of financial cycles. As noted above, other adjustments are called for to account for other factors: the use of public sector money to support balance-sheet repair during the bust; tax and expenditure compositional effects for a given level of output; exchange rate-induced effects on the valuation of debt and on debt-servicing costs; and systematic patterns in the behaviour of interest rates. Consider each in turn.

To adjust the strength of underlying public finances for balance-sheet repair costs, one could use an approach consistent with that used to derive cyclically adjusted balances. This would amount to estimating a time-varying expected contingent liability that is given by the probability of a crisis times the potential financial cost of support. In practice, estimating both items is not straightforward. The probability

---

[21] The literature is growing rapidly but a systematic analysis is not possible, since existing studies provide insufficient information. For example, the real-time properties of the estimates are often not reported. Here are just a few examples. Alberola et al. (2013) adjust the components of the production function by several measures of imbalances, including the current account, and Alberola et al. (2016b) for commodity prices. Albert et al. (2015) employ a similar method in their assessment of potential output in China: the capital stock input to the production function is adjusted for the credit cycle to account for possible overinvestment. Blagrave et al. (2015) and Melolinna and Tóth (2016), in addition to relying on a relationship akin to Equation (3), also include a Phillips curve and an Okun law.

could be estimated based on early warning indicators of crises, while the potential cost could simply be drawn from historical experience.[22] In both cases, relying on cross-country data would be almost inevitable, since crises are rare events. Less ambitiously, the probability of a crisis could be fixed rather than time-varying, and chosen, alongside the costs, to reflect the policymaker's risk tolerance. For instance, a methodology of this kind underlies the top-down approach to the international calibration of bank capital requirements, which is based on their macroeconomic costs and benefits (BCBS, 2010).

Adjustments for the evolution of asset prices could be done in several ways. One method, most consistent with the potential output adjustment, is to estimate asset price elasticities conditional on the output gap (e.g. Price and Dang, 2011). More ambitiously, one could even bypass potential output altogether, estimating directly the co-movements of the key fiscal balance components with the financial cycle proxies. Either method could be coupled with forms of sensitivity analysis. Similar methodologies could be employed to adjust fiscal positions for the impact of the exchange rate.

Adjustments for the systematic behaviour of interest rates are trickier. The main reason is that, as the previous analysis indicates, their behaviour depends on the strategy (reaction function) followed by the central bank and on the market-driven influences on the relevant constellation of rates. In turn, both depend on the constraints, internal and external, that the economy faces, including the sovereign's initial creditworthiness. All this suggests that any adjustment would have to be very country-specific.

That said, a couple of points are worth noting, all inspired by the need for prudence. First, sovereigns with a lower initial creditworthiness would need to be especially alert to the possibility of sharp (non-linear) increases in interest rates should financial busts materialise. The same holds for economies where the policy room for manoeuvre is more limited because of, say, balance-sheet characteristics (e.g. a large share of foreign currency debt, public or private), history (e.g. one of defaults or persistently high inflation) and institutional features (e.g. a tight exchange rate regime, including being a member of a broader currency area).

---

[22] More ambitiously, one could in principle adjust the cost as a function of the financial system's characteristics, such as leverage, concentration etc; see, for example, Arslanalp and Liao (2014, 2015) for one possible approach to estimating time-varying contingent liabilities.

Second, and at the other end of the spectrum, for countries with broad room for monetary policy manoeuvre, it would be imprudent to assess the underlying fiscal strength on the basis of the unusually and persistently low interest rates that may prevail during the post-crisis phase. Rather, it would be important to assess the strength based on some 'normal' long-term level. True, establishing what that level should be is not easy. Even so, using prevailing interest rates is bound to paint too rosy a picture. Worse, it could even pave the way for a self-fulfilling debt trap (BIS, 2015; Borio and Disyatat, 2014; Borio, 2016). Lulled into a false sense of security, the sovereign could loosen its fiscal stance and accumulate further debt. Directly and indirectly, this would make it harder for the central bank to raise rates without causing economic damage. And at some point, regardless of the policymakers' intentions, a sovereign crisis could be triggered by investor fears of a formal default or inflationary finance.

As a final point, it is worth stressing that fiscal balances adjusted for the financial cycle are an important but insufficient statistic for fiscal sustainability. As a result, they need to be complemented with measures of sustainable debt that take full account of future prospects and risks over long horizons. In this regard, a possible but very ambitious avenue for future research would be to build on existing models of debt sustainability (see e.g. D'Erasmo et al., 2015) to incorporate financial risks and the endogenous behaviour of interest rates and other variables in a realistic way. This would also help to understand how the risk of a fiscal crisis could feed back on the financial sector through higher risk premia and by reflection on the rest of the private sector.

5 Conclusion

Financial booms and busts, or financial cycles, can wreak havoc with public finances. It is therefore critical to design fiscal policy in a way that is consistent with this threat, so as not to endanger the sovereign's creditworthiness and retain valuable fiscal space. In this chapter, we have taken a first step in that direction.

Our main focus has been on how to estimate more reliable cyclically adjusted fiscal balances to take into account the nexus between the financial cycle and potential output. Both during financial booms and during financial busts, economists and policymakers tend to overestimate potential or sustainable output, and possibly also its growth rate. This leads to too rosy a picture of the underlying fiscal strength, which risks undermining it further: governments may be tempted to relax needed consolidation and/or to rely too much on fiscal policy to boost disappointing post-crisis growth. The risk is especially high if the cyclical adjustment relies heavily on the premise that rising inflation provides the key signal of sustainability – the typical Phillips curve relationship. As history indicates, dangerous financial booms have built up even in the context of low and stable inflation. The recent global financial crisis is but the latest reminder.

In addition, we have sketched out how policymakers might take into account the other channels through which financial cycles flatter fiscal accounts. During booms, these include the build-up of hidden contingent liabilities associated with the need to support balance-sheet repair if a financial crisis subsequently erupts, effects on the structure of tax receipts and possibly expenditures linked to asset price increases, and the impact of exchange rate appreciation on the valuation of foreign currency debt and debt-servicing costs. Moreover, during busts and for countries with sufficient monetary policy room for manoeuvre, the channels include the effect of unusually and persistently low interest rates, sometimes compounded by central banks' large-scale government bond purchases.

But the ultimate objective should be more ambitious. It should be to design fiscal policy as part of a broader macrofinancial stability framework aimed at taming the financial cycle and ensuring sustainable and balanced growth. Taming the financial cycle is not a task that can be left to macroprudential measures alone (BIS, 2014, 2015; Borio, 2014b). Monetary and fiscal policies also have a role to play. For fiscal policy, this is not just a matter of ensuring that it retains fiscal space to address the financial bust without endangering the sovereign's creditworthiness or having it become a source of macroeconomic instability more generally. Fiscal policy ought to play a more proactive role to restrain financial booms in the first place. This means leaning more deliberately against financial booms, possibly with corresponding targets for deficits and debt, and possibly using the tax code and other fiscal instruments to remove any bias in favour of debt over equity.

In other words, it is a two-way street. We need to protect the sovereign from the financial cycle, but also the financial cycle from the sovereign.

Bibliography

Ahearne, A. and Shinada, N. (2005). Zombie firms and economic stagnation in Japan. *International Economics and Economic Policy*, 2, 363–81.

Alberola, E., Estrada, A. and Santabárbara, D. (2013). *Growth beyond Imbalances: Sustainable Growth Rates and Output Gap Reassessment.* Banco de España. Working Paper No. 1313.

Alberola, E., Kataryniuk, I. , Melguizo, Á. and Orozco, R. (2016a). *Fiscal Policy and the Cycle in Latin America: The Role of Financing Conditions and Fiscal Rules.* BIS Working Papers, No. 543.

Alberola, E., Gondo, R., Lombardi, M. and Urbina, D. (2016b). Output gaps in Latin America and policy stabilisation: the effect of commodity and capital flows cycles. BIS Working Papers, No. 568.

Albert, M., Jude, C. and Rebillard, C. (2015). *The Long Landing Scenario: Rebalancing from Overinvestment and Excessive Credit Growth, and Implications for Potential Growth in China.* Banque de France Document de Travail, No. 572.

Albertazzi, U. and Marchetti, D. (2010). *Credit Supply, Flight to Quality and Evergreening: An Analysis of Bank–Firm Relationships after Lehman.* Bank of Italy Temi di Discussione. Working Paper No. 756.

Amstad, M. and Packer, F. (2015). Sovereign ratings of advanced and emerging economies after the crisis. *BIS Quarterly Review*, December, 77–91.

André, C. and Girouard, N. (2005). *Measuring Cyclically-Adjusted Budget Balances for OECD Countries.* OECD Working Paper No. 434.

Arslanalp, S. and Liao, Y. (2014). Banking sector contingent liabilities and sovereign risk. *Journal of Empirical Finance*, 29, 316–30.

(2015). *Contingent Liabilities from Banks: How to Track Them?* IMF Working Paper No. 15/255, December.

Auerbach, A. (2011). *Long-Term Fiscal Sustainability in Major Economies.* BIS Working Papers, No. 361, November.

Bank of England (2011). *Financial Stability Report*, No. 30, December.

Bank for International Settlements (2010). *The Global Crisis and Financial Intermediation in Emerging Market Economies.* BIS Papers, No. 54.

(2014). *84th Annual Report*, June.

(2015). *85th Annual Report*, June.

Ball, L. (2014). Long-term damage from the Great Recession in OECD countries. *European Journal of Economics and Economic Policies*, 11(2), 149–60.

Basel Committee on Banking Supervision (2010). *An Assessment of the Long-Term Economic Impact of Stronger Capital and Liquidity Requirements*, August.

Baum, A., Checherita-Westphal, C. and Rother, P. (2013). Debt and growth: new evidence for the euro area. *Journal of International Money and Finance*, **32**, 809–21.

Beffy, P., Ollivaud, P., Richardson, P. and Sédillot, F. (2006). *New OECD Methods for Supply-Side and Medium-Term Assessments: A Capital Services Approach*. OECD Economics Department Working Papers, No. 482.

Bénétrix, A. and Lane, P. (2015). *Financial Cycles and Fiscal Cycles*. Trinity Economics Papers, No. 0815.

Bi, H. and Leeper, E. (2013). *Analyzing Fiscal Sustainability*. Bank of Canada Working Paper No. 2013-27.

Bianchi, F. and Civelli, A. (2013). *Globalization and Inflation: Structural Evidence from a Time-Varying VAR Approach*. Economic Research Initiatives at Duke (ERID) Working Papers, No. 157.

Blagrave, P., Garcia-Saltos, R., Laxton, D. and Zhang, F. (2015). *A Simple Multivariate Filter for Estimating Potential Output*. IMF Working Paper No 15/79.

Blanchard, O., Cerutti, E. and Summers, L. (2015). *Inflation and Activity – Two Explorations and Their Monetary Policy Implications*. NBER Working Paper No. 21726, November.

Borio, C. (2014a). The financial cycle and macroeconomics: what have we learnt? *Journal of Banking and Finance*, **45**, August, 182–98.

(2014b). Macroprudential frameworks: (too) great expectations? *Central Banking Journal*, 25th anniversary issue, August. Also available in BIS Speeches.

(2016). Revisiting three intellectual pillars of monetary policy received wisdom. *The Cato Journal*, **36**, 213–38.

Borio, C. and Disyatat, P. (2010). Unconventional monetary policies: an appraisal. *The Manchester School*, 78(s1), 53–89. Also available as BIS Working Papers, No. 292, November 2009.

(2014). Low interest rates and secular stagnation: is debt a missing link? *VoxEU*, 25 June, http://voxeu.org/article/low-interest-rates-secular-stagnation-and-debt

Borio, C., Disyatat, P. and Juselius, M. (2013). *Rethinking Potential Output: Embedding Information about the Financial Cycle*. BIS Working Paper No. 404, February.

(2014). *A Parsimonious Approach to Incorporating Economic Information in Measures of Potential Output*. BIS Working Paper No. 442, February.

Borio, C. and Drehmann, M. (2009). Assessing the risk of banking crises – revisited. *BIS Quarterly Review*, March, 29–46.

Borio, C., Kharroubi, E., Upper, C. and Zampolli, F. (2015b). *Labour Reallocation and Productivity Dynamics: Financial Causes, Real Consequences*. BIS Working Paper No. 534, December.

Borio, C. and Lowe, P. (2002). Assessing the risk of banking crises. *BIS Quarterly Review*, December, 43–54.

Borio, C., Vale, B. and von Peter, G. (2010). Resolving the current financial crisis: are we heeding the lessons of the Nordics? *Moneda y Crédito*, No. 230, 7–49. Also available, in extended form, as BIS Working Papers, No. 311.

Bova, E., Ruiz-Arranz, M., Toscani, F. and Ture, H. (2016). *The Fiscal Costs of Contingent Liabilities: A New Dataset*. IMF Working Paper No. 16/14.

Budina, N., Gracia, B. , Hu, X. and Saksonovs, S. (2015). *Recognizing the Bias: Financial Cycles and Fiscal Policy*. IMF Working Paper No. 15/246, November.

Caballero, R., Hoshi, T. and Kashyap, A. (2008). Zombie lending and depressed restructuring in Japan. *American Economic Review*, 98, 1943–77.

Carnot, N. and de Castro, F. (2015). *The Discretionary Fiscal Effort: an Assessment of Fiscal Policy and Its Output Effect*. Economic Papers, No. 543, February.

Cecchetti, G. and Kharroubi, E. (2015). *Why Does Financial Sector Growth Crowd Out Real Economic Growth?* BIS Working Paper No. 490, February.

Cecchetti, S., Mohanty, M. and Zampolli, F. (2011). The real effects of debt. In *Achieving Maximum Long-Run Growth*, Proceedings from the symposium sponsored by the Federal Reserve Bank of Kansas City, Jackson Hole, August 2011.

Cerra, V. and Saxena, S. (2008). Growth dynamics: the myth of economic recovery. *American Economic Review*, 98, 439–57.

Ciccarelli, M. and Mojon, B. (2010). Global inflation. *Review of Economics and Statistics*, 92, 524–35.

Committee on the Global Financial System (2007). *Financial Stability and Local Currency Bond Markets*. CGFS Papers, No. 28.

(2011). *The Impact of Sovereign Credit Risk on Bank Funding Conditions*. CGFS Papers, No. 43.

Checherita-Westphal, C. and Rother, P. (2012). The impact of high government debt on economic growth and its channels: an empirical investigation for the euro area. *European Economic Review*, 56, 1392–405.

Chudik, A., Mohaddes, K., Pesaran, M. and Raissi, M. (2015). *Is There a Debt-Threshold Effect on Output Growth?* IMF Working Papers, N 15/197, September.

Das, U., Papapioannou, M., Pedras, G., Ahmed, F. and Surti, J. (2010). *Managing Public Debt and Its Financial Stability.* IMF Working Papers, No. 10/280.

D'Erasmo, P., Mendoza, E. G. and Zhang, J. (2015). What is a sustainable public debt? *The Handbook of Macroeconomics*, **2**, April.

de Jong, P. and Penzer, J. (1998). Diagnosing shocks in time series. *Journal of the American Statistical Association*, **93**, 796–806.

Diaz-Alejandro, C. (1985). Good-bye financial repression, hello financial crash. *Journal of Development Economics*, **19**, 1–24.

Drehmann, M., Borio, C. and Tsatsaronis, K. (2012). *Characterising the Financial Cycle: Don't Lose Sight of the Medium-Term!* BIS Working Papers, No. 380.

Drehmann, M. and Juselius, M. (2015). *Leverage Dynamics and the Real Burden of Debt.* BIS Working Papers, No. 501, May.

Eickmeier, S. and Pijnenburg, K. (2013). The global dimension of inflation: evidence from factor-augmented Phillips curves. *Oxford Bulletin of Economics and Statistics*, **75**, 103–22.

Enria, A. (2012). *Supervisory Policies and Bank Deleveraging: A European Perspective.* Speech at the 21st Hyman P Minsky Conference on the State of the US and World Economies, 11–12 April.

Eschenbach, F. and Schuknecht, L. (2004). Budgetary risks from real estate and stock markets. *Economic Policy*, **19**, 314–46.

Fischer, A. and Yeşin, P. (2016). *Undoing CHF Mortgage Loans in Post-Crisis Eastern Europe.* Mimeo, Swiss National Bank.

Furceri, D. and Zdzienicka, A. (2012). The consequences of banking crises for public debt. *International Finance*, **15**(3), 289–307.

Giorno, C., Richardson, P., Roseveare, D. and Van den Noord, P. (1995). *Estimating Potential Output, Output Gaps and Structural Budget Balances.* OECD Economics Department Working Papers, No. 152.

Gosh, A., Kim, J., Mendoza, E., Ostry, J. and Qureshi, M. (2011). *Fiscal Fatigue, Fiscal Space and Debt Sustainability in Advanced Economies.* NBER Working Paper No. 16782, February.

Gourinchas, P. and Obstfeld, M. (2012). Stories of the twentieth century for the twenty-first. *American Economic Journal: Macroeconomics*, **4**(1), 226–65.

Harvey, A. and Trimbur, T. (2003). Generalised model-based filters for extracting trends and cycles in economic time series. *Review of Economics and Statistics*, **85**, 244–55.

Iwaisako, T. (2005). Corporate investment and restructuring. In T. Ito, H. Patrick and D. E. Weinstein, eds., *Reviving Japan's Economy.* Cambridge: MIT Press, pp. 275–310.

Jaimovich, N. and Rebelo, S. (2012). *Non-Linear Effects of Taxation on Growth*. NBER Working Paper No. 18473.

Jordà, Ò., Schularick, M. and Taylor, A. (2013). When credit bites back. *Journal of Money, Credit and Banking*, **45**, 3–28.

(2016). Sovereigns versus banks: credit, crises and consequences. *Journal of the European Economic Association*, **14**, 45–79.

Koopman, S., Shephard, N. and Doornik, J. (2008). Statistical Algorithms for Models in State Space Form: SsfPack 3.0. Timberlake Consultants Press.

Kuttner, K. (1994). Estimating potential output as a latent variable. *Journal of Business and Economic Statistics*, **12**, 361–7.

Kuttner, K. and Robinson, T. (2008). *Understanding the Flattening Phillips Curve*. Reserve Bank of Australia Research Discussion Papers, No. 2008-05.

Lane, P (2003). The cyclical behaviour of fiscal policy: evidence from the OECD. *Journal of Public Economics*, **87**, 2661–75.

Laeven, L. and Valencia, F. (2013). Systemic banking crises database. *IMF Economic Review*, **61**, 225–70.

Leeper, E. (2013). *Fiscal Limits and Monetary Policy*. NBER Working Paper No. 18877.

(2015). *Fiscal Analysis Is Darned Hard*. NBER Working Papers, No. 21822, December.

Martin, R., Munyan, T. and Wilson, B. (2015). *Potential Output and Recessions: Are We Fooling Ourselves?* International Finance Discussion Papers, No. 1145, Federal Reserve Board.

Melolinna, M. and Tóth, M. (2016). *Output Gaps, Inflation and Financial Cycles in the UK*. Bank of England Staff Working Paper No. 585.

Obstfeld, M. (2013). On keeping your powder dry: fiscal foundations of financial and price stability. *Monetary and Economic Studies*, **31** (November), 25–38.

Orphanides, A. and Van Norden, S. (2002). The unreliability of output-gap estimates in real time. *Review of Economics and Statistics*, **84**, 569–83.

Peek, J. and Rosengren, E. (2005). Unnatural selection: perverse incentives and the misallocation of credit in Japan. *American Economic Review*, **95**, 1144–66.

Price, R. and Dang, T. (2011). *Adjusting Fiscal Balances for Asset Price Cycles*. OECD Working Paper No. 868.

Reinhart, C. and Reinhart, V. (2015). Financial crises, development and growth: a long-term perspective. *The World Bank Economic Review*, **29**, Supplement, S53–S76.

Reinhart, C., Reinhart, V. and Rogoff, K. (2012). Public debt overhangs: advanced-economy episodes since 1800. *Journal of Economic Perspectives*, **26**, 69–86.

Reinhart, C. and Rogoff, K. (2009). *This Time Is Different: Eight Centuries of Financial Folly*. Princeton University Press.

  (2011). From financial crash to debt crisis. *American Economic Review*, **101**, 1676–706.

  (2013). Banking crises: an equal opportunity menace. *Journal of Banking and Finance*, **37**, 4557–73.

Santos, T. (2014). *Credit Booms: Implications for the Public and the Private Sector*. BIS Working Papers, No. 481, January.

Talvi, E. and Végh, C. (2005). Tax base variability and procyclical fiscal policy in developing countries. *Journal of Development Economics*, **78**, 156–90.

Tornell, A. and Lane, P. (1999). The voracity effect. *American Economic Review*, **89**, 22–46.

Turner, P. (2012). *Weathering Financial Crises: Domestic Bond Markets in EMEs*. BIS Papers, No. 63, 15–34.

Waldron, M. and Zampolli, F. (2010). The rise in home prices and household debt in the UK: potential causes and implications. In S. Smith and B. Searle, eds., *The Blackwell Companion to the Economics of Housing: The Housing Wealth of Nations*. Oxford: Wiley-Blackwell, pp. 105–25.

Woo, J. and Kumar, M. (2015). Public debt and growth. *Economica*, **82**, 705–39.

14 | Calibrating the Cost of Defaulting in Models of Sovereign Defaults

JUAN CARLOS HATCHONDO AND
LEONARDO MARTINEZ

1 Introduction

We demonstrate how, in a sovereign default model à la Eaton and Gersovitz (1981) with long-term debt, the cost of defaulting can be calibrated to match the average levels of sovereign debt and spread observed in the data.[1] This quantitative success of the sovereign default model makes it an interesting laboratory to evaluate policies for economies that face significant sovereign default risk.

We study a small open economy that receives a stochastic endowment stream of a single tradable good. At the beginning of each period, when the government is not in default, it decides whether to default on its debt. A defaulting government is temporarily prevented from issuing debt and faces an income cost in each period in which it is excluded from the debt market. Before each period ends, the government may change its debt position, subject to the constraints imposed by its default decision. Bonds are priced by competitive foreign risk-neutral investors.[2]

Aguiar and Gopinath (2006) show that a quantitative version of the sovereign default model with one-period debt is successful in generating defaults in equilibrium and countercyclical interest rates and net exports. However, their calibration generates levels of sovereign debt and spreads lower than those observed in the data.

Arellano (2008) also assumes one-period debt but succeeds in generating a spread level similar to the one observed in the data. However,

The views expressed herein are those of the authors and should not be attributed to the IMF, its Executive Board, or its management.
[1] The sovereign spread is the difference between the yield paid by the government when it borrows and a risk-free yield.
[2] Boz (2011), Cuadra and Sapriza (2008), D'Erasmo (2008), Durdu et al. (2013), Hatchondo, Martinez, and Sosa Padilla (2014), Lizarazo (2013, 2012), Roch and Uhlig (2014), and Yue (2010) present extensions of the baseline sovereign default model.

414

her baseline parametrization features low debt levels.[3] The main difference between the models presented by Aguiar and Gopinath (2006) and Arellano (2008) is in the income cost of defaulting. Aguiar and Gopinath (2006) assume that this cost is a constant fraction of income. Arellano (2008) assumes a nonlinear cost: the income cost of defaulting is zero for income levels below a threshold level and is equal to the difference between the income and the threshold for pre-default income levels above the threshold. Thus, with Arellano's (2008) cost of defaulting, the fraction of income lost because of the default is an increasing function of income.[4]

The stronger response of the cost of defaulting to changes in the level of income is what allows Arellano (2008) to generate higher spreads. When the cost of defaulting is a steeper function of income, the probability of a future default is more sensitive to future income realizations than to the current debt chosen by the government. This implies that a given increase in the debt stock generates a lower increase in the spread, which strengthens the government's incentives to choose borrowing levels that command a higher spread in equilibrium.

Hatchondo and Martinez (2009) show that assuming long-term debt instead of one-period bonds allows the model to generate substantially higher spread levels. Hatchondo and Martinez (2009) assume the proportional cost of defaulting that is assumed by Aguiar and Gopinath (2006) and find that when the model is calibrated to a debt duration of four years instead of one quarter, the average spread in the simulations increases from 0.1 percent to more than 2.7 percent. This is because of the debt dilution problem that appears when the government is allowed to issue long-term debt.[5]

---

[3] Arellano (2008) calibrates the model to mimic the ratio of debt service to GDP in the data. With one-period debt, this implies low debt levels.

[4] Mendoza and Yue (2012) show that this property of the cost of defaulting arises endogenously in a setup in which defaults affect the ability of local firms to acquire a foreign intermediate input good.

[5] Debt dilution refers to the reduction in the value of existing debt triggered by the issuance of new debt. Issuing new debt reduces the value of existing debt because it increases the probability of default. Three factors generate the sovereign debt dilution problem: (i) governments issue long-term debt; (ii) the current government cannot control debt issuances by future governments; and (iii) bonds are priced by rational investors. Rational investors anticipate that additional borrowing by future governments will increase the risk of default on long-term bonds issued by the current government and, thus, offer a lower price for these bonds. The current government could benefit from constraining future borrowing

Hatchondo and Martinez (2009) also show that the average debt level in the model simulations increases almost one-to-one with the (constant) fraction of income lost after a default: A cost of defaulting of 10 percent of output generates an average debt-to-output ratio of 10 percent and a cost of 50 percent generates a debt ratio of 51 percent. This hints at how the cost of defaulting could be calibrated to generate observed debt levels. Estimating the output cost of defaulting is a difficult enterprise due to endogeneity bias: it is not easy to disentangle how much of the income falls observed after a default are due to the default itself. In addition, the basic default model abstracts from other costs of defaulting that may be significant. For that reason, many papers in the quantitative literature on sovereign defaults choose to calibrate the income cost of defaulting targeting data moments such as the debt level.

Chatterjee and Eyigungor (2012) present a model with long-term debt and assume the cost of defaulting is a quadratic function of income. Thus, they have two cost parameter values to choose in the calibration. They show that this is sufficient to match exactly their targets for the average levels of debt and spread.

In this article, we assume a quadratic income cost of defaulting and illustrate how the parameters that govern this cost affect the model implications for debt and spread. Following the intuition presented by Arellano (2008), the parameter that determines the sensitivity to the income level of the fraction of income lost after a default affects the spread more than the debt level. Following the intuition presented by Hatchondo and Martinez (2009), the average fraction of income lost after a default affects the debt more than the spread level. We also show that, consistent with these findings, there is a unique combination of the values of these two parameters that allows the model to match both the average debt and spread levels.

In contrast, we show that with one-period bonds and a standard value for the government's discount factor, it is impossible to calibrate the parameters that govern the income cost of defaulting to match the levels of debt and spread observed in the data. Parameter values that generate the level of debt observed in the data imply spread levels that

because this could increase the price of the bonds it issues. However, governments are typically unable to constrain borrowing by future governments, which creates the debt dilution problem.

are an order of magnitude smaller than their data counterpart. This illustrates the importance of assuming long-term debt and thus introducing debt dilution for the quantitative success of sovereign default models.[6]

The rest of the article proceeds as follows. Section 2 discusses the use of sovereign default models for policy analysis. Section 3 presents our model. Section 4 discusses the benchmark calibration. Section 5 explains how we solve the model. Section 6 presents simulation results for the benchmark calibration. Section 7 shows how changes in the value of the cost parameters affect the level of debt and spread in the model simulations. Section 8 presents results for one-period bonds. Section 9 concludes.

2 The Use of Sovereign Default Models for Policy Analysis

There seems to be a consensus among policymakers on the desirability of lower sovereign debt levels. For instance, in an IMF Staff Position Note, Blanchard et al. (2010) argue that "A key lesson from the crisis is the desirability of fiscal space to run larger fiscal deficits when needed." They also note that "Medium-term fiscal frameworks, credible commitments to reducing debt-to-GDP ratios, and fiscal rules (with escape clauses for recessions) can all help in this regard." With the objective of containing sovereign debt levels, an increasing number of countries are adopting fiscal rules that impose (often in laws or in the constitution) restrictions upon future governments' abilities to conduct fiscal policy.

While optimal sovereign debt levels are often at the center of policy debates, these debates are rarely guided by economic theory. The IMF's flagship fiscal publication has recently stated that "the optimal-debt concept has remained at a fairly abstract level, whereas the safe-debt concept has focused largely on empirical applications" (IMF, 2013a). The IMF chief economist has asked: "What levels of public debt should countries aim for? Are old rules of thumb, such as trying to keep the debt-to-GDP ratio below 60 percent in advanced countries, still reliable?" (Blanchard, 2011).

---

[6] In an equilibrium default model with one-period debt, Hatchondo et al. (2009) assume that governments that discount the future at different rates alternate in power, and show that this political turnover could account for high levels of sovereign spreads.

Models of sovereign default could help to answer these questions. These models complement the sustainability analysis (Adler and Sosa, 2013; Ghosh et al., 2011; Tanner and Samaké, 2006) commonly used in policy circles (see for instance IMF, 2013c, and IMF Article IV country reports). In contrast with sustainability frameworks, models of sovereign default feature endogenous sovereign spreads (that, e.g., capture the effects of the expectation of future fiscal adjustments), a welfare criterion, and endogenous borrowing policies (that, e.g., react to fiscal rules).

For example, Hatchondo, Martinez, and Roch (2015) use a default model to quantify the effects of introducing fiscal rules and discuss the optimal value of fiscal rules' targets. Hatchondo, Martinez, and Roch (2015) study fiscal rules that limit the levels of either sovereign debt or the sovereign default premium reflected in spreads. A debt-brake rule imposes a ceiling on the fiscal budget balance to prevent the sovereign debt level going beyond a certain limit. A spread-brake rule imposes a ceiling on the fiscal budget balance that prevents the government from increasing its debt level to push the sovereign spread beyond a limit. Hatchondo, Martinez, and Roch (2015) argue that fiscal rules limiting the sovereign premium may have a significant advantage over rules limiting debt levels.

In an equilibrium default model with long-term debt, without a fiscal rule, the government cannot lower the level of sovereign risk (and thus increase the price of current debt issuances) by committing to lower levels of future debt issuances (the debt dilution problem). Fiscal rules allow the government to solve this problem and thus generate welfare gains.

Hatchondo, Martinez, and Roch (2015) search for a common fiscal rule that maximizes average welfare for a set of economies (i.e., for a set of parameterizations of their model). This is important for two reasons. First, fiscal rules often impose common limits on several economies. According to the IMF fiscal rules database, in 2014, forty-eight of the eighty-five countries with fiscal rules had supra-national rules (perhaps the best known example is the common sovereign debt limit imposed by the Maastricht Treaty). More generally, international organizations often use common fiscal targets to guide policy advice.[7] Second, policy recommendations should acknowledge

---

[7] Common sovereign debt thresholds are used across countries by the IMF as one of the criteria for deciding on the level of scrutiny to be applied in surveillance

that economies may change over time. For instance, the implementation of structural reforms may increase confidence in the future repayment of debt obligations, enhancing the government's borrowing capacity. This introduces a tension in the design of fiscal rules. On the one hand, an effective fiscal rule requires stable fiscal targets that are not too easy to modify. On the other, we would like rules to accommodate for structural changes in the government's borrowing capacity or in its borrowing needs. Furthermore, at any point in time, structural changes make it difficult to identify a government's borrowing capacity and needs, and thus optimal targets for fiscal rules. Our discussion of common fiscal rules that maximize average welfare for sets of economies with different borrowing capacities and needs sheds light on which rules could be stable while still accommodating structural changes.

Hatchondo, Martinez, and Roch (2015) show that a common spread-brake rule performs better than a common debt-brake rule. This result is intuitive. Gains from imposing a fiscal rule arise because the rule achieves a reduction in sovereign risk. A debt limit is too blunt an instrument for that goal. For instance, for economies with high debt intolerance, a debt limit that is too loose fails to achieve the desired risk reduction.[8] For economies with low debt intolerance, a debt limit that is too tight may unnecessarily prevent a government from borrowing. This makes it difficult to use a common debt limit for several economies. In contrast, limits to the sovereign premium directly attack the problem of excessive sovereign risk, and economies with different levels of debt intolerance, and even economies that differ in their eagerness to borrow, benefit from committing to a common low level of risk.

(IMF, 2013b; IMF, 2013c). The IMF 2014 Reform of the Policy on Public Debt Limits in Fund-Supported Programs states that "The reform proposal seeks to accommodate a number of concerns emphasized by Executive Directors and other stakeholders, including: (i) ensuring even-handedness across the membership in the application of the policy, consistent with the principle of uniformity of treatment" (IMF, 2014).

[8] Debt intolerance refers to the relationship between the levels of sovereign debt and spread. Countries with high (low) debt intolerance pay a high (low) spread for low (high) debt levels. Debt intolerance varies across countries and over time (Reinhart et al., 2003; Reinhart et al., 2015). Furthermore, identifying the level of debt intolerance in a particular country and period may be difficult (for instance, what is the relationship between the levels of sovereign debt and spreads that will prevail in Greece after the crisis?).

While policy debates are dominated by sovereign debt levels, the role of market discipline in these debates is growing. For instance, Claessens et al. (2012) argue that "the challenge is to complement fiscal rules affecting quantities most productively with market-based mechanisms using price signals." Juvenal and Wiseman (2015) use the sovereign spread to evaluate Portugal's fiscal position. Recent revisions of the IMF fiscal sustainability framework incorporate sovereign spreads as an additional criteria to guide the level of scrutiny in surveillance (IMF, 2013b).

In practice, debt brakes (for instance, in the 2011 reform of the Maastricht Treaty) impose a constraint on the fiscal budget balance when debt levels are above a threshold. Spread brakes could impose a limit on the budget balance when the sovereign spread is above a threshold. The average spread over a longer period (e.g., the previous fiscal year) could be used to avoid reactions to short-term fluctuations of the spread. Measures of the domestic component of the spread (Juvenal and Wiseman, 2015) could be used to avoid reactions to changes in global factors. Hatchondo, Martinez, and Roch (2015) show that gains from imposing a spread brake are robust to the introduction into the default model of global factors outside the control of the government that affect the spread (in addition to the domestic factors that are also outside the control of the government and affect the spread).

Hatchondo, Martinez, and Sosa Padilla (2016) propose introducing debt covenants as an alternative approach to dealing with the debt dilution problem. In the simulations of an equilibrium default model, eliminating dilution allows the government to increase the duration of sovereign debt by almost two years, which mitigates the government's exposure to increases in the cost of borrowing. They study two covenants that penalize the government for either (i) choosing debt levels above a limit or (ii) borrowing while paying spreads higher than a limit. The implementation of these covenants could help enforce fiscal rules.

Chatterjee and Eyigungor (2015) study how introducing seniority in sovereign debt contracts could help mitigate the debt dilution problem. With seniority, after a default, creditors who lent first suffer a lower haircut. Chatterjee and Eyigungor (2015) present a quantitative exercise in which, in spite of boosting the average debt level by 25 percent, seniority reduces the default frequency by about 35 percent and average spreads by about 50 percent, generating a welfare gain of about 2 percent of flow consumption.

A key difference between fiscal rules and seniority is that rules lower the level of indebtedness and seniority increases it. In fact, Chatterjee and Eyigungor (2015) report that the majority of the welfare gain obtained with seniority is due to the resulting increase of indebtedness. However, the default model favors higher indebtedness because it omits political myopia (Amador, 2012; Azzimonti, 2011; Azzimonti et al., 2010; Cole et al., 1995; Cuadra and Sapriza, 2008; Halac and Yared, 2014, 2015). In fact, Hatchondo, Martinez, and Roch (2015) show that the optimal debt limit decreases with the degree of political myopia. Thus, political myopia may present an important challenge for policy prescriptions that increase the level of indebtedness, as Chatterjee and Eyigungor (2015) show seniority does.[9]

3 The Model

The government has preferences given by

$$\mathbb{E}_t \sum_{j=t}^{\infty} \beta^{j-t} u(c_j),$$

where $\mathbb{E}$ denotes the expectation operator, β denotes the subjective discount factor, and c_t represents consumption of private agents. The utility function is strictly increasing and concave. The government cannot commit to future (default and borrowing) decisions. Thus, one may interpret this environment as a game in which the government making decisions in period t is a player who takes as given the (default and borrowing) strategies of other players (governments) who will decide after t.

---

[9] Considering differences in political myopia would strengthen the advantage of a spread break over a debt brake as a common fiscal rule for different economies. Less advanced economies typically display more debt intolerance and more political myopia (proxied by more polarization, turnover, political risk, or weaker institutions) and would thus require lower debt limits. Applying such lower debt limits to more advanced economies with less debt intolerance and less myopia would not be desirable. In contrast, countries with different degrees of myopia could benefit from common spread limits. Presenting a thorough analysis of the interactions of myopia, dilution, debt intolerance, and fiscal rules is an interesting avenue for future research.

The timing of events within each period is as follows. First, the government learns the economy's income. After that, the government chooses whether to default on its debt. Before the period ends, the government may change its debt position, subject to the constraints imposed by its default decision.

The economy's endowment of the single tradable good is denoted by $y \in Y \subset \mathbb{R}_{++}$. This endowment follows a Markov process.

As in Hatchondo and Martinez (2009), we assume that a bond issued in period t promises an infinite stream of coupons, which decreases at a constant rate δ.[10] In particular, a bond issued in period t promises to pay $(1 - \delta)^{j-1}$ units of the tradable good in period $t + j$, for all $j \geq 1$. Hence, debt dynamics can be represented as follows:

$$b_{t+1} = (1 - \delta)b_t + l_t,$$

where b_t is the number of coupons due at the beginning of period t, and l_t is the number of long-term bonds issued in period t. The advantage of this payment structure is that it enables us to condense all future payment obligations derived from past debt issuances into a one-dimensional state variable: The payment obligations that mature in the current period.

Bonds are priced in a competitive market inhabited by a large number of foreign investors. Thus, bond prices are pinned down by the foreign investors' zero-expected-profit condition. Foreign investors are risk-neutral and discount future payoffs at the rate r.

When the government defaults, it does so on all current and future debt obligations. This is consistent with the observed behavior of defaulting governments and it is a standard assumption in the literature.[11]

---

[10] Arellano and Ramanarayanan (2012) and Hatchondo and Martinez (2013) allow the government to issue both short-term and long-term debt, and study optimal maturity. Bianchi et al. (2012) allow for the simultaneous accumulation of assets and liabilities. Hatchondo et al. (2017) allow the government to issue both defaultable and non-defaultable debt. In Hatchondo and Martinez (2012), we allow the government to issue debt with payments contingent to the level of income.

[11] Sovereign debt contracts often contain an acceleration clause and a cross-default clause. The first clause allows creditors to call the debt they hold in case the government defaults on a payment. The cross-default clause states that a default in any government obligation constitutes a default in the contract containing that clause. These clauses imply that after a default event, future debt obligations become current.

A default event triggers exclusion from the debt market for a stochastic number of periods.[12] In each period after the default period, the government may regain access to debt markets with a constant probability $\psi \in [0, 1]$. In every period in which the government is excluded from the debt market, income is given by $y - \phi(y)$.

3.1 Recursive Formulation

Let b denote the number of outstanding coupon claims at the beginning of the current period, and b' denote the number of outstanding coupon claims at the beginning of the next period. Let d denote the current-period default decision. We assume that d is equal to 1 if the government defaulted in the current period and is equal to 0 if it did not. Let V denote the government's value function at the beginning of a period, that is, before the default decision is made. Let V_0 denote the value function of a sovereign not in default. Let V_1 denote the value function of a sovereign in default. Let F denote the conditional cumulative distribution function of the next-period endowment y'. For any bond price function q, the function V satisfies the following functional equation:

$$V(b, y) = \max_{d \in \{0,1\}} \{dV_1(y) + (1 - d)V_0(b, y)\}, \tag{1}$$

where

$$V_1(y) = u(y - \phi(y)) + \beta \int [\psi V(0, y') + (1 - \psi)V_1(y')]F(dy'|y), \tag{2}$$

and

$$V_0(b, y) = \max_{b' \geq 0} \left\{ u(y - b + q(b', y)[b' - (1 - \delta)b]) \right.$$
$$\left. + \beta \int V(b', y')F(dy'|y) \right\}. \tag{3}$$

The bond price is given by the following functional equation:

---

[12] Hatchondo et al. (2007) discuss the effects of the exclusion assumption in the default model.

$$q(b',y) = \frac{1}{1+r}\int \left[1 - \widehat{d}(b',y')\right] F(dy'|y)$$
$$+ \frac{1-\delta}{1+r}\int \left[1 - \widehat{d}(b',y')\right] q\left(\widehat{b}(b',y'),y'\right) F(dy'|y), \qquad (4)$$

where $\widehat{d}$ and $\widehat{b}$ denote the future default and borrowing rules that lenders expect the government to follow. The default rule $\widehat{d}$ is equal to 1 if the government defaults, and is equal to 0 otherwise. The function $\widehat{b}$ determines the number of coupons that will mature next period. The first term on the right-hand side of Equation (4) equals the expected value of the next-period coupon payment promised in a bond. The second term on the right-hand side of Equation (4) equals the expected value of all other future coupon payments, which is summarized by the expected price at which the bond could be sold next period.

Solving problems (1) and (3), the government finds its optimal current default and borrowing decisions taking as given its future default and borrowing decision rules $\widehat{d}$ and $\widehat{b}$. In equilibrium, the optimal default and borrowing rules that solve problems (1) and (3) must be equal to $\widehat{d}$ and $\widehat{b}$ for all possible values of the state variables.

3.2 Equilibrium Definition

A Markov Perfect Equilibrium is characterized by

1. a default rule $\widehat{d}$ and a borrowing rule $\widehat{b}$,
2. a bond price function q,

such that:

(a) given $\widehat{d}$ and $\widehat{b}$, V, V_1, and V_0 satisfy functional Equations (1), (2), and (3), when the government can trade bonds at q;
(b) given $\widehat{d}$ and $\widehat{b}$, the bond price function q is given by Equation (4); and
(c) the default rule $\widehat{d}$ and borrowing rule $\widehat{b}$ solve the dynamic programming problem defined by Equations (1) and (3) when the government can trade bonds at q.

4 Calibration

The utility function displays a constant coefficient of relative risk aversion, that is,

Table 14.1: *Benchmark parameter values*

Risk aversion	γ	2
Risk-free rate	r	1%
Discount factor	β	0.9745
Probability default ends	ψ	0.083
Debt duration	δ	0.03
Income autocorrelation coefficient	ρ	0.94
Standard deviation of innovations	σ_ε	1.5%
Mean log income	μ	$(-1/2)\sigma_\varepsilon^2$
Income cost of defaulting	λ_0	0.18
Income cost of defaulting	λ_1	1.30

$$u(c) = \frac{c^{1-\gamma} - 1}{1 - \gamma}, \text{with } \gamma \neq 1.$$

The endowment process follows:

$$\log(y_t) = (1 - \rho)\mu + \rho \log(y_{t-1}) + \varepsilon_t,$$

with $|\rho| < 1$, and $\varepsilon_t \sim N(0, \sigma_\varepsilon^2)$.

Table 14.1 presents the benchmark values given to all parameters in the model. A period in the model refers to a quarter. The coefficient of relative risk aversion is set equal to 2, the risk-free interest rate is set equal to 1 percent, and the discount factor β is set equal to 0.9745. These are standard values in quantitative studies of sovereign defaults and business cycles in small open economies. Similar to Mendoza and Yue (2012), we assume an average duration of sovereign default events of three years ($\psi = 0.083$), in line with the duration estimated by Dias and Richmond (2009).

We use data from Mexico, a common reference for studies on emerging economies, for choosing the parameters that govern the endowment process, the level and duration of debt, and the mean spread (Mexico displays the same properties that are observed in other emerging economies; see Aguiar and Gopinath, 2007; Neumeyer and Perri, 2005; Uribe and Yue, 2006). Unless we explain otherwise, we compare simulation results with data from Mexico from the first quarter of 1980 to the fourth quarter of 2011. The parameter values that govern the endowment process are chosen to mimic the behavior of GDP in Mexico during that period.

We set $\delta = 3.3\%$. With this value and our target for the average spread, bonds have an average duration of five years in the simulations, which is roughly the average debt duration observed in Mexico according to Cruces et al. (2002).[13] This value is at the upper end of available measures.

We assume the following functional form for the income cost of defaulting ϕ:

$$\phi(y) = max\left\{y\left[\lambda_0 y + \lambda_1[y - \mathbb{E}(y)]\right], 0\right\}, \tag{5}$$

where $\mathbb{E}(y)$ denotes the unconditional mean income. Equation (5) assumes a non-negative income cost of defaulting. The parameter λ_0 determines the average fraction of income lost during defaults. The parameter λ_1 determines how sensitive the fraction of income lost during defaults is to the income level. Note that the fraction of income lost during defaults observed along the equilibrium path is below λ_0 when defaults tend to be declared at low income realizations. Henceforth, we refer to λ_0 and λ_1 as the average and the slope parameters of the income cost of defaulting, respectively. The parameters λ_0 and λ_1 are calibrated targeting an average debt-to-GDP ratio of 44 percent (Cowan et al., 2006) and a mean spread of 3.4 percent (the average EMBI spread between 1996 and 2011).

In order to compute the sovereign spread implicit in a bond price, we first compute the yield i an investor would earn if it holds the bond to maturity (forever in the case of our long bonds) and no default is ever declared. This yield satisfies

$$q = \frac{1}{(1+i)} + \sum_{j=1}^{\infty} \frac{(1-\delta)^j}{(1+i)^{j+1}}.$$

The sovereign spread is the difference between the yield i and the risk-free rate r. We report the annualized spread

$$r_t^s = \left(\frac{1+i}{1+r}\right)^4 - 1.$$

Debt levels in the simulations are calculated as the present value of future payment obligations discounted at the risk-free rate, that is,

[13] We use the Macaulay definition of duration that, with the coupon structure in this chapter, is given by $D = \frac{1+r^*}{\delta+r^*}$, where r^* denotes the constant per-period yield delivered by the bond. Using a sample of twenty-seven emerging economies, Cruces et al. (2002) find an average duration of foreign sovereign debt in emerging economies – in 2000 – of 4.77 years, with a standard deviation of 1.52.

$b(1+r)(\delta+r)^{-1}$. We report debt levels as a percentage of annualized income.

5 Computation

The recursive problem is solved using value function iteration. The approximated value and bond price functions correspond to the ones in the first period of a finite-horizon economy with a number of periods large enough to make the maximum deviation between the value and bond price functions in the first and second period smaller than 10^{-6}. We solve the optimal borrowing problem in each state by searching over a grid of debt levels and then using the best borrowing level on that grid as an initial guess in a nonlinear optimization routine. The value functions V_0 and V_1 and the bond price function q are approximated using linear interpolation over income (y) and cubic spline interpolation over debt levels (b).[14] We use thirty grid points for debt and income. Expectations are calculated using 100 quadrature points for the income shock.

6 Simulations

Table 14.2 shows that the model simulations match the targeted levels of debt and spread. The model also does a good job in mimicking other non-targeted moments such as the ratio of the volatilities of consumption and income, and the countercyclical spread. Overall, Table 14.2 shows that the model can account for distinctive features of business cycles in Mexico and other emerging economies documented by, for example, Aguiar and Gopinath (2007), Neumeyer and Perri (2005), and Uribe and Yue (2006).

7 Effects of the Cost of Defaulting on the Targeted Moments

In Section 4 we explain that the values of the parameters governing the income cost of defaulting are calibrated targeting the average levels of debt and spread in the simulations. In this section, we explain how the value of these parameters affect the calibration targets and show that there is a unique pair of values that allows the model to match the targets.

---

[14] Hatchondo et al. (2010) discuss the advantages of using interpolation and solving for the equilibrium of a finite-horizon economy.

Table 14.2: *Business cycle statistics*

	Model	Data
Targeted moments		
Mean debt-to-GDP	44	44
Mean r_s	3.4	3.4
Non-targeted moments		
$\sigma(c)/\sigma(y)$	1.4	1.2
$\sigma(tb)$	0.8	1.4
$\sigma(r_s)$	1.8	1.5
$\rho(tb, y)$	−0.7	−0.7
$\rho(c, y)$	0.99	0.93
$\rho(r_s, y)$	−0.6	−0.5
$\rho(r_s, tb)$	0.7	0.6

Note: the standard deviation of x is denoted by $\sigma(x)$. The coefficient of correlation between x and z is denoted by $\rho(x, z)$. The trade balance is denoted by tb. Moments are computed using detrended series. Trends are computed using the Hodrick–Prescott filter with a smoothing parameter of $1,600$. Moments for the simulations correspond to the mean value of each moment in 500 simulation samples. For each sample, we take the last 120 periods (thirty years) without a default episode. Simulation samples start at least five years after a default. Default episodes are excluded to improve comparability with the data. Consumption and income are expressed in logs.

The top panel of Figure 14.1 shows that the average debt level in the simulations increases with the value of the average cost parameter λ_0 and decreases with the value of the slope parameter λ_1. The bottom panel of Figure 14.1 shows that the average spread in the simulations displays the opposite behavior: it decreases with λ_0 and it increases with λ_1. Therefore, as illustrated in Figure 14.2, both the combination of values of λ_0 and λ_1 that allows the model to generate the targeted debt level, and the combination of values of λ_0 and λ_1 that allows the model to generate the targeted spread level, are represented by curves with positive slope.[15] However, Figure 14.2 shows that there is a unique combination of parameter values

---

[15] Let X denote the function that determines the value of moment x in the simulations as a function of the parameters that determine the income cost of defaulting (λ_0, λ_1). The implicit function theorem implies that the combination of parameters (λ_0, λ_1) for which the model simulations replicates the target value for x, denoted by $\overline{X}$, satisfy:

$$\left.\frac{\partial \lambda_1}{\partial \lambda_0}\right|_{X(\lambda_0, \lambda_1) = \overline{X}} = -\frac{\partial X(\lambda_0, \lambda_1)/\partial \lambda_0}{\partial X(\lambda_0, \lambda_1)/\partial \lambda_1}.$$

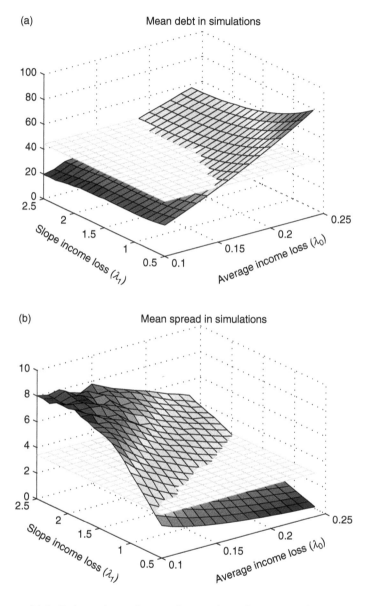

Figure 14.1: Debt ratio and annual spread as functions of income cost parameters

Note: the horizontal planes correspond to the target values for debt and spread.

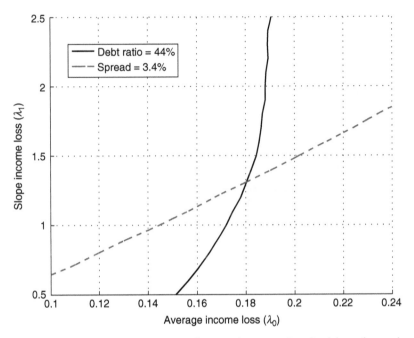

Figure 14.2: Income cost parameters that match target values for debt and spread

that allows the model to match both targets. We explain next that this is a natural outcome in models of equilibrium default because the average cost parameter λ_0 affects the debt level more and the slope cost parameter λ_1 affects the spread level more.

Figure 14.3 illustrates how the average cost parameter λ_0 affects the equilibrium levels of debt and spread (reflected in the equilibrium price at which the government sells bonds). The top panel presents the income threshold at which the government is indifferent between defaulting and repaying.[16] As is standard in equilibrium default models, this threshold is unique. Since the cost of defaulting is an increasing function of income, the government defaults for income realizations below the threshold. The top panel of Figure 14.3 shows that an increase in the value of the average cost parameter λ_0 expands the repayment region – that is, the combination of debt and income levels for which the government would choose to repay its debt. Naturally,

---

[16] Formally, the top panel of Figure 14.3 plots the function y^* that satisfies
$V_0(b, y^*(b)) = V_1(y^*(b))$.

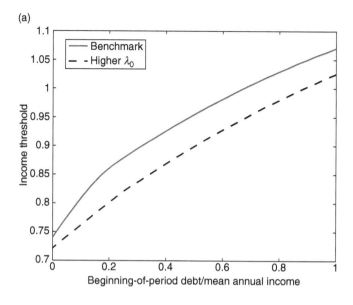

(a)

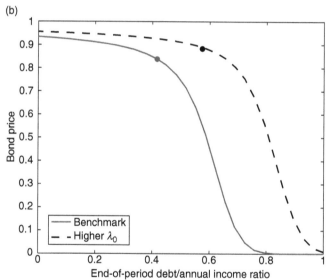

(b)

Figure 14.3: Default regions and bond price menus for different values of λ_0

Note: the top panel presents the income threshold at which the government is indifferent between defaulting and repaying. The government defaults for income levels below this threshold. The bottom panel assumes income is equal to the unconditional mean, and presents the maximum price q lenders would be willing to pay for sovereign bonds. The dashed line assumes $\lambda_0 = 0.23$ ($\lambda_0 = 0.18$ in the benchmark calibration). All other parameter values are the ones in the benchmark calibration. The solid dots in the bottom panel correspond to the optimal choices when the government enters the period with the mean debt level observed in the simulations, for each value of λ_0.

there are states for which the government chooses to default when the cost is lower and chooses not to default when the cost is higher.

The bottom panel of Figure 14.3 presents the bond price function q in a period in which income is equal to its unconditional mean. That is, the panel presents the menu of debt and bond prices available to the government when it chooses the next-period debt level and, in turn, the spread it pays. A higher value of the average cost parameter λ_0 relaxes the government's borrowing constraint. Naturally, since it is more costly for the government to default, for all debt levels, lenders are willing to pay a higher price for sovereign bonds.

The bottom panel of Figure 14.3 also illustrates how the value of the average cost parameter λ_0 has a significant effect on the debt level chosen by the government in the simulations. For each value of λ_0, the panel presents the debt level chosen by the government and the implied bond price when the government enters the period with the mean debt level observed in the simulations. The panel shows that when λ_0 is higher, the government chooses higher debt levels, exploiting the improved borrowing opportunities implied by the higher cost of defaulting.[17] In addition, the panel shows that the debt level chosen by the government when λ_0 is higher implies a higher bond price. This is consistent with the lower spreads in the simulations for higher values of λ_0 presented in Figure 14.1.

Figure 14.4 illustrates how, in comparison with the average cost parameter λ_0, the slope parameter λ_1 has a milder effect on the debt level chosen by the government and a stronger effect on the spread paid by the government. Everything else equal, an increase in the value of the slope parameter λ_1 makes defaulting less costly when income is below the mean and more costly when income is above the mean. This explains the shift of the income threshold at which the government is indifferent between defaulting and repaying depicted in the top panel of Figure 14.4. With a higher value of λ_1, for lower income levels the cost

---

[17] The government is eager to borrow more. In the benchmark calibration (of this and other quantitative studies of sovereign default) the government is assumed to discount the future more than lenders. Therefore, without a borrowing constraint, the government would choose debt levels significantly larger than the ones observed in the data. The inability to commit to repay imposes an endogenous borrowing constraint to the government. Increasing the cost of defaulting relaxes this constraint. Hatchondo, Martinez, and Roch (2015) quantify the increase in borrowing and welfare that would occur if the government could commit to not defaulting in a default model.

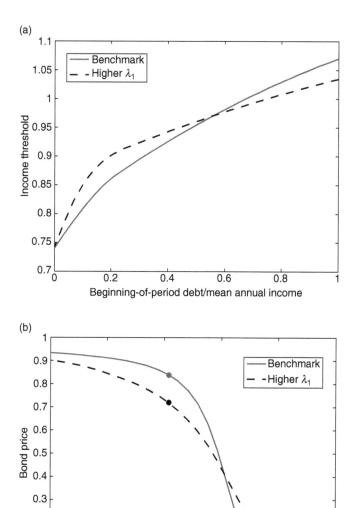

Figure 14.4: Default regions and bond price menus for different values of λ_1

Note: the top panel presents the income threshold at which the government is indifferent between defaulting and repaying. The government defaults for income levels below this threshold. The bottom panel assumes income is equal to the unconditional mean, and presents the maximum price q lenders would be willing to pay for sovereign bonds. The dashed line assumes $\lambda_1 = 2$ ($\lambda_1 = 1.3$ in the benchmark calibration). All other parameter values are the ones in the benchmark calibration. The solid dots in the bottom panel correspond to the optimal choices when the government enters the period with the mean debt level observed in the simulations, for each value of λ_1.

of defaulting is lower and therefore the income threshold (i.e., the maximum income for which the government would choose to default) is higher. Consequently, with a higher value of λ_1, for lower debt levels, the set of income levels for which the government would choose to default is larger (top panel of Figure 14.4). This implies that for these lower debt levels, lenders are willing to pay less for sovereign bonds, as illustrated in the bottom panel of Figure 14.4. In particular, the bottom panel of Figure 14.4 shows that an increase in the value of the slope parameter λ_1 lowers bond prices for the debt levels chosen by the government in the simulations. This is natural because defaults occur in periods of low income and, therefore, the cost of defaulting for low income levels tends to be more relevant for bond prices.[18]

The bottom panel of Figure 14.4 also shows that equilibrium debt levels are very similar for different values of the slope parameter λ_1. However, since with a higher value of λ_1 bond prices are significantly lower, promising to pay the same amount (i.e., the same debt level) allows the government to borrow significantly less.

Overall, the equilibrium choices presented in the bottom panel of Figure 14.4 show that changing the value of the slope parameter λ_1 produces a large effect in the sovereign spread paid in equilibrium (and thus on the bond price), with a mild effect on the debt level. This contrasts with the effect on the equilibrium levels of debt and spread obtained by changing the value of the average cost parameter λ_0, which produces smaller changes in spread and larger changes in debt (bottom panel of Figure 14.3). This illustrates how the value of λ_1 is key for determining the spread level in the simulations and the value of λ_0 is key for determining the debt level in the simulations, which is consistent with the existence of an unique combination of values of these parameters that allows us to match the calibration targets.

8 One-Period Bonds

This section presents results obtained assuming the government can only issue one-period bonds (i.e., $\delta = 1$). The section shows that with one-period bonds, it is impossible to calibrate the parameters that

---

[18] The cost of defaulting for high income levels only becomes relevant for very high debt levels, for which bond prices would be too low (bottom panel of Figure 14.3), implying spread levels inconsistent with those observed in the data.

Mean debt in simulations

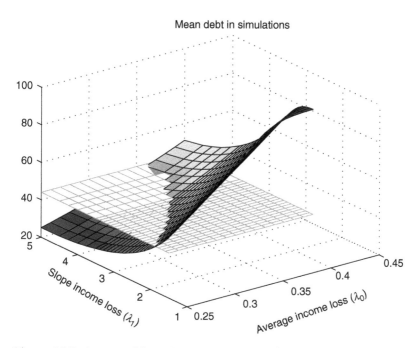

Figure 14.5: Average debt-to-income ratio as a function of income cost parameters

Note: the horizontal planes correspond to the target debt level.

govern the income cost of defaulting to match the levels of debt and spread observed in the data (with our benchmark values for all other parameters).[19] This illustrates the importance of assuming long-term debt and thus introducing debt dilution for the quantitative success of sovereign default models.

Figure 14.5 shows that the model with one-period bonds can replicate the debt level observed in the data and that the relationship between the debt level and the parameters that determine the income cost of defaulting (λ_0, λ_1) is similar to the one observed in the model with long-term debt. However, the top panel of Figure 14.6a shows that

---

[19] Chatterjee and Eyigungor (2012) find that their model with one-period bonds requires an implausible low value for the government's discount factor (β) to match their targets for spread and debt. They also find that parameter values that match their targets with one-period debt lead to severe counterfactual implications in other dimensions such as the relative consumption volatility.

(a)

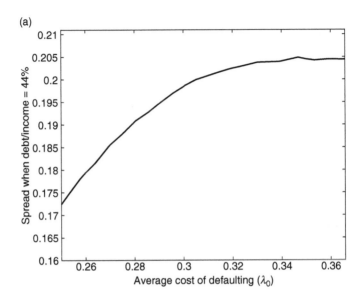

(b)

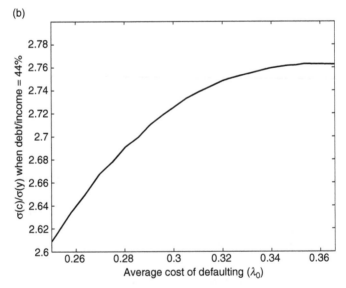

Figure 14.6: Spread and relative consumption-volatility ratio with one-period bonds

Note: panel (a) shows spreads while panel (b) relative consumption-volatility ratios for values of the income cost of defaulting parameters that enable the model with one-period bonds to replicate the ratio of debt to income observed in the data.

for combinations of (λ_0, λ_1) that match the debt target, the average spread is always below 0.21 percent, which is one order of magnitude smaller than the spread observed in Mexico (and other emerging economies). In addition, the bottom panel of Figure 14.6 shows that for these parameter values, the standard deviation of consumption in the simulations is significantly higher than the one observed in the data.

9 Conclusions

We have demonstrated how the income cost of defaulting can be calibrated to match average levels of sovereign debt and spread in a sovereign default framework à la Eaton and Gersovitz (1981) with long-term debt. Furthermore, we have shown how one can expect the combination of parameter values that allow the model to match these targets to be unique. This is because the cost parameter that determines the average fraction of income lost after a default affects the debt level in the simulations more than the spread, while the cost parameter that determines how sensitive that fraction is to the income level affects the spread level more than the debt level. We also showed that, in contrast, it may be impossible for a model with one-period debt to match the average levels of debt and spread in the data.

Bibliography

Adler, G. and Sosa, S. (2013). *External Conditions and Debt Sustainability in Latin* America. IMF Working Paper No. 13/27.

Aguiar, M. and Gopinath, G. (2006). Defaultable debt, interest rates and the current account. *Journal of International Economics*, **69**, 64–83.

   (2007). Emerging markets business cycles: the cycle is the trend. *Journal of Political Economy*, **115**(1), 69–102.

Amador, M. (2012). *Sovereign Debt and the Tragedy of Commons*. Manuscript, Stanford University.

Arellano, C. (2008). Default risk and income fluctuations in emerging economies. *American Economic Review*, **98**(3), 690–712.

Arellano, C. and Ramanarayanan, A. (2012). Default and the maturity structure in sovereign bonds. *Journal of Political Economy*, **120**(2), 187–232.

Azzimonti, M. (2011). Barriers to investment in polarized societies. *American Economic Review*, **101**(5), 2182–204.

Azzimonti, M., Battaglini, M. and Coate, S. (2010). *On the Case for a Balanced Budget Amendment to the US Constitution*. Mimeo, Princeton University.

Bianchi, J., Hatchondo, J. C. and Martinez, L. (2012). *International Reserves and Rollover Risk*. NBER Working Paper No. 18628.

Blanchard, O. (2011). *Rewriting the Macroeconomists' Playbook in the Wake of the Crisis*. IMFdirect, https://blog-imfdirect.imf.org/2011/03/04/2662/

Blanchard, O., Dell'Ariccia, G. and Mauro, P. (2010). *Rethinking Macroeconomic Policy*. IMF Staff Position Note 10/03.

Boz, E. (2011). Sovereign default, private sector creditors, and the IFIs. *Journal of International Economics*, **83**, 70–82.

Chatterjee, S. and Eyigungor, B. (2012) Maturity, indebtedness and default risk. *American Economic Review*, **102**(6), 2674–99.

(2015). A seniority arrangement for sovereign debt. *American Economic Review*, **105**(12), 3740–65.

Claessens, S., Mody, A. and Vallée, S. (2012). *Paths to Eurobonds*. IMF Working Paper No. 12/172.

Cole, H., Dow, J. and English, W. (1995). Default, settlement, and signaling: lending resumption in a reputational model of sovereign debt. *International Economic Review*, **36**(2), 365–85.

Cowan, K., Levy-Yeyati, E., Panizza, U. and Sturzenegger, F. (2006). *Sovereign Debt in the Americas: New Data and Stylized Facts*. Inter-American Development Bank, Working Paper No. #577.

Cruces, J. J., Buscaglia, M. and Alonso, J. (2002). *The Term Structure of Country Risk and Valuation in Emerging Markets*. Manuscript, Universidad Nacional de La Plata.

Cuadra, G. and Sapriza, H. (2008). Sovereign default, interest rates and political uncertainty in emerging markets. *Journal of International Economics*, **76**, 78–88.

D'Erasmo, P. (2008). *Government Reputation and Debt Repayment in Emerging Economies*. Manuscript, University of Texas at Austin.

Dias, D. A. and Richmond, C. (2009). *Duration of Capital Market Exclusion: An Empirical Investigation*. Working Paper, UCLA.

Durdu, C. B., Nunes, R. and Sapriza, H. (2013). News and sovereign default risk in small open economies. *Journal of International Economics*, **91**(1), 1–17.

Eaton, J. and Gersovitz, M. (1981). Debt with potential repudiation: theoretical and empirical analysis. *Review of Economic Studies*, **48**, 289–309.

Ghosh, A. R., Kim, J. I., Mendoza, E. G., Ostry, J. D. and Qureshi, M. S. (2011). *Fiscal Fatigue, Fiscal Space and Debt Sustainability in Advanced Economies*. NBER Working Paper No. 16782.

Halac, M. and Yared, P. (2014). Fiscal rules and discretion under persistent shocks. *Econometrica*, **82**(5), 1557–614.

(2015). *Fiscal Rules and Discretion in a World Economy*. Manuscript, Columbia University.

Hatchondo, J. C. and Martinez, L. (2009). Long-duration bonds and sovereign defaults. *Journal of International Economics*, **79**, 117–25.

(2012). On the benefits of GDP-indexed government debt: lessons from a model of sovereign defaults. *Economic Quarterly*, **98**(2), 139–57.

(2013). Sudden stops, time inconsistency, and the duration of sovereign debt. *International Economic Journal*, **27**(1), 217–28.

Hatchondo, J. C., Martinez, L. and Önder, Y. K. (2017). *Non-Defaultable Debt and Sovereign Risk*. Journal of International Economics, forthcoming. http://dx.doi.org/10.1016/j.jinteco.2017.01.008

Hatchondo, J. C., Martinez, L. and Roch, F. (2015). *Fiscal Rules and the Sovereign Default Premium*. CAEPR Working Paper No. #2015-010.

Hatchondo, J. C., Martinez, L. and Sapriza, H. (2007). Quantitative models of sovereign default and the threat of financial exclusion. *Economic Quarterly*, **93**(3), 251–86.

(2009). Heterogeneous borrowers in quantitative models of sovereign default. *International Economic Review*, **50**, 1129–51.

(2010). Quantitative properties of sovereign default models: solution methods matter. *Review of Economic Dynamics*, **13**(4), 919–33.

Hatchondo, J. C., Martinez, L. and Sosa Padilla, C. (2014). Voluntary sovereign debt exchanges. *Journal of Monetary Economics*, **61**, 32–50.

(2016). Debt dilution and sovereign default risk. *Journal of Political Economy*, **124**(5), 1383–422.

IMF (2013a). *Fiscal Monitor: Fiscal Adjustment in an Uncertain World*. International Monetary Fund, April.

(2013b). *Staff Guidance Note for Public Debt Sustainability Analysis in Market-Access Countries*. Washington: International Monetary Fund.

(2013c). *Staff Guidance Note on the Application of the Joint Bank-Fund Debt Sustainability Framework for Low-Income Countries*. Washington: International Monetary Fund.

(2014). *Reform of the Policy on Public Debt Limits in Fund-Supported Programs*. International Monetary Fund.

Juvenal, L. and Wiseman, K. (2015). *Portugal's Regained Market Access: Opportunities and Risks*. International Monetary Fund, Portugal Selected Issues Papers.

Lizarazo, S. (2012). *Contagion of Financial Crises in Sovereign Debt Markets*. MPRA Paper No. 40623, https://mpra.ub.uni-muenchen.de/40623/2/MPRA_paper_40623.pdf

(2013). Sovereign risk and risk averse international investors. *Journal of International Economics*, **82**(2), 317–30.

Mendoza, E. and Yue, V. (2012). A general equilibrium model of sovereign default and business cycles. *The Quarterly Journal of Economics*, **127**(2), 889–946.

Neumeyer, P. and Perri, F. (2005). Business cycles in emerging economies: the role of interest rates. *Journal of Monetary Economics*, **52**, 345–80.

Reinhart, C., Rogoff, K. S. and Savastano, M. A. (2003). Debt intolerance. *Brookings Papers on Economic Activity*, **34**(1), 1–74.

Reinhart, C. M., Reinhart, V. and Rogoff, K. S. (2015). Dealing with debt. *Journal of International Economics*, **96**, Supplement 1 (July): S43–S55.

Roch, F. and Uhlig, H. (2014). *The Dynamics of Sovereign Debt Crises and Bailouts*. Mimeo, University of Chicago.

Tanner, E. and Samaké, I. (2006). *Probabilistic Sustainability of Public Debt: A Vector Autoregression Approach for Brazil, Mexico, and Turkey*. IMF Working Paper No. 06/295.

Uribe, M. and Yue, V. (2006). Country spreads and emerging countries: who drives whom? *Journal of International Economics*, **69**, 6–36.

Yue, V. (2010). Sovereign default and debt renegotiation. *Journal of International Economics*, **80**(2), 176–87.

PART IV

The Comeback of Discretionary Fiscal Policy

15 | *What Do We Know about Fiscal Multipliers?*

CARLO FAVERO AND MADINA
KARAMYSHEVA

1 Introduction

Fiscal multipliers measure the output effect of fiscal adjustments. This is undoubtedly a controversial issue. Different theoretical models give very different predictions on the magnitude and the sign of the effect of fiscal adjustment on output and other macro variables (see, e.g., Baxter and King, 1993; De Long and Summers, 2012; Christiano et al., 2011). The empirical evidence has produced a plethora of different estimates (see Ramey, 2011b). The fiscal multiplier morass generated by different theoretical specifications has been eminently investigated and remarkably cleared up by Leeper et al. (2015) by tracing differences in estimates of the multipliers to different model specifications. This survey concentrates on the empirical evidence and is aimed at understanding its heterogeneity. We review the available literature by analyzing the design of a relevant empirical experiment that allows the measurement of multipliers.

Our tenet is that the role of empirical analysis of fiscal policy is to establish the evidence relevant to selecting the theoretical model that is capable of matching it. Policy simulation analysis should then be implemented by using the selected relevant model.

It is well understood by now that the validity of experimenting with reduced-form empirical models requires that a number of conditions are satisfied. First, empirical reduced-form models need to be simulated by keeping all parameters constant; in fact, estimated parameters in a reduced-form model might depend on the parameters determining the economic policy rules. Simulating alternative parameterizations of the rules requires a structural model, while simulating deviations from the rules while keeping their systematic component constant makes the empirical evidence robust to the critique of Lucas (1976). However, deviations from the rules must satisfy a number of further conditions

We thank, without implicating them, our discussant, Michal Horváth, and the conference participants for comments and suggestions.

(Ramey 2016) for the investigator to be able to make valid inferences on their effect: (i) they must be exogenous for the estimation of the parameters of interest; (ii) they must be uncorrelated with other relevant structural shocks so that their effect can be assessed by keeping all the other shocks constant and the causal effect of deviations from the rule can be uniquely identified; (iii) they must be unanticipated, because if we want to discriminate among models, we should study responses to unanticipated shocks, for example, when there is a change in the information sets of agents.

We argue that the relevant experiment to measure multipliers is to consider deviation from fiscal rules that come in the form of multi-year corrections: fiscal adjustment plans. Fiscal adjustment plans are a series of multi-period correlated one-period corrections (shocks). They describe closely the way in which deviation from fiscal rules is currently implemented by policy-makers.

Plans consist of the announcement of a sequence of fiscal actions, some to be implemented in the same period of the announcement (unanticipated) and some to be implemented in following periods (announced). Plans are also a mix of measures on government expenditures and revenues. The design of plans generates intertemporal and intratemporal correlations among fiscal variables. The intertemporal correlation is the one between the announced (future) and unanticipated (current) components of a plan. The intratemporal correlation is that between the changes in revenues and spending that determine the composition of a plan.

Traditionally, the empirical fiscal literature concentrates on shocks. Interestingly, plans nest shocks, and taking the perspective of plans will allow us to write down a general empirical model and derive virtually all the different specifications adopted as special cases of this model. The general "nesting" empirical model that we will set out is too heavily parameterized to be estimated empirically, but it is useful in that it allows us to evaluate the different identification and specification strategies adopted in the literature as choices on the relevant dimensions of the empirical models, and therefore to put the heterogeneity of the findings in the empirical evidence in a more general context.

In Section 2 we describe exactly how plans are designed and how the most general empirical model can be constructed. In Section 3 we assess the available literature in terms of the restrictions imposed on such a general model. In Section 4 we shall give an illustration of the relevance of different strategic choices on the measured multipliers. The final section concludes.

2 A General Framework

In this section we build a general framework to describe the empirical evidence on fiscal multipliers. Such a framework is constructed in two steps: the identification of the relevant experiment and the specification of the empirical model to assess its effects.

2.1 The Relevant Experiment: Fiscal Stabilization Plans

The analysis of the output effects of economic policy requires, for the correct estimation of the relevant parameters, identifying policy shifts that are exogenous. If the object of interest is the output effect of fiscal stabilization measures, then exogeneity of the shifts in fiscal policy for the estimation of their output effect requires that they are not correlated with news on output growth.

Fiscal policy is conducted through rare decisions and is typically implemented through multi-year plans: Modeling a standard set of US variables with a medium-scale structural model that allows for foresight up to eight quarters, Schmitt-Grohe and Uribe (2012) find that about 60 percent of the variance of government spending is due to anticipated shocks. A fiscal plan typically contains three components: (i) unexpected shifts in fiscal variables (announced upon implementation at time t); (ii) shifts implemented at time t but announced in previous years; and (iii) shifts announced at time t, to be implemented in future years. Consider, for simplicity, the case in which the forward horizon of the plan is only one year with reference to a specific country i, and assume that corrections exogenous for the estimation of the parameters of interest can be observed. An exogenous plan can be described as follows:

$$f_{i,t} = e^u_{i,t} + e^a_{i,t,0} + e^a_{i,t,1}$$

$$e^u_{i,t} = \tau^u_{i,t} + g^u_{i,t}$$

$$e^a_{i,t+1,0} = e^a_{i,t,1}$$

$$\tau^a_{i,t,1} = \varphi_{1,i}\,\tau^u_{i,t} + v_{1,i,t} \qquad \tau^a_{i,t,1} = \varphi_{2,i}\,g^u_{i,t} + v_{2,i,t}$$

$$g^a_{i,t,1} = \varphi_{3,i}\,\tau^u_{i,t} + v_{3,i,t} \qquad g^a_{i,t,1} = \varphi_{4,i}\,g^u_{i,t} + v_{4,i,t}$$

$$g^u_{i,t} = \varphi_{5,i}\,\tau^u_{i,t} + v_{5,i,t}$$

(1)

Total fiscal corrections in each year consist of increases in taxes and cuts in expenditures. Unexpected shifts in fiscal variables by the fiscal authorities in country i are labeled respectively $\tau^u_{i,t}$ and $g^u_{i,t}$. We define

$\tau^a_{i,t,j}$ and $g^a_{i,t,j}$ as the tax and expenditure changes announced at date t with an anticipation horizon of j years (i.e., to be implemented in year $t+j$). Finally, $\tau^a_{i,t,0}$ ($g^a_{i,t,0}$) denotes the tax (expenditure) changes implemented in year t that had been announced in the previous years. The fiscal plan is completed by making explicit the relation between the predictable and the unpredictable components and the taxation and the expenditure components. The parameters $\varphi_{1,i}$ to $\varphi_{5,i}$ pin down the intratemporal and intertemporal correlations of the different components of the fiscal plan. Note that the framework allows for modifications of an announced measure upon implementation, recording them as an unexpected shift in policy.

2.2 The Empirical Model

Simulation of plans requires that they are embedded in a dynamic model for macroeconomic variables. We consider, for the sake of illustration, an over-parameterized general model that does not have a sufficient number of degrees of freedom to be estimated but nests most of the specification considered in the empirical literature so far. The main purpose of this general model is to make explicit the specification and identification choices adopted by the different authors. Consider modeling the macroeconomic impact of fiscal policy in i countries as follows:

$$
\begin{aligned}
\mathbf{z}_{i,t} = {} & A_{1,i}(L,S_t)\mathbf{z}_{i,t-1} + A_{2,i}(L,S_t)\mathbf{z}^*_{i,t-1} + A_{3,i}(L,S_t)d_{it-1} \\
& + B_1(S_t)\tau^u_{i,t} + B_2(S_t)g^u_{i,t} + C_1(S_t)\tau^a_{i,t,0} + C_2(S_t)g^a_{i,t,0} + \\
& + D_1(S_t)\tau^a_{i,t,1} + D_2(S_t)g^a_{i,t,1} + \mathbf{u}_{i,t}
\end{aligned} \tag{2}
$$

$$
d_{it} = \frac{1+i_{it}}{(1+x_{it})}d_{it-1} + \frac{(g_{it})-(t_{it})}{(y_{it})}
$$

$$
x_{it} \equiv \Delta p_{it} + \Delta y_{it} + \Delta p_{it}\Delta y_{it}
$$

$$
\mathbf{u}_{i,t} \sim N(0,\Sigma_t)
$$

$$
\begin{aligned}
f_{i,t} &= e^u_{i,t} + e^a_{i,t,0} + e^a_{i,t,1} \\
e^u_{i,t} &= \tau^u_{i,t} + g^u_{i,t} \\
e^a_{i,t+1,0} &= e^a_{i,t,1} \\
\tau^a_{i,t,1} &= \varphi_{1,i}\tau^u_{i,t} + v_{1,i,t} \qquad \tau^a_{i,t,1} = \varphi_{2,i}g^u_{i,t} + v_{2,i,t} \\
g^a_{i,t,1} &= \varphi_{3,i}\tau^u_{i,t} + v_{3,i,t} \qquad g^a_{i,t,1} = \varphi_{4,i}g^u_{i,t} + v_{4,i,t} \\
g^u_{i,t} &= \varphi_{5,i}\tau^u_{i,t} + v_{5,i,t}
\end{aligned} \tag{3}
$$

where $z_{i,t}$ is the vector of domestic macro variables that, in order to be able to dynamically simulate (3), must include i_t, the average nominal cost of financing the debt, Δy_t, real GDP growth, Δp_t, inflation, t_t and g_t are, respectively, government revenues and government expenditure net of interest.

From (3) it is immediately obvious that the dynamics of the debt are fully determined at any point in time by the dynamics of a subset of the variables included in the vector $z_{i,t}$, and moreover the relationship between the debt and the variables in $z_{i,t}$ is non-linear.

Several comments on this specification are in order.

(1) The endogenization of the debt–deficit dynamics allows us to check that impulse response functions of diverging paths for fiscal fundamentals are not computed. The explicit inclusion of d_{it} in the dynamic model allows us to pin down explicitly the debt stabilization motive in the fiscal reaction function and the impact of debt in the macro dynamics.

(2) The coefficients in the dynamic macro-model depend on a regime S_t. For example, in a Smooth Transition VAR for $z_{i,t}$, only the regime switch is modeled, as follows:

$$z_t = (1 - F(s_{t-1}))A_1(L, E)z_{t-1} + F(s_{t-1})A_1(L, R)z_{t-1} + u_t$$
$$u_t \sim N(0, \Sigma_t)$$
$$\Sigma_t = \Sigma_E(1 - F(s_{t-1})) + \Sigma_R F(s_{t-1})$$
$$F(s_t) = \frac{\exp(-\gamma s_t)}{1 + \exp(-\gamma s_t)}, \gamma > 0$$
$$var(s_t) = 1, E(s_t) = 0$$

where s_t is an observable (standardized) index of the business cycle.

(3) Foreign variables $z_{i,t}^*$ are allowed to have an impact.

(4) Fiscal plans are modeled as described in the previous section and, for simplicity, the foresight horizon is limited to one period. Exogenous fiscal plans are observable and they are available to the econometricians.

(5) Heteroskedasticity is allowed in the component of fiscal plans and in the model residuals.

(6) The model is non-linear but impulse responses can be computed as the difference between two forecasts:

$$IR(t, s, d_i) = E\left(z_{i,t+s}|v_t = d_i; I_t\right) - E\left(z_{i,t+s}|v_t = 0; I_t\right) \quad s = 0, 1, 2, \ldots$$

Once impulse responses are available, multipliers, as argued by Mountford and Uhlig (2009), Uhlig (2010), and Fisher and Peters (2010), can be calculated as the integral of the output response divided by the integral government adjustment (spending or taxation) response.

3 Empirical Models

The available contributions in the literature can be discussed by classifying them according to the restrictions they impose on the general structure described in the previous section.

3.1 Early SVAR Models

Early studies of the macroeconomic impact on fiscal variables concentrate on shocks by neglecting the intertemporal nature of fiscal plans. The relevant policy shifts are identified with shocks. However, for the correct estimation of the relevant parameters, analysis of the output effects of economic policy requires identifying policy shifts that are exogenous. Exogeneity of the shifts in fiscal policy for the estimation of their output effect requires that they are not correlated with news on output growth. The traditional steps taken to identify such exogenous shifts included, first, estimating a joint dynamic model for the structure of the economy and the variables controlled by the policy-makers (typically estimating a VAR). The residuals in the estimated equation for the policy variables approximate deviations of policy from the rule. Such deviations, however, do not yet measure exogenous shifts in policy, because a part of them represents a reaction to contemporaneous information on the state of the economy. In order to recover structural shocks from VAR innovations, some restrictions are required. So empirical models can be classified via the restrictions they impose on the specification and the identification restrictions.

3.1.1 Traditional SVAR

Blanchard and Perotti (2002) (BP) is the traditional benchmark for the literature on VAR-based investigation of the output effect of fiscal policy.

BP specify the following restricted model to measure fiscal multipliers:

$$\begin{bmatrix} 1 & 0 & -a_{13} \\ 0 & 1 & -a_{23} \\ -a_{31} & -a_{32} & 1 \end{bmatrix} \begin{bmatrix} T_t \\ G_t \\ Y_t \end{bmatrix} = A_1(L) \begin{bmatrix} T_{t-1} \\ G_{t-1} \\ Y_{t-1} \end{bmatrix} + \begin{bmatrix} \sigma^T & b_{12} & 0 \\ b_{21} & \sigma^G & 0 \\ 0 & 0 & \sigma^Y \end{bmatrix} \begin{bmatrix} e_t^T \\ e_t^G \\ e_t^Y \end{bmatrix}$$

where T_t, G_t and Y_t are the log of real quarterly taxes, spending, and GDP, all in real per capita terms. Taxes are net taxes defined as the sum of personal tax and non-tax receipts, corporate profits tax receipts, indirect business tax and non-tax accruals, contributions for social insurance less net transfer payments to persons, and net interest paid by the government. Government spending is defined as purchases of goods and services, both current and capital. Data are quarterly and seasonally adjusted for the period 1947:1 to 1997:4. The e's are non-observable, mutually uncorrelated structural shocks normalized to be of variance 1. However, they can be identified by imposing some restrictions on the a's and the b's. Estimate a reduced-form VAR in the three variables of interest. The VAR residuals u's will be related to the e's as follows:

$$\begin{bmatrix} 1 & 0 & -a_{13} \\ 0 & 1 & -a_{23} \\ -a_{31} & -a_{32} & 1 \end{bmatrix} \begin{bmatrix} u_t^T \\ u_t^G \\ u_t^Y \end{bmatrix} = \begin{bmatrix} \sigma^T & b_{12} & 0 \\ b_{21} & \sigma^G & 0 \\ 0 & 0 & \sigma^Y \end{bmatrix} \begin{bmatrix} e_t^T \\ e_t^G \\ e_t^Y \end{bmatrix}$$

$$A u_t = B e_t$$

from which we can derive the relation between the variance-covariance matrices of u_t (observed) and e_t (unobserved) as follows:

$$E(u_t u_t') = A^{-1} B E(e_t e_t') B' A^{-1}$$
$$= A^{-1} B B' A^{-1} = CC' = \Sigma$$

Substituting population moments with sample moments, we have:

$$\widehat{\Sigma} = \widehat{A}^{-1} \widehat{B} \widehat{IB}' \widehat{A}^{-1} \tag{4}$$

where $\widehat{\Sigma}$ contains $n(n+1)/2$ different elements (where n is the dimension of the VAR), which is the maximum number of identifiable parameters in matrices A and B. Therefore, a necessary condition for identification of the structural shocks is that the maximum number of parameters contained in the two matrices equals $n(n+1)/2$, such a condition making the number of equations equal to the number of unknowns in the system. As usual, for such a condition also to be sufficient for identification, no equation in (4) should be a linear combination of the other equations in the system.

As there are nine parameters in the BP model, at least three identifying restrictions are needed. First, BP rely on institutional information about tax, transfer, and spending programs to restrict the parameters a_{13} and a_{23}. These coefficients, in quarterly data, are assumed to be exclusively driven by the automatic effects of economic activity on taxes and spending and are restricted to the output elasticities of government purchases and net taxes. Using information on the features of the spending and tax and transfer systems, BP set $a_{13} = 2.08, a_{23} = 0$.[1] The last restrictions are obtained by considering two alternative scenarios, $b_{12} = 0$ and $b_{21} = 0$, that are observed to have a negligible impact on the final results.

The identification restrictions are combined with the specification restrictions on the general model. Namely, only one country is considered (US); the vector of variables $z_{US,t}$ consists only of three variables; constant parameters are assumed $A_{1,US}(L, S_t) = A_{1,US}(L)$, no foreign variables enter the specification $A_{2,US}(L, S_t) = 0$; there is no explicit debt feedback $A_{3,US}(L, S_t) = 0$; and the debt dynamics are not modeled, plans are not introduced, and shocks are a combination of announced, unanticipated, and anticipated corrections which are restricted to have the same effect

$$B_1(S_t) = C_1(S_t) = D_1(S_t) = B_1, B_2(S_t) = C_2(S_t) = D_2(S_t) = B_2.$$

Impulse responses are then computed and multipliers calculated by first multiplying the estimates by the sample mean of government spending and net taxes to GDP ratios, and then comparing the peak output response to the initial government spending or tax impact effect. Note that this is different from computing the integral multipliers described in the previous section.

Two sets of empirical results are reported, generated respectively by allowing for stochastic trends (ST) (and specifying the model in first differences) or by considering a specification in level with deterministic trends (DT). The tax multiplier is around one (-1.33 in the case of a ST against -0.78 under DT) and is similar in size to the spending multiplier (0.90 in the ST case against 1.29 under DT). Some evidence

---

[1] Caldara (2011) shows that the sensitivity of estimated multipliers to changes in these elasticities can be very large.

of subsample instability emerges. Follow-up work, such as that by Fatás and Mihov (2001), Perotti (2005), and Gali, Lopez-Salido, and Valles (2007), found similar results.

The BP specification is very restrictive: The set of variables considered is very limited, the model does not allow for debt feedback and tracking of the debt dynamics, and identified shocks are a convolution of unanticipated, anticipated, and announced corrections. The first set of restrictions have not been extensively debated in the literature; the second set can be rationalized by considering that the debt dynamics in the United States have never deviated from stability, and therefore the model can be thought of as including a linearized version of the identity driving the debt dynamics. However, Leeper (2010) stresses the importance of avoiding analyses of "unsustainable fiscal policies" and of making sure that the question "What is the fiscal multiplier" is not asked along a path for the debt dynamics that is at odds with the beliefs of government bond-holders.

As a matter of fact, the restriction that has elicited most debate is the one which implies that identified shocks to government spending and taxation are anticipated. Ramey (2011a, b) argues that distinguishing between announced and unanticipated shifts in fiscal variables, and allowing them to have different effects on output, is crucial for evaluating fiscal multipliers. Leeper et al. (2013) illustrate explicitly that fiscal foresight makes the number of shocks to be mapped out of the VAR innovations too high to achieve identification: Technically, the moving average representation of the VAR becomes non-invertible (see also Lippi and Reichlin, 1994).

3.1.2 SVAR with Sign Restrictions
Mountford and Uhlig (2009) (MU) apply to the analysis of fiscal policy the methodology originally introduced by Uhlig (2005) to identify monetary policy shocks. MU represents the VAR of interest as follows:

$$\mathbf{z}_t = \sum_{i=1}^{p} \mathbf{A}_i \mathbf{z}_{t-i} + \mathbf{u}_t$$

$$\mathbf{u}_t = \mathbf{C}\mathbf{e}_t$$

$$\Sigma = \mathbf{C}E\left(\mathbf{e}_t\mathbf{e}_t'\right)\mathbf{C}' = \mathbf{C}\mathbf{C}'$$

Consider now C as the Cholesky decomposition of Σ.

The impulse response function, given the Cholesky decomposition, could be written as:

$$z_t = [I - A(L)]^{-1} C e_t$$

All the possible rotations of the Cholesky decomposition are obtained as follows:

$$[I - A(L)]^{-1} C Q Q' e_t$$

$$Q Q' = I$$

The impulse response for $Q' e_t$, is then $[I - A(L)^{-1}] C Q$.

The imposition of the sign restrictions then considers Q to generate all possible identification and then select only those that satisfy some restriction on their sign.

The vector y_t contains many more variables than the corresponding one in BP; in fact, Mountford and Uhlig specify a VAR in GDP, private consumption, total government expenditure, total government revenue, real wages, private non-residential investment, interest rate, adjusted reserves, the producer price index for crude materials, and the GDP deflator. These ten variables are considered at a quarterly frequency from 1955 to 2000. The VAR has six lags, no constant or time trend, and uses the logarithm for all variables except the interest rate, which is specified in levels. The definition of the two fiscal variables is the same with BP. Sign restrictions are used to identify shocks of interest: (i) a business cycle shock is defined as a shock which jointly moves output, consumption, non-residential investment, and government revenue in the same direction for four quarters following the shock;[2] (ii) a monetary policy shock, which is taken to be orthogonal to the business cycle shock, moves interest rates up and reserves and prices down for four quarters after the shock; and iii) fiscal policy shocks are orthogonal to business cycle and monetary policy shocks, and government spending shocks and government revenue shocks are identified by a positive response of the corresponding variables; responses are restricted to be delayed (to take into account fiscal foresight) and permanent (to rule out temporary fiscal adjustment).

---

[2] Note that this restriction implies that when output and government revenues move in the same direction, this must be due to some improvement in the business cycle generating the increase in government revenue, not the other way around.

If we interpret MU in terms of our general model, they take a closed-economy, constant-parameters approach; they restrict $B_1 = B_2 = 0$,; they do not track separately the responses upon announcement and upon implementation; and they impose the restrictions that all the φ parameters are positive except those determining the cross correlation between revenue and expenditure adjustments, which are set to zero.

The tax multiplier (deficit-financed tax cuts) is almost three times larger than that computed by BP and stands at 3.57 (with a peak effect after thirteen quarters), while the deficit-spending multiplier is slightly lower than that of BP as it stands at 0.65 (with a peak effect upon impact). Interestingly, by combining their two base fiscal policy shocks in a linear fashion, MU also analyze the effect of a balanced budget tax cut. Comparing these three scenarios, they find that a surprise deficit-financed tax cut is the best fiscal policy to stimulate the economy, giving rise to a maximal present value multiplier of five dollars of total additional GDP per each dollar of the total cut in government revenue five years after the shock.

3.1.3 Expectational VARs

Expectational VARs try and solve the problems posed by fiscal foresight and endogeneity by constructing an instrument for fiscal corrections using information outside the VAR. Ramey and Shapiro (1998) use narrative techniques to create a dummy variable capturing military buildups. *Business Week* is used as a source to isolate political events leading to buildups exogenous to the current state of the economy; the narrative approach is also used to make sure that the relevant shocks were unanticipated. The effect of the "war dates" is measured by estimating single equations for each variable of interest, including current value and lags of the war dates and lags of the left-hand-side variable.

To understand this approach, consider the structural representation of a constant-parameter, closed-economy first-order VAR:

$$\mathbf{A}\mathbf{z}_t = \mathbf{C}\mathbf{z}_{t-1} + \mathbf{B}\mathbf{e}_t. \tag{5}$$

The MA representation of (5) is

$$\mathbf{z}_t = \Gamma(L)\mathbf{e}_t \tag{6}$$

where $\Gamma(L) \equiv \frac{\mathbf{A}^{-1}\mathbf{B}}{\mathbf{I}-\mathbf{A}^{-1}\mathbf{C}}$. The MA representation is not directly estimated in the VAR, but it can be derived by inversion, after having estimated (5).

We re-write (6) as follows

$$z_t = \sum_{j=1}^{M} \Gamma_0^j \Gamma_1 e_{t-j} + \Gamma_1^{M+1} z_{t-(M+1)}$$

$$\Gamma_0 \equiv A^{-1}B, \Gamma_1 \equiv A^{-1}C.$$

and extract from the above system the equation for a variable of interest, say output growth,

$$\Delta y_t = \sum_{j=0}^{M} \gamma_j^{y,t} e_{t-j}^t + \sum_{j=0}^{M} \gamma_j^{y,g} e_{t-j}^g + \sum_{i=1}^{k} \sum_{j=0}^{M} \gamma_j^{y,i} e_{t-j}^i$$

$$+ \Gamma_1^{M+1} z_{t-(M+1)} \tag{7}$$

where

$$\gamma_j^{y,x} = s^x \Gamma_0 \Gamma_1^i s^{t'} \quad x = t, g, x^1, \dots x^k$$

$$s^g = \begin{bmatrix} 1 & 0 & 0 & 0 & 0 \end{bmatrix}, s^t = \begin{bmatrix} 0 & 1 & 0 & 0 & 0 \end{bmatrix}$$

$$s^k = \begin{bmatrix} 0 & 0 & \dots & \underset{2+k}{1} & \dots 0 \end{bmatrix}$$

Consider now the relation between the true unobservable expenditure shocks and the narrative instrument

$$e_t^g = e_t^{WAR} + \varepsilon_t$$

$$\varepsilon_t \sim i.i.d. (0, \sigma_\varepsilon^2) \tag{8}$$

that is, assume that the difference between the expenditure shocks in the VAR and those identified via the narrative method is some error ε_t. This assumption has a number of testable implications, in particular that e_t^{WAR} should be orthogonal to all the lags of all the variables included in the VAR.

We can now write

$$\Delta y_t = \sum_{j=0}^{M} \gamma_j^{y,g} e_{t-j}^{WAR} + \sum_{j=0}^{M} \gamma_j^{y,g} \varepsilon_{t-j}$$

$$+ \sum_{j=0}^{M} \gamma_j^{y,t} e_{t-j}^t + \sum_{i=1}^{k} \sum_{j=0}^{M} \gamma_j^{y,i} e_{t-j}^i$$

$$+ \Gamma_1^{M+1} z_{t-(M+1)} \tag{9}$$

(9) makes clear that the limited information approach adopted by Ramey and Shapiro in which the variable of interest is regressed on a distributed lag of the instrument and lags of the left-hand side variables can be interpreted as a simplified version of (9) that omits variables that are thought of as orthogonal to the regressors (i.e., the distributed lags of other shocks and the measurement error). Within this framework of interpretation there is a potential problem related to the omission of lags M+1 and longer of all the other variables in the dynamic system. This omission is less problematic the more the system is stationary, and the inclusion of lags of the dependent variable might be thought of as a way of swamping this effect.

To overcome the limited information approach, a number of follow-up papers (Edelberg, Eichenbaum, and Fisher, 1999; Burnside, Eichenbaum, and Fisher, 2004; Cavallo, 2005) embedded e_t^{WAR} in a VAR by ordering them first in a Cholesky decomposition. Fisher and Peters (2010) created an alternative forward-looking series of news based on the excess returns of defense contractor shocks for the period starting in 1958. These applications typically found government spending with a multiplier in the range of 0.6–1.5 and therefore slightly higher than that of BP, but comparable, especially after taking into account the effect of fiscal foresight in BP-type models. Ramey (2011a) showed that the shocks from an SVAR were predictable by e_t^{WAR}. After correcting for this effect, the obtained impulse responses become more similar. Barro and Redlick (2011) also use military buildups as an instrument for defense spending, but additionally include in the specification a measure for marginal tax rate and allow for non-linearities making the effects of revenue and expenditure shocks a function of unemployment. Their estimated multiplier for defense spending is 0.6–0.7 at the median unemployment rate (while holding fixed average marginal income tax rates), rising in unemployment to reach 1 when the unemployment rate is around 12 percent. Increases in the average marginal income tax rates have a significantly negative effect on GDP with an implied magnitude of the multiplier of 1.1.

3.2 Narrative Measures

Romer and Romer (2010) (R&R) proceed to non-econometric, direct identification of the shifts in fiscal variables. These are then plugged directly into an econometric specification capable of delivering the

Figure 15.1: Long-run and deficit-driven tax changes in the United States, 1945–2007

impulse response functions that describe the output effect of fiscal adjustments. In this "narrative" identification scheme, a time-series of exogenous shifts in taxes or government is constructed using parliamentary reports and similar documents to identify the size, timing, and principal motivation for all major fiscal policy actions. Legislated tax changes are classified by R&R into *endogenous*, for their estimation of their output effect (induced by short-run countercyclical concerns), and *exogenous* (responses to an inherited budget deficit or to concerns about long-run economic growth, or politically motivated responses). R&R construct time-series for the United States considering quarterly observation over the period 1945–2007. An interesting fact about the two types of exogenous tax changes is evident from Figure 15.1 reported by R&R: The deficit-driven tax changes are almost exclusively positive (episodes of fiscal expansion motivated by inherited surplus are virtually non-existent), while all the long-run tax changes are negative (i.e., expansionary).

If the perspective of plans is adopted to interpret the R&R narrative identification, we can classify their tax shocks as the sum of corrections announced at time t and immediately implemented (therefore unanticipated) and corrections announced at time t to be implemented in future periods:

$$\tau_t^{RR} = \tau_t^u + \tau_{t,1}^a$$

The effect of tax shocks is then measured by running the following single equation specification.

$$\Delta \ln Y_t = \alpha + B(L)\tau_t^{RR} + \varepsilon_t \tag{10}$$

So a truncated constant-parameter, single-country MA representation is adopted, where only the exogenous components of tax adjustments is considered, with the restrictions that unanticipated and announced corrections have the same effect and announced corrections have no impact upon implementation. The resulting evidence is that tax increases are highly contractionary: A tax increase of 1 percent of GDP has a cumulative effect of a reduction of output over the next three years of nearly 3 percent.

The narrative approach has been extended to the United Kingdom case by Cloyne (2013), who constructs a new narrative data-set of legislated tax changes in the United Kingdom to apply the R&R empirical approach and finds that a 1 percentage point cut in taxes as a proportion of GDP causes a 0.6 percent increase in GDP on impact, rising to a 2.5 percent increase over nearly three years.

Devries et al. (2011) (DV) extend the narrative approach to a multi-country sample that identifies episodes for seventeen OECD countries between 1978 and 2009. These authors concentrate on deficit-driven corrections to revenue and expenditure that are not compensated by long-run corrections. Adopting the perspective of plans, the Devries et al. corrections are constructed by adding together two components: unexpected shifts in fiscal variables occurring in year t (i.e. announced when they are implemented), e_t^u, and shifts in fiscal variables which also occur in year t but had been announced in previous years, $e_{i,t,0}^a$

$$e_{i,t}^{DV} = e_{i,t}^u + e_{i,t,0}^a$$
$$e_{i,t}^u = \tau_{i,t}^u + g_{i,t}^u$$
$$e_{i,t,0}^a = \tau_{i,t,0}^a + g_{i,t,0}^a$$

Guajardo et al. (2014) have used these data to estimate fiscal multipliers using constant-parameters panel data techniques on the international sample (and therefore by imposing the restrictions $A_{1,i} = A_1, A_{2,i} = A_{3,i} = 0, B_1 = C_1, B_2 = C_2, D_1 = D_2 = 0$). In practice, in their baseline specification, they estimate the following panel version of the single equation model adopted by R&R:

$$\Delta z_{i,t} = \alpha + A_1(L)\Delta z_{i,t-1} + B_1(L)e_{i,t}^{DV} + \lambda_i + \chi_t + u_{i,t}$$

where λ_i denotes country fixed-effect and χ_t denote year fixed effects.

They estimate that the effect of a fiscal consolidation of 1 percent of GDP has a contractionary effect on GDP with a peak effect of -0.62 percent within two years (t-stat $= -3.82$).

3.2.1 The Government Intertemporal Budget Constraint

Leeper (2010, p. 362) states clearly that "Fiscal policy will shed its alchemy label when the question 'What is the fiscal multiplier?' is no longer asked and detailed analyses of 'unsustainable fiscal policies' are no longer conducted without explicit analysis of expectations and dynamic adjustments."

The traditional VAR literature takes sustainability for granted and interprets the estimated VAR as a linearized model around a stable debt/GDP path. Chung and Leeper (2007) impose this equilibrium condition on an identified VAR and characterize the way in which the present value support of debt varies across various types of fiscal policy shocks and between fiscal and non-fiscal shocks. Favero and Giavazzi (2012) propose an extension of the standard VAR model augmented with observable narrative tax adjustments, e_t^{RR}, capable of explicitly tracking the dynamics of debt/GDP in response to fiscal shocks.

The following empirical specification is introduced for estimating tax multipliers:

$$\mathbf{z}_t = \sum_{i=1}^{k} \mathbf{C}_i \mathbf{z}_{t-i} + \delta e_t^{RR} + \gamma(d_{t-1} - d^*) + \mathbf{u}_t$$

$$d_t = \frac{1 + i_t}{(1 + \Delta p_t)(1 + \Delta y_t)} d_{t-1} + \frac{\exp(g_t) - \exp(t_t)}{\exp(y_t)} \qquad (11)$$

$$\mathbf{z}_t' = \begin{bmatrix} i_t & y_t & \Delta p_t & t_t & g_t \end{bmatrix}$$

where $\mathbf{z}_t$ includes the five variables present in a fiscal VAR. Debt is explicitly introduced in the VAR. The estimated model on US data never delivers "unsustainable debt paths" and the model augmented with debt and the non-linear debt dynamics equation produces results which are very similar to those obtained by including the R&R shocks in a traditional fiscal VAR. US data are drawn from a sustainable fiscal regime: Within this regime it is likely that the feedback between fiscal variables and the (linearized) debt dynamics is captured in a linear VAR specification that includes all the variables that enter into the debt–deficit relationship. Nevertheless, having the possibility of checking that fiscal multipliers are computed along a sustainable path is an important step, which might become relevant for countries other than the United States.

Corsetti, Meier, and Mueller (2012) analyze the effects of an increase in government spending under a plausible debt-stabilizing policy that links current stimulus to a subsequent period of spending restraint. They show that accounting for such spending reversals is of crucial importance to bring the standard New Keynesian model in line with the stylized facts of fiscal transmission.

3.2.2 External Instrument SVARs

Mertens and Ravn (2013, 2014) propose considering the series based on the narrative evidence as a noisy measure of the true unobservable fiscal shock. They identify exogenous tax changes in a VAR model by proxying latent tax shocks with narratively identified tax liability changes.

Given a VAR in n variables, consider again the relationship between the variance covariance of the observed VAR innovations u_t and the unobserved structural shocks e_t:

$$Au_t = Be_t$$
$$E(u_t u_t') = A^{-1}BE(e_t e_t')B'A^{-1}$$
$$= A^{-1}BB'A^{-1} = CC' = \Sigma$$

Substituting population moments with sample moments, we have:

$$\widehat{\Sigma} = \widehat{A}^{-1}\widehat{B}IB'\widehat{A}^{-1}, \tag{12}$$

$\widehat{\Sigma}$ contains $n(n+1)/2$ different elements (where n is the dimension of the VAR), which is the maximum number of identifiable parameters in matrices A and B.

Consider now the availability of a vector m_t of $k \times 1$ observable proxy variables that are correlated with the k structural shocks of interest e_{1t} and orthogonal to the other $n-k$ shocks e_{2t} (where $e_t' = [e_{1t}', e_{2t}']$). The proxy variables have zero mean and satisfy two conditions:

$$E(m_t e'_{1t}) = \Phi, E(m_t e'_{2t}) = 0 \tag{13}$$

where Φ is an unknown nonsingular $k \times k$ matrix.

Consider the following partitioning of C

$$C = \begin{bmatrix} C_1 & C_2 \\ n \times k & n \times (n-k) \end{bmatrix}$$

$$C_1 = \begin{bmatrix} C'_{11} & C'_{21} \\ k \times k & k \times (n-k) \end{bmatrix}$$

$$C_2 = \begin{bmatrix} C'_{12} & C'_{22} \\ (n-k) \times k & (n-k) \times (n-k) \end{bmatrix}$$

with nonsingular C_{11} and C_{22}. Conditions (13), together with the relation between structural shocks and VAR innovations, imply that

$$\Phi C'_1 = \Sigma_{mu'} \tag{14}$$

This system, which is of dimension $n \times k$, provides additional identifying restrictions, but it also depends on the k^2 unknown elements of Φ. If one is not prepared to make any further assumptions on Φ other than nonsingularity, Equation (14) really provides only $(n - k)k$ new identification restrictions. Partitioning $\Sigma_{mu'} = [\Sigma_{mu'_1} \Sigma_{mu'_2}]$, where $\Sigma_{mu'_1}$ is $k \times k$ and $\Sigma_{mu'_2}$ is $k \times (n - k)$ and using (14), these restrictions can be expressed as

$$C_{21} = \left(\Sigma_{mu'_1}^{-1} \Sigma_{mu'_2} \right)' C_{11} \tag{15}$$

which is a viable set of covariance restrictions, as $\left(\Sigma_{mu'_1}^{-1} \Sigma_{mu'_2} \right)$ can be estimated.

In practice, estimation can proceed in three stages:

- Estimate the reduced-form VAR by least squares.
- Estimate $\left(\Sigma_{mu'_1}^{-1} \Sigma_{mu'_2} \right)$ from regression of VAR residuals on m_t.
- Impose (15) and estimate the objects of interest, if necessary in combination with further identifying assumptions.

Mertens and Ravn (2014) apply this methodology to the standard BP VAR to reconcile the apparently different size of multipliers obtained in BP and R&R, while Mertens and Ravn (2013) discriminate between the effects of changes in average personal income tax rates and the effects of changes in average corporate income tax rates to find that unanticipated changes in either tax rate produce large short-run effects on aggregate output. Moreover, tax revenue falls in response to cuts in personal income taxes, while on average the corporate income tax cuts have a minor impact on tax revenues.

3.2.3 The Average Treatment Effect of Fiscal Policy

Jordà and Taylor (2013) (JT) reinterpret fiscal multipliers in the logic of the measurement of treatment effects.

Consider a very simplified version of our general model which includes the narratively identified fiscal correction episodes:

$$z_t = Az_{t-1} + \beta_1 e_t^{DV} + \epsilon_t$$

The MA if the VAR truncated at lag h is

$$z_{t+h} = A^{h+1} z_{t-1} + A^h \beta_1 e_t^{DV} + v_{t+h}$$

$$v_{t+h} = \beta_1 e_{t+h}^{DV} + \ldots + A^{h-1} \beta_1 e_{t+1}^{DV} +$$

$$+ \epsilon_{t+h} + A\epsilon_{t+h-1} + \ldots A^h \epsilon_t$$

The impulse response describing the effect of the fiscal correction on the variable of interest, say output growth, is then

$$E\big(y_{t+h} - y_t | e_t^{DV} = 1, I_t\big) - E\big(y_{t+h} - y_t | e_t^{DV} = 0, I_t\big)$$

$$= \sum_{i=0}^{h} \frac{\partial \Delta y_{t+i}}{\partial e_t^{DV}} = \sum_{i=0}^{h} e^y A^i \beta_1$$

where e^y is a selector vector that extracts output growth for the vector of variables z_t This impulse response can be obtained via a series of h regressions by applying the Linear Projection (LP) method introduced by Jordà (2005):

$$y_{t+h} = \pi'_h z_{t-1} + \theta^h e_t^{DV} + v_{t+h}$$

In practice the conditioning set z_{t-1} can be augmented in LP, as LP is based on a single equation estimation (after the identification of the shocks) and more degrees of freedom are available:

$$y_{t+h} = \gamma'_h w_{t-1} + \theta^h e_t^{DV} + v_{t+h}$$

Note also that the LP method also can easily accommodate non-linear impulse responses. The comparison of the LP regression with the full truncated MA representation makes clear that LP omits all structural shocks between time t and time $t + h$. This omitted variables problem would not lead to inconsistent estimates of the parameters of $A^h \beta_1$ ($p \lim \widehat{H}_h = A^h \beta_1$) only if e_t^{DV} were orthogonal to all omitted variables, or if $\mathbf{w}_{t-1}$ captures the relevant variation in all omitted variables.

The use of LPM to derive IR and multipliers leads naturally to interpreting the effect of fiscal policy as the effect of a treatment. In fact, the average policy effect on a variable y_t at horizon $t + h$ can be written as

$$E\big[(y_{t+h}(d_j) - y_t) - (y_{t+h}(d_0) - y_t)|w_t\big] = \theta^h$$

where d_j is the policy intervention. Jordà and Taylor note that if the fiscal corrections are to be considered as a treatment, then it is crucial that the policy intervention is not predictable to avoid a standard allocation bias problem. As a matter of fact, e_t^{DV} are predictable by their own past, and by past values of debt dynamics (see also Hernandez da Cos and Moral-Benito, 2011). To solve this problem, JT propose to apply LP method after having purged the fiscal actions from predictability. They proceed as follows:

(1) redefine e_t^{DV} innovations as a 0/1 dummy variable;
(2) estimate a *propensity score* deriving the probability with which a correction is expected by regressing it on its own past and predictors;
(3) use the propensity score to derive an Average Treatment Effect (ATE) based on Inverse Probability Weighting.

Denote the policy propensity score $p^j(w, \psi)$ *for* $j = 1, 0$ (the predicted values from a probit projections of the policy indicator on the set of predictors w).

$$\theta^h = E\big[(y_{t+h}(d_1) - y_t) - (y_{t+h}(d_0) - y_t)|w_t\big]$$

$$= E\left[(y_{t+h} - y_t)\left(\frac{1\{D_t = d_1\}}{p^1(w, \psi)} - \frac{1\{D_t = d_0\}}{1 - p^1(w, \psi)}\right)|w_t\right]$$

$$\widehat{\theta}^h = \frac{1}{T}\sum(y_{t+h} - y_t)\widehat{\delta}_t$$

$$\widehat{\delta}_t = \frac{1\{D_t = d_1\}}{\widehat{p}^1(w, \psi)} - \frac{1\{D_t = d_0\}}{1 - \widehat{p}^1(w, \psi)}$$

In the LP framework ATE can be combined with LP in the following LP-IWPRA estimator

$$\widehat{\theta}^{b} = \frac{1}{T}\sum\left[\left(y_{t,b} - y_t\right)\widehat{\delta}_t - \widehat{\phi}_t m\left(w_t, \gamma^b\right)\right]$$

$$\widehat{\phi}t = \frac{1\{D_t = d_1\} - \widehat{p}^1(w, \psi)}{\widehat{p}^1(w, \psi)} - \frac{1\{D_t = d_0\} - (1 - \widehat{p}^1(w, \psi))}{1 - \widehat{p}^1(w, \psi)}$$

where $m(w_t, \gamma^b)$ is the mean of $\left(y_{t,b} - y_t\right)$ predicted by the LP.

By applying the corrected estimator they find an average treatment effect of fiscal consolidation which is not very different from the one estimated by Devries et al., with a peak effect in year 5 after the consolidation that is slightly larger than -1, and a cumulative effect after five years at about -3.

To understand this evidence, two remarks are in order. First, exogeneity in dynamic time-series models is different from predictability. The correct estimation of the effects on output of a fiscal adjustment within our specification requires the use of exogenous fiscal shocks, that is, shocks that cannot be predicted from past output growth. Predictability from past shocks or other variables not directly related to output growth is irrelevant to determine the required exogeneity status. This requirement is satisfied by the original DV shocks. It is no longer satisfied, however, if one transforms those continuous shocks into a 0/1 dummy variable. The reason, as a simple regression shows, is that transformation into a 0/1 dummy, and the loss of information it implies, introduces correlation with past output growth. Notice that the exogeneity required to estimate fiscal multipliers within a dynamic model is different from deriving the effect of a treatment randomly assigned: What matters in our model is weak exogeneity for the estimation of the parameters of interest rather than the random assignment of a treatment.

As a matter of fact, the DV corrections can be predicted from past debt dynamics and from their past history by construction. They are predictable by debt dynamics as they are defined as shifts in fiscal policy, motivated by the objective of stabilizing or reducing the debt ratio. Predictability in this sense is not inconsistent with exogeneity with respect to past output growth: For this reason Romer and Romer (2010), for instance, include tax shocks motivated by the objective of stabilizing or reducing the debt among their exogenous (for the estimation of the output effect of fiscal policy) shocks.

They are predictable from their past, as these corrections are built adding together two components: Unexpected shifts in fiscal variables occurring in year t (i.e. announced when they are implemented), e_t^u, and shifts in fiscal variables which also occur in year t but had been announced in previous years, $e_{t,0}^a$. Dropping the country index,

$$e_t^{DV} = e_t^u + e_{t,0}^a.$$

Based on this definition, the fact that the e_t^{DV} are correlated across time is not surprising.

A fiscal plan is specified by making explicit the relation between e_t^u, $e_{t,0}^a$ and the fiscal corrections announced in year t for years $t+i$ ($i > 1$). Therefore

$$e_{t,1}^a = \varphi e_t^u + v_t \tag{16}$$

$$e_{t+1,0}^a = e_{t+1}^a \tag{17}$$

The first equation describes the style with which fiscal policy is implemented. Plans along which shifts in fiscal variables are persistent will feature a positive value of φ, while temporary plans (i.e., plans along which fiscal actions are reversed, at least partially in the future) feature a negative φ. The second relationship simply states that the announced correction implemented at time t is equal to the correction that had been announced in the previous period with a fiscal foresight of one period.

Then

$$Cov\left(e_t^{DV}, e_{t-1}^{DV}\right) = Cov\left(\left(e_t^u + e_{t,0}^a\right), \left(e_{t-1}^u + e_{t-1,0}^a\right)\right)$$
$$= \varphi Var\left(e_{t-1}^u\right)$$

as

$$e_{t,0}^a = e_{t-1,1}^a = \varphi e_{t-1}^u + v_{t-1}$$

However, in a dynamic time-series model, the requirement for valid estimation and simulation are respectively weak and strong exogeneity, which are different from predictability.

To illustrate the point, consider the following simplified example:

$$\Delta y_t = \beta_0 + \beta_1 e_t^{DV} + u_{1t}$$

$$e_t^{DV} = \rho e_{t-1}^{DV} + u_{2t}$$

$$\begin{pmatrix} u_{1t} \\ u_{2t} \end{pmatrix} \sim N \left[\begin{pmatrix} 0 \\ 0 \end{pmatrix}, \begin{pmatrix} \sigma_{11} & \sigma_{12} \\ \sigma_{12} & \sigma_{22} \end{pmatrix} \right]$$

The condition required for e_t^{DV} to be weakly exogenous for the estimation of β_1 is $\sigma_{12} = 0$, which is independent of ρ. When weak exogeneity is satisfied the existence of predictability does not have any effect on the consistency of the estimate of β_1. Of course, neglecting the existence of predictability of e_t^{DV} under simulation might lead to the consideration of scenarios that were never observed in the data, and therefore to unreliable results.

3.2.4 Fiscal Plans

A natural alternative approach to deal with the predictability of the e_t^{DV} corrections is to specify a dynamic specification for the variable of interests and the fiscal plans.

Mertens and Ravn (2011) take a first step in this direction by studying the different effects of announced and unanticipated adjustments, but they do so without modeling the interdependence between these two components.

Alesina, Favero, and Giavazzi (2014; AFG) use the fiscal consolidation episodes identified by Devries et al. (2011), but propose a methodological innovation. They start from the observation that the shifts in taxes and spending that contribute to a fiscal adjustment almost never happen in isolation: They are typically part of a multi-year plan, in which some policies are announced well in advance while others are implemented unexpectedly and, importantly, both tax hikes and spending cuts are used simultaneously. Also, as these plans unfold, they are often revised, and these changes have to be taken into account as they constitute new information available to economic agents. AFG stress the importance of modeling the connections between changes in taxes and expenditures, and between unanticipated and announced changes. In practice, they consider a restricted version of the general model in which a quasi-panel is estimated allowing for two types of heterogeneity: within-country heterogeneity in the effects of Tax-Based (TB) and Expenditure-Based (EB) plans, and between-country heterogeneity in the style of a plan

$$\Delta z_{i,t} = \alpha + B_1(L)e_{i,t}^u * TB_{i,t} + B_2(L)e_{i,t}^u * EB_{i,t}$$
$$+ C_1(L)e_{i,t,0}^a * TB_{i,t} + C_2(L)e_{i,t,0}^a * EB_{i,t} +$$
$$+ \sum_{j=1}^{3} \gamma_j e_{i,t,j}^a * EB_{i,t} + \sum_{j=1}^{3} \delta_j e_{i,t,j}^a * TB_{i,t} + \lambda_i + \chi_t + u_{i,t}$$

(18)

$$e_{i,t,1}^a = \varphi_{1,i}e_{i,t}^u + v_{1,i,t}$$

$$e_{i,t,2}^a = \varphi_{2,i}e_{i,t}^u + v_{2,i,t}$$

$$e_{i,t,3}^a = \varphi_{3,i}e_{i,t}^u + v_{3,i,t}$$

$$e_{i,t,0}^a = e_{i,t-1,1}^a$$

$$e_{i,t,j}^a = e_{i,t-1,j+1}^a + \left(e_{i,t,j}^a - e_{i,t-1,j-1}^a\right) j \geqslant 1$$

$$\text{if} \left(\tau_t^u + \tau_{t,0}^a + \sum_{j=1}^{horiz} \tau_{t,j}^a\right) > \left(g_t^u + g_{t,0}^a + \sum_{j=1}^{horiz} g_{t,j}^a\right)$$

then $TB_t = 1$ *and* $EB_t = 0,$

else $TB_t = 0$ *and* $EB_t = 1, \forall t$

where λ_i and χ_t are country and time fixed effects. A moving average representation for the variable of interest $\Delta z_{i,t}$ is considered in (18) with no debt feedback and constant parameters. Cross-country restrictions on the B, C, and γ coefficients are imposed, but within- and between-country heterogeneity is allowed for: "Within" because responses of $\Delta z_{i,t}$ to fiscal adjustments will be different for TB and EB plans; "between" because they will also differ across countries as the $\varphi's$ differ, according to each country's specific style. The dynamic effect of fiscal adjustment plans is different across countries because of the different styles of fiscal policy (as captured by the different φ) and within countries as a consequence of the heterogenous effects of plans as determined by their composition. The moving average representation is truncated because the length of the $B(L)$ and $C(L)$ polynomials is limited to three years. The moving average representation is specified to allow for different effects of unanticipated and anticipated adjustments. Shifts in fiscal policy affect the economy through three components: First, unanticipated changes in fiscal stance, $e_{i,t}^u$, announced at time t and implemented at time t; second, the implementation at time t of policy shifts that had been announced in the past, $e_{i,t,0}^a$; third, the anticipation of future changes in fiscal policy, announced at time t, to be implemented at a future date, $e^a_{i,t,j}$ for $j = 1, 2, 3$. Also, different coefficients are allowed for adjustment announced in the past and implemented at time t and adjustments announced at time t for the future. To avoid double counting, lags of future of $e^a_{i,t,j}$ are excluded, as their dynamic effect is captured by $e^a_{i,t+j,0}$. The parameters φ_i, are estimated on a country-by-country basis on the time-series of the narrative fiscal shocks. Note that introducing total adjustment with different labeling (TB or EB) rather than introducing it separately in the specification adjustments in revenue and in expenditure allows a much more parsimonious parameterization of the dynamic system defining the style of fiscal plans, making estimation viable.

The system is put to work by AFG to simulate the effect of TB and EB average plans on macroeconomic variables. Simulation of fiscal plans adopted by sixteen OECD countries over a thirty-year period supports the hypothesis that the effects of consolidations depend on their design. Fiscal adjustments based upon spending cuts are found to be much less costly, in terms of output losses, than tax-based ones and have especially low output costs when they consist of permanent rather than stop-and-go changes in taxes and spending. The difference between tax-based and spending-based adjustments appears not to be explained by accompanying policies, including monetary policy. It is mainly due to the different response of business confidence and private investment.

Alesina et al. (2014) use the system to perform out-of-sample simulations of the austerity plans adopted by different countries over the period 2009–2013. Model projections of output growth conditional only upon the fiscal plans implemented since 2009 do reasonably well in predicting the total output fluctuations of the countries in our sample over the years 2010–2013 and are also capable of explaining some of the cross-country heterogeneity in this variable.

3.3 Non-Linearities

Non-linearities in fiscal multipliers are investigated in a number of papers.

Corsetti, Meier, and Mueller (2012b) study the determinants of government spending multipliers by investigating how the fiscal transmission mechanism depends on three dimensions of economic environment: the exchange rate regime; the level of public debt and deficit; and

the presence of a financial crisis. The analysis is implemented on
annual data for seventeen OECD countries within a sample period
1975–2008. A two-step approach is considered. In the first step the
fiscal policy rule, which links government spending and macroeconomic variables, is identified and estimated. The parameters in fiscal
policy rules are country-specific and fiscal policy shocks are identified
as the innovations in the rules. In a second step, fixed-effects panel
regressions are estimated to trace the impact of the estimated government spending shocks on the relevant macroeconomic aggregates
(output, private consumption, investment, trade balance, and real
effective exchange rate). To study non-linearities, interaction terms of
shocks with dummies capturing the exchange rate regime, the state of
public finances, and the presence of financial crisis are included in the
regression. The estimated system can be represented as follows:

$$g_{t,i} = \phi_i + \eta_i trend_i + \beta_{i,1}g_{t-1,i} + \beta_{i,2}g_{t-2,i} + \gamma_{i,1}y_{t-1,i} + \gamma_{i,2}y_{t-2,i}$$

$$+ \theta_i cli_{t-1,i} + \delta_i b_{t-1,i} + \rho_{i,1}peg_{t-1,i} + \rho_{i,2}strain_{t,i}$$

$$+ \rho_{i,3}crisis_{t-1,i} + \varepsilon_{t,i}$$

$$z_{t,i} = \alpha_i + \mu_i trend_t + \chi_i z_{t-1,i} + \sigma_1\widehat{\varepsilon}_{t,i} + \sigma_2\widehat{\varepsilon}_{t-1,i} + \sigma_3\widehat{\varepsilon}_{t-2,i} + \sigma_4\widehat{\varepsilon}_{t-3,i}$$

$$+ \kappa_1\left(\widehat{\varepsilon}_{t,i}*d_{t,i}\right) + \kappa_2\left(\widehat{\varepsilon}_{t-1,i}*d_{t-1,i}\right) + \kappa_3\left(\widehat{\varepsilon}_{t-2,i}*d_{t-2,i}\right)$$

$$+ \kappa_4\left(\widehat{\varepsilon}_{t-3,i}*d_{t-3,i}\right) + \lambda_1 d_{t,i} + \lambda_2 d_{t-1,i} + \lambda_3 d_{t-2,i} + \lambda_4 d_{t-3,i} + u_{t,i}$$

where $g_{t,i}$ is government spending variable, $y_{t-1,i}, y_{t-2,i}$ – lags of log
per capita output, $cli_{t-1,i}$ lag of a composite leading indicator which
measures the expectation with respect to next-year growth, $b_{t-1,i}$ debt-
to-GDP ratio, $peg_{t-1,i}$ a dummy for an exchange rate, $strain_{t,i}$ – a
dummy for strained public finances, and $crisis_{t-1,i}$ a financial crisis
dummy. $\varepsilon_{t,i}$ – is a fiscal policy shock which measures discretionary
policy change. The methodology does not allow us to disentangle
unanticipated corrections from those announced and implemented;
furthermore, it is assumed that innovations in the projections of gover-
ment spending on past information are orthogonal to deviations of all
other macroecononomic variables (including government revenues)
from their projections. $z_{t,i}$ – is the macroeconomic variable of interest,
$\widehat{\varepsilon}_{t,i}$ is an estimated fiscal shock from the first stage, and $d_{t,i}$ – is a
dummy for specific economic conditions in the particular year.

Importantly, σ parameters measure the baseline dynamic effect of the spending shocks, while κ measures additional marginal effects.

Corsetti, Meier, and Mueller (2012b) use a multi-country economy model; however, $A_{2,i}(L, S_t) = 0$, since foreign variables are not allowed to have an impact. $z_{t,i}$ is not a vector of variables of interest, but it denotes one variable of interest at a time (output, private consumption, private fixed investment, trade balance, the real effective exchange rate, CPI inflation, the short-term nominal interest rate, and government spending itself). There is no debt feedback $A_{3,i}(L, S_t) = 0$. A debt dynamic is also absent in the model. The model does not uses plans, but relies instead on general spending shocks identified by imposing some (strong) restrcitions in the first-stage regression. There are three sources of non-linearities: exchange rate regimes, the state of public finances, and the state of the economy.

Baseline results feature persistency in government spending shocks and a sizeable response of aggregate output by about 0.7 percentage points. Under-the-currency peg multipliers are positive: Impact and maximum is 0.6. Weak public finance produces negative multipliers: Impact is −0.7, maximum 0.2, and cumulative after two years −1.2. The most quantitatively relevant results are for the case of financial crisis: The response of output to a public spending increase is strongly positive, implying a fiscal multiplier of 2.3 for impact and 2.9 for maximum.

Auerbach and Gorodnichenko (2012) make an attempt to assess how the size of fiscal multipliers varies over the cycle by estimating regime-switching SVAR models, with smooth transitions across the relevant states of the economy (i.e., recession versus expansion).

The basic adopted specification is:

$$z_t = (1 - F(s_{t-1}))A_1(L, E)z_{t-1} + F(s_{t-1})A_1(L, R)z_{t-1} + u_t$$

$$u_t \sim N(0, \Sigma_t)$$

$$\Sigma_t = \Sigma_E(1 - F(s_{t-1})) + \Sigma_R F(s_{t-1})$$

$$F(s_t) = \frac{\exp(-\gamma s_t)}{1 + \exp(-\gamma s_t)}, \gamma > 0$$

$$var(s_t) = 1, E(s_t) = 0$$

where $z_t = [G_t, T_t, Y_t]$, following Blanchard and Perotti (2002): G_t is government purchases; T_t government receipts of direct and indirect taxes net of transfers to businesses and individuals; and Y_t gross domestic product. All variables are in logs and are deflated. Estimation uses quarterly data. Structural shocks are identified from VAR innovations by assuming lower triangularity in the matrix that maps shocks into innovations. Importantly, the model allows for contemporaneous differences in the propagation of structural shocks as well as dynamic ones. The first goes through Σ_E and Σ_R, while the second goes through $A_1(L, E)$ and $A_1(L, R)$. s_t is an index, normalized to have mean of 0 and variance of 1, indicating recessions if s is negative and expansion if s is positive. Auerbach and Gorodnichenko (2012) set s_t to a seven-quarter moving average of the output growth rate. γ is calibrated to 1.5, which means that the economy spends around 20 percent of the time in recession, $Pr(F(s_t) > 0.8) = 0.2$, under the assumption that $\gamma > 0$, $A_1(L, E)$ and Σ_E characterizes the economy in expansion and $A_1(L, R)$ and Σ_R – in recession.

In the single-country, closed-economy model of Auerbach and Gorodnichenko (2012), the vector z_t consists of three variables, G_t, T_t, Y_t, and there are two states of the economy: expansion, where $A_1(L, S_t) = A_1(L, E)$ and $\Sigma_t = \Sigma_E(1 - F(s_{t-1}))$ with $F(s_{t-1}) = 0$, versus recession $A_1(L, S_t) = A_1(L, R)$ and $\Sigma_t = \Sigma_R F(s_{t-1})$ with $F(s_{t-1}) = 1$. There is no debt feedback $A_{3, US}(L, S_t) = 0$. The model does not uses plans, but relies instead on shocks restricting announced, unanticipated, and anticipated corrections to have the same effect $B_1(S_t) = C_1(S_t) = D_1(S_t) = B_1(S_t), B_2(S_t) = C_2(S_t) = D_2(S_t) = B_2(S_t)$. As an alternative to the basic model, a more advanced specification is considered. This specification includes professional forecasts of the relevant variable in the vector $z_t = \left[\Delta G_{t,t-1}^{Forecast}, \Delta T_{t,t-1}^{Forecast}, \Delta Y_{t,t-1}^{Forecast}, G_t, T_t, Y_t\right]$.

Because of non-linearities, the estimation as well as the inference is implemented using the Markov Chain Monte Carlo method with Metropolis–Hastings algorithm, where the parameter estimates and confidence intervals are computed directly from the generated chains. Computed multipliers are interpreted as indicating by how many dollars output increases over time if government expenditure increases by \$1. The size of the shock is chosen in such a way that the integral of government spending response over twenty quarters is equal to one.

Baseline results show that in all cases – linear, expansion, and recession – the impact output multiplier is around 0.5 in response to a spending increase of \$1. However, after twenty quarters under the recession regime the multiplier is 2.5 and under the expansion regime the multiplier is -1. The average multiplier under the recession regime is 2.24 and under the expansion regime -0.33. Fiscal policy is considerably more effective in recessions than in expansions. This evidence refers to polar cases, as the initial regime is maintained constant in the computation of impulse responses: the policy innovation cannot cause a shift in s_t.

Ramey, Owyang, and Zubairy (2013) remove this restriction by computing regime-dependent multipliers using the Linear Projections (LP) method of Jordà (2005). In LP non-linearities are easily accommodated and there is no need to impose the restriction that shock does not affect the state of the economy. A state-dependent model is estimated in which impulse responses and multipliers depend on the average dynamics of the economy in each state. These authors address the question of the relevance of non-linearities by analyzing new quarterly historical US data covering multiple large wars and deep recessions. Different from previous studies, they do not find higher multipliers during times of slack in the United States.

Ramey and Zubairy (2014) extend the investigation to consider the effect of two potentially important features of the economy: (i) the amount of slack and (ii) whether interest rates are near the zero lower bound. The main findings indicate no evidence that multipliers are different across states, whether defined by the amount of slack in the economy or by whether interest rates are near the zero lower bound.

Caggiano et al. (2015) also estimate non-linear VARs and address fiscal foresight by appealing to sums of revisions of fiscal expenditure expectations. Their results, based on generalized impulse responses that allow feedback from the simulated policy to the probability of the economy being in expansion and recession, suggest that fiscal spending multipliers in recessions are greater than one, but not statistically larger than those in expansions. However, non-linearities arise when focusing on "extreme" events, that is, deep recessions versus strong expansionary periods.

3.4 Quasi-Natural Experiments and Descriptive Evidence

All the literature that we have discussed so far can be considered as specific cases of our general "encompassing" model. However, there are exceptions that can be described as "case studies" since they do not specify a dynamic model. Such studies are best interpreted as focusing on some direct measure of the causal effect of fiscal policy on output growth.

Acconcia, Corsetti, and Simonelli (2013) exploit the introduction of a law issued to fight political corruption and Mafia infiltration of city councils in Italy that has caused episodes of large, temporary, and unanticipated fiscal contractions that are arguably exogenous for the estimation of their effect on output. Using these episodes as instruments, while controlling for national monetary and fiscal policy and keeping the tax burden of local residents constant, the output multiplier of spending cuts at provincial level is estimated in the range 1.2–1.8.

Alesina and Ardagna (2010), adopting an approach introduced by Giavazzi and Pagano (1990), consider a case study of large changes in fiscal policy stance, namely large increases or reductions of budget deficits, and analyze their effects on both the economy and the dynamics of the debt. In particular, they concentrate on episodes of major changes in fiscal policy. They use a panel of twenty OECD countries with annual data over the sample period 1970–2007. Fiscal variables are cyclically adjusted, computed in period t as a predicted value from a regression of the fiscal policy variable (as a share of GDP) on a constant, a time trend and the unemployment rate, where the unemployment rate at time t is kept at the value observed in time $t-1$. A period of fiscal adjustment (stimulus) is a year in which the cyclically adjusted primary balance improves (deteriorates) by at least 1.5 percent of GDP.

Focusing on these episodes and using mainly descriptive evidence, they find that tax cuts are more expansionary than spending increases in the case of a fiscal stimulus, and fiscal adjustments based upon spending cuts and no tax increases are more likely to reduce deficits and debt over GDP ratios than those based upon tax increases. Finally, adjustments on the spending side rather than on the tax side are less likely to create recessions.

The two very different approaches adopted by Acconcia et al. (2013) and Alesina and Ardagna (2010) have in common the direct analysis of episodes without the specification of a dynamic macro-model. The case of the exogeneity of the chosen episodes for the measurement of the relevant phenomenon is certainly much stronger in Acconcia et al. (2013). In fact, Guajardo et al. (2014) argue convincingly that changes in cyclically adjusted fiscal variables often include non-policy changes correlated with other developments affecting economic activity. For the sake of illustration, they consider a boom in the stock market. Such a boom creates a cyclically adjusted surplus by increasing capital gains and cyclically adjusted tax revenues. This surplus can be associated with an increase in consumption and investment generated by the stock market boom. The resulting measurement error is likely to bias the analysis toward downplaying contractionary effects of fiscal consolidations.

However, even if the exogeneity of the episodes considered by Acconcia et al. (2013) is clearly robust to this type of consideration, the question of how the results produced in the case studies can be extended to the measurement of fiscal multipliers in the presence of different dynamics, initial conditions, and heterogeneity in the mechanism of expectation formation remains unsolved.

4 The Impact of Different Identification and Specification Strategies: An Illustration

To illustrate the relevance of different specification choices, we consider quarterly US data over the period 1978:1–2012:4 and compare the BP SVAR approach with a dynamic model of fiscal adjustment plans. We use National Income and Product Accounts (NIPA) variables described in the Appendix. To be as close as possible to Blanchard and Perotti (2002), we use their definitions of the variables.[3]

The BP specification is as follows:

$$
\begin{bmatrix} 1 & 0 & -2.08 \\ 0 & 1 & 0 \\ -a_{31} & -a_{32} & 1 \end{bmatrix} \begin{bmatrix} T_t \\ G_t \\ Y_t \end{bmatrix} = A_1(L) \begin{bmatrix} T_{t-1} \\ G_{t-1} \\ Y_{t-1} \end{bmatrix} + \begin{bmatrix} \sigma^T & 0 & 0 \\ b_{21} & \sigma^G & 0 \\ 0 & 0 & \sigma^Y \end{bmatrix} \begin{bmatrix} e_t^T \\ e_t^G \\ e_t^Y \end{bmatrix}
$$

where $[T_t, G_t, Y_t]$ is a vector of quarterly taxes, spending, and output. All variables are in the logarithms and in real, per capita, terms.

---

[3] From NIPA tables: Output is nominal GDP (NIPA 1.1.5.1); government spending is General Government consumption expenditures and gross investment (NIPA 1.1.5.21); total tax revenue is General Government Current receipts (NIPA 3.1.1) less General Government Current Transfers to persons (NIPA 3.1.21) less General Government Interest Payments to persons (NIPA 3.1.25) plus General Government Income receipts on assets (NIPA 3.1.8). All series are deflated by GDP deflator (NIPA 1.1.9.1) and by FRED Population (Midperiod, Thousands, Quarterly, and Seasonally Adjusted Annual Rate).

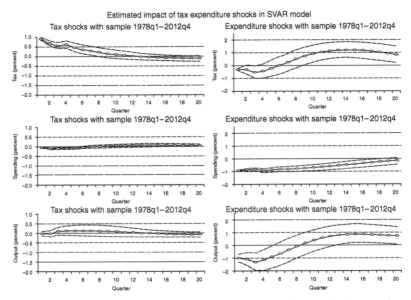

Figure 15.2: Estimated impact of tax and expenditure shocks in the SVAR model

$\mathbf{e}_t = \begin{bmatrix} e_t^T, e_t^g, e_t^y \end{bmatrix}$ are structural shocks, orthogonal to each other. $A_1(L)$ is a lag polynomial with the length of four quarters. Following Blanchard and Perotti (2002), we include constant, linear, and quadratic trends in the model. The sample period is 1978q1–2012q4. Since our sample starts with the first quarter of 1978, we do not need to include a dummy variable for the second quarter of 1975 as in Blanchard and Perotti (2002). BP identifying restrictions are imposed on the matrices relating the unobserved structural shocks to the VAR innovations.

Results are reported in the form of impulse response functions. Note that a unit shock to the structural innovations of taxes transforms into less than a unit change in the reduced-form tax residuals, because output falls in response to the tax increase, and in turn tax revenue falls. Figure 15.2 reports impulse responses where impulse response of output has an interpretation of the tax (expenditure) multipliers, that is, dollar changes in GDP as a ratio of the dollar changes in tax revenues (expenditure). Following BP, multipliers are obtained by expressing impulse responses as shares of average GDP with initial impulse normalized to 1 percent of average GDP. Unless we mention otherwise, we provide confidence intervals of one standard deviation that are computed using a bootstrap algorithm with 1,000 replications. The solid line gives the point estimates, while the dotted lines are confidence bounds.

The BP model produces a response of output that is insignificant and close to zero in response to the 1 percent of structural tax shock. There is a negative response of output in the short run and a positive response of output in the long run in response to a 1 percent cut of structural expenditure innovations.

We compare this impulse response with those obtained from a truncated MA in a model with plans. Plans for quarterly data are reconstructed for the United States on the basis of Devries et al. (2011). In the wording of R&R, we consider only deficit-driven plans, and we adopt the following empirical model to assess their effects:

$$\Delta y_t = \alpha + B_1(L)\left(\tau_t^u + g_t^u\right) * TB_t + B_2(L)\left(\tau_{t,t}^a + g_{t,t}^a\right) * TB_t +$$
$$+ C_1(L)\left(\tau_t^u + g_t^u\right) * EB_t + C_2(L)\left(\tau_{t,t}^a + g_{t,t}^a\right) * EB_t +$$
$$+ \sum_{i=1}^{horz} D_i \left(\tau_{t,t+i}^a + g_{t,t+i}^a\right) * TB_t + \sum_{i=1}^{horz} E_i\left(\tau_{t,t+i}^a + g_{t,t+i}^a\right) * EB_t + \mathbf{u}_t$$

$$\mathbf{u}_t \sim N(0, \Sigma)$$

$$\left(\tau_{t,t+i}^a + g_{t,t+i}^a\right) * TB_t = \delta_i^{TB}\left(\tau_t^u + g_t^u\right) * TB_t + v_{t+i}^1, for\ i = \overline{1, horz}$$

$$\left(\tau_{t,t+i}^a + g_{t,t+i}^a\right) * EB_t = \delta_i^{EB}\left(\tau_t^u + g_t^u\right) * EB_t + v_{t+i}^2, for\ i = \overline{1, horz}$$

$$(19)$$

Δy_t is the growth rate of GDP (quantity index for real GDP, data source National Income and Product Accounts (NIPA), Table 1.1.3).

The specification generalizes the MA adopted by Romer and Romer by allowing different coefficients on the unanticipated expenditure, g_t^u, and revenue, τ_t^u adjustments (announced at time t and implemented at time t), on the anticipated correction currently implemented (announced before time t, and implemented at time t) $\tau_{t,t}^a, g_{t,t}^a$, and on the future corrections (announced at time t, to be implemented in the future), $\tau_{t,t+i}^a, g_{t,t+i}^a$. The length of the polynomials $B_1(L), B_2(L), C_1(L), C_2(L)$ is set to 6. The anticipating horizon is set by considering the median implementation lag, which is again six quarters. The MA representation is then augmented by a number of auxiliary equations that capture the nature of the plan via the

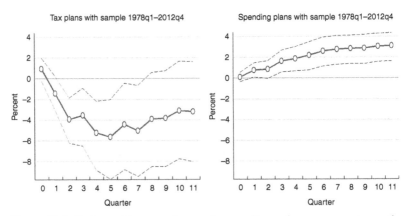

Figure 15.3: Estimated impact of tax and expenditure plans on output growth in the MA model

correlation between the intertemporal and intratemporal components of fiscal adjustments.

EB_t and TB_t are dummies that label plans into expenditure-based or tax-based according to the larger present value of the types of correction.

Results are in the form of the impulse response functions, which are obtained by forward simulation of the model. Since our dependent variable is in differences, we report cumulative impulse response functions. The length of the IRF is limited to the number of lags included in the system. One-standard-deviation confidence intervals are built by bootstrap with 1,000 replications. We use block bootstrap to take into account potential serial correlation in residuals, restricting the length of the block to two. Working with the quarterly data, we give a shock of 1 percent to the total plan. To do so we shock the unanticipated component of the TB plan (-0.58 percent), and the unanticipated component of the EB plan (-0.79 percent). Sample period is from 1978q1 to 2012q4. Figure 15.3 shows the responses of output growth to the TB and EB plans.

A positive shock to the tax-based plan produces a significantly negative effect on the output growth, while the shock to the expenditure-based plan gives a marginally significant exapnsionary effect. These results are very different from those obtained by applying the BP method on the same data-set, with the difference being generated by different identification and specification strategies.

5 What Have We Learned?

This paper represents an attempt to answer the question "what do we know about fiscal multipliers?" by setting up a general "encompassing" model that is flexible enough to consider all the different empirical specifications adopted in the literature as specific cases that can be derived by imposing a set of restrictions on the general model. This framework allows us to take into account two crucial remarks about the empirical analysis of fiscal policy made by Ramey (2016) and Leeper (2010). First, the measurement of fiscal multipliers is a question for which dynamics are all-important, general equilibrium effects are crucial, and expectations have powerful effects. Second, multipliers depend on the type of spending or tax change, as well as on a host of other factors: Expected sources and timing of future fiscal financing; whether the initial change in policy was anticipated or not; how monetary policy behaves; what is the state of the cycle when the policy is implemented. There is no such thing as a unique fiscal multiplier and the evidence obtained by a specific investigation on the multiplier can be understood only within a general dynamic framework which clearly indicates the specification and identification choices made in that investigation.

Bibliography

Acconcia, A., Corsetti, G. and Simonelli, S. (2013). Mafia and public spending: evidence on the fiscal multiplier from a quasi-experiment. *American Economic Review*, **104**(7), 2185–209.

Alesina, A. and Ardagna, S. (2010). Large changes in fiscal policy: taxes versus spending. *Tax Policy and the Economy*, **24**, 35–68.

Alesina, A. and Perotti, R. (1997). The welfare state and competitiveness. *American Economic Review*, **87**, 347–66.

Alesina, A., Ardagna, S., Perotti, R. and Schiantarelli, F. (2002). Fiscal policy, profits and investment. *American Economic Review*, **92**(3), 571–89.

Alesina, A., Barbiero, O., Favero, C. , Giavazzi, F. and Paradisi, M. (2014). *Austerity in 2009–2013*. Paper prepared for 60th panel meeting of Economic Policy, October 2014.

Alesina, A., Favero, C., and Giavazzi, F. (2015). The output effects of fiscal stabilization plans. *Journal of International Economics*, **96**(1), S19–S42.

Auerbach, A. and Gorodnichenko, Y. (2012). Measuring the output responses to fiscal policy. *American Economic Journal: Economic Policy*, 4(2), 1–27.

Bachmann, R. and Sims, E. (2011). *Confidence and the Transmission of Government Spending Shocks*. NBER Working Paper No. 17063, National Bureau of Economic Research, Inc.

Barro, R. J. and Redlick, C. J. (2011). Macroeconomic effects from government purchases and taxes. *The Quarterly Journal of Economics*, 126(1), 51–102.

Ben Zeev, N. and Pappa, E. (2014). *Chronicle of a War Foretold: The Macroeconomic Effects of Anticipated Defense Spending Shocks*. Mimeo, European University Institute.

Baxter, M. and King, R. G. (1993). Fiscal policy in general equilibrium. *American Economic Review*, 83(3), 315–34.

Blanchard, O. and Perotti, R. (2002). An empirical characterization of the dynamic effects of changes in government spending and taxes on output. *Quarterly Journal of Economics*, 117(4), 1329–68.

Blanchard, O. and Leigh, D. (2013). *Growth Forecast Errors and Fiscal Multipliers*. IMF Working Paper No. 13/1. Washington, DC: International Monetary Fund.

Beetsma, R., Cimadomo, J., Fortuna, O. Giuliodori, M. (2015). *The Confidence Effects of Fiscal Consolidations*. ECB Working Paper No. 1770, March 2015.

Bloom, N. (2009). The impact of uncertainty shocks. *Econometrica*, 77(3), 623–85.

Burnside, C., Eichenbaum, M. and Fisher, J. D. M. (2004). Fiscal shocks and their consequences. *Journal of Economic Theory*, 115(1), 89–117.

Caggiano, G., Castelnuovo, E., Colombo, V. and Nodari, G. (2015). Estimating fiscal multipliers: news from a non-linear world. *The Economic Journal*, 125, 746–76.

Caldara, D. (2011). *The Analytics of SVARs: A Unified Framework to Measure Fiscal Multipliers*. IIES Working Paper, http://citeseerx.ist.psu .edu/viewdoc/download?doi=10.1.1.190.4182&rep=rep1&type=pdf.

Cavallo, M. (2005). *Government Employment Expenditure and the Effects of Fiscal Policy Shocks*. Federal Reserve Bank of San Francisco Working Paper No. 2005-16.

Christiano, L. J., Eichenbaum, M. and Evans, C. L. (1998). *Monetary Policy Shocks: What Have We Learned and to What End?* NBER Working Paper No. 6400.

Christiano, L.J., Eichenbaum, M. and Rebelo, S. (2011). When is the government spending multiplier large? *Journal of Political Economy*, 119 (1), 78–121.

Chung, H. and Leeper, E. M. (2007). *What Has Financed Government Debt?* NBER Working Paper No. W12345.

Cloyne, J. (2013). Discretionary tax changes and the macroeconomy: new narrative evidence from the United Kingdom. *The American Economic Review*, **103**(4): 1507–28.

Corsetti, G., Meier, A. and Mueller, G. (2012a). Fiscal stimulus with spending reversals. *The Review of Economics and Statistics*, **94**(4), 878–95.

(2012b). What determines government spending multipliers. *Economic Policy, CEPR;CES;MSH*, **27**(72), 523–64.

de Cos, P. H. and Mora, E. (2012). *Fiscal Consolidations and Economic Growth*. Working Paper, Banco de Espana.

DeLong, J. B. and Summers, L. H. (2012). *Fiscal Policy in a Depressed Economy*. Working Paper.

Drautzburg, T. and Uhlig, H. (2015). Fiscal stimulus and distortionary taxation. *Review of Economic Dynamics*, **18**(4), 894–920.

Dell'Erba, S., Mattina, T. and Roitman, A. (2013). *Pressure or Prudence? Tales of Market Pressure and Fiscal Adjustment*. IMF Working Paper No. 13/170. Washington, DC: International Monetary Fund.

Devries, P., Guajardo, J., Leigh, D. and Pescatori, A. (2011). *A New Action-Based Dataset of Fiscal Consolidations*. IMF Working Paper No. 11/128. Washington, DC: International Monetary Fund.

Edelberg, W., Eichenbaum, M. and Fisher, J. D. M. (1999). Understanding the effects of a shock to government purchases. *Review of Economic Dynamics*, **2**(1), 166–206.

Eggertsson, G. B. (2010). What fiscal policy is effective at zero interest rates? In D. Acemoglu and M. Woodford, eds., *NBER Macroeconomic Annual*. Chicago: Chicago University Press, 59–112.

Eggertsson, G. B. and Krugman, P. (2012). Debt, deleveraging, and the liquidity trap. *Quarterly Journal of Economics*, **127**(3), 1469–513.

Fatás, A. and Mihov, I. (2001). *The Effects of Fiscal Policy on Consumption and Employment: Theory and Evidence*. Mimeo, INSEAD.

Favero, C. and Giavazzi, F. (2012). Measuring tax multipliers: the narrative method in fiscal VARs. *American Economic Journal: Economic Policy*, **4**(2), 69–94.

Favero, C., Giavazzi, F. and Perego, J. (2011). Country heterogeneity and the international evidence on the effects of fiscal policy. *IMF Economic Review*, **59**(4), 652–82.

Fisher, Jonas D. M. and Peters, R. (2010). Using stock returns to identify government spending shocks. *The Economic Journal*, **120** (May), 414–36.

Gal, J., López-Salido, J. D. and Vallés, J. (2007). Understanding the effects of government spending on consumption. *Journal of the European Economic Association*, 5(1), 227–70.

Garratt, A., Lee, K., Pesaran, M. H. and Shin, Y. (2012). *Global and National Macroeconometric Modelling: A Long-Run Structural Approach*. Oxford: Oxford University Press.

Giavazzi, F. and Pagano, M. (1990). Can severe fiscal contractions be expansionary? Tales of two small European countries. *NBER Chapters in NBER Macroeconomics Annual*, 5, 75–122.

Giavazzi, F. and McMahon, M. (2013). The household effects of government spending. In A. Alesina and F. Giavazzi, eds., *Fiscal Policy after the Financial Crisis*. Chicago and London: University of Chicago Press and NBER.

Guajardo, Jaime, Leigh, D. and Pescatori, A. (2014). Expansionary austerity? International evidence. *Journal of the European Economic Association*, 12(4), 949–68.

Hernandez da Cos, P. and Moral-Benito, E. (2011). *Endogenous Fiscal Consolidations*. Working Paper No. 1102, Banco de Espana.

Jalil, A. (2012). *Comparing Tax and Spending Multipliers: It Is All About Controlling for Monetary Policy*. Mimeo, Dept of Economics, Reed College.

Leeper, E. M. (2010). *Monetary Science, Fiscal Alchemy*. Proceedings – Economic Policy Symposium – Jackson Hole, Federal Reserve Bank of Kansas City, pp. 361–434.

Leeper, E. M., Walker, T. B. and Yang, S.-C. (2013). Fiscal foresight and information flows. *Econometrica*, 81(3), 1115–45.

Leeper, E. M., Traum, N. and Walker, T. (2015). *Clearing Up the Fiscal Multiplier Morass*, www4.ncsu.edu/~njtraum/LTW_FMM.pdf

Lippi, M. and Reichlin, L. (1994). VAR analysis, non fundamental representations, Blaschke matrices. *Journal of Econometrics*, 63(1), 307–25.

Lucas, R. (1976). Econometric policy evaluation: a critique. In K. Brunner and A. Meltzer, eds., *The Phillips Curve and Labor Markets*. Carnegie-Rochester Conference Series on Public Policy, 1. New York: American Elsevier, pp. 19–46.

Mertens, K. and Ravn, M. O. (2011). Understanding the aggregate effects of anticipated and unanticipated tax policy shocks. *Review of Economic Dynamics*, 14(1), 27–54.

(2013). The dynamic effects of personal and corporate income tax changes in the United States. *American Economic Review*, 103(4), 2012–47.

(2014). A reconciliation of SVAR and narrative estimates of tax multipliers. *Journal of Monetary Economics*, 68, S1–S19.

Mountford, A. and Uhlig, H. (2009). What are the effects of fiscal policy shocks? *Journal of Applied Econometrics*, **24**, 960–92.

Òscar, J. (2005). Estimation and inference of impulse responses by local projections. *American Economic Review*, **95**(1): 161–82.

Òscar, J and Taylor, Alan M. (2013). *The Time for Austerity: Estimating the Average Treatment Effect of Fiscal Policy*. NBER Working Papers No. 19414, National Bureau of Economic Research, Inc.

Perotti, R. (2005). *Estimating the Effects of Fiscal Policy in OECD Countries*. CEPR Discussion Paper No. 168. Centre for Economic Policy Research, London.

(2008). In search of the transmission mechanism of fiscal policy. In D. Acemoglu, K. Rogoff and M. Woodford, eds., *NBER Macroeconomics Annual 2007*, **22**. Chicago: University of Chicago Press, pp. 169–226.

(2013). The austerity myth: gain without pain. In Alberto Alesina and Francesco Giavazzi, eds., *Fiscal Policy after the Financial Crisis*. Chicago and London: University of Chicago Press and National Bureau of Economic Research, 307–54.

Ramey, V. (2011a). Identifying government spending shocks: it's all in the timing. *Quarterly Journal of Economics*, **126**(1), 1–50.

(2011b). Can government purchases stimulate the economy? *Journal of Economic Literature*, **49**(3), 673–85.

(2013). Government spending and private activities. In A. Alesina and F. Giavazzi, eds., *Fiscal Policy after the Financial Crisis*. Chicago and London: University of Chicago Press and NBER, pp. 19–55.

(2016). Macroeconomic shocks and their propagation. In J. Taylor and H. Uhlig, eds., *Handbook of Macroeconomics*, **2**. Amsterdam: Elsevier, pp. 71–162.

Ramey, V., Owyang, M. and Zubairy, S. (2013). Are government spending multipliers greater during periods of slack? Evidence from 20th century historical data. *American Economic Review, Papers and Proceedings*, **103**(3), 129–34.

Ramey, V. A. and Zubairy, S. (2014). *Government Spending Multipliers in Good Times and in Bad: Evidence from US Historical Data*. Working paper, November.

Romer, C. and Romer, D. H. (2010). The macroeconomic effects of tax changes: estimates based on a new measure of fiscal shocks. *American Economic Review*, **100**(3), 763–801.

Schmitt-Grohe, S. and Uribe, M. (2012). What's news in business cycles. *Econometrica*, **80**(6), 2733–64.

Uhlig, H. (2005). What are the effects of monetary policy? Results from an
    agnostic identification procedure. *Journal of Monetary Economics*, **52**
    (2), 381–419.
    (2010). Some fiscal calculus. *American Economic Review*, **100**(2), 30–4.
    (2012). Economics and reality. *Journal of Macroeconomics*, **34**(March),
    29–41.

16 | Government as Borrower and Innovator of Last Resort

RICHARD C. KOO

1 Introduction

The advent of the Great Recession in 2008 demonstrated that the existence of borrowers cannot be taken for granted when the bursting of a debt-financed bubble leaves the balance sheets of a large section of the private sector underwater. History also shows that a lack of borrowers has traditionally been a bigger constraint on growth than a lack of lenders, except during the early stages of industrialization. When there are no borrowers – whether because of balance-sheet problems or a lack of worthwhile investment opportunities – the government may have to act as borrower of last resort, and possibly even as *innovator* of last resort.

Section 2 discusses potential reasons for a lack of borrowers relative to lenders in a historical context. Section 3 describes the problems stemming from the absence of borrowers, while Section 4 highlights the main causes and consequences of the balance-sheet recession in the euro area. It also presents a number of recommendations for policymakers. The final section concludes.

2 Lenders and Borrowers in a Historical Context

When macroeconomics was developing into an independent academic discipline, starting in the 1940s, investment opportunities for businesses were plentiful as new "must-have" household appliances, ranging from washing machines to televisions, made their appearance. With plentiful demand for funds from the private sector, economists' emphasis was very much on monetary policy and the concern that fiscal policy would crowd out private investment.

The advent of two Great Recessions – in Japan in 1990 and in the West in 2008 – demonstrated that when the broader private sector confronts daunting balance-sheet problems following the bursting of a debt-financed bubble, it may not borrow money at *any* interest rate. As the value of assets purchased during the bubble with leveraged funds collapses, many borrowers fall into negative equity, forcing them to give up profit maximization for debt minimization as they put their financial houses in order.

For businesses, negative equity or insolvency means a potential loss of access to all forms of financing, including trade credits. In the worst case, that means everything will have to be settled with cash. Many financial institutions, such as banks, are also prohibited from rolling over loans to insolvent borrowers. For households, negative equity means savings they thought they had for retirement or rainy days in the future are all gone. Since these are very dangerous conditions to be in for both businesses and households, they will put their highest priority on deleveraging, regardless of the level of interest rates, until they feel safe enough with their financial health.

2.1 The Paradox of Thrift

Such debt minimization is the right and responsible thing to do at the level of individual businesses and households. But when the private sector in aggregate stops borrowing money despite zero interest rates, the economy falls into a deflationary spiral because those saved funds with no borrowers leak out of the economy's income stream and become a deflationary gap. This is because when someone is saving or paying down debt, someone else must be borrowing and spending those funds to keep the national economy going.

For example, if a person with an income of $1,000 decides to spend $900 and save $100, the $900 that is spent becomes someone else's income, which means it is already circulating in the economy. The $100 that was saved would usually be deposited with a bank or other financial institution to be lent to someone else. When that person borrows and spends the $100, total expenditures in the economy equal $900 plus $100, which is the same as the original income of $1,000, and the economy moves forward.

During this process, it is assumed that the financial sector will make sure all saved funds are borrowed and spent, with interest rates rising when there are too many borrowers relative to savers and falling when there are too few. This assumption of automaticity has enabled economists to ignore the financial sector when creating their macroeconomic theories and models.

But if society collectively tries to save $100, or 10 percent of its income, because it cannot find sufficient investment opportunities or has chosen to repair its balance sheet, there will be no borrowers for the saved $100 and total expenditures will drop to $900, which means the economy has contracted by 10 percent. That $900 is now someone else's income. If that person decides to save 10 percent while the rest of the society is still repairing balance sheets, only $810 will be spent, shrinking the economy even further in a process now known as a *balance-sheet recession*. This contractionary process will continue until people have finished repairing their balance sheets or have become so poor that they cannot save any more, in which case the income stream leakage from savings will end.

Keynes called this state of affairs, in which everyone wants to save but is unable to do so because no one is borrowing, the paradox of thrift. Until 2008, the economics profession considered this kind of contractionary equilibrium, which is often called a depression, to be an exceptionally rare occurrence – the only recent example was the Great Depression in the 1930s, when the United States lost 46 percent of its nominal GNP due to the process described above. Although Japan fell into a serious balance-sheet recession when its bubble burst in 1990, its lessons were almost completely ignored by the economics profession until 2008.[1]

2.2 Before the Industrial Revolution

However, a look back over history suggests that such a state was much closer to the norm for thousands of years before the industrial revolution. Economic growth had been negligible for centuries before this technological revolution (Figure 16.1). During this period of essentially zero growth, savers were probably not in short supply because human beings were always worried about an uncertain future. Preparing for old age and a rainy day is an ingrained aspect of human nature. But if it is human to save, then the centuries-long economic stagnation prior to the industrial revolution must have been due to a lack of borrowers.

[1] One exception is the National Association of Business Economists, Washington, DC, which awarded its Abramson Award to my paper entitled 'The Japanese economy in balance sheet recession,' published in their journal *Business Economics* in April 2001.

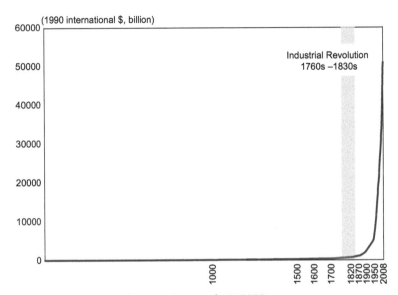

Figure 16.1: Historical economic growth, 0–2008

Since the private sector will not borrow unless it can be sure that it can pay back the debt, it is easy to see why the limited amount of technological innovation before the industrial revolution produced very few borrowers. Because of this dearth of opportunities, the more people tried to save, the deeper the economy fell into the paradox of thrift. The result was a permanent paradox of thrift in which people tried to save but their actions and intentions kept the national economy in a depressed state. This state of affairs lasted for centuries in both the East and the West.

Powerful rulers sometimes borrowed the saved funds and used them to build social infrastructure or monuments. On those occasions, the vicious cycle of the paradox of thrift was suspended because the government borrowed the saved funds and re-injected them into the income stream, generating rapid economic growth. However, unless the project paid for itself, the government would at some point get cold feet in the face of a mounting debt load and discontinue its investment. The whole economy would then fall back into the paradox of thrift and stagnate. Consequently, those regimes often did not last as long as some of the monuments they created. And governments are seldom good at selecting investment projects that pay for themselves.

Countries also tried to achieve economic growth by expanding their territory, that is, by acquiring more land, which was the key factor of production before the industrial revolution. But that was basically a zero-sum proposition for the global economy and also resulted in countless wars and deaths.

2.3 Industrial Revolution and Emergence of Private Sector Borrowers

Today's developed economies were all agrarian societies until the arrival of the industrial revolution finally brought an end to the paradox of thrift. The invention of new products and the machines to make them produced a surfeit of investment opportunities for the first time in history. Private sector businesses, which would not borrow money unless they were sure of being able to pay back the debt, found many projects that would pay for themselves and started borrowing money. This process could continue as long as those debt-financed projects were sound enough to pay for themselves.

This resulted in a virtuous cycle in which investment created new jobs and income, which in turn generated savings that could fund more investment. Unlike government-financed investments in earlier centuries, many of which eventually ran into financing difficulties, private sector-led investments could sustain themselves as long as new products were continuously brought to market. This resulted in the rapid economic growth observed since the industrial revolution.

At the beginning of the industrial revolution, constraints to growth included a lack of transportation networks and other social infrastructure, insufficient savings and underdeveloped financial markets to fund investments, an illiterate work force, and slow technological innovation. But as the emergence of railways and other utilities demonstrates, many of those constraints were soon transformed into investment opportunities themselves. With new household appliances, cars, cameras, and airplanes invented and developed in quick succession, an absence of investment opportunities seldom served as a constraint to growth.

From the perspective of the national economy, household saving became a virtue instead of a vice, and economies in which people felt responsible for their own futures and therefore saved more tended to grow more rapidly than those in which people did not save so much.

		Borrowers (= investors)	
		Yes	No
Lenders (= savers)	Yes	1	3
	No	2	4

Figure 16.2: Four combinations of borrowers and lenders

The availability of such investment opportunities, however, is never guaranteed. It depends on a myriad of factors, including the pace of technological innovation and scientific breakthroughs, the ability of businesspeople to find such opportunities and borrow money to exploit them, the stage of economic development, the availability of financing at reasonable interest rates, the protection afforded to intellectual property rights, and the general state of the economy and world trade.

2.4 *Four Possible Combinations of Borrowers and Lenders*

The discussion above suggests there are four possible combinations of presence and absence of lenders (savers) and borrowers (investors). Either (1) both lenders and borrowers are present in sufficient numbers; (2) there are borrowers but not enough lenders, even at high interest rates; (3) there are lenders but not enough borrowers, even at low interest rates; or (4) both lenders and borrowers are absent. This is illustrated in Figure 16.2.

Of the four combinations, only Cases 1 and 2 are covered in conventional economics, which implicitly assumes there are always borrowers as long as real interest rates can be brought low enough. Of these two, only the first requires the minimum of policy intervention – such as a slight adjustment to interest rates – to keep the economy going.

In Case 2, where there are no lenders, the causes may be found in both non-financial and financial factors. Non-financial factors might include a culture that does not encourage saving or a country that is simply too poor and underdeveloped to save. A restrictive monetary policy may also qualify as a non-financial factor weighing on savers' ability to lend. (If a paradox of thrift leaves a country too poor to save, this would properly be classified as Case 4 because it is actually caused by a lack of borrowers.)

Financial factors might include banks having too many non-performing loans (NPLs), which depress their capital ratios and prevent them from lending. This condition is typically known as a credit crunch. Systemic NPL problems may prompt mutual distrust among banks and lead to a dysfunctional interbank market, a state of affairs typically known as a financial crisis. Over-regulation of financial institutions by the authorities can lead to a similar outcome. An under-developed financial system may also be a factor.

Cultural norms against savings, as well as income (and productivity) levels that are too low for people to save anything, are developmental phenomena typically found in pre-industrialized economies. These issues can take many years to address.

Non-developmental causes of an absence of lenders, however, all have well-known remedies in the literature. For example, the government can inject capital into the banks to restore their ability to lend, or it can relax regulations preventing financial institutions from performing their role as financial intermediaries. In the case of a dysfunctional interbank market, the central bank can act as lender of last resort to ensure the clearing system continues to operate. It can also relax monetary policy.

The conventional emphasis on monetary policy and concerns over the crowding-out effect of fiscal policy are justified in Cases 1 and 2, where there are borrowers but (for a variety of reasons) not enough lenders.

3 Problems Stemming from the Lack of Borrowers

The problem is with Cases 3 and 4, where there are not enough borrowers. If the reason is that businesses cannot find attractive investment opportunities, the government may have to do more to encourage scientific and technological innovation. That may require measures reminiscent of supply-side economics, such as tax incentives and deregulation. Although tax incentives qualify as fiscal policy, these supply-side measures, which are basically microeconomic measures, take a long time to produce results large enough to have macroeconomic impact.

When US President Ronald Reagan lowered tax rates and drastically deregulated the economy in 1980 in the first demonstration of supply-side economics, people with ideas and drive took notice. They began pushing back the technological frontiers of the IT industry, eventually enabling the United States to regain the lead it had lost to Japan in many high-tech fields.

This was a spectacular achievement, but the process took nearly fifteen years. Reagan's ideas were implemented in the early 1980s, but it was not until the Clinton era that those ideas actually bore fruit. During Reagan's two terms and the elder Bush's one, the US economy continued to struggle.

President George H. W. Bush achieved monumental diplomatic successes that included an end to the Cold War, the collapse of the Soviet Union, and victory in the first Gulf War. Yet he lost his re-election campaign to a young governor from Arkansas by the name of Bill Clinton who had only one campaign slogan: "It's the economy, stupid!" The fact that Bush lost this election suggests the economy was still far from satisfactory in the eyes of most Americans in 1992.

Once Clinton took over, however, the US economy began to do much better, even though only a few can remember the details of his economic policies. The economy was doing so well by his second term that the federal government was running a budget surplus. And the surplus was growing so fast that then-Fed Chairman Alan Greenspan worried out loud that a shortage of Treasury bonds might make it difficult for the Fed to conduct monetary policy. The conclusion to be drawn from this is that even though supply-side reforms are essential in encouraging innovation, it takes many years for them to produce macroeconomic results that ordinary citizens can feel and appreciate.

3.1 Absence of Borrowers due to Balance-Sheet Problems

When there are no borrowers because the bursting of a debt-financed bubble has left their balance sheets underwater, the borrowers will not return until their negative equity problems are resolved. This can take many years, depending on the size of the bubble. And the bubbles that burst in Japan in 1990 and in the Western economies in 2008 were very large indeed.

Figure 16.3 compares the US and Japanese bubbles that took place fifteen years apart. It shows that the two bubbles were remarkably

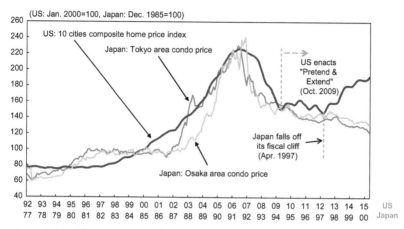

Figure 16.3: House prices in the United States and Japan

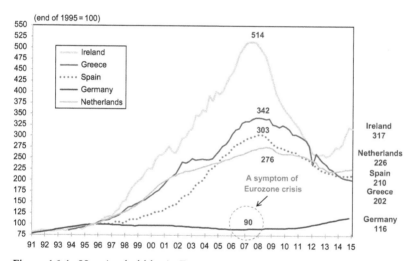

Figure 16.4: Housing bubbles in Europe, 1991–2015

similar both on the way up and on the way down, implying that what the United States experienced is similar to what Japan went through fifteen years earlier. Figure 16.4, which shows the housing bubbles in Europe, indicates the bubbles there were as large as – if not larger than – the US bubble, with only Germany experiencing a fall in house prices over the same period. The subsequent collapse of house prices then pushed all of these economies (except Germany) into severe balance-sheet recessions.

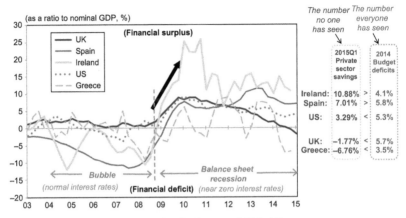

Figure 16.5: Private sector saving in Europe, 2003–15

Figure 16.5 shows the path of private sector savings in these countries as taken from their flow of funds data. It indicates that during the bubble, businesses and households in many of these economies were either saving very little or running a substantial financial deficit, meaning that the private sector as a whole was a net borrower. In other words, they were leveraging up in order to speculate in the housing market.

After the bubble burst, however, the private sectors in these economies changed their behavior dramatically and began running massive financial surpluses, even though interest rates were brought down to record low levels. A large private sector financial surplus at a time of zero interest rates is the prime characteristic of an economy in a balance-sheet recession, where the private sector has been minimizing debt instead of maximizing profits. Conventional economics, which assumes the private sector always seeks to maximize profit, no longer applies in this case.

3.2 Monetary Policy the First Casualty when Borrowers Disappear

The first casualty of this shift has been monetary policy. Although seldom mentioned explicitly in textbooks, the existence of borrowers capable of responding to movements in interest rates is a necessary condition for monetary policy to work. But this fundamental

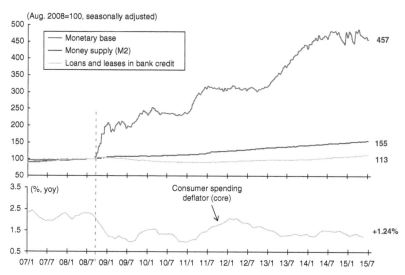

Figure 16.6: Liquidity injections and consumer spending deflator in the United States, 2007–15

assumption is often violated in the aftermath of a bubble, as the private sector is forced to minimize debt no matter how low interest rates go.

When the private sector is minimizing debt because borrowers who had over-leveraged themselves during the bubble are forced to deleverage to fix their balance sheets, the money multiplier turns negative at the margin, causing the central bank to lose control over the money supply.

This is clear from Figure 16.6, which shows the US monetary base, money supply, and bank credit extended to the private sector. According to (outdated?) textbooks, the monetary base, money supply, and credit should have very similar growth rates, that is, a 10 percent increase in the monetary base should result in a 10 percent increase in both the money supply and private sector credit. And such a textbook world did exist in the West until 2008 and in Japan until 1990, where the three monetary aggregates moved together.

After 2008, however, private sector credit grew extremely slowly, despite massive additions of reserves by the Federal Reserve under quantitative easing. This happened because while a central bank can inject any amount of reserves into the banking system, the banks must actually lend money for those reserves to enter the real economy. (Banks cannot *give* money away because the funds belong to depositors.) But when the private sector in aggregate is running a financial

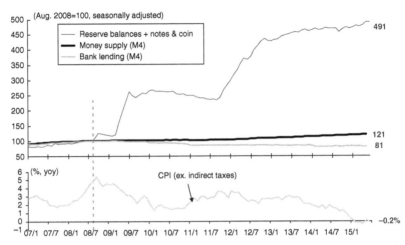

Figure 16.7: Liquidity injections and consumer spending deflator in the United Kingdom, 2007–15

surplus, there are no borrowers and the reserves cannot leave the banking system and enter the real economy. With only a modest increase in money circulating in the real economy, a large part of which was made possible by government borrowing, it is no wonder that inflation failed to pick up, as shown at the bottom of Figure 16.6.

Figures 16.7, 16.8, and 16.9 show the same monetary aggregates for the United Kingdom, eurozone, and Japan. The pattern is the same in all three cases, with growth in the monetary base completely de-coupling from growth in the money supply and credit. Indeed, credit in the United Kingdom has been shrinking since 2008. This means that most of the reserves injected into the banking system by central banks via quantitative easing never made it to the real economy, that is, they remain trapped in the financial system.

This also explains why inflation rates have remained so low. Some asset prices have increased because the funds injected by central banks and deleveraged funds returning to financial institutions had nowhere else to go, but the general level of prices remains low because an absence of borrowers has kept those funds from entering the real economy.

3.3 FX Market Participants Still Assuming Textbook World

Interestingly, even though quantitative easing has had minimal impact on the actual supply of money and credit, those in the foreign exchange market apparently assumed the textbook world was still in effect and

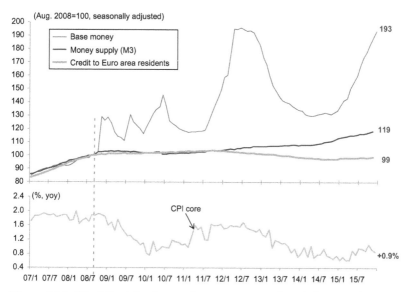

Figure 16.8: Liquidity injections and consumer spending deflator in the euro area, 2007–15

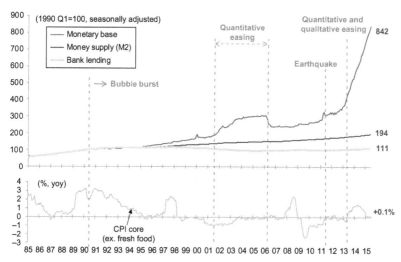

Figure 16.9: Liquidity injections and consumer spending deflator in Japan, 1985–2015

pushed down the value of currencies as soon as their issuing banks announced quantitative easing programs. Thus when the Fed and the Bank of England unveiled QE programs following Lehman's collapse, both currencies fell 30–40 percent against the Japanese yen

Figure 16.10: QE and international exchange rates

(Figure 16.10), effectively making Japan's currency the world's strongest.

That helped both General Motors and Chrysler recover quickly, while Japanese companies struggled under the crushing weight of the strong yen. When Japan's central bank announced its own QE program in late 2012, the yen fell 30–40 percent against the dollar and the pound, completely neutralizing the advantage that US and UK companies had been enjoying.

In all of these cases, however, differences in money supply growth were nowhere near those necessary to justify the observed changes in exchange rates. Indeed, money supply growth failed to accelerate in any of these countries after QE. In other words, QE is basically a zero-sum, beggar-thy-neighbor policy with no real benefit for the global economy. When the high cost of winding down QE is taken into consideration, it is not at all clear whether the whole exercise will have been worth the trouble.[2]

3.4 *Japanese and US Governments as Borrowers of Last Resort*

When balance-sheet problems have forced the private sector to minimize debt, the correct way to avoid a deflationary spiral is for the

---

[2] For further discussion on this topic, see Koo (2014), chapter 2.

government to act as borrower of last resort and borrow and spend the excess savings of the private sector (the $100 amount in the example presented above). By doing so, it can prevent GDP and the money multiplier from shrinking. And by supporting GDP, the government ensures that the private sector has enough income to pay down its debts.

Japan basically followed this path until 1997 and succeeded in keeping GDP at or above bubble-peak levels in spite of an 87 percent fall in commercial real estate prices nationwide. This was an amazing achievement in view of the fact that the country lost national wealth amounting to 1,500 trillion yen, or three times its 1989 GDP, during this period. As a percentage of GDP, this loss of wealth was three times greater than that which the United States sustained during the Great Depression, when the country lost 46 percent of its nominal GNP.

Once the private sector finishes repairing its balance sheet and is ready to borrow again, the government should start fixing its balance sheet, but it has to be in that order. Any attempt to reduce budget deficits before the private sector is ready to borrow will only revive the deflationary spiral and defeat the original purpose of shrinking the deficit.

That was exactly what happened to Japan in 1997 when the country was persuaded to reduce its deficit by the IMF and OECD, two organizations that understood nothing of balance-sheet recessions at that time. The result was a complete collapse of the economy and the banking system that led to a 72 percent *increase* in the deficit in spite of higher taxes and lower spending. This mistake lengthened the recession by at least five years, and it took Japan nearly ten years to bring the deficit back to pre-1997 levels, as shown in Figure 16.11.

US policymakers from Ben Bernanke to Larry Summers recognized in the first two years of the GFC that they were facing a balance-sheet recession, the same sickness that had afflicted Japan. This was amply demonstrated when Larry Summers, then the NEC chairman in the Obama administration, indicated in July 2009 that fiscal stimulus must have the "three S's": it must be sufficient, sustained, and speedy.[3] It must be sufficient to fill the deflationary gap and stabilize the economy. It must be sustained until the private sector has finished its balance-sheet repairs. And it must be implemented speedily to pre-empt a

---

[3] Summers (2009).

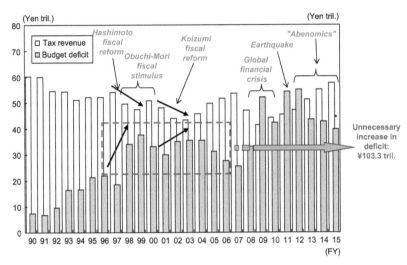

Figure 16.11: Japan's fiscal cliff, 1990–2015

deflationary spiral. Doing any less risks creating a deflationary spiral when the private sector in aggregate is not borrowing.

US policymakers also issued strong warnings against premature fiscal consolidation using the phrase "fiscal cliff," which in turn allowed the United States to avoid the Japanese mistakes of 1997. Although the United States came very close to falling off the fiscal cliff on a number of occasions, including the debt ceiling debate, sequester, and the government shutdown, it ultimately managed to avoid that outcome. The private sector therefore had the income needed to pay down debt, to the extent that some US households are now starting to borrow again. The United States success in avoiding Japan's mistakes was why US house prices diverged from the path of Japanese house prices after 1997, as shown in Figure 16.3.

Figure 16.12 shows the financial assets and liabilities of the US household sector. In this chart, the shaded bars represent growth in financial liabilities (scale inverted) and the white bars growth in financial assets. It shows that Americans were borrowing heavily to invest in houses during the bubble era, but after the bubble burst they stopped borrowing altogether and dramatically increased savings in spite of zero interest rates. There has been a modest recovery in borrowing, starting around 2013 as some households finished repairing their balance sheets. Although the new borrowing is still small relative to the past trend and

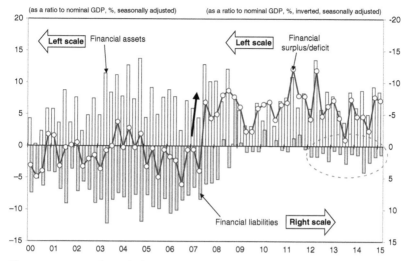

Figure 16.12: US household sector borrowings, 2000–15

the household sector in aggregate continues to run a substantial financial surplus, progress is being made, which explains the better economic performance of the United States compared to Europe.

4 European Ignorance of Balance-Sheet Recessions Leads to Fiasco

In Europe, unfortunately, policymakers never understood that they were confronting a newly recognized disease called balance-sheet recession and never issued any warnings about the fiscal cliff, in spite of the fact that eurozone household sectors borrowed huge sums during the bubble era and were then forced to engage in massive deleveraging despite zero and even negative interest rates. Figures 16.13, 16.14, and 16.15 show the household sectors of Spain, Ireland, and Greece, the three countries where house price increases were particularly pronounced. In all three countries, the shaded bars are mostly above the zero line after 2008, indicating that households in these countries are paying down debt at a time of zero interest rates.

Unfortunately, when the common currency was being designed in the 1990s, nobody outside Japan knew anything about balance-sheet recessions, and the Maastricht Treaty ended up making no provision for this type of recession. In particular, the Treaty prohibits member

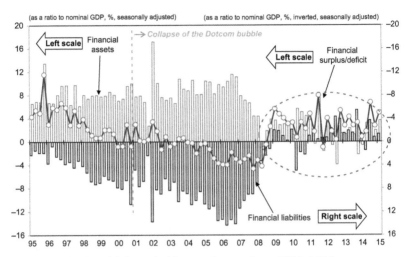

Figure 16.13: Spanish household sector borrowings, 1995–2015

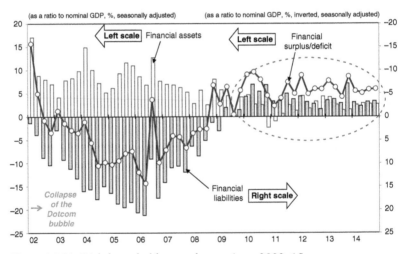

Figure 16.14: Irish household sector borrowings, 2002–15

governments from running sustained budget deficits of more than 3 percent of GDP *regardless* of the size of private sector savings. This means that even if the private sector is saving 7 percent of GDP, the government can borrow only 3 percent of GDP, leaving the remaining 4 percent of GDP as un-invested savings to start the deflationary spiral.

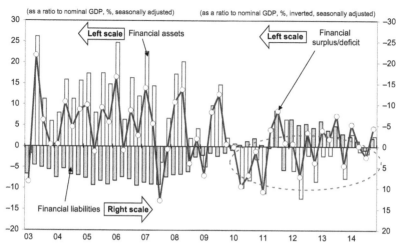

Figure 16.15: Greek household sector borrowings, 2003–15

The Spanish private sector, for example, was saving 7.0 percent of GDP in the twelve months that ended in the 1st quarter of 2015, as shown in Figure 16.13. That was over *six* years after the bursting of the bubble in 2008. For the Irish private sector, savings six years after the bubble amounted to 10.8 percent of GDP. Although not included in the graph, the private sectors in Italy and Portugal were saving 6.3 percent and 6.8 percent of GDP, respectively, six years after 2008. Given the size of their housing bubbles prior to 2008, however, both the magnitude and duration of their deleveraging are not at all surprising.

The amount of time the peripheral private sectors are taking to repair their balance sheets is far beyond anything that was anticipated by the Maastricht Treaty. With eurozone member governments forced to comply with the 3 percent rule, the large and unfilled deflationary gaps between private sector savings and public sector borrowings triggered deflationary spirals. That effectively pushed these countries off the fiscal cliff, with devastating consequences for their economies and their peoples.

4.1 Dotcom Bubble Collapse Triggers Balance-Sheet Recession in Germany

This tragedy – a result of European policymakers' lack of understanding of balance-sheet recessions – did not start in 2008. It actually began

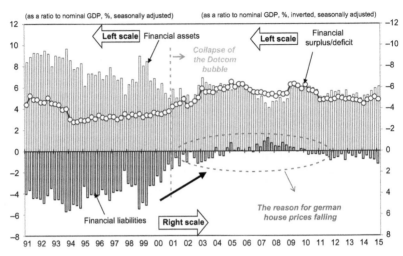

Figure 16.16: German household sector borrowings, 1991–2015

in 2000 when the German private sector, which was heavily involved in the dotcom bubble, stopped borrowing money altogether after the bubble burst.

Figure 16.16 shows that until 2000, German households were large net savers but were also borrowing money to buy houses and so forth. But after the spectacular rise and subsequent 97 percent fall in the Neuer Markt, the German equivalent of Nasdaq (Figure 16.17), borrowing disappeared altogether. German households are still not borrowing much today, fully fifteen years after the collapse of the dotcom bubble. Although there is no evidence to suggest that German households were heavily leveraged during the dotcom bubble, the losses they incurred nonetheless prompted them to stop borrowing and rebuild savings. This explains why German house prices fell and remained stagnant until 2011, as shown in Figure 16.4.

Even though German private sector savings reached as much as 10 percent of GDP in the wake of the dotcom bubble collapse, the Maastricht Treaty kept the German government from borrowing more than 3 percent of GDP, creating a large deflationary gap. The resultant weakness in the post-2000 German economy then prompted the European Central Bank (ECB) to bring interest rates down to a postwar low of 2 percent. As neither households nor businesses in Germany were borrowing money, the ECB's lower interest rates had no impact on the country's economy. In fact, the German economy continued to lose

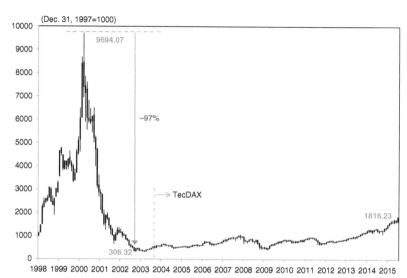

Figure 16.17: The Neuer Markt collapse in 2001

momentum, prompting many to call the country the "sick man of Europe" because of its failure to respond to monetary easing.

While the German economy and money supply growth stagnated, the peripheral economies that had sidestepped the dotcom bubble and therefore enjoyed clean balance sheets responded enthusiastically to the lowest interest rates in generations by borrowing and investing in real estate. With strong demand for funds, the money supply grew rapidly, pushing wages and prices in those countries higher. In contrast, anemic demand for funds in Germany led to low money supply growth and stagnant wages and prices (Figure 16.18), making Germany highly competitive relative to the rest of the eurozone and enabling it to export its way out of the balance-sheet recession (Figure 16.19).

When the housing bubble burst in 2008, the private sectors of the peripheral countries all had to deleverage while the Germans continued to pay down debt, plunging the entire eurozone into a massive balance-sheet recession.

Greece was already in a balance-sheet recession when revelations about the manipulation of deficit data in late 2009 threw the country into a massive fiscal crisis. To make the matter worse, the IMF, which came up with a "rescue" package for the country in 2010, had no

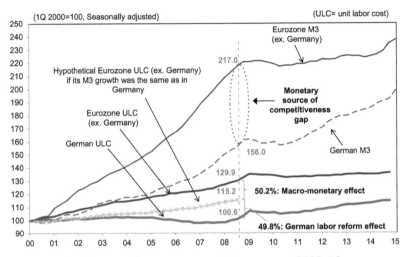

Figure 16.18: Germany–Eurozone competitiveness gaps, 2000–15

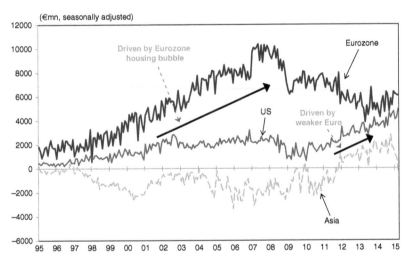

Figure 16.19: German balance of trade, 1995–2015

understanding of balance-sheet recessions at that time. In contrast to
the mild contraction forecasted by the IMF, the austerity program
imposed by the Troika (the EU, ECB, and IMF) in the midst of
balance-sheet recession ended up shrinking Greek GDP by 26 percent,
as indicated in Figure 16.20. With 26 percent less income, businesses

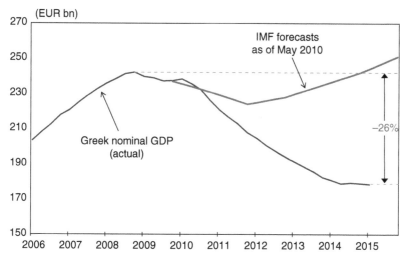

Figure 16.20: Greece's nominal GDP, 2006–15

and households are forced to draw down savings in order to survive. This is indicated by the white bars below zero in Figure 16.15. A country whose private sector must dis-save simply to stay alive naturally cannot pay back its foreign creditors.

The huge gap that developed between the IMF's forecasts of Greek GDP and the actual performance also led to massive distrust of the Troika among a suffering Greek public, further complicating an already difficult situation.

4.2 Japanese "Structural Reform" Blunder Repeated in Europe

The European policymakers also repeated the Japanese error of mistaking structural problems for balance-sheet problems. Both the Hashimoto administration (1996–8) and the Koizumi administration (2001–6) in Japan thought the economic stagnation was a result of structural problems within the Japanese economy and embarked on ambitious programs of reforms while refusing to put in fiscal stimulus. This was an understandable mistake, to the extent that balance-sheet problems were never taught in economics while structural issues were popularized since 1980 by President Reagan in his supply-side reforms.

Although all economies suffer from structural rigidities of one type or another, they cannot explain the sudden loss of momentum and prolonged stagnation these economies suffered in the wake of the bubble collapse. More importantly, structural remedies are no substitute for fiscal remedies in balance-sheet recessions because the former can easily take a decade or more to produce macroeconomic impacts, as mentioned above, whereas balance-sheet problems can trigger the $1000–$900–$810–$730 deflationary spirals almost from day one.

The reform efforts of Prime Ministers Hashimoto and Koizumi in Japan and Chancellor Gerhard Schroeder in post-dotcom Germany, as well as of peripheral governments in the post-2008 eurozone, are not without merit. But they all failed to produce the recovery these leaders promised because their economies were suffering from a completely different disease. Until European leaders recognize that perhaps 70–80 percent of their problems are balance sheet-driven and only about 20–30 percent are structural in nature, it is difficult to see how European economies would return to anything resembling normalcy anytime soon. Interestingly, the United States, led by the Obama administration, was the only country in balance-sheet recession that managed to avoid the "structural reform trap" that afflicted both Japan and Europe.

The German government's inability to use fiscal policy to fight its balance-sheet recession after 2000 and peripheral governments' inability to use fiscal policy to address their balance-sheet recessions after 2008 caused Europe's on-going tragedy. A significant part of the competitiveness gap between Germany and the rest of the eurozone was also due to inappropriate Maastricht restrictions on German fiscal policy that forced the ECB to ease monetary policy, which in turn created housing bubbles as well as higher wages and prices in peripheral countries.

Europe is likely to stagnate until policymakers in the core countries realize they are facing a highly unusual kind of recession that occurs only after a bubble bursts and that was not previously discussed in university economics courses. In particular, the Maastricht Treaty must be revised to enable it to deal with both ordinary downturns and balance-sheet recessions. In countries where the private sector is saving more than 3 percent of GDP in spite of zero interest rates, the government should be allowed – if not required – to borrow and spend those excess savings to stabilize its economy. Such a provision is also needed to prevent countries in balance-sheet recession from causing distortions in ECB monetary policy.

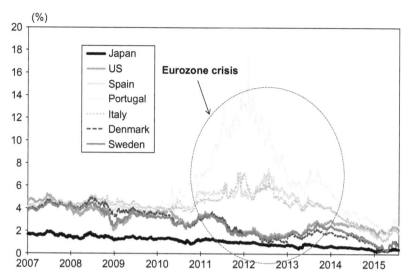

Figure 16.21: Euro-area periphery bond yields, 2007–15

4.3 *Deficits Easily Financed during Balance-Sheet Recessions Except in Eurozone*

It should be noted that, except in the eurozone, there is no reason for governments in balance-sheet recession to face financing problems. This is because the amount the government must borrow and spend to stabilize the economy is exactly equal to the excess (i.e., unborrowed) savings of the private sector. From the perspective of fund managers entrusted with those savings, increased government borrowing is a welcome development because there are no borrowers in the private sector. Those fund managers who are not allowed to take on too much foreign exchange risk or principal risk will rush to purchase government bonds during this type of recession, pushing bond yields down to levels that would be unthinkable under ordinary conditions.

This happened first in Japan after 1990 and spread to other countries in balance-sheet recession after 2008, including small and open economies such as Denmark and Sweden (Figure 16.21). These ultra-low government bond yields are the market's way of telling the government it needs to act as the borrower of last resort to support the economy and the money supply. If the government heeds the market's message and increases its fiscal stimulus, both GDP and money multiplier will be supported to speed up the economic recovery. If the government refuses to heed the market's message, both GDP and money multiplier will suffer, with terrible consequences for the economy and its people. In this sense, ultra-low government bond yields seen during this type of recession are the key manifestations of the self-corrective mechanism of economies in balance-sheet recessions.

In the eurozone, however, fund managers can choose from nineteen government bond markets that are all denominated in the same currency. As a result, peripheral countries' excess private sector savings often ended up in German government bonds, pushing up the yields of peripheral government bonds while lowering yields on Bunds. Foreign exchange risks which ring-fenced government bond markets and allowed self-corrective mechanisms to work in all economies suffering from balance-sheet recessions outside the eurozone could not ring-fence government bond markets in the eurozone.

This intra-zone capital flight that is unique to the eurozone effectively robbed the peripheral countries of the fiscal space they would have had if they had stayed outside the eurozone. If Spain or Ireland stayed outside the eurozone, their government bond yields would have come down to those ridiculous levels seen elsewhere because their private sector savings have been so large. Low government bond yields, in turn, would have given those countries plenty of fiscal space to fight their balance-sheet recessions.

To fix this problem of destabilizing capital flight between government bond markets, incentives might have to be introduced to encourage the excess savings of peripheral countries to stay in their own government bond markets so that those economies' self-corrective mechanisms would work properly.

Unfortunately, European policymakers, who still have no understanding of balance-sheet recessions, naturally have no appreciation of the economy's self-corrective mechanism against such a recession. They have also failed to notice that peripheral countries' private sector savings are dangerously large relative to their government deficits.

Based on this ignorance, they are trying to limit domestic financial institutions holding their own government bonds for the fear of so-called "diabolic loop." If they succeed in their proposals, the self-corrective mechanism of individual countries will be made inoperable and the EU will be forced to come up with a mechanism to recycle

Spanish savings in Germany back to Spain, and Irish savings in the Netherlands back to Ireland. But such a task will be politically far more difficult than simply giving some incentives for domestic institutions to hold domestic government bonds (e.g., by giving lower risk weights for holdings of own government bonds). Indeed, if such incentives existed from the beginning of the euro, the peripheral government bond crisis might never have happened, since there are more than sufficient private sector savings to finance deficit in all post-2008 peripheral countries except Greece.

4.4 Debt Aversion Must Be Overcome

When countries finally emerge from their balance-sheet recessions, they will be saddled with huge public debt because they had to use fiscal stimulus to fight the recession. The natural tendency of policymakers and orthodox commentators faced with a large national debt is to raise taxes wherever possible. But such wanton tax hikes may discourage businesses from investing aggressively in new innovations, thus prolonging the period of subpar economic growth.

This is because borrowers who go through a long and painful period of balance-sheet repairs typically become traumatized by debt even after their balance sheets have been cleaned up. This aversion to borrowing was observed in the United States after the Great Depression, when both short- and long-term interest rates took a full thirty years to return to the average levels of the 1920s (Figure 16.22). The same aversion can be observed in Japan today even though the private sector had completed its balance-sheet repairs by 2005. Many countries in the post-2008 West are likely to witness the same private sector aversion to borrowing after completing their balance-sheet repairs. To overcome this aversion, governments must introduce accelerated depreciation allowances and other incentives to encourage traumatized businesses to borrow and invest again.

The point is that all countries emerging from balance-sheet recessions need to resist the temptation to raise taxes, which may thwart both innovation and borrowing. Only in this way can their economies gain sufficient growth velocity to escape the gravity of the debt trap and the debt trauma. Maintaining innovator- and borrower-friendly tax regimes at a time when the public debt is so large will be a major challenge for all of these countries.

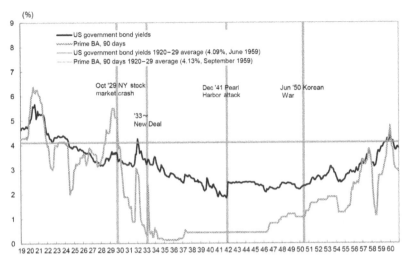

Figure 16.22: US interest rates, 1919–60

The huge increase in public debt that results from fighting a balance-sheet recession should be viewed as the cost of medical care needed to cure the injury sustained as a result of reckless behavior during the bubble. As in the treatment of any injury, uninterrupted application of necessary medication until the patient is ready to move on is the best way to minimize both the downtime needed as well as the final bill for the treatment.

Japan was the first country since the 1930s to face this type of recession, starting in 1990, but because its policymakers did not understand the disease until way after 1997, it ended up chasing two hares at the same time, losing both in the process. In particular, it was willing to put in fiscal stimulus to get the economy moving, but as soon as the economy responded to the stimulus and showed signs of life the government was too willing to end the stimulus and strive for a balanced budget, even though its private sector was far from finished with its balance-sheet repair. The resultant economic downturn then forced the government to implement fiscal stimulus again, only to repeat the same mistake over and over again.

The net result was on-again, off-again treatment, which is the worst type of treatment for any injury or disease. The government also lost precious time dealing with structural issues when the problem was with balance sheets. Even though Japanese GDP never fell below the peak of the bubble and its unemployment rate has never risen higher than 5.5 percent in the past twenty-five years thanks to government's fiscal actions, the net result was a hugely lengthened recession and a massive build-up of public debt.

The Obama administration in the United States, which understood the lessons from Japan, strove to avoid the Japanese mistake of 1997 by issuing strong warnings on premature fiscal consolidation via the term "fiscal cliff." Indeed, the United States is the only country that managed to avoid Japan-like double-dip recessions and policy diversion to less urgent structural issues. As a result, its private sector balance sheets have improved significantly, and its public sector deficit has shrunk to a quarter of the post-GFC peak.

The Europeans who completely ignored the Japanese lesson and went straight for fiscal consolidation thanks to the defective Maastricht Treaty ended up with huge losses of output and employment, with unemployment rates many times higher than those observed in Japan. The inability of center-left and center-right parties to question the wisdom of the fiscal straitjacket imposed by the Treaty is also forcing many desperate voters to seek help elsewhere – a dangerous sign in any democracy.

The above experiences of Japan, the United States, and the eurozone suggest that even though smaller deficits are more desirable than bigger deficits, there really is no choice when it comes to fighting balance-sheet recessions. Although commentators who never understood balance-sheet recessions will continue to bash large deficits, uninterrupted application of sufficient fiscal stimulus until private sector financial health is restored is the fastest and lowest-cost treatment to overcome this economic malaise. Any attempt to save on medical care when it is needed only prolongs the suffering of the people, while increasing the final bill for the treatment.

5 Conclusion

Most conventional debate on economic growth assumes that there are always borrowers, and that those borrowers will step forward if only the central bank lowers real interest rates far enough. This kind of thinking prompted Paul Krugman, a Nobel laureate, to propose a 4 percent inflation target when the original 2 percent target failed to produce the expected results.[4] Although he was also a strong advocate

---

[4] Robb (2015).

of fiscal stimulus after 2008, his reliance on monetary policy assumes that there are always investment opportunities worth borrowing for, and that there are always borrowers with clean balance sheets. Because of these two assumptions, it is assumed that constraints on growth are chiefly on the lenders' side. Economists have therefore emphasized the use of monetary easing to remove possible constraints for lenders while remaining cautious about excessive fiscal stimulus to avoid crowding out private sector investments.

These assumptions held up reasonably well in the postwar era. But by assuming there are always borrowers, economists have assumed away the most critical challenges to economic growth, that is, the questions of whether there are sufficient investment opportunities and whether there are enough businesspeople who are able and willing to take the risks entailed in those investments.

Instead, they simply *assumed* a rate of long-term potential growth based on the trend growth of capital and labor and argued that policy-makers should strive to bring the economy back to that growth path. They also *assumed* rates of long-term productivity growth and techno-logical innovation without specifying how they were derived. But such potential growth rates mean absolutely nothing when businesspeople on the ground are either unable (because of balance-sheet concerns) or unwilling (because of a lack of investment opportunities) to borrow money and invest it. This also suggests that conventional economics has no valid theory of economic growth.

The advent of the balance-sheet recession in Japan in 1990 and in Western economies starting in 2008 has finally awakened some econo-mists to the possibility that borrowers can disappear when faced with daunting balance-sheet challenges, even at zero interest rates. Policy-makers who understood this, such as former Fed Chair Ben Bernanke and current Chair Janet Yellen, issued strong warnings about the fiscal cliff to ensure that the government served as "borrower of last resort" to keep the economy and money supply from shrinking. Japanese Finance Minister Taro Aso also recognized this danger and made a point of making fiscal stimulus the second "arrow" of Abenomics. Their actions helped the post-2008 Japanese and US economies in no small way.

In contrast, the utter failure of European policymakers to under-stand the danger of balance-sheet recessions has led to extended suffering on the part of the European populace, many of whom are beginning to lose hope in their center-left or center-right governments. However, if the Europeans accept two modifications to Maastricht, not will only their economies recover, but their single currency can also look forward to a long and bright future. These are: (1) allow member governments to borrow more than 3 percent of GDP when their private sectors are saving more than 3 percent of GDP at zero interest rates and (2) introduce preferential risk weights for financial institutions holding their own government bonds.

These two minor modifications will make the Treaty amenable to both ordinary and balance-sheet recessions by providing plenty of fiscal space to member countries so that their self-corrective mechanisms will work properly to bring recovery to their economies. Since the proposed differentiated risk weights apply only to holdings of domestic rather than foreign *government* bonds, they will not affect the efficient allocation of resources in the private sectors of nineteen countries that is made possible by the single currency.

Within economics circles, there is still not enough appreciation of the fact that, apart from the early stages of industrialization, where there are plenty of low-hanging investment opportunities, shortages of borrowers have always had far more serious consequences than shortages of lenders. There is also no reason to believe that there will be sufficient borrowers in the future. This means the tax regimes that were appropriate in earlier years, when there were numerous attractive investment opportunities, may no longer be optimal when those opportunities are exhausted and the country is at the forefront of technological advances.

This may be particularly relevant in advanced countries, where worthwhile investment opportunities are much more difficult to find than is the case in emerging economies. In this case, the government must consciously direct fiscal spending toward the development of cutting-edge technology – in effect, serving as the innovator of last resort.

Finally, there is a possibility that borrowers are absent because many of them have balance-sheet problems and those who do not have balance-sheet problems cannot find innovations in which to invest. In that case, government must act as both innovator and borrower of last resort by directing sustained and sufficient fiscal stimulus toward the development of cutting-edge technology. Here it is hoped that modern governments are better than the emperors and kings of the past at selecting projects that will ultimately pay for themselves.

Instead of assuming away the key challenges of economic growth and hiding behind assumptions about the potential growth rate, it is time for the economics profession to face this problem head-on. Availability of borrowers should never be taken for granted.

Bibliography

Bank for International Settlements (2014). *84th Annual Report*, www.bis.org/publ/arpdf/ar2014e.htm

Board of Governors of the FED (1976). *Banking & Monetary Statistics, 1914–1970*, 2 vols. Washington DC.

The Economist (2005). The global housing boom: in come the waves. June 16, www.economist.com/node/4079027

European Central Bank (2012). *Mario Draghi's Interview with Le Monde.* July 21, www.ecb.europa.eu/press/inter/date/2012/html/sp120721.en.html

Eurostat (2014). *Provision of Deficit and Debt Data for 2013 – First Notification.* April 23, http://epp.eurostat.ec.europa.eu/cache/ITY_PUBLIC/2-23042014-AP/EN/2-23042014-AP-EN.PDF

International Monetary Fund (2010). *IMF Executive Board Approves €30 Billion Stand-By Arrangement for Greece.* Press Release No. 10/187, May 9, 2010. www.imf.org/external/np/sec/pr/2010/pr10187.htm

(2013a). *Global Financial Stability Report: Old Risks, New Challenges.* April.

(2013b). *Unconventional Monetary Policies – Recent Experience and Prospects*, www.imf.org/external/np/pp/eng/2013/041813a.pdf

(2013c). *Unconventional Monetary Policies – Recent Experience and Prospects – Background Paper.* www.imf.org/external/np/pp/eng/2013/041813.pdf

Koo, R. (2001). The Japanese economy in balance sheet recession. *Business Economics*, 36(2), 15.

(2003). *Balance Sheet Recession: Japan's Struggle with Uncharted Economics and Its Global Implications.* Singapore: John Wiley & Sons.

(2008). *The Holy Grail of Macro Economics: Lessons from Japan's Great Recession.* Singapore: John Wiley & Sons.

(2014). *The Escape from Balance Sheet Recession and the QE Trap: A Hazardous Road for the World Economy.* Singapore: John Wiley & Sons.

Koo, R. and Fujita, S. (1997). Zaisei-saiken no Jiki wa Shijo ni Kike: Zaisei-saiken ka Keiki-kaifuku ka (Listen to the bond market for the timing of fiscal reform). *Shukan Toyo Keizai*, February 8, 52–9.

Krugman, P. (1998). It's baaack: Japan's slump and the return of the liquidity trap. *Brookings Papers on Economic Activities*, 2, 137–205.

Maddison, A., *Historical Statistics of the World Economy: 1–2008 AD*, www.ggdc.net/maddison/Historical_Statistics/vertical-file_02-2010.xls

Robb, G. (2015). Krugman: "Meh" is grade Fed gets on QE. *Market Watch*, November 9, www.marketwatch.com/story/krugman-meh-is-grade-fed-gets-on-qe-2015-11-09

Summers, L. H., (2009). *Rescuing and Rebuilding the US Economy: A Progress Report*. Prepared remarks at the Peterson Institute for International Economics, Washington DC, July 17, 2009, www.piie.com/publications/papers/paper.cfm?ResearchID=1264

17 | *Fiscal Consolidation Strategies*

CHRISTIAN KASTROP, BORIS
COURNÈDE, FALILOU FALL AND
ANNABELLE MOUROUGANE

1 Introduction

Fiscal positions have markedly worsened since the crisis. In the euro area, the general government balance has more than doubled in the post-crisis period, with the debt-to-GDP ratio over 100 percent since 2015. Other OECD countries, such as the United States and Japan, also experienced a marked deterioration in their fiscal balances and a rise in public debt.

In the short run, growth prospects in the major economies have improved, but a return to the pre-crisis growth path remains elusive for a majority of OECD countries. The near- to medium-term outlook is still one of moderate, rather than rapid, GDP growth and inflation (OECD, 2016). In most advanced economies, potential growth has been revised down and in some cases there are growing concerns that persistently weak demand is pulling potential growth down further, resulting in a protracted period of stagnation. Risks of persistent stagnation concern mainly the euro area and Japan, but many of the underlying challenges, such as slowing productivity, high long-term unemployment and falling labour force participation, are common to other advanced economies.

After a few years of dismal growth and austerity, countries have faced social discontent and reform fatigue. This is a common feature of consolidation episodes: there is evidence that the longer an episode lasts, all things being equal, the greater the likelihood of the adjustment being reversed (von Hagen, 2002; Guichard et al., 2007).

Against this background, this chapter reviews consolidation strategies in OECD countries, with a special focus on euro-area countries, along

This chapter draws on analyses undertaken by Boris Cournède, Falilou Fall, Debbie Bloch, Jean-Marc Fournier, Antoine Goujard, Peter Hoeller, Asa Johansson and Alvaro Pina, all of whom work at the OECD Economics Department. Special thanks to Sylvie Foucher-Hantala for excellent statistical work.

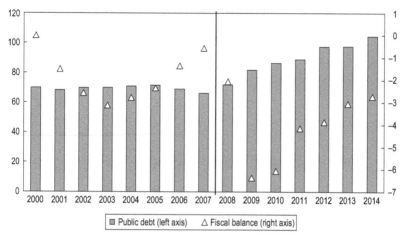

Figure 17.1: Budget deficit and public debt in the euro area, 2000–14
Note: percent of GDP.
Source: OECD Economic Outlook No. 98 database (OECD, 2015)

several dimensions. It first examines past and planned consolidation policies. It subsequently discusses the appropriate timing and pace of consolidation, before identifying a hierarchy of instruments. It then investigates the scope for raising the quality of public finances, before taking a longer-term perspective and looking at fiscal rules.

2 Consolidation: Recent Past and Plans

After the 2009 fiscal stimulus, sizeable fiscal consolidation in most euro-area countries has weighed on activity. Efforts have been particularly stringent in Southern euro-area economies, such as Portugal, Spain and Greece, and in Ireland. Fiscal policy has, on average, been less restrictive in other OECD countries, and has surely contributed to explain part of the cross-country differences in growth.

For the coming years, fiscal policy in the euro area as a whole is expected to be broadly neutral compared with the sharp tightening of earlier years (OECD, 2016). On average in 2015 and 2017, fiscal consolidation was less than one-eighth of its value in the 2012–15 period in euro-area countries. While euro-area growth has strengthened in 2015–17, domestic demand has been persistently weak since the crisis, and strong policy support to demand remains

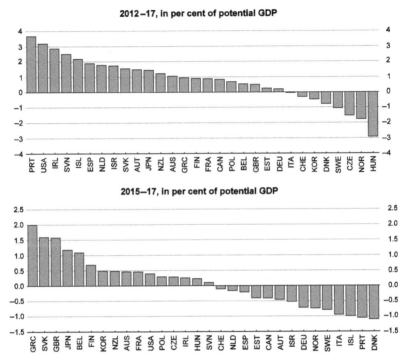

Figure 17.2: Change in the underlying primary balance in OECD countries, 2012–15

Source: OECD Economic Outlook No. 98 database

warranted. With the ECB undertaking exceptional policy stimulus, and given the considerable progress already made in fiscal consolidation since the crisis, fiscal policy can be more supportive of demand.

In addition to the change in speed, there has been a noticeable change in the composition of fiscal consolidation. While consolidation relied to a large extent on increases in taxes in the 2012–15 period, most countries did not raise household, production and import taxes and social security contributions in 2015–17. By contrast, countries are now focusing on restraining current primary spending.

3 The Appropriate Timing and Pace of Consolidation

There is now a consensus in the literature that weak public finance conditions are an important trigger of consolidation (Barrios et al., 2010; Guichard et al., 2007; von Hagen and Strauch, 2001).

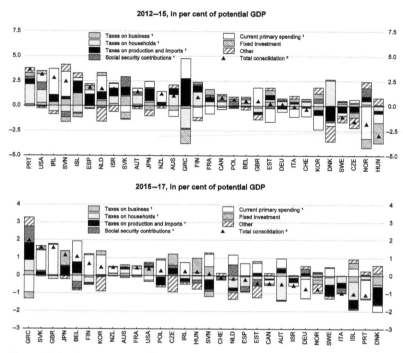

Figure 17.3: Composition of consolidation in OECD countries, 2012–17

Note: 1. Cyclically adjusted. A positive number means expenditure restraint.

2. Based on underlying primary balance.

Source: OECD Economic Outlook No. 98 database

But the economic situation also matters in the timing of consolidation: a survey of thirteen consolidation episodes indicates that consolidation was often implemented in an economic environment that had already turned favourable (Blöchliger et al., 2012). Typically, growth rates picked up before fiscal tightening began and became relatively robust, with the output gap beginning to close around the trough and unemployment rates starting to decline a bit after the trough. In the same vein, von Hagen and Strauch (2001) found that positive output gaps increase the probability of launching a retrenchment. Von Hagen and Strauch (2001) also identified a negative impact for the international environment, which, combined with the positive coefficient on domestic cyclical conditions, implies that governments are more likely to undertake consolidation efforts when the domestic economy is doing well relative to other economies.

In addition to these factors, the political environment is critical. Henriksson (2007) underlines the importance of strong political leadership in starting consolidation episodes. Past country experiences suggest that many consolidation episodes started within one year of the election of a new government, with several of the newly elected governments having declared during the election campaign that they intended to consolidate (Blöchliger et al., 2012).

3.1 The Appropriate Pace of Consolidation Is Country-Specific

Estimating the optimal consolidation pace is challenging, given the interactions between fiscal policy, financial markets and economic growth. On the one hand, large, front-loaded adjustment can reduce GDP growth with negative fallout for the fiscal situation. Such effects are more likely when output and unemployment gaps are large, effectiveness of monetary policy is reduced with interest rates close to the zero lower bound and credit constraints are binding (Galí et al., 2007; Christiano et al., 2009; Woodford, 2011; Auerbach and Gorodnichenko, 2012; Blanchard and Leigh, 2013). In addition, depressed output can damage long-term growth through hysteresis effects (De Long and Summers, 2012). On the other hand, postponing consolidation may undermine markets' confidence in the solvency of a government, risking, in a benign scenario, sluggish growth due to pass-through of higher sovereign risk to borrowing conditions in the broader economy and, in the worst-case scenario, disruptive sovereign default (Rawdanowicz, 2014). Interactions between these different factors are likely to be non-linear and give rise to multiple equilibria. Consequently, their quantification is highly uncertain.

In practice, the appropriate pace of fiscal adjustment depends on a number of country-specific factors (Mann, 2015; Henriksson, 2007):

(i) *Initial fiscal position*: the worse the initial debt dynamics, the greater the need to consolidate swiftly.

(ii) *Policy credibility*: front-loading fiscal consolidation may be inevitable in countries that have lost market access, such as euro-area programme countries, and necessary in countries with low policy credibility, where it serves to signal seriousness about fiscal adjustment and reduces the risks of a confidence crisis.

(iii) *Fiscal rules*: with embedded expenditure targets, fiscal rules tend to be associated with larger and longer adjustment, and higher success rates. This could reflect that well-designed fiscal rules are effective or that governments committed to prudent fiscal management are more likely to institute a rule.

(iv) *Present and expected future economic conditions*: fiscal multipliers are typically higher when excess capacity is large, monetary policy is impaired and credit conditions are poor, so countries in this position should, other things being equal, consolidate more slowly than otherwise. Moreover, fiscal consolidation in some economies may aggravate hysteresis effects and depress long-term potential output.

(v) *Political economy considerations*: the redistributive effects of fiscal adjustment across income classes are crucial for the political sustainability of fiscal consolidation. A fiscal adjustment that is too costly to vulnerable groups may be difficult to sustain once the immediate threat of government default has disappeared, especially following a financial and fiscal crisis that has already exacerbated income inequality.

3.2 The Interplay between Structural and Fiscal Policy

Policy strategies that explicitly combine fiscal and structural efforts in a common framework are desirable to take full advantage of their complementarities. International experience suggests that, in fast-paced consolidation episodes, the need for quick spending reductions often tends to be at odds with efficiency objectives. In particular, when the main objective is to achieve fiscal results quickly, it appears very difficult to introduce effective structural reforms in areas such as pension and health care, where long lead times are required.

Furthermore, during a consolidation period or in a context of weak demand, some structural reforms can have an adverse short-run impact. For instance, reforms putting downward pressures on wages and markups are more likely to further depress demand. Reforms increasing labour supply are also less effective. By contrast, increases in the retirement age, spending on job-search assistance, training, childcare support or investment in knowledge-based capital are likely to have stronger effects (Caldera Sanchez et al., 2015).

Finally, changes in tax and spending items that are presented to the public as needed mainly for fiscal adjustment can meet strong, sometimes successful, pressure to reverse them once consolidation is achieved. These lessons indicate that effective structural reform does not necessarily ensue from fiscal consolidation.

4 Choice of Instruments

The choice of consolidation instruments determines how various policy objectives, such as short-term growth, long-term prosperity and equity, are affected.

Using a qualitative assessment (Table 17.1) and putting equal weights on short and long-term growth and equity objectives, Cournède et al. (2014) identify a generic hierarchy of consolidation instruments (Figure 17.4). They find that:

- The most appropriate consolidation measures are cutting subsidies, reducing pension outlays and increasing inheritance, capital gains and other property taxes.
- The least appropriate measures are spending cuts in the areas of education, health care and family policies, as well as hikes in social security contributions.
- Other consolidation instruments, which involve sharper trade-offs between growth and equality, move more in the ranking when the weights given to growth and equality vary. Hikes in corporate and personal income taxes, for instance, fall rapidly in the ranking when growth receives a rising weight relative to equality.

While the impact assessments underpinning Table 17.1 and Figure 17.4 have been found to hold in general across advanced countries, they will not apply in all countries; as such, they need to be treated with caution. Countries may have ample or limited scope to use favourable instruments depending on their tax and spending structures. For example, a government with very high income tax rates has more limited scope to increase them than one starting from low tax rates.

The framework therefore sets criteria to capture the limited scope that countries have for using different instruments. More specifically, the assumption is that each measure, say a spending cut, can proceed as long as it does not take the country into the group of ten OECD countries that spend least in this area as a share of GDP. The calculations impose the additional constraint that the cut cannot be excessively large.

Many G-20 advanced countries have significant scope to meet fiscal challenges with limited adverse side effects for growth and equity if

Table 17.1: *Summary assessment of growth and equity effects of fiscal consolidation instruments*

	Growth		Equity	
	Short-term	Long-term	Short-term	Long-term
Spending cuts				
Education	−	−	−	−
Health services provided in kind	−	−	−	−
Other government consumption (excluding family policy)	−	+	−	
Pensions		++		
Sickness and disability payments	−	+	−	−
Unemployment benefits	−	+	−	
Family	−	−	−	−
Subsidies	−	++	+	+
Public investment	−	−		
Revenue increases				
Personal income taxes	−	−	+	+
Social security contributions	−	−	−	−
Corporate income taxes	−	−	+	+
Environmental taxes	−	+	−	
Consumption taxes (other than environmental)	−	−	−	
Recurrent taxes on immovable property	−			
Other property taxes	−		++	+
Sales of goods and services	−	+	−	−

Source: Cournède, Goujard and Pina (2014)

instruments are well chosen (Figure 17.5). It is estimated that France, Germany, Japan, Korea, Spain and the United States could improve their primary balance by more than 3 percent of GDP using only spending reductions and revenue increases that are in the top half of the least damaging measures. Slovak Republic could increase its primary balance by almost 8 percent. By contrast, Australia and the United Kingdom, where tax and spending structures are already relatively well aligned with the hierarchy implied by this approach, have less potential to improve growth and equity through adjusting their policy mix.

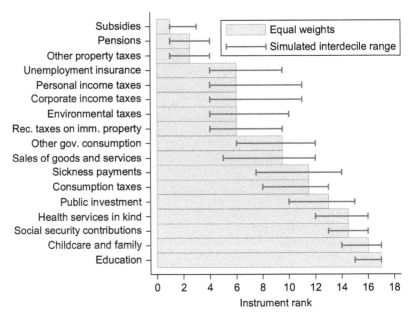

Figure 17.4: Ranking of instruments of consolidation

Note: all consolidation measures have been assessed for their Keynesian effects on short-term growth, their supply effects on long-term growth and their consequences for income distribution, before and after behaviour adjusts. A score of −2 to +2 is given to the effect of each instrument on each objective. Growth and equity effects are weighted equally. Short- and long-term effects are weighted equally. Combining scores and weights yields an indicator for each instrument, which is used to rank them. Stochastic simulations provide a measure of the sensitivity of ranks to the assessment of instrument effects on growth and equity. In 10,000 random draws, each individual instrument score along each objective is kept with a probability of ¾ or increased by +1 with a probability of ⅛ or reduced by −1 with a probability of ⅛. The sensitivity range displays the 10th and 90th percentiles of the instrument rankings in the stochastic simulations.

Source: Cournède, Goujard and Pina (2014)

Corporate and personal income taxes are favourable instruments if putting a strong weight on equity considerations, but less so if giving overriding priority to long-term growth. Corporate or personal income taxes take different places in the ranking of instruments depending on the weights given to objectives, as they raise acute trade-offs between output and equity considerations. They are relatively good candidates to create fiscal space in countries where income dispersion is wide. The ranking of fiscal instruments can also take into account their effect on

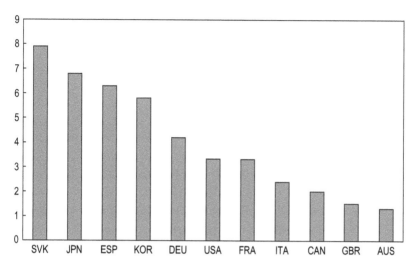

Figure 17.5: Scope to use relatively favourable consolidation instruments
Note: in percent of GDP.
Source: Cournède, Goujard and Pina (2014)

external imbalances. To pick one example, this approach suggests favouring increases in consumption taxes over social security contributions in countries that experience large current account deficits.

Reductions in public expenditure become more attractive when taking a long-term perspective. The hierarchy of instruments can look through near- and medium-term considerations and focus on the very long term, say 2030 – a horizon at which Keynesian demand effects lose relevance. The framework can produce an illustrative long-term ranking at this horizon by dropping short-term considerations. Public expenditure cuts move up the ranking when switching to the long run. Symmetrically, personal and corporate income taxes, which generate distortions that durably reduce growth, drop to low places in the long-term rankings.

5 Improving the Quality of Public Finances

Reforms that improve the quality of public finances, while desirable in their own right, can also ease the trade-offs between consolidation, equity and long-term growth objectives. In the most favourable cases, those reforms can even eliminate trade-offs and bring fiscal improvements, as well as progress along growth or equity goals. As a result, they also have the potential to make fiscal consolidation more likely to succeed. Two main types of reforms are discussed in this section: those that enhance the allocative efficiency of spending and those that improve the design of instruments.

5.1 Raising Efficiency in Expenditure Allocation

Recent reviews of country experiences have identified a range of reforms that could foster efficiency and allow a better allocation of resources.

There is now a widespread consensus on the need to improve expenditure prioritisation in a context where governments need to be careful and systematic in how they allocate their limited resources. One reason why expenditure prioritisation has been relatively weak thus far in OECD countries has been that spending reviews were mostly confined to new rather than baseline spending (Robinson, 2015). Vandierendonck (2014) identifies key success factors for spending reviews. They include political commitment, ownership by the administration, clear objectives and governance, integration in the budgetary process, anticipation of implementation, building of transformation capability and a performance culture at all levels of public service. More specifically, past experience suggests that spending reviews should be designed in a flexible way and should not substitute for political decisions. In this regard, it is preferable to have politically led reviews and to deliver savings options to political authorities rather than making decisions about cuts on their behalf. In most countries there is also probably a need for a greater budgetary role for centres of government (central budget administration) at the expense of individual spending ministries.

Performance-based budgeting, which establishes performance targets for budget lines, can also improve the cost-effectiveness of public spending by improving budgetary allocation across policy areas. Past attempts, however, have not had much impact on budget decision-making, with little use of performance indicators developed as part of the reform. One reason is that performance budgeting was generally more focused on performance management than on budgeting (Robinson, 2015). Moreover, most often, performance indicators were not complemented by a thorough evaluation. Further investigating these issues would be useful for countries to reap the full benefits of performance-based budgeting.

Finally, reforms that transform public administration structures or processes (e.g. cutting red tape) can rapidly generate efficiency gains and savings, as evidenced by a review of case studies on France, the Netherlands, Sweden and Austria undertaken by the European Commission in 2012. Conditions of success appear to be that these reforms are prepared by rigorous spending reviews and that their implementation is tightly monitored.

5.2 *Improving the Design of Expenditure and Tax Tools*

At a general level, structural reforms that improve efficiency in the delivery of public services can reduce the adverse growth impact of spending cuts in productive areas of government spending. Similarly, the negative equity impact of spending cuts can be headed off by structural reforms that ensure a better targeting of public services and transfers and stimulate labour supply.

There is scope to enhance the delivery of essential public services while saving resources. In health care, efficiency gains could permit improvement or maintenance of service provision while containing the cost to the public purse, therefore mitigating adverse growth and equity impacts (Hagemann, 2012). Although they are subject to considerable uncertainty, quantitative estimates suggest that the scope for efficiency gains in the health sector has the potential to be very large (European Commission, 2012). Previous OECD work emphasised that, while structural reforms to realise potential efficiency gains vary depending on the structure of health systems, some apply to most countries. In particular, better priority-setting, improved consistency in responsibility assignment across levels of government and better user information on the quality and price of services would be reform options to consider in many OECD countries (Joumard et al., 2010).

The potential for efficiency gains is also large in education and quasi-fiscal activities. For instance, introducing higher education tuition fees coupled with means-tested grants or loan guarantees can improve public finances, possibly spur growth by encouraging tertiary schooling completion and educational investment in areas with greater economic potential and help to correct the regressive impact of public spending on tertiary education (Hagemann, 2012). Both earlier and more recent OECD studies have suggested that more performance monitoring, more school autonomy and greater user choice is associated with greater efficiency in the public provision of primary and secondary schooling (Sutherland and Price, 2007; Frederiksen, 2013). With the exception of the United States, countries with the greatest potential for efficiency gains are generally not the ones with the largest consolidation needs. However, in the United States, the need to address widening skill gaps points to a case for allocating efficiency gains to providing more and better education rather than cutting expenditure (OECD, 2012).

On the tax side, the growth impact of hikes can be reduced through the closing of loopholes and base broadening (including by curbing fraud and evasion) rather than via rate increases. Indeed, recent OECD research found robust evidence that multinational enterprises (MNEs) engage in international tax planning (OECD, 2013). MNEs shift profit from higher to lower-tax rate countries. Large MNEs were also found to exploit mismatches between tax systems (e.g. differences in the tax treatment of certain entities, instruments or transactions) and preferential tax treatment for certain activities or incomes to reduce their tax burden. Tax planning was estimated to reduce the effective tax rate of large MNEs by 4–8½ percentage points on average. Overall, the net tax revenue loss from tax planning is estimated at 4–10 percent of global corporate tax revenues.

As regards personal and corporate income taxes, tax expenditures often distort resource allocation and hamper productivity growth. They can also result in a less equal income distribution. The preferential tax treatment of owner-occupied housing and the dispersion of effective corporate tax rates are typical examples.[1] Estimates of tax expenditures vary widely across countries, and harmonised information is missing (Figure 17.6). In the mid-2000s, those expenditures were estimated at 8½ percent of GDP in the United Kingdom, 6 percent in the United States and below ½ percent in Germany (OECD, 2010). Since then, there seems to have been some base broadening, resulting in a stabilisation of revenues despite the observed cuts in tax rates (OECD, 2013).

---

[1] OECD research shows that corporate tax has a lower impact on investment and productivity in small firms, and concludes that general cuts in corporate taxes are more effective in raising investment and productivity that a preferential treatment for SMEs (Johansson et al., 2008).

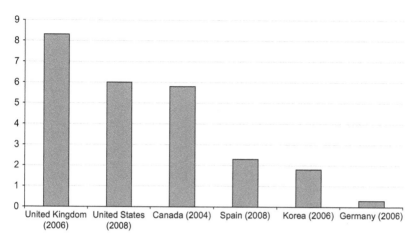

Figure 17.6: Estimated personal and corporate income tax expenditures in selected countries

Note: in percent of GDP.

Source: OECD (2010), *Tax Expenditures in OECD Countries*

In the area of consumption taxes, base-broadening reforms can bring in additional proceeds and reduce distortions detrimental to growth. If accompanied by targeted measures towards poorer households, abolishing reduced value-added or consumption tax rates may improve public finances without negative consequences for equity, at a comparatively low cost for growth. Although crude and subject to important caveats, the so-called VAT revenue ratio is the most readily available indicator to provide illustrative estimates, on a cross-country basis, of the scope for base broadening. The ratio compares actual VAT revenue to the standard VAT rate multiplied by final consumption expenditure. Despite its caveats, the indicator suggests that, even after factoring in the costs of accompanying distributional measures, base broadening can yield substantial additional revenues in many countries while reducing cross-sector distortions (Figure 17.7).

As regards property taxes, broadening bases by regularly aligning real estate taxable values to market valuations could yield equity gains in addition to bringing in additional revenues and reducing distortions. In many countries cadastral values have become outdated, often by a large margin. By way of example, Austria, Belgium, France and Germany last carried out a housing valuation exercise three or more

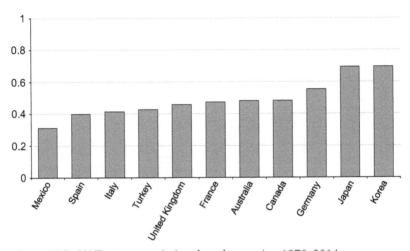

Figure 17.7: VAT revenue ratio in selected countries, 1970–2014

Note: the VAT revenue ratio is calculated as total VAT receipts divided by an estimate of the tax base and the standard VAT rate. This measure provides an indicator of the effect of exemptions, reduced rates and non-compliance on government revenues.

Source: OECD Consumption Tax Trends 2014

decades ago (Andrews et al., 2011; Johannesson-Linden and Gayer, 2012; OECD; 2011). Updated property taxes could also alleviate the regressive impact of mortgage interest deductibility. Though the redistributive impact of updating is complex, being felt across individuals, generations and territorial units, it will tend to be progressive at least if account is taken of the distribution of wealth, and not merely of current income. Even on the basis of the latter, equity gains will ensue if those residing in buildings with more outdated values tend to enjoy above-average income. Admittedly, updating cadastral values will raise difficulties for old people living on low pensions in large old houses, but this issue could be addressed by offering those taxpayers the option of paying this part of taxes in a deferred manner on their estate after their death. More generally, making the property tax structure more progressive would be an option to help offset harmful equity effects from other consolidation measures.

Overall, quality of public finance is multi-dimensional. It refers to how well fiscal policies achieve governments' macroeconomic and socio-economic objectives. In most countries a key policy concern is to sustain long-term economic growth while at the same time addressing redistributive objectives and ensuring sound public finances. This underlines the importance of understanding how public spending and tax systems could best be designed to promote inclusive long-term growth. Reflecting this, ongoing research at the OECD is currently examining in more detail the quality of public finances and its relation with growth and inequality. The research will bring together various dimensions of revenue and spending and analyse their linkages with growth in a comprehensive setting. This allows taking into account that the growth effect of a change in a certain spending item will depend on the way it is financed.

Existing research has shown that complementarities may exist between fiscal policies and institutions, which can have implications for the impact of fiscal policy on growth. For instance, Agénor (2010) showed that, in countries with weak public investment management processes, public investment is unlikely to fully translate into growth effects. Drawing on this literature, ongoing OECD research explores whether certain institutions and design features (e.g. budgeting practice, degree of decentralisation, degree of progressivity, etc.) alter the effect of fiscal policy on growth. As discussed, apart from affecting growth, the structure and design of public finance also has implications for equity. Some fiscal policies may raise both long-run growth and equity (e.g. spending on education for disadvantaged groups), while others create trade-offs (e.g. reduction in the progressivity of personal income taxes). The research will empirically assess the role of tax and spending structure for income distribution in order to highlight potential trade-offs between growth and equity.

6 Taking a Longer Perspective: Designing Growth-Friendly Fiscal Rules

The sharp rise in debt experienced by most OECD countries has raised questions about the fiscal frameworks needed to accommodate cyclical fluctuations along the path towards a prudent debt target, creating fiscal space to react to future shocks and taking into account countries' specificities. In particular, the euro-area fiscal rules are essential to the stability of the monetary union, but their complexity has created uncertainty in recent years (see also Chapter 7 of this volume), not least because of the repeated resort to *ad hoc* extensions of deadlines for corrective budgetary action. This uncertainty reduces the demand impact of expansionary changes in policy. Open discussion of how to make the rules more effective and more credible is needed.

Fiscal rules should have two objectives:

- *A discipline objective*: anchoring fiscal policy expectations by targeting a prudent debt level (see Box 17.1).
- *A stabilisation objective*: allowing for macroeconomic stabilisation that enhances economic growth.

Box 17.1: Setting a Prudent Debt Level

Defining a prudent debt target is not easy. First, there is a need to assess the impact of debt on the economy, and in particular to find out whether there is any turning point above which negative effects of debt dominate its positive effects. The turning point or debt threshold serves as a reference point in the determination of a prudent debt level. Second, countries should set debt targets that avoid overshooting the debt threshold, and the degree of prudence required to achieve this depends on country-specific shocks and risks.

To minimise the risk of missing a debt target, which could undermine credibility, a prudent target for future deficit developments needs to be set, accounting for uncertainties surrounding the development of the main macroeconomic variables and therefore debt dynamics. OECD analysis uses a stochastic macroeconomic framework to quantify those uncertainties. The framework can also be used to assess the risk of hitting a debt threshold and to calculate the cushion needed so that adverse macroeconomic shocks do not push debt beyond the level at which adverse effects of debt on economic activity set in.

In practice, this can be achieved by keeping the probability that debt goes above this threshold level sufficiently low. In this framework, the probability of debt going above 85 percent for non-euro-area OECD countries and 65 percent for euro-area countries is calculated. The prudent debt target is the median debt by 2040, such that there is less than a 25 percent risk of going beyond the debt thresholds, and the corresponding fiscal deficit trajectory is calculated. Larger uncertainties in a given country are associated with a lower prudent target.

From this analysis, the prudent debt target is on average 50 percent of GDP for euro-area countries and 70 percent of GDP for the rest of the OECD, with some heterogeneity among countries. Reaching the prudent debt target by 2040 would require a primary surplus in nineteen OECD countries.

SOURCE: FALL ET AL. (2015)

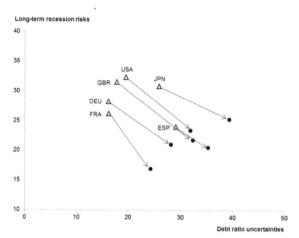

Figure 17.8: The trade-off between counter-cyclicality and hitting the debt target

Note: the long-term recession risk is the probability of GDP per capita growth becoming negative. The uncertainty surrounding the debt trajectory is assessed by the interquartile range of the debt level in 2040. The 'constant primary balance' simulation is a stylised scenario in which the actual primary balance is kept constant such that the prudent debt target is reached, with no automatic stabilisers. In the scenario labelled 'Automatic stabilisers', a 1 percentage point negative surprise in the output gap is associated with 0.4 percent of GDP stimulus.

Source: Fall et al. (2015)

Drawing on Fall et al. (2015), four types of fiscal rules are reviewed in this chapter: a budget balance rule; a structural (balance budget) rule; an expenditure rule; and a revenue rule. These rules differ in their ability to fulfil the competing stabilisation and discipline objectives. For instance, fiscal stimulus through the effect of an automatic stabiliser mitigates recessions but, compared with a strict primary balance rule, increases uncertainties surrounding the debt path (Figure 17.8).

The structural budget balance rule combines, in principle, the capacity of meeting the two objectives, but it has important drawbacks in terms of observability and real time assessment. Structural balance measures, despite some progress on measurement, are highly dependent on volatile and often biased estimates of the output gap and subject to frequent revisions (Hers and Suyker, 2014). Indeed, a number of studies have highlighted the fact that the sign and the magnitude of the output gaps estimated in real time are subject to large revisions as new information becomes available (Turner et al., 2016; European

Table 17.2: *Synthesis of the effects of rules with respect to fiscal discipline and stabilisation*

	Budget balance	Structural balance	Expenditure rule	Revenue rule
Fiscal stabilisation	–	+	+	–
Fiscal discipline	++	+	+	-+
Side effects and risks	–	–	–	–

Source: Fall et al. (2015)

Commission, 2015; Bundesbank, 2014). For instance, for Slovakia, Klein et al. (2013) report that the structural deficit in 2010 using pre-crisis estimates of potential growth would have been nearer to 4 percent than 8 percent of GDP.

Therefore, the best combination may be the adoption of a budget balance rule observed over the medium run, complemented by an expenditure rule. As shown in Table 17.2, the combination of the two rules responds to the two objectives. A budget balance rule ensures hitting the debt target and well-designed expenditure rules appear decisive in ensuring the effectiveness of a budget balance rule (Guichard et al., 2007). The marginal benefit of adding a revenue rule is likely outweighed by its costs in terms of complexity and reduction in fiscal flexibility.

For most countries, simulations using a four-equation model on GDP, inflation and short- and long-term interest rates confirm the good performance of a combined budget balance and spending rule (Fall et al., 2015). The combined budget balance and spending rules lead to a higher primary balance surplus and, thus, to a lower public debt path (Figure 17.9). This is the case in particular for countries which have a relatively high level of government spending (see below for the example of France), but is also true in countries with a low level of spending but where fiscal policy is moderately effective in dampening shocks. In these countries an expenditure rule is useful to ensure adherence to the debt target (see Canada and the Czech and Slovak Republics). By contrast, adding a spending rule to the budget balance rule appears to be unnecessary in countries with low levels of government spending and high fiscal policy capacity to mitigate short-term fluctuations (Australia, Israel, Korea, New Zealand, Poland, Switzerland and the United States).

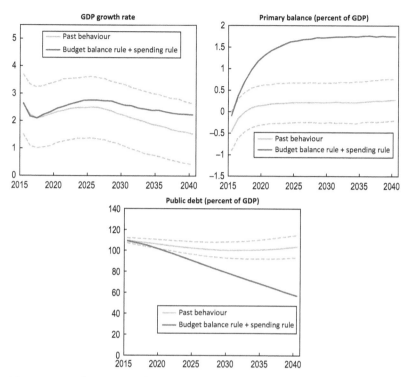

Figure 17.9: Illustration of a budget balance rule combined with a spending rule, France

Source: Fall et al. (2015)

Tail events happen, but they need not undermine credibility. Clear escape clauses should be set allowing the temporary suspension of fiscal rules. A temporary suspension should be conditional on exceptional events such as natural catastrophes or a sharp output contraction. However, the definition of these clauses must be clear to make sure they cannot be used in normal times. To cope with tail events, a 'rainy day' fund can underpin respect of the rule over the cycle and would allow greater room for stabilisation. Unexpected surpluses would be saved and used later to finance unexpected deficits or short-term stabilisation policies.

7 Conclusion

The current policy debate on austerity has underlined that there is no one-size-fits–all rule. While common triggering factors to consolidation can be found, the appropriate pace of consolidation appears to be country-specific. Political economy considerations play a prominent role in this regard, and the redistributive effects of fiscal adjustment across income classes are crucial for the political sustainability of fiscal consolidation.

Against this background, fiscal policy in the euro area as a whole is expected to be broadly neutral in the coming years, compared with the sharp tightening of earlier years. In many countries, there will be a significant change in the composition of fiscal consolidation from tax increases to expenditure restraints, objective which may be more challenging to achieve.

Many OECD countries have significant scope to meet fiscal challenges with limited adverse side effects for growth and equity if instruments are well chosen. In general, the most appropriate consolidation packages involve cutting subsidies and reducing pension outlays while increasing inheritance, capital gains and other property taxes. The least appropriate measures are spending cuts in the areas of education, health care and family policies, as well as hikes in social security contributions.

In addition, improving the quality of public finance is key to ease the trade-offs between consolidation, equity and long-term growth objectives. Country experiences in raising the efficiency of spending allocation have been mixed thus far. There is scope to enhance the delivery of essential public services such as health care or education while saving resources. On the tax side, the growth impact of hikes can be reduced through closing loopholes and broadening tax bases rather than raising rates.

From a longer-term perspective, fiscal consolidation strategies should be guided by prudent debt targets and framed by fiscal rules. Most OECD countries could fulfil the competing stabilisation and fiscal discipline objectives by adopting a budget balance rule observed over the medium run, complemented by an expenditure rule.

Bibliography

Agénor, P.-R. (2010). A theory of infrastructure-led development. *Journal of Economic Dynamics and Control*, 34(5), 932–50.

Andrews, D., Caldera Sanchez, A. and Johansson, A. (2011). *Housing Markets and Structural Policies in OECD Countries*. OECD Economics Department Working Papers, No. 836.

Auerbach, A. J. and Gorodnichenko, Y. (2012). Measuring the output responses to fiscal policy. *American Economic Journal: Economic Policy*, 4(2), 1–27.

Barrios, S., Langedijk, S. and Pench, L. (2010). *EU Fiscal Consolidation after the Financial Crisis-Lessons from Past Experiences*. Paper presented at the 12th *Banca d'Italia* Public Finance Workshop, Fiscal Policy: Lessons from the Crisis, Perugia, 25–27 March.

Blanchard, O. and Leigh, D. (2013). *Growth Forecast Errors and Fiscal Multipliers*. IMF Working Paper No. 13/1, Washington, DC.

Blöchliger, H., Song, D. and Sutherland, D. (2012). *Fiscal Consolidation: Part 4. Case Studies of Large Fiscal Consolidation Episodes*. OECD Economics Department Working Papers, No. 935. doi: http://dx.doi.org/10.1787/5k9fdf5xptlq-en

Bundesbank (2014). *On the Reliability of International Organisations' Estimates of the Output Gap*. Deutsche Bundesbank Monthly Report, April.

Caldera Sanchez, A., de Serres, A. and Yashiro, N. (2015). *Reforming in a Difficult Macro Context: What Should Be the Priority?* OECD Economics Department Working Papers, No. 1297.

Christiano, L., Eichenbaum, M. and Rebelo, S. (2009). *When Is the Government Spending Multiplier Large?* NBER Working Papers, No. 15394.

Cournède, B., Pina, A. and Goujard, A. (2014). Reconciling fiscal consolidation with growth and equity. *OECD Journal: Economic Studies*, 2013(1), 7–89.

De Long, J. B and Summers, L. H. (2012). *Fiscal Policy in a Depressed Economy*. Paper prepared for the Spring 2012 Brookings Panel on Economic Activity, 22–23 March, Washington, DC.

European Commission (2012). *The Quality of Public Expenditure in the EU*. Occasional Paper 125, December.

———— (2015). *An Assessment of the Relative Quality of EU Gap Estimates*. Quarterly Report on the Euro Area, Vol. 14.

Fall, F., Bloch, D., Fournier, J.-M. and Hoeller, P. (2015). *Prudent Debt Targets and Fiscal Frameworks*. OECD Economic Policy Papers, No. 15.

Fredriksen, K. (2013). *Decentralisation and Economic Growth – Part 3: Decentralisation, Infrastructure Investment and Educational Performance*. OECD Working Papers on Fiscal Federalism, No. 16, Paris.

Galí, J., Lopez-Salido, D. and Valles, J. (2007). Understanding the effects of government spending on consumption. *Journal of the European Economic Association*, 5(1), 227–70.

Guichard, S., Kennedy, M., Wurzel, E. and André, C. (2007). *What Promotes Fiscal Consolidation: OECD Country Experiences*. OECD Economics Department Working Papers, No. 553.

Hagemann, R. (2012). *Fiscal Consolidation: Part 6. What Are the Best Policy Instruments for Fiscal Consolidation?* OECD Economics Department Working Papers, No. 937, OECD, Paris.

Hers, J. and Suyker, W. (2014). *Structural Budget Balance: A Love at First Sight Turned Sour.* CPB Policy Brief, 2014/07.

Henriksson, J. (2007). Ten lessons about budget consolidation. *Bruegel Essay and Lecture Series,* http://bruegel.org/wp-content/uploads/imported/publications/el_010607_budget.pdf

Johansson, Å., Heady, C., Arnold, J., Brys, B. and Vartia, L. (2008). *Tax and Economic Growth.* OECD Economics Department Working Papers, No. 620.

Johannesson-Linden, A. and C. Gayer (2012). *Possible Reforms of Real Estate Taxation: Criteria for Successful Policies.* European Economy: Occasional Papers, No. 119, European Commission, Brussels.

Joumard, I., Hoeller, P. André, C. and Nicq, C. (2010). *Health Care Systems: Efficiency and Policy Settings.* OECD Economics Department Working Papers, No. 769.

Klein, C., Price, R. W. and Wörgötter, A. (2013). *Improving the Fiscal Framework to Enhance Growth in an Era of Fiscal Consolidation in Slovakia.* OECD Economics Department Working Papers, No. 1018. doi: 10.1787/5k4c9kv6b7f2-en

Mann, C. (2015). *Budget Deficit and Austerity.* Paper prepared for the Institute for New Economic Thinking Conference on 9 April.

OECD (2010). *Tax Expenditures in OECD Countries.* Paris: OECD.

(2011). *OECD Economic Surveys: France.* Paris: OECD.

(2012). *OECD Economic Surveys: United States.* Paris: OECD.

(2013). *Addressing Base Erosion and Profit Shifting.* Paris: OECD.

(2015). *Economic Outlook* Vol 2015/2. Paris: OECD.

(2016). *Economic Outlook* Vol 2016/2. Paris: OECD.

Rawdanowicz, Ł. (2014). Choosing the pace of fiscal consolidation. *OECD Journal: Economic Studies,* **2013**, 91–119.

Robinson, M. (2013). Aggregate expenditure ceilings and allocative flexibility. *OECD Journal on Budgeting,* **12**(3), 1–19.

Robinson, M. (2015). *Budget Reform before and after the Global Financial Crisis.* Paper presented at the 36th Annual OECD Senior Budget Official Meeting, 11–12 June 2015.

Sutherland, D. and Price, R. (2007). *Linkages between Performance and Institutions in the Primary and Secondary Education Sector.* OECD Economics Department Working Papers, No. 558.

Turner, D., Cavalleri, M. C., Guillemette, Y., Kopoin, A., Ollivaud, P. and Rusticelli, E. (2016). An investigation into improving the real-time reliability of OECD output gap estimates. OECD Economics Department Working Papers, No. 1294.

Vandierendonck, C. (2014). Public spending reviews design, conduct, implementation. *Economic Papers*, 525 (July), http://ec.europa.eu/economy_finance/publications/economic_paper/2014/pdf/ecp525_en.pdf.

Von Hagen, J., Hallett, A. H. and Strauch, R. R. (2002). Budgetary consolidation in Europe: quality, economic conditions and persistence. *Journal of the Japanese and International Economies*, 16, 512–35.

Von Hagen, J. and Strauch, R. R. (2001). Fiscal consolidations: quality, economic conditions and success. *Public Choice*, 109, 327–46.

Woodford, M. (2011). Simple analytics of the government expenditure multiplier. *American Economic Journal: Macroeconomics*, 3(1), 1–35.

18 | Discretionary Fiscal Policy and Recessions

FABRIZIO CORICELLI, RICCARDO
FIORITO AND FRANCESCO MOLTENI

1 Introduction

The depth of the output fall during the Great Recession has revived interest in the role of fiscal stimulus, which has been endorsed even by paladins of fiscal rigour such as the IMF (IMF, 2010, 2012a). The broad consensus on the need for a fiscal stimulus has surely been affected by the fact that the last crisis was not a normal cyclical downturn but a deep recession – a rare event in OECD countries during the post-war era. However, the simple observation of large budget deficits and soaring government debts during the Great Recession cannot be taken as a signal of expansionary discretionary action by governments, since a large share of the deterioration in the fiscal accounts originated from the endogenous adjustment to the recession.

The debate on the fiscal stimulus initially focused on fiscal multipliers. However, with the passage of time, the nature of the stimulus and its temporary characteristic has taken center stage, as exemplified by the debate on exit from fiscal stimulus. The early (or too early) abandonment of fiscal stimulus has been considered a main cause of the double-dip recession and the slow and anaemic recovery of the eurozone. For several European countries, rather than exit from fiscal stimulus, fiscal policy tightening was forced by the sharp deterioration in confidence in their debt, which led to a jump in the cost of servicing public debt. Generally – with Italy as the best example – the tightening took place through increasing tax revenues rather than reducing government expenditure.

Neglecting the fact that reducing expenditure would have been undesirable in the context of the deepest recession since the Great Depression, it is worth noting that the reliance on revenues in many austerity programs reveals that governments face severe obstacles in cutting back expenditure, which proves to be largely inertial, in contrast with textbook analyses and common approaches to cyclically adjusted budgets, which depict expenditure as almost entirely discretionary. Focusing on OECD countries, in this chapter we use the measure of discretionary expenditure derived in Coricelli and Fiorito (2013) to try to shed light on the behavior of discretionary expenditure during the Great Recession, and during previous recessions.[1] Identifying truly discretionary expenditure is a crucial precondition to carry out meaningful analysis of the effects of changing expenditure on GDP.

Our definition of discretion implies that expenditure has to be temporary, not inertial (thus easily reversible), and not automatic.

In analyzing the role of fiscal policy in relation to economic fluctuations, not long-run growth, one should focus on temporary expenditure, which can be easily reversed as economic conditions change. By contrast, a large component of expenditure reflects entitlements associated with social contracts or political exchanges, which are hard to modify. Not only are these types of expenditures, such as health, education, and pensions, hard to change, but also their use to achieve short-term stabilization is debatable.

Isolating discretionary policies is complicated as every spending component combines automatic, inertial, and discretionary elements. Undoubtedly, every item has at one point in time resulted from discretionary decisions, but once decisions are implemented they involve inertial dynamics, which vary depending on the type of expenditure. Automatic components, such as unemployment benefits and income subsidies, respond at least in principle to the cyclical conditions of the economy. However, often the automatic components are significantly modified during downturns and thus become discretionary rather than automatic. A typical example is the lengthening of the period of entitlement for unemployment benefits during recessions.

As we illustrate in Section 2, three main approaches have been followed in the literature. First, discretionary expenditure is derived as expenditure adjusted for the component determined by cyclical fluctuations. Traditionally, such an approach identifies only unemployment benefits as non-discretionary expenditure.[2] Second, discretionary

---

[1] Our notion of discretion is based on economic grounds and it goes beyond the legal/institutional aspects relating to the budgetary process, which are nevertheless extremely important (Elmendorf, 2011).

[2] Larch and Turrini (2009) indicate that the European Commission approach to evaluating fiscal stance still relies on a cyclically adjusted budget in which the only automatic expenditure is associated to unemployment benefits.

expenditure is obtained from the estimated residuals of a regression for total expenditure (usually consumption, or consumption plus investment), determined by lagged expenditure (inertial component) and some subjective measure of economic activity to approximate cyclical components. Third, discretionary expenditure is obtained through a "narrative" approach, focusing on a few selected episodes, mostly related to policy or administrative decisions.

The cyclically adjusted budget balance assumes that, except for unemployment benefits, all expenditure is discretionary and contributes to determining the so-called fiscal stance. At the other extreme we find the identification of discretionary expenditure with the (possibly) white noise residuals of an estimated expenditure equation. In this approach, discretionary expenditure is thus a negligible proportion of total expenditure.

Identifying discretionary expenditure as residuals from an estimated equation has major drawbacks as it fails to distinguish the nature of different components of expenditure, which have different degrees of inertia or dependence on the cycle. Moreover, in contrast with the above definition, discretionary spending may well react to the state of the economy. Discretion and unpredictability are not synonymous.

Finally, the "narrative" approach, which isolates the policy decisions from a review of the actual behavior of policymakers, is closer to our approach, as it emphasizes the diversity of various spending interventions. However, the narrative approach is usually applied to a few large changes in policy decisions and does not apply to more systematic changes in spending to be evaluated on a cyclical basis, using macro-economic spending variables. Furthermore, the narrative approach requires detailed information on actual decisions taken by governments and assumes that decisions taken are then implemented. In fact, in the phase of implementation, fiscal plans are likely to change and the gaps between *de jure* and *de facto* measures may vary across countries depending on institutional and political features. According to Elmendorf: "Congress specifies the amount of budget authority provided each year, but does not directly control when outlays occur" (Elmendorf, 2011, p. 3).

We develop a different measure of discretionary expenditure, which tries to avoid some of the drawbacks of the measures associated with the three approaches discussed above. In particular, we evaluate individual components of spending to identify those components that

qualify as discretionary, assuming that a necessary condition for discretion is that expenditure has a low degree of inertia. We then aggregate these components to derive our overall measure of discretionary
expenditure. This definition is consistent with the view that discretionary spending used to affect short-term output fluctuations has to be
temporary.

One of the main findings from our analysis is that discretionary
spending is a small component of overall primary expenditure, at
around 30 percent in OECD countries. This implies that, when faced
with the need to use fiscal policy to smooth temporary shocks to
output, governments tend to have a small margin of maneuver. Economists have generally indicated public debt as a burden for the freedom
of maneuver of future governments. We identify an additional source
of constraint on governments' room to maneuver, which is the high
share of inertial and rigid expenditure.[3] Interestingly, we find that
during recessions discretionary spending does not always move more
than non-discretionary spending and, moreover, in many instances it
moves pro-cyclically.[4] Furthermore, during recessions, including the
Great Recession, this pro-cyclicality appears stronger for countries
facing tight fiscal constraints.

Of course, we do not claim that changes in expenditures that are
persistent are irrelevant. In fact, large changes in what we define non-
discretionary spending are associated with fiscal reforms, often carried
out in the wake of crises. We have several examples of these phenomena during the Great Recession, especially in countries facing deep
financial crises and debt crises.[5]

Large contractions in public sector employment and public sector
wages occurred in these countries.[6] According to our approach, these
measures cannot be classified within the realm of short-term measures
aimed at stabilizing the economy. The fact that these changes occur
during major crises indirectly confirms our view that non-discretionary

---

[3] Steuerle (2013) denotes the large share of rigid expenditure as lack of "fiscal
democracy," as it imposes tight constraints on action of future governments.
[4] In general, government spending has been shown to be acyclical or even
procyclical also in developed countries (Fiorito, 1997; Lane, 2003).
[5] Examples are the GIIPS and Iceland in the OECD area, and Latvia for the
emerging countries.
[6] Table 18.5 shows how large contractions in the compensation of employees, and
therefore also in government consumption, were in Iceland and Ireland.

spending is hard to modify in the short run, except in exceptional circumstances.

In conclusion, we provide a measure of discretionary spending that is driven by the properties of different components of expenditure. Our approach leads to a transparent and easy way to compute a measure of discretionary expenditure.

The remainder of the chapter is organized as follows. In Section 2 we discuss major alternatives in measuring fiscal discretion set out in recent research. In Section 3 we summarize the approach of Coricelli and Fiorito (2013). Section 4 presents stylized facts on both traditional fiscal aggregates and discretionary versus non-discretionary expenditure. Section 5 analyzes the behavior of the different components of expenditure during recessions, including the Great Recession. Section 6 concludes.

2 Discretion in the Empirical Literature

In this section we discuss in some detail the three main approaches to measuring fiscal discretion in the literature: (1) the cyclically adjusted government balances; (2) residuals from feedback equations; and (3) event chronology ("narrative approach").

2.1 Cyclically Adjusted Balances

The first approach refers to cyclically adjusted balances as a simple device for removing automatic stabilization from fiscal variables (Girouard and André, 2005). Despite their wide use in both empirical studies and official documents, adjusted balances have several limitations.[7] First, they do not account for recessions. Second, both corrected and uncorrected balances do not account for differences in government size, which are important for characterizing fiscal policy in a structural way. Finally and most importantly, adjusted balances' ability to remove cyclical fluctuations is clearly overstated.

---

[7] Cyclically adjusted balances (CAB) or cyclically adjusted primary balances (CAPB) are widely used in IMF, OECD and European Commission documents. Recently, the IMF structural balances (SB) have added to CAB other transitory factors such as commodity and asset price fluctuations. However, except for 2009, the differences between the CAB and the more subjective SB indicator are not empirically relevant (IMF, 2012b).

Table 18.1: *Primary balances and cyclically adjusted primary balances, 1980–2014*

Country	Range	(1) Primary balances		(2) CAPB		Correlation
		Volatility	Persistence	Volatility	Persistence	(1)–(2)
Austria	1990–2011	1.44	8.4 (5)	1.10	8.5 (5)	0.84
Belgium	1980–2011	3.80	54.1 (8)	3.41	46.0 (8)	0.97
Denmark	1980–2011	3.82	49.4 (8)	2.93	49.7 (8)	0.97
Finland	1980–2011	3.99	45.5 (8)	2.54	51.6 (8)	0.95
France	1980–2011	1.54	24.3 (8)	1.12	37.2 (8)	0.88
Iceland	1990–2011	4.32	9.7 (5)	4.06	5.2 (5)	0.94
Ireland	1990–2011	6.48	15.7 (5)	3.75	35.7 (5)	0.84
Italy	1980–2011	3.37	89.0 (8)	3.81	75.0 (8)	0.97
Japan	1980–2009	3.34	60.3 (7)	3.00	64.5 (7)	0.99
Netherlands	1980–2011	2.20	12.5 (8)	2.00	6.9 (8)	0.91
Norway	1980–2012	2.35	46.1 (8)	2.36	43.3 (8)	1.00
Spain	1980–2011	3.63	37.8 (8)	2.84	37.4 (8)	0.96
Sweden	1980–2012	4.09	58.1 (8)	3.13	43.1 (8)	0.95
UK	1980–2013	3.36	38.7 (8)	2.90	44.4 (8)	0.96
US	1980–2014	3.17	31.5 (8)	2.71	40.3 (8)	0.98

Source: OECD, *Economic Outlook 90* (EO90), November 2011. Primary balance and CAPB are percentage ratios to actual and potential GDP, respectively. As in the rest of the paper, persistence is measured via the Ljung–Box (LB) 2-statistics. The number in parenthesis refers to the number of autocorrelations for time series having a different length

As Table 18.1 shows, the adjusted (CAPB) and unadjusted primary balances (CAB) are strongly correlated. Moreover, even though – as expected – adjusted balances are in most cases less volatile, adjusted and unadjusted budgets display similar degrees of persistence. This is a severe limitation, as variables associated with discretionary short-term policies should be less persistent than the unadjusted balances (see Section 3). Of course, if one interprets the adjusted budget as the structural budget, which reflects long-run structural features of expenditure and taxes – such as, for instance, the generosity of the social welfare system and the relevance of public education – one should also expect a higher degree of persistence of the adjusted than the unadjusted budget. However, in this interpretation, the use of the adjusted balance as an indicator of short-term discretionary measures taken by governments is meaningless.

2.2 *Residuals from Estimated Spending Equations*

The seminal contribution of this approach is that of Fatás and Mihov (2003), who estimate percentage changes in the government consumption/GDP ratio as a function of its lag, of real GDP changes, and of a set of controls approximating institutional factors. Since the estimated residuals should be free from cyclical components, the authors interpret them as a measure of the discretionary spending in each country. As in Galí (1994), this measure is then shown to be destabilizing in the resulting cross-section estimate. Finally, Fatás and Mihov include in their panel both developed and developing countries, even though, as shown in more recent studies, the two groups of countries seem to respond differently to the same fiscal stimuli (Ilzetzki et al., 2011).

Afonso et al. (2010) follow a similar approach, estimating government expenditure and revenues in levels, analyzing both developed and developing countries in the same panel. As in Fatás and Mihov (2003), government consumption is labeled "government spending" and the estimated residuals are interpreted as discretionary impulses. The same residual approach is also followed in a recent paper by Corsetti et al. (2012), which focuses on a more homogeneous sample of OECD countries. In line with previous studies, in Corsetti et al., estimated residuals from a government consumption equation are supposed to provide a reliable measure of the discretionary spending interventions.

In general, approximating discretion through the estimated residuals of a subjective equation confines discretionary spending to an unpredictable shock, and this happens in a single equation that cannot produce SVAR impulses, regardless of whether they are more or less appropriate for the purpose. Moreover, the fact that properly estimated residuals are not cyclical does not imply per se deliberate discretion. Indeed, it is plausible that discretionary spending aims at improving the economy, that is, that discretionary interventions should only be less cyclical than automatic stabilizers, but nevertheless responsive to and oriented toward economic conditions.

Two additional objections could be raised to the approach of identifying discretionary expenditure with residuals from a simple regression. First, aggregating components of expenditure characterized by sharply different persistence and responsiveness to GDP changes crucially affects the residuals. Second, expenditure rules are specified in terms of ratio of expenditure to GDP. This, as discussed below, creates a serious problem of identification of discretionary policy, as the denominator of the variable depends on GDP, which in turn depends on expenditure. More generally, it is not clear how one can interpret as a choice variable the ratio of a policy variable (expenditure) and an endogenous variable such as GDP. At most, policymakers could decide on a rule that specifies the ratio of expenditure with respect to *expected* rather than *actual* GDP.

2.3 Event Studies

The third approach measures discretionary policy from policy interventions or intentions, taken directly from laws, government interventions, presidential speeches, and the like. This "narrative approach" was first used by Ramey and Shapiro (1998) to extract data from announcements and policy decisions. The approach was also adopted by Romer and Romer (2010) in their post-war reconstruction of tax legislation in the United States, which shows that discretionary interventions have stronger effects than those obtained by cyclical adjustments.[8] Finally, this methodology was used by Ramey (2011) to evaluate the impact of "spending news," which appears more reliable than SVAR impulses.

The narrative approach is surely promising, as it directly measures policy decisions that are unlikely to be captured by cyclically adjusted balances or particular regression residuals. However, the approach has some limitations, because laws and policy statements identify policy intentions that do not always result in approved budget decisions. Moreover, some of the proposals are not precise enough in terms of the involved funding to be approved, and approved budget decisions do not necessarily imply that actual spending is the same as the approved spending in the reference year (Elmendorf, 2011). Additionally, accrual accounting complicates the analysis of government spending in relation to GDP and other macroeconomic variables.

All these limitations make subjective and possibly arbitrary the reconstruction of the selected episodes, as it is difficult to separate

---

[8] In general, the reconstruction of events is costly, especially when the sample includes countries with different languages. This explains why until recently the approach was mainly used for the United States. However, two recent IMF studies (IMF, 2010; Devries et al., 2011) provide cross-national evidence.

actual decisions from mere announcements. In addition, announcements, even if not immediately or consistently followed by corresponding decisions, may equally affect expectations and then market outcomes.

Finally, even if the proposed events can at least produce reasonable dummies, it is difficult to reconstruct in this way how fiscal policy can exert discretion more continuously, as the magnitude of discretionary expenditure depends on the composition of expenditure and on the working of inside and outside lags, which affect actual policy outcomes (Blinder, 2006).

3 Discretionary Spending: A New Measure

Coricelli and Fiorito (2013) constructed a new measure of discretionary spending. Discretionary and non-discretionary spending are artificial constructs, as they do not have any reference to the national accounts. However, they play a key role in representing how fiscal policy works. Automatic stabilizers do not require policymakers to have knowledge of the current state of the economy; more importantly, they do not require political consensus. By contrast, discretionary spending assumes an adequate knowledge of the current and prospective economic conditions. Furthermore, discretion is generally based on the political commitment to improve, more or less immediately, the state of the economy.

A possible clue for separating discretionary from automatic expenditures arises from the fact that legal and political constraints make most components of expenditure de facto unavailable for deliberate control. Indeed, several types of government spending reflect some sorts of obligations, which go beyond the interest payments on debt. Our main assumption is that discretionary expenditure is not compatible with rigid obligations, which make outlays inertial after a spending decision is made. Looking at disaggregate expenditures classified by *uses* would help to identify the degree of potential inertia in different spending categories. However, this approach has the potential to be arbitrary.

To reduce the scope for arbitrariness, rather than the legalistic approach often used by the event methodology, we adopt an economic perspective relying on the time-series properties of various components of expenditure. Given that obligations derived from social contracts lead to persistent spending, we distinguish discretionary from non-discretionary spending by evaluating the persistence and volatility derived from the univariate time-series properties of each expenditure component. Given that our focus is on short-term changes in expenditures, each expenditure component is de-trended.

We base our definition and measurement of discretionary spending on a few, rather intuitive, assumptions:

(i) *Discretion cannot be inertial.*

Since current policy decisions do not simply, or necessarily, complete past decisions, discretionary spending should be less persistent than automatic stabilizers. In addition, there is no reason that discretionary spending must behave like a white noise process.[9]

We test persistence by applying Ljung–Box statistics to the univariate cyclical components of each type of spending. Our candidate discretionary variables should be less persistent than the other spending variables.

(ii) *Discretion does not imply obligations.*

Discretionary spending should rest more on choice than on *obligations.* In reality, several expenditures imply several types of obligations (e.g., debt payments, compensation of employees, social security pensions), regardless of whether these obligations are legal, contractual, or plainly moral in nature.[10] Empirically, the absence or presence of less stringent obligations should not only imply a *lower* persistence but also a *higher* volatility relative to more automatic types of spending, due to cyclical factors and to the transmission of previous shocks. Thus, combining low persistence and high volatility could provide a reasonable signal for detecting discretion, independently of any particular theoretical assumption.

(iii) *Discretionary expenditure must be temporary.*

Policy interventions should reflect discrete and reversible choices, that is, temporary spending decisions that democratic governments

---

[9] For instance, public investments or other time-to-build projects need more than one period to be implemented and completed.

[10] Conversely, in an analysis of discretionary spending trends in the United States, for instance, "essentially all spending on federal wages and salaries is discretional" (Austin and Levitt, 2010, p. 3). We do not follow this wide "legal" definition here, instead favoring a more economic interpretation to be tested against detailed cyclical evidence.

can legally start and cancel.[11] Therefore, *temporary* decisions reconcile the lack-of-persistence requirement with the assumption that (well-behaved) discretionary spending should pursue temporary and reversible goals. Furthermore, temporary decisions do not have to behave like a white noise process because temporary interventions are not necessarily instantaneous interventions to be completed in the same period in which a decision is taken: Outside lags in general and time-to-build technologies for capital spending imply some persistence, required at least by the completion time.

3.1 Candidates for Discretion

Given the above assumptions, we identify ex ante discretionary expenditure on the basis of its purpose, since certain outlays per se reflect fewer obligations than others, including the need to be protracted over time. However, for empirical analysis, general government spending is considered here by NIPA variable (see Table 18.2) rather than by function (e.g., defense, health, etc.), though spending variables such as wages, investment, interest, etc. are easily related to economic purposes, which are more or less likely to reflect implicit or explicit obligations.[12]

3.2 Criteria for Identifying Discretion: Persistence and Volatility of Expenditure Series

We first compute the cyclical component of each expenditure item using the HP filter. Our chosen series relate to real expenditure variables rather than to expenditure-to-GDP ratios as in Fatás and Mihov (2003) and Afonso et al. (2010). Scaling expenditure by GDP, while ensuring the stationarity of the series, is not an innocuous normalization if the objective is to identify discretionary policy. Indeed, the expenditure-to-GDP ratio varies as a result of changes in GDP. Moreover, as GDP itself is affected by government expenditure, scaling

---

[11] In principle, government could also establish ex ante rules ensuring that the relevant expenditure is implemented when certain conditions occur, for instance a fall in GDP, an increase in unemployment, or an increase in inflation. Musgrave (1959) defined such rule-based discretion as "formula flexibility," which recently regained consensus in the literature.

[12] This is less obvious in the case of government consumption that includes several functions or types of services.

Table 18.2: *Government revenues, spending, and debt, 1980–2014*

Country	TY	GY	GSIZE	BY	Country	TY	GY	GSIZE	BY
Austria					**Japan**				
1980–9	48.12	47.93	96.05		1980–9	30.89	30.86	61.75	66.54
1990–9	49.65	49.13	98.79	68.59	1990–9	31.80	33.10	64.89	88.10
2000–8	48.69	46.10	94.79	75.16	2000–8	32.18	35.93	68.10	158.7
2009–14	48.92	47.25	96.17	92.71	2009–14	33.34	40.48	73.57	208.8
Belgium					**Netherlands**				
1980–89	47.03	56.36	103.4	122.1	1980–9	56.10	38.64	94.74	38.73
1990–99	47.49	50.02	97.51	146.4	1990–9	50.28	52.27	102.6	75.86
2000–8	48.37	46.53	94.90	109.4	2000–8	46.70	46.43	93.13	82.48
2009–14	49.79	50.93	100.7	*115.7*	2009–14	42.80	40.05	82.85	56.52
Denmark					**Norway**				
1980–89	51.42	51.48	102.9	67.49	1980–9	52.02	38.77	90.79	31.12
1990–99	54.43	51.22	105.7	75.05	1990–9	53.41	42.42	95.83	30.87
2000–8	54.40	46.81	101.2	49.72	2000–8	57.12	36.60	93.73	46.07
2009–14	55.46	51.39	106.8	56.95	2009–14	56.10	38.64	94.74	38.73
Finland					**Spain**				
1980–9	48.00	38.72	86.72	16.93	1980–9	33.94	37.17	71.11	40.51
1990–9	55.04	49.68	104.7	50.25	1990–9	38.56	42.07	80.63	62.79
2000–8	52.40	41.63	94.04	46.16	2000–8	38.71	37.26	75.96	52.94
2009–14	53.75	48.14	101.9	60.35	2009–14	36.56	43.63	80.19	85.81
France					**Sweden**				
1980–9	47.65	46.97	94.62	37.92	1980–9	56.39	50.16	106.6	56.83
1990–9	48.97	49.33	98.30	60.82	1990–9	58.03	53.23	111.3	68.93
2000–8	49.57	48.57	98.14	77.07	2000–8	53.74	46.97	100.7	54.11
2009–14	51.43	52.72	104.1	105.9	2009–14	51.74	47.70	99.43	46.39
Iceland					**UK**				
1980–90	34.26	33.42	67.69		1980–9	41.17	41.30	82.47	44.59
1990–9	37.70	38.10	75.80	45.14	1990–9	36.82	37.92	74.74	44.23
2000–8	43.05	38.50	81.55	39.96	2000–8	39.12	37.14	76.26	50.01
2009–14	40.82	41.54	81.86	90.38	2009–14	38.78	42.32	81.10	96.89
Ireland					**USA**				
1990–99	39.35	37.45	76.80	55.62	1980–9	31.66	34.75	66.42	52.56
2000–08	34.90	32.17	67.07	34.18	1990–9	33.16	34.70	67.86	64.45
2009–14	34.12	44.02	78.14	102.6	2000–8	32.52	33.80	66.31	61.65
Italy					2009–14	31.60	38.10	69.70	105.3
1980–9	36.98	46.73	83.71	89.71					
1990–9	44.38	50.10	94.47	116.7					
2000–8	44.04	45.72	89.76	116.2					
2009–14	46.84	49.19	96.03	135.7					

Note: TY = total revenues/GDP; GY = total government spending/GDP; GSIZE = (TY + GY)/GDP; BY = government debt/GDP. All variables are in nominal terms and refer to general government.

expenditure by GDP creates circularity in the measure of expenditure dynamics.

We analyze the autocorrelation function for each cyclical expenditure component and for two aggregate measures, discretionary and non-discretionary spending, defined according to our priors based on persistence and volatility patterns. If a series lacks any persistence – that is, if the series is a white noise process – the coefficients of autocorrelation will be zero at all lags. We then evaluate the presence of persistence in the series through the Ljung–Box statistics, whose value increases along with the degree of persistence. However, the persistence of a time series affects its variance. Consider the simplest case of an AR(1) process $y_t = \rho\, y_{t-1} + \varepsilon_t$, with finite variance of the disturbance term $\left(0 < \sigma^2(\varepsilon) < \infty\right)$. The volatility of any covariance-stationary variable (y) increases with the persistence of the process, defined in this case by the parameter $\rho : var(y) = \frac{\sigma^2(\varepsilon)}{(1-\rho^2)}, 0 < \rho < 1$.

In addition, we use the standard deviation as a comparable, scale-free measure of volatility for cyclical, zero-mean variables. As the volatility of a series is affected by the degree of persistence, we construct as our preferred measure of the degree of discretion an indicator of volatility corrected for the persistence of the series. Therefore, our summary criterion of "deflated volatility" is simply obtained by dividing the volatility of each variable (standard deviation) by the Ljung–Box statistics, which measure the degree of persistence of the series.

Discretion is characterized here by low persistence *and* high volatility.

We consider the volatility and persistence of each spending variable. Such analysis is then applied to an ex ante distinction between discretionary and non-discretionary expenditures based on our priors. The analysis of volatility/persistence is crucial to validate our priors. Starting from an individual expenditure series for each country, we derive total discretionary expenditure simply adding up the individual discretionary series.

Our candidate variables satisfying the lack of obligation requirement are *subsidies, purchases*, and *capital spending*. Thus, we exclude from discretion not only interest payments but also compensation of employees and transfers, which are in most cases dominated by pensions. This means that we exclude from discretionary spending the non-pension components as well (e.g., mainly unemployment and welfare benefits), which behave more as a persistent cyclical component than as an occasional labor market intervention (see Coricelli and Fiorito, 2013 for details).

4 Stylized Facts

We first describe the evolution of the main fiscal variables during the period 1980–2014, focusing on ten-year intervals prior to the Great Recession and on the first years of the Great Recession (Table 18.2). All variables used are defined in Appendix 2.

4.1 Government Revenues, Expenditure, and Debt

One can note from Table 18.2 that in the 2000s, prior to the Great Recession, government spending declines in most countries. Such a decline is reversed at the outset of the Great Recession, except in the case of Spain. We next report for the same time interval the behavior of discretionary and non-discretionary expenditure.

4.2 Trends in Discretionary and Non-Discretionary Spending

On the basis of the Coricelli–Fiorito definition, the share of discretionary spending (GD) is about one third of total government spending in the OECD (Figure 18.1). This is much larger than the discretionary expenditure obtained from estimated residuals, but is much smaller than typically assumed in the earlier econometric models where government spending was by definition an exogenous, controlled variable.[13] Moreover, although there are significant differences across countries, the share of discretionary spending (GD) in total expenditure sharply dropped in the period 1970–2014.

Table 18.3 illustrates the behavior of GD, GN, and total expenditure (GY) as ratios to GDP over four time intervals during the period 1980–2014. Until 2008, the ratio of GD/GDP declines in most countries. Therefore, not only does discretionary expenditure declines as a share of total expenditure, but it also declines as a share of GDP. Interestingly, this tendency is reversed in the Great Recession, with a

---

[13] Common identification schemes of a government spending shock in SVAR models with Cholesky decomposition or using institutional information on fiscal elasticity à la Blanchard and Perotti (2002) assume that total public expenditure or the sum of public investment and public consumption do not respond within the same period to variations in other macroeconomic variables, namely GDP.

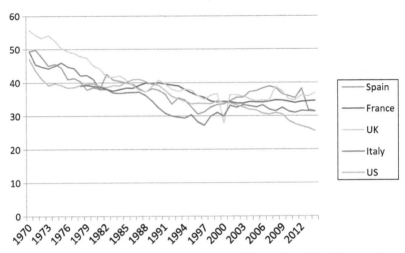

Figure 18.1: Share of discretionary expenditure in selected countries, 1970–2014

Note: in percent.

significant increase in discretionary spending, especially in those countries that entered the recession phase with less stringent debt constraints.[14] However, during the Great Recession GN/GDP increased more than GD/GDP, suggesting that automatic stabilizers responded more to the decline in GDP. Furthermore, the inertial components of GN induced an increase in the GN/GDP ratio in the face of a contraction of GDP. Finally, as we will discuss in Section 5, the increase in the GD-to-GDP ratio does not necessarily imply an increase in discretionary expenditure, as it may reflect the drop in the denominator (GDP).

5 Discretionary and Non-Discretionary Expenditure over the Business Cycle

In this section we present stylized facts for discretionary (GD), non-discretionary (GN), and aggregate expenditure (GT), which is the sum of these two components. We focus on the cyclical component of the variables, obtained by subtracting from each component its respective trend. We first illustrate univariate properties of each type of spending, in

---

[14] This increase was particularly high in Ireland and – for different reasons – in the Netherlands, where the discretionary share is always increasing, eventually reaching about half of total outlays, as in Japan.

Table 18.3: *Discretionary and non-discretionary spending, 1980–2014*

Country	1980–9			1990–9			2000–8			2009–14		
	GD	GN	GY	GD	GN	GY	GD	GN	GY	GD	GN	GY
Austria	17.05	30.88	47.93	15.80	33.34	49.13	14.46	31.64	46.10	15.22	32.03	47.25
Belgium	19.04	37.33	56.36	14.60	35.42	50.02	15.60	30.93	46.53	18.82	32.10	50.93
Denmark	14.20	37.27	51.48	13.44	37.79	51.22	13.71	33.10	46.81	16.38	35.01	51.39
Finland	13.50	25.22	38.72	14.92	34.77	49.68	13.21	28.42	41.63	15.75	32.39	48.14
France	16.39	30.58	46.97	16.60	32.73	49.33	16.06	32.51	48.57	17.98	34.74	52.72
Iceland	17.30	16.12	33.42	16.67	21.43	38.10	16.84	21.66	38.50	16.36	25.18	41.54
Ireland	–	–	–	11.21	26.23	37.45	12.61	19.57	32.17	15.98	28.04	44.02
Italy	15.28	31.45	46.73	13.80	36.30	50.10	14.34	31.38	45.72	15.05	34.14	49.19
Japan	15.50	15.36	30.86	17.71	15.38	33.10	18.00	17.93	35.93	19.47	21.01	40.48
Netherlands	19.24	33.04	52.27	18.26	28.17	46.43	18.96	21.09	40.05	22.83	21.84	44.67
Norway	15.04	23.73	38.77	15.44	26.99	42.42	13.14	23.47	36.60	14.07	24.56	38.64
Spain	14.94	22.23	37.17	14.61	27.46	42.07	13.91	23.34	37.26	14.77	28.86	43.63
Sweden	19.51	30.65	50.16	20.76	32.47	53.23	17.93	32.47	46.97	19.65	28.05	47.70
United Kingdom	13.67	27.63	41.30	11.89	26.03	37.92	12.78	24.37	37.14	15.24	27.08	42.32
United States	11.30	23.46	34.75	9.934	24.76	34.70	10.05	23.75	33.80	10.70	27.40	38.10

Note: average data; GD = discretionary spending; GN = non-discretionary spending; GY = general government spending/nominal GDP.
Source: OECD Economic Outlook No. 97 (Edition 2015/1), OECD Economic Outlook: Statistics and Projections (database)

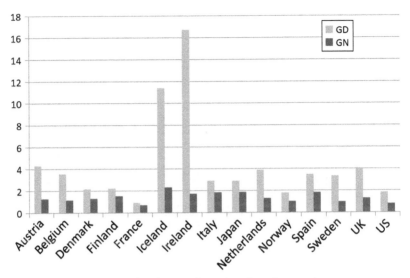

Figure 18.2: Volatility of real expenditure in selected countries
Note: standard deviation of the cyclical data.

particular in terms of volatility. We then evaluate the co-movements of each component of expenditure with real GDP cycles at different leads and lags. Such co-movements give us an indication of the pro- or counter-cyclical, or else acyclical, properties of each component of expenditure.

5.1 Volatility of Expenditure

In this section we verify whether our priors on the selection of discretionary and non-discretionary components are confirmed by analysis of the volatility of these two types of spending. Figure 18.2 clearly illustrates the fact that discretionary expenditure is consistently more volatile than non-discretionary expenditure (and primary and total expenditure).

Furthermore, in ten out of fifteen cases, non-discretionary expenditure is more persistent than discretionary expenditure (Table 18.4).

However, volatility and persistence are related, as volatility is increased by the propagation mechanism of the shocks, especially if they are persistent. Even when we adjust volatility for the different persistences of the expenditure series in each country, discretionary expenditure is more volatile than non-discretionary expenditure.

In summary, the estimated discretionary GD variable conforms well enough to our definition of a type of spending that is more volatile not

Table 18.4: *Persistence and volatility of spending categories*

	Vol	LB	Dvol		Vol	LB	Dvol		Vol	LB	Dvol
Austria				**Belgium**				**Denmark**			
1990–2011				1980–2011				1980–2011			
GD	4.28	5.03	0.85	GD	3.54	17.3	0.20	GD	2.16	8.1	0.27
GN	1.28	7.24	0.18	GN	1.16	16.0	0.07	GN	1.30	26.2	0.05
GDP	1.55	7.77	0.20	GDP	1.62	12.9	0.13	GDP	1.31	28.2	0.05
GT	1.41	6.14	0.23	GT	1.49	4.36	0.34	GT	1.28	27.8	0.05
Finland				**France**				**Iceland**			
1980–2011				1980–2011				1990–2011			
GD	2.22	13.8	0.16	GD	0.91	6.6	0.14	GD	11.4	5.1	2.23
GN	1.54	17.6	0.09	GN	0.69	12.1	0.06	GN	2.31	5.6	0.41
GDP	1.14	13.5	0.08	GDP	0.61	3.8	0.16	GDP	5.77	3.9	1.48
GT	1.22	23.1	0.05	GT	0.56	10.5	0.05	GT	5.34	4.5	1.17
Ireland				**Italy**				**Japan**			
1990–2011				1980–2011				1980–2008			
GD	16.7	3.94	4.25	GD	2.90	16.4	0.18	GD	2.88	12.3	0.23
GN	1.72	7.23	0.24	GN	1.84	13.9	0.13	GN	1.88	12.6	0.15
GDP	7.7	2.80	2.75	GDP	1.01	3.3	0.30	GDP	2.3	14.4	0.16
GT	7.34	2.90	2.53	GT	1.15	5.6	0.20	GT	2.54	12.8	0.20
Netherlands				**Norway**				**Spain**			
1980–2011				1980–2011				1980–2011			
GD	3.87	11.3	0.34	GD	1.79	26.2	0.07	GD	3.46	14.6	0.24
GN	1.31	15.2	0.09	GN	1.02	12.6	0.08	GN	1.83	14.5	0.13
GDP	1.97	12.9	0.15	GDP	1.11	26.4	0.04	GDP	1.93	23.6	0.08
GT	1.81	10.8	0.17	GT	1.16	20.2	0.06	GT	1.84	18.6	0.10
Sweden				**UK**				**US**			
1980–2011				1980–2011				1980–2011			
GD	3.33	11.3	0.29	GD	4.05	10.5	0.39	GD	1.83	12.7	0.14
GN	0.98	4.6	0.21	GN	1.31	17.4	0.08	GN	0.80	17.0	0.05
GDP	1.57	11.8	0.13	GDP	1.87	9.9	0.19	GDP	1.23	24.6	0.05
GT	1.49	9.5	0.16	GT	1.64	10.0	0.16	GT	0.90	22.6	0.04

Source: OECD Economic Outlook No. 97 (Edition 2015/1), *OECD Economic Outlook: Statistics and Projections* (database). All indicators refer to deflated cyclical deviations from an annual HP trend; Vol is the standard deviation of the cyclical data. LB(p) is the Ljung–Box statistics where p = T/4 is the number of autocorrelations and T is the number of data points. The LB(p) statistics are used as an indicator of persistence (the higher the index, the higher is persistence); Dvol = Vol/LB is an indicator of deflated volatility, i.e., of the volatility not induced by the estimated persistence.

because of its dependence on the past (persistence), but because it mostly reflects punctuated policy changes, characteristic of highly volatile variables.

5.2 Co-Movements between Expenditure and GDP

In this section, we evaluate the cyclical co-movements between the two government spending components (GD, GN) and real GDP. As is commonly done in the real business cycle literature (Kydland and Prescott, 1990), these cross-correlations are evaluated at different leads and lags to assess whether expenditure variables anticipate, are synchronous, or follow real GDP fluctuations.

All variables are measured in real terms and as cyclical deviations from a smooth trend, obtained using the Hodrick–Prescott filter for annual data.[15] Given the small sample size (1980–2014), we restrict co-movements to a small range (t−3, t+3) with respect to contemporaneous real GDP cycles.[16]

Results are summarized in Tables 18.5, 18.6, and 18.7 for discretionary (GD), non-discretionary (GN), and total government spending (GT). A few general findings stand out.

First, GD is not contemporaneously correlated with GDP or is mildly counter-cyclical in all countries of the sample, except in Norway and Sweden, where it is strongly counter-cyclical. Furthermore, the correlation between GDP and GD at one lead is also weak, thus ruling out a delayed discretionary response of fiscal authorities to business cycle fluctuations. By contrast, GN is contemporaneously strongly counter-cyclical in the majority of countries, with the exceptions of Austria, Italy, Japan, and Sweden. This finding is common to previous studies of OECD countries. For instance, Darby et al. (2008) show that not only unemployment compensation, but also age- and health- related social expenditure and incapacity benefits, which are included in social security benefits, have high elasticity to output and react to the cycle in a stabilizing manner. Fiorito (1997) analyzes the cyclical fluctuations of public outlays and finds that transfers and the wage component of government spending are counter-cyclical and act as timely cyclical stabilizers. By contrast, Finn (1998) calculates that US cyclical fluctuations of government investments and government consumption, which are largely contained in the discretionary aggregate (investments and purchases), do not co-move with GDP.

---

[15] The smoothing parameter is 6.25, a number which is often used for annual data (Ravn and Uhlig, 2002).

[16] For countries with a shorter sample (Austria, Iceland and Ireland have data only for the period 1990–2011) we focus on a smaller interval (t−2,..., t+2).

Table 18.5: *Cross-correlations between discretionary spending and real GDP*

Leads/Lags	GD(−3)	GD(−2)	GD(−1)	GD	GD(+1)	GD(+2)	GD(+3)	LB−	LB+
Austria		−0.049	−0.152	−0.023	−0.018	0.054		0.511	0.068
Belgium	0.279	0.122	0.062	−0.158	0.117	−0.206	0.110	3.076	2.114
Denmark	0.102	−0.056	0.039	0.022	−0.078	0.0056	−0.131	0.477	0.831
Finland	0.188	0.063	−0.133	−0.096	−0.068	−0.246	−0.114	1.788	2.432
France	0.163	−0.099	−0.067	−0.148	0.143	0.297	0.311	1.291	6.453
Iceland		−0.595	−0.468	0.264	0.471	0.297		11.804	6.278
Ireland		−0.001	−0.174	−0.247	−0.218	0.454		0.604	5.277
Italy	0.025	0.193	0.076	−0.094	0.121	−0.184	0.0018	1.348	1.499
Japan	0.066	0.339	−0.166	−0.259	0.164	0.159	0.099	4.528	1.904
Netherlands	0.253	−.225	−0.195	−.008	0.251	0.210	0.089	4.764	3.509
Norway	0.361	−0.002	−0.541	−0.600	−0.124	0.385	0.301	12.955	7.965
Spain	0.396	−0.279	−0.083	−0.078	0.222	0.581	0.476	7.654	19.216
Sweden	0.047	0.101	−0.175	−0.411	−0.302	0.065	0.313	1.305	6.010
UK	0.154	−0.104	−0.518	−0.166	0.308	0.042	−0.026	9.138	2.919
US	0.296	0.021	−0.282	−0.384	0.113	0.530	0.306	5.210	12.097

Table 18.6: *Cross-correlations between non-discretionary spending and real GDP*

Leads/Lags	GN(−3)	GN(−2)	GN(−1)	GN	GN(+1)	GN(+2)	GN(+3)	LB−	LB+
Austria		−0.058	−0.14	−0.226	0.001	0.222		0.462	1.035
Belgium	0.071	−0.117	−0.333	−0.386	0.350	0.597	0.323	3.909	18.069
Denmark	0.572	0.493	0.184	−0.594	−0.539	−0.003	0.264	19.054	10.944
Finland	0.365	0.117	−0.267	−0.525	−0.201	0.247	0.226	6.838	4.742
France	0.123	−0.178	−0.291	−0.413	−0.140	0.292	0.526	4.006	12.114
Iceland		−0.166	−0.475	−0.072	0.397	0.405		5.080	6.589
Ireland		0.027	−0.389	−0.517	−0.016	0.573		3.034	6.900
Italy	0.126	−0.449	−0.439	−0.067	0.398	0.377	0.068	12.535	9.297
Japan	0.026	0.054	0.079	0.091	−0.066	−0.089	−0.486	0.299	7.960
Netherlands	0.009	−0.098	−0.379	−0.41	0.087	0.496	0.449	4.605	14.326
Norway	0.161	−0.323	−0.636	−0.578	0.041	0.275	0.067	16.188	2.539
Spain	−0.06	−0.311	−0.565	−0.377	0.399	0.72	0.455	12.680	27.488
Sweden	0.002	−0.088	−0.069	0.192	0.087	−0.024	−0.272	0.383	2.62
UK	0.468	0.459	0.082	−0.502	−0.568	−0.091	0.282	13.765	12.478
US	0.304	0.216	−0.211	−0.651	−0.305	0.200	0.259	5.748	6.181

Table 18.7: Cross-correlations between total government spending and real GDP

Leads/Lags	GT(−3)	GT(−2)	GT(−1)	GT	GT(+1)	GT(+2)	GT(+3)	LB−	LB+
Austria		−0.104	−0.268	−0.158	−0.027	0.177		1.660	0.672
Belgium	0.198	0.044	−0.118	−0.329	0.284	0.172	0.280	1.736	5.851
Denmark	0.383	0.333	0.152	−0.457	−0.468	0.045	0.160	8.840	74.480
Finland	0.418	0.165	−0.287	−0.529	−0.228	0.091	0.145	8.922	2.490
France	−0.197	−0.189	−0.258	−0.409	−0.022	0.404	0.591	4.348	16.289
Iceland		−0.595	−0.468	0.264	0.471	0.297		11.804	6.278
Ireland		0.018	−0.2	−0.313	−0.229	0.492		0.805	6.130
Italy	−0.135	−0.299	−0.36	−0.13	0.443	0.204	0.047	7.240	7.242
Japan	−0.06	0.342	−0.161	−0.239	0.165	0.149	0.001	4.518	1.504
Netherlands	−0.264	−0.263	−0.321	−0.164	0.273	0.409	0.268	7.470	9.725
Norway	0.289	−0.187	−0.655	−0.638	−0.057	0.341	0.188	16.622	4.837
Spain	−0.317	−0.392	−0.423	−0.287	0.398	0.821	0.548	13.352	35.284
Sweden	0.04	0.05	−0.169	−0.253	−0.213	0.032	0.136	0.985	1.985
UK	0.373	0.132	−0.44	−0.405	−0.003	−0.011	0.119	10.809	0.459
US	0.462	0.136	−0.285	−0.605	−0.102	0.455	0.317	9.860	9.956

Second, there are a few results for which classification is difficult, since there are also cases of *twofold* peak values, that is, correlations that are about the same in absolute terms but holding a different *sign* in a different *phase*: this happens in two cases for discretionary (Italy, Netherlands) and for non-discretionary spending (Austria, Denmark), and in one case (France) when co-movements refer to the total of general government spending.

Generally, with respect to leads and lags, results are mixed. Nevertheless, it is worth noting that, in line with our notion of non-discretionary expenditure, GN never positively leads GDP. Indeed, a positive lead would signal that GN is driven by an object-ive to affect expected developments in GDP – an objective that would conflict with our view of mainly automatic or inertial types of expenditure.

In summary, from the analysis of co-movements it clearly emerges that different types of expenditure behave very differently in relation to output fluctuations. This suggests caution in using aggregate measures of expenditure in analyses of fiscal stance and of the impact of govern-ment expenditure on economic activity.

5.3 Granger Causality Test

In the previous section we have shown that discretionary and non-discretionary expenditures exhibit, contemporaneously and at different leads and lags, different correlations with GDP. We proceed one step further in the analysis of the relationship between components of public expenditure and economic activity by testing the Granger caus-ality of GDP on public expenditures – discretionary (GD), non-discretionary (GN), and total (GT) – and vice versa. The purpose of this analysis is to assess whether adding past values of GDP in the autoregressive process of fiscal variables helps their prediction. In the case of a positive result, public spending reacts significantly to business cycle fluctuations either because it incorporates automatic stabilizers or because fiscal authorities intervene, modifying the outlays in response to the state of the economy. Otherwise, public spending could be inelastic to economic activity, for instance because it has been modified to meet a fiscal target. Overall, our prior is that non-discretionary expenditure, including automatic components, should respond more to GDP fluctuations than discretionary expenditure. Therefore, we

Table 18.8: *Granger causality test (a)*

Country	GDP → GD		GDP → GN		GDP → GT	
	F statistics	Critical value	F statistics	Critical value	F statistics	Critical value
Austria	1.096	4.160	2.259	3.295	1.745	4.130
Belgium	2.058	4.085	14.676	2.634	5.103	4.091
Denmark	0.504	4.113	3.892	2.874	4.420	3.259
Spain	2.738	4.085	5.321	4.085	8.574	4.085
Finland	4.387	4.105	10.818	2.626	4.785	2.650
France	3.136	3.305	4.477	2.743	7.281	2.960
Great Britain	0.827	4.085	7.616	2.650	2.022	4.085
Ireland	6.534	3.160	1.579	4.351	7.470	3.160
Iceland	6.244	4.171	4.852	2.759	12.106	4.171
Italy	4.181	3.252	6.447	2.641	7.126	3.252
Japan	4.909	3.245	11.771	2.859	5.263	2.874
Netherlands	1.396	4.085	3.395	2.852	0.773	4.085
Norway	2.722	4.085	1.387	4.085	0.671	4.085
Sweden	3.305	4.085	4.478	3.259	2.745	4.085
USA	9.537	3.238	7.158	2.626	6.758	2.626

Note: the table shows pairwise Granger causality tests. Series are deflated and in rate of growth. The number of lags is selected to maximize the BIC and alpha is 0.05.

expect that GDP Granger-causes non-discretionary expenditure more frequently than discretionary expenditure.

Tables 18.8 and 18.9 report the results of the Granger causality test for real series in rates of growth.[17] In order to make comparable the F statistics for the tests between GDP and GN, GDP and GD, and GDP and GT, we select series with the same length. If the F statistics are higher than the critical value, we reject the null hypothesis that GDP does not Granger-cause GD, GN, or GT.

GDP Granger-causes GN in most countries, with the exceptions of Austria, Ireland, and Norway. GDP Granger-causes GD in a much smaller set of countries (Finland, Ireland, Iceland, Italy, Japan, and the United States). It is interesting to note that for the latter countries GN is

[17] The number of lags is selected to maximize the Bayesian Information Criterion (BIC) fixing the maximum number of lags to four, given that the size of the sample is not very large (maximum forty-five observations).

Table 18.9: *Granger causality test (b)*

Country	GD → GDP		GN→ GDP		GT → GDP	
	F statistics	Critical value	F statistics	Critical value	F statistics	Critical value
Austria	3.961	4.149	2.127	4.149	3.971	4.149
Belgium	5.183	2.641	5.447	2.866	5.758	2.866
Denmark	5.076	3.245	6.976	2.634	3.958	2.634
Spain	3.951	2.634	3.867	2.634	4.037	2.634
Finland	0.122	4.091	0.260	4.091	0.343	4.091
France	0.201	4.149	0.228	4.149	0.228	4.149
Great Britain	1.929	4.105	0.835	4.105	1.693	4.105
Ireland	0.662	4.351	1.187	4.351	0.435	4.351
Iceland	4.285	3.328	1.500	4.171	4.442	3.328
Italy	6.010	2.626	4.926	2.626	5.332	2.626
Japan	0.757	4.105	2.376	4.105	1.137	4.105
Netherlands	0.215	4.085	0.077	4.085	0.095	4.085
Norway	1.880	3.238	4.175	2.852	3.496	2.852
Sweden	2.493	4.085	0.578	4.085	2.229	4.085
USA	1.268	4.085	5.455	2.852	4.498	2.852

Note: the table shows pairwise Granger causality tests. Series are deflated and in rate of growth. The number of lags is selected to maximize the BIC and alpha is 0.05.

very persistent, except in Iceland and Japan (see Table 18.4). This suggests that where non-discretionary expenditure is highly persistent, fiscal authorities may tend to intervene more on discretionary expenditure in response to variations in GDP. Furthermore, the F statistics are generally lower for GD than GN, indicating a weaker predictive power of GDP for discretionary expenditure. These results confirm that non-discretionary expenditure is relatively more counter-cyclical than discretionary expenditure, and that the latter is acyclical in many countries.

6 Discretionary Spending during Recessions

In this section we analyze the behavior of expenditure during recessions, focusing on a subset of representative countries: Three members of the euro area, one member of the EU, and, finally, the United States. First we look at the growth rates of real government

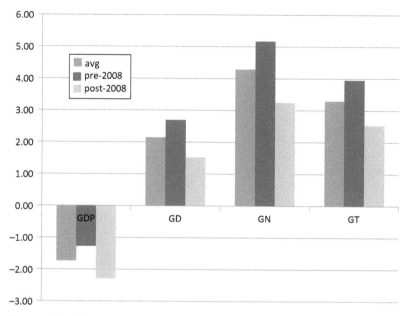

Figure 18.3: Real expenditure during recessions

expenditure during recession episodes, thus focusing on periods of negative GDP changes. Figure 18.3 contains the simple average of expenditure variables and of GDP across countries during recession periods, also distinguishing the pre-Great Recession and Great Recession periods. A few stylized facts stand out.

The experience of individual countries is displayed in Table 18.10. First, during recessions total real government expenditure increases in all countries. Interestingly, non-discretionary expenditure grows faster than discretionary expenditure, except for Italy. The experience of the Great Recession is revealing. Growth rates of total real expenditure are lower than in previous recessions for EU countries, and especially for countries belonging to the euro area, in spite of a much deeper recession in these countries. Only for the United States can one detect a significantly higher rate of growth of total expenditure during the Great Recession, relative to previous recessions.

In addition to the behavior of expenditure during the recession years, it is useful to put the recession episodes in a long-term horizon. Figure 18.4 describes the behavior of GD and GN throughout the whole sample period, highlighting the recession years with a shaded

Table 18.10: *Growth of public expenditures and GDP in recessions*

Country	Recessions	GD	GN	GT	GDP
France					
	All	2.902	6.196	3.419	−1.509
	Before 2008	3.119	7.666	3.780	−0.815
	After 2008	2.685	3.255	3.058	−2.897
Italy					
	All	2.249	1.311	1.692	−2.103
	Before 2008	5.229	4.047	4.713	−1.547
	After 2008	1.058	0.217	0.484	−2.325
Spain					
	All	−0.246	3.919	2.389	−1.098
	Before 2008	4.654	6.116	5.421	−0.399
	After 2008	−3.186	2.600	0.570	−1.518
UK					
	All	2.631	5.234	3.786	−1.829
	Before 2008	0.139	6.386	3.423	−1.606
	After 2008	8.862	2.356	4.695	−2.389
USA					
	All	3.829	4.840	4.447	−0.913
	Before 2008	2.871	4.347	3.778	−0.649
	After 2008	6.224	6.072	6.118	−1.572

Note: all variables are expressed in real terms, deflated by their relevant price deflator. Recessions are defined as years in which the rate of growth of real GDP is negative.

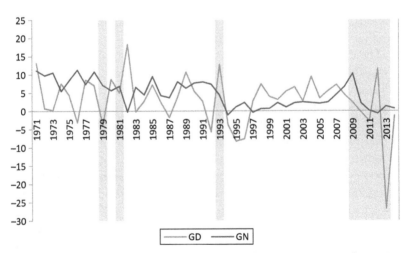

Figure 18.4: Growth of discretionary and non-discretionary expenditures in the United States, 1970–2014

Note: in percent.

area. This permits evaluation of the behavior of expenditure before and after recessions – a theme particularly relevant to the debate on exit from fiscal stimulus. Two main facts support our view on the sharp differences in the nature of GD and GN. First, around recession episodes, GD shows a clear pattern of reversibility: Following the recessionary years, during which GD tends to increase, the growth rates of GD turn negative. This almost never happens for GN, confirming the much stronger inertial nature of this component of expenditure, in spite of the fact that GN also includes automatic stabilizers.

7 Concluding Remarks

The Great Recession has revived the debate on the role of fiscal policy to support economic activity in the short run. A large consensus has emerged regarding the need for exceptional fiscal stimuli. Much of the debate has concentrated on the size of fiscal multipliers. We believe that before econometric results on the effects of fiscal interventions are derived, a better measure of truly discretionary policy is needed. This chapter is a step in that direction. Focusing on the expenditure side, we analyze how the measure of discretionary spending derived in Coricelli and Fiorito (2013) behaved during recession episodes, including the recent Great Recession.

Coricelli and Fiorito (2013) provide a measure of discretionary spending defined on the basis of three features of expenditure that can be easily approximated for empirical purposes: First, the lack of inertia; second, the lack of prior obligations; third, temporariness or reversibility. Given the persistence of macroeconomic fluctuations, a lack of inertia implies that discretionary spending variables should have relatively lower persistence and higher volatility.

They found that, indeed, discretionary spending is always more volatile than non-discretionary spending. According to their definition, discretionary expenditure accounts for about one third of total expenditure. Given that the bulk of government expenditure has little flexibility, the ability of governments to swiftly respond with counter-cyclical policy is sharply reduced. Analyzing co-movements of expenditure with GDP at business cycle frequency, we found no evidence of counter-cyclical expenditure, either for discretionary or non-discretionary expenditure. From a different perspective, Granger causality tests indicate that non-discretionary expenditure tends to be caused by GDP movements, whereas such causality is much more rare for discretionary expenditure. This is consistent with the fact that non-discretionary expenditure includes automatic components that respond to output fluctuations, whereas no systematic response to output is found for discretionary expenditure, at least in a large number of countries. However, when we restrict our attention to episodes of recession, we find that both forms of expenditure play a counter-cyclical role. Interestingly, during the Great Recession, in spite of the large drop in GDP, such counter-cyclical roles have been muted, especially for discretionary spending. This behavior, particularly evident in European countries, raises a puzzle regarding the policy choices of governments during the Great Recession.

Bibliography

Adema, W., Fron, P. and Ladaique, M. (2011). *Is the European Welfare State Really More Expensive? Indicators on Social Spending (1980–2012) and a Manual to the OECD Social Expenditure Database.* OECD Working Paper No. 124.

Afonso, A., Agnello, L. and Furceri, D. (2010). Fiscal policy responsiveness, persistence and discretion. *Public Choice*, **145**, 503–30.

Austin, D. A. and Levit, M. R. (2010). *Trends in Discretionary Spending.* Congressional Research Service, September.

Blanchard, O. J. (1990). *Suggestions for a New Set of Fiscal Indicators.* OECD Working Paper No. 79.

Blanchard, O. J. and Perotti, R. (2002). An empirical characterization of the dynamic effects of changes in government spending and taxes on output. *The Quarterly Journal of Economics*, **117**(4), 1329–68.

Blinder, A. S. (2006). The case against the case against discretionary fiscal policy. In R. W. Kopcke, G. M. B. Tootell and R. K. Triest, eds., *The Macroeconomics of Fiscal Policy*, MIT Press, 25–61.

Coricelli, F. and Fiorito, R. (2009). *Output Gap, Recessions and Fiscal Discretion.* Case Conference, Warsaw, November.

   (2013). *Myths and Facts about Fiscal Discretion: A New Measure of Discretionary Expenditure.* Document de travail du Centre d'Economie de la Sorbonne, 13033.

Corsetti, G., Meier, A. and Miller, G. J. (2012). *What Determines Government Spending Multipliers?* IMF Working Paper No. 12/150.

Darby, J., Melitz, J. and Masten, I. (2008). Social spending and automatic stabilizers in the OECD. *Economic Policy*, **23**(56), 715–56.

Devries, P., Guajardo, R., Leigh, D. and Pescatori, A. (2011). *A New Action-Based Data Set of Fiscal Consolidation.* IMF Working Paper No. 11/128.

Elmendorf, D. W. (2011). *Discretionary Spending.* Testimony before the Joint Select Committee on Deficit Reduction, US Congress, October 26.

Fatás, A. and Mihov, I. (2003). The case for restricting fiscal policy discretion. *Quarterly Journal of Economics,* 118(4), 1419–47.

Finn, M. (1998). Cyclical effects of government's employment and goods purchases. *International Economic Review,* 39(3), 635–57.

Fiorito, R. (1997). *Stylized Facts of Government Finance in the G-7.* IMF Working Paper No. 97/142.

Galí, J. (1994). Government size and macroeconomic stability. *European Economic Review,* 38, 117–32.

Girouard, N. and André, C. (2005). *Measuring Cyclically Adjusted Budget Balances for OECD Countries.* OECD Working Paper No. 434.

Granger, C. W. J. (1969). Investigating causal relations by econometric models and cross-spectral methods. *Econometrica,* 37(3), 424–38.

Ilzetzki E., Mendoza, E. G. and Végh, C. A. (2011). *How Big (Small) Are Fiscal Multipliers?* IMF Working Paper No. 11/52.

IMF (2010). Will it hurt? Macroeconomic effects of fiscal consolidation. In *World Economic Outlook,* October, pp. 93–124.

(2012a). *World Economic Outlook,* October.

(2012b). *Fiscal Monitor,* October.

Kydland, F. and Prescott, E. (1990). Real facts and monetary myth. *Federal Reserve Bank of Minneapolis Quarterly Review,* 1345–70.

Lane, P. R. (2003). The cyclical behaviour of fiscal policy: evidence from the OECD. *Journal of Public Economics,* 87, 2661–75.

Larch, M. and Turrini, A. (2009). *The Cyclically-Adjusted Budget Balance in EU Fiscal Policy Making: A Love at First Sight Turned into a Mature Relationship.* European Economy, March.

Levy-Yeyati, E. and Sturzenegger, F. (2005). Classifying exchange rate regimes: deeds vs. words. *European Economic Review,* 49(6), 1603–35.

Musgrave, R. (1959). *The Theory of Public Finance.* New York: McGraw Hill.

Ramey, V. A. (2011). Identifying government shocks: it's all in the timing. *Quarterly Journal of Economics,* 126(1), 1–50.

Ramey, V. A. and Shapiro, M. D. (1998). Costly capital reallocation and the effects of government spending. *Carnegie-Rochester Conference on Public Policy,* 48(1), 145–94.

Ravn, O. and Uhlig, H. (2002). On adjusting the HP filter for the frequency of observations. *Review of Economics and Statistics,* 84(3), 71–5.

Romer, C. and Romer, D. (2010). The macroeconomic effects of tax changes: estimates based on a new measure of fiscal shocks. *American Economic Review*, 100, 763–801.

Steuerle, E. (2013). *Dead Men Ruling: The Decline of Fiscal Democracy in America*. Urban Institute, video commentary, January.

Appendix 1

Table A1: *List of countries*

Algeria	Finland	Mali
Angola	France	Mexico
Argentina	Gabon	Moldova
Armenia	Gambia, The	Mongolia
Australia	Germany	Morocco
Austria	Ghana	Namibia
Azerbaijan	Greece	Netherlands
Bahrain	Guatemala	New Zealand
Bangladesh	Guinea	Nicaragua
Belarus	Guinea-Bissau	Niger
Belgium	Haiti	Nigeria
Bolivia	Honduras	Norway
Botswana	Hungary	Oman
Brazil	India	Pakistan
Bulgaria	Indonesia	Panama
Burkina Faso	Iran, Islamic Rep.	Papua New Guinea
Canada	Ireland	Paraguay
Chile	Israel	Peru
China	Italy	Poland
Colombia	Japan	Portugal
Congo, Rep.	Jordan	Qatar
Costa Rica	Kazakhstan	Romania
Cote d'Ivoire	Kenya	Russian Federation
Croatia	Korea, Rep.	Saudi Arabia
Czech Republic	Kuwait	Spain
Denmark	Latvia	Sri Lanka
Dominican Republic	Lebanon	Sudan
Ecuador	Lithuania	Switzerland
Egypt, Arab Rep.	Madagascar	United Arab Emirates
Estonia	Malawi	United Kingdom
Ethiopia	Malaysia	

Table A2: *Monetary unions*

Monetary union	Established	Members
CFA	1945	Benin, Burkina Faso, Côte d'Ivoire, Guinea-Bissau, Mali, Niger, Senegal, Togo, Cameroon, Central African Republic, Chad, Republic of the Congo, Equatorial Guinea, Gabon
CFP	1945	French Polynesia, New Caledonia
East Caribbean dollar	1965	Anguilla, Antigua and Barbuda, Dominica, Grenada, Montserrat, Saint Kitts and Nevis, Saint Lucia, Saint Vincent and the Grenadines
Euro	1999 2011	Austria, Belgium, Cyprus, Estonia, Finland, France, Germany, Greece, Ireland, Italy, Latvia, Lithuania, Luxembourg, Malta, Netherlands, Portugal, Slovakia, Slovenia, Spain, Monaco, San Marino, Vatican City Andorra
Hong Kong dollar	1977	Hong Kong, Macau
Singapore dollar	1977	Brunei, Singapore
Australian dollar	1966	Australia, Kiribati, Nauru, Tuvalu
South African rand	1974	Lesotho, Namibia, South Africa, Swaziland

Table A3: Correlation matrix of regressors

	Democracy	Federalism	Checks and balances	Government stability	Monetary union	Fixed exchange rate	Inflation targeter	Capital acc. openness	Financial development	Economic development	Cost of fiscal rules I	Cost of fiscal rules II	Government balance	Dependency ratio	Pro-cyclicality of gov. exp.
Democracy	1.00														
Federalism	0.21	1.00													
Checks and balances	0.81	0.25	1.00												
Government stability	0.22	0.07	0.26	1.00											
Monetary union	-0.00*	-0.05	-0.02*	0.06	1.00										
Fixed exchange rate	-0.19	-0.10	-0.11	0.09	-0.55	1.00									
Inflation targeter	0.29	0.08	0.26	0.07	-0.11	-0.21	1.00								
Capital account openness	0.28	0.11	0.33	0.24	-0.01*	0.16	0.22	1.00							
Financial development	0.36	0.19	0.47	0.21	-0.00*	0.07	0.24	0.48	1.00						
Economic development	0.43	0.17	0.58	0.29	-0.03*	0.08	0.24	0.61	0.67	1.00					
Cost of fiscal rules I	-0.33	-0.07	-0.32	-0.09	-0.15	-0.10	0.26	-0.23	-0.45	-0.39	1.00				
Cost of fiscal rules II	-0.15	-0.08	-0.08	-0.02*	0.02*	0.04	-0.17	0.01*	-0.07	-0.01	0.56	1.00			
Government balance	-0.08	-0.05	-0.03	0.17	0.05*	0.05	0.04	0.12	0.03*	0.16	-0.27	-0.28	1.00		
Dependency ratio	-0.34	-0.11	0.46	-0.37	0.17	-0.07*	-0.25	-0.47	-0.58	-0.71	0.27	0.01	-0.16	1.00	
Pro-cyclicality of gov. exp.	-0.13	-0.03*	-0.16	-0.11	-0.03*	-0.06	-0.06	-0.21	-0.16	-0.18	0.09	-0.03	-0.04	0.15	1.00

Note: (*) statistically insignificant at 90% confidence.

Table A4: *Data definition and sources*

Variables	Definition	Source
Democracy	Polity2 measure of democracy which ranges from −10 (strongly autocratic) to 10 (strongly democratic).	Polity IV Project (2010)
Political checks and balances	The Polcon V index is a quantitative measure of the institutional constraints faced by authorities and evaluates the extent to which any one political actor or the replacement for any one actor (e.g. the executive or a chamber of the legislature) is constrained in his or her choice of future policies.	Henisz and Zelner (2010)
Federalism	Dummy variable taking value 1 if the country has a *de jure* federal system and zero otherwise (unitary countries).	Feld and Schnellenbach (2010)
Political stability	ICRG stability index: Defines government stability as government's ability to carry out its declared program and its ability to stay in office. The ICRG stability index ranges from 1 (the lowest level of government strength) to 12 (the highest level).	ICRG (2015)
Monetary regime	We build a binary variable that takes value 1 if the country formally belongs to a monetary union and 0 otherwise.	Own elaboration

Table A4: (*cont.*)

Variables	Definition	Source
Exchange regime	Dummy variable taking value 1 if the country has a fixed exchange system and zero if it has a floating or intermediate regime. Fixed exchange systems include dollarization, currency boards, and monetary unions.	Reinhart and Rogoff (2004), extended to 2013 using IMF country reports.
Inflation targeting	Dummy variable taking value 1 if the country has an explicit inflation targeting regime and 0 otherwise.	Elbadawi et al. (2015)
Capital account openness	Index of the *de jure* openness of an economy measured by which the degree of restrictions on cross-border financial transactions as reported in the IMF's Annual Report on Exchange Arrangements and Exchange Restrictions.	Chinn and Ito (2008 and extended by the authors to 2014)
Financial development	Outstanding stock of domestic credit to the private sector (as a share of GDP).	World Bank, World Development Indicators (2015)
Overall development	GDP per capita in constant US$ of 2000.	World Bank, World Development Indicators (2015)
Costs of fiscal rules I	Three-year moving average of the coefficient of variation of government revenue (as share of GDP).	IMF Database 2015
Costs of fiscal rules II	Three-year moving average of the coefficient of variation of government balances (as share of GDP).	IMF Database 2015

Table A4: (*cont.*)

Variables	Definition	Source
Fiscal policy conditions	Fiscal balance of the central government.	Fiscal accounts obtained from the databases of the IMF, ECLAC, the African Development Bank, and the Asian Development Bank
Dependency ratio	Population below 15 and above 64 years of age to the labor force.	World Bank, World Development Indicators (2015)
Pro-cyclicality of government expenditure	Five-year rolling correlation of the HP-filtered government consumption expenditure (% of GDP) and HP-filtered GDP (both at constant prices).	World Bank, World Development Indicators (2015)

Appendix 2

Data are from the OECD *Economic Outlook* No. 97 (December 2011). Except for GD, GN, and WELFARE (our definitions), all variables and acronyms are those used by the OECD.

NOMINAL VARIABLES:

CGNW: Government final non-wage consumption expenditure
CGW: Government final wage consumption expenditure
IGAA: Government fixed capital formation
SSPG: Social security benefits
SUB: Subsidies to firms
TKPG: Capital Transfers paid and other capital payments
INTERESTS   gross government interest payments
(GGINTP):
PENSIONS =   old age + survivors spending cash benefits (Social
                 expenditure database)
WELFARE =   Welfare spending (SSPG Pensions) [Our definition]

DEFLATORS:

PCG: Government final consumption expenditure, deflator
PCGW: Government final wage consumption expenditure, deflator
PCP: Private final consumption expenditure, deflator
PGDP: Gross domestic product, deflator, market prices
PIG: Government fixed capital formation, deflator; PIT: Gross
         total fixed capital formation, deflator

REAL VARIABLES:

Using the nominal defnition: CG = CGW + CGNW and the OECD deflated total consumption variable (CGQ), real purchases (CGNWQ) have been obtained using the definition CGNWQ = CGQ CGWQ where the real compensation of employees (CGWQ) is obtained by using the private consumption deflator: CGWQ = CGW/ PCP (Fiorito, 1997). The other cases are explained in the chapter.

CGQ = CGNWQ + CGWQ

IGAAQ = IGAA / PIG

CGWQ = CGW/ PCP

TSUBQ = TSUB / PGDP

SSPGQ = SSPG / PCP

GDPQ = GDP / PGDP

TKPGQ = TKPG / PIG

PENSIONSQ = PENSIONS/PCP

WELFAREQ = WELFARE / PCP

GGINTQ = GGINT/PGDP

AGGREGATE SPENDING:

Aggregates in volume are obtained by summing the appropriate variable in volume.

GD = IGAA + CGNW + TKPG + TSUB

GN = SSPG + CGW + GGINTP.

Index